Did Moses Exist?
The Myth of the Israelite Lawgiver

D.M. *Murdock*

STELLAR HOUSE PUBLISHING
SEATTLE, WASHINGTON

StellarHousePublishing.com

ALSO BY D.M. MURDOCK a.k.a. ACHARYA S

The Christ Conspiracy: The Greatest Story Ever Sold
Suns of God: Krishna, Buddha and Christ Unveiled
Who Was Jesus? Fingerprints of The Christ
Christ in Egypt: The Horus-Jesus Connection
The Gospel According to Acharya S
The Astrotheology Calendar Series

DID MOSES EXIST? THE MYTH OF THE ISRAELITE LAWGIVER
Copyright © 2014 by D.M. Murdock a.k.a. Acharya S
All rights reserved. Printed in the United States of America.
No part of this book may be used or reproduced in any manner whatsoever—electronic, mechanical, photocopy, recording, or otherwise—without written permission except for brief quotations in articles and reviews. For information, address Stellar House Publishing, LLC, 93 S. Jackson St., Ste. 57463, Seattle, WA 98104; www.stellarhousepublishing.com

Library of Congress Cataloging in Publication Data
Murdock, D.M./Acharya S
 Did Moses Exist? The Myth of the Israelite Lawgiver.
 1. Moses—Historicity 2. Judaism—Origin
Includes bibliographical references and index
ISBN: 0-9799631-8-4
ISBN13: 978-0-9799631-8-6

Design and layout by D.M. Murdock; cover by Mark Chiacchira and D.M. Murdock. Cover images (clockwise from upper left): Moses mosaic in the Cathedral Basilica of St Louis; Michelangelo, *Moses with horns*, San Pietro in Vincoli, Rome; cuneiform *muš*, Sumerian for "snake" or "serpent"; Hebrew text of Exodus verses; Hero (Gilgamesh?) holding lion, palace of Sargon II at Khorsabad, 713-706 BCE; *Epic of Gilgamesh* in cuneiform; Dionysus coin; *Moses and the Burning Bush* by Mark Chiacchira; Moses holding tablets by José de Ribera (1591–1652).

Biblical quotes herein are from the Revised Standard Version or "RSV," except where otherwise noted. Revised Standard Version of the Bible, copyright © 1946, 1952, and 1971 the Division of Christian Education of the National Council of the Churches of Christ in the United States of America. Used by permission. All rights reserved.

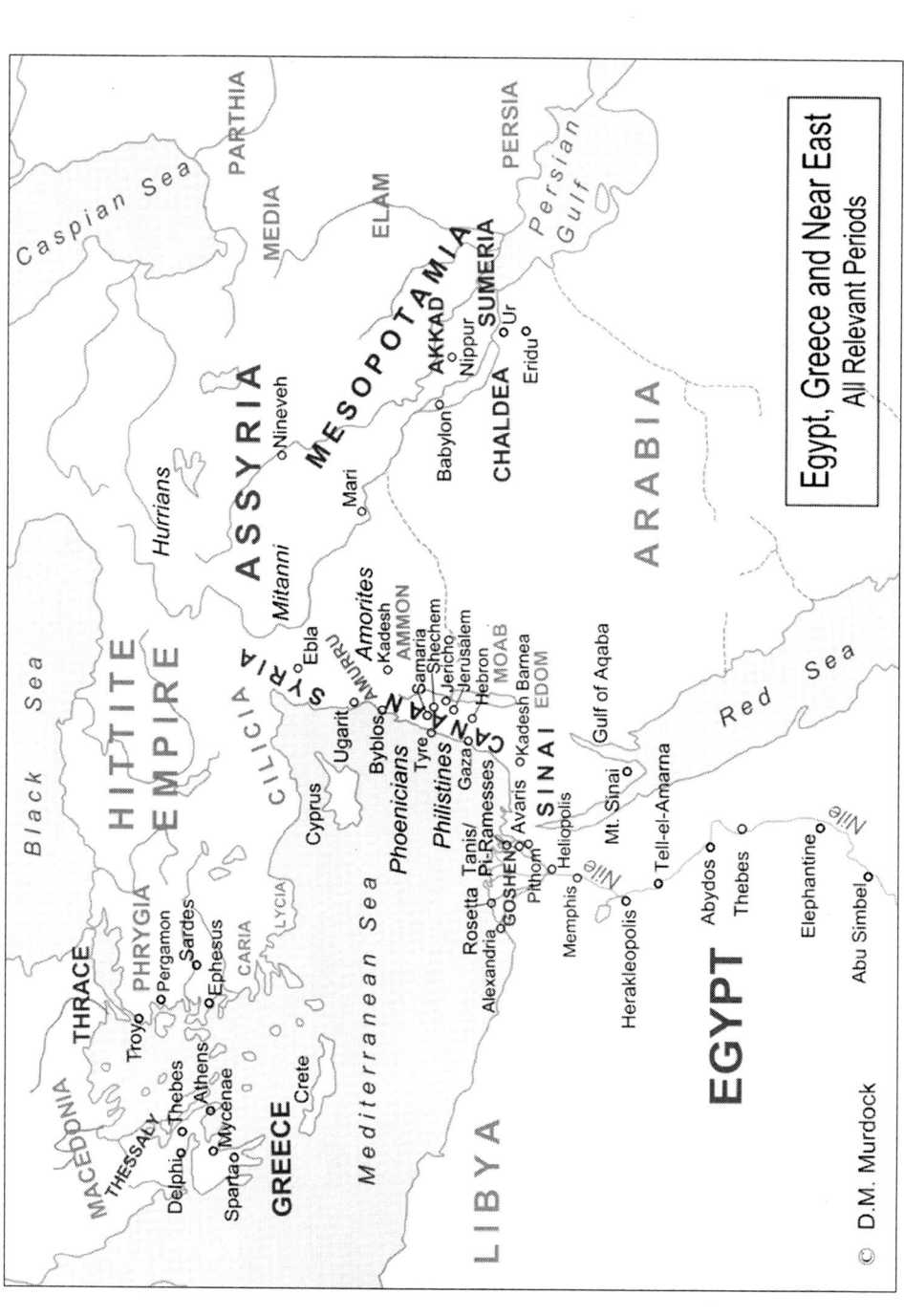

Table of Contents

List of Illustrations — viii

Preface — 1
- The Book of Enoch and Talmud — 2
- Comparative Religion Suppressed — 3
- Meaningful Mythology — 3
- Primary Sources and Translations — 4
- Pioneering Scholarship — 5
- Modern Discoveries — 5
- Space Consideration — 6
- Unprecedented Access — 7

Introduction — 9
- Greek Scriptural Knowledge? — 11
- Philo Judaeus of Alexandria — 12
- Mythological, Not Historical — 13
- The Mysterious Milieu of the Day — 14
- Many Lawgivers and Law Codes — 16
- Jewish and Pagan Syncretism — 17
- Major Crossing — 18
- Egypt and the Levant — 19
- Byblos — 19
- Osiris in Jerusalem — 21
- Differences Irrelevant — 22
- Biblical Special Pleading — 23

Who Wrote the Pentateuch? — 25
- Mosaic Attribution — 26
- Anachronisms and Contradictions — 26
- Book of the Wars of the Lord — 29
- Moses's Era — 30
- No Moses Before the Exile? — 30
- Divine Revelation and Authority — 31
- No Archaeological Evidence — 33
- Wellhausen and the Documentary Hypothesis — 34
- Exodus Composition — 37
- Earlier Folklore — 38
- The Book of the Law — 42
- Found or Fabricated? — 45
- Josiah's Yahwism — 46
- Ezra's Memories — 48
- Ancient Egyptian Words — 49
- Hebrew Emergence — 52
- Conclusion — 53

Was Moses an Egyptian Pharaoh or Priest? — 55
- Exodus Date — 56
- Akhenaten the Monotheist? — 56
- Atenism — 59
- Hebrew Henotheism — 60
- Yahweh Supremacy — 62

Great Hymn to Aten and Psalm 104	64
Thutmose II	65
Etymology of Moses	66
Pharaoh Thutmose III	67
King Tut	68
Ramesses I	68
Seti I	69
Ramesses II	69
Nectanebo II	70
A Priest of Aten?	70
Historical Fiction	71
Conclusion	72

The Exodus as History? — 75

Nonbiblical References	76
Logistic Implausibility	76
Modern Gatherings Irrelevant	79
Geography and Archaeology	79
The Burning Bush	82
Rods to Serpents	82
Bricks without Straw	83
Elderly Leaders	85
The 10 Plagues	85
Unleavened Bread	89
Mass Communication	89
The Route of the Exodus	90
The Philistines	91
Pillars of Cloud and Fire	94
Parting the Red Sea?	94
Exodus Encampments?	95
Mt. Horeb and Mt. Sinai	97
Serabit el-Khadim	98
Gulf of Aqaba	99
Baal Zephon and Migdol	100
Water Sources	101
Heavenly Manna	102
29 Trillion Quails?	105
Tents or Booths?	105
Striking the Rock	106
The Amalekites and the Magic Rod	106
Judging According to What Statutes?	107
Priests before Priests?	107
The Ten Commandments	108
The Ark of the Covenant	109
Golden Calf	111
Magical Wood?	113
Cannibalism	113
Disposition of the Dead	113
Giants in the Promised Land	113
No Edomites	114
Holy Genocide	114
Time Compression	116

TABLE OF CONTENTS   iii

    Canaanites and Amorites   116
    Magical Clothes   117
    Conquest of Canaan   117
    Jericho   118
    Apologies   119
    Conclusion   121

The Exodus in Ancient Literature   125

    Circular Reasoning   125
    Song of the Sea   126
    The Baal Cycle   129
    The Deep and Other Allegories   133
    Song of Moses   135
    The Song of Deborah   136
    Exodus in the Prophets   140
    Absent Egyptian Record   141
    The Ipuwer Papyrus   141
    Amarna Letters   144
    Conclusion   145

Hyksos and Lepers   147

    Conquerors or Captives?   148
    Religious Conflict?   150
    History or Fiction?   151
    Ahmose I   152
    Jerusalem Founding   154
    Hyksos as Greeks of Argos   154
    Proto-Israelite Amorites   155
    Osarseph and the Lepers   160
    Syrians from Palestine   162
    Antiochus IV   164
    Lysimachus and Chaeremon   165
    Tacitus on Jewish Origins   167
    Flight of Saturn   169
    Thieving Son of Joseph?   171
    Conclusion   174

Who Were the Israelites?   177

    El Prevails   178
    Merneptah Stele   179
    Hapiru   182
    Shasu of Yhw   186
    Yhw is Yahweh?   190
    Early Israelite Religion   192
    Conclusion   193

The Exodus as Myth   195

    The Slaughter of Innocents   196
    The Flight Archetype   197
    The Great Mendes Stele   198
    The Exodus from Egypt of Osiris   200
    The Exodus of Jesus   202

Pagan Exoduses	203
Exodus as Midrash	205
Magical Rod	205
The 10 Plagues?	206
600,000 as a Mystical Number	211
Mythical Pillars	216
Parting and Crossing the Sea	217
Controlling the Waters	221
Storm and Sun God	228
Wandering the Wilderness	232
12 Wells and 70 Palms	233
Manna and Heavenly Bread	234
Water from a Rock	236
Forty Days, Nights and Years	240
The Many Arks	241
Covenants and Testaments	246
The Golden Calf Redux	247
Mythical Giants	248
Conclusion	250

The Lawgiver Archetype — 253

The Hero's Birth	254
Divine Legislators	258
Ur-Nammu	262
Menes/Manes, Manis and Mannus	262
Menu/Manu	263
Minos	264
Law Code/Tablets of Law	264
Pygmy Lawgiver	269
Conclusion	271

The Dionysus Connection — 273

Early History	274
Sumerian Dionysus?	276
Dionysus in Literature	277
Homer	280
Hesiod	280
Homeric Hymns	281
Anacreon	282
Pindar	283
Herodotus	283
Orphic Hymns	286
Euripides	288
Aristophanes	291
Plato	291
Megasthenes	292
Artapanus	294
Apollodorus	296
Maccabees	296
Varro	298
Cicero	299
Diodorus	299

TABLE OF CONTENTS

Horace	301
Ovid	302
Seneca	302
Pliny the Elder	302
Plutarch	303
Pausanias	306
Arrian	306
Justin Martyr	307
Lucian of Samosata	307
Clement of Alexandria	307
Polyaenus	308
Philostratus	309
Porphyry	309
Eusebius	310
Sepphoris Mosaics	311
Macrobius	312
Hermias	313
Nonnus	314
Sanford	317
Vossius	317
Bochart	318
Gale	319
Thomassin	320
Patrick	321
Danet	321
Huet	322
Voltaire	323
Edwards	324
Bell	324
Dupuis	324
Hort	325
Le Brun	325
Bellamy	326
Clarke	327
Higgins	328
Darlington	328
Taylor	328
Massey	328
Conclusion	329

The Life of Dionysus — 331

Bacchic Attributes	331
God of Nysa	336
Drawn from the Nile	338
Mises	339
Twice-Born Grapevines	341
Marriage to Zipporah	341
Burning 'Bush'	343
Land Flowing with Milk and Honey	343
Smiting Unbelievers	343
Passover, Vernal Equinox and Wilderness	345
Exodus into the Sea	347

Food of the Gods	349
Women Celebrating	349
Water Manifestation	351
Jehovahnissi	351
Dian-nisi, Great Judge of Heaven and Earth	353
'Dog' as Companion	355
Sun Standing Still	356
Conclusion	356

The Vine and Wine — 359

Early History	360
Egypt's Vineyards	361
Wine Goddesses	363
Greek Viniculture	364
Blood and Resurrection	365
Wine Epithets and Roles	366
Elixir of Love	367
Baal's Cup	368
Sacred Drinking Banquet	369
Biblical Grape Reverence	371
Water to Wine	379
Ass and Foal	380
The Shoot of Jesse	382
Sacred Serpents	386
Conclusion	388

The Great God Sun — 391

Shamash, Lord of the World	392
Semitic Sun Goddess	393
King, Shepherd and Raiser of the Dead	396
El the Canaanite High God	397
The God of Exodus?	400
Holy Mount of Elohim	402
Yahweh as El's Son	404
El's Wives Asherat and Anat	405
El Shaddai	408
Enlil and Ellil	410
Adad/Hadad	411
Conclusion	412

Yahweh and the Sun — 414

Origins and History	415
Solar Yahwism	418
Mazzaroth/Mazzaloth	422
Jewish Zodiacs	425
Ezekiel's Godly Visions	425
Tammuz and the Sun	429
Lunar Deity	430
Ieuo	430
Iao	431
Adon-Adonai-Adonis	435
Conclusion	436

Moses as Solar Hero — 439

- Moses as God — 440
- Solar Aspects — 442
- The Tent of the Sun — 443
- Moses's Shining Face — 446
- Etymology of Moses Revisited — 449
- Masu the Hero — 451
- Gilgamesh and Mt. Mašu — 456
- Twin Mountains — 459
- The Moses Connection — 461
- Mŝ the Sacred Serpent — 470
- Ningishzida the Mush — 474
- Mosheh and the Serpent — 476
- Jebusite Serpent Cult at Jerusalem? — 479
- Mašmašu Priesthood — 480
- Conclusion — 484

Conclusion — 491

- Biblical Anachronisms and Errors — 492
- Brutal Literalism — 494
- Allegorical Fall — 496
- Political Fiction — 496
- Moses versus Jesus Mythicism — 498
- Preventing Armageddon — 499

Bibliography — 502

Index — 533

List of Illustrations

Fig. 1. Map of the Levant and surrounding areas (after MapMaster)   4

Fig. 2. Rosetta Stone with Egyptian hieroglyphs, Demotic and Greek, c. 196 BCE. Louvre Museum, Paris   6

Fig. 3. King Og riding giant unicorn behind Noah's ark. (Landa, *Jewish Fairy Tales and Legends*, 30)   8

Fig. 4. Wise and learned giant frog, "fairy son" of Adam and Lilith found at Passover, "wrote out the Law" and taught Rabbi Hanina "the whole Torah." (Landa, *Jewish Fairy Tales and Legends*, 252)   8

Fig. 5. Egyptian lawgiver Menes (?) on Narmer Palette, c. 2925–c. 2775 BCE. Siltstone tablet, Egyptian Museum, Cairo   16

Fig. 6. Prehistoric bull carving, c. 15,000 BP. Stele from Gobekli Tepe, Turkey (after Teomancimit)   18

Fig. 7. Dwelling foundations from Early Bronze Age, c. 3300-2100 BCE. Tell es-Sultan, Jericho, Israel   24

Fig. 8. Hammurabi receiving the law from Shamash, 18th cent. BCE. Stele from Susa, Louvre (Fritz-Milkau-Dia-Sammlung)   32

Fig. 9. Cuneiform clay tablet, 3rd millennium BCE. Found at Ebla, Syria   40

Fig. 10. Stylized palm tree or *asherah*, like those torn down by Josiah (2 Kings 23)   43

Fig. 11. Aramaic letter from Jewish community, 407 BCE. Papyrus, Elephantine, Egypt   47

Fig. 12. Israelite reformer king Hezekiah and his men destroy idols, including Moses's brazen serpent (2 Kings 18)   54

Fig. 13. Josiah smashes the idols of Baal (2 Ki 23). (*Holman Bible*, 1890)   54

Fig. 14. Hieroglyphs for 'Asari.' (Budge, 1973:1.25)   57

Fig. 15. Akhenaten worshipping solar disc Aten, rays extend as hands holding life-giving ankhs or Egyptian crosses, 14th cent. BCE. Alabaster carving from tomb of Akhenaten, Amarna, Egypt   59

Fig. 16. Hebrew tetragrammaton signifying 'YHWH,' 'Yahweh'   62

Fig. 17. Egyptian words *mes* and *mesu* denoting 'born.' (Budge, 1848:149)   67

Fig. 18. Ramesses II's victory in the Siege of Dapur, 13th cent. BCE. Mural at Thebes, Egypt (*Nordisk familjebok*)   69

Fig. 19. Akhenaten, Nefertiti and children with Aten and his rays/hands holding ankhs, c. 1350 BCE. Staatliche Museen in Berlin, Germany   74

Fig. 20. *God Appears to Moses in Burning Bush*, 1848. Painting from Saint Isaac's Cathedral, Saint Petersburg, Russia   82

Fig. 21. Gustave Doré, *Moses and Aaron Before Pharaoh*, 1866. (*Doré's English Bible*)   82

Fig. 22. Doré, *The Murrain of Beasts*, 1866. (*Doré's English Bible*)   86

ILLUSTRATIONS ix

Fig. 23. Doré, *The Plague of Darkness*, 1866. (*Doré's English Bible*) 87

Fig. 24. Egypt's firstborn destroyed. (de Hondt, *Figures de la Bible*, 1728) 88

Fig. 25. Yahweh's pillar of cloud. Bible card by Providence Lithograph Company, c. 1896-1913 94

Fig. 26. Israel's escape through the Red Sea. Bible card by Providence Lithograph, 1907 95

Fig. 27. Moses brings water out of the rock, (de Hondt, *Figures de la Bible*, 1728) 106

Fig. 28. Doré, *Moses Breaking the Tables of the Law*, 1866. (*Doré's English Bible*) 108

Fig. 29. Henry Davenport Northrop, *The Ark and the Mercy Seat*, 1894. (*Treasures of the Bible*) 110

Fig. 30. Exodus route bypassing the Red Sea, showing supernatural parting as unnecessary for flight from Egypt (Möller) 124

Fig. 31. Golden Calf worship (Exod 32:1-35). Bible card by Providence Lithograph Co, 1901. 124

Fig. 32. Deity labelled either 'YHW' (Yahu) or 'YHD' (Judea), seated on winged chariot wheel, holding bird, 4th century BCE. Silver coin from Gaza, British Museum 133

Fig. 33. Jael killing Sisera. (*Speculum Humanae Salvationis*, c. 1360) 140

Fig. 34. Map of Near East during Amarna period showing regional powers: Egyptians, Hittites, Mitanni, Kassites (after *Historical Atlas*, fig. 6) 146

Fig. 35. Ahmose I battling the Hyksos, 16th cent. BCE 152

Fig. 36. Saturn in a chariot drawn by winged, serpent-like dragons. Engraving by Pietro Bonato (1765–1820), Rome, Italy 169

Fig. 37. Migrations of Semitic peoples out of Africa into Arabia, Levant, Mesopotamia and Asia Minor (after 'Ancient Mesopotamia,' Worldology.com) 176

Fig. 38. 'Asiatics' (Semites) entering Egypt, c. 1900 BCE. Relief from the tomb of Khnumhotep II at Beni Hasan, Egypt. 176

Fig. 39. Merneptah Stele, 13th cent. BCE. Cairo Museum (after Webscribe) 179

Fig. 40. Egyptian hieroglyphs on Merneptah stele transliterated as 'Ysrir' 181

Fig. 41. Shasu prisoner bound around arms and neck, 12th cent. BCE. Line drawing of relief by Ramesses III at Madinat Habu, Egypt 186

Fig. 42. Map with shaded areas showing hill settlements of Samaria and Judea, in between Jordan River/Dead Sea and Mediterranean coast (Smith, G.A.) 194

Fig. 43. Seth-Baal (top), Baal-Seth and the sun god (bottom left two), and Seth with Amun name (bottom right), c. 16th-11th cents. BCE. Seal amulets (after Keel and Uehlinger, 115) 198

Fig. 44. Great Mendes Stele, 3rd cent. BCE. Formerly in Bulaq Museum, Egypt 199

Fig. 45. Benjamin West, *The Brazen Serpent*, 1790. BJU Art Gallery and Museum, Greenville, SC — 206

Fig. 46. Joshua commanding the sun to stand still. (*Treasures of the Bible*, 1894) — 211

Fig. 47. 'Rama's Bridge' between India (top) and Sri Lanka (bottom). (NASA) — 218

Fig. 48. Doré, *Destruction of Leviathan*, 1865 — 226

Fig. 49. Mose's rod turned into a serpent, (*Holman Bible*, 1890) — 228

Fig. 50. Horus of Edfu spearing the crocodile Set (Budge, 1920:16) — 232

Fig. 51. Mithra shooting an arrow into a rock to produce water, c. 2nd cent. AD/CE. Mithraeum at Neuenheim, Germany — 237

Fig. 52. The ark, bark, barque or boat of Amun, carried in procession at the Opet Festival — 241

Fig. 53. Ass-headed man crucified, with inscription "Alexamenos worships his god," c. 3rd cent. AD/CE. Graffito found at Rome — 252

Fig. 54. Chaos ocean monster battled by Semitic sun god, c. 7th cent. BCE? (Layard, plate 19/83) — 252

Fig. 55. Sumerian king Ur-Nammu approaches the god Enlil, c. 21st cent. BCE. Stele from Mesopotamia — 262

Fig. 56. Enki, Sumerian god of wisdom and fresh water, c. 2200 BCE. Cylinder seal, British Museum — 265

Fig. 57. Sunrise over Luxor, Egypt, as the baby sun god Horus emerges from the reeds of the Nile. (RaniaHelmy) — 272

Fig. 58. Mary A. Lathbury, *Pharaoh's Daughter Finding Moses*, drawing the baby from the reeds of the Nile, 1898. (*Child's Story of the Bible*) — 272

Fig. 59. Vinča symbols, c. 5300 BCE. Clay amulet from Tărtăria, Romania — 277

Fig. 60. Beth Shean, here called by Greek name, Scythopolis (Nichalp) — 278

Fig. 61. Celtic head with tonsure, c. 3rd century BCE. Stone carving from Czech Republic (CeStu) — 286

Fig. 62. Possibly proto-Pelasgian Vinča script, c. 5th millennium BCE, Romania — 287

Fig. 63. Bacchus and serpent, 1st cent. AD/CE. Fresco from Pompei, National Archaeological Museum, Naples, Italy — 290

Fig. 64. Bacchic staff or thyrsus — 294

Fig. 65. *Obv.* Turreted head of Cybele; *rev.* 'BACCHIVS IVDAEVS,' with camel and bearded man (Aristobolus II?) holding palm or olive branch, 55 BCE. Silver coin of A. Plautius, Babelon Plautia 13 — 297

Fig. 66. Herakles and Dionysus, 3rd-4th cents. AD/CE. Mosaic at Sepphoris/Tzippori, Israel — 311

Fig. 67. Hermes's winged caduceus with two snakes — 313

ILLUSTRATIONS xi

Fig. 68. Michiel van der Borch, *Spies return from Canaan with grapes*, 1332. Vellum, National Library of The Netherlands, The Hague — 321

Fig. 69. *The Dance of Cogul*: Small black 'Dionysus' with enormous genitals appears at center right; of 45 dancers, nine are women, c. 10,000 BP? Rock drawing, Lleida, Spain (Henri Breuil) — 330

Fig. 70. Territory of the Pelasgians, 2nd millennium BCE (Megistias) — 330

Fig. 71. Venus (?), dubbed the "Mona Lisa of Galilee," c. 4th cent. AD/CE. Mosaic from Sepphoris, Israel — 341

Fig. 72. Ashurnasirpal II holding a wine cup, 9th cent. BCE — 355

Fig. 73. Dionysian maenads or women with thyrsi and drums dancing around an idol of Bacchus as a pillar with branches (not shown), c. 420 BCE. Red figure stamnos by Dinos painter, Museo Nazionale Archeologico, Naples, Italy — 358

Fig. 74. Moses's sister, Miriam, dancing with a timbrel. (André, 1884) — 358

Fig. 75. Egyptian grape cultivation and wine production, c. 1500 BCE. Tomb painting from Thebes, Egypt — 361

Fig. 76. King David as Orpheus with harp and snake, 508 AD/CE. Synagogue mosaic from Gaza, Israel Museum — 370

Fig. 77. Cornelis Cort, *The Mocking of Noah*, c. 1560. Engraving (*The Story of Noah*, pl. 6) — 372

Fig. 78. Israelite spies bringing back huge grape cluster from Canaan. (*Treasures of the Bible*) — 373

Fig. 79. *Rev.* grape bunch between two grape leaves; *obv.* head of Dionysus (not shown), c. 530 BCE. Silver coin, Naxos, Greece — 374

Fig. 80. Charles Foster, *Offering to Molech*, 1897. (*Bible Pictures and What They Teach*) — 374

Fig. 81. Engraved sterling silver kiddush cup (Dimitri) — 378

Fig. 82. Dionysus with kantharos or cup reclining on ass, c. 460-423 BCE. Coin from Macedonia, Schonwalter Collection — 380

Fig. 83. Hermes with winged boots and caduceus, c. 480 BCE. Red figure lekythos, Metropolitan Museum, New York (David Liam Moran) — 383

Fig. 84. Bacchus, born from Zeus's thigh, holds a sprouting grapevine, c. 460 BCE. Museo Nazionale di Spina, Ferrara, Italy — 386

Fig. 85. Pinecone staff of Osiris, 1224 BCE. Egyptian Museum, Turin, Italy — 386

Fig. 86. Rod of Asclepius — 386

Fig. 87. Storm god Tarhunta holding grapes and vines, 'in Dionysian fashion,' while propitiated by the king of Tyana, c. 8th cent. BCE. Relief from Ivriz, Turkey, Archaeological Museum, Istanbul — 389

Fig. 88. Bacchus holds a fruiting grapevine in his left hand and a wine jar in his right, facing his wife, Ariadne, or a nymph, c. 520-510 BCE. Amphora by the Andokides and Lysippides painters, Louvre Museum, Paris — 389

Fig. 89. Dionysus holding a thyrsus and sprouting grapevine, c. 490-480 BCE. Kylix by Makron, Antikenmuseen, Berlin — 389

Fig. 90. Giovanni Lanfranco, *Moses and the Messengers from Canaan*, carrying grapes, 1621-1624. Getty Center, Los Angeles, CA — 390

Fig. 91. Hephaistos led back to heaven by Dionysos, riding an ass, c. 430 BCE. Attic Red Figure oinochoe, Metropolitan Museum, New York — 390

Fig. 92. Shapash/Shipish, sun goddess of Ugarit and Ebla, winged and in cruciform or cross shape, 2nd millennium BCE — 393

Fig. 93. Egyptian winged sun disk, like the biblical 'Sun of Righteousness' (Mal 4:2), surrounded by two serpents, like the caduceus or symbol of healing — 397

Fig. 94. Shamash between Mashu's Twin Peaks, wearing a horned helmet and with solar rays from shoulders and arms, 3rd millennium BCE. Akkadian, British Museum — 413

Fig. 95. Storm god Baal-Zephon holds a thunderbolt and stands on two mountains, with a serpent below, c. 16th cent. BCE. Cylinder seal from Tell el Daba/Avaris — 413

Fig. 96. Mount Sinai (right), with St. Catherine's monastery at foot of Horeb (left), 1570-2. Oil painting by El Greco, Historical Museum of Crete, Iraklion — 413

Fig. 97. Cuneiform 'Yahwè is god' tablets from Babylon, 18th cent. BCE. (Rogers, R.W., 91) — 416

Fig. 98. Cuneiform of North Semitic 'Jau is God,' 18th cent. BCE. (Rogers, R.W., 91) — 416

Fig. 99. Winged sun disk, c. 700 BCE. LMLK seal, Judea — 420

Fig. 100. Anonymous, *Ezekiel's Vision*, 1670. Copy from *Iconum Biblicarum* by Matthaeus Merian the Elder — 426

Fig. 101. Apollo/Helios in his quadriga chariot with four horses. Roman mosaic — 428

Fig. 102. Soli-lunar Osiris syncretized to Aah or Iah, the moon god. (Budge, 2010:1.83) — 430

Fig. 103. Yahweh written as IAO (inset), c. 1st cent. BCE. Dead Sea Scroll fragment 4Q120, Rockefeller Museum, Jerusalem — 433

Fig. 104. Sun god Helios surrounded by 12 zodiacal signs, with four solstices and equinoxes in corners, 6th cent. AD/CE. Synagogue mosaic from Beit Alpha, Israel (NASA) — 438

Fig. 105. Zodiac with Helios in center, 6th cent. AD/CE. Synagogue mosaic, Tzippori/Sepphoris, Israel. (G.dallorto) — 438

Fig. 106. Michelangelo, *Moses* with horns, c. 1513-1515. Marble, San Pietro in Vincoli, Rome — 447

Fig. 107. Amarna tablet no. 6. (Sayce, 1888:10.500) — 454

Fig. 108. Old Babylonian for 'Gilgamesh' (*Epic* 11.322) — 458

Fig. 109. Cuneiform *muš*, Sumerian for 'snake' or 'serpent' — 471

Fig. 110. *Mušḫuššu* or "reddish/fierce snake," originally 6th cent. BCE. Reconstructed Ishtar Gate from Babylon, Pergamon Museum, Berlin — 472

Fig. 111. Libation vase of Gudea with dragon Mušḫuššu, 21st cent. BCE. Louvre — 475

ILLUSTRATIONS xiii

Fig. 112. Mór Than, *Moses and the Nehushtan*, 1879. Plan for stained glass window, Ferencváros Church, Hungarian National Gallery 476

Fig. 113. Egyptian wine and snake goddess Renenutet, Renenet, Rennut, Ernutet, Thermuthis, Thermouthis, Hermouthis or Parmutit 478

Fig. 114. Bronze menorah with seven (phallic) serpents, Roman period (?) (after Charlesworth, 16) 479

Fig. 115. Robert Anning Bell, *The Brazen Serpent*, c. 1890. Reproduction of wood engraving, Wellcome Library no. 18284i 480

Fig. 116. French School, *Moses Receives the Tablets of the Law from God on Mount Sinai*, 19th cent. Color lithograph, Private Collection 486

Fig. 117. Jean-Léon Gérôme, *Moses on Mount Sinai*, revealing solar aspects, 1895-1900. Private collection, USA 486

Fig. 118. Moses's shining, solarized face on Mt. Sinai. Artist unknown, c. 20th cent. AD/CE 487

Fig. 119. Carl Heinrich Bloch, *Transfiguration of Jesus*, with Moses and Elijah, 19th cent. AD/CE 487

Fig. 120. Gilgamesh between two 'Bull Men with Sun-Disc,' 10th-9th cents. BCE. Relief from Kapara, Tell Halaf, Syria 488

Fig. 121. Parallels between Gilgamesh and Moses. (*Literary Digest*, 35.54) 488

Fig. 122. Egyptian priests and Aaron change their rods into a serpent in front of pharaoh (Exod 4:1-5). (*Foster's Bible Pictures*) 489

Fig. 123. Moses and the plague of fiery serpents upon Israel (Num 21:6-9). (*Treasures of the Bible*) 489

Fig. 124. Hezekiah removes the bronze serpent (2 Ki 18:4). (Charles Horne, *The Bible and Its Story*) 490

Fig. 125. Moses orders the Levites to slaughter all those worshipping the Golden Calf. Woodcut by Julius Schnoor von Carolsfeld (*Das Buch der Bücher in Bilden*, 1920) 501

Fig. 126. James Tissot, *The Women of Midian Led Captive by the Hebrews*, 1900. Watercolor, Jewish Museum, New York. 501

Preface

"I will open my mouth in a parable: I will utter dark sayings of old..."

Psalm 78:2

"The Bible is like water, the Mishna like wine: he that has learned the scripture, and not the Mishna, is a blockhead."[1]

Rabbinical saying from the Gemara[2]

"The learned may penetrate into the significance of all oriental mysteries, but the vulgar can only see the exterior symbol. It is allowed by all who have any knowledge of the scriptures that everything is conveyed enigmatically."[3]

Church father Origen, *Contra Celsus* (1.12)

"We must not understand or take in a literal sense, what is written in the book on the creation [Genesis], nor form of it the same ideas, which are participated by the generality of mankind, otherwise our ancient sages would not have so much recommended to us, to hide the real meaning of it, and not to lift the allegorical veil, which covers the truth contained therein. When taken in its literal sense, that work gives the most absurd and most extravagant ideas of the Deity. Whosoever should divine its true meaning, ought to take great care in not divulging it."[4]

Rabbi Moses Maimonides, *Guide for the Perplexed* (2.29)

T HE BIBLE has fascinated an enormous segment of humanity during the past many centuries to millennia. As esteemed American mythologist Joseph Campbell artfully implied, the Bible has been perceived widely as a sacrosanct subject that alone among

---

[1] Translator Lightfoot (1.1) combines two different sources here. The first part can be found in Stehelin (1.39). The latter part is from Wagenseil (516): *Alii dicunt, utut quis maxime Scripturam & Mischnam ad didicerit, si tamen Sapientibus non ministraverit, nihilo minus pro plebejo habendus. Caeterum qui solam Scripturam sine Mischnam didicit, bardus est...*

[2] In the Jewish text called the Talmud, the Gemara (גמרא) represents commentary and analysis of what is called the "Mishnah," existing in two versions, one published in 350-400 and another in 500 AD/CE. Also part of the Talmud and called the "Oral Torah," the "learning" and the "second law," the Mishna or Mishnah (משנה) constitutes a written composition based on oral debates between Jewish sages/rabbis from the first century BCE to the second AD/CE, redacted around 200 or 220 by Rabbi Yehudah haNasi. Jewish tradition claims that, like the Torah, the Mishnah was "delivered to Moses on Mount Sinai." (Barclay, 1) The 63 tractates of the Mishnah explicate biblical laws, rituals and traditions, such as concerns religious festivals and the status of women.

[3] This translation by lay Egyptologist Gerald Massey (2007:2.184), who cited the passage as appearing in *Contra Celsus* (4.1), is paraphrased from a lengthier exposition specifically on the Egyptian, Persian, Syrian and Indian priests and vulgar masses. (See my *Study Guide for Did Moses Exist?* for the full quote from Origen.)

[4] This translation is from the English rendering of Dupuis, 226. For another translation from the Arabic, see Maimonides/Friedländer, 211.

the world's religious literature and traditions must be treated as if it has no mythology in it.[1] In accepting various implausible if not impossible biblical tales as "history," we are asked likewise to agree that the ancient Hebrews, Israelites and Jews had no mythology whatsoever, whereas practically all other ancient cultures on Earth assuredly have possessed mythology to one degree or another.

In reality, ancient Jewish priests, intellectuals, scribes and bards most certainly did engage in mythmaking, and, as it turns out and as one might have supposed logically, the biblical stories about the Israelite lawgiver Moses rate as chief among these allegorical efforts. Because of this fact and the popularity of the biblical stories, there exists a great need to peer clearly and without blinkers at these tales, in order to analyze their origin and meaning; hence, the purpose for this present work.

The Book of Enoch and Talmud

To discover whether or not ancient Jews were engaged in mythmaking, we need only look at various non-biblical Jewish texts, such as 1 and 2 Enoch (c. 300 BCE-1st cent. AD/CE), with their bizarre, supernatural and otherworldly tales.[2] Very few scholars of today or yesteryear would argue that the adventures of the Old Testament patriarch Enoch (Gen 5:18) in these texts or other Enochian writings record "history" or "biography." The Enochian revelations represent obvious mythmaking, as do several other apocryphal and intertestamental texts.

This same fiction-writing can be found in the prominent Jewish text called the Talmud (c. 200-500 AD/CE):

> ...The Talmud informs us that "a young unicorn one day old is as large as Mount Tabor." Consequently Noah had great difficulty in saving an old one alive. He could not get it into the ark, so he bound it by its horn to the side of the ark. At the same time Og, King of Bashan (being one of the antediluvians), was saved by riding on its back. We are further informed that he was one of the giants who came from the intermarriage of angels with the daughters of men. His footsteps were forty miles long, and one of his teeth served to make a couch for Abraham. When the Israelites came against him under the command of Moses, he inquired the size of their camp, and hearing that it was three miles in extent he tore up a mountain of that size to hurl it upon them. Grasshoppers were, however, sent to bore holes in it, so that it fell over his head on to his neck. His teeth also grew and were entangled in the rocks, as the Psalmist says, "Thou hast broken the teeth of the ungodly" (Ps. [3:7]). He is

---

[1] Campbell, 141. See discussion in text below.
[2] Enoch's "prophecies" are mentioned in the New Testament book of Jude (1:14), in a reference that appears to be citing the known Book of Enoch, which is pseudepigraphic and not written by the OT prophet.

also said to be identical with Eliezer the servant of Abraham, and to have been, like Enoch, translated to Paradise.[1]

This tale is farfetched to say the least, and, as the Talmudic text called the Gemara suggests, we would be "blockheads" to understand it literally. As it turns out, the same can be said of the supernatural and miraculous story of Moses and the Exodus, neither of which entities finds its place in the historical record but exists only in the Bible.

In this regard, famed Jewish philosopher Baruch Spinoza (1632-1677) "looked with a cold eye on the myths of the Hebrews but accepted them as 'extremely necessary...for the masses whose wits are not potent enough to perceive things clearly and distinctly.'"[2]

In addition, a favorite Roman adage was *Vulgus vult decipi; ergo, decipiatur.* "The common people want to be deceived; therefore, let them be deceived."[3]

Comparative Religion Suppressed

As we examine the facts in this book, we may be tempted to ask why this important information is not known better in the world at large. Why are not the tales of the Akkadian king Sargon, the Mesopotamian demigod Gilgamesh and the Greek god Dionysus, for example, which resemble those of Moses, taught from the pulpit and in seminaries, Bible colleges and universities, alongside with the biblical stories?

By revealing the myths behind biblical stories, particularly that of Moses, we are not simply tearing down supposed "history" but also restoring the lost, hidden or suppressed mythology and religious ideas and traditions of other cultures. We are a lopsided world religiously, as a significant part of the globe is under the domination of intolerant monotheism that has swallowed up much local color. This destruction of indigenous communities and their cultural traditions is unfortunate and should be rectified, particularly for the sake of the harmony with our natural surroundings, the source of much of the world's great religious traditions.

Meaningful Mythology

In this regard, few of the facts casting doubt upon the historicity of various biblical figures are known to the populace, who do not benefit from reading ancient texts in their original languages, context and milieu. Nevertheless, one need not throw out the baby with the bathwater and simply dismiss these traditions because they are myth, as myth is not meaningless. Quite the opposite is true,

---

[1] Barclay, 23.
[2] Allen, D., 301.
[3] An alternate rendering is: *Mundus vult decipi, ergo decipiatur*—"The world wants to be deceived; thus, let it be deceived."

because myth is pregnant with meaning, more so than is understood, despite the extraordinary efforts of such thinkers as Joseph Campbell and so many others.

Here I will discuss not only the lack of historicity to these biblical tales—that analysis is merely the beginning—but also the lost, hidden or suppressed meanings behind the myths, wherever possible. The path is not always clear, because of the massive destruction of past cultures, including and especially by the megalomaniacal and fanatical monotheism out of the Levant[1] that spread throughout Europe and beyond, destroying and devouring much in its path. We certainly can make the effort not only to enlighten ourselves as to the connotation of the ancient religion and mythology but also to provide some justice for the attempted annihilation of non-monotheistic cultures globally.

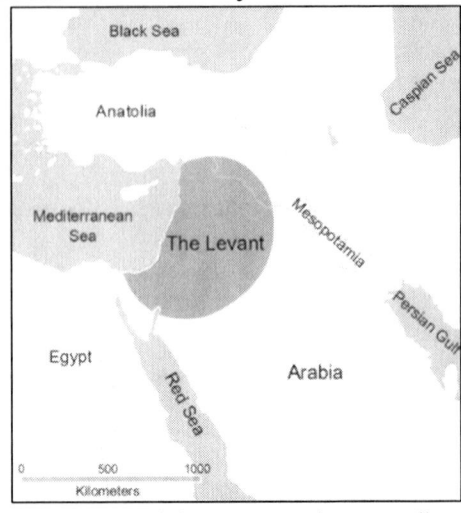

Fig. 1. Map of the Levant and surrounding areas (after MapMaster)

Primary Sources and Translations

The present work provides a few excerpts from several of my other books but mostly new material, including quotes from both primary sources and the works of credentialed scholars in relevant fields. In my citations and bibliography appear numerous ancient sources such as the Bible, Anacreon, Apollodorus, Aristides, Aristophanes, Arrian, Cicero, Clement of Alexandria, Diodorus, Euripides, Eusebius, Herodotus, Hesiod, Homer, Josephus, Justin Martyr, Megasthenes, Origen, Ovid, Pausanias, Pindar, Plato, Plutarch, Porphyry, Seneca, Strabo, Varro, Virgil and others, often in the original languages, mostly Greek, Hebrew and Latin. There is a reason these ancient texts are called "classics," as they retain their worth despite their great age. Hence, it is not the age of a text or lack thereof alone that determines its value.

I also discuss texts and words in Akkadian, Arabic, Assyrian, Babylonian, Canaanite, Phoenician, Ugaritic and other Semitic languages, along with Egyptian, Sumerian, Vedic and Sanskrit. As concerns my original translations herein, breaking with the past tradition of flowery, poetic language designed to reproduce the "feel" of a composition, and in line with more current methodology, I have

---

[1] The term "Levant" is used to designate the land in the east Mediterranean comprising Israel, the Palestinian territories, Lebanon, Syria, southern Turkey and Jordan.

rendered texts so that the lay reader will be able to see the correspondent words and learn the language in question for him or herself. Note also in this regard that I have chosen to include Hebrew consonants only, without vowel points, in order to simplify the text for the reader, who is reminded that Hebrew is written from right to left.

Pioneering Scholarship

In this process, I have employed the most modern works from experts in relevant fields by the best publishers in English, such as E.J. Brill, de Gruyter, Routledge and major universities and colleges. In several instances, quotes from an earlier era of scholars and researchers are juxtaposed with the words of more modern scholars, to demonstrate how reliable were these older writers.

Indeed, many of the earlier scholars' perceptions remain remarkably accurate and insightful, confirmed and validated numerous times by discoveries in the historical and archaeological record since their time. This prior generation is thus validated in numerous of its perspectives and should not be dismissed automatically as "outdated," a specious generalization that deprecates both the older authorities and individuals capable of distinguishing between illogical, unscientific or incorrect contentions and those that are accurate, truthful and factual.[1]

In this same regard, the quotes at the top of each chapter are cited not as proofs but as premises, demonstrated by the rest of the chapter or book.

In the end, we can see from the contents of the current work that the previous generation of scholars often was intelligent and precise, with or without more modern discoveries and knowledge, in this case correctly surmising that Moses and the Exodus can be sustained as mythical tales, not as history.

Modern Discoveries

In general, when it comes to ancient and enduring mythology, major scientific breakthroughs do not happen very often, and much of what we know now we have understood since antiquity through the literary record and other artifacts. Of course, our knowledge is added to on a regular basis, with striking archaeological discoveries over the centuries, such as the Rosetta Stone, which opened up

---

[1] There has been a trend in the study of history, religion, mythology and archaeology to dismiss out of hand all research prior to the middle of the 20th century, except for primary sources, translations and, perhaps, excavation reports. In other words, according to this unscientific and illogical affectation, no conclusions, interpretations or insights by these earlier generations are valid, and thus should not be considered. One can only hope that future generations do not behave so rashly and irresponsibly with the works of *our* time, including blithely dismissing and disparaging those of current writers advocating this post-1950 methodology.

Egypt to the world as never before, or the Sumerian civilization, both of which finds have led to a tremendous amount of profound comparative-religion material.

Those discoveries occurred 150 to nearly 200 years ago, and our knowledge now, although still lacking because of the tremendous loss of culture over the *millennia*, is relatively solid as concerns numerous important aspects of ancient religion and mythology. The great volume of archaeological finds since the late 17th century until today has also led to a large amount of speculation, some of which indeed has been slightly or entirely inaccurate.[1]

Fig. 2. Rosetta Stone with Egyptian hieroglyphs, Demotic and Greek, c. 196 BCE. Louvre Museum, Paris

To reiterate, we also have seen verified significant insights from the pioneers and discoverers. Indeed, scholars have built entire paradigms upon these pioneers' work, and dismissing these respectable earlier authorities out of hand, therefore, is not advisable. Ignoring a massive body of literature that reflects the history of a particular subject, dating back thousands of years, does not make of one an expert in the field. On the contrary, such condescension merely makes one ignorant of the subject.

Space Consideration

The sources here are cited and annotated in over 1800 footnotes, with a bibliography of some 700 resources, drawing from eras of scholarship beginning thousands of years ago to today. Because this subject is so extensive, however, with a great deal of relevant literature composed over the past 2,500 years or so, this treatise could not be exhaustive on every issue but seeks to present the most scientific analyses in sum for the most part.

For example, entire monographs can be and have been written on the biblical "manna from heaven" or "Song of the Sea." Hopefully, I will be excused for any oversights within this vast body of scholarship.

Also because of such space constraints, I have not included a complete table of contents or the appendices. These features can be obtained, however, as a separate document by going to my website

---

[1] For example, many people today adhere to a form of von Danikenism or Sitchinism, the so-called Ancient Alien or Astronauts Theory. However, the major players in this paradigm, such as the Sumerian gods, are not aliens but astronomical or atmospheric entities or attributes, personified and anthropomorphized. For more information, see my book *Suns of God: Krishna, Buddha and Christ Unveiled* for a detailed study of the astronomical or astrotheological origins of religion and mythology.

DidMosesExist.com for *The Study Guide to Did Moses Exist?*, a PDF file.

In some places, repetition has been necessary, as in the chapter "The Dionysus Connection," a key piece of the puzzle that requires emphasis. Readers may skip this repetition and view this chapter as a reference resource.

Biblical quotes here are from the Revised Standard Version or "RSV," unless otherwise noted. Also included are 126 illustrations utilized according to United States' public domain, copyright and fair use laws.

Unprecedented Access

The need for this book highlighting the best and most scientific scholarship on this subject is great. Although past scholars in general have done an outstanding job with the tools they possessed, never before in history has there been such availability of data as we have today, with the internet and millions of texts in a variety of languages opened up to scholars globally. In this electronic era, we now have instant access at our fingertips to texts long lost in the bowels of collections in far-distant lands, as well as originals too precious to expose to the public, such as the Codex Sinaiticus, now available online for anyone with internet access.

Combine this unprecedented availability of data with a facility for languages, and it is likely that there has never been a volume quite like this one. This book is necessary in order to bring forth the lost information, which in reality has a very unifying effect on humanity, helping to transcend biases and prejudices that divide and separate us. One of the major cultural artifacts that separate us is religion. However, understanding the mythological, non-blockheaded meaning of religion can go a long way in increasing harmony among all the world's peoples.

D.M. Murdock
April 2014
U.S.A.

Fig. 3. King Og riding giant unicorn behind Noah's ark. (Landa, *Jewish Fairy Tales and Legends*, 30)

Fig. 4. Wise and learned giant frog, "fairy son" of Adam and Lilith found at Passover, "wrote out the Law" and taught Rabbi Hanina "the whole Torah." (Landa, *Jewish Fairy Tales and Legends*, 252)

Introduction

"The existence of Moses as well as the veracity of the Exodus story is disputed amongst archaeologists and Egyptologists, with experts in the field of biblical criticism citing logical inconsistencies, new archaeological evidence, historical evidence and related origin myths in Canaanite culture."

"Moses," *Wikipedia*[1]

"We cannot be sure that Moses ever lived because there are no traces of his earthly existence outside of tradition."

Dr. Jan Assmann, *Moses the Egyptian* (2)

"There is no historical evidence outside of the Bible, no mention of Moses outside the Bible, and no independent confirmation that Moses ever existed."[2]

Dr. Michael D. Coogan, lecturer on the Old Testament at Harvard Divinity School

"The life of Moses contains elements—canonical and apocryphal—that mark him as a true mythic hero, and certainly he is Judaism's greatest hero and the central figure in Hebrew mythology."

Dr. David Leeming, *The Oxford Companion to World Mythology* (270)

"...the stories of the creation, of the flood, of Abraham, of Jacob, of the descent into and the exodus from Egypt, of the career of Moses and the Jews in the desert, of Joshua and his soldiers, of the judges and their clients, are all apocryphal, and were fabricated at a late period of Jewish history."

Dr. Thomas Inman, *Ancient Faiths and Modern* (5)

IN THE BIBLE, famed Israelite prophet Moses is credited with bringing the Hebrew slaves out of Egypt to the edge of the "Promised Land" of Israel, after supposedly taking 40 years to cross the Sinai Peninsula, a stretch of desert 130 miles or so wide. Before leaving Egypt, Moses is portrayed as performing various miracles with his magical rod, in order to defeat the Egyptian pharaoh so that the Hebrews can flee the country. While simultaneously hardening

---

[1] The citation of the internet resource Wikipedia.org serves to demonstrate that the current mainstream consensus leans towards Moses mythicism, evincing the lawgiver to be a mythical figure. The *Wikipedia* articles in the present work's bibliography are used as a starting point for research, because they often mention the most up-to-date scholarship, which then can be studied directly. These articles are not cited as authorities in themselves. Moreover, it should be recalled that the paragraphs at the beginning of chapters serve as summaries of the chapter's premise, which then will be demonstrated within the chapter using primary sources and the works of credentialed experts in relevant fields. It should be noted that *Wikipedia* changes regularly, and some of the wording therefore may be altered at some point from what can be found here. The statements are included here, however, because they are accurate, in our estimation.

[2] Quoted in Zalan, "Moses Is Revered by Three Faiths."

the pharaoh's heart, the biblical god Yahweh mercilessly sends a series of deadly supernatural plagues upon Egypt, massacring hundreds of thousands, including innocent men, women and children. Eventually, after the firstborn of all people and animals throughout Egypt are slaughtered, the remaining Egyptians beg the Israelites to leave, taking with them a mass of Egyptian gold, jewels and other booty.

Extrapolating from the number of 600,000 Israelite men alone, according to the Old Testament, a possible two to three million people are depicted as leaving Egypt, hunted by a fickle pharaoh's army. These millions of refugees narrowly escape after Moses supernaturally parts the Red Sea, which crashes down upon the pursuing Egyptians, drowning them. During the flight in the desert, God miraculously leads the Israelites with pillars of cloud and fire, and throughout the four-decade period in the wilderness, Yahweh supernaturally feeds this massive mob with "manna from heaven" and provides water that he magically purifies with wood and draws from rocks. From a perpetually burning bush, Yahweh also calls Moses upon Mt. Horeb, generally taken to be Mt. Sinai or a plateau thereupon, where with his almighty finger the Lord carves the Ten Commandments on two tablets of stone.

From these implausible tales and others, we can assert that, like other biblical figures, the Hebrew lawgiver appears to be not a historical person but a mythical character found in a number of cultures, significantly as an archetypal solar hero or deity.

The conclusion of Moses's mythical nature has been reached many times over the centuries, and, despite the continued fervent bibliolatry or Bible-worship, modern scholars basically have thrown their arms in the air while trying to salvage some historicity. For example, archaeologist Dr. William G. Dever attempts to be "theologically sensitive and responsible" by reconciling, "if possible, the probably mythical Moses of the texts with a possible Moses-like figure who may have been historical."[1] Referring to his article, "Is There Any Archaeological Evidence for the Exodus?," Dever further comments:

> On Moses as the putative "founder of the Israelite religion," see, e.g., Susan Niditch, *Ancient Israelite Religion...*, which barely mentions the possibility of a historical Moses...[2]

After centuries of Bible criticism and scientific analysis, today's scholars are disinclined to represent Moses as a historical personage. To their credit, numerous scholars of previous generations also were well aware of this doubtful historicity, centuries ago, having noticed the dearth of historical evidence and the preponderance of mythical and religious prototypes and parallels.

---

[1] Dever (2003), 235.
[2] Dever (2001), 99.

Greek Scriptural Knowledge?

In reality, there exist so many correspondences between paganism and the purported religion founded by Moses, Judaism, that not a few individuals beginning with the early Church fathers have attempted to claim that famous Greek philosophers, poets, mythographers and others in antiquity were familiar with the Old Testament.

For example, in noting the similarities between the Bible and the texts of Greek poet Homer (9th cent. BCE[1]), *The Iliad* and *Odyssey*, famed English explorer Sir Walter Raleigh (c. 1552-1618) wrote that "it cannot be doubted but that Homer had read over all the books of Moses, as by places stolen thence almost word for word may appear...."[2]

Despite this claim, which appears to be asserting that the Homeric epics plagiarized *verbatim* from the Hebrew books, there exists no hard, scientific evidence that the Homeric composer(s) had ever seen the Jewish texts. Although there are place-names and other appellations for Asian Minor locations, not one clear word in Hebrew, no Hebrew names of prophets, kings or otherwise, no Israelite locations, not even a Hebraistic phrase can be found in the Greek books. The only purpose for such a comparison is because the stories are similar, an admission we are certain to be true, for the simple reason that we are dealing not with "history" but with shared mythical archetypes.

Others who had seen these correspondences between Greek religion/philosophy and biblical tales included early Christian writers Justin Martyr (c. 100-c. 165 AD/CE), Tatian (c. 120-c. 180 AD/CE), Theophilus of Antioch (d. c. 183 AD/CE) and Clement Alexandrinus (c. 150-c. 215 AD/CE), who "were of the opinion that both Plato and Pythagoras had gone into Egypt to read the books of Moses."[3]

When the evidence is analyzed in detail, with as much data as possible, it appears that, rather than serving as a historical prophet and patriarch of the Jewish people, the figure of Moses represents a Judaic rendition of an archetype at the traditional basis of many nations. This fact of commonality in pre-biblical mythology may explain why the supposedly "historical" Israelite foundational story apparently was unknown until a few centuries before the beginning of the common era.

---

[1] The present work uses the abbreviation "BCE" for "Before the Common Era," denoting the time period commonly styled "B.C." or "Before Christ." For the period designated "Anno Domini," I have employed the phrase AD/CE, "CE" standing for "Common Era." The abbreviation in dates of "fl." stands for "flourished," referring to the period in which a ruler or other authority was in power. The abbreviation "b." connotes "born," while "d." means "died."

[2] Raleigh, 1.195.

[3] Allen, D., 21.

Philo Judaeus of Alexandria

By the time of Jewish writer Philo of Alexandria (20 BCE–50 AD/CE), Moses either was ignored widely or disparaged by non-Jewish cultures, such that the philosopher felt the need to write an extended biography of the lawgiver. Philo provides a lengthy and detailed account of Moses's "life," drawing from the Bible and other sources, but also apparently relying on his own imagination, engaging in the Jewish practice of interpreting or adding to texts called "midrash."[1]

In his attempt at raising Moses above all other divine prophets of antiquity, Philo (*Moses* 62-63) discusses the reasons for a king to serve as "shepherd" of his people and claims Moses was the "most skillful herdsman of his time."[2] In other words, the Jewish lawgiver was the greatest shepherd of his day who could lead his flock expertly, a skill valued in that era and location.

In his account exalting the Jewish lawgiver, Philo (23) also relates of Moses that "philosophers taught him Assyrian literature,"[3] indicating the connection between biblical traditions and that culture. Moreover, the Jewish apologist (*Moses* 2.3.12) brags that the patriarch is the greatest of all lawgivers and his law the most divine,[4] demonstrating that there were other lawgivers and laws in other cultures before Philo's time.

Philo's inflation of Moses's character is unrelenting, obviously designed to make of the Israelite legislator a more moral and formidable figure than any other man since his time, so great that the one and only God of the cosmos—eschewing all other great men and women of old—spoke directly to this superior man and bestowed upon him the highest honors. Philo (*Moses* 2.51.288) even goes so far as to claim that the patriarch is serving immortally in heaven with Yahweh, ruling the world and commanding the elements![5]

History or Propaganda?

Philo was a member of what has been claimed to be the wealthiest family in the Roman Empire, and thereby one of the most powerful. Philo's brother, Alexander the Alabarch (10 BCE-? AD/CE), was a builder of the Jerusalem temple, while the writer's nephew, Tiberias Julius Alexander (10-70 AD/CE), served as a procurator of Judea and later a prefect of Egypt. After inheriting the Alabarch's fortune, Tiberias later helped the Roman emperors Vespasian (9-79 AD/CE) and Titus (39-91 AD/CE), along with the Jewish general and

---

[1] Dictionary.com, based on *Random House Dictionary*, defines "midrash" as "an early Jewish interpretation of or commentary on a Biblical text, clarifying or expounding a point of law or developing or illustrating a moral principle."
[2] Philo/Yonge (2000), 465.
[3] Philo/Yonge (2000), 461.
[4] Philo/Yonge (2000), 492.
[5] Philo/Yonge (2000), 517.

historian Josephus (37-100 AD/CE), to destroy his father's sacred building.

Because of the enormous financial resources, Philo's works—very large and expensive to produce—apparently were disseminated widely during his lifetime, a fairly rare occurrence that only happened with a well-oiled and extensive distribution system, such as a brotherhood network, including the various collegia, sodalicia and other fraternities around the Mediterranean.[1]

These texts were highly influential on the Christian effort, which patently built upon many Philonic notions, themselves in turn representing a synthesis of Judaism and paganism, specifically Platonism in significant part, the philosophical system named for the renowned Athenian thinker Plato (428/427-348/347 BCE). It is clear that Philo's campaign on behalf of the Jewish *genos* or "race," as he calls it,[2] and its religion, including Moses as the great lawgiver, was extremely successful, as many of Judaism's ideas have been spread around the world via Christianity, which holds up Moses as one of the greatest men of God who ever lived.

Magical Papyri

Indicating how successful was his expensive propaganda campaign, after Philo's time there erupted great interest in Moses, with a number of magical papyri written in his name, such as the "Eighth Book of Moses." This book comprises several earlier texts, such as the "Key of Moses" and "The Hidden Book of Moses on the Great Name, that for Everything, in which is the Name of the One Who Rules All."[3] Any complaint that the Jewish lawgiver was being ignored or derogated obviously was remedied.

It is noteworthy that, in these magical texts, the Jewish tribal god is invoked as "Iao," the Hellenized version of the Semitic Yahweh, as likewise identified by the Greco-Sicilian writer Diodorus Siculus (1.94) in the first century BCE. Also in these writings appear pagan gods and goddesses likewise beseeched and syncretized with the Jewish prophets.

Mythological, Not Historical

Despite ongoing efforts to anchor it into history, the Bible constitutes a cultural artifact containing large swathes of mythology and some history that should be viewed on the same level as the mythological and historical accounts of other cultures, not a

---

[1] See Murdock (2009), 438ff, etc.
[2] In "On the Confusion of Languages" (De Confusione Linguarum/Περι συγχυσεως διαλεκτων 20), Philo writes about Moses as from τὸ θεοφιλὲς γένος or "the god-loved genus." *Oxford Classical Greek Dictionary* (68) defines γένος genos as: "birth, descent, race, family, kindred; descendant, child; sex, gender; one's own country; kind, species; generation; a tribe (subdivision of a phatry)."
[3] See, e.g., Bromiley, 4.217.

sacrosanct subject to be raised above all others. Let us therefore give the biblical authors leeway and accept that the Jewish authorities quoted at the beginning of this chapter are correct in asserting that there is much allegory in the Bible. Essentially, therefore, to believe in the book as literal is the sign of a "blockhead," again as the Talmudic text the Gemara states.

For example, among the numerous biblical implausibilities stands out the description of God at Exodus 24:9-10:

> Then went up Moses, and Aaron, Nadab, and Abihu, and seventy of the elders of Israel: And they saw the God of Israel: and [there was] under his feet as it were a paved work of a sapphire stone, and as it were the body of heaven in [his] clearness.

Are we to believe this scene represents a historical occurrence? Yet, at John 1:18, we read: "No one has ever seen God,"[1] and at 1 John 4:12, it is asserted: "No man has ever seen God."[2] How can we reconcile this apparent contradiction with the verse in Exodus above, along with many others in which Moses, his older brother, Aaron, and others convene with the Lord in the tabernacle or tent for the divine presence? Do these passages truly represent history?

The Mysterious Milieu of the Day

In an analysis of what transpired in antiquity, it is important to know as much as possible about the milieu or environment of the place and era. In this quest, we need to study not only Jewish and Christian texts and history but also those of the many other relevant cultures, such as ringed the Mediterranean and beyond, east into India and as far west as Ireland. When Bible enthusiasts exhort us that we need to read the holy texts in their original languages, they often do not know precisely what they are advocating, because, in doing so, immediately we will be struck by the commonalities in language between the Judeo-Christian and pagan ideologies.

Indeed, when the Greek of the Bible and patristic writings is examined, we can see numerous terms used in pre-Judaic and pre-Christian philosophy, religion, mythology and mysteries. For example, one Greek word for "mysteries," τελεταί *teletai*, appears in a variety of forms many times in the writings of Greek-speaking pagans, such as Andocides, Aristides, Aristophanes, Aristotle, Demosthenes, Dio Chrysostom, Diodorus, Dionysius, Euripides, Herodotus, Isocrates, Josephus, Julian, Lucian, Pausanias, Pindar, Plato, Plutarch, Strabo and others.

The Sacred Sanctuary

The word *teletai* is also used in the Greek Old Testament or Septuagint ("LXX"), to describe, for instance, the "sanctuaries of

---

[1] Θεὸν οὐδεὶς ἑώρακεν πώποτε
[2] Θεὸν οὐδεὶς πώποτε τεθέαται.

INTRODUCTION

Israel" (Amos 7:9): αἱ τελεταὶ τοῦ Ισραηλ. The original Hebrew rendered *teletai* in the LXX is מִקְדָּשׁ *miqdash,* meaning:

1) sacred place, *sanctuary,* holy place
   a) sanctuary
      1) of the temple
      2) of the tabernacle
      3) of Ezekiel's temple
      4) of Jehovah[1]

The Hebrew word *miqdash* is also rendered "holy place," "chapel" and "hallowed place."

In the biblical book of Ezekiel, the prophet (c. 622-c. 570 BCE?) has a strange vision of the Jerusalem temple, in which appears a detailed discussion of the mysteries held there involving peculiar beasts and other elements that resemble typical pagan worship, as concerns the Babylonians, Canaanites and Egyptians, for example. The term *miqdash* or "sanctuary" appears many times in Ezekiel, more than any other book of the Bible, rendered in the LXX as, for example, τὰ ἅγιά μου or "my holy things."[2]

Miqdash is not translated again in the Greek OT or Septuagint as *teletai,* however, and various forms of *teletai* have been used to render terms other than *miqdash,* such as 1 Kings 15:12, in which the phrase τὰς τελετὰς is employed to describe the קְדֵשִׁים *qadeshim* or "male cult prostitutes."

Qadesh in Ugaritic

The word *qadesh* appears in the Northwest Semitic language of Ugaritic, as *qdš,* meaning "holy" and used in reference to the god Ilu, "head of the Ugaritic pantheon and father of mankind and the gods."[3] Obvious cognates of the god-name Ilu are El and Allah.

Comparable to Canaanite and related to Hebrew, Ugaritic is from the area now known as Ras Shamra, Syria, where were discovered thousands of texts dating from the 12th to 14th centuries BCE. The pantheon and religion discussed in the texts are Canaanite and share many commonalities with biblical traditions. Scholars differentiate between Canaanite and Ugaritic, as there exist subtle distinctions between the cultures and languages, but both belong to the Northwest Semitic family, along with Amorite, Hebrew and Phoenician.[4]

We further discover that Qdš is the name of a Semitic goddess mentioned in Egyptian texts of the Ramesside period and that this term, *qdš,* is identified possibly with Ilu's consort, the Canaanite goddess Aṭiratu (compare, Ashtar, Ishtar, Asherah).[5] The plural word

---

[1] Strong's H4720.
[2] See, e.g., Ezek 5:11, 8:6, 9:6, 21:7; 23:38-9, etc.
[3] Rahmouni, 208.
[4] Rainey (1965), 107.
[5] Rahmouni, 208.

qadeshim is related also to the Arabic *quddūsun* or "All Holy."[1] The tradition of *qadeshim* as male temple prostitutes may extend well back into pre-Israelite times.[2]

As we can see, placing the various Bible stories into their proper context reveals much about Jewish worship, including the fact that the faith did not arise in a vacuum but was highly influenced by or dependent upon the traditions of the pre-Israelite peoples, such as the Canaanites, including the residents of the cosmopolitan city of Ugarit. Indeed, so obvious is this influence that, assuming Moses to be a historical personage, scholars of the past concluded, "Moses quoted some heathen Canaanite poetry."[3]

In this same regard, biblical and Near Eastern studies scholar Dr. William M. Schniedewind remarks that a number of biblical Psalms, such as Ps 29, "borrow quite directly from Canaanite literature, as we now perceive through our study of Ugaritic literature."[4]

Many Lawgivers and Law Codes

Rather than serving as that of a historical Hebrew prophet, the legend of the divine lawgiver is found in germ around Europe and Africa, as well as the Near, Middle and Far East, as are other biblical tales. In this archetype, the main character possesses different names, races and ethnicities, depending on the locale: "Menu" is the Indian legislator;[5] "Mises" appears in Syria and Egypt, where also the first king, "Menes the lawgiver," takes the stage;[6] "Minos" is the Cretan reformer;[7] and "Mannus" the Teutonic lawgiver.[8]

Moreover, the Ten Commandments represent the Jewish version of the Babylonian Code of Hammurabi, the *Egyptian Book of the Dead* and other texts. Like Moses, other figures such as Sargon the Great and the Indian son of the sun god, Karna, were placed by their mothers

Fig. 5. Egyptian lawgiver Menes (?) on Narmer Palette, c. 2925–c. 2775 BCE. Siltstone tablet, Egyptian Museum, Cairo

---

[1] Rahmouni, 209.
[2] While the Bible gives the impression of the Canaanites as licentious, it is claimed that "there is no evidence of sacred prostitution in ancient Canaanite cities." ("Canaanite religion," *Wikipedia*)
[3] Allen, D., 39, discussing the work in the 17th century by the priest Louis Thomassin.
[4] Schniedewind, 28.
[5] See, e.g., Franklin, Ketkar. Variant transliterations are "Manu" and "Manou."
[6] Bennett, 2.121; *Journal of the North China Branch of the Royal Asiatic Society*, 8-9:24. Variations include "Men" and "Manes."
[7] See, e.g., Rollin, 438.
[8] Tacitus, *Germania* (2); *JNCBRAS*, 24.

in reed boats and set adrift in a river, to be discovered by others.[1]

This identification of Moses with other lawgivers was recognized in antiquity. As Johns Hopkins professor Dr. Don Cameron Allen says, "The historian Diodorus Siculus and the geographer Strabo associate the Hebrew lawgiver with Mercurius, Minos, Lycurgus, Amphiaraus, Orpheus, Musaeus, Zamolxis and other leaders and prophets of various shades of respectability."[2]

In *The World's Great Religion Leaders*, Francis Potter includes the lawgiver archetype in his summary of the mythicist case or mythicism[3] concerning Moses:

> The reasons for doubting his existence include, among others, (1) the parallels between the Moses stories and older ones like that of Sargon, (2) the absence of any Egyptian account of such a great event as the Pentateuch asserts the Exodus to have been, (3) the attributing to Moses of so many laws that are known to have originated much later, (4) the correlative fact that great codes never suddenly appear full-born but are slowly evolved, (5) the difficulties of fitting the slavery, the Exodus, and the conquest of Canaan into the known chronology of Egypt and Palestine, and (6) the extreme probability that some of the twelve tribes were never in Egypt at all.[4]

The Pentateuch refers to the first five books of the Bible, also called the Torah or the Humash, the latter from the Hebrew word for "five," comprising Genesis, Exodus, Leviticus, Numbers and Deuteronomy.

We would add to this list the dearth of archaeological evidence for the Exodus of possibly three million people spread around a 130-mile-wide desert, in spite of numerous attempts over the centuries by archaeologists and the faithful alike to find such artifacts.

Jewish and Pagan Syncretism

In our quest, we must keep in mind the syncretism or merging together of divine figures, such as these various lawgivers, practiced not only by pagans with their numerous gods and goddesses but also by Jews. Regarding the Greco-Roman period (332 BCE-284 AD/CE), for example, British New Testament scholar Dr. Ralph P. Martin (1925-2013) and American theologian Rev. Dr. Peter H. Davids state:

> Nowhere is syncretism illustrated more clearly than in the magical and astrological beliefs of the era. In this realm, power takes precedence over personality. Commitment to one deity or fidelity to one cult gives way to rituals of power that work. Thus many gods and goddesses could be invoked at the same time by one person. Yahweh (or Iao) could be invoked in the same breath as Artemis and

---

[1] Buitenen, 779.
[2] Allen, D., 107.
[3] A part of mythicism is the perspective that, rather than representing historical figures, certain prominent biblical characters may be mythical in nature, including Abraham, Elijah, Jesus, Joshua, Moses, Noah and possibly David and Solomon, et al.
[4] Potter, 27-8.

Hekate. Palestinian and diaspora Jews participated in this form of syncretism. Numerous Jewish magical amulets, spells and astrological documents attest to the prevalence of syncretistic Jewish magic.[1]

It is by just this sort of syncretism, we submit, that the Moses figure was created, along with other biblical characters, including Noah, Abraham, Joshua and Jesus.

Major Crossing

As concerns the spread of ideas in this particular region, it should be recalled throughout this book that the corridor via the Sinai and Red Sea area has represented one of the main avenues by which mankind has passed from Africa to the rest of the world. As such, it is estimated that humanity has been traversing this very region for at least 70,000 years, with constant traffic along the Mediterranean coast from Egypt to the Black Sea and points east and west.

As part of this route, the Nile Valley has been occupied by humans for many thousands of years, with current paleoanthropological studies revealing "campsites of the period 16,000 to about 9000 B.C. of a community subsisting on intensive hunting and fishing."[2]

In Israel, we find Neanderthal remains from 45,000 years ago, as well as very ancient *Homo sapiens* fossils.[3] In Asia Minor and the Near East in general appear several extremely archaic archaeological sites, such as at Çatalhöyük (c. 9,000 BP[4]) and Göbekli Tepe (c. 10-13,000 BP) in Turkey, as well as the earliest strata of sites such as the village of Jericho, dating to around 10,000 years ago, populated by a people called by anthropologists "Natufians."[5] Prior to that

Fig. 6. Prehistoric bull carving, c. 15,000 BP. Stele from Gobekli Tepe, Turkey (after Teomancimit)

---

[1] Martin, 1147.
[2] Redford (1992), 5.
[3] A 45,000-year-old Neanderthal skull was discovered in 1961 at Amud, Israel, by Hisashi Suzuki. Researchers at Tel Aviv University claim to have found *Homo sapiens* teeth at Qesem cave near Rosh Ha'ayin, Israel, that date to some 400,000 years ago. The contention remains controversial, however, as the current mainstream evolutionary paradigm suggests humankind arose some 200,000 years ago, a figure that may be pushed back. (See Daniel Estrin's "Have the oldest human remains been found in Israel?")
[4] The abbreviation BP refers to "Before Present," representing the number of "years ago."
[5] Mann, "Gobekli Tepe: The Birth of Religion": "In the Levant—the area that today encompasses Israel, the Palestinian territories, Lebanon, Jordan, and western Syria—

ethnicity was the "highly nomadic" Stone Age culture styled "Kebaran," named for the Kebara Cave, south of Haifa, Israel, where human cultural remains have been found dating from around 18,000 to 12,500 BCE.

What would be surprising is if any group, tribe or culture in that region arose in isolation, in consideration of this long history of crisscrossing the region by numerous peoples since remote antiquity. Crossing the Red Sea region at some point or another thus appears to have been a common migration route for tens of thousands of years by numerous tribes of people.

Egypt and the Levant

As might be expected, during this millennia-long migration period, a relationships and clashes developed between several civilizations, cultures and ethnicities of the region. Regarding archaic interaction between the Levant and Egypt, Egyptologist Dr. Donald B. Redford remarks:

> Evidence of Egyptian involvement in the affairs of Palestine and Syria during the 1st and 2nd Dynasties is unmistakable. In the surviving fragments of annals from the reigns of the immediate successors of Menes, one often encounters an entry such as "smiting the Asiatics," or "first occasion of smiting the east," as an identifying event by which to designate a year. Artistic motifs sometimes incorporate a shaggy-haired, kilted foreigner, with arms manacled, who is glossed by the simple hieroglyphs for "Asia." And the archaeological record confirms the textual evidence. First Dynasty cenotaphs from Abydos throw up clear examples of Early Bronze (EB) II pottery [3000-2700 BCE], and attest to the use of Lebanese timber in their construction....[1]

That Egyptians were attracted to the region of southern Palestine and Sinai is beyond question. Most prominent in the surviving record looms the turquoise- and copper-rich terrain of western Sinai, as at Serabit el-Khadim, where for nearly two thousand years from the early third millennium BCE the Egyptians expended immense energies in the mining and transportation of these minerals.[2]

Byblos

The relationship between Egypt and the northern coastal Levantine people later called "Phoenicians" began possibly 6,000 or more years ago. Redford calls these early Phoenicians "Byblians," after their most renowned city of Byblos, called "Gebal" in Semitic,

---

archaeologists had discovered settlements dating as far back as 13,000 B.C. Known as Natufian villages (the name comes from the first of these sites to be found), they sprang up across the Levant as the Ice Age was drawing to a close, ushering in a time when the region's climate became relatively warm and wet."
[1] Redford (1992), 33.
[2] Redford (1992), 33-34.

situated in order to exploit the famed cedars of Lebanon. In this regard, the Egyptologist remarks:

> Byblos in the third millennium dominated that part of the coast from which access to the forest was easiest, and thus it comes as no surprise that the Byblians should have become both excellent seafarers and shrewd timber merchants.
>
> Precisely when contact was established between Egypt and Byblos is not known, but the date must have been very early indeed. Byblian tradition took pride in the belief that it was the oldest city in the world, founded by El, high god of the Canaanite pantheon; and the French operations at the site have revealed a Neolithic stratum.[1]

The use of the timber from the Lebanese cedars was vital to the building programs of Egypt, one aspect of sustained exchange between the Egyptians and the Byblians over a period of centuries to millennia. At Hierakonpolis, one of Egypt's oldest known temples, a sanctuary of the Egyptian god Horus, was built with massive Lebanese cedars.[2]

Egypto-Semitic Religious Exchange

The influence from Egypt to Byblos is also laid plain, with Egyptian architectural motifs in Phoenician buildings and the myths of the two cultures intertwined, as in the story of the Egyptian goddess Isis seeking the slain god Osiris's body parts at Byblos.[3] A counterpart of Isis, the Egyptian goddess Hathor too was a favorite of the Byblians, originally appearing as Astarte[4] or Astoreth, and so on.

Concerning the theological exchange, Redford remarks:

> The pantheon of the Phoenicians gives prominence of place to a god "Taut" who is none other than the Egyptian god of writing Thoth; and the Canaanite craftsman god Kothar is said to have his seat in HKPT—that is, Ḥwt-kз -Ptḥ, "Memphis."[5]

Found in the texts from Ebla, Syria, dating to around 2250 BCE, Kothar or Kuṭaru is a very ancient "craftsman god,"[6] a role assumed by the gospel Jesus when he is said to be a "carpenter" or *tekton*. Kothar or *kṯr* in the Ugaritic texts and *kašāru* in Akkadian also means "skillful," cognate with the Hebrew כשר *kasher/kosher*.[7]

The Egyptian name for the city of Memphis literally translates as "Temple of the Ka of Ptah," this latter term the moniker of the craftsman, mason and carpenter god. It is logical for the Byblians to take interest in the craftsman or carpenter god, in consideration of

---

[1] Redford (1992), 38.
[2] Holst, 31.
[3] See, e.g., Griffiths, 28.
[4] Redford (1992), 45.
[5] Redford (1992), 40.
[6] Emerton, 131. Another Ugaritic term for "craftsman" is *ḥrš* or *ḥarrāšu*, cognate with the Hebrew חרש *charash* (H2796).
[7] Schniedewind, 195; Strong's H3787.

their role as suppliers of the most desired wood around the Mediterranean, used for ships and temples in particular.[1]

Moreover, the well-known Semitic god Baal, Ba'al or Balu, a meteorological deity controlling weather and storms,[2] was compared in antiquity with the Egyptian crocodile deity Arsaphes, and with the Greco-Phoenician god Herakles, two millennia later,[3] among others.

The close relationship between the Byblians and Egyptians lasted from at least the fourth millennium BCE until Roman times, producing significant cultural exchange, including technology, language and religion.

Osiris in Jerusalem

The Egyptian cultural exchange extended to many other Semitic and Near Eastern peoples as well, including those who became the Israelites. In this regard, the pre-Israelite and Amoritish city of Jerusalem also hosted an Egyptian temple.[4] During separate studies, Israeli archaeologist Dr. Gabriel Barkay and biblical archaeologist Dr. Peter van der Veen discovered a number of Egyptian artifacts in Judaism's holiest city, including "statues, architectural elements and texts attesting to their presence in the city."[5]

One of these artifacts contains an inscription mentioning "the illuminated Osiris."[6] Another is a red granite statue of an Egyptian queen, dating to the 13th century BCE, while other statues of the Egyptian war and healing goddess, Sekhmet, have been found also at Jerusalem, including in early Iron Age strata.[7]

By the time King David purportedly conquered the city, sometime between 1000 and 800 BCE, the Egyptians seem to have disappeared, leaving the outpost vulnerable to the Israelites. As van der Veen comments, "In short, the Egyptians apparently ruled the area in the period before the Israelites consolidated their grip on the central highlands during Iron Age I (1200–1000 B.C.E.)."[8]

In this same regard, van der Veen remarks that the "Jerusalem highlands were an ideal hideout for bandits and soldiers of fortune; the Egyptian garrison at Manahat was no doubt an effort to control them."[9] Situated some two miles southwest of Jerusalem, Manahat was a fortified village where archaeologists unearthed scarabs from

---

[1] For a discussion of the carpenter-god motif, see my books *Suns of God* (298-299, 366-368), and *Christ in Egypt* (210-211).
[2] See, e.g., Rahmouni, 131.
[3] Redford (1992), 45.
[4] See Barkay's "What's an Egyptian Temple Doing in Jerusalem?" and van der Veen's "When Egyptian Pharaohs Ruled Bronze Age Jerusalem."
[5] Wiener.
[6] van der Veen (2013), 48.
[7] van der Veen (2013), 45.
[8] van der Veen (2013), 48.
[9] van der Veen (2013), 44.

the pharaohs Amenophis/Amenhotep III (d. 1353 BCE) and Ramesses II (1303-1213 BCE).

It would appear, therefore, that the bandits and brigands of the highlands—the eventual Israelites—waited for an opportunity to conquer the city after the Egyptian forces had left. Jerusalem held strategic value, and it would provide a financial boon to these semi-nomadic peoples, much like the important merchant city of Constantinople provided its Muslim conquerors centuries later.

Differences Irrelevant

Throughout this present work, we will be discussing comparative religion and numerous parallels between the Bible and the mythology of preceding cultures. Along with commonalities created through cultural exchange, this field of study also recognizes the differences between the various belief systems analyzed. Of course, there will always be dissimilarities, because legends and myths are highly organic and have much to do with era and location, milieu and environment, as well as culture, ethnicity, race, gender, climate, flora, fauna and so on.

Therefore, no one is claiming that all aspects of a myth are lifted wholesale and transferred to another time and culture. If these aspects were plagiarized entirely, they would constitute the exact same myth, and there would be no need to do comparative mythological studies of them in the first place.

The contention is not being made that the myths were copied or plagiarized wholesale. What we are asserting is that popular religious, spiritual and mythological ideas often float between cultures during contacts of a wide variety, from conquest of peoples to cross-cultural royal marriages, deliberate exchanges between educated priesthoods and traveling merchants, as well as the lowliest illiterate slaves sharing their faiths with each other. Among the masses, naturally, there will be a set of attributes, practices, doctrines and so on that appeal to the less scholarly and intellectual, as noted in the quotes above discussing one understanding for initiates and the other for the common people. These exoteric and esoteric mysteries include very basic understandings, as well as profound philosophical ideas and wisdom.

To illustrate how syncretism works, we use dressmaker's patterns to create clothing, the expression of which may differ from place to place and era to era, but the pattern remains the same. In the same manner, human beings typically have two arms, two legs, a head and a torso; however, their skin color and various other characteristics differ around the world. Nevertheless, they are all still human beings. The same thing can be said of the basic pattern or archetype of religious and mythological ideas.

INTRODUCTION

Biblical Special Pleading

In any event, we know that religions are constantly trading attributes with one another; hence, the special pleading when it comes to the Bible and its singularly sacrosanct subjects constitutes a fallacy. As previously noted, mythologist Joseph Campbell knew that major biblical tales, such as that of Moses and the Exodus, were mythical. In his book *Occidental Mythology*, following a discussion of the Bible, Campbell turns to the "Gods and Heroes of the European West," and says, with apparent resentment:

> Fortunately, it will not be necessary to argue that Greek, Celtic or Germanic myths were mythological. The peoples themselves knew they were myths, and the European scholars discussing them have not been overborne by the idea of something uniquely holy about their topic.[1]

The people themselves knew they were myths; hence, they were not *bardus*, per the Latin rendition of the Gemara, meaning "blockheaded," "stupid," "slow" and "dull."[2] Let us proceed, therefore, with our *scientific* examination of the Exodus story and the identity of Moses, without the unscientific, *a priori* assumption that these subjects constitute both "history" and "something uniquely holy."

---

[1] Campbell, 141
[2] *Cassell's*, 26.

Fig. 7. Dwelling foundations from Early Bronze Age, c. 3300-2100 BCE. Tell es-Sultan, Jericho, Israel

Who Wrote the Pentateuch?

"Biblical scholars have long known that all the books of the Hebrew Bible were written long after the events that they purported to describe, and that the Bible as a whole was produced by composite writers and editors in a long and exceedingly complex literary process that stretched over a thousand years."

Dr. William Dever, *Who Were the Early Israelites and Where Did They Come From?* (1)

"During the 17th and 18th centuries, the voices became louder which contested the traditional view that the Pentateuch in its entirety had been written by Moses. Scholars pointed to numerous passages which seem to reflect events, customs, etc., of periods after Moses. Among other things, it was time and again pointed out that Moses could not possibly have described his own death (Deut. 34:5-12)."

Dr. Paul Sanders, *The Provenance of Deuteronomy 32* (2)

"No direct connections have been found between the abundant documentary evidence from the ancient Near East for the second millennium and the biblical narrative of Israel's ancestors and origins found in the first seven books of the Bible. As a result, it is impossible to determine whether or not the individuals and events described in the Bible existed, and, if they did, when they should be dated."

Dr. Michael D. Coogan, *A Brief Introduction to the Old Testament* (21)

"...the early date of Pentateuchal sources according to the Documentary Hypothesis is entirely lacking in external corroboration, since archaeological evidence, including an analysis of written finds in Judea and at Elephantine, does not support the existence of any written Pentateuchal materials prior to the third century BCE."

Russell E. Gmirkin, *Berossus and Genesis, Manetho and Exodus* (2)

THE STORY OF MOSES is contained in the first five books of the Bible, called the Pentateuch or Torah, consisting of Genesis, Exodus, Leviticus, Numbers and Deuteronomy, as noted. Although many people still believe that the Bible is a monolithic product of the Almighty God himself, infallibly recorded by the authors purported, the evidence indicates that Moses was not the writer of the Pentateuch, as is maintained by tradition.

Like several books of the New Testament as well, various other Old Testament texts are pseudepigraphical: In other words, they were not written by those in whose names they appear. Also like the NT, over the centuries the texts of the OT were redacted many times, which is to say they were edited, interpolated, mutilated and forged.

Even though the text contains archaicisms from earlier eras, much of the Old Testament seems to have been composed during the first millennium BCE, with the older language akin to quotes from the King James Bible, Shakespeare or Chaucer in a modern book in English.

Mosaic Attribution

The question of whether or not Moses wrote the Pentateuch has been circulating within academia since at least the 17th century, when the French Catholic priest Richard Simon (1638-1712) composed his *Critical History of the Old Testament*, which "reasoned that Moses could not have written the Pentateuch because it contains historical details and refers to events about which he could not have known."[1] This questioning of the Torah's traditional authorship continued over the next centuries, with the result that today most mainstream authorities doubt this Mosaic attribution.

Concerning modern scholarly consensus regarding Moses and the Torah, Bible expert Dr. Richard E. Friedman remarks, "At present...there is hardly a biblical scholar in the world actively working on the problem who would claim that the Five Books of Moses were written by Moses—or by any one person."[2]

Again, this fact of non-Mosaic authorship for the Pentateuch has been discussed for hundreds of years, and the earlier, pioneering critics have proved to be accurate, as they were with many other issues. The details of their theses have been worked over since their time, with tweaks and alterations here and there. However, these earlier scholars were substantially correct, and their work has been *built and improved upon*, not dismissed and forgotten.

Anachronisms and Contradictions

In 1679, Spinoza already had "observed that in the Pentateuch certain towns and places bore names that were not given to them until several centuries after Moses."[3] This fact has been borne out by a great deal of scholarship and scientific analyses since Spinoza's time.

Regarding the many anachronisms of the Pentateuch, lawyer Joseph Wheless (1868-1950) comments:

> The first and most obvious proof that the so-called Five Books of Moses were not written by Moses, but date from a time many centuries after his reputed life and death, is very simple and indisputable. This proof consists of very numerous instances of what are called *post-Mosaica*, or "after-Moses" events, related in those books under the name of Moses as their inspired author; events of which Moses of course could not have known or written, as they occurred long after his death.[4]

---

[1] Coogan, 42.
[2] Friedman (1989), 28.
[3] Busenbark, 79.
[4] Wheless, 34.

These post-Mosaica elements are summarized thus:

> Several details point to a 1st millennium date for the Book of Exodus: Ezion-Geber, (one of the Stations of the Exodus), for example, dates to a period between the 8th and 6th centuries BCE with possible further occupation into the 4th century BCE, and those place-names on the Exodus route which have been identified— Goshen, Pithom, Succoth, Ramesses and Kadesh Barnea—point to the geography of the 1st millennium rather than the 2nd. Similarly, Pharaoh's fear that the Israelites might ally themselves with foreign invaders seems unlikely in the context of the late 2nd millennium, when Canaan was part of an Egyptian empire and Egypt faced no enemies in that direction, but does make sense in a 1st millennium context, when Egypt was considerably weaker and faced invasion first from the Persians and later from Seleucid Syria.
>
> The mention of the dromedary in Exodus 9:3 also suggests a later date of composition, as domesticated camels had not been introduced to Egypt until Cambyses II's invasion in 525 BCE.[1]

Camels?

For decades now, many people have contended that the mention of camels in the Bible represents an anachronism, because remains of domesticated camels do not appear in the archaeological record until centuries after their purported use by the patriarch Abraham described in Genesis (37:25).[2] Hence, it is claimed the Bible could not have been written until the beginning of the first millennium BCE at the earliest, when the first signs of camel domestication emerge in Israel, long after Abraham's purported era (c. 2000 BCE).

The rebuttal or apology for this alleged error is that camels have existed for millions of years and that evidence from northern Arabia points to their domestication by 2000 BCE.[3] However, the claim is not being made that there were no camels on Earth previous to the first millennium BCE, as the earliest known type existed some 40 to 50 million years in North America, where it became extinct 10 to 12,000 years ago. Nor is it denied that camels evidently were in some domestic use in *Arabia* as early as 4,000 years ago.

However, it is maintained, for example by Old Testament scholar Dr. John Van Seters in *Abraham in History and Tradition*, that "only with the first millennium B.C. was the camel fully domesticated as a riding and burden-carrying animal."[4] In this regard, camel bones appear to have been introduced suddenly into the relevant *biblical* areas during the 10th century BCE.[5]

---

[1] "The Exodus," *Wikipedia*.
[2] See, e.g., Finkelstein and Silberman (2001), 37.
[3] See, e.g., Bradshaw, "Archaeology & the Patriarchs."
[4] van Seters, 17.
[5] Mintz, "Oldest Camel Bones Undergo Carbon Dating, 'Direct Proof' Bible Was Written Centuries After Events Described."

Moreover, since camels evidently were domesticated in *Arabia* by the 20th century BCE, when most scholars place Abraham's supposed time, and if the patriarch had packs of these beasts of burden (Gen 24), it seems inexplicable that they were never used again after he allegedly arrived with them in Israel and that domesticated camel bones discovered there would date only from a thousand years later.

Genealogies

In addition to the camel anachronism, Wheless also points out that the genealogies at Exodus 6:14-27 take pains to identify Moses and Aaron with other figures of tradition, an identification that would only be necessary for scribes centuries later clarifying the tale and trying to tie these legendary founders in with the contemporary Jewish kingdom. Says he:

> It is recognized by scholars that all these elaborate genealogies inserted in the Five Books are post-exilic compositions. Their exact duplicates are found in the post-exilic Books of the Chronicles and some in Ezra.[1]

In other words, the lists attempting to depict Moses's historical lineage are very late, up to the time of the biblical scribe Ezra in the fifth century BCE.

Christian apologists who admit that these anachronisms occur after Moses nevertheless insist that the patriarch Joshua, immediate successor to the lawgiver who led the chosen into the Promised Land, "was responsible for some, if not all, of the post-Mosaica under the same divine utterance as Moses," interpolating the Pentateuch "under the direction and inspiration of the Holy Spirit."[2] Appeal to supernatural intervention aside, the bottom line suggested here is that significant portions of the Pentateuch were not composed or redacted until the eighth to fourth or, possibly, third centuries BCE.

Oily or Honeylike Manna?

As one example of the numerous contradictions in the Bible, at Exodus 16:31 the miraculous manna from heaven for the Israelites to eat in the desert is described as tasting like "wafers made with honey," while at Numbers 11:8, the substance's taste is that of "fresh oil." Wheless points out that this discrepancy was written supposedly by one person, Moses, whose vague and brief descriptions of this divinely sent food he had purportedly eaten daily for 40 years appear inexplicable, if he really wrote the Pentateuch.[3]

Moreover, Exodus 16:35 states that, upon Joshua's entrance into the Promised Land, the diet of the chosen people switched from the manna to the local grain (Jos 5:11-12). Wheless rightly asks how the

---

[1] Wheless, 35; 1 Chr 5: 3. See also Gen 46:9.
[2] Kaiser, 22.
[3] Wheless, 39-40.

supposed author, Moses, could have known that alleged fact, if he had died previously?[1] It is obvious that Moses did not write this pericope or passage of text. In his critical analysis, *Is It God's Word?* Wheless gives many other evidences of the fact that an allegedly historical Moses could not have composed the Pentateuch.

Moses's Death

Another profusely proffered proof that the Pentateuch was not written by a historical Moses is the fact that the text itself speaks of the lawgiver in the third person and asserts that "no man knows the place of his burial to this day." (Deut 34:6) Obviously, "to this day" implies a passage of time, and the deceased Moses surely was not writing about how his own grave had become lost since his death many years previously.

This temporal clarification also negates the apology that Moses could have been prophesying his own death in writing this passage. Most literalists today argue that Joshua composed this post-Mosaic verse, but that claim too would make little sense, since, again, "to this day" implies a length of time, and since Joshua surely would know where his predecessor was buried.

The fact that the author of the Pentateuch speaks in the third person is important to note, as not only does it sound strange in numerous instances, but also there are other contradictions indicating authorship by someone else. For example, at Exodus 11:3, we read that Moses was "very great in the land of Egypt"; yet, at Numbers 12:3, he is "very meek, more than all men that were on the face of the earth." Wheless remarks, "So meek a man would not probably have made such immodest boasts of himself."[2]

Book of the Wars of the Lord

Moreover, Numbers 21:14 mentions an earlier text upon which the Mosaic author(s) evidently drew:

> Wherefore it is said in the book of the wars of the LORD, What he did in the Red sea, and in the brooks of Arnon...[3]

If Moses wrote this text, it is inexplicable why he would refer to himself in the third person and to a previous composition for his account. Apparently, this "book of the wars of the LORD" was copied by the Pentateuch writers and then destroyed or lost.

Because of such difficulties, outside of Christian and Jewish fundamentalist circles, relatively few scholars today believe Moses actually wrote the Pentateuch, reflecting a doubt that has lingered

---

[1] Wheless, 40.
[2] Wheless, 38.
[3] King James Bible, which follows the Vulgate: *unde dicitur in libro bellorum Domini sicut fecit in mari Rubro sic faciet in torrentibus Arnon.* Other editions render "Red Sea" as "Waheb in Suphah," while "brooks" is also translated as "valleys" or "wadis."

Moses's Era

Even in ancient times, it was evident to various writers that Moses did not write the Pentateuch and that there was not a clear period in which the Hebrew prophet may have lived. In this regard, in *Against the Christians* (176), Greco-Phoenician philosopher Porphyry (234–c. 305 AD/CE) remarked:

> ...nothing Moses wrote has been preserved; for, all his writings are said to have been burnt with the temple. All those [books] written under his name afterwards were composed inaccurately one thousand one hundred and eighty years after Moses's death by Ezra and his followers.[1]

If Moses's purported era was the 13th century BCE, Porphyry has placed the prophet Ezra at around the first to third centuries BCE, while mainstream scholarship generally dates him to around 480–440 BCE. It seems that in Porphyry's time Moses was considered to have lived at a more remote date, as is believed to this day by certain Christians and Jews.

In the fourth century AD/CE, Church father Jerome (*Chronicon*) contended that the Israelite lawgiver was born in 1592 BCE. Other authorities place his birth in 1491 BCE. Mainstream Jewish scholars today put the period when Moses supposedly lived to around 1391–1271 BCE, with Rabbinic Judaism traditionally favoring 1313 BCE for the Exodus.[2] Some modern Christian apologists reckon Moses's birth to 1526 BCE, based on Exodus 7:7, which makes Moses 80 years old and Aaron 83 when they asked pharaoh to let their people go, an advanced age to be leading hundreds of thousands of warriors in battle.

In any event, we can see the difficulty here, as Moses's date was uncertain even in antiquity. In that time also, it was understood Moses did not compose the Pentateuch or first five books of the Bible, as tradition holds.

No Moses Before the Exile?

One major problem with the tradition of Moses composing the Pentateuch and Exodus story of Israel's founding comes from the fact that several other Old Testament texts omit the patriarch largely or entirely, even when discussing the law or other foundational myths. These texts are attributed to prophets who traditionally thrived before the Babylonian Captivity or Exile (598/7-538 BCE), the period when significant numbers of Jews purportedly were held captive in

---

[1] Berchman, 198.
[2] See the text *Seder Olam Rabbah*, composed during the second century AD/CE.

Babylon. These books include: Amos, Habakkuk, Hosea, Isaiah, Jeremiah, Jonah, Micah, Nahum and Zephaniah.

Regarding the absence of Moses in these biblical texts, Bible scholar Dr. Margaret Baker remarks:

> Why is Moses not a part of the religion of the pre-exilic prophets? It has even been suggested that Moses is not mentioned in any genuinely pre-exilic writing.[1]

Baker also states that "the authors of the pre-exilic literature of the Old Testament outside the Pentateuch appear to know virtually nothing of the patriarchal and Mosaic traditions of the Pentateuch..."[2]

Danish Old Testament professor Dr. Niels Peter Lemche (b. 1945) agrees that "Moses is also not mentioned by the pre-exilic prophets."[3] It appears, therefore, that the biblical character was created for the most part not until after or during the Exile.

Hosea

For example, the author of the book of Hosea, Lemche remarks, "knows nothing of Moses, since Hos 12,14 is secondary."[4] As an instance of how an earlier text may have been redacted to create the fictional tale, although Hosea thus makes no mention of Moses, it apparently was used by later editors (e.g., "J" and "E") to compose the Pentateuch.[5]

Isaiah

The major prophet Isaiah's book contains the word "Moses" one time each in two verses (63:11-12), but these too could be secondary interpolations into a typical recitation of what originally comprised *Yahweh's* miraculous works, not those of Moses. The rest of this very long book has no other mention of the patriarch. Indeed, these verses in Isaiah 63 appear to reflect the *mythical* core of the Exodus story, obviously of great importance to the Israelites in their national identity, and built upon over the centuries to incorporate a *fictional* founder.

Divine Revelation and Authority

Despite these 15 or so pre-exilic prophets who seem to be oblivious to the existence of Moses, apologists cite the 21 biblical books with 71 references to the Mosaic authorship of the Pentateuch.[6] This number may appear impressive, but it merely reflects a *tradition* continued throughout the history of the Bible and Judaism. This tradition exists to give the text and religion authority

---

[1] Baker (1992), 13.
[2] Baker (1992), 16-17.
[3] Lemche (1985), 315.
[4] Lemche (1985), 314.
[5] See the "Documentary Hypothesis" discussion below.
[6] See, e.g., Möller, 300.

under a divine legislator who allegedly received his law directly from the finger of God.

In consideration of the fervent biblical contention of the Jews as the "chosen people" of *the* God of the cosmos, a holy nation of priests, it is not surprising that this claim of the religion being codified by a "prophet of the Lord" is made repeatedly, as it continues to be today, in order to justify Judaism as the "true religion."

Thus, the books are attributed to Moses in order to give them authority: The patriarch is the inspired lawgiver and possesses supernatural and miraculous capacities, demonstrating that the Lord God indeed is working with and through him.

Hammurabi

Again, such contentions were common in antiquity, with numerous divine legislators cited in other cultures, such as the Babylonian-Amorite king Hammurabi (d. 1750 BCE),[1] who allegedly received his law from the sun god Shamash. As noted, several of the Ten Commandments are similar to the earlier Code of Hammurabi, a brutal law requiring the death penalty for transgressions such as theft and adultery, as does the Mosaic law. If we are to accept that Moses received the law supernaturally on Mount Sinai during the 13th or 15th century BCE, then we must also accept the claim that Hammurabi received his code from Shamash in the 18th century BCE, indicating that the Babylonian deity is as real as the Israelite god.

Fig. 8. Hammurabi receiving the law from Shamash, 18th cent. BCE. Stele from Susa, Louvre (Fritz-Milkau-Dia-Sammlung)

Cosmic Understandings or Petty Concerns?

Throughout the Pentateuch/Torah, Yahweh is depicted as communicating with and appearing in person to Moses, Aaron and assorted other persons, in detailed dialogue over a period of years. Moses becomes so comfortable with God that he speaks as a child to a parent, running the gamut from subservience to insolence.

One is left wondering a number of things from these discussions, including what was happening in the rest of the cosmos while the God of the universe was occupied by chit-chatting with Moses and his select representatives in a tiny backwater of the miniscule earth, off to the side of one of numberless galaxies? A cosmos, in fact, that is described as infinite? And why would such a massive entity be

---

[1] The West Semitic spelling of this name "Hammurabi" from an Ugaritic text is *'mrpi*, transliterated as "Ammurapi" (Rainey, 1965:112) or "Hamurapi."

fascinated by these few puny humans of no significant material substance, no grand buildings, no real art, no navy or even a country—why choose such a contingent out of a seemingly infinite choice?

Animal Sacrifice

In accepting this claim, we are also to believe all the mind-numbing and absurd commandments, ordinances and instructions in the Bible on how to behave and prepare the tabernacle and other priestly accoutrements and rituals, including page after page concerning bloody sacrifices of various animals.

Indeed, what does the God of the cosmos convey to this chosen people? The cure for disease? Blueprints for the combustible engine—or, better yet, Tesla technology? A plan for a space station? The Almighty in his ultimate and infinite wisdom spends years repeating over and over again mind-numbing and grotesque details about the sacrifice of animals. Stone Age animal sacrifice designed to please his omnipotent nose![1]

Much of the Torah, especially Deuteronomy, constitutes a tedious set of detailed ordinances governing everyday life that would seem unfathomable for the Lord of the universe to be concerned with above all else.

Human Bloodshed

The absurdity of the creator of the cosmos being obsessed with animal sacrifice is evident enough, but a significant part of the rest of the biblical tale is likewise repugnant. For example, the founding of Israel as the "Promised Land" is rife with bloodshed and slaughter, as God—again, speaking quite personally with Moses, Aaron and others for months or years on end—commands his "chosen" to massacre one people after another, such as the Amalekites, Canaanites, Midianites and Moabites. This bloodshed was followed by Joshua's slaughter all around Canaan, proudly boasted about throughout the book of Joshua, part of the Hexateuch or first six biblical books.

No Archaeological Evidence

The unreal air of the Pentateuch is obvious also from the lack of archaeological evidence, which continues to elude discovery, despite numerous efforts to find it over a period of centuries to millennia. Concerning this mythical appearance, lay Egyptologist Gerald Massey (1828-1907) remarks:

> As history, the Pentateuch has neither head, tail, nor vertebrae; it is an indistinguishable mush of myth and mystery. Had it been a real history, Palestine and Judea ought to have been found overstrewn

---

[1] See, e.g., Gen 8:21; Exod 29:18, 25, 41; Lev 1:9, 13, etc. Exod 29:18: "and burn the whole ram upon the altar; it is a burnt offering to the LORD; it is a pleasing odor, an offering by fire to the LORD."

with implements of warfare and work, both of Hebrew manufacture and of that of the conquered races, whereas outside the book, it is a blank. The land of a people so rich that King David, in his poverty, could collect one thousand millions of pounds sterling towards building a temple, is found without art, sculptures, bronzes, pottery or precious stones to illustrate the truth of the Bible story of the nation of warriors and spoilers of nations who burst away from their captivity in Egypt two millions strong. Nor will the proofs be found, not if Palestine be uprooted in the search....

The chief Jewish teachers have always insisted on the allegories of the Pentateuch, and the necessity of the oral interpretation of the books by those who were in possession of the key. No confession could be more explicit than that of the Psalmist: "I will open my mouth in a parable: I will utter dark sayings of old which we have heard and known, and our fathers have told us...." [Psalm 78:2] Parables and dark sayings of old are the allegories of mythology, and enigmas of the ancient wisdom of Egypt uttered emblematically; the wisdom with which Moses is accredited by Jewish writers. Foremost amongst these parables and mystical sayings are the Exodus, the dividing of the waters, smiting of the rock for drink, and opening of the heavens to let down manna for food. These things which to the modern ignorance are miracles, are parables expressed in dark sayings of old, that is, they are the myths put forth in the manner of the mysteries.[1]

Since Massey's time and even before it, artifacts have been discovered that demonstrate there were inhabitants of Israel, but none that provides verification of the supernatural tales of the Torah, or of the massive warfare with huge numbers of fighters. Thus, this independent scholar, although maligned, was substantially correct in his perception of Moses and the Exodus, without the benefit of modern discoveries but based on the extant literary record of the day, the ideas of Egypt, and his own common sense.

Wellhausen and the Documentary Hypothesis

Instead of attributing the Pentateuch to a historical lawgiver of the 17th to 13th centuries BCE—which represents the wide range of dates given for Moses's era, reflecting its lack of solid historical foundation—some scholars support dates for certain books and authors ranging from the 10th to seventh centuries BCE, with parts of it possibly older. Others consider the majority of the Pentateuch to have been committed to writing between the Babylonian exile/captivity (6th cent.) and the third century BCE, with other OT books, such as Esther (5th-1st cents. BCE) and Daniel (c. 165 BCE), redacted, interpolated or composed later.[2]

---

[1] Massey (2007), 2.178-179. For more information on Gerald Massey, including the fact that his works were peer-reviewed by some of the most respected authorities of the time, see my book *Christ in Egypt*, 13ff.

[2] The late dating of the Book of Daniel remains debated; however, the book reflects a genre and style of the third and second centuries BCE, not the sixth century, when it is

WHO WROTE THE PENTATEUCH?

In discussing the "Yahwist's Primeval Myth," Dr. Bernard F. Batto summarizes current mainstream scholarship on who actually wrote the Torah, specifically concerning the "Documentary Hypothesis":

> "The Yahwist" is, of course, part of the so-called Documentary Hypothesis, which is currently under attack from a number of quarters. Nonetheless, this theory remains in its broad outline the best and most widely accepted explanation of the development of the Pentateuch, the first five books of the Bible. To be sure, numerous aspects of the theory as originally formulated in the classical statement by Julius Wellhausen toward the end of the nineteenth century must be revised in light of more recent research. But as an explanation for the many doubles and apparently contradictory narratives of the Pentateuch, the Documentary Hypothesis remains unsurpassed....
>
> Rather than scrap the whole Documentary Hypothesis as some have suggested, it seems more in keeping with the literary data of the Pentateuch to modify the Documentary Hypothesis along the lines suggested by Frank Cross. Cross maintains the basic four pentateuchal traditions, but posits that the early epic traditions (J and E) were subsequently reworked by P, who added his own editorial structure and priestly materials to form a Tetrateuch (viz., Genesis through Numbers).... P never existed as a separate source...[1]

The complex construction of the Pentateuch has been worked out over a period of centuries, including famously by the renowned German biblical scholar and theologian Rev. Dr. Julius Wellhausen (1844-1918), one of the originators of the Documentary Hypothesis. Wellhausen's hypothesis is as follows:

1. The Yahwist source ("J"), possibly written around 950 BCE in the southern kingdom of Judah;
2. The Elohist source ("E"), c. 850 BCE in the northern kingdom of Israel;
3. The Deuteronomist ("D"), c. 600 BCE in Jerusalem during a period of religious reform; and
4. The Priestly source ("P"), c. 500 BCE by *kohanim* (Jewish priests) who had been in exile in Babylon.[2]

Thus, according to this theory, J was first, followed by E and D, and all were redacted together by P.[3]

Jesuit priest Rev. Dr. William W. Meissner (d. 2010) elaborates the lettering system developed by Wellhausen and maintained in the

---

traditionally placed. Several scholars have noted the similarity between Daniel and Dan'el, the chieftain hero of an Ugaritic epic. (See, e.g., Schniedewind, 27.)

[1] Batto, 41-42.

[2] Adapted from the *Wikipedia* article, "Documentary Hypothesis." Friedman (2003:15-16) shows that there are many parallels in language between the D source and the book of Jeremiah, as well as between P and Ezekiel. J and E are closest to the book of Hosea, previously mentioned.

[3] See also the chart in Coogan, 45.

current documentary hypothesis, along with the reasons for doubting the attribution of the Pentateuch to Moses:

> ...modern scholarship has revealed variations in style, disruptions of sequence, and narrative repetitions that argue against a single author. Following Wellhausen, modern scholars have regarded the Pentateuch as an amalgam of four documents, all written much later than the time of Moses. There were initially two narrative sources, the Yahwistic (J), which uses the divine name (Yahweh) that was given to Moses, and the Elohistic (E), which uses the common name for God, Elohim. J was written in Judah in the tenth century B.C., and E followed a little later in Israel. After the fall of the Northern Kingdom (following the fall of Samaria in 722 B.C.), J and E were combined. After the period of Josiah, the Deuteronomic (D) source was added; the Priestly Code (P), made up of laws for the most part, with a smattering of narrative, was joined to the existing compilation (JED) after the exile. The redactional steps by which the Deuteronomic and Priestly traditions were later joined to JE are still matters of scholarly debate, but it is clear that the entire Pentateuch had reached its present form by the period of the exile or shortly thereafter.[1]

In *Who Wrote the Bible*, Friedman dates P to the time of the brutal Israelite reformer king Hezekiah (fl. 715-686 BCE), because the hypothesized text reflects a strong centralizing tendency of the priesthood, which was the reformer's major thrust. In this regard, P diminishes Moses's role and raises Aaron and his priesthood to dominance. This supremacy is reflected in Hezekiah's destruction of the Mosaic serpent in the temple at 2 Kings 18:4.

As Meissner states, a number of later redactors over the centuries have been proposed as well. The hypothesized individual who combined J and E in the eighth century is styled the "Redactor of JE" or "RJE."[2] The person who apparently combined all five texts after Deuteronomy was composed is called the "Redactor" or "R." Another redactor/editor is posited as having reworked the texts during the second century BCE, when it appears the book of Daniel was composed.[3]

Nevertheless, Pentateuchal scholarship remains fractured by multiple alternative theses.[4] For example, Van Seters has argued for a sixth-century date for J and no E at all, making D the earliest layer,

---

[1] Meissner, 118.
[2] Friedman (2003), 4.
[3] See, e.g., Lacocque, 9-10.
[4] See, e.g., "Pentateuchal Studies Today" by Gordon Wenham and "Dating the Bible" at *Wikipedia*. Note that the dating on *Wikipedia* for the Old Testament includes scientific analysis, whereas the dating in the same article for the New Testament is inadequate and rests solely on internal evidence and the *a priori* assumption that the gospel story represents "history" that actually occurred during the era in which it was set. For a more scientific discussion of the dates of the canonical gospels as we have them, see my book *Who Was Jesus?*

dating to the late seventh century.¹ Other biblical scholars such as Dr. Roger N. Whybray see the Pentateuch as a "collection of fragments assembled into its present form in the post-exilic period by a single author."² Many writers have averred this single author to be the prophet Ezra (fl. 480-440 BCE). For reasons discussed below, American scholar Russell E. Gmirkin dates the Pentateuch's final composition to the third century BCE.

Moreover, the documentary hypothesis remains debated, naturally, by Bible literalists, who maintain the biblical Mosaic attribution as actual history of the second millennium, as well as by the most skeptical critics called "minimalists," who push the book's composition into the latest possible period, around the middle to the last quarter of the first millennium BCE. However, arguments for the antiquity of at least certain parts of the Pentateuch include linguistic studies revealing Hebrew at "several distinct periods,"³ which suggests that some of the texts were composed, orally at least, centuries earlier.

Exodus Composition

Concerning the date of the Exodus story's composition, *The Oxford Companion to the Bible*, edited by biblical scholar Dr. Bruce M. Metzger (1914-2007), states:

> The account of the Exodus in the Pentateuch is multilayered, being composed of various traditions, some very ancient, such as the "Song of the Sea" in Exodus 15, and the bulk a prose narrative combining the Pentateuchal sources J, E and P, to be dated from the tenth to perhaps as late as the sixth century BCE.⁴

Theologian and biblical studies professor Dr. Brian D. Russell calls the "Song of the Sea," a pericope at Exodus 15:1-18, "perhaps the oldest literary or textual element extant in the Hebrew Bible,"⁵ citing as evidence the text's "archaic grammar and syntax, lack of prosaic particles, the use of staircase parallelism, and phrases and word pairs in common with Ugaritic prosody."⁶

Theologian Dr. Michael D. Oblath concludes that the Exodus epic was "created and given its original life" during the "foundational era" of the period of David and Solomon⁷ (10th to ninth cents. BCE). Egyptologist Redford argues for the time of the drama's composition to after the Babylonian Exile, during the Late Egyptian/Saite era (c.

---

¹ Hoffmeier (2011), 8.
² Hoffmeier (2011), 8.
³ Friedman (2003), 7.
⁴ Metzger, 210.
⁵ Russell, 47.
⁶ Russell, 59. "Prosody" refers to the style of speech, including its rhythm, emphasis and tone. Russell (66) cites as an example of Ugaritic influence on the Bible the verse at Psalm 92:10.
⁷ Oblath, xvi.

712-332 BCE) or Persian period (539-334 BCE).[1] Based on the fact that the pre-exilic texts are virtually devoid of Moses, it would appear that the bulk of his story was composed during or after the Exile, using an older *mythical* core such as the Song of the Sea, as will be discussed in detail here.

Regarding the date when the Exodus story was composed significantly, Israeli archaeologist Dr. Israel Finkelstein and archaeology writer Neil Asher Silberman conclude:

> All of these indications suggest that the Exodus narrative reached its final form during the time of the Twenty-sixth Dynasty, in the second half of the seventh and first half of the sixth century BCE. Its many references to specific places and events in this period quite clearly suggest that the author or authors integrated many contemporary details into the story.... Old, less formalized legends of liberation from Egypt could have been skillfully woven into the powerful saga that borrowed familiar landscapes and monuments. But can it be just a coincidence that the geographical and ethnic details of both the patriarchal origin stories and the Exodus liberation story bear the hallmarks of having been composed in the seventh century BCE?[2]

The Exodus story is highly anachronistic and reflects the topography of much later centuries, the era when it evidently was composed. The seventh century, of course, was the time of the violent reforms of the Israelite king Josiah (fl. c. 640-609 BCE), on the heels of those by Hezekiah, when Josiah's high priest Hilkiah "discovered" or, possibly, composed the "Book of the Law."

This date of about 650 to 550 BCE for the composition of this part of the tale makes sense in light of all the data, as presented here, including access to texts in Babylon before and during the Babylonian exile.

While the language of some texts in significant part may be older than the Babylonian Exile, with later interpolations, there remains no credible evidence that Moses even existed as depicted, much less wrote any part of the first five books of the Bible.[3] If we allow that someone else wrote about Moses's death and grave, such as his successor Joshua, we can suggest likewise that other individuals wrote other parts of the Pentateuch, which is what skeptical scholarship and biblical criticism have held for a number of centuries now.

Earlier Folklore

As we can see, there remains a lack of consensus as to the dates of relevant biblical texts, but it would appear that later dates for most

---

[1] Oblath, 21.
[2] Finkelstein and Silberman, 68.
[3] See also my article "Did the Exodus Really Happen? A Review of Lennart Möller's *The Exodus Case*." (See the Bibliography here. Some of the paragraphs here are excerpted from there.)

of the texts rank as the most scientific analysis, with older strata representing folklore and myth not only from the Hebrews but also from earlier cultures such as the Akkadians, Amorites, Assyrians, Babylonians, Canaanites, Eblaites, Egyptians, Greeks, Hittites, Indians, Mitanni, Phoenicians, Persians, Sumerians, Ugaritians and others.

The Allegorical 'Dark Sayings' of Old

In consideration of the fact that "chief Jewish teachers have always insisted on the allegories of the Pentateuch," we may do likewise in recognizing the various "dark sayings of old" (Ps 78:2)[1] as *mythical*, not historical. Indeed, we would suggest that these parables and dark sayings are the myths, lamentations, psalms, hymns, scriptures and poems of pre-Israelitish peoples of the area.

In this regard, for the past couple of centuries, archaeologists have been excavating sites of Egyptians and Levantine peoples, unearthing numerous important artifacts, including tens of thousands of texts. From these discoveries, we now know that many of the stories in the Pentateuch represent not "history" but mythology found in these previous cultures. The biblical myths that have counterparts in these earlier cultures include the Creation, the Garden of Eden, the Tower of Babel, Noah's Ark, Abraham's Trial, Jacob's Ladder, the Exodus, Job's Trial, and Samson and Delilah. A single redactor of the Old Testament such as Ezra would have utilized fragments of just such tales from pre-biblical times.

After this mass of textual evidence began to be discovered, these precursor myths and stories were scrutinized so thoroughly in the 19th century that among the many books on this subject written at that time was one titled *Bible Myths and Their Parallels in Other Religions*. Since then, archaeology and other disciplines have demonstrated that the biblical renditions are continuities and adaptations of these earlier tales and myths. Yet, the bulk of humanity remains unaware of these mythical precedents, as they are rarely taught from the pulpit and continue largely to be buried within the hallowed halls of academia.

Sumeria

During the past century, discoveries from the pre-Semitic civilization of Sumer or Sumeria have shed an enormous amount of light upon the Bible. The Sumerians' use of writing to record literature began around 2500 BCE, and their cuneiform script was used for many hundreds of years afterwards, adapted to a number of

---

[1] Strong's (H2420) defines the relevant Hebrew term חידה *chiydah* as: "riddle, difficult question, parable, enigmatic saying or question, perplexing saying or question; riddle (dark obscure utterance); riddle, enigma (to be guessed…"

other languages, including Akkadian, Eblaite, Ugaritic and other Semitic tongues.

Significant Sumerian myths also were passed from one culture to another throughout the region, changed to suit the ethnicity, location and era, and eventually ended up in the Bible as purported Hebrew cosmology.

Ebla

Home of the Eblaites, the city of Ebla, Syria, has yielded thousands of cuneiform texts that reveal a bustling trade, educational and religious center over a thousand years before the supposed conquest of Canaan. Ebla is the first known area in which a Semitic language—now called Eblaite—was recorded in cuneiform,[1] using a simplified Sumerian script.

These Eblaite compositions date to around 2250 BCE and include a legal code, which has been compared in particular to Leviticus 16. Names of various biblical characters also have been discovered at Ebla, such as Abraham and David, long predating any "historical" individuals by those names and indicating their probable *mythical* nature instead. A hypothesized "ya" god-name has been posited in one of these texts; however, the suggestion has been refuted by biblical apologists.

Fig. 9. Cuneiform clay tablet, 3rd millennium BCE. Found at Ebla, Syria

In "Old Testament Mythology in Its Ancient Near Eastern Context," British Near Eastern archaeologist Dr. Wilfred G. Lambert (1926-2011) comments on Sumerian texts found at Ebla:

> ...virtually from the beginning personal names reveal names of deities and occasionally their attributes. The remains of the earliest group of literary myths have been recovered from three Sumerian sites from about the middle of the 3rd millennium... Only a few individual phrases or sentences have been deciphered so far, but two of these express the widespread myth of the separation of heaven and earth, which appears, somewhat transformed, in Gen. i as the dividing of the cosmic waters. The period of these Sumerian myths is also the period of the Ebla archives, and some Sumerian literature has been found at Ebla... The only original literary texts in Semitic from Ebla...are incantations...[2]

Lambert also states:

> One of the most striking things from the study of Near Eastern myth is the essential similarity of so much from different civilizations,

---

[1] Snell, 133.
[2] Emerton, 129-130.

despite differences in detail. From the Aegean to Pakistan striking similarities constantly occur to the attentive reader.[1]

It is significant that Ebla is fairly close to the areas of Ugarit and the Mitanni kingdom, as these later cultures share similar mythical archetypes with the earlier Eblaites. In the end, there is significant "biblical" tradition, doctrine and ritual in the Sumero-Semitic literature, and it remains logical and scientific to suggest that such earlier culture represents the real foundation of scriptural tradition, rather than the myths purporting supernatural divine revelation.

Mari

Another highly influential, literate Semitic group was that of the Amorites, who left many texts at Mari in eastern Syria, on the western bank of the Euphrates River. Some 25,000 cuneiform tablets (1800-1750 BCE) from Mari reveal the extent of the Amorite civilization there. The official language of the tablets is Akkadian, but there are "hints in syntax" that Mari's citizens spoke Northwest Semitic,[2] essentially Amorite/Canaanite.

Ugarit

To reiterate, at the Canaanite city of Ugarit or Ras Shamra were discovered thousands of cuneiform tablets in the local dialect of Ugaritic, dating to the 14th to 12th centuries BCE. The occupation of Ugarit began in the Neolithic (c. 6500 BCE) and continued to the end of the second millennium BCE, including the arrival around 1900 BCE of the Amorites to settle its lands. Because of its location on the eastern Mediterranean, Ugarit became a commercial hub and "attracted merchants and foreigners from nearby maritime towns as well as more distant locations like Egypt, Cyprus, Syria and Mesopotamia," encompassing "Phoenicians, Hittites, Egyptians, Assyrians, Canaanites, Cypriots and other Aegeans."[3]

It is surmised that the Ugaritic epics were passed along orally for hundreds of years before being written down initially during the reign of the king Niqmaddu II (c. 1350 BCE).[4] Schniedewind remarks that Ugarit as a scribal center was "particularly important when we reflect on the significant parallels between Ugaritic and biblical literature…" He further states: "Such scribal schools were undoubtedly a conduit for some of the literary and poetic similarities between Ugaritic and biblical literature."[5]

Regarding these texts, Russell concurs that "there are many parallels between the literature unearthed at Ras Shamra and the

---

[1] Emerton, 126.
[2] "Mari, Syria," *Wikipedia*.
[3] Schniedewind, 8.
[4] Schniedewind, 13.
[5] Schniedewind, 10, 12.

Old Testament literature of all periods."[1] These various Semitic texts, along with Egyptian, Greek and others, will be discussed throughout this present work.

In addition to shared god-names and divine epithets, the languages of Canaanite and Hebrew themselves are largely indistinguishable for most of Israel's early history. Much temple terminology and many sacred rituals believed to be Hebrew from their repeated discussion in the Bible are actually Canaanite/Ugaritic/Western Semitic or Phoenician.[2] These Ugaritic/Canaanite terms that made their way into the Bible included "priest" (*kōhēn*) and "tent of meeting," which were "derived from Canaanite prototypes."[3]

The Book of the Law

Since the Pentateuch is clearly not a historical text written by Moses, the biblical story at Deuteronomy 31:24, purporting the patriarch's composition of the Mosaic or Jewish law is thus unsustainable factually: "When Moses had finished writing the words of this law in a book, to the very end…" There simply exists no evidence for the law's genesis as depicted in the Bible. The reality is that the evidence, including the Bible itself, indicates the law was composed long after Moses's purported time.

In this regard, we read in 2 Kings 22 and 2 Chronicles 34 about the alleged discovery of the "Book of the Law," in Hebrew תורה *towrah*.[4] Although it refers to the entire Pentateuch in general, the term "torah" is understood often to signify the individual biblical book of Deuteronomy or "Second Law."

Purging Paganism

The biblical story contends that, after Hezekiah's death (687 BCE), his son Manasseh (c. 697/6-642/64 BCE) returned the local "pagan" worship to the people. However, the fanatical and violent reformers struck back with their favorite king, Josiah, who was even more vehement than his grandfather Hezekiah in his assaults on the old religion.

In order to explain why the Israelites kept "whoring after" other gods[5] after Yahweh supposedly chose them for his monotheistic revelation, Bible writers pretended that Moses's "Book of the Law" had been "lost," to be found 600 years later (622 BCE) by Hilkiah, a "son of Zadok" or proto-Sadducee, one of the two main sects of Jewish priests in later times. After reading the law—or before, depending on which of the contradictory accounts in the "inerrant word" one reads—Josiah goes on a rampage and purges the high

---

[1] Russell, 71.
[2] Smith, M. (2002), 22-23.
[3] Smith, M. (2002), 23-24.
[4] Strong's H8451.
[5] See, e.g., Exod 34:15, etc.

WHO WROTE THE PENTATEUCH?

places in the same violent manner that Hezekiah had done previously.[1] This destruction is described at 2 Kings 23:4-11:

> And the king commanded Hilki'ah, the high priest, and the priests of the second order, and the keepers of the threshold, to bring out of the temple of the LORD all the vessels made for Ba'al [בעל *Ba'al*], for Ashe'rah [אשרה *'asherah*],[2] and for all the host of heaven; he burned them outside Jerusalem in the fields of the Kidron, and carried their ashes to Bethel.
>
> And he deposed the idolatrous priests whom the kings of Judah had ordained to burn incense in the high places at the cities of Judah and round about Jerusalem; those also who burned incense to Ba'al, to the sun, and the moon, and the constellations, and all the host of the heavens.
>
> And he brought out the Ashe'rah from the house of the LORD, outside Jerusalem, to the brook Kidron, and burned it at the brook Kidron, and beat it to dust and cast the dust of it upon the graves of the common people. And he broke down the houses of the male cult prostitutes which were in the house of the LORD, where the women wove hangings for the Ashe'rah.
>
> And he brought all the priests out of the cities of Judah, and defiled the high places where the priests had burned incense, from Geba to Beer-sheba; and he broke down the high places of the gates that were at the entrance of the gate of Joshua the governor of the city, which were on one's left at the gate of the city.
>
> However, the priests of the high places did not come up to the altar of the LORD in Jerusalem, but they ate unleavened bread among their brethren. And he defiled To'pheth, which is in the valley of the sons of Hinnom, that no one might burn his son or his daughter as an offering to Molech.
>
> And he removed the horses that the kings of Judah had dedicated to the sun, at the entrance to the house of the LORD, by the chamber of Nathan-melech the chamberlain, which was in the precincts; and he burned the chariots of the sun with fire.

Fig. 10. Stylized palm tree or *asherah*, like those torn down by Josiah (2 Kings 23)

In his fanaticism, Josiah reversed the policies of Manasseh, who, again, had restored ancient pagan polytheistic worship shared in by the Israelites. Sacred objects were immolated, priests killed, a "grove"

---

[1] Cf. 2 Kings 22:8-11ff and 2 Chron 34:3, 14ff.
[2] Strong's (H1168) defines Baal both as "lord" and as "supreme male divinity of the Phoenicians or Canaanites." Asherah is defined (Strong's H842) as: "groves (for idol worship)"; "a Babylonian (Astarte)-Canaanite goddess (of fortune and happiness), the supposed consort of Baal, her images"; "the goddess, goddesses"; and "sacred trees or poles set up near an altar."

(*asherah*) from the "house of the Lord" burned, and the "houses of the sodomites" inside the temple were destroyed.

From this one pericope alone, we can learn a great deal about the Israelite worship, including that it was essentially the same as that of the Canaanites and other peoples of the Levant, as well as that it was largely astrotheological in nature, here having to do with sun worship. It also incorporated male cult prostitutes or *qadeshim*, previously mentioned.[1]

Priestly Payoff

The obsession with preventing people from worshipping other gods is motivated by a priesthood that desires power and enrichment. The monetary aspect of the biblical scenario is punctuated throughout the foundational tale, with constant offerings to the Jewish priesthood, such as exemplified in the tithe, as at Deuteronomy 14:28-29. The politics are obvious from Deuteronomy 16:16-18:

> Three times a year all your males shall appear before the LORD your God at the place which he will choose: at the feast of unleavened bread, at the feast of weeks, and at the feast of booths. They shall not appear before the LORD empty-handed; every man shall give as he is able, according to the blessing of the LORD your God which he has given you. You shall appoint judges and officers in all your towns which the LORD your God gives you, according to your tribes; and they shall judge the people with righteous judgment.

Concerning this development, Dever remarks:

> The Deuteronomistic history...is almost certainly the work of a school of Mosaic reformers (thus "Deuteronomy" or "Second Law") under Josiah (650-609 B.C.), with final additions concerning the end of Judah added during the exile in the 6th century B.C.[2]

That Josiah's grandfather Hezekiah had a hand in creating the scriptures is contended biblically at Proverbs 25:1, in which it is claimed that "Solomon's" proverbs were "copied" by Hezekiah's men. This verse probably recounts the writing down of sayings traditionally and pseudepigraphically attributed to "Solomon" that had been passed along for centuries, originally claimed to have emanated from a deity or deities. Since we have not discovered any such texts as Hezekiah's Solomonic composition, it is possible they were written in perishable materials, such as papyrus scrolls, rather than cuneiform tablets. These latter would be cumbersome for nomadic peoples, which the Israelites originally were.

In any event, at Proverbs 25:1 we have a clear admission of Hezekiah's hand in the composition of the Bible, and we are wise to

---

[1] For more information on the male cult prostitutes, see my *Study Guide for Did Moses Exist?*
[2] Dever (2003), 8.

suspect that such influence did not end there and that the effort continued for centuries afterwards. In this same regard, concerning the hypothesized source text "P," Friedman shows that it "has elements that connect it to the time of Hezekiah..."[1]

Found or Fabricated?

To reiterate, in the story of Josiah, the "stiff-necked chosen people" were "whoring after" the gods in their old ways, as if no previous censure had ever happened, whether with Hezekiah two generations before, or with Moses and Aaron centuries previously. Both of these patriarchs' lineages were supposed to uphold the law given by Yahweh over a significant period of time, during a 40-year indoctrination camp in the desert, in which the Almighty allegedly appeared in person many times. According to the Torah, the Lord had expended much energy with one supernatural, miraculous and magical event after another to ensure his law would be imposed upon his chosen.

It is inexplicable why God would have gone to so much trouble to talk regularly with Moses and Aaron—both pious workers of miracles and founders of priestly lineages—give them an enormous amount of painstaking and detailed instructions, and then just let them put it all away for 600 years. Where was Yahweh during this time? He was purportedly involved in every little detail of Israelite life; yet, he never reminded his prophets and priests of the long-lost law?

Seven-Year Recitation

Moreover, at Deuteronomy 31:10-13 Moses instructed the priestly tribe of Levites to read the law once entirely to the Israelite congregation every seven years, so, again, why was it lost for 600 years? It seems odd that the Levites or their following would not remember any of it, especially since centuries later Ezra was claimed to have done just that, purportedly recalling from memory all the books of the Old Testament or "Tanakh," as it is called in Hebrew, written by his time.

Yet, in the end it was all for naught, as the people—including a highly trained and organized priesthood whose very livelihood depended on the law—simply forgot all about it.

This tale of the finding of the law is obviously fictitious, as, in reality, it cannot be explained why, if Moses had been real and had such a dramatic and impactful life, his law would have been "lost" in the first place. And if it had been lost, how did Hezekiah know to follow it, when he made his purges and reforms?

---

[1] Friedman (2003), 21.

Temple Texts

The finding of the book of the law under the temple recalls the location of religious libraries such as that of the high priest at Ugarit/Ras Shamra, discovered in between the city's two main temples, one to Baal and the other to Dagan.[1] The Ugaritic library also provides an example of a legal text dedicated to a god, *El's Marzeah* or *Marzihu*, reflecting the rules of a wine cult festival, to be discussed below.

In consideration of the numerous tablets at Ugarit and elsewhere, it is possible that one or more older Semitic text indeed was found in Jerusalem, from a pre-Israelite temple or shrine, eventually used as the basis of some of the Pentateuch. It is also possible that religious law texts of this sort were deliberately buried in such sacred spaces as talismans or objects dedicated to a god or gods.

Josiah's Yahwism

From the biblical tale about the discovery of the book in the Jerusalem temple, as well as various anachronisms and artifacts in the Pentateuch, it has been surmised that "Moses's" law was written down first during the reign of Josiah, apparently based in significant part on his predecessor Hezekiah's actions. Those two rulers used religion and God to justify both of their violent assaults, designed to slaughter competitor priests and leaders, and to subordinate their peoples under Yahwistic rule.

While it is claimed Moses discovered or developed monotheism, from the numerous biblical references to the Jews worshipping other gods it appears that it was under Hezekiah and then Josiah that fanatical, intolerant monotheism began to be imposed upon the masses, starting around 690 BCE. Although there is no mention of Moses in the other pre-exilic prophets, it is possible that a germ tale of a tribal lawgiver was elaborated piously to some extent at this time, in order to give a more ancient, godly foundation to Hezekiah/Josiah's fanatical and harsh legal reforms, under the intolerant and oppressive monotheism. This tale would have been embellished and altered continuously until it was finally written down in the form found in the Old Testament.

Part of this Yahwism was the imposition of onerous laws as in Leviticus and Deuteronomy, about which Dever comments: "Much of the incredibly complex priestly legislation (especially throughout Leviticus) can only reflect the later institutional cult of urban life in the Monarchy, not the experience of desert wanderers."[2]

In this same regard, discussing Yahweh's law, Redford remarks:

> The rules he laid down, unilaterally in fact—the human party to the contract had no say in the matter—were Draconian in the extreme,

---

[1] Schniedewind, 9-11.
[2] Dever (2003), 19.

WHO WROTE THE PENTATEUCH? 47

and the deity's will utterly barbaric. Alien groups whose actions or even presence were deemed in opposition to Israel are consigned to genocidal slaughter at the behest of Yahweh (Exod. 17:14; Num. 31; 1 Sam. 15:3); even fraternization with foreigners brings the plague (Num. 25:9, 18). Anyone who dissents, Yahweh burns up (Num. 11:1-3; 16:35); anyone who complains he strikes with plague (Num. 11:33; 14:37; 16:49), or sends poisonous snakes after (Num. 21:6). Aberrant cultic practices, even though indulged in innocently, bring death (Exod. 32:35; Num. 15:37-40).[1]

When reading this tedious mass of oft-cruel instructions about issues currently irrelevant to the bulk of humanity, it becomes obvious why Christianity was created as a sort of "Judaism Lite," with no need to follow the law in all its mind-numbing and draconian details.

To summarize, although parts of it are older, it has been surmised by many scholars that, during Josiah's time around 621 BCE, someone such as the high priest Hilkiah and his scribal underlings composed and/or combined much of the Pentateuch. This work evidently was redacted during the Babylonian exile in the sixth century and afterwards.

Elephantine Papyri

Throwing a wrench into the works of solving this puzzle of authorship and late dating of the Pentateuch's emergence, Gmirkin remarks:

> ...archaeological evidence fails to support the historicity of Josiah's reforms, essential for Wellhausen's theory of the historical circumstances which produced—and dated—D. The Elephantine Papyri show no evidence of the existence of any Pentateuchal writings as late as 400 BCE.[2]

Dating to between 494-400 BCE, the Elephantine Papyri "confirm the Jewish worship of the god Ya'u (alongside 'Anath, Bethel, Ishum and Herem); the Jewish observation of the Days of Unleavened Bread and (probably) Passover (related ostraca referred to both Passover and sabbath); and the religious authority of the Jewish high priest at Jerusalem from whom the Elephantine colonists sought support for the rebuilding of the Jewish temple at Elephantine."[3]

Fig. 11. Aramaic letter from Jewish community, 407 BCE. Papyrus, Elephantine, Egypt

As we can see, even in the fifth century, the Jews in Egypt remained polytheistic, continuing to worship their ancestral Canaanite/Semitic deities, cultic practices similar to

---

[1] Redford (1992), 276.
[2] Gmirkin, 5. See also Na'aman, 278.
[3] Gmirkin, 29-30.

those Jews in "other preexilic Jewish sanctuaries, notably at 7th-century Kuntillet 'Ajrud."[1] It should be kept in mind that, even after the fifth century, Jews in general continued to revere deities other than Yahweh, including syncretizing him with the gods Zeus, Dionysus and others.

Furthermore, the texts are devoid of the Mosaic writings, as Gmirkin points out:

> Yet when the Elephantine Papyri are scoured for evidence of the existence of the Pentateuch or any portion thereof, the results are emphatically negative. There is no evidence that the priests at Yeb were of Aaronide descent. Indeed, there is no mention of Aaron or Levites in the papyri. Of over 160 Jews at Elephantine mentioned in the papyri, not one name comes from the Pentateuch. Nor is there any reference in the papyri to the Exodus or any other biblical event. Reference to laws of Moses or other authoritative writings is entirely absent....
>
> ....The extraordinary absence of any reference to the contents of the Pentateuch in the Elephantine Papyri is all the more remarkable given the friendly contacts between the Jews of Elephantine and the priests of the temple of Jerusalem.[2]

It would seem that the Pentateuch was unknown to these Jews and those at Jerusalem in the fifth century BCE. If so, it remains to be explained, if Hezekiah and Josiah were real people, what they did instead of these biblical accounts and why they were singled out for this falsification of history.

Ezra's Memories

Also purportedly written in the fifth century, at 2 Kings 23 we read that the Torah was lost once more, to be reproduced reputedly from memory around 425 BCE by Ezra. For various reasons, including the entire Old Testament/Tanakh's apparent emergence in the historical record during this era, it was suggested by Porphyry and others that Ezra himself composed much of the text. As we have seen, there are apparently even later strata in some parts of the text, however, indicating composition and/or redaction after Ezra's time, particularly in light of the Elephantine papyri's omissions.

After Ezra, once more these books disappear, supposedly destroyed by Greco-Syrian king Antiochus IV Epiphanes in 180 BCE, to reappear yet again. With all this destruction, it would be difficult to believe that we possess the true words of Moses from over a thousand years earlier, unless they were preserved orally, as was the original divinely revealed instruction to the priests. Again, how could the law be lost for 600 years if there was a continuous oral tradition from Moses's day?

---

[1] For more on the Elephantine papyri, see the entry in Freedman, et al., 391.
[2] Gmirkin, 30.

Alexandria?

In his book *Berossus and Genesis, Manetho and Exodus*, Gmirkin "argues that the Hebrew Pentateuch was composed in its entirety about 273-272 BCE by Jewish scholars at Alexandria that later traditions credited with the Septuagint translation of the Pentateuch into Greek."[1] Gmirkin's theory of the Pentateuch's late date is "demonstrated by literary dependence on Berossus and Manetho," priests of Babylon and Egypt, respectively, during the third century BCE, and essentially constitutes the "definitive overthrow of the chronological framework of the Documentary Hypothesis."

He concludes:

> ...these multiple lines of evidence are consistent with the composition of the Pentateuch having taken place in 273-272 BCE. Analysis of the sources utilized in the Pentateuch point to Jewish access to Greek manuscripts of the Great Library in Alexandria. Authorship of key portions of the Pentateuch by Jewish scholars knowledgeable in Greek, and having access to Alexandria's library in 273-272 BCE, points to the identity of the authors of the Pentateuch with the team of seventy (or seventy-two) Jewish scholars whom tradition credited with having created the Septuagint translation about this same time through the generous patronage of Ptolemy II Philadelphus.[2]

We would not be surprised if Alexandria played a greater role then the mere translation of the Hebrew text into Greek. Yet, the Hebrew text clearly contains older sections composed centuries before this era, which could be passed along orally or in individual texts. In any event, Mosaic attribution cannot be sustained.

Ancient Egyptian Words

In attempting to assert that Moses did write the Pentateuch, Christian apologists claim that "50 words in the Torah are ANCIENT EGYPTIAN and that authentic Egyptian details are present in the text that no later redactor could know." The fact is that it would be quite easy for a later redactor to know much about Egypt, since not only was it close by and in constant communication with the Levant—having occupied the territory on and off for centuries—but also there existed many thousands of Egyptian writings from which to draw.

If the writers of the Torah knew 50 ancient Egyptian words, then some of these scribes likely were able to read the ancient Egyptian texts to a certain extent, which means the terms could have been copied from these writings, including various "historical" details. However, even then the Bible writers are very vague and do not present discernible historical details, such as dates or pharaohs' names.

---

[1] From the book's summary on Amazon.com, etc.
[2] Gmirkin, 3.

Savior of the Age

One of the Egyptian terms in the Bible, צפנת פענח *Tsaphnath phanehh* or *Zaphnathpaaneah* (Gen 41:45), is essentially the same as the Coptic: *Psontom phanech*,[1] which appears at a much later date, demonstrating the term's continued currency, such that it could have been known to scribes during the late first millennium BCE. The Septuagint renders this Egyptian title Ψονθομφανηx *Psonthomphanex*, while Josephus has it as Ψοθομφάνηxον *Psothomphanechon*, one of some 11 different variations in copies of the historian's works.[2]

Strong's Concordance (H6847) defines this term as "treasury of the glorious rest," while the New Living Translation (NLT) renders the name as "God speaks and lives." In his Vulgate Bible, St. Jerome/Hieronymus (347-420 AD/CE) translates the phrase into Latin as *Salvatorem mundi* or "savior of the world," while *Gesenius's Lexicon* relates the connotation of "savior of the age."

In consideration of the popularity of the Egyptian religion, this appellation, which Massey traces to Egyptian myth, may have been used commonly for many centuries. What it also reflects is that the Egyptians had the concept of a "world savior" long before Christianity. Indeed, one of these saviors was the god "Shu," whose name resembles "Yeho*shu*a," "Ye*shu*a" and "Jo*shu*a," a moniker denoting "salvation" or "Yahweh saves"[3] and rendered later as "Jesus."

Even if this Egyptian word is very ancient, there is little reason a writer centuries later could not have known terms from more archaic Egyptian to utilize for realism, particularly if the term was important and still in use. Fiction writers often use archaicisms and assorted other period pieces in placing their fictions in a historical setting.

Semitic and Egyptian Language Connections

Oddly enough in consideration of their physical proximity, a misconception lingers that the Semitic and Egyptian languages have little in common. Contradicting this erroneous impression, renowned Egyptologist Dr. Alan Gardiner (1879-1963), who specialized in Egyptian language, states:

> Unfortunately the origin of the EGYPTIAN LANGUAGE lies so far back in the uncharted past that only little that is certain can be said about it. Since it is generally agreed that the oldest population of Egypt was of African race, it might be expected that their language should be African too. And in fact many affinities with Hamitic and in particular with Berber dialects have been found, not only in vocabulary, but also in verbal structure and the like. On the other

---

[1] Allen, D., 122, citing Kircher.
[2] Massey (2007), 2.304.
[3] See *Christ in Egypt*, 329.

WHO WROTE THE PENTATEUCH?

hand, the relationship with Semitic (Hebrew, Arabic, etc.) is equally unmistakable, if not greater.[1]

Shem

As I relate in *Christ in Egypt* (256), one important apparent etymological connection between Israel and Egypt occurs in the word *shm* or *shem*, which in the languages of both nations is a title of divinity, meaning "mighty one" or "Power" in Egyptian, and "Name" as in the "Name of God" in Hebrew.[2]

Furthermore, in Egypt the sun often was deemed *shm* or "power" in the "eulogies of the offering" of the sun hymns.[3] Hence, there exists a solar correlation between the Egyptian *shm* and Semitic *shmsh* or Shamash, the Babylonian sun god. This fact could not have been lost on the Jews, who looked for pithy puns with cosmic connections demonstrating divine order.

Bilingual?

Even with this proximity and commonality, Bible apologists claim that the Pentateuch must have been written by Moses, because he was bilingual and knew both Hebrew and Egyptian, whereas "a thousand years later no Jews would have known that language" and that the Jews "might have known Coptic, but not hieratic or hieroglyphics which by this time were lost."

The contention is made by Messianic/Netzari Jewish minister Andrew Gabriel Roth:

> Psalm 104 was written 400 years before David was even born and found on the tomb wall of Akenaten, the first known Egyptian king to worship a single deity. EA Wallis Budge, one of the leading Egyptoligists [sic] of the 19th century, translated the tomb text and confirmed this was nearly verbatim. Moses even knew how long it took to embalm Jacob Egyptian style—70 days. That little nugget isn't even suggested until a thousand years after Moses by Herodotus, and his earliest mss [manuscripts] are hundreds of years after him. Not even the most liberal scholars date the Torah books as post-exilic. Similarly, burying someone in the sand was an ancient Egyptian ritual that pre-dates their writings. Only someone reared in the royal court could have known these things, and even if he [may] disagree with these details, there are many more examples where they came from.

All of these details would have been knowable and readily available centuries later, because of the huge literary record of the Egyptians, and the emulation of their religious traditions and practices, as well as their previous long-term presence in Canaan. It is noteworthy that Psalm 104 is recognized to have a relationship with the writings of the Egyptian pharaoh Amenhotep IV or

---

[1] Gardiner, 19.
[2] Strong's H8034; Hornung, 63; Faulkner (1962), 241.
[3] Assmann, (1995), 121.

Akhenaten (d. c. 1336 BCE), a correlation we will revisit later. This fact of "borrowing" in the Bible is highly significant and reveals the reliance on non-Israelite texts and themes, as we assert happened also with the bulk of the Pentateuch.

Egyptian Burial

In consideration of the fact that possibly half a billion or more people followed the Egyptian religion over its 3,000 years of popularity, the detail of the Egyptian burial likely was known widely by the time the Pentateuch actually was written. Burial in sand especially would have been known quite readily since, by that era, millions of poor people in particular would have been buried in the desert. This burial is logical for people of the deserts, especially those focused on preservation, as such entombment was the least expensive way to desiccate and mummify remains.

The reality is that a people subjugated in a foreign country for hundreds of years would include much *more* Egyptian in their language after all that time, particularly as concerns whatever tools or accoutrements they needed as supposed slave laborers during that long period. All innovations in Egypt proper likely would be termed in Egyptian, and if the Israelites had taken any of these novelties with them, they surely would import their Egyptian names as well.

The same might be said of at least some of the mass of booty the Israelites reputedly obtained from the Egyptians, including images of deities with Egyptian names. If the Exodus were true, and the Israelite slaves had lived in Egypt for centuries, with Moses purportedly having been born and raised in an Egyptian household, one would expect many more than just 50 Egyptian terms in the Pentateuch, which contains some 14,691 Hebrew words.

Hebrew Emergence

Moreover, since the Hebrew alphabet developed only after the "Phoenician" alphabet was created around 1050 BCE, Moses could not have written the Pentateuch in it some 200 or more years earlier. Prior to that development, cuneiform and Egyptian hieroglyphs/alphabet were used, with the latter "adapted for use with Semitic writing systems as early as 2000 BCE."[1] It seems highly improbable that Moses would have written in Hebrew in the second millennium using cuneiform, hieroglyphs or the apparently primitive Semitic script called "Proto-Sinaitic" (c. 1700-c. 1400 BCE). Nor is there evidence of any such edition of the Pentateuch or its progression towards the Hebrew text as we have it.

In addition, Hebrew as a spoken language was confined largely to the period between the 10th and seventh centuries, long after Moses's alleged time. Thus, we can look towards this era for the composition

---

[1] Schniedewind, 34.

of various oral traditions that many have made it into the Bible. After that point, Aramaic became the lingua franca among Semites, extending into other regions, especially north and east.

Furthermore, according to scholarly consensus, while archaicisms do appear in the text, the written language used in the Old Testament/Tanakh, Classical Hebrew, flourished mainly during the sixth century, "around the time of the Babylonian exile." Hence, it is not possible that centuries earlier Moses wrote in Classical Hebrew when recording his Pentateuch.

In reality, the oldest alphabetical text found in Judea appears on a jar discovered near the Temple Mount in Jerusalem that dates to the tenth century.[1] However, the inscription is Canaanite, not Hebrew, which does not emerge in the extant archaeological record until the eighth century. As pre-Israelite, the artifact may have belonged to a Jebusite or pre-Davidic inhabitant of Jerusalem, named "Jebus" at the time.[2]

Conclusion

In the end, there exists no credible, scientic evidence for the biblical story of Moses writing the Torah or receiving the law from the Most High God. Rather, the Pentateuch evidently comprises compositions possibly from the tenth century BCE to the third, having their origin in the pretended divine attribution of the newly fanatical monotheism under Yahweh.

During the exile in the sixth century, Jewish priests evidently studied Babylonian texts in the library there, learning much about Mesopotamian and Persian religions, which, it is contended, they incorporated into Judaism. Many parts of the Old Testament can be found in older writings such as the Canaanite, Sumero-Babylonian and Egyptian, and a redaction of these texts at that time would explain much of the religious syncretism in the Bible. It is possible, of course, that Jews at Alexandria also had access to these earlier texts, explaining a possible later redaction there during the third century as well.

---

[1] See "Oldest Alphabetical Written Text Found Near Temple Mount."
[2] Jos 15:63; 2 Sam 5:6.

Fig. 12. Israelite reformer king Hezekiah and his men destroy idols, including Moses's brazen serpent (2 Kings 18)

Fig. 13. Josiah smashes the idols of Baal (2 Ki 23). (*Holman Bible*, 1890)

Was Moses an Egyptian Pharaoh or Priest?

"An Egyptian priest named Moses, who possessed a portion of the country called the Lower [Egypt]..., being dissatisfied with the established institutions there, left it and came to Judæa with a large body of people who worshipped the Divinity. He declared and taught that the Egyptians and Africans entertained erroneous sentiments, in representing the Divinity under the likeness of wild beasts and cattle of the field; that the Greeks also were in error in making images of their gods after the human form. For God [said he] may be this one thing which encompasses us all, land and sea, which we call heaven, or the universe, or the nature of things."[1]

Strabo, *Geography* (16.2.35)

"Was Akhenaten the Egyptian Moses? Was the Biblical image of Moses a mnemonic transformation of the forgotten pharaoh? Only 'science fiction' can answer these questions by a simple 'yes.' But mnemohistory is able to show that the connection between Egyptian and Biblical monotheism, or between an Egyptian counter-religion and the Biblical aversion to Egypt, has a certain foundation in history; the identification of Moses with a dislocated memory of Akhenaten had already been made in antiquity."

Dr. Jan Assmann, *Moses the Egyptian* (24)

"Before much of the archaeological evidence from Thebes and from Tell el-Amarna became available, wishful thinking sometimes turned Akhenaten into a humane teacher of the true God, a mentor of Moses, a Christlike figure, a philosopher before his time. But these imaginary creatures are now fading away one by one as the historical reality gradually emerges. There is little or no evidence to support the notion that Akhenaten was a progenitor of the full-blown monotheism that we find in the Bible. The monotheism of the Hebrew Bible and the New Testament had its own separate development—one that began more than half a millennium after the pharaoh's death."

Dr. Donald B. Redford, "Aspects of Monotheism," *Biblical Archaeology Review*

ALTHOUGH THERE is no hard evidence that Moses was a historical personage who composed the Pentateuch based on his actual experiences, over the centuries it has been posited that the alleged Israelite founder was one or another of a number of Egyptian pharaohs, priests or other notables from the land of the Nile. The pharaoh most commonly identified as Moses has been Amenhotep IV (d. 1336/4 BCE), whose later pseudonym was Akhenaton/Akhenaten,

---

[1] Strabo/Hamilton, 3.177.

associated with the patriarch primarily because both the Egyptian and the Hebrew are attributed with "discovering" monotheism. Another pharaoh identified as Moses was Thutmose II (fl. 1493-1479 BCE). The purportedly historical pharaoh of the biblical story has been posited variously to be Ahmose I (fl. c. 1550–1525 BCE), Thutmose III (fl. 1479-1425 BCE), Akhenaten's son Tutankhamun (fl. c. 1332-1323 BCE), Ramesses I (fl. c. 1295/2-1290 BCE) and Ramesses II (c. 1303-1213 BCE). All of these individuals thrived at different periods, a fact that indicates the swampy "historical" ground upon which the Exodus tale has been set.

Exodus Date

We have seen already that Moses's era has been dated variously during the second millennium BCE. In order to determine the date of Moses and the pharaoh or priest he is suggested to be, if any, we need to know the date of the Exodus itself. However, numerous dates also have been put forth as the time of the "historical" Exodus, ranging across several centuries during the second millennium BCE, including 1960, 1796, 1776, 1738, 1700, 1683, 1598, 1582, 1570-1550, 1561-1542, 1555, 1552, 1523, 1513, 1446, 1290 and others.[1] This plethora of dates reveals the murky depths we encounter when trying to place the Exodus into history.

At 1 Kings 6:1, we learn that Solomon's temple was constructed in the 480th year after the Exodus, possibly built around 961 BCE, which would thus date the flight out of Egypt to 1441 BCE.[2] Yet, there has been not found a single artifact or stone to indicate where Solomon's Temple existed, or *if* it existed. This edifice supposedly was destroyed in 587 by the Neo-Babylonian conqueror Nebuchadnezzar II (c. 605-562 BCE), but no substantiating Babylonian record has been discovered.

Akhenaten the Monotheist?

Despite being incompatible with the date of 1441, the pharaoh Amenhotep IV/Akhenaten (13th cent.) is believed widely to have been the "historical Moses" because both individuals purportedly discovered monotheism. Akhenaten set up a new capital at a place called Amarna and went on a massive building campaign to establish his chosen god, the solar Aten, as the main Egyptian deity. However, Akhenaten did not discover monotheism as we know it; rather, he

---

[1] See Stephen Meyer for a survey of the numerous possible dates for the Exodus. The date of 1446 has been proposed by theologian Dr. Bryan G. Wood, among others. The date of 1960 reflects the story of the priest Sinuhe's flight from Egypt upon the death of the pharaoh Amenemhet I, which some have sought to identify with the Exodus. (See discussion below.)
[2] 1 Kings 6:1: "In the four hundred and eightieth year after the people of Israel came out of the land of Egypt, in the fourth year of Solomon's reign over Israel, in the month of Ziv, which is the second month, he began to build the house of the LORD."

focused on one god as chief above all the others, who nevertheless remained real. This perception of a god above all others already existed within Egyptian religion but was not necessarily a fanaticism among the ruling elite until Akhenaten.

Monolatry and 'Polytheistic Monotheism'

The practice of favoring one god over all others is called "monolatry" or "henotheism."[1] The original Egyptian idea of "monotheism" or, rather, *monolatry*, represented one main god (e.g., Ptah as creator) whose attributes were "limbs" or "auxiliaries," perceived as other deities.

Among other appellations, these auxiliary or prototype gods have been said to be "Ari" or "Ali,"[2] an Egyptian word, or , meaning "to make, to do, to create, to form," "to be made" and "to be used as an auxiliary."[3] It is claimed that all other deities proceed from the Ari, a term that is part of the name *Aus-ar(i)* or Osiris,[4] among many other Egyptian usages. The "enthroned eye" hieroglyph is also the symbol of Horus and the sun.[5]

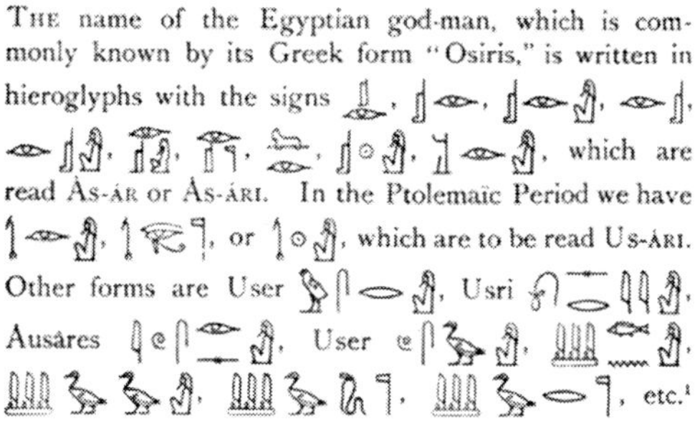
THE name of the Egyptian god-man, which is commonly known by its Greek form "Osiris," is written in hieroglyphs with the signs , , , , , , , , , which are read Ás-Ár or Ás-Ári. In the Ptolemaic Period we have , , or , which are to be read Us-Ári. Other forms are User , Usri , Ausàres , User , , , , , etc.[1]

Fig. 14. Hieroglyphs for 'Asari.' (Budge, 1973:1.25)

---

[1] Monolatry is "the worship of only one god, although other gods are recognized as existing" or "the exclusive worship of one god without excluding the existence of others." Henotheism is "the worship of a particular god, as by a family or tribe, without disbelieving in the existence of others" or "ascription of supreme divine attributes to whichever one of several gods is addressed at the time."

[2] Massey (1883:2.22): "The *Ari* in Egyptian are the companions, the watchers who became the seven Kab-ari, as the Ari of Kheb (Egypt)..." See also Massey (1907:1.421-422): "This first company of the gods in the fields of heaven were the Ali or Ari (as in the seven Kab-ari) by name, and the Ali are a group of companions who are herein set forth as co-creators of all that exists in heaven and earth." Citing Louvre Papyrus 3283, Egyptologist Sir Peter Renouf (217) relates various invocations, such as: "Hail to you, ye gods, ye associate gods, *who are without body* who rule that which is born from the earth and that which is produced in the house of your cradles [in heaven]... Ye prototypes of the image of all that exists, ye fathers and mothers of the solar orb, ye forms, ye great ones (*uru*), ye mighty ones (*āaiu*), ye strong ones (*nutriu*), first company of the gods of Atmu, who generated men and shaped the form of every form, ye lords of all things: hail to you, ye lords of eternity and everlasting!" In Canaanite/Ugaritic, as in Arabic, *'ali* means "exalted one," serving as a title for Baal. (Redford, 1992:109; Albright, 57) The comparable Hebrew term is עלה `*alah* (H5927), "to exalt," etc.

[3] Budge (2003a), 1.65.

[4] Budge (1973), 1.25

[5] Grant Bey states that "As-ari" or Osiris means "the enthroned eye," as in the "all-seeing eye," an emblem often representing the god's son, Horus, and symbolic of the

Concerning this "polythestic monotheism," as it were, Dr. James A.S. Grant Bey (1840-1896) summarizes:

> The one God of the Egyptians was nameless; but the combination of all the other good divinities made up His attributes, which were simply powers of nature.... In the ancient Egyptian religion, therefore, we have clearly depicted to us an unnamed almighty Deity, who is uncreated and self-existent.[1]

Yahweh eventually possessed similar attributes but appears as such much later in the literary record.

German Egyptologist Dr. Jan Assmann (b. 1938) likewise comments that "most polytheisms known to the history of religion are complex in the sense that they reckon—or better, live—with a divine realm beyond which there is a 'god' or 'highest being' who created the world and its deities."[2]

As I state in my book *Christ in Egypt* (56), although it is widely believed that monotheism was introduced essentially by Akhenaten, the consensus of earlier Egyptologists was that monotheism and polytheism existed side by side at least as early as the Fifth Dynasty,[3] around 2500 BCE. We would venture that such concepts may have been devised much earlier in humankind's long history, possibly tens of thousands of years previously, as among the world's oldest peoples such as the Pygmies or Ituri people of the Congo.[4]

The notion of "polytheistic monotheism," reflecting one divine whole with many auxiliaries or "gods," can be found within Hinduism as well, which posits the figure of Brahman, the transcendent, supreme universal being from whom all creation emanates and is expressed as the numerous deities. An example of Indian monolatry can be found in *Rigveda* Hymn 10.121, a text little different from what we find in Genesis as concerns the biblical god, but which dates to some 3,000 years ago at the latest.[5]

Syncretism and Oneness

Discussing the sacred fusion of Egyptian gods, Egyptologist Dr. James P. Allen states:

> Although the Egyptians recognized most natural and social phenomena as separate divine forces, they also realized that many of

---

sun. (Houghton, 265) It is also speculated that Osiris/Ausari is related to "Asari," an epithet of the Babylonian god Marduk. (See, e.g., Griffiths, 91)

[1] Houghton, 265. Grant Bey's essay in Houghton rates as one of the best summaries of the Egyptian religion. An esteemed lay Egyptologist, Grant spent many years as a physician in Cairo and was awarded the title of "Bey," meaning "Lord."
[2] Assmann (2001), 11.
[3] Budge (1967/1895), xciii.
[4] See, e.g., Hallet, 70.
[5] Conservative scholarship places the composition of various parts of the Rigveda between 1700 and 1000 BCE. Indian scholars push the text's date back thousands of years, based upon the geography and astronomy found therein. (See, e.g., Tilak.) For a copy of Hymn 10.121, see *The Study Guide for Did Moses Exist?*

these were interrelated and could also be understood as *different aspects of a single divine force*. That realization is expressed in the practice known as "syncretism," the combining of several gods into one.[1]

Egyptian monolatry appears in the Coffin Texts (c. 2181-2041 BCE), which repeatedly refer to the "primeval god" or the "Primeval One," who is "superior to the primeval gods" (Coffin Text Spell 39)[2] and who is "older than the gods" (CT Sp. 317).[3]

Concerning the concept of oneness within the Egyptian faith, Assmann remarks, "Time and again the Egyptian sources predicate the oneness/singleness/uniqueness of a god."[4] In this regard, in the Egyptian religion the great God Sun is "the One Alone with many arms."[5]

Atenism

Rather than discovering such "monotheism," already a concept well developed by his ancestral Egyptians and others previously, Akhenaten emphasized the Aten, also transliterated as "Aton," said to be the "primal god"[6] and represented by the disk of the sun. Aten worship was called "Aten monolatry," "Atenism" or the "Amarna heresy." Initially, Akhenaten was not a monotheistic fanatic who destroyed all other symbols of deity, but he did become increasingly intolerant, going almost as far as the Israelites, as depicted in the Old Testament.

The record shows Akhenaten, like a good Yahwist king, eventually defacing and closing temples, especially those of the old supreme god Amun, as well as destroying idols, while declaring in his "Great Hymn to the Aten": "O Sole God beside whom there is none."[7] However, we do not find accounts of the pharaoh ordering his troops to purge the land of heathens, as we do throughout the

Fig. 15. Akhenaten worshipping solar disc Aten, rays extend as hands holding life-giving ankhs or Egyptian crosses, 14th cent. BCE. Alabaster carving from tomb of Akhenaten, Amarna, Egypt

---

[1] Allen, J.P. (2000), 44. (Emph. added.)
[2] Faulkner (1973), 1.31.
[3] Faulkner (1973), 1.241.
[4] Assmann (1995), 134.
[5] Assmann (1995), 153.
[6] Bromiley, 4.104.
[7] See *The Study Guide* for the entire hymn.

Pentateuch with Moses and the "chosen people," commanded to slaughter entire cultures, such as the Midianites at Numbers 31.

Prophet of God or Megalomaniac?

The same megalomaniacal fanaticism by which Akhenaten declared himself the sole god's only mediator can be seen also in the stories of Jesus and Mohammed, as well as to a certain extent that of the Persian divine lawgiver Zoroaster, among many others who professed to speak for God or a god. Rather than representing a historical Moses who did the same, Akhenaten appears to be the most visible individual in a long line of religious fanatics. He also seems to be one of the relatively few megalomaniacal "prophets" who actually was historical. The conclusion is that, while Atenism started out as monolatristic or henotheistic, worshipping one god among many, the pharaoh subsequently became increasingly fanatical, asserting superiority and dominance of the Aten.

Hebrew Henotheism

While proselytizing the most fanatical type of monotheism, the Bible also depicts the Israelites and Jews as worshipping many other gods, and an apparent henotheism or monolatry develops out of this behavior, as in: "Thou shalt have no other gods before me." The Hebrew word for "gods" in this verse at Exodus 20:3 is אלהים *'elohiym,* the plural of אל *'el,* this latter denoting "god" but also, importantly, the name of the Canaanite high god, El or Ilu.[1]

The resemblance between the Semitic Elohim/Elim[2] and the Egyptian Ari/Ali has been noted.[3] In this regard, the Egyptian "First Dynasty of Gods" often has been equated with the Elohim,[4] a plural word frequently rendered as the singular "God." As Grant Bey says: "The Elohim of the Hebrews was exactly the same as the gods of the Egyptians, i.e., a unity in plurality and vice versa, and God with many attributes."[5]

---

[1] Gray (1965:161) shows that "El" is most often if not exclusively used in the Ugaritic texts not as a general moniker for "god" but as the name of the preeminent Ugaritic god. (See the discussion of El below.)

[2] Daniel 11:36 and Isaiah 57:5 read אלים *elim* for "gods."

[3] Speaking of the creation stories in Genesis 1 and 2, Massey (1907:1.424) remarks: "All through [the first] chapter the creators are the associate-gods, the Egyptian Ali, the Phoenician Elohim. In the second chapter, one of the Elohim is individualized by name as Iahu or Iahu-Elohim, translated as 'the Lord God,' which might be rendered the god Iahu = Iu-em-hetep." Derived from the Phoenician 𐤀, the Hebrew letter א *aleph*—the first letter in the word אל *'el*—is equivalent to an "a" and is pronounced here as "āl," as in "ale." As such, the word has been transliterated also as *al,* in which can be seen the Ali and the Arab deities Allat and Allah. While Ilu is the main Ugaritic god, the Arabic word for "god," as in "a god" or "a deity," is generally transliterated as *illah,* while *the* God, Allah, is a contraction of Al-Ilah.

[4] See, e.g., Houghton, 262.

[5] Houghton, 265.

As we can see, the plural Elohim represent the same type of monolatry or "polytheistic monotheism," eventually serving as a single title for Yahweh, culminating in the Hebrew henotheism.

It has been contended thus that Moses was a henotheist or monolatrist, rather than a strict monotheist, since, in the biblical tale, he acknowledges the existence and power of other gods. The monolatry and henotheism of the Old Testament are made clear in the passages in which Yahweh competes with other deities, defeating them but nevertheless maintaining that they are real and indeed have supernatural powers.

This depiction of other gods as "real" can be found also in biblical contests with other humans, such as at 1 Kings 17:1, when the Hebrew prophet Elijah (9th cent. BCE?) cuts off Baal's life-giving water, connoting the dew and/or rain. This miracle is reiterated in the New Testament epistle of James (5:17), in which Elijah is portrayed as praying successfully for a drought. There are many such instances in the Bible in which the gods of other cultures are depicted as real beings, including where the word *elohim* is used.

Regarding the claim of Mosaic monotheism, Jewish studies professor Dr. Frank Eakin concludes:

> ...the highest claim to be made for Moses is that he was, rather than a monotheist, a monolatrist.... The attribution of fully developed monotheism to Moses is certainly going beyond the evidence.[1]

Hence, again, Moses may be viewed as a monolatrist or henotheist, rather than a monotheist. If we accept that some of the Pentateuch was composed up until the third century, it is possible that Jewish monotheism or henotheism with the Judean tribal god becoming transcendent was influenced by Plato, rather than discovered by a historical Moses.

Abraham's Polytheism?

As further evidence, if Moses were the "discoverer" of pure monotheism, then what was his predecessor patriarch, Abraham? If Moses were the first "monotheist," then Abraham was not, and his god is one of many. Is Abraham to be admitted as having been polytheistic? If so, he could be viewed as a follower of El Elyon, the "God Most High," *a separate deity*, rather than simply a god-name of Yahweh, as at Genesis 14:19:

> And he blessed him and said, "Blessed be Abram by God Most High, maker of heaven and earth...

The original Hebrew for this verse is:

ויברכהו ויאמר ברוך אברם לאל עליון קנה שמים וארץ:

Here we discover not only this figure of אל עליון *'el 'elyown* but also שמים *shamayim*, rendered "heaven." *Shamayim* or *šmym* is a Ugaritic/

---
[1] Eakin, 107-108.

Canaanite name, meaning "celestials"[1] or "celestial beings," related to the West Semitic god of the heavens, transliterated *Šmm*.[2] In these words *shamayim* and *šmm*, we may also see inferences of the Semitic term שמש *sh.m.sh*, a vowel-less word frequently transliterated as *shemesh* or *shamash*, "sun." These heavenly words also are related evidently to the Indo-European root *sm* denoting "sun,"[3] a logical premise in consideration of the fact that the sun dominates the heavens.

El Shaddai

At Genesis 17:1, Abraham is depicted as worshiping another of the Elohim, El Shaddai:

> When Abram was ninety-nine years old the LORD appeared to Abram, and said to him, "I am God Almighty; walk before me, and be blameless."

The Hebrew here for "God Almighty" is אל שדי *'el Shadday*, the latter word used 48 times in the Old Testament.[4] El Shaddai is evidently an Ugaritic/Canaanite god, one of the 70 Elohim or "sons of El," like the limbs of the main god within the religious philosophy of Egypt and India, for example.

El Shaddai is also an epithet used at Exodus 6:3 to describe "one of the patriarchal names for the tribal god of the Mesopotamians"[5]:

> I appeared to Abraham, to Isaac, and to Jacob, as El Shaddai, but by my name YHWH I did not make myself known to them.
>
> וארא אל־אברהם אל־יצחק ואל־יעקב באל שדי ושמי יהוה לא נודעתי להם:

Jacob is the patriarch whose offspring represented the 12 tribes of Israel (Gen 47-49).

Yahweh Supremacy

Thus, Exodus 6:3 introduces us to Yahweh on Mt. Horeb, while various other verses likewise depict him as coming from Horeb/Sinai.[6] In this verse, the Hebrew word usually translated "Lord" is the tetragrammaton יהוה *Yĕhovah*.[7] The inference is that, prior to this moment in the Israelite story, God never had been known by this name יהו YHWH. The term here for "my name" is שם *shem*, as in השם *HaShem* or "the Name," the

Fig. 16. Hebrew tetragrammaton signifying 'YHWH,' 'Yahweh'

---

[1] Sanders, 364.
[2] Tsumura (2005), 61; Gordon (1990), 2.83. Tsumura notes that *šmm* or *šamuma* corresponds to the Sumerian sky god, An.
[3] *Gesenius*, 174.
[4] Strong's H7706.
[5] "El Shaddai," *Wikipedia*.
[6] E.g., Deut 33:2; Jdg 5:5; and Ps 68:8.
[7] Strong's H3068.

code word for the theonyms Yahweh and Adonai, which pious Jews are loathe to pronounce (Lev 24:11).

Yet, despite this purported introduction in Exodus, the writer of Genesis evidently erred with an anachronism by including Yahweh in the verse at 15:7, in which the god appears to Abraham:

> And he said to him, "I am the LORD who brought you from Ur of the Chalde'ans, to give you this land to possess."

ויאמר אליו אני **יהוה** אשר הוצאתיך מאור כשדים לתת לך את־הארץ הזאת לרשתה:

In this Genesis verse, God goes by the tetragrammaton יהוה *Yĕhovah*, even though at Exodus 6:3 it is claimed Abraham did not know the deity by that name. In addition, at Genesis 21:33 we find Abraham planting a tree at Beersheba and calling on Yahweh:

יהוה אל עולם or "YHWH El Everlasting."

The Hebrew word here for "everlasting" is עולם *'owlam*.

In spite of the claims of Yahweh being unknown to Abraham, the sacred tetragrammaton is used throughout Genesis, attributed by modern scholarship not to Moses but to an unknown scribe or scribes. This disparity of when Yahweh first emerges on the scene is one of those problems addressed by the Documentary Hypothesis, which evinces that the discussions of Yahweh in Genesis emanate from the hand of "J" or the "Jahwist" source text, while the Exodus introduction was composed by the "E" or "Elohist" a century or so later.[1]

Amos

In any event, the Bible itself makes it clear that Yahweh as a dominant force is a later development in the Israelite pantheon of earlier Semitic gods. The biblical book of Amos (4:13, 5:8) insists on Yahweh's supremacy, and it would seem that it was during this Hebrew prophet's era (c. 750 BCE) that the push for domination and exclusion was intensified, with the result of Hezekiah's purges, Manasseh's "relapse" and Josiah's renewed violent Yahwist fanaticism. The northern kingdom of Samaria is the particular area of interest for Amos's Yahwist diatribe, since the god was special to the south, which attempted constantly to force him upon the north, as the latter continued to "whore after" or worship the gods of their forebears and neighbors.

From Sun Disc to Cosmic God

Yahweh's development from tribal war and volcano god[2] to *the* God of the universe is similar to the earlier monolatristic progression

---

[1] Friedman (2003:10): "The sources in the text are then nearly 100 percent consistent on this matter. The E and P sources identify God as El or simply as 'God' (Hebrew: Elohim) until the name is revealed to Moses. After that, they use the name YHWH as well. The J source meanwhile uses the name YHWH from the beginning."

[2] See, e.g., Acharya (2004), 119f.

of Aten from a sun disc to a universal deity. Moreover, Akhenaten's later fanaticism of banning religious images other than the solar disc resembles Jewish law, but predates its formulation by many centuries. Hence, if borrowing there be, it would be from the Egyptian to the Israelite.

In the final analysis, it is surmised that the Jews were not monotheistic until the time of the Maccabees (2nd cent. BCE).[1] Nevertheless, they continued well into the common era to feature Greek gods and others in their mosaics and other depictions, as well as in spells syncretizing Yahweh to these numerous other deities, as we shall see.

Great Hymn to Aten and Psalm 104

Within this syncretism appear solar concepts as in the biblical Psalm 104, based on the same genre as Akhenaten's famous "Great Hymn to Aten."[2] While Akhenaten flourished in the 14th century BCE, the earliest psalm by conservative dating was written during the First Temple Period, which traditionally began around 950 BCE, with the latest psalm perhaps composed during the sixth century BCE. Critical scholars date the composition or compilation of biblical texts to later centuries, although these scriptures may represent more ancient writings and oral traditions to some extent, as is surely the case with Psalm 104.

Concerning the relationship between the Egyptian and Hebrew texts, Redford remarks:

> Certain affinities have long since been pointed out between the hymn to the sun-disc and Psalm 104, and the parallels are to be taken seriously. There is, however, no literary influence here, but rather a survival in the tradition of the northern centers of Egypt's once great empire of the *themes* of that magnificent poetic creation.[3]

Rather than direct dependence, Psalm 104 may have been based on a widespread and enduring genre of solar hymns with the same or similar themes, possibly themselves based on Akhenaten's hymn.

However, Oxford Old Testament professor Dr. John Day outlines various commonalities between the two texts and remarks:

> ...Psalm 104 is indeed dependent on Akhenaten's hymn to the Sun but...this dependence is confined to Ps. 104.20-30. This is because the parallels here are especially impressive, all of them with one exception occurring in the same order, a point often overlooked, which seems too much to attribute to coincidence.[4]

Day concludes that "it very much looks as if the author of Psalm 104 did indeed have access to Akhenaten's hymn to the Sun in some

---

[1] See, e.g., "Asherah," *Wikipedia*.
[2] See *The Study Guide* for the complete hymn.
[3] Redford (1987), 233.
[4] Gillingham, 213.

form."[1] He further cites the close relationship between the Canaanites and Egyptians of the era, including Akhenaten's two "high officials of Canaanite or Syrian origin."[2] He also surmises that the hymn may have passed into the Near East during the reign of Akhenaten, when Canaan was part of the Egyptian empire. Here it was translated into Northwestern Semitic at some point, ending up as Psalm 104.

Other than the megalomania and fanatical monolatry or henotheism, a characteristic shared by many other individuals over the millennia, there exists little resemblance between the lives of Akhenaten and Moses. Akhenaten is not recorded as having been chased by a pharaoh across the miraculously parted Red Sea with some two or three million people in tow, to be led through the desert by pillars of cloud and fire, and sustained for 40 years by the Jewish tribal god Yahweh's miraculous creation of manna from heaven and water from a rock, and so on.

Moreover, the timing of Akhenaten (d. c. 1336/4 BCE) does not correspond to the traditionally posited dates of 1441, 1290 or others proffered over the centuries for the Exodus. For these reasons, the historical correlation between the two figures has been dismissed by scholarly consensus. Furthermore, it is the opinion of Israeli archaeologists such as Finkelstein that the Israelites emerged from the Samaritan and Judean hill country at the beginning of the Iron Age, centuries after Akhenaten.

Thutmose II

Because of his name and the dating in 1 Kings of 1441, some researchers have surmised that the pharaoh who ruled previous to that time, Thutmose II (fl. 1500/1493-1489/79 BCE), was Moses himself. For example, after attempting to locate various places cited in the Mosaic account, Christian physician Dr. Lennart Möller tries to identify the "historical Moses" with Thutmose II, whose Egyptian name *dhwty-ms* is transliterated also as Thutmosis, Tuthmose, Tutmosis, Thothmes, Tuthmosis, Djhutmose and so on.

Möller gives a long list of correspondences between the two individuals, but there exists no corroborative evidence that Thutmose II did magic tricks and miracles or was aided by the Jewish tribal god Yahweh in plaguing Egypt, and so on. We have no record of Thutmose II fleeing Egypt with the current pharaoh in pursuit, subsequently drowned with his entire army.

Nor is Thutmose II recorded as having parted supernaturally the Red Sea or been guided by massive pillars of cloud and fire showing the way. We hear nothing about magical manna falling from heaven during Thutmose II's life, or about his settling "the Promised Land." This association represents speculation based on the assumption

---

[1] Gillingham, 221.
[2] Gillingham, 222.

that the Bible story is true, that Moses was a historical personage, and that he was raised in the Egyptian royal house.

Regarding this contention, a reviewer of Möller's book, Christian scholar van der Veen, comments:

> If Moses had ruled Egypt as Pharaoh for some time, one would expect the biblical writers/redactors to have known. Also, Thutmosis II was not the son of an Israelite by the name of Amram (Moses' father according to Exodus 6:20), but in reality the son and successor of Pharaoh Thutmosis I by his lesser wife Mutnofret. Nor did he reach the mature age of over [a] hundred years as Moses apparently did, but died at a tender age of not more than thirty years. His mummy was found in the Royal Cache at Deir el-Bahri in Upper-Egypt. This find has allowed scholars to establish that he indeed was Thutmosis I's blood-related heir. The suggestion that Thutmosis II was in reality the Israelite Moses is therefore simply nonsensical.

Indeed, if Moses truly wrote the Pentateuch—as the devout Möller believes—the patriarch surely would have known that he himself was the pharaoh.

Möller also has a lengthy comparison of Moses with other individuals,[1] and, while the characteristics he lays out do seem to be valid parallels, they are not so extraordinary as to indicate exclusivity, which is obvious from the fact that Möller can make these comparisons between Moses and *several* historical persons.

Etymology of Moses

One of the reasons for associating Moses with various pharaohs is because of the shared name "mose" or "moses" in their monikers. The biblical definition of "Moses," משה *Mosheh* in the Hebrew, is given simply as "drawn,"[2] as at Exodus 2:10:

> And the child grew, and she brought him to Pharaoh's daughter, and he became her son; and she named him Moses, for she said, "Because I drew him out of the water."

Subsequent commentators have denoted the term to mean "drawn from the waters," although this latter part is based on the lawgiver's birth circumstances, not the root word, which means only "to draw." It remains to be explained why the Egyptian pharaoh's daughter would name a child with a Hebrew moniker in the first place.

In his book *On Moses*, Philo (1.17) averred that *mos* was Egyptian for "water,"[3] so it seems that even during the Jewish writer's time there was confusion as to the origin and connotation of the name Moses.

---

[1] See, e.g., Möller, 114ff.
[2] Strong's H4872.
[3] Philo/Yonge (2000), 460.

WAS MOSES AN EGYPTIAN PHARAOH OR PRIEST?

The archaic word משה *mshh* lacks vowels and therefore can be transliterated elsewise as well, however. *Mosheh* is said to derive from the root word essentially spelled the same: משה *mashah*.[1] The same word משה *mashah* is used at Psalm 18:16 to describe the psalmist as being "drawn out of many waters." It would appear that this motif in the Moses myth was incorporated from old, allegorical songs and verses such as this one, rather than representing a "historical fact" about the patriarch's nativity.

The name in the Greek Bible, both Old and New Testaments, is Μωυσῆς, transliterated as *Mōusēs* or *Möÿsēs*, whence "Moses," which is also how the name is written in the Latin Vulgate, revealing that the word was seen to end with an "s" in antiquity. Hence, it was perceived also as deriving from the Egyptian term ms or *mes/mesu*, which means "born of" or "birth."

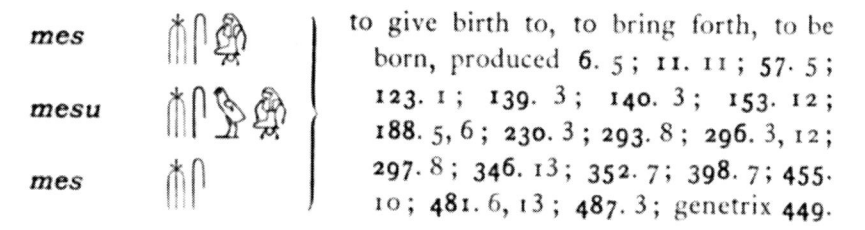

mes	𓄟𓇋𓇋𓀀	to give birth to, to bring forth, to be born, produced 6. 5; 11. 11; 57. 5; 123. 1; 139. 3; 140. 3; 153. 12; 188. 5, 6; 230. 3; 293. 8; 296. 3, 12; 297. 8; 346. 13; 352. 7; 398. 7; 455. 10; 481. 6, 13; 487. 3; genetrix 449.
mesu	𓄟𓇋𓇋𓀁	
mes	𓄟𓇋𓇋	

Fig. 17. Egyptian words *mes* and *mesu* denoting 'born.' (Budge, 1848:149)

In the Bible, the pharaoh's daughter raised Moses as her own after the baby was fished out of the river (Exodus 2:10); her other son is thus the older stepbrother of Moses, with the theory that the name Ahmose means "brother of Moses," and therefore it was during the reign of pharaoh Ahmose I that the patriarch lived. Despite claims to the contrary, the etymology of Ahmose, Amasis or Iahmes as "brother of Moses" is not sustainable, however, as Egyptologists are certain that the name means "born of the moon" or "the moon has given birth."[2] Furthermore, if the date for a "historical" Moses in the 15th or 13th century were accurate, then he could not have been the brother of a pharaoh from the 16th century.

Pharaoh Thutmose III

As concerns the identity of the pharaoh of the Exodus, to reiterate, the biblical date of 1441 would place the event in the reign of the pharaoh Thutmose III (fl. c. 1479-1426/5 BCE),[3] but no such massive event can be discovered in the historical or archaeological

---

[1] Strong's H4871.
[2] Vernus, et al., 2.
[3] The dating used in the present work follows the "low chronology," which posits the reign of Thutmose III to have begun in 1479 BCE, while the middle and high chronologies suggest his reign began in 1490 or 1504 BCE, respectively. (See, e.g., Redford 1992:xxiii)

record in Egypt or elsewhere at this time. This lack of record ranks as even more puzzling in consideration of the fact that Thutmose III has been considered "Egypt's greatest conqueror" and "the Napoleon of Egypt," whose many exploits were well and proudly documented.

Thutmose III went so far as Babylon, but in all contemporary texts there is no mention of any "Jews" or "Israelites" in Egypt or "Hebrews" in the Levant along the way. Nor can we equate Moses himself with Thutmose III, for the reasons that there is no evidence of any Exodus events in the life of this pharaoh and that Moses is clearly a mythical figure, as will be demonstrated abundantly in the present work.

It is possible that some details or bitter memories of Thutmose III's incursions into Canaan and Syria, such as the battle at Megiddo against the prince of Kadesh (c. 1479 BCE), were incorporated into the Exodus story many centuries later. However, the fact remains that the biblical account represents myth historicized, not history mythologized, as will be laid plain in the present work.

It is also noteworthy that, after this pharaoh's expansion, the Levant would have been full of Egyptian presence, thus refuting the impression given by the Exodus tale of being able to flee Egypt to there.

King Tut

As it was with Thutmose III, the suggestion of King Tutankhamun (fl. 1335-1325/3) as the pharaoh of the Exodus is likewise unsustainable. If the Israelites were supernaturally rewarded all of Egypt's wealth, where did Tut's magnificent treasures come from? Especially with such a devastated economy as would surely have followed the plagues and exodus from Egypt of some two million slaves who purportedly did all the work? And, if Tut were drowned in the Nile, how could his mummy be entombed in the Valley of the Kings? Moreover, the teen Tut was far too young to have been the stepbrother of the 80-year-old Moses.

Like these others, Tut too is not recounted as engaging in any of the events of the Exodus story, and we can say safely he is not the pharaoh of a historical Exodus.

Ramesses I

One scholarly tradition places the Exodus around 1290 BCE,[1] reducing the time between that and the accepted date of Solomon's temple to a mere 329 years, not the 480 of God's Inerrant Word. In this timeline, the pharaoh of the Exodus has been identified as Ramesses/Rameses/Ramses I (fl. 1292–90).[2] The same dearth of evidence for this contention in the historical/archaeological record

---

[1] E.g., the Revised Standard Version of the Bible ("RSV"), "Time Chart of Bible History."
[2] Harl has the dates for Ramesses I's reign as 1293-1291.

occurs in this era as well, but now the apology is that, since the Exodus represented a military defeat, it could have been ignored, because Egyptian rulers "never recorded their reverses and, in fact, transformed some of them into victories."[1]

If Egyptian rulers were prone to transforming defeats into victories, in such an extreme case as the Exodus tale one would expect that the pharaoh would boast loudly about having vanquished such a mighty foe with its powerful god. Nothing of the sort occurred, however, and there remains no other outside verification for any event of the Exodus, either during the time of Ramesses I or at all.

Seti I

Because the low chronology as proposed by American historian Dr. Kenneth W. Harl also places Seti I as Egypt's ruler during the period between 1292-1279,[2] this famous king likewise becomes a candidate for the Exodus pharaoh. While there indeed may have been resentment towards Seti I for his aggressions in Canaan against the various nomadic brigands there, no "historical" Exodus can be traced to his era.

Ramesses II

Over the centuries, Ramesses II (c. 1303-1213 BCE) has been the favored pharaoh of the Exodus. If Ramesses II was indeed the Exodus pharaoh, and if the Exodus actually occurred and the pharaoh was drowned during it, the event must have happened in 1213, when the Egyptian ruler died. That purported fact would mean that Ramesses II was 90 years old while chasing the 80-year-old Moses and 83-year-old Aaron through the desert (Exod 7:7), a rather implausible notion and one certainly not depicted in the popular film with the vigorous Charlton Heston and Yul Brynner!

Fig. 18. Ramesses II's victory in the Siege of Dapur, 13th cent. BCE. Mural at Thebes, Egypt (*Nordisk familjebok*)

The same objections apply here as previously about the other candidates for the Exodus pharaoh: There simply exists no historical or archaeological evidence for such a claim.

---

[1] Josephus/Maier, 95.
[2] The chronology of Egypt and the Near East is complicated, and several alternates have been proposed to the conventional "middle chronology" used throughout the present work. In addition to this middle chronology are the long/high, short/low and new, the latter proposed by Egyptologist Dr. David M. Rohl. Rohl's "New Chronology" may possess merit in various elements, but professional Egyptologists and historians have not embraced it as a whole. There are also the "ultra-high" and "ultra-low" chronologies sparsely employed.

Nectanebo II

If the Pentateuch was constructed during the third century BCE, using older texts and including much new material to glue it together, then some characteristics could have been borrowed from the pharaoh Nectanebo/Nakhthorheb II (fl. 360-342 BCE) as well, as proposed by Gmirkin. It is possible that characteristics from this pharaoh—the last native Egyptian to hold that position—were combined along with others to create an archetypal pharaoh for the purpose of playing the foil in the Exodus story. In this regard, Gmirkin evinces that "the geography of the Exodus reflects toponyms of the early Ptolemaic period and may allude to certain features of the Ptolemaic Nile-to-Red-Sea canal in place in ca. 273 BCE."[1]

It should be kept in mind, however, that there is evidence from the Song of the Sea and other apparently archaic writings that this archetypal designation of pharaoh as villain had been created hundreds of years earlier. This fact would not exclude a retelling centuries later with embellishments from subsequent Egyptian kings.

A Priest of Aten?

As previously seen, the ancient Greek geographer Strabo (c. 64/63 BCE-c. 23 AD/CE) contended Moses to be an Egyptian priest who, disgusted with the bizarre representations of the Egyptian gods, left Egypt with a band of followers to establish his new cult in Palestine.[2]

This alternate theory also was proposed in *Moses and Monotheism* by famous Viennese psychoanalyst Dr. Sigmund Freud (1856-1939), who suggested that the Hebrew lawgiver was a priest of Aten who, with his followers, escaped the purges subsequent to Akhenaten's death, eventually to found Judaism. This theory has been discounted as well, for the same reasons as applied to the Akhenaten thesis itself, such as incompatible dating and no real evidence, especially in the case of this hypothesized priest for whom there is no historical record.

Adon-Adonis

Freud's study remains useful, nevertheless, such as for his discussion of the numerous lawgiver myths and comparison of the Aten/Aton to Adon/Adonai and the Greco-Syrian god Adonis,[3] the latter an assessment discussed below.

---

[1] Gmirkin, 3.
[2] Assmann (1997), 38. Strabo (*Geo.* 16.2.35) "identifies Moses as an Egyptian priest holding part of Lower Egypt. As a result of his dissatisfaction with theological expressions there, Moses led a flight from Egypt." (Oblath, 28)
[3] Freud, 27. For other comparisons, see "The Connection of the Aton Religion with Older Religions" by Christian apologist Sir Arthur Weigall in *The Life and Times of Akhnaton Pharaoh of Egypt* (117). See also Redford (1992:45): "...in the case of the hero-god of Byblos [Baal], his 'lordship' tended, as the centuries passed, to find

As will be demonstrated in greater detail, rather than Moses representing Akhenaten or a priest of Aten, the Israelite lawgiver is more akin to Akhenaten's *god*, as the latter symbolizes significantly a solar entity or sun god, the actual disk of the solar orb, in fact, as well as the cosmic power behind it.

Historical Fiction

In this analysis, it is important to remember that, although they appear anciently in the historical record, many of the stories of these various pharaohs would have been forgotten to some extent by most people, probably, by the time the Bible was composed centuries later. Thus, it is unlikely that the Moses pharaoh would have been based entirely on any one of them. In this regard, some legendary exploits may have been passed along over the centuries, and certain rulers like Seti I and Ramesses III possibly would have been recalled with animosity for their alleged aggressions in Canaan.[1] As we shall see amply, the basic, archetypical motif existed first and was elaborated upon with mundane detail. The biblical story thus ranks as historicized fiction, rather than fictionalized history. The difference may be subtle but is important.

As another example, the fictional character of Gulliver by English author Jonathan Swift is placed into a historical setting, England, and certainly reflects aspects of one or more real people, since he acts like a human being, specifically a man. However, in no way could we claim that Gulliver is a "historical person" who has been fictionalized. Rather, he is a fictional character who has been placed into a historical setting.

Euhemerism/Evemerism

In certain instances, the opposite has occurred, and history has been fictionalized. The tradition of elevating a historical individual to the status of a deity, for example, is called "euhemerism" or, for pronunciation's sake, "evemerism." This perception is named after the Greek philosopher Euhemeros (4th cent. BCE), who posited that the gods originally had been the kings, queens, heroes and assorted other individuals from antiquity who were deified. This process is also styled "apotheosis," and, again, such deification of mortals *has* happened in the past, although less frequently than generally is believed.

This evemerism/apotheosis occurred, for example, with Alexander the Great (356-323 BCE), who was asserted by an oracle/priest to

---

expression in the local vernacular word for 'lord,' namely *Adon*, whence the classical 'Adonis.'" Egyptologist Assmann disagrees with the etymological connection between Aton/Aten and Adon.

[1] In reliefs at the site of Medinet Habu, Ramesses III brags about his purported incursion into the Amurru kingdom to fight back the Sea Peoples, but some modern historians doubt this battle occurred.

have been born of a mortal woman and the Greek god Zeus Ammon,[1] making him the son of God. Another instance of evemerism evidently transpired with the Egyptian architect and physician Imhotep (2650-2600 BCE), who was so esteemed that he was deified and worshipped as the god of medicine. Many historical rulers have been viewed as "gods on earth," "sons of God" or another divine concept, including among the ancient Israelites, whose kings were said to be the "begotten sons of Yahweh" as at Psalm 2:7:

> I will tell of the decree of the LORD: He said to me, "You are my son, today I have begotten you.

This same psalmist—traditionally King David—is not only the son of God but also the "anointed," styled *Christos* or "Christ" in the Septuagint, centuries before Jesus purportedly lived.

Astral Religion

The fact remains, however, that the bulk of those figures whom human beings have perceived or created as "gods" and "goddesses" were never real people who walked the earth before having a series of fabulous fairytales added to their biographies, as in the process of evemerism.

On the contrary, many deities are cosmic, allegorical and mythical entities based on nature worship, including the sun, moon, planets, stars, constellations and so on, anthropomorphized or personified, given human attributes and adventures that explained their characteristics, movements, phases and influences. This nature worship revolving around celestial bodies is called astral religion, astrolatry, astromythology or astrotheology.

In this regard, Bible scholar and mythicist Dr. Robert M. Price proclaims that "many, many of the epic heroes and ancient patriarchs and matriarchs of the Old Testament were personified stars, planets, and constellations..."[2] This assessment includes Moses, whose "life" is laden with solar mythology and astrotheology, as we shall see abundantly.

Conclusion

Since antiquity, attempts at identifying Moses in the historical record have included his equation with a variety of individuals from Egyptian history, such as various priests and pharaohs. Over the centuries, the Akhenaten thesis in particular has been hit upon in order to provide a historical background for the Hebrew patriarch, who is otherwise glaringly absent from the historical record. However, the Egyptian pharaoh Amenhotep IV, also known as Akhenaten, did not discover monotheism but only focused on one god in an overall

---

[1] See, e.g., Plutarch, *Life of Alexander* (3.1); Plutarch/Perrin, 7.229; Strabo 17.1.43: τοῦτο μέντοι ῥητῶς εἰπεῖν τὸν ἄνθρωπον πρὸς τὸν βασιλέα ὅτι εἴη Διὸς υἱός.
[2] Price, "Review of *Christ in Egypt* by D.M. Murdock."

religious ideology that had been in existence for centuries, if not millennia. Other than that fact of a religious disruption having to do with Egypt, there is little correspondence in the Akhenaten story to the life of Moses as found in the Old Testament. Nor can we say with any confidence that the Moses-Exodus tale is rooted in the escape of a priest of Aten during the purges that followed the death of Akhenaten. In reality, the Israelite lawgiver's purported biographical details find their place for the most part not in history but in myth.

Fig. 19. Akhenaten, Nefertiti and children with Aten and his rays/hands holding ankhs, c. 1350 BCE. Staatliche Museen in Berlin, Germany

The Exodus as History?

"They answered him, 'We are descendants of Abraham, and have never been in bondage to any one. How is it that you say, "You will be made free"?'"

John 8:33

"...After a century of exhaustive investigation, all respectable archaeologists have given up hope of recovering any context that would make Abraham, Isaac or Jacob credible 'historical figures.'... [A]rchaeological investigation of Moses and the Exodus has similarly been discarded as a fruitless pursuit. Indeed, the overwhelming archaeological evidence today of largely indigenous origins for early Israel leaves no room for an exodus from Egypt or a 40-year pilgrimage through the Sinai wilderness. A Moses-like figure may have existed somewhere in the southern Transjordan in the mid-late 13th century B.C., where many scholars think the biblical traditions concerning the god Yahweh arose. But archaeology can do nothing to confirm such a figure as a historical personage, much less prove that he was the founder of the later Israelite religion."

Dr. William G. Dever, *What Did the Biblical Writers Know and When Did They Know It?* (98-99)

"The exodus from Egypt is unknown to history save what is written in the Hebrew Bible. Outside of the most meager of circumstantial evidence we possess nothing to substantiate the text."

Dr. Michael D. Oblath, *The Exodus Itinerary Sites* (7)

"No direct evidence [of] the Israelite sojourn in Egypt and the Exodus can be extracted from archaeology."

Drs. Israel Finkelstein and Amihai Mazar, *The Quest for the Historical Israel* (59)

"The consensus among biblical scholars today is that there was never any exodus of the proportions described in the Bible, and that the story is best seen as theology, a story illustrating how the god of Israel acted to save and strengthen his chosen people, and not as history..."

"The Exodus," *Wikipedia*

IN THE BIBLE story of the Exodus, we are asked to believe that possibly two or three million fleeing people tromped through the desert from Egypt to Israel, requiring four decades to make this relatively short journey of 130 miles or so, set on the path by Yahweh speaking through a burning bush and led by supernatural pillars of cloud and fire. Somehow this massive and spectacular event failed to be noticed by any Egyptian scribe or other ancient writers, who relate not one word of the affair, even though it could and should have been recorded by any number of cultures with whom these historians and geographers came into contact, such as the Egyptians, Canaanites, Babylonians, Phoenicians and so on.

Nonbiblical References

The earliest unambiguous, nonbiblical reference to the Exodus account is averred to be in the writings of the Greek historian Hecataeus of Abdera (c. 4th cent. BCE),[1] who is surmised to have had the Pentateuch before him, based on what appears to be a direct quote from Deuteronomy. However, we know about Hecataeus's supposed description only from texts of the first century BCE, and Gmirkin argues that Theophanes of Mytilene (62 BCE) is the real origin of this passage attributed to the earlier historian. Since the relevant parts of Hecataeus's writings are not extant but appear in the later recounting by Diodorus (fl. c. 60-30 BCE), we cannot be certain that the early writer actually referred to the Exodus story at all.[2] Gmirkin does suggest, however, that Hecataeus knew about the "law of Moses" but not the "books of Moses."[3]

The Egyptian priest Manetho (fl. 285 BCE) follows the period of Hecataeus and appears to refer to the Exodus. Yet, again, we do not possess his originals, only reports by Josephus and others. Going against mainstream scholarship, Gmirkin concludes that the earliest account of the Exodus is the Greek translation of the Pentateuch (c. 270 BCE), which is not a rendering from an older Hebrew text but which, in reality, was based significantly on the writings of Manetho and the Babylonian priest Berossus (fl. 278 BCE), as could be found in the library of Alexandria.

In any event, the fact remains that there exists no contemporary literary record of any sort depicting the Exodus as a historical event, and this silence was maintained for many centuries, until stories started circulating after the Jewish scriptures began to emerge publicly in the latter half of the first millennium BCE.

Logistic Implausibility

The improbable nature of the Exodus tale has been recognized many times in past centuries, by earlier generations of scholars, such as Bible scholar and Anglican bishop Dr. John William Colenso (1814–1883):

> ...Bishop Colenso's...mathematical arguments that an army of 600,000 men could not very well have been mobilized in a single night, that three millions of people with their flocks and herds could not very well have drawn water from a single well, and hundreds of other equally ludicrous inaccuracies of a similar nature, were

---

[1] Assmann (1997), 34.
[2] See, e.g., Gmirkin, 39ff.: "That so many writers on the Jews who were familiar with Hecataeus knew nothing of the contents of Diodorus Siculus, *Library* 40.3.1-8 suggests that the latter passage did not derive from Hecataeus."
[3] Gmirkin, 49, 65.

THE EXODUS AS HISTORY?

popular points which even the most unlearned could appreciate, and therefore especially roused the ire of apologists and conservatives.[1]

The apologists and conservatives have little choice in the matter, however, as there exists no evidence for the Exodus and wandering in the desert as historical. To begin with, Wheless's lengthy analysis shows the impossibility of even 600,000 male descendants of Jacob during the alleged four generations of Hebrew sojourn in Egypt (Gen 46). He calculates that the most the Hebrews in Egypt could have produced over those generations would be fewer than 7,000 males.[2]

Putting aside for the moment the dearth of literary or archaeological records for the events in the Pentateuch, let us examine the story itself to evaluate its merits as "history." Even if we grant the impossible number of two to three million Hebrews in the time since Jacob entered Egypt, we can look at this issue logistically and propose that, marching single file, about 2,000 people will fit comfortably into a mile, with no belongings and little space between them. If three million people—not just the 600,000 men mentioned in the Bible but also women, children (Exod 12:37) and non-Hebrew men, among them the Israelites' own *slaves*[3]—were lined up single file, the route would require an estimated 1,500 miles. In order to fit into the 130-mile-broad Sinai, the Israelites would need to line up more than 10 abreast, without belongings such as wagons and animals.

The Septuagint of Exodus (LXX 13:18) relates that the "children of Israel went up by five in a rank out of the land of Egypt,"[4] which, if composed of two to three million individuals, has been calculated to equal a column of people some 280 miles long, more than twice the width of the desert.[5]

---

[1] Mead, 27.
[2] Wheless, 90ff.
[3] See, e.g., Exod 21:2; Lev 25:44; Deut 15:12. Apologists proffer the argument that the Hebrew word for "thousand," אלף 'eleph, can be interpreted as meaning simply a "group" or "troops," thereby reducing this impossible number to a more practical size, such as 600. In the first place, the word is translated "thousands" some 500 times in English editions, demonstrating consensus as to its connotation. Secondly, Jewish tradition and extrabiblical writings themselves assert six hundred *thousand*—see the discussion in the chapter "The Exodus as Myth," below.
[4] The translations with the number five (AV/NAV/TMB) are based on the Septuagint/LXX: καὶ ἐκύκλωσεν ὁ Θεὸς τὸν λαὸν ὁδὸν τὴν εἰς τὴν ἔρημον εἰς τὴν ἐρυθρὰν θάλασσαν πέμπτη δὲ γενεὰ ἀνέβησαν οἱ υἱοὶ Ισραηλ ἐκ γῆς Αἰγύπτου. Matthew Henry relates: "They went up in five in a rank, some; in five bands, so others..." Bible commentators Jamieson, Fausset and Brown (1.57) clarify a marginal note that "five in a rank" denotes "obviously five large divisions, under five presiding officers, according to the usages of all caravans; and a spectacle of such a mighty and motley multitude must have presented an imposing appearance, and its orderly progress could have been effected only by the superintending influence of God." Some translations of this LXX passage render the phrase "fifth generation," as the Greek word πέμπτος pemptos (G3991) connotes "fifth," rather than "five."
[5] Wheless, 97.

It would be inexplicable why, if such an improbable event occurred, the Israelites could not have continued their shoulder-to-shoulder march into the Promised Land but required 40 years to cross this desert, except that the period is described biblically as a time of conditioning the "chosen people" to follow the Mosaic law (Num 32:13).

Four Decades of Desert Traumatization

According to the Exodus story, millions of escaped slaves were traumatized and tortured in the desert for four decades by Yahweh playing all manner of scary tricks and mind games on them. If the tale were true, such behavior would be condemnable as the practice of a bizarre and anti-human cult with an evil god. If the "chosen people" were so "stiff-necked" that they needed 40 years of being terrorized and abused in the desert, while alternately astonished by mind-bending miracles, one wonders why the all-powerful God would choose them in the first place.

We would consider such a cult leader to be completely sinister who takes his followers out into the desert and subjects them to severe deprivations and interchangeably terrorizes and astonishes them, all for the purpose of training them to be obedient. What kind of "father" would such a tyrant be? Moreover, knowing that the Promised Land was not far away, is it truly logical that not a single Israelite left, escaping Moses's cult, during the entire 40-year period in the desert?

Animals and Booty

Add to this tale a couple hundred thousand animals, as well as the mass of booty supposedly acquired from the Egyptians, and the tale become even more implausible. How was this huge amount of animals fed in the desert? What plant matter would they be able to eat, in the enormous quantities needed?

Additionally, how could this huge mass of livestock have been pastured in Egypt to begin with? Wheless calculates that the amount of lambs needed to fulfill the Passover decree at Exodus 12:21 would be something on the order of at least 240,000, slaughtered in one night. If those were only the lambs, how many other animals were there, including all the adult sheep, cattle, goats and horses, all spared miraculously during the plagues? Wheless also calculates that the pasture lands needed for such a mass would be equivalent to the size of the American state of Rhode Island.[1]

At Exodus 3:22 and 12:35, the Israelites are to flee through the desert with the enormous wealth of Egypt, taking a mass of silver and gold. Why carry all that weight to live in the desert, where it has no value? Could not Yahweh instantly transport the gold and silver into

---

[1] Wheless, 94.

THE EXODUS AS HISTORY?

a safer place in Israel? Was he not capable of hiding it and giving it to the Israelites later? Why would they need this wealth in the first place, since Yahweh is purported to be omnipotent and able to take care of all their needs?

Moreover, such an amount of pillaged booty would leave the nation of Egypt bankrupt and destitute, and the Israelites extremely wealthy, a situation not borne out by the historical and archaeological record. Archaeologists have found no evidence of such wealth among the hill settlers who became the Israelites.

Modern Gatherings Irrelevant

One argument seeks to prove that this large number of people could have fit into the 130-mile-wide Sinai Peninsula, because in the modern era we have rock concerts, religious gatherings such as at the Vatican, and political rallies that number in the hundreds of thousands to millions. In the first place, these events are *temporary* gatherings, not 40 years of attempting to live in such a space. Nor do these modern mass meetings try to move a couple of hundred miles or so through a desert, with hundreds of thousands of animals, carts and other belongings, such as a vast treasure.

Secondly, today we benefit from modern technology that provides resources for such temporary gatherings; we cannot rely on God to supply manna and water miraculously. And how would all those people fare socially with each other under such conditions for four decades? Modern events do not require such long-term co-habitation.

The bottom line is that, while such numbers may be sustainable in cities with modern technology, as in the case of Mexico City, New York, Tokyo and so on, again there are no large amounts of animals, and the people are not living in tents in a desert, depending on miraculously provided food and water.

Geography and Archaeology

Although the Exodus story appears to demonstrate a "good knowledge of the geography and natural conditions of the eastern Delta, the Sinai peninsula, the Negev and Transjordan," archaeologists "cannot provide any clues to the Exodus as an event that indeed happened." They cannot "identify Mount Sinai and many other place-names in the story; nor were any remains from this period found anywhere in the Sinai, including at the oasis of Kadesh-barnea, which plays such an important role in the story."[1]

Pithom and Pi-Ramesses

At Exodus 1:11, we read about the purported construction by Hebrew slaves of the Egyptian cities of Pithom and Raamses/

---

[1] Finkelstein (2007), 60. "Transjordan" here refers to the east of Israel, biblically designated as "beyond the Jordan" but also referring to Ammon, Moab and Edom.

Rameses/Ramesses. Pithom or the "House of Atum," called by the Greeks Heroöpolis, was a well-known city dedicated to one of Egypt's major gods. In recent decades, archaeologists have discovered the massive city of Pi-Ramesses, built under the pharaoh Ramesses II, which construction may be reflected in the Exodus tale as a long-distant memory. However, any "slaves" purportedly involved in its building could be designated as "Western Semites," not Israelites *per se*.[1]

Moreover, the Septuagint rendering of Genesis 46:29 includes an anachronism, by changing the location of Jacob in Egypt from "Goshen" to Ἡρώων πόλιν or Heroöpolis, where Jacob's 11th son, Joseph, purportedly went to meet his father. As we know now, Heroöpolis or Pithom did not exist at the time when Jacob traditionally was in Egypt, but it was an important trading station at the time when the LXX was composed (3rd-2nd cent. BCE). In this regard, Redford states that the biblical names of Pithom and Ramesses date from the Saitic period (7th-6th cents. BCE);[2] hence, they could not have been part of a tradition from the second millennium.

Indeed, Pithom may have been included because of its popularity among the Greeks and Romans of the apparent time of this biblical passage's composition, during the seventh to possibly third centuries BCE. The city's proximity to the Red Sea gives the Exodus tale legitimacy, possibly explaining its inclusion in the story.

The construction of Pi-Ramesses was ordered during a period when Egypt lost its colonization of Canaan, because of constant attacks by groups of raiders called the "sea peoples." In this regard, Redford remarks:

> In the wake of the retreating Egyptians [under Ramesses II], all Canaan flared into open revolt. For the first time in over two hundred years Egypt could scarcely lay claim to any territory beyond Sinai. The building of a "great and awesome new residence," Pi-Ramesses ("the House-of-Ramesses") in the northeastern Delta, was now hurried forward with all dispatch, "to strengthen the borders of Egypt."[3]

Here seems to be a real, historical detail from the Exodus tale, and it has been surmised therefore that one of the small groups of slaves who helped build Pi-Ramesses retained a memory that was fleshed out to become the biblical drama in later centuries. In this regard, Dr. Michael B. Rowton, a professor of Near Eastern Languages and Civilizations at the University of Chicago, relates that a relatively new Ramesside text recounts that laborers from the group

---

[1] Finkelstein (2007), 59.
[2] Sivertsen (2), citing Redford, "Exodus I 11," *Vetus Testamentum* 13 (1963): 406-13.
[3] Redford (1992), 185.

called *'apiru* or "Hapiru" were used in construction work,[1] providing a clue as to the true origin of the Israelites, as we will see.

Despite this correlation between Pi-Ramesses and Ramesses II, many researchers and scholars continue to posit other pharaohs as the one in Exodus, once again revealing the difficulty in taking this text as a "historical" account.

Psusennes I and Tanis

A renowned wine-producing region that "lay in the centre of a great vineyard,"[2] Pi-Ramesses remained famous centuries later, as it was moved by the priest-king Psusennes I (fl. 1047-1001 BCE) to the city of Tanis, apparently created for this very purpose, thus keeping its memory alive. For hundreds of years, priests maintained the pharaohs' divine legacies through inheriting these rulers' property specifically for this reason.

Tanis was situated in the Nile Delta on the Mediterranean along the popular Horus Way, in between Jerusalem and Alexandria. It was built evidently for the purpose of maintaining the memory of Pi-Ramesses and Ramesses II, and, since the city survived into the second century AD/CE, it is likely that Jews during the millennium of Pi-Ramesses's existence were aware of its connection to the pharaoh and, therefore, knew about him as well. Psalm 78, written in post-exilic times, recounts that the Israelites toiled "in the fields of Tanis," thereby appearing to recognize that Pi-Ramesses was in Tanis.[3]

The city's inclusion biblically may explain why, over the centuries, the famous Ramesses II has been the favored pharaoh associated with the Exodus. In any event, biblical writers may have known about Pi-Ramesses and used it as a historical detail to flesh out their tales.

On/Heliopolis

In addition, it is significant that the Septuagint of Exodus 1:11 includes another city, "On, which is Heliopolis." This fact of an additional location also indicates the fictional nature of the tale, changed over the centuries in order to suit the needs of the writers and their sponsors. Literalists may argue, nonetheless, that the LXX translators were "correcting" God's inerrant Word by adding the name On, the city of the sun god, or that they were simply wrong and not inspired by the Holy Spirit. It is possible nonetheless that the Septuagint translators wanted Israel to take credit for what ranked as a very popular tourist and pilgrim spot at the time of the translation.

---

[1] Rowton, 19. See below for a detailed discussion of the Hapiru.
[2] Osman (2002), 109.
[3] The Hebrew of Psalm 78:12 for "Tanis" is צֹעַן *Tso'an*, which Strong's H6814 defines as "place of departure" and "an ancient city of lower Egypt called Tanis by the Greeks."

The Burning Bush

In addition to the various problems already discussed, from the start of the Exodus story we encounter implausible tales best viewed as myth. At Exodus 3:2ff, for example, the Lord God of the universe is depicted as speaking to Moses through a burning bush. Surely, we cannot be expected to accept this tale as historical, particularly since, if the Almighty could appear to Moses in such a form, he could take care of shepherding his people out of Egypt much more easily than the plan he purportedly came up with for the lawgiver.

Fig. 20. *God Appears to Moses in Burning Bush*, 1848. Painting from Saint Isaac's Cathedral, Saint Petersburg, Russia

Exodus 3:5 gives the scene an even more unreal air, as the omnipotent Lord of the universe is concerned about Moses wearing shoes to walk on the patch of dirt in front of him: "Then he said, 'Do not come near; put off your shoes from your feet, for the place on which you are standing is holy ground.'" Thus, Yahweh appears in a finite form on a small piece of ground, a tale that differs little from the Greek or Roman myths about Zeus/Jupiter or any number of gods and goddesses manifesting themselves to humans over the millennia.

Adding to the primitivism of sacred concepts in the Bible, at Exodus 3:19 the Lord says unto Moses, "I know that the king of Egypt will not let you go unless compelled by a mighty hand." Knowing this fact, Yahweh hardens pharaoh's heart, thereby increasing the suffering beyond all comprehension, when he just as easily could have softened it.

Rods to Serpents

In the story about the battle of wits and brawn that follows, we are asked to accept that Aaron and the Egyptian priests truly turned their staffs into serpents (Exod 4:3, 7:10), an impossible tale as "history" that finds its miraculous counterpart in pagan myth, discussed below. As is the case with the exodus theme as a whole, many individual elements

Fig. 21. Gustave Doré, *Moses and Aaron Before Pharaoh*, 1866. (*Doré's English Bible*)

THE EXODUS AS HISTORY? 83

of the biblical drama likewise find their parallels in other and often earlier texts and traditions.

Bricks without Straw

One example of a fictional literary device occurs with the element of the bricks without the straw at Exodus 5:7ff, which is pointed to as a sign of the tale's historicity. In this story, the pharaoh is so cruel that he will not give the slaves a material supposedly vital to their brickwork but forces them to labor harder in order to procure the straw themselves. Christian apologists explain this passage both in historical terms, claiming that such bricks without straw found in Egypt serve as proof that the Exodus happened, and in spiritual terms, signifying that, with the help of God, bricks can be made without straw.[1]

This *fictional* element may have been included also for realism, in order to show that the scribe (and by extension the Hebrews) knew how to make bricks and therefore their role as brickmakers is given credibility. Again, fiction writers include such details on a regular basis, in order to produce a setting for their stories.

Biblical literalists frequently cite the remarks of British clergyman Rev. Henry Villiers Stuart (1827-1895) observing purported straw-free bricks at the then newly excavated site of Pithom.[2] Villiers Stuart exclaimed that he had never seen such bricks anywhere outside of this site, a discovery therefore lending credibility to the Exodus story. However, Egyptologist Dr. James H. Breasted (1865-1935) responded, "We can only say that Mr. Stuart's observations cannot have been very extended, for ancient bricks without straw were common enough in Egypt."[3]

Nevertheless, Villiers Stuart's insights are recited to this day as evidence of the Exodus; yet, he was not a professional Egyptologist or archaeologist, and his pronouncements in this regard rate as flawed, outdated and irrelevant.

In reality, the verses in Exodus do not say that the Hebrews could not *use* straw; the relevant passage states that the people must gather their own, which means they could have done so and not had strawless bricks at all, thus negating this purported "proof." Moreover, even where such strawless bricks have been found, they serve only as evidence that at times there was no available straw. They do not have stamped on them, "Made by Hebrew Slaves," and they do not serve as evidence that Exodus actually occurred.

---

[1] See, e.g., Caiozzo, "The Secret of Making Bricks without Straw."
[2] Villiers Stuart, 81ff.
[3] Breasted (1898/9), 8.30.

Rare Straw

In fact, such strawless bricks appear to have been typical, and this apology is erroneous. Ancient mud brickmaking required much the same as it does today, including straw added to the mold to prevent sticking, but not for the bricks themselves. In this regard, Rupert Furneaux remarks:

> The denial of supplies of straw to the Israelites often leads to the speculation as to how they could have made bricks without straw. But straw or stubble was not used in the bricks themselves: it was sprinkled on the workmen's hands to prevent the mud bricks from sticking, and the withdrawal of the straw issue made their task more difficult.[1]

Discussing the subject of ancient brickmaking, evangelical archaeologist Dr. Joseph P. Free states:

> On the basis of the biblical record, it has usually been assumed that straw was necessary as binding material, that bricks could not be made satisfactorily without straw, and the Egyptian bricks generally contained a certain amount of straw.
>
> On the contrary, T. Eric Peet, Egyptologist of the University of Liverpool, stated that the use of straw in making bricks was "somewhat rare" in ancient times and that the Nile mud coheres so well that any binding material would be quite unnecessary... He added that the reference to the use of straw in brick making is often used to demonstrate the biblical writer's acquaintance with Egyptian customs, but that it actually proves his ignorance of Egyptian practice... Peet's treatment of the matter leaves one with the impression that the Bible was wrong in implying that straw was necessary in making bricks.[2]

As does Free, Bible literalists will claim that Peet's declarations are overstated, because ancient mud bricks are found commonly enough with straw both visible and invisible in them; hence, we know that straw was used to make them. Again, it is true that straw was used to make mud bricks, and evidence of it may exist on the outside from the molds. However, there are also mud bricks without much if any straw in many places, evidence that does not prove the Exodus to be historical. Moreover, many people in antiquity would probably know that much about brickmaking, without being brickmaking slaves themselves.

This motif also may be from pre-biblical mythology, for example possibly concerning the Egyptian creator god Ptah.[3] Even if this Egyptian story was not employed to create the biblical tale, this one element does not serve to prove historicity of any sort, as it simply may be a literary device for the purposes of the plot.

---

[1] Furneaux, 47.
[2] Free, 80.
[3] Massey (2007), 2.194.

Elderly Leaders

To reiterate, at Exodus 7:7 we learn that Moses was 80 years old and Aaron 83 when they purportedly endured the strenuous and grueling events of the Exodus. How plausible is it for an 80-year-old man to be doing the things attributed to Moses either then or from that point forward, living in the harsh desert until he was 120 years old, at a time when the average lifespan was less than half that?

The 10 Plagues

Exodus 7-12 contains a detailed account of the 10 plagues supposedly sent by Yahweh to force the Egyptians to let the Israelites go. In order to make the plot interesting, apparently, God hardens pharaoh's heart so he will not let Moses's people leave. Then come the plagues, one after another, relentlessly tormenting not just the hard-hearted king but also all of his people, thousands upon thousands of innocent men, women and children.

Plague One

The Bible says that in the first plague all the water was turned to blood and that it killed all the fish in Egypt. How could this singular event escape the notice of Egyptian writers or the many travelers from abroad? The death of all the fish, as well as the undrinkability of water everywhere in Egypt, would lead to tremendous hardship that would resound well beyond the Egyptian borders. But, we hear nary a word of such "historical" events in literature of the time. Nor is there any solid, scientific proof of any extraordinary mass fish die-off or water spoiling at that time.

Plague Two

We are told that frogs "covered Egypt" during the second plague. Again, there exists no historical account anywhere of such an extraordinary event. The economic cost of a pandemic frog invasion would be enormous, as would the potential illness when these hundreds of millions to trillions of frogs died and rotted away.

Plague Three

In the third plague, lice or gnats spread everywhere. This pestilence might be considered "historical" in the sense that lice and gnats thrive in Egypt and many other places globally. But the biblical event is well beyond anything known to occur naturally, because the Lord God purportedly was behind it and made it quite *super*natural. If the lice/gnat infestation was beyond the norm to this extent, one would think the Egyptians and other cultures would mention it somewhere. Again, such a pestilence would be very costly to their economy, as would all of these plagues, and there exists no scientific evidence for this claim.

Plague Four

A scourge of flies next covers Egypt, according to the Bible, although it is difficult to believe there is anything left to plague at this point. Only Egypt proper is affected, and Moses is able to stop this pestilence, proving that it is the supernatural Jewish Lord behind it. Once more, there exists no scientific evidence that it happened.

Many cultures in antiquity perceived a deity who controlled anything that flew, as was the role of the Philistine god Baal Zebub, "Lord of the Flies" or "Lord of Flying Things." In this regard, it seems that each of these plagues may have been included in order to demonstrate the superiority of Yahweh as the controller of all these various elements.

Plague Five

Livestock are beset with disease during the fifth plague (Exod 9:3-6), which is directed at the animals belonging to the Egyptians but not to the Hebrews. However, it is claimed at Exodus 3:6 that *all* the Egyptian cattle had died already, so they could not have been killed later in the fifth plague. Again, the economic cost would be staggering, as would be the resultant epidemic, and no scientific evidence has been found for this event.

Fig. 22. Doré, *The Murrain of Beasts*, 1866. (*Doré's English Bible*)

Plague Six

Because all the preceding horror still did not destroy Egypt and soften pharaoh's heart—which Yahweh hardened in the first place and continued to do throughout the plagues—God next abuses the people and beasts with incurable boils. This sixth plague could not be natural, as how could it affect beasts and *Egyptian* humans but not Hebrews? Moreover, if all or most of the Egyptian animals were killed off during the fifth plague, how were there any left to abuse with boils?

Again, there is no account of such an event in the Egyptian or other historical record, and this disaster would bring Egypt to its knees financially, as would the first five the country had already endured. There simply would be nothing left at this point to plague.

Plague Seven

Next we are supposed to believe that huge hailstones fell in Egypt, killing every living thing that remained outdoors, as if there could be anything left by that time! The Hebrew area of Goshen remained unaffected as usual. There is no evidence that "every living thing" was killed at any point in Egyptian history, whether by hail or any of the other plagues here.

Plague Eight

Adding to the utter destruction already contended in the biblical account is the plague of locusts, which may seem plausible at first glance, since locust plagues are not uncommon in various regions. However, we should note that the biblical account has Moses supernaturally controlling this plague by stretching forth his hand. He is also able to end the plagues upon request of the pharaoh, by asking Yahweh to stop sending them.

Furthermore, the previous plague of hail would have killed much of the foliage, leaving little for the locusts to destroy.

Despite all of this torment and the witnessing of Moses controlling this plague, pharaoh still does not relent—but how could he, since the Lord is controlling his "heart?"

Plague Nine

Next we read about three days of darkness, but it is difficult to believe that there would be anyone left to endure this frightening period. According to the text, the pharaoh himself must have been so strong and resilient that he suffered plague after plague relatively unharmed, having lived through bloody water and mosquitoes, overcome incurable boils and coincidentally remained inside during the hailstorm that killed every other living thing caught outdoors. He also survived the famine that likely would have followed the locust plague.

Fig. 23. Doré, *The Plague of Darkness*, 1866. (*Doré's English Bible*)

Obviously, there is no corroborating account of this purported three-day blackout, which also would have interrupted life significantly in Egypt and elsewhere. Moreover, this triduum or three-day period can be found in the myths of other cultures.[1]

In addition, Wheless sensibly asks, if Egypt was plagued with three days of darkness, why did the Hebrews not flee under this cover, especially since they were the only ones who could see lights during that time, according to Exodus 10:23?[2]

---

[1] See below and the chapter "Burial for Three Days, Resurrection and Ascension" in my book *Christ in Egypt*, 376ff.
[2] Wheless, 88.

Plague Ten

Finally, the 10th plague (Exod 12:12-29) is the infamous event commemorated during Passover: The killing of all first-born humans and other living things, except the Israelites who put a mark in lamb's blood upon their doors. It remains to be explained why the all-knowing Lord would need such a guide marker.

Yahweh claimed initially to Moses that he had heard the cries of his people in Egypt; yet, he did not know where they were? And how did some two million Israelites all receive word in such short notice to mark their door lintels with blood? Moses had no organization at that time, an era long before there were telephones, text-trees, internet, email, social or other mass media. Again, whence did the Israelites immediately obtain an estimated 240,000 or so lambs necessary for this mass sacrifice? Additionally, if all the animals had already been killed in the other plagues, how were there any first-born to be slaughtered in the 10th plague (Exod 12:29)?

Fig. 24. Egypt's firstborn destroyed. (de Hondt, *Figures de la Bible*, 1728)

Like the other plagues, this episode of the slaughter by God of the firstborn of Egypt, both human and animal, is never mentioned in the historical record. If such a massively traumatic event had occurred, the Egyptians surely would have felt a huge ripple effect in their very social structure. Thousands of people and animals would have died suddenly, and the survivors would likely have feared the Israelite god and incorporated his worship into their pantheon. However, we find nothing of the sort happened.

One is tempted, moreover, to ask what kind of God is this to cause such suffering? The plagues story ranks as a horrible tale unworthy of a good and just divinity. If one were the all-powerful God, why not just snap one's fingers and simply remove the Israelites to the Promised Land?

Furthermore, why did the omnipotent Yahweh allow Israel to serve as captives in Egypt for six hundred years before sending Moses along? Why go to all the trouble and cause so much hardship and suffering? These stories are "object lessons," not historical facts. This tale of sending pestilence is sadistic as "history," but as myth it serves as a cultural artifact that can be found in the myths of other cultures as well.

In addition, the Egyptian population itself, throughout the entire nation, was only an estimated three to three and a half million, so how could there be such an enormous population of "slaves?" After the utter decimation of the Egyptians by Yahweh, why would the "slaves" need to flee and from whom would they be escaping? Who would pursue them at that point? Who would keep them in the land and in thrall?

If Egypt were so devastated, with nearly every living thing killed, including most able-bodied men, it would be easy for the millions of spared Hebrews to overwhelm the remnants of the Egyptians and take over the entire country, rather than fleeing into the relatively poor and inhospitable wilderness.

As we can see, the plagues story is hopeless as "history," but there have been attempts to trace these episodes to the eruption of the Greek island of Santorini or Thera, which apparently occurred around 1600 BCE.[1] While some of these efforts may appear exhaustive, and while it is tempting to look in the historical record for such a massive event, which would have effected life around the Mediterranean for years, this argument remains unconvincing for the many reasons stated above, such as when the Exodus tale itself first appears in the historical record and the obvious use of allegorical biblical verses in its construction. Another major reason to suggest the plagues tale as myth—*pagan* pestilence mythology—will be discussed below.

Unleavened Bread

At Exodus 12:8, we read about the unleavened bread (מצות *matstsah*) and bitter herbs (מרר *mĕror*) to be eaten as Passover, before the Israelites flee Egypt. In this regard, attempts at explaining the Feast of Unleavened Bread as representing a "real Exodus" in which the Israelites fled so quickly that they did not have time for their bread to rise are simplistic and anachronistic. The Bible (Gen 19:3) records the use of unleavened bread by Abram's nephew, Lot, centuries earlier, according to the story.

Moreover, the Egyptian religion had its own "unleavened bread" in the form of "buns," which were "unleavened, like the shewbread of the Hebrews, eaten by priests only, and offered to them in piles."[2]

Mass Communication

It must be asked further how the Israelites knew to leave Egypt and to take the booty from their Egyptian neighbors (Exod 12:35), since it would require a very long time for any message passed mouth

---

[1] See, e.g., Sivertsen.
[2] Massey (2007), 2.65; Budge (1991), 401.

to ear to spread through the households of hundreds of thousands. Exodus (12:41, 51) tells us that this feat of organizing all these people and animals, for their departure from Egypt, required only *one day*:

> And at the end of four hundred and thirty years, on that very day, all the hosts of the LORD went out from the land of Egypt....
>
> And on that very day the LORD brought the people of Israel out of the land of Egypt by their hosts.

It is extremely unlikely that such an event with so massive a population could have occurred in a single day. Not even with our modern technology could such a "flash mob" be put together in that time.

No Formal Organization

According to the Bible, the Israelites had no formal and centralized organization until *after* they were already settled in the desert. How could any of the Exodus events have been organized, with millions all wandering around aimlessly with no chain of command?

Moreover, the military training of the hundreds of thousands of Israelite "warriors" (who were raised as slaves) does not occur until after they arrive at Mt. Sinai, although Exodus 13:18 claims the Israelites left Egypt "equipped for battle." Regardless, how could Moses have executed "brilliant" military tactics with a mass of untrained fighters? Where did these supposed "slaves" learn these military tactics, then, and obtain their enormous amount of weapons?

Such a massive force on the move would surely have left some mark on the desert. Yet, despite the wishful attempts by various devout researchers, not a single unambiguous and scientifically verified artifact has been found from such a vast and long-term migration.

The Route of the Exodus

There are three major routes through the Sinai Peninsula: 1. Along the coast at the north, as a continuation of the "Horus Way," which becomes the "Way of the Philistines"; 2. the "Way of Shur" in the middle of the peninsula; and 3. the longer Egypt-Arabia route or "Way of the Wilderness," which cuts diagonally south, to the "King's Highway." There is also the south coastal route, which is closer to what the Israelites traditionally are purported to have taken, according to the ambiguous biblical tale.

Egyptian Waystations

Along the northern "Horus Road" route, there were more than 20 fortified Egyptian waystations;[1] hence, fleeing slaves would not

---
[1] Finkelstein (2007), 60.

THE EXODUS AS HISTORY?

escape via that path, but it remains to be understood why this specific fact was not mentioned by the Bible writers. They were concerned not with Egyptians along the route but with Philistines, an ethnicity who did not exist yet in Canaan at the supposed time of Moses. Indeed, the Egyptian waystations were no longer in use by the time of the Philistines; thus, we have an anachronism that reveals the story was not composed until centuries after the era in question.

As we can see from the map at the end of this chapter, which represents only one of many attempts at tracking the Exodus, rather than taking the short routes across the desert, the Israelites wandered about aimlessly having adventures that could have been compressed considerably if Yahweh were truly all powerful. The whole event has the feel of a fictional drama of the sort we enjoy reading in epics or watching in theaters and on television.

Certain researchers have attempted to address various problems in this tale by tracing the Exodus route along the southern coast of the Sinai Peninsula,[1] placing Mt. Sinai in Arabia. However, the Bible itself indicates that Mt. Sinai was not in Arabia/Midian.[2] In any event, this effort reflects how nebulous is the purported "history" of the biblical account, indicating it to be fictional and certainly not "God's inerrant Word." If one is endeavoring to be scientific, one may wish to question whether or not this tale truly took place before assuming *a priori* that it occurred and then trying to outline the "correct" route.

The Philistines

At Exodus 13:17, it is claimed that, by taking the desert route, the Israelites were attempting to avoid the Philistines or *pelistīm*, a supposedly barbarous and violent warrior ethnicity who may have come from Crete as part of the confederation of "sea peoples." This invasion of sea peoples occurred during the Bronze Age collapse (1550-1200 BCE), which comprised the purported time of Moses. Contrary to the barbaric impression given by the Bible, the Philistines, a non-Semitic, apparently Indo-European people, possessed fine pottery, artwork, furniture and architecture, and were relatively civilized. The Philistines evidently arrived in the Levant around 1175 BCE, the year of the supposed defeat of the sea peoples by Ramesses III, claimed to have destroyed Amor/Amurru, ancestral homeland of the Amorites in Syria.[3]

As we can see, the homeland of the Amorites was one source and waystation of these migrating and rampaging hordes of sea peoples. It was into this fray that Moses supposedly stepped, but these

---

[1] See, e.g., Rudd, Möller.
[2] See, e.g., Exod 18:27 and Num 10:29-31, wherein Mt. Sinai and Midian—"Arabia"—are separate locations. See also Sparks, B., "Problems with Mt. Sinai in Saudi Arabia."
[3] Rainey (2001), 58. Robbins (289f) expresses doubt that this military action by Ramesses III ever took place.

destroyers of the land and conquerors of Canaan were not Israelites, as the Bible claims.

Greeks to Canaanites?

While their pottery, loom weights and other artifacts indicate a relationship to the Mycenaean Greeks,[1] by the 10th century or so the Philistines evidently were speaking Canaanite. Where the Philistines came from continues to be debated, however, with suggestions not only that they were displaced Pelasgians or Greeks[2] but also, as identified by Xanthus in the fifth century BCE, that they emanated from Lydia in western Asia Minor or what is now Turkey.[3] Redford notes that "both 'Carians' and 'Cretans' appear as ethnic indicators in the lists of bodyguards of Judaean kings recruited from Philistia."[4]

Even if the Philistines had lived in the Promised Land during the century earlier when the Israelites purportedly conquered Canaan, the latter allegedly had more than 600,000 "warriors" among them, and it seems odd they would not simply swoop down and crush the Philistines along the way, destroying their cities, stealing their booty and virgin girls, and slaughtering all the rest, as the chosen people are depicted later in the Old Testament as doing repeatedly.

Moreover, we must ask why there would be so much fear of the Philistines, when the express goal of leaving Egypt was the military conquest and destruction of the peoples of Canaan (Deut 7:1), of which the Philistines were but one?

It remains inexplicable that the two-million-strong nation of Israel would be terrified of the Philistines, a fairly civilized people in reality, especially with the Almighty Yahweh on the Israelites' side. If Yahweh could decimate the mighty nation of Egypt with plagues and drown the pharaoh and his army with the supernaturally parted Red Sea, he easily could defeat the Philistines.

In any event, when Moses was purportedly alive, there were no Philistines *per se*, and this motif is yet another anachronism, which basically proves that the biblical tale is fiction composed long after the purported facts.

Sea Peoples

The sea peoples appear to have been a "disparate mix of Luwians, Greeks and Canaanites, among others."[5] The earliest extant mention of the sea peoples occurs in an obelisk from Byblos that may date to

---

[1] See, e.g., "Historical Philistines were not philistines, archaeologists say."
[2] The pre-Greek Pelasgians may have been in Athens as early as the 6th millennium BCE, with ancient remains there similar to those found in Thessaly. This term appears to designate several different ethnicities, and some claim that one of the main languages defining the Pelasgian culture was closest to what is now called Albanian.
[3] Redford (1992), 252.
[4] Redford (1992), 252.
[5] "Bronze Age collapse," *Wikipedia*.

around 2000 BCE, some 2,500 years after that city's settlement by the ancestors of the Phoenicians.[1]

Regarding their arrival along the southern coast of Canaan during the eighth year of the reign of Ramesses III, Redford remarks, "The invasion of year 8 was sudden and unique; and all references to 'Philistines' in the Bible must postdate it."[2] Depending on which chronology one uses, the eighth year of Ramesses III would fall around 1178 BCE or some other time during the 12th century, decades or centuries after the Israelites purportedly were encountering "Philistines" in the Promised Land. This invasion and destruction by the sea peoples at the end of the 12th century led to the Iron Age.

Summarizing the sea peoples' era, Redford states:

> The contemporary, as well as the classical, evidence permits us to draw the following sketchy picture. At the end of the thirteenth century B.C. a desperate effort to reunite the disintegrating Mycenaean community directed a loose coalition of former member states against Troy, the former leader of the erstwhile Ionian confederation against the Hittites. In the years immediately following the reduction of Troy some of the members of the Mycenaean expedition, under the leadership of enclaves in Caria, banded together in a loose federation and moved east along the southern coast of Asia Minor, along with their families, to settle in the plains of Cilicia and North Syria. Branch movements spread far and wide. Sardis was occupied by Greeks around 1200 B.C., and ships of the movement made for Cyprus...
>
> The end was near. In truth, no one could stand before these raiders. Hattusas was destroyed, and the Hittite empire swept away in one stroke. Tarsus was laid waste, as was Enkomi on Cyprus. Alalakh and Ugarit were razed to the ground, never to be rebuilt. The Late Bronze Age of the Levant vanished in an instant: archaeology gives a graphic dimension of the terror conveyed by the written record.
>
> From their camp in Amurru—that is, in the Eleutheros Valley—the confederacy trundled south, women and children in oxcarts, while the ships kept pace offshore.[3]

Sardis or Sardes is an ancient site in Turkey, southeast of Troy and northeast of Ephesus, here claimed by Redford to have been occupied by Greeks by around 1200 BCE. Hence, we have Greek culture in the region before the Israelites emerge as an ethnicity, an important fact when considering the possible influences on the Bible and Jewish doctrines.

---

[1] Holst, 33.
[2] Redford (1992), 250.
[3] Redford (1992), 253-255.

Pillars of Cloud and Fire

In the Exodus story, we are supposed also to believe in the miracle of the pillars of cloud and fire accompanying and leading the Israelites through the desert (Exod 13:21). If the Almighty God can do all that, why did he not just instantly transport the Israelites into the Promised Land and spare us all the drama, suffering and bloodshed? Also, one would have thought that God could come up with better technology than fire to light the night, perhaps a giant halogen spotlight, but such is the view from the mind of a *human* writing thousands of years ago, without knowledge of modern technology.

Fig. 25. Yahweh's pillar of cloud. Bible card by Providence Lithograph Company, c. 1896-1913

Parting the Red Sea?

At Exodus 14, we read about the famous supernatural and dramatic parting of the Red Sea, during which time Moses controls the waters with the stretching out of his magic rod and hand. While uncritically accepting the *supernatural* explanation of the pillar of fire, biblical apologists and devout military experts alike attempt to explain the Red Sea crossing *naturalistically* by placing it in the shallow "Sea of Reeds," a shallower, swampy area to the north. In this naturalistic explanation, a wind conveniently reduces the water, allowing passage to the Israelites and all their animals and wagons laden with a mass of booty, while inexplicably the lighter chariots of the Egyptians are mired in the exposed muck.

Sea of Reeds

None of the Exodus routes actually needs to cross the Red Sea, so in the biblical story the Israelites must go out of their way to pass through the waters. To explain this strange situation, some researchers have suggested that the Israelites actually crossed the Sea of Reeds and that the term thus probably refers to a "sweet-water lake."[1]

The theory goes that the original Hebrew refers not to the "Red Sea" but to the "*Reed* Sea," ים סוף *Yam Suph* in the Hebrew, the first word meaning "sea," while the latter, *suph* or *cuwph*, is defined as: "1) reed, rush, water plant; a) rushes; b) sea of rushes."[2] The word

---

[1] Finkelstein (2007), 60-61.
[2] Strong's H5488.

THE EXODUS AS HISTORY?

"Yam" is also the name of the Semitic god of the sea, Yamm, equivalent to Poseidon and Neptune in the Greek and Roman mythologies, respectively.

This idea of the "Reed Sea" has been rebutted, however, by scholars such as Batto, who claims that the "whole Reed Sea hypothesis is nothing more than a figment of scholarly imagination."[1] Russell prefers the "hybrid form 'Re(e)d' as a way to acknowledge the complexity of deciding between 'Reed Sea'/'Sea of Reeds' and the traditional 'Red Sea.'"[2]

Despite the many convoluted and contorted efforts at explaining the miraculous parting of the Red Sea,[3] the fact remains that there is no solid scientific evidence of such a magical event in history and that supernatural water control and crossing can be found in the myths of other cultures, as we shall see.

Fig. 26. Israel's escape through the Red Sea. Bible card by Providence Lithograph, 1907

Exodus Encampments?

Bible literalists claim that purported ancient encampments along the supposed Exodus route, now visible using technology such as Google Earth, prove the biblical story to be true. Firstly, if these were the biblical sites, they would need to be enormous. Regarding the massive encampments of the Israelites and their animals, the latter of which is estimated to be at least the same as the number of Israelites, over 2 million,[4] Wheless remarks:

> Every one of the forty-two times the camp was pitched [Num 33], there must be suitable space found for some 250,000 tents, laid out [Num 2] regularly four-square around the holy tabernacle, after that was constructed, and with the necessary streets and passages, and proper spaces between the tents. A man in a coffin occupies about twelve square feet, six feet by two. Living people would not be packed in their tents like corpses in sardines; they must have at least, say, three times that space, thirty-six square feet or four square yards each. A tent to house ten persons with minimum decency must occupy therefore an average of forty square yards.
>
> If the 241,420 such tents were set one against another, with no intervening space or separating streets, they would occupy

---

[1] Batto, 115.
[2] Russell, 13.
[3] See, e.g., Möller.
[4] Wheless, 93.

9,656,800 square yards, or over 1995 acres of ground, a little more than three square miles.[1]

Secondly, where did all the tents come from? Were they part of the booty hauled all the way from Egypt, where the Israelites supposedly lived in wooden houses with lintels? Wheless estimated the amount of tents needed for his proposed 2,414,200 refugees would be at least 241,420.[2] Who would have owned so many tents, or, if new, how did the Hebrews construct them all in the desert wilderness? Exodus 12:39 says the Israelites fled in a hurry, without even their bread; yet, they are depicted as hauling a huge amount of Egyptian gold and other precious artifacts, along with a mass of animals and, apparently, an enormous quantity of tents.

It is difficult to believe that the Israelites could find 42 different locations with that kind of space in this small desert. In this same regard, Leviticus 8:3-5 tells us that Yahweh commanded his congregation—the whole of Israel—to gather at the tabernacle doors; but to have two to three million people gather in that manner would seem impossible. Regarding this tale, Dever concludes, "There is simply no way that the Sinai Desert, then or now, could have supported more than a very few thousand nomads."[3]

Moreover, each one of these encampments would need to be excavated to show whether or not there are any artifacts from the proper time period, to determine if they were encampments also in antiquity. Any such artifacts would need to be linked scientifically to the biblical tale, in order to provide evidence of the story's alleged historicity.

Even if there were an archaeological stratum from the proper era, the existence of these sites might suggest that whoever wrote the Exodus tale had taken or knew of a similar route, an act that could have occurred hundreds of years after the purported event. We highly doubt, however, that this individual(s) had with him two or three million people.

It is more likely that the route was devised centuries later, when the tale was composed, using known encampments. Or, possibly, some of these encampments were created as tourist spots, like those springing up whenever a sacred story is believed by a certain percentage of people. The fact that one of the more prominent encampments of the Exodus, Rephidim (Exod 17:1), is translated as "Resting Places" serves as an indication that we are dealing with a mythical tale.

---

[1] Wheless, 108.
[2] Wheless, 92, 107.
[3] Dever (2003), 9.

Simple Place-Names

People often name locations and objects simply, such as a place called "Elkland" where elks once may have roamed. Frequently in stories, however, place-names like "Bitter Water" or "Rest Stop" indicate we are looking at a fairytale or myth, to be passed along easily from generation to generation. In instances where such appellations would serve as a warning to other travelers, such as "Place of the Bitter Water," these names may be found in a number of sites. Hence, we cannot be certain of a location based merely on such simplistic names.

Like the designation "Resting Places," other monikers in various Bible stories also serve as fictional elements of similar primitiveness, including Kadesh Barnea, where the Israelites purportedly ended up camping for 38 years, after leaving Mt. Sinai (Num 20). The name means "Holy Wandering," and, since the traditional site dates to the Iron Age,[1] it certainly was styled *after* the purported Exodus, rather than previously existing as some miraculously named location where the Israelites just happened to land. All in all, the whole Exodus story has an air of fiction, even beyond the miraculous and supernatural events.

Mt. Horeb and Mt. Sinai

As another example, the alternate or "twin" name for Mt. Sinai is "Mt. Horeb" (חרב *Choreb*), which means "desert" an appropriate designation for a mountain in a tale occurring in the desert. In this regard, there are many "desert mountains" in the area in question, so trying to pinpoint one of them from over 3,200 years ago could be difficult indeed.

Gesenius's Lexicon delineates Horeb as "a lower summit of Mount Sinai," from which one "ascends Mount Sinai properly so called." The name "Sinai" (סיני *Ciynay*) itself simply means "thorny" and thus could be used to refer to *any* thorny area, plenty of which can be found from Egypt to Arabia.

According to the Bible, the Israelites spend two years at Mt. Sinai before encamping at Kadesh Barnea. Mt. Sinai is said in Exodus 16:1 to be located in the "wilderness of Sin," a name meaning "clay."[2] Conventionally, this wilderness is situated between "Elim and Sinai." According to tradition, Sin has been located on the eastern edge of Egypt, while Mt. Sinai has been placed on the Sinai peninsula.

Even if the traditional Mt. Sinai where sits St. Catherine's monastery were "real," in the sense that it is indeed the mountain in the biblical tale, its existence would not make the Exodus story true,

---

[1] Redford (1992), 265.
[2] Strong's H5512.

any more than the tales of Mt. Olympus, a real place in Greece, prove the Greek gods sat thereupon and their myths were historical.[1]

Serabit el-Khadim

Because there exists no evidence of the Exodus or any Mosaic behaviors on the traditional site of Mt. Sinai, researchers have looked elsewhere and struck upon other locations, such as Serabit el-Khadim in the western Sinai. Serabit is renowned for its turquoise mines discovered by at least 3500 BCE and mined by the Egyptians during the fourth to second millennia BCE. These mines at Serabit were worked in the second millennium by Semitic prisoners of war evidently significantly from the Northwest Levant, and it has been surmised that Serabit's advanced metallurgical and smelting facilities would have been used by Moses to create the ark, tabernacle and other artifacts.

Moreover, there existed at the site a temple to the horned Egyptian goddess Hathor the Cow, leading to speculation that her worship by these Semites is the source of the biblical "Golden Calf" story. Also, there appear several ancient inscriptions in Proto-Sinaitic, hypothesized to be the alphabet used by Moses to compose the Pentateuch.

Despite these claims, the Serabit Canaanites cannot be equated with the Hebrews of Exodus, as some have done, based on the writings of the site's first archaeologist Dr. Flinders Petrie and his assistant, Canadian researcher Lina Eckenstein (1857-1931).[2] Eckenstein's work on the subject is published by the Society for Promoting Christian Knowledge and treats the Pentateuch as a historical text.[3] Nevertheless, this Serabit thesis contradicts the Bible in a number of ways, including that the Torah makes no mention of a Hathor temple and active priesthood waiting to greet Moses on Mt. Sinai.

As Petrie cautioned: "It must not be imagined that the Semitic ritual of the temple at Serabit had any direct connection with the Exodus some centuries later. I do not suppose the Israelites ever saw either the temple or the mines."[4]

Certain traditions from their Egyptian sojourn, such as the worship of assorted deities, may have been passed into the folklore of possible proto-Israelite Semites at Serabit. However, the supposition that the goddess of the region, Hathor, was the "Golden Calf" would appear erroneous, because the northwestern Semitic Phoenicians, for one, were already Hathor worshippers for centuries to millennia without any type of bondage in Egypt. Hence, such worship by

---

[1] Wheless, 111.
[2] Eckenstein, 67, etc.
[3] E.g., Eckenstein, 26.
[4] Petrie, ix.

Canaanites would not necessarily be the result of a particular stay in Egypt, whether voluntary or conscripted.

There appears to be a long history of Canaanite presence at the site, leaving behind Proto-Sinaitic writing, centuries before Moses would have arrived in the area, according to accepted dates. In addition, these inscriptions have not been translated, save for one possible reconstruction by Egyptologist Gardiner, and they have not been shown to have any relationship to Moses or the Pentateuch.

Furthermore, Eckenstein relates that Ramesses IV (fl. 1155-1149 BCE) was the last pharaoh for centuries at Serabit,[1] activity postdating the purported time of Moses both traditionally and as a hypothesized friend of Akhenaten.[2] Hence, Serabit would have been occupied over several centuries by many Egyptians, at least seasonally, as no permanent garrison was found there.[3] In any event, there had been Egyptians at Serabit on and off for centuries, but there exists no evidence that these were heretical followers of Akhenaten chased there by other Egyptians, as is surmised in this hypothesis.

Even if the Israelites moved along the traditional route, the Serabit region is much farther north and west than the traditional site of Mt. Sinai, so they would have passed right through this territory, thus possibly encountering hundreds of Egyptians working an organized mining operation in existence for centuries to millennia. Yet, this historical detail is missing from the Exodus account.

There simply is no direct evidence of Israelite occupation of Serabit or even Israelite existence at all during the time when Moses is hypothesized to have visited the site. What the discovery of Serabit in the Sinai does prove, however, is that the desert was not the desolate wasteland depicted in the biblical account and that the Egyptians could not have been escaped by this flight into the Sinai region, as they were already there and had been for centuries.

The Exodus story may have been placed deliberately near this important "country of blue stone," as it was called in antiquity,[4] but it remains a mythical motif historicized, not history, mythologized or otherwise, as we will continue to see in the present work.

Gulf of Aqaba

Alternative locations for the Mosaic desert account include east of the Gulf of Aqaba, which brings up many new problems. Despite the dearth of evidence and presence of clearly mythical motifs, Christian apologist videos, books and websites go so far as to claim that in the "ancient 'Yam Suph' (modern day 'Gulf of Aqaba' aka the 'Red Sea')"

---

[1] Eckenstein, 83.
[2] Eckenstein, 65.
[3] Petrie, viii.
[4] Eckenstein, 8.

there are "hundreds of Egyptian chariots...strewn across the sea floor." It is further contended that robotic submarine cameras have revealed "an underwater battlefield where the coral encrusted remains of Pharaoh's army still litter the ocean floor like an ancient chariot junkyard."[1]

This theory also contends that, along with these chariot parts, human and horse bones likewise have been found in the Gulf of Aqaba. Regarding one of these purported discoveries, a supposed chariot wheel from the Gulf, we read:

> The hub had the remains of eight spokes radiating outward and was examined by Nassif Mohammed Hassan, director of Antiquities in Cairo. Hassan declared it to be from the 18th Dynasty of ancient Egypt, explaining the eight-spoked wheel was used only during that dynasty around 1400 B.C.
>
> Curiously, no one can account for the precise whereabouts of that eight-spoked wheel today, though Hassan is on videotape stating his conclusion regarding authenticity.[2]

The supposed underwater "chariot wheels" in question are not accepted by mainstream scientists as existing in the Gulf of Aqaba. Moreover, Prof. Yigal Yadin writes that "the Egyptian chariot in the first half of the XVIIIth Dynasty is exactly like the Canaanite chariot."[3] The 18th Dynasty is dated to around 1550 to 1292 BCE, the era in which Moses was said to have lived. Hence, this wheel, if indeed it is such, could be from a *Canaanite* chariot, not from the Exodus event at all.

As concerns such claims, let us quote archaeologist Dever, who goes out of his way to be "theologically responsible and sensitive" in order to salvage something "historical" from the Bible: "In fact, no one had ever found any archaeological evidence for the Exodus from Egypt."[4]

Baal Zephon and Migdol

Bible literalists contend that the Ugaritic and Hyksos god-name Baal Zephon at Exodus 14:2, meaning "lord of the north," reflects a historical detail proving the veracity of the Exodus tale. However, it could be simply an old term that maintained its currency for many centuries after its first usage, apparently during the 19th Dynasty or Late Bronze Age (1550-1200 BCE).[5] The fact that this god-name was known later to the Greeks as Zeus Kasios, reflecting Mt. Casius, demonstrates that his worship continued into the Hellenistic period

---

[1] Michael Rood, "The Red Sea Crossing & The Exodus Revealed."
[2] Kovacs, J., "Pharaoh's chariots found in Red Sea?"
[3] Yadin, 186.
[4] Dever (2003), 5. For more on the purported Exodus discoveries by amateur archaeologist Ron Wyatt, see my article "Did the Exodus Happen?," a review of *The Exodus Case* by Lennart Möller.
[5] Hoffmeier (1996), 190; Scolnic, 99.

(323-32 BCE), spanning the centuries when much of the Bible were composed. While this name's inclusion may reflect the memories of proto-Israelite nomads kept alive in folklore later used to create the Exodus epic, its employment in the tale nevertheless could have been incorporated in much later centuries than the purported time of the event.

The retention of god-names for many centuries does not prove that texts in which they appear emanate from the monikers' earliest usage, obviously. In this same regard, modern texts using the English god-name "Jehovah," first popularized by the King James Bible in the 17th century AD/CE, do not date from that era.

Nor does the geographical detail of the Canaanite city of Migdol in this same verse indicate that the story is true, any more than the presence of Cambridge or London in *Gulliver's Travels* demonstrates that historicized fiction to be true. The same can be said of other biblical demonyms that reflect real places.

Furthermore, Baal Zephon, the "protector of sailors,"[1] has been equated with the storm god Baal Hadad, an identification important for our discussion of the water-controlling, storm-god *myths* below.

Water Sources

During the desert sojourn, two or three million people and hundreds of thousands of animals would require a huge amount of water. One must ask why the good Lord initially gives these thirsty travelers "bitter water," as is the name of the well, Marah, where the Israelites end up at Exodus 15:25? Here apologists try to excuse Yahweh's abuse of his chosen by claiming God is "testing" them. But they have already endured enough, so why let them suffer in this manner?

In *The Exodus Case*, Möller calculates that the Israelites and their livestock would have needed some 8,000 cubic meters of water *per day*.[2] This massive requirement Moses supposedly achieved by throwing the wood from a particular tree into the bitter waters at Marah. However, no such magical tree can be discerned, and water-producing miracles can be found within the realm of mythology.

The 12 Wells

In addition, the 12 wells at Elim ("palms") as discussed at Exodus 15:27 served as the last natural source the Israelites would come across for the next 38 years, as they eventually relied on other miracles of Moses to provide them with water. Again, the story has an unreal air about it and possesses mythical elements, to be discussed later.

---

[1] Hoffmeier (1996), 190.
[2] Möller, 237.

Heavenly Manna

At Exodus 16:4 appears the story of "bread from heaven," elsewhere known as "manna,"[1] which has fascinated humanity for hundreds to thousands of years. For centuries now, theologians and others thus have puzzled over the meaning of this story about magical manna from heaven, which purportedly appeared supernaturally all over the desert, in order to feed the Israelites miraculously during their grueling 40-year desert entrapment.

We saw previously that this mysterious "food" is described variously, as a wafer "made with honey" or tasting also like "fresh oil." Manna is explained also as a "flake-like thing," "round thing"[2] or "coriander seed"[3] with an appearance like "bdellium," a gum resin,[4] revealed in the frost on the ground as the dew evaporates in the morning. Philo (*Moses* 1.37.200, 208) muddies the waters further by claiming that the manna is like both a grain such as millet and "honey cheesecake."[5] Adding to the confusion, the KJV of Psalm 78:24 styles manna as "corn of heaven," an erroneous rendering because corn or maize was not brought to the "Old World" until after Columbus.

The biblical word rendered *manna* is מן *man*, which Strong's (H4478) defines as:

1) manna
a) the bread from Heaven that fed the Israelites for 40 years of wilderness wanderings
b) means "What is it?"

This "what is it?" word is used 14 times in the Old Testament.[6] Gesenius gives the naturalistic explanation of this "heavenly bread":

> ...*manna Arabica*, a sweet gum-like honey, which, in Arabia and other Oriental regions, exudes from the leaves of several trees and shrubs, especially those of the tamarisk kind; this takes place mostly in July and August, before sunrise. ...British naturalists have proved that certain insects...aid in producing the manna ... the manna flows out after the leaves are punctured by insects.

However, Gesenius notes in brackets:

> No one who simply credits the inspired history of the giving of the manna can doubt that it was something miraculously given to the Israelites, and that it differed in its nature from any thing now known.

---

[1] See also Exod 14-15, 16:31-35; Num 11:6-7, 9; Deut 8:3, 16; Jos 5:12; Neh 9:20; Ps 78:24.
[2] Exod 16:14: חספס *chacpac* (H2636), from a root meaning "to peel," "to flake off" or "to strip off."
[3] Exod 16:31.
[4] Num 11:7; Strong's H916.
[5] Philo/Yonge (2000), 478.
[6] E.g., Exod 16, Num 11, Deut 8, etc.

THE EXODUS AS HISTORY?

Hence, although the Bible states manna is like coriander seed and bdellium, biblical fundamentalism excludes any naturalistic explanation such as this "gumlike honey" from plants like the tamarisk.

Natural or Supernatural?

Attempts at identifying manna as a lichen, secretion of the tamarisk or hamada plant, insect excretion or other natural substance thus have not been received universally.[1] According to Bible literalists, the naturalistic explanation fails, because it cannot account for manna's ubiquity: "The fact that manna has been provided through all the different terrains that Israel has passed through suggests something far different from what the various natural explanations can provide."[2]

Needless to say, no one has discovered the location of these supernatural miracles, which would have produced an estimated 10,000 cubic meters of manna falling from heaven *every day*. Is this miraculous tale truly credible as history, even if there were a naturalistic source of manna, which could never produce such a massive amount on a daily basis?

Who or What?

Speaking of the pre-Hebraic Semitic word *manna*, Near Eastern and biblical scholar Dr. Edward Lipiński (b. 1930) remarks:

> In Amorite, *ma-an-na*, "who?", and *ma-a*, "what?", are both attested in proper names.... there is an interrogative *ma-an-na*..., "what?", certainly related to the Ugaritic *mn*, "what?", which can be explained in the light of Minaic mhn, "what?", as *mahna* > *manna*.[3]

The word *manna* in Amorite means "who?," while in Old Canaanite it means "what?"[4] Thus, although this term seems mysterious to us, giving its air of supernaturalism a boost, *manna* was commonly and mundanely used in pre-Hebraic antiquity, including as a name. As we shall, a similar "divine food" folktale can be found in pre-Hebraic Ugaritic or Canaanite mythology.

No Sheep, Goats and Cattle?

In order to bring about the need for miraculous manna from heaven to feed the two million Israelites, Yahweh must make them starve. Although many apologies have been put forth, it remains to be explained adequately why, if the Israelites had so many oxen, sheep

---

[1] See the discussion in Houtman, 1.143f. Eckenstein (72) asserts that manna "appears under the name mennu in the contemporary records of Egypt, and is still collected in Sinai and exported." However, Rev. Herbert Lockyer (66) points out that *mennu* in Egyptian simply means "food."
[2] Walton, et al. (2000), 217.
[3] Lipiński, 336.
[4] Lipiński, 337.

and goats with them, they needed to be fed through miraculous means.[1]

Bird Sacrifice

Moreover, in the Pentateuchal book of Leviticus, we read about the numerous animal sacrifices, including thousands upon thousands of birds per day, but we are not told where these birds come from in the middle of the desert.[2] Indeed, throughout the Pentateuch appear detailed instructions on how to sacrifice all these animals, repeated abundantly; yet, the common people apparently were kept out of that feasting and were fed flake-like round things found on rocks instead.

Shewbread

While the Israelites were starving and subsisting off manna and water, Yahweh required not only the sacrifice of thousands of animals and but also heaps of "shewbread" or "bread of the Presence"[3] (Exod 25:30) made with "fine wheat flour" (Exod 29:2, 40). From where, one might ask, did the Israelite priests obtain this "fine flour" out in the middle of the desert, where the people were starving?

Is it believable that 600,000 warriors would subsist solely on manna, watching their wives and children also go hungry, while thousands of food animals were being immolated, and expensive and difficult to procure fine wheat flour was given as bread to Yahweh?

Sabbath Establishment

The apology/excuse for the starvation of the chosen avers it a deliberate "test" from Yahweh, to see if the "stiff-necked" will follow his law, especially as concerns the sabbath, which the god himself observes by not providing the massive amount of needed manna that day.

Thus, the heaven-sent manna represents a literary device to train people in the six-day week (Exod 20:10-11), with a non-working sabbath, the manna's six-day delivery providing an example from God himself. The mythical manna tale serves to give origin and authority to a law already in existence, however, as the six-plus-one work week and Sabbath formula could be found also in Babylon,[4]

---

[1] One apology, for example, suggests that the Israelites may have been influenced by Egyptian animal worship, but why would Yahweh encourage this blasphemous error, especially when he himself requires an endless stream of animal sacrifice?
[2] See, e.g., Wheless, 121.
[3] Heb. לחם lechem.
[4] In discussing the disparate biblical accounts of the Sabbath's origin (Exod 20:11, Deut 5:15), Delitzsch (38) comments: "The Babylonians also had their Sabbath day (shabattu), and a calendar of feasts and sacrifices has been unearthed according to which the 7th, 14th, 21st and 28th days of every month were set apart as days on which no work should be done, on which the king should not change his robes, nor mount his chariot, nor offer sacrifices, nor render legal decisions, nor eat of boiled or roasted

where the Jews purportedly were exiled for decades during the sixth century BCE. After its adoption into Yahwism, the custom apparently was given Jewish authority by creating this story about Moses.

29 Trillion Quails?

In one initial act of relief from the starvation, at Exodus 16:13 Yahweh brings a huge amount of quails from the sea to feed his chosen. First of all, during that time were there even quails at the sea *at all*, much less millions upon millions of them? Secondly, we read at Number 11:31 that these quails were "stacked up on the face of the earth" to a height of two cubits, equivalent to about 44 inches high, in a row the length of "a day's journey round the camp." Wheless calculates that, based on the settlement's descriptions at Numbers 2 and 24, the camp's total mass would be 4,569.76 square miles or 452,404,727,808 cubic feet of birds![1] He further computes that such a mass of quails would be equivalent to almost 29 trillion individual birds.[2]

Even if these calculations are off by a factor of 99 percent, we would still be discussing 290 million birds, to be picked up immediately, cleaned, cooked and consumed by a couple of million people, providing dozens or hundreds of quails per person. Where did they get all the wood to cook with, and what did they do with the birds' remains?

One also may ask reasonably, since there are billions of hungry people in the world today, why doesn't God do the same for them, bringing trillions of birds and manifesting manna from heaven? The all-powerful Lord miraculously feeds two million in the desert for 40 years, but he cannot end world hunger?

Tents or Booths?

Another biblical contradiction occurs in repeated encampment episodes, presumably in "tents" as at Exodus 16:16, using the Hebrew word also employed to describe the Lord's tabernacle. Yet, at Leviticus 23:40-43 we read that the Israelites were housed in the "booths" (סכה *cukkah*)[3] later used for spiritual retreat, particularly during the time of the fall Feast of the Tabernacles. These "booths" are made of "fruit of goodly trees, branches of palm trees, and boughs

---

meats, on which not even a physician should lay hands on the sick. Now this setting apart of the seventh day for the propitiation of the gods is really understood from the Babylonian point of view, and there can therefore be scarcely the shadow of a doubt that in the last resort we are indebted to this ancient nation on the banks of the Euphrates and the Tigris for the plenitude of blessings that flows from our day of Sabbath or Sunday rest."

[1] Wheless, 103.
[2] Wheless, 103.
[3] The same term סכה *cukkah* is used at Genesis 33:17 to describe the "booths" Jacob built for his cattle.

of leafy trees, and willows of the brook," none of which grows in the desert.

As we have seen, the quantity of tents needed would have been enormous—if these were all booths instead, there could not have been enough foliage in the desert to create them all.

Striking the Rock

At Exodus 17:6, Moses is depicted as striking a rock, from which fresh water magically issues forth. At Numbers 20:11, thirty-eight years after the first rock-smiting, the prophet is portrayed as repeating this water-producing miracle. Regarding these two episodes of producing water miraculously, Wheless remarks:

> Here we have the desert of Sin [Exod 16:1-3] and the desert of Zin, and two waters Meribah, but thirty-eight years apart, and each with entirely different circumstances.... In either event, so far as revealed, this is about all the water that the millions of Chosen and their millions of cattle had to drink in the terrible wilderness for almost forty years.[1]

We can hardly be expected to accept these supernatural tales as "historical facts," and we shall see that this motif is mythical, found in the traditions of other cultures.

Fig. 27. Moses brings water out of the rock, (de Hondt, *Figures de la Bible*, 1728)

The Amalekites and the Magic Rod

In Exodus 17:8ff, the Israelites are depicted as battling a "giant" people called the Amalekites—identified by later Arab chroniclers as Amorites and Canaanites—at a site where the children of Israel settled, again, conveniently called Rephidim or "Resting Places." The Amalekites are portrayed as defeating the Israelites whenever Moses lowered his magic rod, while losing to them when he raised his stick.

If we discount the magic tricks and assume the story has some basis in reality, is it possible that, no matter how tall, the Amalekites could have held off the 600,000 Israelite men at any point? How many people would they have needed to do so? How were all these heathens able to stay alive in the desert without manna and miraculously provided water, as happened with Moses and the Israelites? And why could not the all-powerful Yahweh make the

---

[1] Wheless, 100.

Amalekites magically disappear, rather than putting Moses to all the trouble, costing Israelite lives?

Judging According to What Statutes?

Another anachronism occurs at Exodus 18:16, when Moses is to judge the people according to "the statutes of Elohim and his torah." Yet, according to the Bible this event occurred before Moses had received the commandments on Mt. Sinai (Exod 20). Earlier at Exodus 15:26, Yahweh had spoken of his commandments and statutes, but he had not given them all to Moses yet, such that the latter could act as a judge using the Torah.

Because Moses is worn out, however, his Midianite father-in-law, Jethro, suggests that he appoint judges to do this work for him (Exod 18:17-25), again even though they did not have the Torah to judge by. Moses takes Jethro's advice but later lays claim to the idea himself (Deut 1:9-19).

Priests before Priests?

Exodus 19:22 and 24 anachronistically speak of "priests" before any such individuals ever had been ordained. The first ordination of Aaron and his two sons—the only priests during the Exodus—occurs at Exodus 28:1. At this point, Wheless remarks:

> As further proof of there being no priests yet, we find Moses, after delivering the first batch of "law" [Exod 24:4-5], himself building an altar under the hill, and twelve phallic *mazzeboth*, and sending "young men of the children of Israel" to do the priestly job of making burnt offerings and sacrificing peace-offerings unto Yahweh; for all the Chosen were at that time a "kingdom of priests" [Exod 19:6]—every man his own priest. And Brother Aaron, as a priest, during Moses' next forty-day sojourn up on the mountain, made gods of the golden calves, and sacrificed to them, thus again proving that there was no "law" as to "priests of Yahweh," and that "Thou shalt have no other gods before me" was not yet law.[1]

The word מצבה *matstsebah* is rendered generally as "pillar," here taken to be a phallic symbol, which indeed were common in antiquity, including in the Levant.[2]

Despite the declaration at Exodus 19:6 that the Israelites as a whole were a "nation of priests," at Exodus 28 we are told that only Aaron and his sons can be priests. There follows in Exodus 28 and elsewhere a long description of the fancy, gold-laced vestments with jewels that the starving Israelites must put together, all in the desert. One wonders, of course, where the resources for these costly priestly accoutrements came from, perhaps part of the Egyptian booty, the

---
[1] Wheless, 113.
[2] See, e.g., Ben-Gedalyahu, "Evidence of Stone Age Cultic Phallic Symbols Found in Israel."

latter a clearly fictional detail possibly included in order to explain where this finery came from in the desert.

The Ten Commandments

At Exodus 20-32 appears the story of Moses and the Ten Commandments or Decalogue, in which the prophet, while in the wilderness after fleeing Egypt, is claimed to receive a unique, divine revelation endorsing the notion of the Israelites as Yahweh's "chosen people." In the story, Moses spends 40 days and nights on the mountain of Sinai, during which time the commandments are purportedly written by the very finger of God on two tablets of stone. The patriarch brings the tablets down the mountain to the people, but he angrily smashes them upon seeing the Israelites "whoring after" other gods, specifically the Golden Calf.

Moses's solution to this transgression of his fellow sectarians is bloodletting, so he orders the Levitical priestly tribe to slaughter all the men, women and children. (Exod 32:27) Apparently, this godly gang could only manage to massacre 3,000 people before losing steam, but Moses was not done with the genocidal mania, as, when finally he and his merry band arrived in Canaan, they massacred everyone in their path who would not kowtow or serve them somehow.

So emerges the biblical picture of the great prophet esteemed by the three Abrahamic religions of Judaism, Christianity and Islam. One does not wonder why there has been so much suffering on Earth when the world's esteemed heroes are known for one event of slaughter and genocide after another. It would be better for everyone if we accept that this story is not historically true but represents legend, folklore, fiction and myth.

Fig. 28. Doré, *Moses Breaking the Tables of the Law*, 1866. (*Doré's English Bible*)

No Archaeological Evidence

There simply exists no credible, scientific evidence for the alleged events on Mt. Sinai, despite claims otherwise:

> For years, scholars have speculated as to the location of the actual Mount Sinai where Moses received the Ten Commandments from God. At least 13 sites have actually been claimed on the Sinai peninsula as being the correct spot.[1]

---

[1] Kovacs, J.

If the holy mountain location were so concretely established, there would not be so many candidates. This fact of multiple locations lends credence to the contention that the Exodus is fictional.

To make "history" of these implausible events, we are told that "world maps will need to be redrawn" to relocate Mount Sinai and that "[h]istory books, travel guides and biblical commentaries will need to be rewritten."[1] At this point, of course, we must ask why God never clearly revealed any of these previous mistakes in interpreting his Word all these many centuries.

Second Set

In addition, there is another set of "ten commandments" at Exodus 34:28: "We have the ten commandments in two different revisions neither of which is based upon the tables themselves, but upon other versions."[2] The J and E sources of this story differ, as in the Elohist, Moses never retrieves a second set of tables/tablets; hence, there is nothing to put inside the famous "Ark of the Covenant" and, indeed, the ark is never mentioned in E at all,[3] as if it never existed.

Slavery?

Included in this biblical discussion of the commandments is one concerning slavery, at Exodus 21, in which the Lord does not forbid it but, rather, qualifies how it should be carried out. This fact casts doubt on this passage as representing anything more than the will of the moneyed elite of the time.

In reality, as mentioned and as we shall see further, the legislator receiving the law code on a mountain or elsewhere represents a fictional foundation archetype found in other cultures as well.

The Ark of the Covenant

Exodus 25 discusses the Ark of the Covenant, including detailed instructions on how to build this gilded and jewel-encrusted box designed to carry around godly energy and objects such as the tablets with the 10 commandments. Housed in the tent/tabernacle, the ark was used to lead the Israelites in their conquest of the Promised Land, according to the Bible. The ark was utilized also to fell Jericho, carried around the city for six days before horns were blown on the seventh, to take down the walls.

---

[1] Kovacs, J., citing "Cambridge University physicist Colin Humphreys," who is quoted also as declaring: "The Exodus of the ancient Israelites from Egypt really is one of the greatest true stories ever told." It is difficult to fathom how a sober scientist could make such an unfounded and unscientific statement.
[2] Delitzsch, 96.
[3] Friedman (2003), 177, 11.

The marvelous ark was covered with a blue cloth and animal skins, and, as with the priestly vestments, one wonders where in the desert all the fine materials came from to build it, with its precious metals and splendid appointments. Was it too created out of the mass of Egyptian booty, implausibly dragged around the desert for four decades?

According to the Bible, the ark's lid was used as Yahweh's footstool and "mercy seat." Exodus 25:22 claims God spoke to Moses from "above the mercy seat, from between the two cherubim" decorating the "ark of the testimony" (ארן העדת *'arown 'eduwth*).[1]

Fig. 29. Henry Davenport Northrop, *The Ark and the Mercy Seat*, 1894. (*Treasures of the Bible*)

This odd imagery is vivid enough to have been taken literally by many over the centuries, including those who see in the ark a type of short-wave radio, possibly from extraterrestrials. Because of the story at 1 Samuel 6:19, in which some men of Beth Shemesh ("House of the Sun") are struck down after looking into the ark, a mythology has been created that this "alien" artifact contained some type of weapon of mass destruction, possibly a laser. Among other magical powers, the ark was said also to levitate,[2] another miraculous attribute used to assert its divine or "alien" origin.

Philistine Capture

According to the Bible (1 Sam 5), the Philistines eventually captured the ark but returned it after a series of plagues was sent upon them by Yahweh. After King David defeated the Philistines and took over Jerusalem, his son Solomon built his temple and put the ark in the "holy of holies" with the 10 commandments, after which point there are no references to the ark, until the seventh century BCE.

We next learn that Manesseh's pagan idols drove away the ark, after the Judean king built the altars to "all the host of heaven" (2 Ki 21:3). As stated, this latter term שמים *shamayim* is the same as the heavenly deities in Canaanite mythology. Manasseh also set up the *asherah* or sacred groves dedicated to the Semitic goddess of the

---

[1] Numbers 10:33 uses the phrase "ark of the covenant" or ארון ברית *'arown běriyth* in the Hebrew, the latter word, ברית *běriyth* (H1285), meaning "covenant, alliance, pledge," etc.
[2] See, e.g., Singer, Is. (1925), 2.105.

same name. It is hard to fathom how the powerful ark could be driven off by these false pagan deities.

Speaking of the ark, German theologian and Hebraist Dr. Friedrich Delitzsch (1813-1890) comments:

> When the Philistines capture the ark of the covenant and place it in the temple of Dagon at Ashdad, they find on the second morning following the image of the god Dagon lying in fragments before the ark of Yahveh [1 Sam 5ff] and then when it is brought to the little Jewish border-town of Beth Shemesh and the inhabitants look at it, seventy of them pay for their presumption by death—according to another account fifty thousand (!) [1 Sam 6:19]. Even one who touches the ark from inadvertence is slain by the wrath of Yahveh (2 Sam. 6-7 f.).
>
> But as soon as we touch the soil of the historical period, history is silent. We are told in detail that the Chaldaeans carried away the treasures of the temple at Jerusalem and the gold, silver and copper furnishings of the temple, the fire pans and basins and shovels [2 Kings 24:14, 25:13ff], but no one is concerned about the ark with the two God-given tables; the temple goes down in flame, but not a single word is said of the fate of the two miracle-working tables of the Almighty God, the most sacred treasure in the Old Covenant.[1]

The fertility and fish god Dagon or Dagan was a popular Eblaite, Amorite and Ugaritic deity whose reverence extended from at least 2250 BCE into the first millennium BCE. One can see that the biblical pericope serves to demonstrate Yahweh's dominion over this powerful Semitic god.

As concerns the ark, for thousands of years, it has been asked, how could this centerpiece of Jewish religion disappear? After all the detailed instructions for its design purportedly given by the Lord himself in a series of dramatic meetings in the tabernacle, the ark simply vanishes and is forgotten. And, if it were real and truly so powerful as to kill tens of thousands, why does the hypothesized textual source E or "Elohist" make no mention of it?

Over the centuries, many people have looked for the lost ark all over the world, from Ethiopia to Japan to America. Even if the most famous of these, the supposed ark of Ethiopia, truly exists and dates to a relevant period—the 13th to 15th century BCE, not the seventh century when the ark disappears or later—and can be proved to be Hebrew in origin, it would not represent a unique and specially magical artifact above all others, which we will see have been commonplace. The powers of the ark are *mythical* attributes, no more real than Zeus's thunderbolts or Thor's hammer.

Golden Calf

The pericope at Exodus 32 about the Golden Calf, worshipped when Moses goes up the mountain for too long, is peculiar in that it

---
[1] Delitzsch, 95-96.

is the lawgiver's own brother, Aaron, who institutes this idolatry while Moses is away. Again, the prophet orders the slaughter of all the Israelites but only manages to get through a few thousand. However, the instigator of this illicit worship, Aaron, remains unpunished and, as noted, subsequently receives the only priestly ordination, along with his sons, who are slaughtered by Yahweh later.

Curiously, Philo (*Moses* 2.28.142) claims Moses chose Aaron as high priest because of his "great virtue."[1] Why would Yahweh make the initiator of the most infamous episode of idol worship his sole priest afterwards?

One also wonders why, if the Israelites took with them a vast treasure from Egypt, Aaron would need to use the Hebrews' rings and earrings for the calf (Exod 32:2), rather than melting down the Egyptian gold? This element indicates the writer of this passage was not conscious of the motif of Egyptian booty, possibly because it had not yet been woven into the *fictional* story, which evidently was embellished over a period of centuries.

As concerns cattle graffiti purportedly found in the Sinai and held up as evidence by literalists as proof of the Golden Calf episode, these markings in fact could have been scratched by any number of nomadic, desert-dwelling Bedouins or others who have passed through the area over the past 70,000 years or so, including during more recent centuries.

Supremacist Propaganda

In the quest for Yahwist supremacy over these cultic beliefs, Exodus 32:27 records Moses forcing his men to slaughter their own brothers, companions and neighbors because they were revering the Golden Calf, suggesting that murdering one's best friends and family members is morally superior to idol worship.

Rather than representing an actual, illogical and irrational, if not evil, act, it appears that this "object lesson" was composed during a time when the intended audience evidently *was* worshipping the Golden Calf. Hence, this Israelites and Jewish behavior required this harsh theological lesson from the Yahwist author(s), who essentially threatened these worshippers with death or other grievous punishment.

According to the Bible (1 Ki 12:25-33), the first Israelite king Jeroboam (fl. 10th century BCE?) set up golden calves in the Northern Kingdom at Dan and Bethel, asserting these deities to be the gods that Israel had brought out of Egypt, completely oblivious to Moses's purported proscription, despite the alleged memory-searing bloodshed just a few centuries earlier. Hence, this deadly Mosaic episode evidently was composed after Jeroboam's era, centuries later

---

[1] Philo/Yonge (2000), 503.

THE EXODUS AS HISTORY? 113

than when Moses purportedly lived. This theme appears to reflect the southern kingdom Yahwists' attempt at intimidating the northerners into the former's version of the Israelite religion, possibly beginning in the reigns of Hezekiah and/or Josiah.

Magical Wood?

Once encamped for four decades, the Israelites were instructed to offer up mass sacrifices of animals, which must be burned. (Lev 4:11-12) Where did the wood come from for these enormous holocausts, which were attended by a handful of priests, the elderly Aaron and his two sons, before the latter were struck down for looking into the ark, thus leaving only Aaron? And what about all the remains and ashes? How were they disposed of, as Yahweh demanded ritual cleanliness? (Deut 23:12-14)

Cannibalism

At Leviticus 26:29, Yahweh threatens his chosen people with the cannibalism of their own children if they do not obey him, a threat repeated elsewhere biblically.[1] With such an atrocious punishment for disobedience and/or apostasy, we must question whether or not Yahweh is truly the God of the cosmos and the "Good Book" actual history faithfully recording God's concerns and words.

Disposition of the Dead

In other such episodes of Yahwist bloodthirstiness, after the second manna miracle (Num 11:7-9), at Numbers 11:33-34 the god decides to punish Israel for its "lust" by slaying huge numbers of his people with a "great plague." This bloody episode raises up the issue of the burial of Israel's dead during the 40 years in the desert:

> ...as Yahveh got angry with his chosen, whom he had repeatedly promised to bring into Canaan, and he caused every one of them, except Joshua and Caleb, to die in the wilderness, there were on the average 1700 deaths and funerals per day for forty years, at the rate of 72 per hour, more than one for every minute of every day; and all the corpses must also be carried "without the camp" for burial, an average of six miles going and returning. And as the census taken at the end of the forty years shows but a slight decrease in numbers from that taken at the beginning, the entire host was renewed by a birth-rate of over one a minute for forty years; and all the debris must be lugged without the camp and disposed of.[2]

As can be seen, the biblical tale once more ranks as implausible.

Giants in the Promised Land

At Numbers 13:33, the Bible contends the Israelites were terrified of "Nephilim" (sg. נפיל *nĕphiyl*) or giants occupying the Promised Land,

---

[1] See Deut 28:53-57; Lev 26:29; Jer 19:9; Ezek 5:10; Lam 4:10.
[2] Wheless, 110.

suggested as one reason the chosen sojourned for so long in the Sinai.[1] These Nephilim are mentioned also at Genesis 6:4 as the offspring of the "sons of God" (*bene Elohim*) and "daughters of men."

We need to ask why the all-powerful Yahweh could not rid Israel of the giants but instead made millions of his people suffer in the desert for 40 years. Additionally, if there were so many giants, where are their tens of thousands of remains, all dating to the second millennium BCE?

It is clear that this giants detail is a literary device used to drive the Israelites into the desert, where they could be brainwashed into the Mosaic cult/law, which is the stated purposed of this latter motif.

Anakim

At Deuteronomy 1:28, we read the story about more Canaanite "giants," the sons of Anakim (ענקים *'Anaqiym*), descendants of Anak and part of the Nephilim. These intimidating giants supposedly lived in huge fortified cities; yet, archaeology tells us that these cities were non-existent, in decline or destroyed by the time of the Exodus.[2]

The Anakim were apparently the smiths of the Philistine people, who were also evidently the Kenites.[3] In this regard, their presence in the story would constitute another anachronism.

No Edomites

Another biblical anachronism occurs when the Israelites are depicted as negotiating with the king of Edom to cross his land (Num 20:14). Although the name "Edom, Edomites" appears in the Ugaritic Keret epic or *Krt Text* (15th cent. BCE) as 'Udm or Udumu,[4] there evidently existed no *kingdom* in Edom before the time of the Assyrians in the seventh century BCE.[5] Moreover, the kingdom was short-lived, destroyed by the Babylonians in the next century, which would indicate that this part of the Exodus tale was cobbled together during that period, which is the time of Hezekiah, Josiah and the Babylonian exile.

Holy Genocide

Amid all the wanton biblical bloodshed and genocide, one sanguine episode stands out for its gruesome detail and matter-of-fact recounting: The massacre of the Midianites in Numbers 31. This pericope represents a chronicle of horrors:

---

[1] The abbreviation "sg." refers to "singular."
[2] See, e.g., Finkelstein and Silberman, 323.
[3] The Kenites (קיני *Qeyniy*) were a tribe evidently related to but preceding the Midianites, as Moses's father-in-law, Jethro, was considered to be a Kenite (Jdg 1:16), a "priest of Midian" (Exod 3:1) and a "Midianite" (Num 10:29).
[4] *Bulletin of the American Schools of Oriental Research*, vols. 81-92, 14. Russell (76) states that "Moab and Edom are both mentioned in thirteenth-century Egyptian texts."
[5] Finkelstein and Silberman, 68.

The LORD said to Moses, "Avenge the people of Israel on the Mid'ianites..."

And Moses said to the people, "Arm men from among you for the war, that they may go against Mid'ian, to execute the LORD's vengeance on Mid'ian. You shall send a thousand from each of the tribes of Israel to the war."...

They warred against Mid'ian, as the LORD commanded Moses, and slew every male. They slew the kings of Mid'ian with the rest of their slain...

And the people of Israel took captive the women of Mid'ian and their little ones; and they took as booty all their cattle, their flocks, and all their goods.

All their cities in the places where they dwelt, and all their encampments, they burned with fire, and took all the spoil and all the booty, both of man and of beast.

Then they brought the captives and the booty and the spoil to Moses, and to Elea'zar the priest, and to the congregation of the people of Israel, at the camp on the plains of Moab by the Jordan at Jericho. Moses, and Elea'zar the priest, and all the leaders of the congregation, went forth to meet them outside the camp.

And Moses was angry with the officers of the army, the commanders of thousands and the commanders of hundreds, who had come from service in the war. Moses said to them, "Have you let all the women live? Behold, these caused the people of Israel, by the counsel of Balaam, to act treacherously against the LORD in the matter of Pe'or, and so the plague came among the congregation of the LORD.

Now therefore, kill every male among the little ones, and kill every woman who has known man by lying with him. But all the young girls who have not known man by lying with him, keep alive for yourselves...."

The LORD said to Moses, "Take the count of the booty that was taken, both of man and of beast..."

And Moses and Elea'zar the priest did as the LORD commanded Moses. Now the booty remaining of the spoil that the men of war took was: six hundred and seventy-five thousand sheep, seventy-two thousand cattle, sixty-one thousand asses, and thirty-two thousand persons in all, women who had not known man by lying with him....

Here we see that the God of the universe orders Moses to slaughter men, women and children, after which the Hebrew leader is angry because his men have left the women alive. The excuse here is that the women and children—*all* of them, apparently—have been acting against Israel, a deed punishable by death. Evidently, the omnipotent Lord cannot find another solution except to slaughter every last one of them. Moses and his men are able to keep all the virgin girls as sex slaves, to be counted among the booty, upon which there is great focus throughout the biblical conquest.

Anachronism

Fortunately for the Midianites, the biblical account could not have happened, as the area of Midian was not settled in any significant way until the eighth to seventh centuries BCE,[1] leaving us with yet another anachronism. Hence, in Moses's alleged era there could not have been such numbers amassed in a kingdom for the Israelites to have slaughtered.

This revolting account is, again, simply one of the most outrageous of many in the Old Testament, in which the chosen people are depicted repeatedly as slaughtering and pillaging their way around the region for decades to centuries.

The Midianite story appears to be designed to intimidate Israel's neighbors into submission, woven possibly by Hezekiah in his quest at centralized power. This element as a later innovation explains how Moses could be depicted as the son-in-law of a Midianite priest yet responsible for the subsequent genocide of the Midianites.

Time Compression

In Deuteronomy (1:6ff, 2, 3), the manner in which Moses is made to speak to the "hosts of Yahweh" 38 years after the Israelites left Mt. Sinai is as if these were the same individuals who had left Egypt. However, at Numbers 26:64-65 we learn that almost all of the original refugees were dead, and only Joshua and Caleb remained of the original group of chosen who left Egypt 40 years earlier, indicating that in these speeches we are seeing fictional accounts erroneously compressed into a short period by their authors.

Canaanites and Amorites

In another bloodthirsty act, Deuteronomy 2:34, 3:3 and 3:6 depict the massacre of all the people of Heshbon and Bashan, including innocent men, women and children. Although Genesis 14:13 says that certain Amorites were confederates of Abraham, Deuteronomy 20:17 lays out once again the planned genocide of Canaanitish peoples, including the Amorites:

> Then I brought you to the land of the Amorites, who lived on the other side of the Jordan... And you went over the Jordan and came to Jericho, and the men of Jericho fought against you, and also the Amorites, the Per'izzites, the Canaanites, the Hittites, the Gir'gashites, the Hivites, and the Jeb'usites; and I gave them into your hand.

This genocide subsequently was accomplished allegedly by Joshua (Jos 24:8, 11).

Also in Deuteronomy (1:20), Moses states that the Amorites were in the "hill country" promised to the Israelites by Yahweh. However, we now know that the Israelites were themselves Canaanites and

---

[1] Dever (2003), 34.

Magical Clothes

Deuteronomy 29:5 asserts that the clothing the Hebrews fled with miraculously remained the same during the entire 40 years in the desert, also continuing to fit the children as they grew up during this time:

> I have led you forty years in the wilderness; your clothes have not worn out upon you, and your sandals have not worn off your feet...

Thus, the Israelites had supernatural clothes and shoes that never wore out and that grew with the children born during the four decades, comprising the garments of those who died, which magically shrank to fit the younger generation.

Conquest of Canaan

Concerning the biblical account of the founding of Israel by the conquest of the Canaanitish peoples, Redford comments:

> If we examine what evidence we have for the Israelite appearance and settlement in Canaan, we shall find that it falls into three disparate and unequal bodies of material. In the first place we have the historical traditions preserved in parts of Numbers, Joshua and Judges, which far outweighs in sheer volume the other two; second, the extra-Biblical textual evidence; and finally, the archaeological data of excavation....
>
> ...even a cursory reading of this account is bound to excite suspicion. Cities with massive fortifications fall easily to rustic nomads fresh off the desert..., a feat Pharaoh's armies had great difficulty in accomplishing. Some cities are taken twice in the record..., suggesting conflicting traditions poorly integrated. ...
>
> A detailed comparison of this version of the Hebrew takeover of Palestine with the extra-Biblical evidence totally discredits the former. Not only is there a complete absence...in the records of the Egyptian empire of any mention or allusion to such a whirlwind of annihilation, but also Egyptian control over Canaan and the very cities Joshua is supposed to have taken scarcely wavered during the entire period of the Late Bronze Age. Far more damaging, however, than this argument from silence is the archaeological record. Sites such as Hormah, Arad, Jericho, 'Ai and Jarmuth had indeed suffered violent destruction, but this had been during the Early Bronze Age or at the end of the Middle Bronze, and during the Late Bronze Age they had lain unoccupied (save for squatters); others such as Kadesh Barnea, Heshbon and Gibeon were not to be settled until the Iron Age. Those sites that do show massive destruction at the transition from the Bronze to the Iron Age, about 1200 B.C., can as easily be explained as victims of the movement of the Sea Peoples.[1]

---

[1] Redford (1992), 263-265.

In portraying the conquest of Canaan, Joshua 8:28 uses the term "to this day," indicating the verse was written long after the purported facts. Adding to this fictional air, Joshua 10 depicts an impossible military move, and the important city of Gibeon probably would have been guarded by the Egyptians at that time, a fact unknown to the biblical scribe centuries later.

Regarding the purported conquest, Israeli archaeologists Drs. Finkelstein and Amihai Mazar conclude:

> ...it has become obvious that this was not the historical reality. Archaeological investigations have shown that many of the sites mentioned in these conquest stories turned out to be uninhabited during the assumed time of the Conquest, ca. 1200 B.C.E. This is the case with Arad, Heshbon, 'Ali and Yarmuth. At other sites, there was only a small and unimportant settlement at the time, as at Jericho, and perhaps Hebron....
>
> It is thus now accepted by all that archaeology in fact contradicts the biblical account of the Israelite Conquest as a discreet historical event led by one leader. Most scholars of the last generation regard the Conquest narratives as a literary work of a much later time, designed to create a pan-Israelite, national saga.[1]

Concerning the conquest of Ai (Joshua 8), Finkelstein and Mazar surmise that the germ tale may have been created as the hill tribes began to settle into agricultural communities during the 12th to 11th centuries BCE.[2] Such germ tales would have been developed as fictionalized tribal folklore, embellished over the centuries.

Tin?

At Gilgal, Joshua magically acquires bronze weapons for his hundreds of thousands of warriors, made with tin, a metal rare in the Middle East. One wonders, of course, where all that tin could have come from at that time, making the story highly implausible.

Jericho

The conquest of Canaan allegedly destroyed the town of Jericho and annihilated all living things within the walls, including babies. Yahweh devised this plan, but one could ask why he did not just make the Canaanites disappear, rather than commit brutal genocide?

It is claimed that the massive force of Israelites eventually arrived at the city of Jericho (Jos 6:1-27), nevertheless requiring the horn-blowing miracle from the Lord to knock down the walls.

Rahab?

What is the need of the treasonous woman in the tale (Jos 2:3, 6, etc.), Rahab the prostitute, to hide the Israelites and give them access to the city, if the walls are going to be destroyed supernaturally?

---

[1] Finkelstein (2007), 62.
[2] Finkelstein (2007), 62.

Oddly enough, this "harlot" is listed in the New Testament as one of Jesus's ancestors *(Mt 1:5)*.

Anachronism

As concerns Jericho and the excavations in the late 1950s by archaeologist Dame Kathleen Kenyon, Dever states:

> ...Kenyon showed beyond doubt that in the mid-late 13th century B.C.—the time period now required for any Israelite "conquest"—Jericho lay completely abandoned. There is not so much as a Late Bronze II potsherd of that period on the entire site. This seems a blow to the biblical account indeed.... Simply put, archaeology tells us that the biblical story of the fall of Jericho, miraculous elements aside, cannot have been founded on genuine historical sources. It seems invented out of whole cloth.[1]

Hence, in the story of Jericho we possess another biblical anachronism. Moreover, there exists at the site no extant evidence of any enormous and sudden occupation by huge amounts of Israelites with an enormous amount of Egyptian booty.

No Evidence of Conquest

Under such circumstances as the Canaanite inhabitants of Jericho being vastly outnumbered and easily defeated, as well as the fact that by the time of the supposed conquest (c. 13th cent. BCE), the city was uninhabited, it is evident that no such thing as the massive Israelite incursion into Canaan depicted in the Bible ever occurred.

Like other biblical stories, this Joshua tale too has precedent in other cultures, such as the Egyptian and Canaanite, as Joshua appears to be a localized version of a syncretized solar deity of the Egyptians and Canaanites, the "god of salvation."

Unfortunately, this story has been used to justify the modern Israeli state, with the slaughterers of unarmed men, women and children in Jericho's conquest labeled "special ops forces" by modern military strategists.[2]

Apologies

Christian apologists attempt through convoluted "reasoning" to insist that the Exodus *could* have happened as described in the Bible. They appeal to other incredible stories in the Bible, such as Noah's ark and Jonah and the whale, as if these patent fairytales somehow prove the implausible Exodus also could have occurred. It is contended that "God works in mysterious ways" and is omnipotent, therefore capable of pulling off *anything*, including all manner of natural law-bending miracles. For example, here is an apology about how this reason-defying event could have come about:

---

[1] Dever (2003), 46-47.
[2] For example, Canadian historian Dr. Richard A. Gabriel, as cited in the History Channel's "Bible Battles."

The exodus population were sustained by miracles: Pillar of fire provided light; cloud provided shelter and water (Isa 4:4-6); manna provided food, their cloths [sic] and shoes did not wear out; (Deut 8:4) God gave them supernatural strength in fleeing Egypt and crossing the Red Sea.[1]

Such tortured attempts prove little more than the ability of the human mind to cling to things programmed into it at an impressionable age. After continued labored reasoning, the conclusion by the same individual is: "The Bible is God's inspired word. Trust it!" The *a priori* assumption is that the Bible is true, therefore the Exodus happened, regardless of how implausible or impossible that story may be.

Political Fiction and National Epic

The Exodus as political fabrication was asserted as early as 1790-1800 in *Critical Remarks on the Hebrew Scriptures* by Reverend Dr. Alexander Geddes (1737-1802), a concept confirmed by modern thinkers almost 250 years later. Once again, the assessment of another older scholar has proved to be intelligent, insightful and accurate. The fact will remain that, not only is this migration an absurd notion for the reasons given here, but also, after over a century of intense exploration, there remains no unambiguous artifact for such a mass movement. Moreover, this tale of an exodus or desert sojourn can be found in ancient *mythology.*

In this "minimalist" or "mishnaic" analysis, the Exodus resolves itself to a national epic central to Jewish identity. As Oblath remarks:

> ...if we remove the exodus story, all references and allusions to it and all ethics and laws that derive from it, the Bible would indeed be a barren document. How do we explain its prominence in history and text, if indeed the events described never occurred?[2]

As we can see, modern scholarship indicates the Exodus not to be a historical account, and the answer to this question is that this national epic ranks as little different from the foundational myths of other cultures. These other national epics too can be seen to permeate the culture they purportedly spawned. Much of the daily life of the huge nation of India, for example, is tied into its creation myths as concerns the world, its ethnicity, religion and general culture(s).

In reality, the Exodus story "cannot be accepted as an historical event and must be defined as a national saga."[3] As Finkelstein and Mazar state, "We cannot perceive a whole nation [wandering] through the desert for forty years under the leadership of Moses, as presented in the biblical tradition."[4]

---

[1] Rudd, "The Number of the Exodus Jews."
[2] Oblath, 16-17.
[3] Finkelstein (2007), 60-61.
[4] Finkelstein (2007), 60.

They leave room however, for the tradition to be "rooted in the experience of a certain group of West Semitic slaves who fled from the northeastern Delta region into the Sinai during the late-thirteenth century, as paralleled by events recorded on papyri from the New Kingdom in Egypt."[1]

We are reminded that there have been *many* ingresses and exoduses to and from Egypt over the many centuries preceding the biblical era: "Papyri describe small groups of slaves escaping to the Sinai through the eastern fortification system of Egypt..."[2] Finkelstein and Mazar suggest that such stories may have served as "typological parallels to the genesis of the Exodus narrative."[3]

The Exodus story constitutes epic myth, possibly with details added from any one or more of these various sojourns, up to the point when the biblical account was composed, parts of which possibly as late as the sixth century BCE, if not later, such as the time of Ezra (5th cent. BCE), with alterations into the third century BCE.

Conclusion

In the end, scholarly consensus asserts that "there is no archaeological evidence to support a Late Bronze Age exodus" and that "no historical kernel for the exodus can be placed within any specific period."[4] To reiterate, not a shred of credible physical evidence has been discovered anywhere in over a century of scientific excavations, scouring the Sinai Desert for any sign of the Israelites' 40-year sojourn there.

As seen, the entire Exodus story appears unreal, even beyond the supernatural miracles. The pharaoh is never named, in dozens of pages of text, despite the fact that Egyptian kings were well known and inscribed their names all over monuments. According to the Bible, Moses himself was raised as a brother of the pharaoh; yet, the account is vague and ambiguous, written in the third person. None of the individuals is clearly distinguished in history; no dates are given, and place-names, again, are primitive.

While Egyptian chronology remains problematic in its minute details, the general eras of various pharaohs is known through a number of scientific means, including: chronologies in texts; linguistics; DNA evidence; Carbon-14 dates; styles of artifact such as pottery; building styles; climate studies; technological and metallurgic advancement; comparisons with other chronologies such as those of Canaan and Mesopotamia; and so on. The lack of specifying the pharaoh and era in the biblical tale is therefore inexplicable.

---

[1] Finkelstein (2007), 60.
[2] Finkelstein (2007), 59.
[3] Finkelstein (2007), 60.
[4] Oblath, 21.

Furthermore, the biblical text contains abundant anachronisms, including the names of peoples such as the Philistines, Edomites and Midianites who did not exist as such at the purported time. The inclusion of these anachronisms fits in with political issues during the seventh century.

Clearly, the Exodus account was written long after the purported events, revealed in its anachronisms and simplicity in many instances. The setting reflects an era centuries later and unfamiliarity with the milieu of the purported Exodus period.

We have seen also numerous elements of the tale clearly implausible or impossible. Many other nonsensical aspects of the Exodus story can be found in the skeptical analysis by Wheless in his book *Is It God's Word?*

The problems with the Exodus account were summarized by Michael D. Lemonick in a *TIME* magazine article entitled "Are the Bible's Stories True?":

> But even scholars who believe [the events] really happened admit that there's no proof whatsoever that the Exodus took place. No record of this monumental event appears in Egyptian chronicles of the time, and Israeli archaeologists combing the Sinai during intense searches from 1967 to 1982—years when Israel occupied the peninsula—didn't find a single piece of evidence backing the Israelites' supposed 40-year sojourn in the desert.
>
> The story involves so many miracles—plagues, the parting of the Red Sea, manna from heaven, the giving of the Ten Commandments—that some critics feel the whole story has the flavor of pure myth. A massive exodus that led to the drowning of Pharaoh's army, says Father Anthony Axe, Bible lecturer at Jerusalem's Ecole Biblique, would have reverberated politically and economically through the entire region. And considering that artifacts from as far back as the late Stone Age have turned up in the Sinai, it is perplexing that no evidence of the Israelites' passage has been found. William Dever, a University of Arizona archaeologist, flatly calls Moses a mythical figure. Some scholars even insist the story was a political fabrication, invented to unite the disparate tribes living in Canaan through a falsified heroic past....
>
> ...If the general line of interpretation is correct, El, not Yahweh, was the original god of the Israelites who came out of the land of Egypt. Only later, under the impetus of contact with the southern tradition of Edom, does Yahweh come to be associated, and then assimilated, with El.[1]

To sum further:

> A century of research by archaeologists and Egyptologists has found no evidence which can be directly related to the Exodus captivity and the escape and travels through the wilderness, and most

---

[1] Lemonick, *TIME*, 147:68.

archaeologists have abandoned the archaeological investigation of Moses and the Exodus as "a fruitless pursuit."[1]

The Exodus is not a historical event fictionalized but a mythical motif historicized. Again, the difference may seem subtle but is highly important. The archetypal myth existed first and was utilized as a framework upon which to build a national epic. This sort of mythmaking is abundant enough—and easily identified as such—in the foundational stories of other cultures. Who, for example, would believe that the legendary founders of Rome, Romulus and Remus, indeed were suckled by a she-wolf?[2]

As concerns the creation of the Exodus myth, Finkelstein and Mazar conclude, "During several centuries of transmission, it was constantly changed and elaborated on until it received the form known to us from the Hebrew Bible."[3]

---

[1] "The Exodus," *Wikipedia*.
[2] The story of twins—twin "culture-heroes"—founding an ethnicity or nation is common, evidently reflecting an astral or astrotheological archetype symbolized popularly by Castor and Pollux. In antiquity, the legend of Romulus and Remus was identified with that of Pelias and Neleus, the sons of Poseidon and Tyro. (Gaster, 367)
[3] Finkelstein (2007), 61.

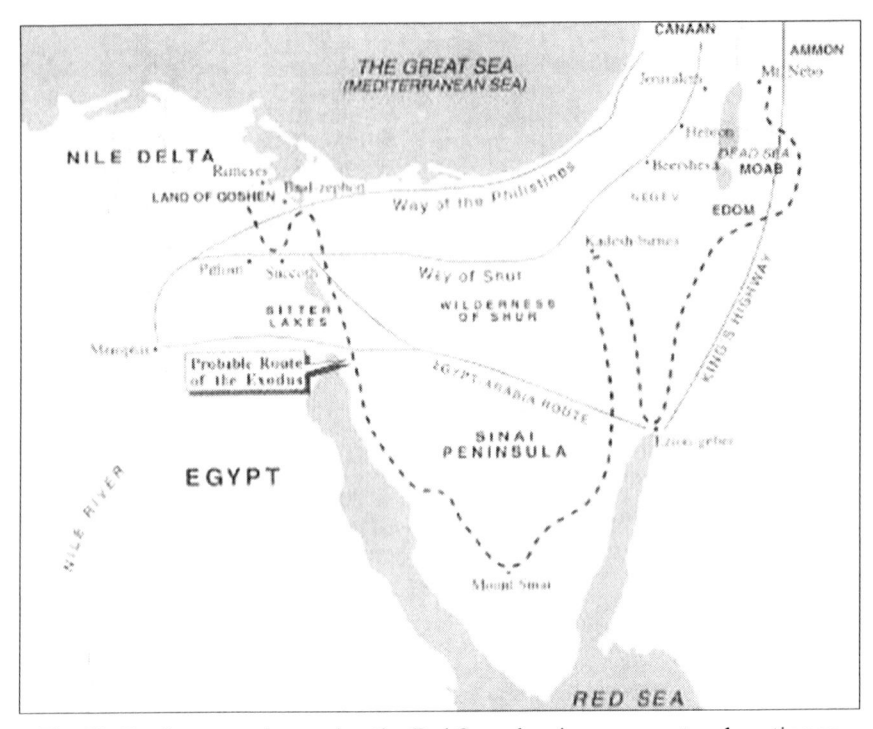

Fig. 30. Exodus route bypassing the Red Sea, showing supernatural parting as unnecessary for flight from Egypt (Möller)

Fig. 31. Golden Calf worship (Exod 32:1-35). Bible card by Providence Lithograph Co, 1901.

The Exodus in Ancient Literature

"Except for the biblical story there is no literary evidence that there was ever an Egyptian Sojourn and Exodus as described in the Bible. This is true regardless of the date one assumes for the event, if there was such an 'event' at all."

Dr. John C. H. Laughlin, Archaeology and the Bible (87)

"The *incipit* of the Song of Moses, in Exodus 15.1—'I will sing to the Lord, for he hath triumphed gloriously: the horse and his rider hath he thrown into the sea'—clearly is to be counted as among the oldest compositions in the whole Bible. It seems very likely that the whole sequence of verses comprising the song [of the sea] contains in poetic form the germ of the narrative that becomes the full-blown story of the Exodus."

Dr. William Franke, Universality and History: Foundations of Core
(63)

"Contrary to those who claim that the Song of the Sea describes a historical battle, whatever historical core the exodus may have had, it is already thoroughly transformed into mythic proportions even in this early poetic composition. The Song exhibits the same basic structure as *Enuma elish* and the Ugaritic Baal cycle. The Divine Warrior overcomes his watery foe of chaos, creating a new order in the process... As in the Combat Myths, the Divine Warrior then retires to his (newly constructed) mountain sanctuary, from where he eternally rules his newly ordered cosmos (vs. 17-18).... Yahweh's mountain sanctuary here is of course the temple on Mount Zion—Yahweh's eternal 'resting place'..."

Dr. Bernard F. Batto, Mythmaking in the Biblical Tradition: Slaying
the Dragon (113-114)

THE LACK OF archaeological evidence demonstrating the Exodus story has led to the literalist apology that the text proves itself, regardless of extraneous circumstances. A more skeptical view such as evemerism claims that the oldest strata of the story contain an orally transmitted germ folktale recording a historical exodus of a much smaller scale, embellished over time with supernatural miracles and other mythical motifs. A closer scrutiny of the evidence, however, points to neither view as entirely correct. The third perspective or "mythicist position" posits that the story existed first as a mythical motif and was embellished over the centuries with many other non-historical elements, along with some historical or literal details, such as place-names or ethnic designations.

Circular Reasoning

In the literalist argument, it is believed that the biblical scribes were honest, God-fearing men; therefore, what they have written must be historically correct.

As Oblath remarks:

> With a recognition that direct archaeological evidence does not exist, supporters often turn to the exodus narrative itself for reinforcing its own historicity. Scholars such as Albright and R. Cohen have recounted the assumed scribal accuracy and pure conscientiousness in preserving this tale.[1]

The same argument could be made for the composers of any number of ancient texts, including the Homeric and Indian epics: Are we to suppose that these other stories bursting with miracles and supernaturalism represent "true history," because their scribes presumably were precise, full of integrity and truly transmitting history as it actually occurred? Moreover, shall we ignore the commentary by those who continued the lineage of the biblical scribes, the Jewish rabbis—presumably also possessing integrity—who speak openly about the Bible containing *allegory*?

Regardless of the belief in the biblical text, there exists no solid scientific evidence of the Exodus as a historical event, as depicted in the Old Testament. Hence, this argument is not scientifically based but is circular.

Moreover, if the core represents a historical memory, it has been reproduced only as a hatred towards Egypt and its pharaohs overall, possibly for a number of perceived transgressions over a period of centuries, rather than a single historical event with accurately recorded details.

Song of the Sea

This literalist perspective is not held by skeptics, of course, who nonetheless may assert that there is a historical core to the tale, with mythical embellishment. One biblical pericope or "discrete literary unit" that allegedly demonstrates a "historical" core is the "Song of the Sea" or "Song of Moses" at Exodus 15:1-18.[2] This song purportedly was sung on the day of the crossing of the Red Sea, a contention for which there is no evidence, since the crossing itself appears to be mythical.

This allegedly older text is pointed to by critical scholars as the possible basis and "historical" nucleus of the Exodus story, elaborated upon for centuries before being written down during the later centuries. It is significant that, while the verses in chapter 14 immediately preceding the Song tout Moses as Yahweh's mouthpiece and equal, the patriarch is not named at all in the Song, other than at Exodus 15:1a, at the very beginning and easily interpolated. The

---

[1] Oblath, 15.
[2] See *The Study Guide* for the present work.

purpose for this core text seems to be to demonstrate the superiority of the Jewish god over the esteemed deities of the region.[1]

In his monograph on the subject, Christian theologian Russell argues for the song's composition between the 12th and eighth centuries BCE, mostly long after the purported events of the Exodus:

> ...the poetry of Exod 15:1-21 (specifically vv. 1b-18) was most likely composed during the mid-twelfth century B.C.E. (ca. 1150 B.C.E.)....
>
> ...the late eighth century B.C.E. is established as the *terminus ad quem* for Exod 15:1b-18 on the basis of compelling evidence for the date of composition of Ps 78 during the time of Hezekiah.[2]

As concerns source text criticism, Russell recounts that current scholarship tends to assign verses 1-18 and 20-21 to J and E, respectively, while verse 19 has been ascribed to the priestly redactor or P.[3]

Oblath avers the song's composition around the 10th century,[4] while others contend for a post-Exilic effort, after the middle of the sixth century and even into the late fourth century BCE.[5]

Psalm 78

Russell cites Psalm 78 along with several others as influenced by the Song of the Sea at Exodus 15,[6] contending for a composition date in the late eighth century BCE, "following the fall of the Northern Kingdom."[7] Thus, Psalm 78 may have been reworked during Hezekiah's reign, based on the Song, created centuries earlier.

Psalm 78 contains the verse that opens this present work regarding the utterance of "dark sayings from on old" (חידה *chiydah*),[8] a reference evidently to *allegorical* stories, in other words *myths*. The "old" qualification suggests we are discussing pre-Israelite and largely Canaanite myths. After this introduction comes a detailed summary of the Exodus story (Ps 78:12ff). Oddly enough, Moses is never named in this Exodus psalm, as was the case with the pre-exilic prophets.

In Psalm 78, it is not Moses but the *Lord God* who splits the rock for water and does other major acts of the Exodus. God is named in Psalm 78 as יהוה Yĕhovah/YHWH; אל *'el*/El; אלהים *'elohiym*/Elohim;

---

[1] See, e.g., Russell (30) regarding verses 1b-11: "On the basis of Yhwh's triumphant victory over the Egyptians, the poet asserts that there is no other god like Yhwh. This is indeed the center of the Song of the Sea. This verse [11] boldly and openly declares in a polytheistic world that Yhwh has no rivals."
[2] Russell, 2, 5, 113, 149.
[3] Russell, 33.
[4] Oblath, 14.
[5] Russell, 1.
[6] Russell, 73. Other verses include Psalms 74, 77, 118 and Isaiah 11:11-12:6.
[7] Russell, 128, 129.
[8] Strong's H2420: "1. riddle, difficult question, parable, enigmatic saying or question, perplexing saying or question; a. riddle (dark obscure utterance); b. riddle, enigma (to be guessed); c. perplexing questions (difficult)..."

עליון *'elyown*/Elyon; and אדני *'Adonay*/Adonai, comprising major god epithets and pre-Yahwist deities. Most of the time, the word for "God" is El, while YHWH is employed only in two places (78:4, 78:21).

Hence, this text appears to be the remake of a Canaanite composition exalting the high god El and interpolated to favor the southern kingdom of Judah, as opposed to the Israel of the north. Instead of Moses, Aaron or any other supposedly historical personages of the Exodus tale, Psalm 78 mentions Jacob, Joseph, Ephraim and Judah, the latter one raised above the former three northerners. The psalm is based apparently on Jacob's purported sojourn in Egypt and the domination of the southern Israelites or Judahites over the northern kingdom, especially the Ephraimites.

In any event, there is no indication in Psalm 78 of any "historical Moses," despite the fact that the text provides a detailed summary of the Exodus story. It would appear that the creators of the Moses myth used texts like Psalm 78 and the Song of the Sea to compose their foundational epic centuries later, creating a fictional "patriarch" to accomplish the miraculous tasks originally attributed to God. Hence, the psalm speaks of "dark sayings of old," possibly denoting pre-Israelite Canaanite scriptures and pre-Mosaic core folklore.

Anachronisms

The Song of the Sea contains a few Exodus story elements interspersed with hymns of praise for the god. The mention at 15:14 of the "inhabitants of Philistines" is an anachronism, as is the next verse (15:15) about the "chiefs of Edom." It would seem that at least those parts of the text postdate the arrival of the Philistines and creation of the Edomite *kingdom,* centuries after the purported Exodus events. Again, these peoples were troublesome especially during the era of Hezekiah and Josiah, indicating the song's propagandist refitting at that time.

First or Second Temple?

As one reason for his late dating of the song, theologian Dr. Charles F. Pfeiffer claims that Exodus 15:17 identifies the Second Temple, built in 516 BCE.[1] Wheless points out the same anachronism, although he allows for it to be the First Temple, supposedly built sometime during the 10th to eighth centuries:

> ...the significant proof of long post-Mosaic authorship in these anachronic strophes of the Song: "Thou shalt bring them in, and plant them in the mountain of thine inheritance, in the place, O Yahveh, which thou *hast made* for thee to dwell in, in the Sanctuary [מקדש *miqdash*], O Yahveh, which they hands *have established*" [Exod 15:17]... This mountain was Zion, at Jerusalem, and the sanctuary was Solomon's temple; and Jerusalem did not come into the hands of

---

[1] Russell, 1.

the Chosen until partly captured by David. The temple was built by his son Solomon, some five hundred years after the so-called Song of Moses at the Red Sea, wherein these things are spoken of as already existing. So this reputed Song of Moses was written centuries after the death of Moses.[1]

Hence, this part of the song may not be as old as other sections. It should be noted that there has never been found any evidence of the First Temple, and David and Solomon's historicity as in the Old Testament is questionable.

Regarding the song as reflecting a historical Exodus, Oblath concludes:

> It is evident that the Song of the Sea refers to a flight from an aggressive, pursuing enemy. It tells of a sea crossing at Yam Sûp [סוּף יָם *yam cuwph*, meaning "red sea"], events strongly associated with the exodus from Egypt. Considered in isolation, however, it implies no more than a flight from "Pharaoh." Any battle could be described in the song. There is no evidence within the song that would support a flight from Egyptian slavery.[2]

Although it may represent a core text upon which the rest of the Exodus tale was built, the core too shows few signs of being "historical." On the contrary, it has the earmarks of a typical mythological epic of the era.

It is possible the Song of the Sea is a Canaanite/Amorite poem reworked after the alleged destruction by Ramesses III of Amurru or one of many other perceived transgressions by Egypt, to cast the land of the Nile and its rulers in a bad light as the "villain" in ancient mythology. Therefore, the core story may have been committed eventually to writing in Hebrew but nonetheless reflects an ancient Semitic mythological tradition. The inclusion of Moses in the Song would post-date Psalm 78 and Hezekiah.

The Baal Cycle

Another biblical text that appears to have been influenced by Ugaritic mythology is Psalm 29, about which Schniedewind remarks that the biblical text's storm imagery "has strong parallels with the Baal imagery of a Ugaritic epic." Schniedewind also states that Psalm 29 "shares much with the 'Song of the Sea' (Exodus 15:1-18), which is in many ways a polemic against Baal and the Canaanite religion."[3]

Stripped of its historical anachronisms, the Song of the Sea possesses parallels with the Canaanite "Baal cycle," which lends the core biblical text credibility as an older composition, borrowed from Canaanite *mythology*, not a historical tradition.

---

[1] Wheless, 39.
[2] Oblath, 15.
[3] Schniedewind, 30.

As Russell states:

> Exodus 15:1b-18 resembles the Baal cycle in a number of striking ways.... The Baal narrative may be summarized around the themes of conflict, order, kingship and palace (or temple) building. There is an initial conflict between Baal and Yamm. Yamm represents watery chaos and thus threatens the order of the cosmos. Baal is victorious and is declared king... The victory of order over chaos has cosmological overtones. A palace is then built for Baal as a symbol of his authority... Conflict, however, arises again with a new threat, Mot. Baal is initially defeated, but he inevitably is victorious and his kingship is again declared.
>
> The overall movement in the Song of the Sea from a conflict involving Yhwh's use of the sea in the defeat of Pharaoh's hordes to references about Yhwh's holy place, and finally to the declaration of Yhwh's eternal kingship roughly follows this sketch of the Baal cycle.[1]

It is further noteworthy that the focus of Baal is his "holy mountain," the "beautiful hill of my might," while Exodus revolves around Mount Sinai, holy hill of Yahweh.[2]

Regarding this correspondence, Schniedewind comments that the "story concerning Baal and Yamm is in many ways typical of Near Eastern cosmological stories (cp., *Enuma Elish*; Exodus 15) and marks Baal's rise to power with his defeat of Yamm (cp. Marduk's victory over Tiamat)." He also reminds that "Baal was worshipped throughout Syria-Palestine, and the Baal cycle necessarily is a primary source for understanding the religious beliefs of the entire ancient Near East."[3]

Although Russell admits that the parallels are striking, even to certain phrases, he maintains that the differences are significant: To wit, the Baal cycle is mythology, whereas the "events of the Song of the Sea take place on the plains of human history."[4] However, it appears that the Song in reality is the *mythical* core of the later historicized Exodus story, constructed around the Baal cycle and turned into pretended "history."

In this regard, speaking of Exodus 15, Dutch theologian Dr. Carola Kloos states that "the Reed Sea story originates in the myth of the combat with Sea, which has been 'historicized,' i.e. turned into pseudo-history, by the Israelites."[5] Kloos also concurs that Psalm 29 is dependent in significant part on Baal mythology, and she concludes that the psalm "pictures Yhwh throughout as Baal..."[6]

The Canaanite Baal-cycle core dates to earlier than the 12th century, and it may have been reworked during the subsequent

---

[1] Russell, 39.
[2] See, e.g., Russell, 41.
[3] Schniedewind, 26-27.
[4] Russell, 40.
[5] Kloos, 11.
[6] Kloos, 11.

THE EXODUS IN ANCIENT LITERATURE

centuries to revolve around the emerging Israelites, as a demonstration of how their henotheistically elevated god Yahweh was superior to the Egyptian pantheon.

Salvation Cultus

In the Baal cycle, the protagonist defeating the sea or sea god "Yamm" is considered the savior, reflected also at Exodus 15:2:

> The LORD is my strength and my song, and he has become my salvation; this is my God, and I will praise him, my father's God, and I will exalt him.

The original Hebrew is:

עזי וזמרת יה ויהי־לי לישועה זה אלי ואנוהו אלהי אבי וארממנהו:

The Hebrew here for "salvation" is ישועה *yĕshuw'ah*, essentially the same as Yehoshua or Yeshua, "Joshua" or "Jesus."

All of these terms derive from the root word ישע *yasha'*, which is used some 200 times in the Old Testament,[1] reflecting a frequent focus on deliverance and salvation. With such an emphasis, it is not difficult to understand why a salvation cult eventually would be created, apparently as an extension of a Yeshua/Joshua cult based on this Israelite's salvific and messianic role as leader of the conquest of Canaan and entry into the Promised Land.

In this same regard, ישע *yasha* is used to describe the Lord God, rendered as "savior" at 2 Samuel 22:3 and Psalm 106:21, for example. At 2 Samuel 22:2-3, we read about David singing:

> The LORD is my rock, and my fortress, and my deliverer, my God, my rock, in whom I take refuge, my shield and the horn of my salvation, my stronghold and my refuge, my savior; thou savest me from violence.

The original Hebrew is:

יהוה סלעי ומצדתי ומפלטי־לי: אלהי צורי אחסה־בו מגני וקרן ישעי משגבי ומנוסי משעי מחמס תשעני:

The word here for "the LORD" is יהוה *Yĕhovah* or Yahweh, while "God" is אלהים *'elohiym*, the plural word for "gods," in the Ugaritic/Canaanite pantheon. "Salvation" is expressed by ישע *yesha'*, while "savior" and "savest" or "to save" are both denoted by forms of ישע *yasha'*.[2] Note the word for "rock" in the LXX is πέτρα *petra*, the same as the name "Petros" or "Peter."

As we can see, there is a heavy emphasis in the Old Testament on salvation and Yahweh as a savior. Again, this fact of reverence for salvation explains why a salvific cult was created in Christianity, with the "savior," Yeshua, as its mythical founder.

---

[1] Strong's H3467.
[2] Strong's H3468 and H3467.

Yahh

The term for "Lord" at Exodus 15:2, יה *Yahh*,[1] is used generally in later poetic texts, tending to cast doubt on an early date for this important passage. Russell proffers Psalms 68:5 and 19 as examples of an early usage of יה *Yahh*; however, might not these examples also be later interpolations? Russell also points out that the terms for "strength and protection" in Exodus 15:2—עז *'oz* and זמרה *zimrah*, the latter rendered generally as "song"—are found in the exact form as a divine epithet in the Ugaritic texts, thereby also giving them antiquity.[2] This fact serves to demonstrate that the core text drew upon Canaanite literature and cosmology.

In the next verse, Exod 15:3, "Moses" also calls the Lord a "man of war" and names him as יהוה *Yĕhovah* or Yahweh, and so on. Hence, Yahweh is a warrior and war god, as well as a savior.

Semitic Influence on Egyptian Texts

The Canaanite myth of the battle between Baal and Yamm/Yam spread well beyond the borders of the Levant, making its way to Egypt. As concerns the cultural exchange between the Levant and Egypt, Redford remarks:

> A number of Asiatic myths appear rendered with very little modification into Egyptian. The aforementioned story of Yam and the Goddess, so well known from Ugarit and the Phoenician cities of the Levantine coast, has turned up in a beautiful, though fragmentary, papyrus now in the J.P. Morgan library. Yam exacts tribute from the gods, who reluctantly acknowledge him as overlord.... it would appear that Seth (Ba'al) eventually championed the gods' cause and defeated Yam. Other papyri deal with the sex life of Anath and her lusty paramour of the Ba'al-type of deity. Here again Seth adopts the role of Ba'al....[3]

Thus, the Baal-Yam myth migrated to Egypt, with the Egyptian god Set/Seth substituting for Baal. It is significant to note also the similarity between Seth and Jacob, "the supplanter," possibly representing not a historical patriarch but a god, "in Egypt."[4]

Redford cites other writings that reveal Near Eastern influence on Egyptian culture, including language, remarking:

> The impact Levantine and Mesopotamian culture made on Egypt of the New Kingdom is nowhere more vividly reflected than in the lexicon of the Egyptian language. Hundreds of Canaanite words turn up in New Kingdom documents...[5]

---

[1] Strong's H3050.
[2] Russell, 20.
[3] Redford (1992), 234-235.
[4] See, e.g., Acharya (2004), 506-507, etc.
[5] Redford (1992), 236.

Again, for centuries the cultural exchange between Canaan and Egypt included myths and language.

The Deep and Other Allegories

The Song of the Sea thus appears to be derived from Semitic and Egyptian mythology, not a "historical" Exodus of whatever size. Referring to Exodus 4-5, Russell remarks that "Yhwh uses the primordial waters as his weapon."[1] In this regard, Exodus 15:5 employs the word תהום *tĕhowm* for the "deep waters" that supposedly cover the pharaoh; as we shall see, this term is utilized within the context of the great sea monster or leviathan.[2] The same word is used at Exodus 15:8 to describe the "deeps...congealed in the heart of the sea."

As Batto says:

> The creation myth structure of the Song alone should be confirmation enough that Pharaoh and his hosts are viewed in larger-than-life proportions, that Pharaoh-Egypt has been metamorphosed into the primeval foe of the Creator. For this reason the poet has Pharaoh and his army cast into the sea and sunk to its abyssal depths. Pharaoh and the sea merge as a single entity. This explains why in verses 6-8 Yahweh's ire seems to shift from Pharaoh to the sea itself...[3]

Again, the Hebrew word for "sea," ים *yam*, is essentially the same as the Canaanite/Ugaritic name for the sea god, Yamm, battled against in the Baal cycle. Hence, in YHWH/Moses's control of the Yam Suph or "Red Sea" we have an echo of this battle.

Chariots

Preceding this *yam* pericope, the word for "chariots" at Exodus 15:4 is מרכבה *merkabah*,[4] in the singular, a term popular within the mystical and allegorical Jewish tradition called the Kabbalah. An associated concept is the mysterious and otherworldly "wheel within a wheel" of the biblical prophet Ezekiel (1:4-26), to be discussed below. The same term מרכבה *merkabah* is used to describe Yahweh's "throne-chariot" in the Dead Sea Scrolls and elsewhere.[5]

Fig. 32. Deity labelled either 'YHW' (Yahu) or 'YHD' (Judea), seated on winged chariot wheel, holding bird, 4th century BCE. Silver coin from Gaza, British Museum

---

[1] Russell, 28.
[2] See, e.g., Isaiah 27:1; 51:9-10
[3] Batto, 114.
[4] Strong's H4818.
[5] Barnstone, 705-706.

Moreover, 2 Kings 23:11 employs the same term to describe the רכבות השמש *merkabah hashemesh*: "chariots of the sun" or "Shamash's chariots." Hence, the word's use in the Exodus story need not concern a historical or actual chariot but could represent an allegorical concept associated with deity.

In this regard, Dr. Jan van Goudoever remarks:

> The Merkaba (chariot)-theology is developed in the Qumran writings and in the Enoch traditions, especially in the Third Enoch. There it is said "And the appearance of its splendour is like unto the splendour of the sunshine in the summer solstice."[1]

The word "chariot" appears in Semitic texts in a poetic context,[2] while real charioteers in the Levant attained an esteemed class, called by the Indo-European term *maryannu*, or *mrynm* in the Semitic. Interestingly, one of these charioteers in the Ugaritic texts is called *ysril* or "Israel."[3] In any event, the inclusion of chariots in the Song is a reflection of a mythical motif, not history.

Reed Sea?

Previously, we discussed the notion of the "Red Sea" and that Batto disagrees with its literal association with the Exodus. Regarding the reference to the "Red Sea" at Exod 15:4-5, Batto reiterates his observations:

> It has been fashionable to translate *yam sûp* as "Reed Sea" and to suggest that we have preserved here an authentic historical memory that Israel escaped from Egypt by wading across a shallow papyrus marsh—hence the name "Reed Sea/Marsh"—which their Egyptian pursuers were unable to negotiate in their heavy horse-drawn chariots. Elsewhere I have argued that the presence of *yam sûp* here cannot be due to authentic historical memory that the battle occurred at some "Reed Sea." The whole Reed Sea hypothesis is nothing more than a figment of scholarly imagination. Biblical *yam sûp* always and everywhere refers to that body of water which we today identify as the Red Sea or one of its extensions...[4]

Batto also states that "it is not likely that the placement of Israel's deliverance from Pharaoh in or near the Red Sea in the Song of the Sea derives from authentic historical memory," continuing:

> Rather, the presence of *yam sûp* here is explained by the mythological connotations inherent in the name itself. *Yam sûp* literally means "the Sea of End/Extinction"... To these ancient Israelites *yam sûp* really was the sea at the end of the world. As such it was heavily freighted with all the mythological connotations associated with primeval sea.[5]

---

[1] van Goudoever, 73.
[2] See, e.g., Mark Smith (2009:2.297) for a discussion of Baal's chariot and Marduk's "storm chariot" in the *Enuma Elish*.
[3] Botterweck, 399.
[4] Batto, 115.
[5] Batto, 115.

Thus, the Red Sea was employed to historicize an ancient myth, the Baal cycle-type battle between the hero and Yamm, while Yahweh and Moses control Yam.

Ruach

At Exodus 15:10, we read about the "wind" that the Lord blew in order to control the waters, which some have tried to find in "history." The Hebrew term used in this verse is רוח *ruwach*, which also refers to God's "breath" and the Holy Spirit.[1] Again, this entire song seems to be a typical allegorical and mythological poem, not the recounting of a historical event. In other religions and mythologies, the wind is personified, considered to be a deity, as in the Egyptian god Shu, also an Egyptian lawgiver and vine deity. Here we can see a germ, perhaps, of the personified "Holy Spirit."

Underworld

The word for "earth" or "land" at Exodus 15:12—"Thou didst stretch out thy right hand, the earth swallowed them"—is ארץ *'erets*,[2] which can refer also to the "underworld."[3] Russell cites the Akkadian and Ugaritic cognates for ארץ *'erets*, indicating the term's pre-Hebrew significance.[4] Hence, again, this song could be viewed as poetic allegory based on older Canaanite underworld myths.

Philistines

Exodus 15:14 refers to the inhabitants of פלשת *Pēlesheth*, rendered in English "Philistia" and in Greek Φυλιστιιμ *Phulistiim*, referring to the Philistines. As we have seen, the Philistines did not exist during the time when the Exodus is purported to have happened, so this verse represents one of the anachronisms previously mentioned.

All in all, there remains little reason to insist that the Song of the Sea recounts a historical event. It may well be an older Canaanite poem, reworked by the later Jews, utilized as the basis for their foundational tradition.

Song of Moses

Current scholarship demonstrating the non-historicity of the Pentateuch includes discussion of the "Song of Moses" at

---

[1] Strong's H7307 for רוח ruwach: "1) wind, breath, mind, spirit... Spirit of God, the third person of the triune God, the Holy Spirit, coequal, coeternal with the Father and the Son..." The LXX is πνεῦμα pneuma, employed in other parts of both the Old and New Testaments to describe the "Holy Spirit." See, e.g., Ps 51:11, Isa 63:10-11, Mt 10:20 and Lk 1:35 for examples of πνεῦμα pneuma (G4151), which is used 385 times in the New Testament. This Greek word is the root of "pneumonia" and "pneumatic," etc.
[2] Strong's H776.
[3] Russell, 16. See also Gen 2:6, 1 Sam 28:13, Isa 29:4 and Jon 2:6.
[4] Russell, 16.

Deuteronomy 32:1-43, a lengthy recitation clearly not composed by a historical Moses. Concerning the song's attribution to Moses as asserted in Deuteronomy 31:19 and 31:22, biblical scholar Dr. Paul Sanders remarks that "present-day scholars almost universally deny the historicity of these claims" and that "Deut. 32 would have been composed in a later period of Israel's history."[1]

In his monograph *The Provenance of Deuteronomy* 32, Sanders provides the scholarship for this contention of non-Mosaic origin for the "Song of Moses." Likewise, we can assert that the rest of the Pentateuch too was not written by a historical Moses but was composed many centuries after his supposed existence, for a variety of reasons, not the least of which was political, to compete with the founding myths of other nations.

As we do here with various Exodus themes, Sanders demonstrates that elements of the Song of Moses are pre-Mosaic, emanating from Ugaritic/Canaanite mythology. These pre-Israel and mythical elements in turn were drawn upon to flesh out of the Exodus story.

The Song of Deborah

As important as the texts claimed to contain germ verses about a supposed "historical" exodus are various records of relevant eras devoid of such tales. For example, along with Psalm 78—which attributes the miracles in the Exodus account to Yahweh himself and never mentions Moses—a peculiar lack of the Exodus in the literary record occurs in the biblical book of Judges, which purports to record the first organized era after the Israelites' arrival in Canaan. Moses and Joshua barely are mentioned in Judges, only briefly in order to give some "historical" basis.

Part of Judges (5:2-31), the "Song of Deborah" recounts the conquest of peoples in Canaan by the Israelites, representing a summary of germane themes in the Pentateuch. However, the actual foundational story itself is never mentioned in any specifics. Like the Song of the Sea, Deborah's ditty contains anachronisms such as victory over the Edomites, reflecting once more the enemies of Hezekiah and Josiah centuries later.

The date of Deborah's song has been estimated to be 1200 to 900 BCE, making it very old and predating the Hebrew script. The older date is based on internal evidence only, such as linguistic forms, the supposed "history" it contains and when Deborah purportedly lived (c. 1200-c. 1124/1067 BCE), according to the biblical chronology. In reality, these older linguistic forms could represent archaicisms from an underlying oral tradition, originally Canaanite, since they evidently were in existence before the emergence of Hebrew as a separate Semitic dialect.

---

[1] Sanders, 1.

No Moses or Joshua

Neither of Israel's purported national founders, Moses and Joshua, is included in Deborah's song about Canaan's conquest. The limited discussion in Judges of Moses, the purported divine lawgiver who allegedly appointed Israel's first judges, is very strange. Throughout the text, there were many opportunities that, had the writer known the Exodus story and Moses's receipt of the law on Mt. Sinai, he or she would have taken to bring up these themes. Moreover, the song contradicts or differs from a number of reputed "facts" in the preceding chapter 4 of Judges; hence, one or both of these accounts could not be historically accurate.

No Evidence of the Exodus

In the entire book, there are only a few references to Yahweh's deliverance of Israel out of Egypt, as at Judges 2:1, where the angel of the Lord mentions the Israelites "brought up from Egypt" and given the Promised Land. There remains no extant, corroborating archaeological or literary evidence for the existence of Israelites in any meaningful manner during Deborah's purported time.

In any event, Deborah's song provides no evidence of the Exodus, which, if she were truly the great heroine of a mere generation later, is inexplicable. As Oblath points out:

> ...the Song of Deborah mentions nothing about an exodus from Egypt. Nor does the text say anything concerning Moses, nor a war waged between YHWH and Pharaoh. In short, the song does not describe how Israel arrived inside the land of Canaan. Given no biblical account of an exodus, such an event could not be concluded, or even inferred, from the text in Judges.[1]

If genuinely ancient to whatever extent, the Deborah poem would represent only a repeated tradition of Israel in Canaan and would not prove any of the events of the Exodus.

Sisera and the Chariots of Iron

An example of where Moses surely would be recalled, were the Exodus historical and had involved the patriarch, can be found in the account of the Canaanite general Sisera's defeat. In this story, Yahweh routes Sisera and his 900 "chariots of iron" (Jdg 5:15), a scene reminiscent of the Red Sea drowning of the pharaoh and his army in chariots. Yet, the writer of Judges appears to be oblivious to this important and decisive moment in Israel's alleged history.

Instead, the figure of Samson is the book's most famous hero, defeating the Philistines, into whose hands the Israelites had been delivered for 40 years (Jdg 13:1), the familiar length of time used repeatedly in the Exodus story. Samson may have been the epithet of a local solar, fertility and wine-vine god at Timnah, in the vineyards

---
[1] Oblath, 10.

of which the hero kills a lion, to discover a beehive full of honey inside the animal (Jdg 14:5-9). It should be evident that this implausible tale does not reflect a historical event.

Astral Symbolism

The Song of Deborah has been analyzed as reflecting astral religion or astrotheology, focusing on the pericope (Jdg 5:20) which states that the stars were part of the victorious Israelite army:

> From heaven fought the stars, from their courses they fought against Sis'era.

> מן־שמים נלחמו הכוכבים ממסלותם נלחמו עם־סיסרא:

Here the Hebrew word for "heaven" is שמים *shamayim*,[1] the same term used to describe the "sky" as well as "God's heaven," along with the sky deities in Canaanite myth, previously noted. *Shamayim* appears over 400 times in the Old Testament, including at Isaiah 47:13, combined with the verb הבר *habar*, "to divide," indicating "astrologers."

The Hebrew term for "stars" in this passage is כוכב *kowkab*, also used in conjunction with another word, חזה *chozeh*, "seer," to indicate "stargazers." (Is 47:13) The same term כוכב *kowkab* is employed to denote the "star of Messiah" or "star out of Jacob" (Num 24:17).

This story follows on the heels of Joshua's conquest of Canaan, which is demonstrably fictional and is omitted from Judges, and there is little reason to suspect that the song of Deborah itself is historical.

Nonhistoricity of Deborah

In this regard, Deborah herself may represent not an ancient historical personage but a mythical character, possibly a demoted goddess or anthropomorphized divine epithet. This sort of mythmaking turning tribal gods into demigods, heroes, patriarchs, prophets, elders, saints, disciples and so on was common in antiquity, as cultures and ethnicities merged, and as monotheistic supremacism or henotheism were developed.

Massey equates Deborah, along with her seven princes and companions, with the "goddess Seven" of Egypt:

> Deborah was the first, the primordial Word, the oracle of the beginning, identical as such with Tep (Eg.), the tongue, and Teb, a name of Typhon, the living Word; one with Wisdom of the seven pillars, and Arke of the beginning. Her name also identifies Deborah with the north, or hinder part. Before her time, we are told that the highways were unoccupied, and the travellers walked through the byways. There was no celestial chart, no roads mapped out, no inhabitants in heaven. Hers was the time of the SHEPHT, the judges (princes) the seven companions who are the Elohim of Genesis,

---

[1] Strong's H8064.

whose judgment-seat was the mount, and who rode on white asses. Following Deborah, "They chose new gods; there was war in the gates." [Jdg 5:8] Hers was the reign of Peace. Hept (Khept) means peace and plenty. Hers was the time when mankind were of one tongue, the golden age associated with the name of Sut or Saturn.

Her consort is Lapidoth (לפידות), the lightner; his name signifies lightnings. Another Hero is Barak, whose name has the same meaning. Barak is Sutekh; Bar the Son, the Ar, is one of Sut's names. Sutekh or Barak was the glorious war-god, fierce as fire, the fulminator against the powers of darkness, one of the first, as the star Sothis and son of the Sabean mother, to pass through the Hades of death...[1]

Massey was of the opinion that, like much else in the Bible, this story takes place not on earth but in the heavens, in emulation of Egyptian myth. The number seven, it should be recalled, frequently represented in antiquity the Pleiades or "Seven Sisters."

The Bee Goddess

Deborah also may be the bee goddess who came with the tribe of Issachar when the early Iron Age hill settlements were established.[2] Honey, it should be noted, was a "substance of resurrection-magic," with the dead embalmed in it and "ready for rebirth."[3] In this regard, independent scholar of mythology Barbara G. Walker relates:

> Myths presented many symbolic assurances that the Goddess would restore life to the dead through her magic "bee-balm." Worshippers of Demeter called her "the pure mother bee," and at her Thesmophoria festivals displayed honey-cakes shaped like female genitals. The symbol of Aphrodite at Eryx was a golden honeycomb. Her priestess bore the name of Melissa, "Queen Bee," the same as the Jewish Queen Deborah, priestess of Asherah, whose name also meant "bee."[4]

Elsewhere Walker states:

> "Queen Bee," a ruler of Israel in the matriarchal period, bearing the same name as the Goddess incarnate in early Mycenaean and Anatolian rulers as "the Pure Mother Bee." Deborah lived under a sacred palm tree that also bore her name, and was identified with the maternal Tree of Life, like Xikum, the Tree of Ishtar. The Bible called her a "prophetess" or "judge" to disguise the fact that she was one of the governing matriarchs of a former age (Judges 4:4).
>
> One of Deborah's alternate names was Jael, "the Goddess Jah," possibly the same one patriarchal Persians called "Jahi the Whore," an earlier feminine form of Yahweh.[5]

---

[1] Massey (2007), 2.145.
[2] Speaking of biblical pests, Alfred Ely Day states: "Both hornets and wasps are abundant in Palestine (compare Zorah, which may mean 'town of hornets'). A large kind is called in Arabic *debbur*, which recalls the Hebrew *debhorah*, 'bee.'"
[3] Walker (1983), 407.
[4] Walker (1983), 407.
[5] Walker (1983), 217.

Writing about Jael (Jdg 4:22), Walker further states:

> "Wild She-Goat," alternate name for the Israelite queen Deborah as a mate of the scapegoat-god, Baal-Gad or Pan, Ja-El was the same as the Persians' primal Goddess Jahi, adopted by tribal queens of the pre-patriarchal period. Jael sacrificed Sisera in a strange way, nailing his head to the ground (Judges 4:21), which may be likened to the priestess of Artemis Tauropolis nailing the heads of their victims to crosses.[1]

Fig. 33. Jael killing Sisera. (*Speculum Humanae Salvationis*, c. 1360)

Concerning the Persian goddess Jahi the Whore, Walker comments:

> Oddly enough, some of the earliest forms of the name of the Jewish God seem to have been masculinized versions of the name of Jahi. Variations include Jahu, Jah, Yahu, Iau, Jaho. Some myths indicate that this God like Ahriman once had a serpent form and may have played the part of the Great Mother's serpent.[2]

The emergence of Yahweh as perhaps a masculinization of the old Persian serpent and fertility goddess Jahi is significant, as is his possible early role as the serpent of the Goddess.

As part of her magical and godly attributes, Walker contends, Jael/Deborah was said to "cast victory spells" for the Israelites (Jdg 4:8). She was said also to rule for 40 years, another usage of the ubiquitous number 40, discussed below.

Exodus in the Prophets

Absent in Judges, the earliest that traces of the Exodus story can be discerned is the eighth century, in the writings of the biblical prophets:

> The earliest mentions are in the prophets Amos (possibly) and Hosea (certainly), both active in 8th century BCE Israel. In contrast, Proto-Isaiah and Micah, both active in Judah at much the same time, never do. It thus seems reasonable to conclude that the Exodus tradition was important in the northern kingdom in the 8th century, but not in Judah.[3]

Evidently by this time, the southern kingdom Judeans had not adopted the Canaan-conquest foundational myth, which makes sense since Joshua was significantly a northern kingdom hero. Indeed, he evidently was originally a Semitic "god of salvation" remade into a patriarch; hints of his esteem as a god can be seen in

---

[1] Walker (1983), 459.
[2] Walker (1983), 460.
[3] "The Exodus," *Wikipedia*.

the Joshua cult of the Samaritans and Dead Sea Zadokites, as well as the New Testament Jesus.[1]

Absent Egyptian Record

We have seen that there exists no real evidence of the Exodus story in the Bible until the time of the prophets at the earliest, and no evidence for Moses until post-Exilic times. Nor is there any extrabiblical record of this supposedly historical occurrence. Literalist apologies for why there exists no specific Egyptian documentation of these extraordinary events include that people suffering so would not be interested in writing things down, as they scrambled to stay alive—and to protect their beloved children, undoubtedly, who were being slaughtered mercilessly by Yahweh.

On the contrary, all over the world people have felt compelled to chronicle their suffering, and the Exodus story itself is a record of Israelite misery. By this logic, the Exodus story would not have been written down by those who purportedly experienced the distress; hence, it must be either hearsay or fictional.

As we have seen, another excuse for the lack of a corroborative historical record is that the Egyptians naturally would be humiliated completely and try to erase such a resounding defeat from their memories and history. This last part is difficult to believe, as by the 10th biblical plague, for instance, the country would be completely decimated, and refugees would be fleeing to other parts, where they assuredly would tell others about what supposedly had happened to them. Of course, the apology at that point might be that *nobody* survived to escape and tell anyone. In this case, there would also not be anyone to pursue the fleeing mass of slaves.

Moreover, such reasoning does not take into account the Egyptian outposts such as in Canaan and elsewhere, which certainly would be aware that everyone in their country was either dead or enduring a horrendous calamity which likewise would have destroyed the economy, including as far as these very colonies.

The bottom line is that these numerous devastating supernatural events would have reverberated well into the Near and Middle East, and possibly farther, into India and even China. The Bedouin and other travelers through the Sinai also likely would have heard about a mass of two to three million people camping there for 40 years, and the flight of so many laborers from Egypt would have destroyed the economy as well.

The Ipuwer Papyrus

Even though it has been contended that the Egyptians were too "humiliated" by the Exodus to include it in their written records,

---

[1] For more on the cult of Joshua as a pre-Judaic god, see *Suns of God*.

some researchers have pointed to the Egyptian text called the Ipuwer Papyrus as "probably a description of these events."

The Ipuwer Papyrus, also called the "Admonitions," describes the usurpation of wealth from the Egyptians to their slaves; hence, it is similar to the biblical story that the Hebrews were given the "unimaginable" riches of the Egyptians to take with them on their journey to the Promised Land. It remains difficult to explain how the Hebrews could carry all that booty—and who would give it to them, since most of Egypt was dead.

The papyrus has been dated either to several centuries before the Exodus supposedly happened, possibly between 1850-1600 BCE, or to the 13th century at the latest. Current scholarship also avers that some of the text may be as old as the time of the pharaoh Khety I (c. 2130–2080 BCE). As we can see, there is no consensus as to its date, much less what it purportedly contains as "history." Because of its apparent age, however, the text would predate the era of Moses by centuries and thus could not be relating the Exodus tale.

The Ipuwer text is directed at the sun god and names foreigners as *bedu* or Bedouins, typical Asiatic hordes, like the *shasu* and *'apiru*, to be discussed below.[1] The Egyptians had been dealing with these "vile Asiatics" for over a thousand years before the Exodus purportedly happened.[2] To reiterate, during this time there were numerous ingresses and exoduses by Asiatics from the east, who came and went countless times over the centuries.

Lamentations Genre

The Ipuwer papyrus's writer appears to be lamenting the destruction of the scribe's country by these alien Asiatics, whom some have surmised were the Hyksos, the Semitic peoples who occupied part of Lower Egypt during the second millennium BCE. Christian apologist Dr. Stephen C. Meyer avers that the lamentations refer to the "second intermediate period when the Hyksos rose to power."

Since this text was composed evidently over a period of centuries, it may be part of a genre of "lamentations," like similar texts of the Egyptians and Sumerians. In this regard, German Egyptologist Dr. Ludwig D. Morenz (b. 1965) comments:

> In respect of their content and form...the "Admonitions" are strikingly close to the Sumerian city laments (Quack 1997), and, from Egypt itself, to the laments for the dead.... In the "Lamentation over the Destruction of Sumer and Ur," the decline of the land and its (capital) city is bewailed first, while that of the cities follows.[3]

---

[1] Redford (1992), 67.
[2] Redford (1992), chap. 3.
[3] Tait, 111.

Morenz further surmises that, as had these earlier Sumerian writings, the Ipuwer text serves as propaganda to justify a power shift from Memphis to Hieracleopolis.[1] The changeover occurred at the end of the Old Kingdom, around 2150 BCE, many centuries before the alleged historical Exodus.

There are lamentations in the Bible as well, with an entire book by that title bemoaning Jerusalem, like the Sumerian texts lamenting a city. For decades since various pagan lamentations texts were discovered, there has been within academia a debate about whether the biblical version drew directly from Mesopotamian compositions or represents an independent manifestation of a "broad literary tradition of laments."[2]

As Morenz concludes: "Whatever their historical relationship may be, Mesopotamian lament literature and the book of Lamentations obviously share similar motifs, themes and images."[3] Hence, if it has any significance in this matter, the Ipuwer text would demonstrate the non-historical nature of the Exodus, as part of a *genre*.

Early Messianism

The Ipuwer text also exemplifies very ancient messianic ideas reflected in the much later Jewish and Christian ideology. In discussing Ipuwer's laments for instance, Breasted remarks:

> The peculiar significance of the picture lies in the fact that, if not the social programme at least the social ideals, the golden dream of the thinkers of this far-off age already included the ideal ruler of spotless character and benevolent purposes who would cherish and protect his own and crush the wicked. Whether the coming of this ruler is definitely predicted or not, the vision of his character and his work is here unmistakably lifted up by the ancient sage—lifted up in the presence of the living king and those assembled with him, that they may catch something of its splendor. This is, of course, Messianism nearly fifteen hundred years before its appearance among the Hebrews.[4]

In recalling this "golden age," Ipuwer mourns the reign of the king under Re or Ra, reflecting the solar divinity as "savior," a very ancient and widespread notion.

As we can see, significant "biblical" ideas find their place in much older literature, which is not "historical" but represents a genre, including lamentations and messianism. In any event, the Ipuwer papyrus cannot be said to reflect a historical account of the biblical Exodus. If there is any relationship, it may be that parts of the Exodus story started out as an allegorical and/or propagandistic lamentation such as we find in this *type*.

---

[1] Tait, 111.
[2] Berlin, 27.
[3] Berlin, 27.
[4] Breasted (1912), 212.

Amarna Letters

Discovered in the 19th century at the headquarters of Akhenaten's cult and written using cuneiform in Akkadian, the oldest known Semitic language, the Amarna letters date from Amenhotep III's reign until the demise of his "monotheistic" successor, Akhenaten (14th cent. BCE). The letters represent a cache of about 200 cuneiform tablets that address the rulers of many different regions in the Near and Middle East, including the Assyrian, Babylonian, Canaanite, Cypriot, Hittite, Mitanni, Phoenician, Syrian and Ugaritian. True to the nature of the Akhenaten cultus, the Amarna texts constantly invoked the sun as Lord, in phrases such as "the eternal sun," "the sun, god of my father," "my sun" and so on.

Thus, the Amarna letters are not all administrative or diplomatic, as they also contain religious ideas, such as the following solar hymn:

> To the King my lord, my sun, my god, the breath of my life... your slave and dust under your feet. At the feet of the King my lord, my sun, my god, the breath of my life, I bowed down seven times seven times. I heard the words of the tablets of the King my lord, my sun, my god, the breath of my life, and the heat of your slave and the dust under the feet of the King, my lord, my sun, my god, the breath of my life, is exceeding glad that the breath of the King my lord, my sun, my god has gone out to his slave and to the dust under his feet.[1]

This 30-year correspondence comprising some 400 letters and spanning two Egyptian kingships also involves kings and other rulers in lesser or more obscure areas such as Amurru, Beruta, Gezer, Megiddo, Qadesh, Qatna, Taanach, Zidon and elsewhere. Yet, in all this mass, we find not a single recognition of any certain Israelite presence but, instead, reference to nomadic Semitic "robbers" called 'apiru or Hapiru/Habiru. In all this correspondence dealing with these Levantine peoples who would have been surrounding the Israelites, there is no mention of the Hebrews in Egypt or elsewhere whatsoever, as if they did not exist or were of so little consequence as to be unrecognized.

According to some of the numerous dates assigned to the purported events of the Exodus, these letters were composed around the time of, or decades to centuries after, the biblical texts. Yet, they make no mention of the horrendous destruction of the plagues and deaths, even though they highlight many other problems. They also show that the Canaan of this theorized Exodus era and even decades later was full of Egyptian influence. As Redford says, "The occupation by Egyptian troops of Canaanite towns is well attested in the Amarna Letters and in Egyptian inscriptions."[2]

---

[1] Pritchard, 486.
[2] Redford (1992), 204, 206.

At this same time, Canaanites were engaged in Egypt, as they had been for centuries, including and especially those later called Phoenicians:

> Asiatics are found as goldsmiths, coppersmiths and shipwrights, and one even rose to superintendent of all construction work of the king. One young Canaanite, Pas-Ba'al, possibly taken prisoner under Thutmose III [c. 1479-c. 1425 BCE], became chief draftsman in the Temple of Amun, and six generations later his descendants are still occupying this office. Scribes of Syrian extraction turn up commonly, especially in the treasury. A chief physician Ben-'anath is known, belonging to the prestigious "Mansion-for-Life."[1]

Thus, the Amarna letters reveal abundantly the longtime and intimate cultural interchange between the Levant and Egypt, before and/or during the purported time of the Exodus.

Ilimilku and the Legend of Keret

In one Amarna letter, mention is made of a man named Ilimilku (fl. 1350-1335 BCE), also transliterated as Milkilu, Milk-ilu or Milku-ilu, who "caused the loss of all the territories of the king."[2] There did exist a prominent Ilimilku, an Ugaritic high priest who wrote down the Canaanite myths of Baal and of El in the *Legend of Keret* found at Ugarit/Ras Shamra. The name appears to signify Ilu-milkom, or "King Ilu/El," reflecting a common tradition of theophoric or "god-bearing" names for priest-kings.

The *Legend of Keret* (c. 1500-1200 BCE) describes the trials of a king—a purported son of the god El—the solution of which sounds very biblical, as a precursor of various OT tales, such as making war on the neighboring kingdom to demand a wife and booty. This tale, however, is devoid of Hebrew influence, as are the Amarna texts.

In the end, it is obvious that, at the time of the Amarna correspondence, there was no significant proto-Israelite "Hebrew" people.

Conclusion

As was the case with the archaeology and scientific analysis, the extant literature of the Levant and Egypt does not reveal a historical Exodus, whether biblical or otherwise. In the end and as was the case with the archaeology, the literary record does not provide evidence of a "historical" Exodus. Rather, the core story appears to be mythical, based on Canaanite and Egyptian religion, mythology and tradition, altered in order to cast Egypt and its rulers as the villains of ancient cosmological battling. A number of biblical scriptures support this view, including the Song of the Sea, Song of Moses and Song of Deborah.

---

[1] Redford (1992), 225.
[2] "A Letter from Abdu-Heba of Jerusalem," EA 286.

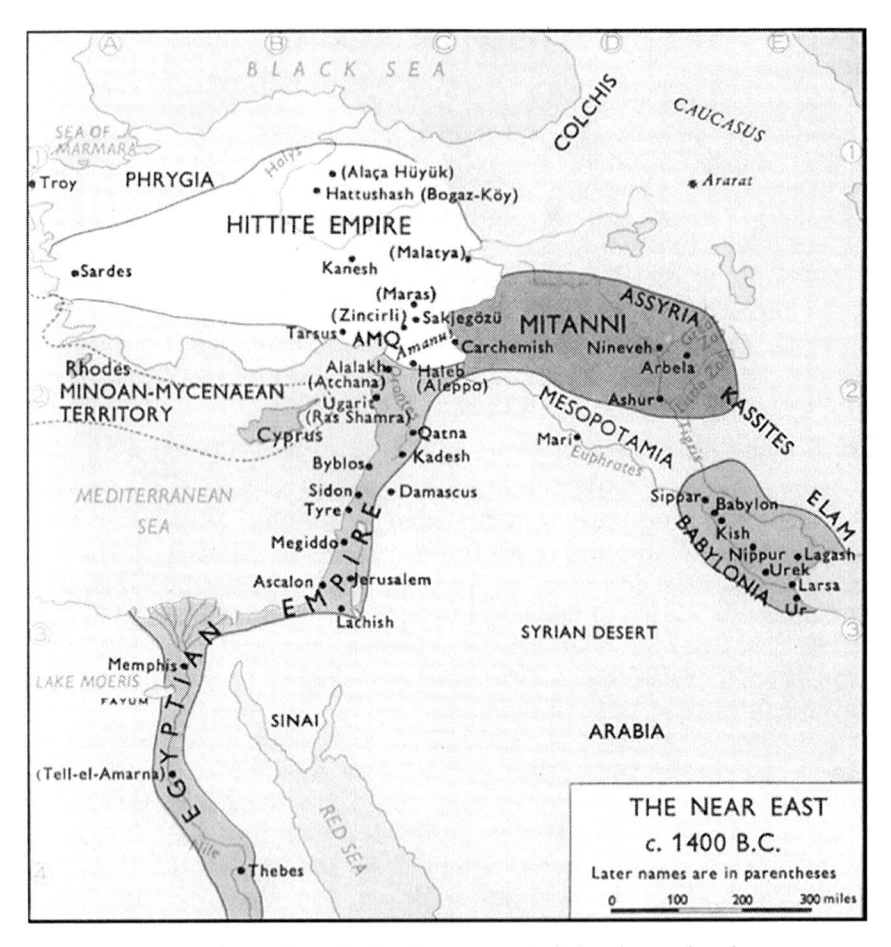

Fig. 34. Map of Near East during Amarna period showing regional powers: Egyptians, Hittites, Mitanni, Kassites (after *Historical Atlas*, fig. 6)

Hyksos and Lepers

"This is Manetho's account [of the Hyksos]; and evident it is from the number of years by him set down to belong to this interval, if they be summed up together, that these shepherds, as they are here called, who were no other than our forefathers, were delivered out of Egypt, and came thence, and inhabited this country..."[1]

Josephus, *Against Apion* (1.16/1.103)

"...it must be apparent that the Hebrews were never in Egypt, and that the story in the Book of Exodus had its foundation in the exploits of the Hyksos."

Judge Parrish B. Ladd, "The Hebrews, Egypt, Moses and the Exodus," *The Humanitarian Review* (5.159)

"...The Jewish historian Flavius Josephus saw the ancestors of Israel in these foreign rulers of Egypt. But there was certainly no religious conflict between the Hyksos and the Egyptians. The Hyksos were neither monotheists nor iconoclasts. On the contrary, their remaining monuments show them in conformity with the religious obligations of traditional Egyptian pharaohs, whose role they assumed in the same way as did later foreign rulers of Egypt such as the Persians, the Macedonians, and the Romans. They adhered to the cult of Baal, who was a familiar figure for the Egyptians, and they did not try to convert the Egyptians to the cult of their god. The whole concept of conversion seems absurd in the context of a polytheistic religion."

Dr. Jan Assmann, *Moses the Egyptian* (24)

ALTHOUGH THE NOTION contradicts many details in the Bible, it has been surmised since antiquity that a "historical" germ of the Exodus tale may revolve around the expulsion from Egypt in the 16th century BCE of the Semitic group called the Hyksos. In this scenario, it is proposed that much material was added to the Hyksos story in the seventh century BCE, with other layers in subsequent centuries as well, to create the fictionalized Exodus tale. Scholars such as William F. Albright, Stephen Meyer, Redford, David M. Rohl, Finkelstein and Silberman, among others, support a Hyksos historical framework for the biblical tale.

The Hyksos were an Asiatic people or peoples who purportedly conquered Lower Egypt from the east during the Second Intermediate Period (c. 1700 or 1650–c. 1550 or 1441 BCE). The name has been thought since ancient times to mean "shepherd kings," as proffered by Manetho in the third century BCE,[2] according to Josephus, who believed the Hyksos to be his Jewish forebears. However, modern

---

[1] Josephus/Whiston, 612.
[2] Manetho's original writings are lost to us, and what we know from him comes through others, such as Africanus, Eusebius, Josephus, Philo and Plutarch.

Egyptologists prefer the reading "rulers of foreign lands" or "chiefs of foreign lands" for the meaning of "Hyksos," or *heqa khoswe* in the Egyptian. Israeli psychohistorian Dr. Avner Falk submits that the name "Hyksos" derives from the phrase *hiq shasu* or *shosu*,[1] which would provide an interesting clue as to their identity.

According to Josephus (*Against Apion* 1.14), Manetho recounted that this barbarous and violent people from the east invaded Egypt, burned Egyptian cities, destroyed temples and slaughtered the natives. Constructing a capital in the Nile Delta at Avaris, a city dedicated to the god Set/Apophis/Typhon, these barbarians terrorized the locals, until they were expelled by the pharaoh, Ahmose I (fl. c. 1550–1525 BCE). These Hyksos occupying Lower Egypt were identified by the Jewish historian (*Ap.* 1.14.74ff) as the "children of Jacob who joined his son Joseph in Egypt to escape the famine in the land of Canaan."[2]

The Hyksos included the spectrum of society, from politicians to religious leaders to lawyers, doctors, merchants and skilled laborers, as well as riffraff with whom the bulk were identified by Manetho, who called the Hyksos "men of ignoble birth out of the eastern parts."[3] Or so complained Josephus, who likewise cited the Egyptian priest as associating these Hyksos with the people who settled Jerusalem.

Hence, according to the Jewish historian, Manetho's Hyksos were the Israelites of the Exodus, although the Egyptian writer never uses the terms "Hebrews," "Israelites" or "Jews" to describe these Asiatics. In this regard, Gmirkin remarks, "Despite a superficial resemblance to the Jewish Exodus story, it can be demonstrated that Manetho relied entirely on native Egyptian records and literature."[4] In other words, Manetho's account was not based on the Old Testament and did not identify the Hyksos with the Israelites/Jews.

Conquerors or Captives?

In another book, Josephus claims, the Egyptian priest remarked that "this nation, thus called shepherds, were also called captives, in their sacred books."[5] After naming various Hyksos kings, Manetho comments:

> And these six were the first rulers among them, who were all along making war with the Egyptians, and were very desirous gradually to destroy them to the very roots. This whole nation was styled *Hycsos*, that is, *Shepherd-kings*...[6]

---

[1] Falk, 78, 53.
[2] "Hebrews," *Wikipedia*.
[3] Josephus/Whiston, 614.
[4] Gmirkin, 37.
[5] Josephus/Whiston, 611.
[6] Josephus/Whiston, 611.

Josephus relates that "in another copy it is said that this word does not denote *kings*, but, on the contrary, denotes *captive shepherds...*"[1] Thus, the Jewish historian equates these slaughtering invaders and supposed conquerors with the pitiful and oppressed "slaves" of the Exodus. The fact that these Hyksos were an autonomous nation led by a king would negate this equation, however.

Sacred Books?

In describing the Hyksos' "sacred books" in which this "captive" claim allegedly appeared, it would seem at first glance that Manetho is talking about the Jewish texts, although, again, he does not name them as such. As concerns purported literature, the Hebrew language was not distinct and had no alphabet by this time; hence, the Hyksos could not have possessed any part of the Pentateuch, which would not have been written down until possibly a millennium after their expulsion. Thus, these texts, if Manetho's account is factual, could not have been the Torah, as also believed by many since antiquity.

If these Hyksos books existed, they may have been akin to the Ugaritic/Canaanite or Sumero-Babylonian texts, with religious stories such as the Baal cycle, *Enûma Eliš* or *Enuma Elish* (18th-12th cents. BCE) and *Epic of Gilgamesh*. If these sacred books had any relevance to the later Israelites, it would be as sources for the core myths in the Old Testament. Moreover, the Hyksos were not adverse to absorbing Egyptian religious ideas, which also may have been incorporated into their sacred writings. Indeed, this mix would constitute a near-perfect combination to produce elements of the later biblical texts.

Not Wandering Slaves

Relevant Egyptian texts from the traditional time of the Hyksos do not equate these Semites with the Israelites or match the Exodus either chronologically or in detail, as the Hyksos in fact were not "captives."

The differences between the accounts, including that the Hyksos were not slaves and did not spend 40 years wandering around in the desert, demonstrate that the story was not used as the core of the Exodus tale, although elements of the era—perhaps bitter memories of eviction and defeat—may have been woven later into extant myths.

Invaders or Infiltrators?

Moreover, the archaeological record, as revealed by archaeologist Dr. Janine Bourriau's excavation at Memphis, proves the ingress of Canaanites/Syro-Palestinians into Egypt as gradual, rather than as a massive invasion force, since there exists no evidence of the sudden

---

[1] Josephus/Maier, 942.

introduction of Hyksos pottery or other artifacts. As we can see, Manetho's account of the Hyksos as a massive force of invaders could not be true; nor would it be applicable to the Israelites, either way.

Religious Conflict?

Although they may have had proto-Yahwist tribalists among them, the Hyksos were not followers of the Israelite god Yahweh, as depicted in the Exodus story. Indeed, the Hyksos were never actually at odds with the Egyptians religionwise and did not leave Egypt because of religious persecution. According to the Egyptian accounts that preceded Manetho by many centuries, these foreigners were Canaanites who adopted the host's religious customs, as noted. The Hyksos themselves had Canaanite names that included Semitic gods and goddesses, such as Baal and his virgin lover Anath/Anat. While Baal was equivalent to the Egyptian god Seth, Set, Apophis or Typhon, Anath was associated in turn with "a number of sexually oriented Egyptian deities, Min, Hathor and Set."[1]

The Hyksos were known to revere the "Mistress of the Two Trees," a type of Hathor, the Egyptianized goddess of Byblos, indicating their origin near Phoenicia.[2] It is noteworthy that, at the beginning of the second millennium BCE, the Amorites ruled Byblos,[3] a desired status evidently reflected in their most famous literary work, the *Epic of Gilgamesh*. After this era, the Late Bronze Age collapse occurred, along with the invasion in the south of the sea peoples; yet, the Phoenician cities were not decimated during this period of destruction.[4]

Another Canaanite deity adopted into the Egyptian pantheon was the goddess Astarte, who during the New Kingdom was "made a consort of Set and a daughter of Re"[5] or Ra, the sun god.

Yet another important deity possibly brought to Egypt by the Hyksos was Reshef, "a Canaanite god of war and thunder" and "king of the netherworld." Reshef was "thought to bring plague and war upon humanity,"[6] strongly resembling the role of Yahweh in the Exodus tale. Rashap/Reshef is a very old god, as he was also the Eblaite deity of "desert drought and destruction, a warrior associated with death,"[7] found in texts dating to the middle to latter half of the third millennium BCE.

---

[1] Aling and Billington.
[2] Redford (1992), 117.
[3] Moscati, 125,
[4] See, e.g., Holst.
[5] Aling and Billington.
[6] Aling and Billington.
[7] Snell, 133.

Servants of Horus

Manetho also claimed the Hyksos were "servants of Horus," which would represent a strange appellation for Hebrews, unless they were followers of the "Golden Calf," although this idol is associated biblically not with Horus but with the northern kingdom of Samaria, as a Canaanite god (Hos 8:4-6). Yet, the Bible also says the Golden Calf worship came with the Israelites out of Egypt (Exod 32:4).

As evidence of biblical knowledge of Horus, Egyptologist Dr. Raymond Faulkner notes that the "Waterway of Horus" is the "Biblical Shihor."[1] Written שיחור *Shiychowr in Hebrew,* Shihor or Sihor is the name of a stream or river—some guess the Nile—that also serves as the border between Israel and Egypt.[2] According to *The Theological Dictionary of the Old Testament,* the "Hor" is a reference to Horus, Shihor denoting also the "Waters of Horus" or "Pool of Horus."[3] Thus, we know that ancient Hebrews were aware of Horus, as they would have to be, since the major thoroughfare from Israel to Egypt was called the "Horus Road."

In any event, we can see how tolerant and inclusive was the polytheism of both the Semites and Egyptians, welcoming with relative ease the deities of other cultures, and increasing the peace and understanding between peoples. In contrast, the Egyptians were at enmity with the Israelites on several occasions and do not seem to have accepted the Jewish tribal god Yahweh into their pantheon. The fact remains that, religiously, the Hyksos did not resemble the later intolerant Yahwists, and the rift between the Hyksos and Egypt was not based on religion, as is the focus of the Pentateuchal tales.

History or Fiction?

The disentangling of the accounts of Manetho and the Pentateuch, as well as the problem of the Egyptian priest himself not associating the Hyksos with the Jews, as if he had not heard of the latter, might be solved by a reworking of the chronology of when the Torah clearly emerges in the historical record. Pushing the Pentateuch's final redaction into the third century BCE, Gmirkin proposes the solution lies in Manetho's account predating the composition of the Exodus tale and serving as a source thereof:

> ...the Exodus story was based on Manetho's account of the expulsion of foreigners from Egypt into Judea. The traditions in Manetho can be demonstrated to have drawn exclusively on native Egyptian sources and display no awareness of the biblical account. The Exodus story, meanwhile, shows considerable knowledge of Manetho's accounts regarding Hyksos and expelled Egyptians, showing systematic agreement with Manetho in all details favorable

---

[1] Faulkner (1973), 1.275
[2] Jos 13:3; 1 Chr 13:5; Isa 23:3; Jer 2:18.
[3] Botterweck, et al., 5.359.

or neutral to the Jews but containing polemics against precisely those points in Manetho that reflected unfavorably on the Jews. The Exodus story thus appears to have originated in reaction to Manetho's Aegyptiaca written in ca. 285 BCE.[1]

Whether or not the biblical Exodus account drew in any way from Manetho, rather than the other way around, the Egyptian's writing does not serve as an independent identification of the Hyksos with the Israelites. Indeed, it appears that Josephus intertwined biblical stories into Manetho's historical core, the latter's work devoid of mention of Israel or Jews.

Were it not for the fact that Josephus was answering the charge that the Jews were a young and insubstantial nation, it would be difficult to understand why anyone would wish to claim heritage of the Hyksos legacy as described by Manetho. Yet, the Hyksos portrayed by Manetho as rampaging throughout Egypt and destroying sacred sites exhibit the same sort of violent religious intolerance as found throughout the Bible, especially in the Conquest tale. In this regard, if we read Numbers and Deuteronomy, the terrible description of the Hyksos indeed would reflect that of Yahweh and his Israelites engaging in one aggressive act after another, at times for the most petty of reasons. Again, however, evidence shows the Hyksos were not invaders, conquerors, captives or at odds religiously, accounting for their expulsion.

Ahmose I

Once more according to Josephus, Manetho identified the pharaoh who finally rid Egypt of the Hyksos as "Alisphragmuthosis," commonly accepted to be Ahmose I (fl. 16th cent. BCE), the father of "Thumomosis" or Thutmose I who "made an attempt to take them by force and by siege."[2] It is for this reason that Ahmose has been identified as the "brother of Moses," previously mentioned.

Fig. 35. Ahmose I battling the Hyksos, 16th cent. BCE

Manetho related that, at Ahmose's insistence, the Hyksos finally agreed to leave Egypt and exited with "their whole families and effects, not fewer in number than two hundred and forty thousand, and took their journey from Egypt, through the wilderness, for Syria; but that as they were in fear of the Assyrians, who had then the dominion over Asia, they built a city in that country which is now

---

[1] Gmirkin, 3.
[2] Josephus/Maier, 942.

called Judea, and that large enough to contain this great number of men, and called it Jerusalem."[1]

After discussing Manetho's description of the Hyksos expulsion, Finkelstein and Silberman bring up "an Egyptian source of the sixteenth century BCE that recounts the exploits of Pharaoh Ahmose, of the Eighteenth Dynasty, who sacked Avaris and chased the remnants of the Hyksos to their main citadel in southern Canaan—Sharuhen, near Gaza—which he stormed after a long siege. And indeed, around the middle of the sixteenth century BCE, Tell el-Daba/Avaris was abandoned, marking the sudden end of Canaanite influence there."[2] This straightforward, unembellished Egyptian account existed long before the Bible was written and therefore was unaffected by it.

From the Egyptian narration of the Hyksos expulsion, the fleeing foreigners were chased all the way to Canaan. There exists no record of any parting of the Red Sea, drowning of the Egyptians or wandering in the desert for four decades before reaching the "Promised Land." Nor, again, were these Hyksos "slaves," as depicted in the Old Testament concerning the Israelites in Egypt. Also, there is no evidence of a massive ingress into the Levant of two to three million Israelites at this time, so this event cannot be equated with the Exodus and Conquest.

Tempest Stele

It is to Ahmose I that the so-called Tempest or Storm Stele (c. 1550 BCE) is attributed, which some claim has to do with the Hyksos, although the fragment we possess make no mention of them. Others have speculated the text represents the eruption of Thera/Santorini, but the Tempest Stele sounds more like the archetypal battle between the sun/storm god and the sea, resembling also the mythical control of a meteorological phenomenon.

Considering that other rulers likewise engaged in recording this type of disaster and relief, including the female pharaoh Hatshepsut (1508-1458 BCE) at Speos Artemidos, this storm-destruction theme in the Tempest Stele appears to be a genre, like lamentations, rather than a historical record. Ahmose I is Hatshepsut's son, and it would be a simple matter for him to copy her storm-destruction record during his own reign. There appears to be little reason to associate this text with the Hyksos as an allegorical representation of the "storm" of their eviction. Nor can we identify their removal with the biblical Exodus or Ahmose with the pharaoh thereof.

---

[1] Josephus/Maier, 942.
[2] Finkelstein and Silberman, 55-56.

Jerusalem Founding

The Hyksos who purportedly founded Jerusalem could be said to be the predecessors of the Jews in that city, but they were not the Israelites of the Exodus. The Bible itself states that these Jerusalemites were conquered by the Jewish king David, who then turned the city into a Jewish enclave. It would make little sense for David to conquer his own Israelites, if the Jerusalem-founding Hyksos in reality were Moses and Joshua's Hebrews. At most, we could say that among the Hyksos were proto-Israelites whose descendants centuries later inhabited the Samaritan and Judean hill country, ending up in Jerusalem.

In reality, the city of Jerusalem was pre-Hebraic, pre-Israelite and pre-Jewish, with remains dating to the fourth millennium BCE, long before the Hyksos. In the Amarna texts, the city was called *Urušalim* in Akkadian. It was dedicated sometime during the Bronze Age (3600-1200 BCE) to the god Salem, meaning "peace," also styled Shalim, the Canaanite "dusk" god or evening aspect of Venus. Linguistic analysis supports the idea that the original inhabitants emanated largely from Northwest Semitic lands.

It appears Jerusalem eventually was inhabited by proto-Israelite Semitic peoples such as Amorites, Edomites, Jebusites and Kenites/Qenites. In this regard, Ezekiel 16:3 identifies the Jerusalemites as an Amorite-Hittite mixture of Canaanite origin:

> ...Thus says the Lord GOD to Jerusalem: Your origin and your birth are of the land of the Canaanites; your father was an Amorite, and your mother a Hittite.

Jerusalem's "Jewish" history purportedly began with David around 1000 BCE, although the city's conquest has been dated to several eras, from 1003 to 869 BCE. Despite the biblical embellishment, by this time Jerusalem was still a small village, and Judea as a whole continued to be sparsely populated until the late eighth century BCE.[1]

Hyksos as Greeks of Argos

Although the evidence thus points to a Semitic origin, the Argive Greeks also claimed that the Hyksos were *their* ancestors, contending that the story referred to the "expulsion of Belus (Baal?) and the daughters of Danaos"[2] or Danaus, the mythical Egyptian king who supposedly founded the Greek city of Argos.

Obviously, not all these scenarios can be correct, especially since the Hyksos were clearly Semites, while the Greeks were not. What this tale reveals, however, is that various different groups claimed

---

[1] Finkelstein and Silberman, 324-325.
[2] "Hyksos," *Wikipedia*.

some sort of "exodus" out of Egypt, which could be true, based on the "out of Africa" genetics studies.[1]

Concerning who the Hyksos were, Redford remarks:

> The true identity of the Hyksos can now easily be ascertained through the examination of two bodies of evidence: archaeological and linguistic... recent excavations at such Hyksos sites in the eastern Delta as Tel-ed-Dab'a and Tel el-Mashkuta have revealed an intrusive culture whose ceramic and artifactual content differs not at all from the culture of contemporary MB IIb Palestine and Phoenicia. The linguistic picture is wholly consistent. Contemporary Egyptian texts...call the invaders...speakers of a West Semitic tongue.... It is abundantly clear from such an analysis that we are dealing with personal names from a West Semitic dialect—all but two names sustain a West Semitic derivation, and none permit a Hurrian.[2]

"MB IIb" refers to the Middle Bronze Age IIb, around 1750 to 1650 BCE in the Near East. Thus, the Hyksos were essentially "Palestinians" and "Phoenicians," West Semites largely along the coastal regions.

Proto-Israelite Amorites

A major candidate for the identity of the Hyksos is the Amorites, described biblically as "sons of Canaan," son of Ham (Gen 10:16). "Amorite" is a name scholars such as Ugaritic language expert Dr. John Gray aver is a more appropriate moniker for the "Canaanites."[3]

Redford comments that "in their family tradition the Hyksos again demonstrate their unmistakable origins in a Middle Bronze 'Amorite' kingship..."[4] This family tradition is reflected in the fact that "most of the Hyksos personal names are west-Semitic, in the same language group as Amorite and the Canaanite and Aramaic dialects."[5]

The Hyksos-Amorites connection is suggested further by the moniker of one of the Hyksos rulers, Khyan, interpreted as the Amorite name "Hayanu," which appears in the Assyrian king-lists as belonging to a "remote ancestor" of the powerful king Shamshi-Adad I (1813-1781 BCE), who ruled much of Near East and Asia Minor. Son of an Amorite father, Shamshi-Adad was a contemporary of Hammurabi, who defeated him in battle.

---

[1] DNA studies determining that humanity is descended from one "Genetic Eve" traceable to South Africa have been challenged, but currently represent the most widely accepted scientific theory of human origins. Even if *Homo sapiens* did not originate exclusively in Africa, there still have been many exoduses out of that continent over the millennia.
[2] Redford (1992), 100. Redford's contention differs from the common perception that there *were* Hurrian names among the Hyksos, to which assertion he remarks also that the Hurrians appear not to have been in existence at this point.
[3] Gray (1964:16): "Actually, as an ethnic term denoting the Semitic substratum of the population of Syria and Palestine in the second millennium, 'Amorite' is more appropriate than 'Canaanite'."
[4] Redford (1992), 107.
[5] "Hyksos," *Jewish Virtual Library*.

History and Domination

Thriving for thousands of years beginning in at least the 25th century BCE, the Amorites were called *MAR.TU* in Sumerian, identified as nomads to the west before they migrated east and contributed to the downfall of the Sumerian civilization. The Akkadian term for them, *Amurru*, was also the name of their principal deity and of the Amorite kingdom in the Northwest Semitic region allegedly destroyed by Ramesses III.

The rough and barbaric Amorites' description is similar to that of both the Hyksos and the Israelites/Jews, the latter as described in the Bible and by Greek and Roman writers of a later period. Initially, the Amorites were aggressive nomadic herdsmen who took over lands as they wished, causing friction and dislike of them by other peoples, such as the Akkadians:

> By the time of the last days of the Sumerian Ur III empire, immigrating Amorites had become such a force that kings such as Shu-Sin were obliged to construct a 170 miles (270 km) long wall from the Tigris to the Euphrates to hold them off. These Amorites appear as nomadic clans ruled by fierce tribal chiefs, who forced themselves into lands they needed to graze their herds. Some of the Akkadian literature of this era speaks disparagingly of the Amorites, and implies that the Akkadians and Sumerians viewed their nomadic way of life with disgust and contempt...[1]

As early as the middle of the 20th century BCE, the Amorites had become a powerful kingdom, previously having lived a "rustic, nomadic life on the Syrian steppes," before being influenced by the Akkadian culture.[2] Says Redford, "In Palestine and Syria too by the mid-nineteenth century Amorite communities were in the ascendancy."[3] It was Amorites who founded the city of Babylon, and the legendary figure of Gilgamesh was one of their heroes.

One of their main cities was Mari, named for a Semitic goddess, which flourished as first a Sumerian and then an Amorite town between 2900 and 1759 BCE, when it was conquered by Hammurabi. Amorite dominance in Mesopotamia was ended in the early 16th century by attacks from the Assyrians and Hittites, who introduced the Kassites into the region. After dominating since about 2000 BCE, around 1595 the Amorites were expelled from Babylon and forced back to Syria/Canaan.

The tall Amorites have been equated also with the Amalekites, said to be "giants" (Exod 17:8ff). After Joshua supposedly defeated the Amorites, their descendants became the Gibeonites, and they appear also to have spawned the Ammonites and many other tribes.

---

[1] "Amorites," *Wikipedia*.
[2] Redford (1992), 93.
[3] Redford (1992), 94.

Amurru and Hapiru

In close proximity to Byblos and other Canaanite cities, the outlaw Amorite kingdom of Amurru was home to the Hapiru, who may have been among the Hyksos. Regarding Amurru and the Hapiru, Redford remarks:

> Beginning in the reign of Amenophis III, Amurru became a favorite haunt for those "cossacklike" bands of outlaws known as 'Apiru, as well as seminomadic West Semitic speaking clans. Under the leadership of a family of Canaanite-speaking individuals headed by their sheikh Abdi-ashirta, Amurru grew into a warlike canton that posed a political threat to its neighbors. It was Amurru's struggle for recognition and its perceived "manifest destiny" to expand to the Phoenician coast and the Orontes that posed the major problem in the northern empire for Egypt.
>
> ...Amurru was an 'Apiru community, but lately graduated from that type of stateless, lawless brigandage for which 'Apiru bands throughout the Levant were notorious.[1]

Amenophis is Greek for Amenhotep III, who may have reigned from 1391/88/86 to 1353/51/50/39 BCE or other times, depending on the chronology.

Mitanni

In order to protect itself from Egypt, the Amorite kingdom turned to the Mitanni, who imposed "excessive taxation" on Amurru to that end.[2] The Mitanni were a people occupying part of Turkey whose leaders followed Indian/Vedic gods, among others. The Mitanni royalty of evident Perso-Indian ancestry had married into Amenhotep III's family, bringing with them their deities.

Amorite Deities

We have noted that the Amorites had a goddess named Mari, significant to Christian myth studies as well, and a god styled Amurru. Biblical and Hebrew scholar Dr. Frank M. Cross (1921-2012) relates that the "Amorite deity called Amurru and Ilu Amurrū...in cuneiform sources has a particularly close relation to a mountain or mountains..."[3]

Cross further recounts the conclusion that Amurru is a storm god, like the Semitic Hadad/Adad, as well as a "divine warrior," roles taken on by the later Yahweh.[4] Modern scholarship proposes that Amurru is the same as Shaddai, the Canaanite "god of the fathers" worshipped biblically by Abraham.[5] Cross also suggests that Ilu Amurrū is the Amorite El.

---

[1] Redford (1992), 170-171.
[2] Redford (1992), 171.
[3] Cross, 57.
[4] Cross, 58.
[5] Cross, 57-58.

After the Amorites usurped the Sumerian and Akkadian civilizations during the first half of the second millennium BCE, they adopted the region's earlier deities in significant part: "They continued to worship the Sumerian gods, and the older Sumerian myths and epic tales were piously copied, translated, or adapted, generally with only minor alterations."[1] It is through the Amorites that the Sumerian gods were retained within the Babylonian pantheon. Hence, those passing along Sumerian myths, such as the OT writers, are spiritual descendants of the Amorites as well.

Migration

While their Northwestern Semitic language indicates their place of origin to be northern Syria/Canaan, the Amorites eventually occupied much of the Near East from the Levantine coastline to the Euphrates River and into southern Syria/Canaan and Transjordan, the area east of the Jordan River to Mesopotamia, as well as the hill country that became Samaria and Judea.

Aramaeans

These West Semites evidently settled in Jerusalem and, with other Canaanite/Amorite tribes such as the Yahwistic Kenites and Jebusites, eventually became the Israelites, as well as other ethnicities such as the Aramaeans: "They appear to have been displaced or absorbed by a new wave of semi nomadic Semites, the Arameans, from circa 1200 BCE onwards, and from this period the region they had inhabited became known as Aram (Aramea)."[2] In other words, after their collapse in the 12th century BCE, the Amorites "re-emerge as a vibrant and energetic people, known as the Aramaeans."[3]

Jebusites and Jerusalem

The Amorites were said to "dwell in the mountains," evidently as the early hill settlers in Israel (Jos 10:5-6). At Numbers 13:29, we read that they shared the hill country with Hittites and Jebusites, and the *Apocryphon of Joshua* essentially equates the Amorites and Jebusites.[4] The Bible claims that both the Jebusites and Amorites (Jos 10:5, etc.) occupied Jerusalem before its conquest. These two are listed both as separate peoples and as interchangeable, indicating the Jebusite tribal status within the Amoritish peoples overall:

> These Amorites seem to have been linked to the Jerusalem region, and the Jebusites may have been a subgroup of them. The southern slopes of the mountains of Judea are called the "mount of the Amorites" (Deut. 1:7, 19, 20).[5]

---

[1] "Amorites," *Wikipedia*.
[2] "Amorites," *Wikipedia*.
[3] "Amorites," *The British Museum*.
[4] Paul, et al., 188.
[5] "Amorites," *Wikipedia*.

The Jebusites have been surmised to be Amoritish and/or Hurrian, the latter based on the Hurrian name of their ruler,[1] who might have been a member of an elite Hurrian class or a Semite influenced by Hurrian religion. The non-Semitic and non-Indo-European Hurrians occupied the region of northern Mesopotamia and Anatolia, and the multiethnic Mitanni constituted one of their kingdoms.

The Jerusalem rulers Melchizedek and Adonizedek were said to have been Jebusites. Hence, the Jebusites appear to have been the Amorite occupants of Jebus/Jerusalem, claimed to have been "founded" by the Hyksos. Thus, these Jebusites evidently were descendants of the Amoritish Hyksos.

Amorites and Jebusites were among the peoples destined to be slaughtered to the last one by the Israelites, as at Deuteronomy 20:16-17:

> But in the cities of these peoples that the LORD your God gives you for an inheritance, you shall save alive nothing that breathes, but you shall utterly destroy them, the Hittites and the Amorites, the Canaanites and the Per'izzites, the Hivites and the Jeb'usites, as the LORD your God has commanded...

These chronicles or legends represent significantly what amounts to internecine battling between related Semitic Amoritish tribes.

Arabians

According to Josephus (*Ap.* 1.14.82), Manetho related that the Hyksos were also believed by some to have been "Arabians." If a significant portion of the Hyksos were Amorites, that fact could explain also the "Arabian" label, as the Amorites spoke a northwest Semitic dialect related to the later Hebrew (10th cent. BCE) but had migrated to the lower Mesopotamian area, near Arabia.

Regarding this description of "Arabia," Redford points out that the "constant use" of the term refers to "the East," employed by classical writers to "designate the regions of Asia closest to the Suez frontier, regions that in pharaonic times would have been known collectively as 'the northern countries,' namely Palestine and Syria."[2] Moreover, it is claimed that all Semites, including the Amorites, emanated originally from Arabia, a contention evidently borne out by DNA evidence.[3]

The equation of the Hyksos with Amorites would explain the variety of ethnicities, within a Semitic-speaking framework, as the Amorites apparently swirled around the Near and Middle East for centuries. The Amorites are labeled distinctly in Egyptian as *Amar*,

---

[1] See, e.g., Collins, 202.
[2] Redford (1992), 99.
[3] For a discussion on the out-of-Arabia theory for the Amorites in specific, see Haldar, 7f.

rather than Hyksos or *hiq shasu*, however, but that fact does not negate the identification with the Hyksos, as these latter had many names pertaining to tribes or ethnicities.

Vintners

Another correlation between Amurru and the Hyksos comes through viniculture. As an important part of their economy and significant to this present work, the Hyksos enjoyed wine produced from the vineyards to the east of their Egyptian kingdom.[1] Amurru too was considered a good wine-producing region, while Palestine was renowned for its grapes.[2]

Although the story cannot be said to represent the Hyksos' historical expulsion, one could suggest that the Exodus myth was created as Amorite propaganda expressing resentment at being dominated and evicted by Egypt, casting the pharaoh as the villain in ancient myths because of enduring enmity and ancient hostilities.

Osarseph and the Lepers

In another muddled tale by Manetho in Josephus (*Ap.* 1.26), the Hyksos reappeared two or three centuries later regarding another exodus in which an Egyptian priest of Osiris named "Osarsiph" or "Osarseph" supposedly led a rebellion of some 80,000 "lepers" and heretics against the pharaoh "Amenophis," and subsequently named himself "Moses." Josephus and others understood this exodus also to be that of Israelites, which would mean that we have two exoduses from Egypt, out of many for humanity as a whole over a period of thousands of years.

When these "unclean people" were displaced to Avaris, their leader, Osarseph, sent an invitation to the "shepherds" who had settled in Jerusalem, the Hyksos, expelled from Egypt a few centuries earlier, asking them to return to their Egyptian city.[3] From Avaris, according to Josephus, the 200,000 Hyksos who answered the call pillaged and raped the land, fanatically destroying the Egyptian gods and temples, as the Israelites are depicted throughout the Old Testament as doing to the Canaanites and other Levantine peoples. Here we can see again that the Hyksos are portrayed as very much at odds with the Egyptians, but, as discussed, Egyptologists such as Assmann contend otherwise.

Amenophis/Akhenaten

At this point in Josephus's tale, Amenophis (Amenhotep) and his son Ramesses expel the Hyksos from Egypt once more. Since

---

[1] Redford (1992), 122.
[2] Redford (1992), 227.
[3] Assmann (1997), 32.

Akhenaten originally was named Amenhotep, it has been surmised that Osarseph was a fanatical priest of Aten run amok.[1]

Thus, a prevailing theory among Egyptologists is that this "rather fantastic story about lepers and Jews preserved in Manetho's *Aigyptiaka* could refer only to Akhenaten and his monotheistic revolution."[2] Regarding Manetho's "Jews" and lepers tale, Assmann comments:

> The story as told by Manetho and others integrated many different historical experiences, among them the expulsion of the Hyksos from Egypt in the sixteenth century B.C.E But the core of the story is a purely religious confrontation, and there is only one episode in Egyptian history that corresponds to these characteristics: the Amarna period.[3]

As we can see, Assmann avers the Akhenaten rift would be an event most appropriately compared to the Osarseph narrative. From the comparison, the conclusion also has been made that Osarseph must have been named "Moses," since it is obviously the latter's story being told, which means that Moses was a priest of Aten, explaining his intolerant monotheism.

However, Josephus's chronology places Osarseph after Ramesses II (fl. 1279-1213 BCE), long succeeding the time of Akhenaten, and the Jewish historian calls Manetho's Amenophis a "fictitious person."[4]

Concerning the Osarseph tale, we read:

> Three interpretations have been proposed for the story: the first, as a memory of the Amarna period [Akhenaten's era]; the second, as a memory of the Hyksos; and the third, as...anti-Jewish propaganda. Each explanation has evidence to support it: the name of the pharaoh, Amenophis, and the religious character of the conflict fit the Amarna reform of Egyptian religion; the name of Avaris and possibly the name Osarseph fit the Hyksos period; and the overall plot is an apparent inversion of the Jewish story of the Exodus casting the Jews in a bad light. No one theory, however, can explain all the elements. An influential proposition by Egyptologist Jan Assmann suggests that the story has no single origin but rather combines numerous historical experiences, notably the Amarna and Hyksos periods, into a folk memory....
>
> Some modern scholars have suggested that the Osarseph story, or at least the point at which Osarseph changes his name to Moses, is a later alteration to Manetho's original history made in the 1st century BCE, a time when anti-Jewish sentiment was running high in Egypt; without this, Manetho's history has no mention of the Jews at all....[5]

---

[1] See, e.g., Greenberg, 175.
[2] Assmann (1997), 30.
[3] Assmann (1997), 30.
[4] Greenberg, 171-172.
[5] "Osarseph," *Wikipedia*.

It would seem that the conclusion of a garbled, fictitious mishmash, rather than a single historical event, ranks as the most scientific analysis of this story. We would add the observation that the tale possesses a mythical framework or core as well. In any case, these events do not correspond to the Exodus story beyond large numbers of Semites leaving Egypt, although some of the details may have been used to historicize the central myth.

A Forgery?

It has been asserted that the reference purportedly in Manetho equating Osarseph/Osarsiph with Moses was "undoubtedly an interpolation—a forgery, which famed French Middle Eastern scholar Dr. Joseph Ernest Renan (1823-1892) evinced was made at Alexandria by a Hebrew priest after the death of Manetho, for it is well known that there are some spurious books ascribed to him."[1]

American judge Parrish B. Ladd (d. 1912) concluded that the purported equation of the two figures in Manetho was forged in order to give historical legitimacy to the Exodus tale: "This interpolation was intended to support the biblical story of the exodus, and is in keeping with the tactics of the priesthood everywhere when they need further proof to support their religion."[2] In any event, in Osarseph and the lepers we will not find a historical Moses and his chosen people, as depicted in the Old Testament.

One could argue thus that the focus on the Hyksos ranks as yet another attempt to anchor the Exodus into history. The Hyksos are too early to be Israelites *per se*, but the Iron Age hill settlements evidently included some of their descendants, such as those who ended up in Jerusalem over a period of several centuries.

These various Hyksos stories were latched onto in antiquity in order to provide historicity to the biblical tale, confounded and embellished so that they would appear more like the Exodus account. Moreover, it is clear that Josephus and other Jews glommed onto them in order to disprove the widespread contention that the Jews were a young people; hence, the historian's work *Antiquities of the Jews*. In reality, the older Egyptian sources of the Hyksos story are devoid of this overt connection, as there were no Israelites or Jews at the time when these earlier accounts were written and when the Hyksos were in Egypt.

Syrians from Palestine

Although Josephus asserts that the Hyksos were "Jews," no word for "Jew" in any language appears in the historical record until a thousand years after the initial Hyksos expulsion and several centuries after the second one. Also averring the Osarseph tale to be

---

[1] Ladd, 5.159.
[2] Ladd, 5.159.

HYKSOS AND LEPERS

a conflation of not only Akhenaten but also others, Assmann states that the earliest any specific tribe of "Jews" could have encountered the Egyptians is the sixth century BCE.[1]

In the fifth century BCE, the Greek historian Herodotus (2.104) referred to the circumcised "Phoenicians and Syrians of Palestine," the latter of whom since the Greek historian's time have been surmised to be Jews, although he did not call them by that name. At 3.5, Herodotus also states:

> The only entrance into Egypt is through the desert. From Phoenicia to the boundaries of Gaza the country belongs to the Syrians known as "Palestinian"...[2]

At 3.91, Herodotus refers to "that part of Syria which is called Palestine," using the Greek word Παλαιστίνη *Palaistinē*,[3] evidently derived from פלשתים *Pĕlishtim*, meaning "immigrants."[4] These "Syrians," again, are not specified as "Jews," and we possess no indication that Herodotus had ever heard of such a tribe, much less the *kingdom* of Judea.

At 7.89, the Greek historian discusses a battle that involves, among many other peoples such as the Persians under King Xerxes the Great (519–465 BCE), the "Phoenicians, with the Syrians of Palestine" as allies of one another. This reference to a "Syrian" alliance with Phoenicians seems unlikely to signify Jews from the Israelite tribe of Judah.

Regarding this issue, Herodotus editor Rev. Dr. George Rawlinson remarks:

> By the "Palestine Syrians," or "Syrians of Palestine" [2.104, 7.89], Herodotus has been generally supposed to mean exclusively the Jews; but there are no sufficient grounds for limiting the term to them. The Jews in the time of Herodotus must have been a very insignificant element in the population of the country known to him as Palestine Syria [3.91]... Palestine Syria means properly "the Syria of the Philistines," who were in ancient times by far the most powerful race of *southern* Syria..., and who are thought by some to have been the Hyksos or Shepherd-invaders of Egypt... Even in southern Syria the Jews were but one of many tribes, and the Philistines continued powerful down to the time at which Herodotus wrote. (Zech. [9:5-6]). The common notion that Herodotus by his "Syrians of Palestine" means the Jews rests chiefly upon the statement [2.104] that they practiced circumcisions, which is thought to have been an exclusively Jewish rite. But it may be questioned whether the surrounding nations had not by the time of Herodotus adopted to some extent the practice from the Jews.[5]

---

[1] Assmann (1997), 32.
[2] Herodotus/de Selincourt, 155.
[3] Herodotus/de Selincourt, 192.
[4] Strong's H6430.
[5] Herodotus/Rawlinson, 334. (Emphasis added.)

As we know also from Herodotus, these Syrians took their practice of circumcision from the Egyptians, so it is this latter people, rather than Jews, to whom we should look for the custom's origin among other Levantine ethnicities. Thus, the designation of "Syrians" by Herodotus may not represent Jews after all, but even if we allow that it does, we can see that the latter tribe was evidently so small and insignificant as not even to be known by name by the fifth century BCE.

In the fifth century BCE, the "Jews" (יהודימ *Yehudim*) as such indeed were a fairly new development as the dominant tribe of the region, and it is surmised that monotheistic Judaism or Yahwism as such was not created until the Seleucid period (323-64 BCE), which might explain why the Elephantine Jews were not instructed in strict monotheism in their communiques from the Jerusalem priesthood.

After Jews began to appear in the historical record, there followed a series of commentaries depicting them as descendants of brigands and lepers, shunning and opposing the rest of humanity. This perception has been averred to represent anti-Jewish propaganda and xenophobia. The stranger among them was indeed new, however, demonstrating that, previously, Jews had been unknown to these commentators, indicating that biblical "history," with its grandiose dramas purportedly dating back thousands of years, is largely fictitious. Moreover, the xenophobia seems to have been perceived by Gentiles as coming from the Jews initially, and even the Jewish Josephus eventually asserted that the general perception seems to have been that the Jews were descended from Hyksos marauders and "unclean people."

Antiochus IV

Putting Manetho together with Jewish history of the succeeding second to first centuries BCE, Diodorus (34.1) discussed the siege of Jerusalem by the Greek king Antiochus IV Epiphanius (fl. 175-164 BCE):

> King Antiochus besieged Jerusalem, but the Jews stood it out for some time: but when all their provision was spent, they were forced to send ambassadors to him, to treat upon terms. Many of his friends persuaded him to storm the city, and to root out the whole nation of the Jews; For they only of all people hated to converse with any of other nations and treated them all as enemies; and they suggested to him that their ancestors were driven out of Egypt, as impious and hateful to the gods: for their bodies being overspread, and infected with the itch and leprosy, (by way of expiation) they got them together, and as profane and wicked wretches, expelled them out of their coasts: and that those who were thus expelled seated themselves about Jerusalem, and being after embodied into one nation (called the nation of the Jews) their hatred of all other men descended with their blood to posterity. And therefore they made

strange laws, and quite different from other people: never will eat nor drink with any of other nations, or wish them any prosperity.[1]

Diodorus evidently viewed the Jews as Manetho's leprous Hyksos, and he associated their dislike of all other nations with their wretched diseased state.

Describing a statue found in the temple by Antiochus, Diodorus related that the king thought it was "Moses who built Jerusalem, and settled the nation, and established by law all their wicked customs and practices, abounding in hatred and enmity to all other men."[2]

The Greco-Sicilian historian continues:

Antiochus therefore abhorring this, their contrariety to all other people, used his utmost endeavour to abrogate their laws. To that end he sacrificed a great swine at the image of Moses, and at the altar of God that stood in the outward court, and sprinkled them with the blood of the sacrifice. He commanded likewise that the sacred books, whereby they were taught to hate all other nations, should be besprinkled with the broth made of the swine's flesh: And he put out the lamp (called by them immortal) which was ever burning in the temple. Lastly he forced the high priest and the other Jews to eat swine's flesh. When Antiochus's friends had debated and considered of these things, they were very earnest with him to root out the whole nation, or at least that he would abrogate their laws, and compel them to change their former manner of living and conversation. But the king being of a generous spirit, and mild disposition received hostages and pardoned the Jews; but demolished the walls of Jerusalem and took the tribute that was due.[3]

Antiochus's alleged harsh measures represent an extreme reaction to the Yahwists' absolute separation from and derogation of the non-Jewish populace expressed in the Old Testament and in contemporary life. This xenophobic supremacism extended to Antiochus's time and was obviously noticeable and greatly offensive to "the nations" or גויהם *goyim*,[4] as the non-Jewish cultures are described throughout the Tanakh.

Following Diodorus in the first century BCE, Strabo (16.2.34) was of the impression that the Jews were descendants of Egyptians, naming Moses as a dissatisfied Egyptian priest.[5]

Lysimachus and Chaeremon

According to Josephus, the Osarseph/Moses-led leper story was repeated by the ancient chroniclers Lysimachus of Alexandria (1st cent. BCE) and Chaeremon of Alexandria (1st cent. CE/AD), apparently

---

[1] Diodorus/Booth, 2.543-544.
[2] Diodorus/Booth, 2.544.
[3] Diodorus/Booth, 2.544.
[4] Among other definitions, such as "nations" or "peoples," appears the derogatory figurative meaning of *goyim* as "swarms of locusts or other animals." (Strong's H1471)
[5] Strabo/Hamilton, 3.177.

basing their accounts not only on Egyptian writings such as Manetho but also on the Jewish texts.[1] These chroniclers also evidently regarded Osarseph/Moses as originally *Egyptian*, not Hebrew or Hyksos.

Josephus (*Ap.* 1.34) quotes Lysimachus as saying:

"The people of the Jews being leprous and scabby, and subject to certain other kinds of diseases, in the days of Bocchoris, king of Egypt, they fled to the temples, and got their food there by begging: and as the numbers were very great that were fallen under these diseases, there arose a scarcity in Egypt. Hereupon Bocchoris, the king of Egypt, sent some to consult the oracle of [Jupiter] Hammon about this scarcity. The god's answer was this: That he must purge his temples of impure and impious men, by expelling them out of those temples into desert places; but as to the scabby and leprous people, he must drown them, and purge his temples, the sun having an indignation at these men being suffered to live; and by this means the land will bring forth its fruits. Upon Bocchoris's having received these oracles, he called for their priests, and the attendants upon their altars, and ordered them to make a collection of the impure people; and to deliver them to the soldiers, to carry them away into the desert: but to take the leprous people, and wrap them in sheets of lead, and let them down into the sea. Hereupon the scabby and leprous people were drowned, and the rest were gotten together and sent into desert places, in order to be exposed to destruction. In this case they assembled themselves together, and took counsel what they should do; and determined that, as the night was coming on, they should kindle fires and lamps, and keep watch; that they also should fast the next night, and propitiate the gods, in order to obtain deliverance from them. That on the next day there was one Moses, who advised them that they should venture upon a journey, and go along one road till they should come to places fit for habitation: that he charged them to have no kind regards for any man, nor give good counsel to any, but always to advise them for the worst; and to overturn all those temples and altars of the gods they should meet with: that the rest commended what he had said with one consent, and did what they had resolved on, and so travelled over the desert. But that the difficulties of the journey being over, they came to a country inhabited, and that there they abused the men, and plundered and burnt their temples, and then came into that land which is called Judea, and there they built a city, and dwelt therein, and that their city was named *Hierosyla*, from this their robbing of the temples; but that still, upon the success they had afterwards, they in time changed its denomination, that it might not be a reproach to them, and called the city *Hierosolyma*, and themselves *Hierosolymites*."[2]

---

[1] See, e.g., Assmann (1997), 35.
[2] Josephus/Whiston, 621. The pharaoh of the 24th dynasty known by the Greek name "Bocchoris" or "Boccharis," the Egyptian Bakenranef (c. 722–c. 715 BCE), is far too late for this tale to serve as having to do with Moses and the Israelites' exodus out of Egypt. Therefore, Evangelical theologian Stephen Meyer speculates that Diodorus's "Boccharis

Rather than serving simply as anti-Jewish propaganda, many of these contentious remarks undoubtedly are based not only on Manetho's Hyksos but also on the Jews' own scriptures, which depict them repeatedly engaging in destructive acts, especially the overthrowing of temples and ruination of high places of worship belonging to the non-Jewish tribes, including the polytheistic Israelites of the Northern Kingdom.

Josephus states that Chaeremon gave the number of "afflicted persons" banished to the Avaris area as not 80,000 but 250,000,[1] who meet up with another 380,000 at a place called Pelusium. Hence, here we have one of several discrepancies that make the tales difficult to sort through and to analyze conclusively. It is interesting that the two numbers add up close to 600,000, the alleged number of Israelite men who left Egypt during the Exodus.

Chaeremon subsequently related that, unable to defeat this enormous rabble, Amenophis fled to Ethiopia, while his deserted wife gave birth to their son Ramses/Ramesses, who grew up to drive the now-diminished Jewish population of 200,000 into Syria. This tale sounds reasonably like the Exodus, especially because the pharaoh in question is a Ramesses, and centuries-long tradition has placed the biblical flight during the time of Ramesses II. However, Josephus demonstrates discrepancies, and questions the story's veracity. The tale seems to be a garbled account of several pharaohs, possibly including Amenhotep III, whose mother was an Ethiopian sun worshipper and who was said to have passed along her passion for Aten to his apparent son, Amenhotep IV or Akhenaten.

Tacitus on Jewish Origins

In his *Histories* (5.2-4), Roman historian Tacitus (56-117 AD/CE) repeats the prominent theories of Jewish origins in his day, including the story of Boccharis/Bocchoris and the disfiguring disease, as well as the need for the king to "convey into some foreign land this race detested by the gods." The Roman then summarizes an account of Moses and his wandering the desert, seeking and finding water. Next we read: "After a continuous journey for six days, on the seventh they possessed themselves of a country, from which they expelled the inhabitants, and in which they founded a city and a temple."

Leprosy

Tacitus also mentions the "leprosy" from pigs that purportedly afflicted Moses's followers, which may refer to trichinosis, a parasitic disease developed from eating raw or undercooked pig products. This alleged disease state may explain why the affected Israelites became

---

the Wise" was another, "much older" lawgiver of renown who devised his own code. (Epsztein, 17, 144)
[1] Greenberg, 177.

so xenophobic and antagonistic towards swine. Assmann believes these lepers displaced to Avaris, the capital of the Hyksos, developed an "enclave culture" attempting to prevent any assimilation that would destroy their distinct ethnicity.[1] An example of an enclave culture is Judaism itself, with its extreme "purity" laws.

Obviously, few Jews would like to believe that the Israelite prophet Moses was the "king of the lepers," and, again, this tale has been dismissed as "anti-Jewish propaganda."

Other writers to whom Tacitus refers as discussing the leprosy-like disease are surmised to be Chaeremon, Diodorus, Lysimachus, Manetho and the Roman historian Pompeius Trogus (1st cent. BCE).[2] Citing his grandfather Lamprias, the ancient Greek historian Plutarch (46-120 AD/CE) expressly attributes the Jewish hatred of pigs to "leprosy" (*Quaes. Conv.* 4.5.3):

> But the Jews do hate swine's flesh, because all the barbarians are naturally fearful of a scab and leprosy, which they presume comes by eating such kind of flesh.[3]

In this same passage, Plutarch also relates that Callistratus, Athenian archon and procurator of the Amphictyons (3rd-2nd cent. BCE), believed the Jewish abstention from pork flesh was based on veneration of that animal.

Fugitives from Crete?

Tacitus further addresses Jewish origins:

> Some say that the Jews were fugitives from the island of Crete, who settled on the nearest coast of Africa about the time when Saturn was driven from his throne by the power of Jupiter. Evidence of this is sought in the name. There is a famous mountain in Crete called Ida; the neighbouring tribe, the Idæi, came to be called Judæi by a barbarous lengthening of the national name. Others assert that in the reign of Isis the overflowing population of Egypt, led by Hierosolymus and Judas, discharged itself into the neighbouring countries. Many, again, say that they were a race of Ethiopian origin, who in the time of king Cepheus were driven by fear and hatred of their neighbours to seek a new dwelling-place. Others describe them as an Assyrian horde who, not having sufficient territory, took possession of part of Egypt, and founded cities of their own in what is called the Hebrew country, lying on the borders of Syria. Others, again, assign a very distinguished origin to the Jews, alleging that they were the Solymi, a nation celebrated in the poems of Homer, who called the city which they founded Hierosolyma after their own name.

In the passage above, Tacitus relates the thesis that the Jews were from Crete, specifically Mount Ida, whence their name. The

---
[1] Assmann (1997), 32.
[2] Tacitus/Church, 229.
[3] Plutarch/Goodwin, 3.309.

Cretan connection may reflect the origin of the Philistines, possibly Mycenaeans fleeing that island, evidently indistinguishable from Jews by Tacitus's day, after having adapted the local culture and language centuries before.

The Roman historian also reported the claim that the Jews were part of the "overflowing population of Egypt," which spilled out into southern Palestine, under the direction of the eponymous leaders Hierosolymus (Jerusalem) and Judas (Judah). Another theory contended that the Jews were part of the "Assyrian horde," which could reflect their status as Hyksos and Amorites. Finally, the inhabitants of Jerusalem were equated with Homer's Σόλυμοι Solymi (*Il.* 6.184), predecessors of the Lycians,[1] the *Lukka* mentioned in Egyptian records to have been among the sea peoples.

Tacitus also says of the exiles:

> ...We are told that the rest of the seventh day was adopted, because this day brought with it a termination of their toils; after a while the charm of indolence beguiled them into giving up the seventh year also to inaction. But others say that it is an observance in honour of Saturn, either from the primitive elements of their faith having been transmitted from the Idæi, who are said to have shared the flight of that God, and to have founded the race, or from the circumstance that of the seven stars which rule the destinies of men Saturn moves in the highest orbit and with the mightiest power, and that many of the heavenly bodies complete their revolutions and courses in multiples of seven.[2]

Tacitus points out that the Israelites under Moses developed a "novel form of worship, opposed to all that is practised by other men." Because of their strict sectarianism and xenophobia towards nonbelievers, devout followers of Judaic law left a similar impression on several writers of antiquity, including Roman philosopher and statesman Lucius Annaeus Seneca (c. 4 BCE-65 AD/CE) Seneca. It is noteworthy that Tacitus's Exodus account occurs only during a week, as opposed to 40 years.

Flight of Saturn

Tacitus recounts the myth of the flight of "Saturn," Latin name of the Greek god Kronos, who is syncretized with Typhon, Apophis, Set or Seth, fleeing after his defeat by Horus. The Roman historian's translators Drs. Alfred John Church and William Jackson Brodribb remark that he follows a tradition which "represents

Fig. 36. Saturn in a chariot drawn by winged, serpent-like dragons. Engraving by Pietro Bonato (1765–1820), Rome, Italy

---

[1] Herodotus 1.173.2.
[2] Tacitus/Church, 193-195.

the Idaei [Judeans] as an old Cretan race who shared in Saturn's expulsion."[1]

Typhon or Set/Seth, the god of desert and pestilence, was the main deity of the Hyksos, and, again, their eviction is equated with his flight from Egypt. This escape of Typhon-Seth "from the battle" is associated with Jewish origins, a tale told also by Plutarch, a "senior priest" of the oracle at the temple of the sun god Apollo at Delphi, Greece, who objected to this connection.

Nevertheless, it is this *mythical* story that Tacitus and others have believed is at the heart of the biblical exodus. The Exodus narrative in part may be in emulation of these gods' journeys from Egypt, to compete with their myths.

The Saturn-Jupiter timeline follows post-deluge divisions wherein Saturn ruled over the "Golden Age," the first 100 years after the Flood, before being replaced by Jupiter/Zeus, who reigned over the Silver Age.[2] Moreover, Yahweh has been identified with Saturn/Kronos since antiquity in many instances outside of this episode.[3] This fact explains why the Jewish sabbath was said to be held on the day of Kronos, which came to be called "Saturday."[4]

There is also the myth of the flight of other gods *from* monstrous Typhon, who chases them *to* Egypt, where they hide themselves as animals.

The story about the main Hyksos god, Baal, identified with Seth/Typhon and Saturn, likewise may represent a *mythical germ* of the Exodus tale. The fact that both Hyksos and Jews revered Typhon-Seth/Baal adds to the association of these groups with each other.

The Sacred Ass

Seth's flight occurred mythically on the back of an ass, an animal with which the Egyptian god was identified. Regarding Tacitus's comment about the Jews worshipping the animal of their deliverance from Egypt, his translators remark:

> It was a widely spread notion that an ass or an ass's head was an object of Jewish worship. We are told in one of the fragments of Diodorus' history that Antiochus Epiphanes entered the inner part of the temple, and found there the image of a man with a long beard, seated on an ass, holding a book in his hand, and that he conjectured it to be an image of Moses who had founded Jerusalem and established the nation. Tertullian and Minucius Felix both allude to this erroneous conception about the Jews (Tert. *Apol.* 16, Minuc. Felix *Oct.* 28).[5]

---

[1] Tacitus/Church, 229.
[2] See, e.g., Gale, 24.
[3] Smallwood, 130, citing Varro (l.c.), Tibullus (1.3.18), Tacitus (*Hist.* 5.4.4), Diodorus (37.16.2-4, 17.3; 49.22.4; 66.7.2) and Plutarch (*Symp.* 4.6).
[4] Cassius Dio, Historiae Romanae 37.17.3: ...καὶ τὴν ἡμέραν τὴν τοῦ Κρόνου καλουμένην ἀνέθεσαν...
[5] Tacitus/Church, 229.

In consideration of the fact that the Israelites were engaged in the worship of many gods, and that the ass was a symbol of Typhon-Seth, who was syncretized with Baal, the supposition of ass-worship may not be an "erroneous conception," and Antiochus may indeed have found such a statue. As Gmirkin says:

> The ass was a symbol of Seth-Typhon, who in Egyptian reliefs of the Ptolemaic period was sometimes pictured as a man with the head of an ass. According to one Egyptian tradition, after Seth-Typhon's defeat by Horus, he fled Egypt on the back of an ass and then fathered two sons, Hierosolymus and Judaeus. The alleged discovery of a statue of Moses astride an ass was doubtless intended to equate Moses, the founder of the Jewish nation, with Typhon.[1]

It is significant that Moses—identifiable with Seth-Typhon-Baal—is depicted as riding on the ass, as so too were Dionysus and Hephaistos/Hephaestus, to be discussed below. Also like these two, the Egyptian solar-atmospheric god Shu is portrayed in the tomb of Seti I as "riding on an ass."[2]

Osarseph Redux

In the later Hyksos tale of Osarseph, rather than a historical account of Moses and the Exodus, following Tacitus and others Gary Greenberg too sees the myth of Osiris, Isis, Set and Horus:

> The similarity between the Horus-Set theme and the Moses/Osarseph stories should be obvious. Iconographically, Osiris is the displaced king, Set is the usurping king, Isis is the mother who hides the child away, and Horus is the returning son who defeats the usurping king.[3]

Thus, the Exodus could be analyzed in terms of Egyptian mythology, reworked as a national epic. This analysis is interesting, especially when one considers that in Egypt the sitting king/pharaoh was deemed Horus on Earth. This fictional Osarseph story also could have incorporated real events, as conquests of this nature have occurred continually throughout history. In addition, there is reason to bring up Osiris and Moses in the same discourse, as we shall see later.

Thieving Son of Joseph?

While relating in *Historicae Philippicae* (c. 7 AD/CE) a more developed tale about the "scabby lepers" following Moses, expelled from Egypt because of their disease, Pompeius Trogus recounts another story in which the lawgiver is made to be the son of the Hebrew patriarch Joseph. In this tale, Moses not only brings disease and epidemics to Egypt but also steals Egyptian sacred objects, while the Egyptians pursuing him are driven off by storms.

---

[1] Gmirkin, 285.
[2] Green, 17.452.
[3] Greenberg, 181.

If Moses were Joseph's son and truly wrote the Pentateuch, why did he not identify himself as such? The author(s) of the Torah describes Joseph's life in great detail but never says a word to indicate his relationship to the patriarch. One would think that Moses would proudly declare such an affiliation, but he does not. Instead, the writer of Exodus 2:1, speaking of Moses in the third person, identifies the future lawgiver's father as an anonymous "man from the house of Levi." In the same passage, the writer describes Moses's mother only as "a woman," very odd if the patriarch himself wrote these verses.

Moreover, the historicity of the biblical Joseph tale itself has been questioned:

> Modern day scholars believe the historicity of the events in the Joseph narrative cannot be demonstrated. Hermann Gunkel, Hugo Gressmann and Gerhard von Rad identified the story of Joseph as a literary composition, in the genre of romance, or the novella. As a novella, it is read as reworking legends and myths, in particular the motifs of his reburial in Canaan, associated with the Egyptian god Osiris. Others compare the burial of his bones at Shechem, with the disposal of Dionysus's bones at Delphi. For Schenke, the tradition of Joseph's burial at Shechem is understood as a secondary, Israelitic historical interpretation woven around a more ancient Canaanite shrine in that area. The reworked legends and folklore were probably inserted into the developing textual tradition of the Bible between the 8th and 6th centuries BCE. Most scholars place its composition in a genre that flourished in the Persian period of the Exile.[1]

Thus, it appears that the Joseph story was created also during the eighth to sixth centuries or later, possibly producing a later myth conflating Osiris or Ausar and Joseph, as a syncretized "Osarseph." It is noteworthy that Joseph's wife's name, Asenath (Gen 41:45), means "holy to Anath," the popular Semitic goddess also transliterated as Anat, worshipped by the Canaanites/Western Semites, including the Hyksos. The goddess Anat-Yahu/Yahweh is mentioned in a Jewish papyrus from Elephantine from the fifth century that claims the deity was "worshiped in the temple to Yahweh originally built by Jewish refugees from the Babylonian conquest of Judah."[2]

Egyptian Wisdom

Regarding the tale of sacred objects in Pompeius, Assmann comments:

> Therefore, the cult of Moses founded in Jerusalem must have been the cult of these "sacra"—a veritable "translatio religionis."[3]

The Latin word *sacra* means "sacred things," while the phrase *translatio religionis* connotes a "translation," "transferring" or

---

[1] "Joseph (son of Jacob)," *Wikipedia*.
[2] "Anat," *Wikipedia*.
[3] Assmann (1997), 36.

"handing over" of religion. In other words, the Jews took many of their religious ideas and sacraments from Egypt. Two thousand years ago, the connection between Judaism and Egypt was so obvious that a tale depicted Moses as stealing his religion from the land of the Nile.

As is said in the New Testament book of Acts (7:22):

> And Moses was instructed in all the wisdom of the Egyptians, and he was mighty in his words and deeds.

The Greek word in this New Testament verse for "wisdom" is σοφία *sophia*, the name of a personified female divinity within Gnosticism and Wisdom literature, as in the Hebrew Hokhmah concept,[1] as well as Platonic and Egyptian mystical tradition.

During the period in which this verse in Acts was written—sometime towards the end of the *second* century,[2] as indicated by the extant evidence—the Gnostic Sophia was well known, particularly as treated by Valentinian Gnostics at Alexandria, Egypt. Thus, someone reading this biblical verse in Greek might understand that the author is trying to assert expertise in the subject of the gnostic Sophia, important in this era.

The correlation between the wisdom of the Egyptians and Moses subsequently being "mighty in his words and deeds" is noteworthy, as it reveals significant esteem for Egyptian knowledge and sagacity, as well as serving as a blatant admission that Jewish traditions were based significantly on Egyptian religion and mythology.

We would disagree, of course, with the assumption that Moses was a historical character who, in fact, could spread disease or carry off stolen religious artifacts. Rather than making such an assumption, we can conclude that the Egyptian origin of much Judaism is indicated in this apocryphal tale.

Egyptian Cultural Influence

Despite the tale that they rampaged against the Egyptians, slaughtering and pillaging, destroying temples and believers, the Hyksos adopted many of the Egyptian manners, as noted, including their religious ideas, although they preferred their "Asiatic" rendition of Baal-Seth, called by them "Apophis," also the name of one of their kings. It is therefore probable that the Hyksos took Egyptian religious ideas back with them whence they came. If some of this group subsequently became Israelites, that fact would explain in significant part why there is so much Egyptian religion and mythology in the Old Testament. This fact evidently is expressed later in the fictional tale of Moses stealing sacred objects and fleeing to establish a cult with them.

---

[1] See, e.g., Husain, 89-90, etc.; Strong's H2451.
[2] See my book *Who Was Jesus?* for a discussion of the late dating of the canonical gospels and Acts.

The Hyksos surely picked up some Egyptian language during their hundreds of years in Egypt. It is possible that some of it was passed along in folklore, songs, poems and other oral traditions for centuries until written down.

Conclusion

The Hyksos or Amorites/Jebusites of Jerusalem were pre-Israelite Western Semites or Canaanites who worshipped Semitic, Sumero-Babylonian and Egyptian deities, such as Baal-Seth. Among the Hyksos may have been ancestors of various peoples who came together to create the nation of Israel centuries later:

> A number of theories have been put forward to account for the origins of the Israelites, and despite differing details they agree on Israel's Canaanite origins. The culture of the earliest Israelite settlements is Canaanite, their cult-objects are those of the Canaanite god El, the pottery remains in the local Canaanite tradition, and the alphabet used is early Canaanite, and almost the sole marker distinguishing the "Israelite" villages from Canaanite sites is an absence of pig bones, although whether even this is an ethnic marker or is due to other factors remains a matter of dispute. There is archeological evidence of the Canaanite Hyksos people moving into and out of northern Egypt, though the relation of their dates to the biblical account is debated by scholars.[1]

The morphing from Hyksos to Israelites did not happen as depicted either in the Torah or in the writings of ancient historians such as Manetho. There was no burning bush, no divine lawgiver with a magical rod, no miraculous and supernatural contests or plagues, no pillars of cloud and fire, no parting of the Red Sea, no manna or marvelous water, no divine voice speaking from a mountain or finger carving commandments into tablets of stone, no 40-year-old desert sojourn, no conquest of a promised land and so on.

By the time of the Amarna letters (c. 1350-1330 BCE), the Hebrews were not a significant presence, if they even existed as a tribe or ethnicity. It is obvious that the later Israelites were likewise nothing like the hyperbole by which they are described in the Old Testament. The same can be said of the Jewish tribe of Judah, which even by Herodotus's time (fifth cent. BCE) was so insignificant as to merit no notice from the Greek historian. The closest he comes is describing "Syrians" and those who circumcise in emulation of Egypt.

The Exodus epic represents an elaboration of a mythical event with historical or quasi-historical details added to it, not the other way around. Could the storytellers have incorporated some historical journeys, such as the expulsion of the Hyksos? In fact, the Exodus composers did set the story in real places, such as Egypt, the Red

---

[1] "The Exodus."

Sea, the Sinai and Canaan/Israel. So too had the mythographers of other myths in a wide variety of locations, including Saturn/Seth-Typhon's flight from Egypt and Crete. Are we to accept these similar *myths* as "history?"

Such a development in reality would be called "historical fiction" and would constitute mythmaking little different from that of other cultures, such as the Greeks with the Homeric epics, or the Indians with the *Ramayana* and *Mahabharata*, or the Scandinavian *Eddas* and so on. Rather than accepting a typical mythical foundation story as "history," in the next chapter we will peer more closely at the real origin of the Israelites.

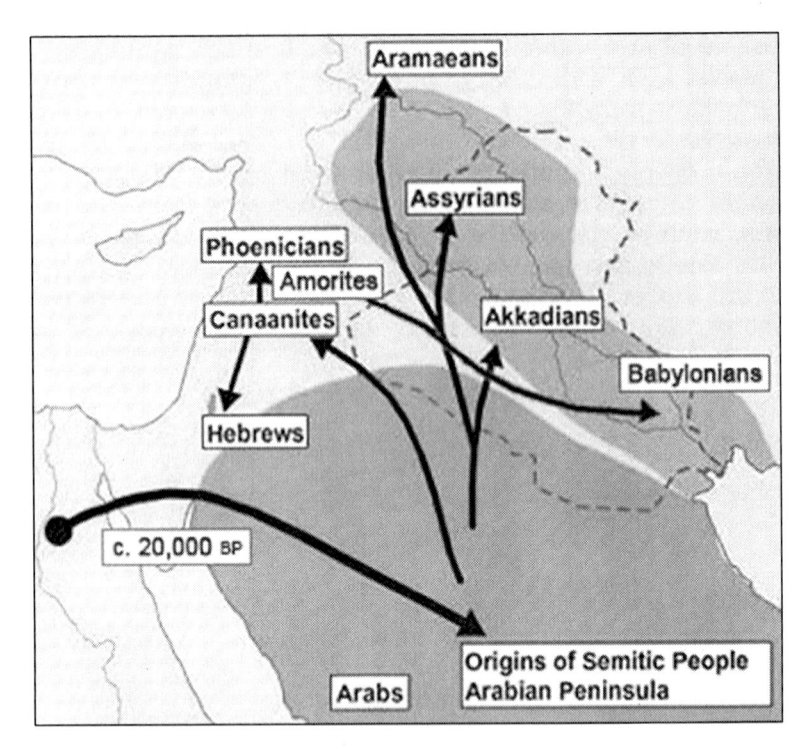

Fig. 37. Migrations of Semitic peoples out of Africa into Arabia, Levant, Mesopotamia and Asia Minor (after 'Ancient Mesopotamia,' *Worldology.com*)

Fig. 38. 'Asiatics' (Semites) entering Egypt, c. 1900 BCE. Relief from the tomb of Khnumhotep II at Beni Hasan, Egypt.

Who Were the Israelites?

"Who were the Semites in Egypt? Can they be regarded as Israelite in any meaningful sense? No mention of the name Israel has been found in any of the inscriptions or documents connected with the Hyksos period. Nor is it mentioned in later Egyptian inscriptions, or in an extensive fourteenth century BCE cuneiform archive found at Tell el-Amarna in Egypt, whose nearly four hundred letters describe in detail the social, political and demographic conditions in Canaan at that time.... the Israelites emerged only gradually as a distinct group in Canaan, beginning at the end of the thirteenth century BCE. There is no recognizable archaeological evidence of Israelite presence in Egypt immediately before that time."

Dr. Israel Finkelstein and Neil Silberman, *The Bible Unearthed* (57)

"No archaeological traces can be attributed to the early Israelites in Canaan before the early Iron Age (after 1200 B.C.E.), and there is no evidence of a distinct population of early Israelites in Egypt. The area west of the Jordan River reveals an archaeological picture quite at odds with the biblical accounts of the Israelite journey to the Promised Land, and there is little to no evidence of the Conquest, as it is described in the book of Joshua, in the archaeological record of the Late Bronze Age (1550-1200 B.C.E.) Canaan."

Dr. Barbara J. Sivertsen, *The Parting of the Sea* (xiv)

"The elements making up Israel derived from Canaanite and Amorite stock, spoke a South Canaanite dialect, and preserved old North Mesopotamian traditions and Canaanite traditions rooted in the second millennium B.C. They did not emerge from the desert as newcomers to Canaanite culture, nor did they speak the language of North Arabia."

Dr. Frank M. Cross, *Canaanite Myth and Hebrew Epic* (99)

"...Israel is a confederation of Hapiru tribes in the hill country of Canaan that formed the nation of Israel in the Iron Age. Originally, Abraham was part of an Amorite migration south into Canaan from Mesopotamia which continued down to Egypt, climaxing in the Hyksos rule...."

Dr. Stephen C. Meyer, "Biblical Archaeology: The Date of the Exodus According to Ancient Writers"

WE HAVE SEEN that Moses and the Exodus as depicted in the Bible cannot be considered scientifically to be historical, despite a number of theories proposing to identify the patriarch and Israelites with known historical individuals and peoples, including and especially the Amoritish Hyksos. While there evidently were proto-Jerusalemites and proto-Israelites among them, however, the Hyksos expulsion does not explain satisfactorily the foundation of the Israelite nation, as portrayed in the Exodus tale. How exactly did the Israelites come into being? Who were they originally?

The term "Israel" can be found in pre-Hebraic Canaanite texts as a person's name, in such forms as I-šar-il, Iš-ra-il and Išra'il, discovered in tablets from Ebla and Ugarit dating to the Bronze Age (4th-2nd millennia BCE).[1] Thus, the *name* "Israel" appears in pre-Israelite Semitic writings, including not only as a renowned charioteer, previously mentioned, but also in Amorite kings' cylinder seals,[2] another indication of the Amorite connection to the Israelites.

As a people and nation, we find no significant presence of an Israel until a century or more into the Iron Age (c. 1300-600 BCE). Archaeological evidence from the Canaanite hill settlements points to the emergence of Israel as a tribal ethnicity, although not by that name, around 1200 BCE,[3] close to the time of the Philistines' arrival on the coast, at the end of the Late Bronze Age destruction.

Jacob to Israel

The name "Israel" is encountered biblically first at Genesis 32:28, in the story of Jacob, subsequently styled "Yisrael." The moniker "Jacob," meaning "supplanter," is a common Amorite name, and the patriarch is said at Deuteronomy 26:5 to be a "wandering Aramean," an anachronistic term said to connote also "Amorite." Like Abraham, Isaac and others, Jacob too appears to have been a nonhistorical figure, possibly a deity such as Seth, the Egyptian usurper.[4] Jacob's sojourn in Egypt (Gen 46) could represent the time when Baal-Seth's Hyksos followers lived in the Nile Delta, and the "patriarch's" name change to "Israel" might indicate a later period when the *god's* devotees were subordinated or converted to El as their high god.

El Prevails

The word "Israel" itself is an indication of where some of the Israelites originated. Indeed, the name ישראל *Yisra'el* represents a combination of שרה *sarah*[5] and אל *'el*, to produce "Isra*el*," meaning "El prevails." Genesis 14:18 declares El to be the "most high God," whose priest was the biblical character Melchizedek, also a supposed "high priest" of Yahweh.

In this regard, Near Eastern studies professor and biblical scholar Dr. Mark S. Smith (b. 1956) analyzes whether or not the Canaanite high god El, therefore, was the original deity of Israel and the Exodus:

---

[1] Gnuse (1997), 195; van der Veen, et al., 19. The term "Zion" is also a Canaanite name. (*Mercer Commentary on the Bible*, 2.159)
[2] Clay, 90.
[3] Finkelstein and Silberman, 110.
[4] See Gen 4:25 for the sense of supplanting in the Hebrew name "Seth": "And Adam knew his wife again, and she bore a son and called his name Seth, for she said, "God has appointed for me another child instead of Abel, for Cain slew him." (Strong's H8352) See *Suns of God* for more on the Jacob-Set/Seth connection.
[5] Strong's H8280: "contend, have power, contend with, persist, exert oneself, persevere."

WHO WERE THE ISRAELITES?

Because the name of the god El appears as the divine element in the name of Israel, it has been supposed that El was the original god of Israel. Some evidence may point to El as the god associated with the Exodus from Egypt in some early biblical tradition.[1]

Canaanite text expert Gray comments that Israel's focus on El continued into the time of the monarchs and that "we should emphasize the influence of the Canaanite ideology of Baal as King, as well as the sovereignty of El, in the new royal ideology in Israel under the House of David."[2]

Although apologists attempt to make the Israelites contemporaneous with the Ugaritians, Smith unhesitatingly states that the latter are the predecessors of the former.[3] Contrary to popular notions and the impression given by the Bible itself, in many ways the Israelites were little different from their Canaanite forebears and neighbors.

Smith also asserts that the adoption of Yahweh as Israel's sole or most dominant god was a long and gradual development, meaning that the Exodus tale on Mt. Sinai with its abrupt introduction of Yahweh as the head divinity is a fictional account.[4] This contention is demonstrated additionally by the fact that Yahweh purportedly was introduced earlier to Abraham, who built the god an altar at Shechem (Gen 12:6-7).

Merneptah Stele

On all the many monuments and in the countless texts of Egypt, we find a purported mention of the word "Israel" only once,[5] and this one reference does not validate the biblical tales of the Israelites, including the Exodus. The reference to a "Ysrir," interpreted to be "Ysrael," on a stele/stela by the pharaoh Merneptah (fl. 1213-1203 BCE) indicates this "foreign people" was devastated by the Egyptian leader during his fifth year in Canaan. The brief inscription (KRI IV, 19) has been

Fig. 39. Merneptah Stele, 13th cent. BCE. Cairo Museum (after Webscribe)

---

[1] Smith, M. (2001), 9.
[2] Gray (1965), 158.
[3] Smith, M. (2001), 14.
[4] Smith, M. (2001), 14.
[5] van der Veen, et al., propose that the same or similar word as *Ysrir* may appear on a statue pedestal now housed at the Berlin Museum (no. 21687). The hieroglyph is fragmentary and the data inconclusive. If the word is the same as in the Merneptah inscription, it would present the same difficulties, including that it is undetermined whether or not it represents "Israel." Even if genuinely the Semitic word "Israel," this term is found as a personal *name* within pre-Israelite Canaanite texts and would not connote necessarily the ethnicity or people we picture as the nation of Israel.

rendered: "Israel is laid waste; its seed/grain is no more."[1] This one sentence has been enough for the seekers of historical validation for Israel to declare the Exodus as "historical fact."[2]

If Merneptah had the stele composed just a few decades after Israel supposedly escaped Egypt in an enormous and dramatic manner, following a tremendous decimation of the Egyptian nation, why would he not clarify his "Ysrir" with a comment? Surely, the entire country would be resounding with the name of Moses and Israel, if the Exodus truly had happened!

If the Hebrew slaves had been so involved in Egyptian daily life, doing much of the labor for the natives, including making the very bricks of their buildings, one would think that the pharaoh might indicate that highly important fact as well.

No Exodus

In this Egyptian text, there exists no mention of any enslavement in Egypt of Moses and the chosen people, whether as bricklayers or otherwise. Merneptah says nothing about the plagues, the devastation of the nation, the taking of all the Egyptian wealth, the miraculous parting of the Red Sea, or the destruction of the previous pharaoh and his army. All of this ruination purportedly had taken place during the previous decades, but Merneptah did not find it expedient to include one word of reference to it, while raising up his supposed routing of "Israel." Not "Israel, who destroyed our land," nothing of the sort, just one ambiguous word.

A literal Exodus would have caused a vast repercussion throughout the entire Mediterranean world, dependent on Egypt for many things. No doubt, this pharaoh would brag proudly about how he destroyed the mighty nation that nearly had annihilated Egypt during the previous century! Yet, he did not, and if this stele does refer to the tribe of Israel, it refutes the Exodus account by virtue of its minimalism.

Jewish scholars such as Israeli archaeologist Dr. Ze'ev Herzog (b. 1941) contend that "there is no evidence in the archaeological record that Israel was a powerful force, whether at the time of the stele's creation or at any other time during that general period."[3] In other words, there exists no evidence of the descendants of some two or three million people occupying Canaan for the past decades or centuries, according to the Conquest myth.

'His Seed is Not'

Regarding "Israel's seed," Egyptologist Breasted contended that its context and the common use of the phrase "his grain is not" was

---

[1] See Hasel, 76.
[2] See, e.g., Oblath, 10.
[3] "Merneptah Stele," *Wikipedia*.

WHO WERE THE ISRAELITES?

applied in antiquity also to other peoples, meaning that "the phrase cannot refer to an incident peculiar to the history of Israel, but that we have in it a conventional, stereotyped phrase, which could be and was applied to any conquered and plundered people." He continues: "It indicates nothing more than the loss of their supplies of grain or produce incident to some defeat."[1]

People, Not Land

Despite efforts to identify this term "Ysrir" with known locations such as "Jezreel" and "Syria," the hieroglyph indicates a "socio-ethnic" group or people, not a city-state or land, and the seed in the context of El may indicate not agriculture but procreation. Semitic language specialist Dr. Anson Rainey demonstrates that the "seed" in the Merneptah stele refers not to crops but to offspring, as in the "seed of Abraham." The slaughter of Israel's progeny, nevertheless, does not reflect the biblical massacre of the firstborn, as some have surmised.[2] Rather, destroying one's seed or fruit has been a common expression in the eastern Mediterranean.[3]

Fig. 40. Egyptian hieroglyphs on Merneptah stele transliterated as 'Ysrir'

Rainey avers that the inscription denotes "Israel" as a widespread semi-nomadic people of the hill country: "The group thus designated might be living on the level of a village culture, or could be pastoralists still in the nomadic stage."[4] This nomadic group has been surmised to comprise the Shasu, discussed below.

'Poetic Text,' Not Israel?

However, the stele is not accepted by all as proof of an Israelite people by this time. Finkelstein and Mazar call the Merneptah stele a "poetic text" and state that the purported mention of "Israel" as a "people" is "puzzling," asking:

> Was Israel at the end of the thirteenth century B.C.E. a sizeable confederation of tribes posing a threat to an Egyptian empire that had ruled Canaan for almost three hundred years? And if so, where did this Israel live? The answers to these questions continue to be disputed. Revisionist scholars who do not accept the traditional reconstruction of the early history of Israel attempt to dismiss the reference to Israel in this text.[5]

Since the personal name "Israel" already was present in Eblaite and Canaanite literature for centuries by Merneptah's time, and since much Semitic language was known by Egyptians of that era, one

---

[1] Breasted (1898/9), 8.35.
[2] Rainey (2001), 64.
[3] E.g., Amos 2:9; 2 Kings 19:30; Isa 37:31; Mal 3:19.
[4] Rainey (2001), 66.
[5] Finkelstein (2007), 93.

wonders why the stele's scribe appears so unfamiliar with the moniker as to spell it so obtusely. This oversight would be especially peculiar if the people using this name were considered troublesome and notorious enough to merit a record of their defeat. Surely the scribe(s) would have understood the name to mean "El Prevails" and would have rendered it properly in Egyptian. The sense is that the term on the stele is not the known Canaanite name of "Israel."

Mesha Stele

In any event, there exists no other mention of Israel as an ethnicity, nation or land in the extant historical record until the 9th century BCE, with the Mesha Stele or Moabite Stone. The monument was set up around 850 by the Moabite king Mesha to commemorate the god Chemosh's victory over Israel, which previously had subjugated Moab. This stele confirms the bitter feuding between these Amoritish peoples that continued into the reigns of Hezekiah and Josiah, leading to the Moabites as villains in the anachronistic Pentateuchal tales.

Hapiru

A century prior to Merneptah, the Amarna letters referred to the people called ʿpr.w or 'Apiru/Hapiru/Habiru, who have been identified with the Hyksos and Hebrews. The Amarna correspondence includes a missive (EA 286) to Abdi-Heba of the small highland village of Jerusalem (fl. c. 1330's), a pre-Israelite chieftain whose name indicates he was a follower of the Hurrian goddess Hebat. Abdu-Heba complained about these nomadic brigands sacking his village, with the result that all the territories of the pharaoh had been lost. He blamed the Hapiru leader and Egyptian vassal Labayu/Labaya for giving away the lands to the ruffian tribes.

In Sumerian, Egyptian, Akkadian, Hittite, Mitanni and Ugaritic texts dating from around 1800 to 1100 BCE, the Hapiru are portrayed as "nomadic or semi-nomadic, rebels, outlaws, raiders, mercenaries, and bowmen, servants, slaves, migrant laborers" and so on. Concerning the Hapiru, Redford remarks:

> Whatever the reason, the 'Apiru, as their name suggests ("dust makers," i.e. people who vacate the premises with speed) display a gypsylike quality, and proved difficult for the state authorities to bring under effective control. Their heterogeneous nature is vividly illustrated by the census lists from Alalakh, wherein one 'Apiru band includes an armed thief, two charioteers, two beggars and even a priest of Ishtar.[1]

The Hapiru are described essentially as "a loosely defined, inferior social class composed of shifting and shifty population elements

---

[1] Redford (1992), 195.

without secure ties to settled communities."[1] Rowton traces the development of the 'apiru class to nomadic tribes whose impoverished members needed to move into cities to survive, "very often entering military service."[2] Some of these nomads may have formed "into more or less predatory bands, which urban society [viewed] as little better than gangs of bandits."

As other examples of this sort of societal fringe, Rowton discusses the terms "turk," "kurd," "kazak," "mawali" and, probably, עברים or "'Ibrîm," the Old Testament word for "Hebrews."[3] Another term used to describe West Semitic nomads is "Sutean" or "Sutû warriors," referring to those who thrived in Syro-Palestine during the middle of the second millennium.[4]

Multiethnic Mob

The Hapiru are identified in Sumerian by the logogram SA.GAZ and in Akkadian sources as ḫabbātu, meaning "robber, bandit, raider." The Hapiru included many individuals with Akkadian names, while others are West Semitic, indicating an Amoritish origin that spread eastward. In this regard, Rowton remarks:

> ...the term 'apiru is of West Semitic origin, and it first appears in Mesopotamian urban society at a time when that society was being penetrated by Amorites. This suggests that it was brought in by the Amorites and that it originally denoted some aspect of tribal society...the economically and socially uprooted....[5]

Contributing to this multiethnic picture, documents from the ancient city of Nuzi in Mesopotamia describe the local Hapiru as "predominantly Hurrian, while approximately 2/3 of the Habiru names are Semitic; of these, all are East Semitic (Akkadian), none West Semitic."[6] While there evidently were proto-Hebrews among them, the word "Hapiru" thus seems to identify a multiethnic grouping engaged in a nomadic "gypsy" style of living, rather than a specific ethnos or people.

Adding to the mix, the king of the Mitanni, Idrimi of Aleppo (c. 1500-1450 BCE), fled the Amorite city of Emar in Syria[7] to join with the Hapiru at "Ammija in the land of Canaan," evidently located near Byblos. Perhaps at this point or earlier, Indian ideas were introduced to these Semites; in this regard, the word evidently "Syria:Surya"

---

[1] "Hapiru," Wikipedia.
[2] Rowton, 14.
[3] Rowton, 15ff; 1 Sam 4:9, etc. Strong's H5680: עברי 'Ibriy, meaning "one from beyond."
[4] Rahmouni, 224.
[5] Rowton, 17.
[6] "Habiru," Wikipedia.
[7] Excavations at Emar revealed a temple dedicated to the Canaanite god Baal and, possibly, his consort Astarte, dating to the 13th and 12th centuries BCE. Tablets at Emar include about 1,100 in Akkadian language, 100 in Hurrian and one in Hittite.

derives from the Vedic word "Surya," meaning "sun,"[1] demonstrating the Indic influence in the region.

Shechem

In the 14th century, the Hapiru leader Labayu enlisted a group of men to attack the Levantine town of Megiddo, for which effort he rewarded his supporters with the village of Shechem (שכם *Shēkem*), which had not been occupied previously, during the Intermediate Bronze Age.[2] This latter town is an important locale in the Bible, serving as the capital of the Northern Kingdom (1 Ki 12:25), where the altar allegedly was established by Abraham and dedicated to יהוה *Yĕhovah*/YHWH. Thus, it is at Shechem that the ethnicity of Israel swore allegiance to Yahweh, even though the book of Exodus contradictorily claimed Abraham did not know the god, who was introduced first to *Moses* on Mt. Sinai.

It is possible that this gang of Hapiru who joined Labayu were the predecessors of the northern Israelites in significant part, mixed with other Semites.[3] Another group of these rough nomads was composed significantly of centralized Semites, as in the records by the Egyptian pharaoh Seti I (d. 1279 BCE) of Hapiru attacks from "Mt. Yarmuta."[4] As noted, there were also many Hapiru in the kingdom of Amurru, ancestral homeland of the Amorites, who eventually occupied pre-Israelite Jerusalem as Jebusites.

In the Amarna correspondence of the 14th century, the Hapiru had become such a nuisance to the Egyptians in the Levant that the authorities there had complained these wandering nomads would eventually take over the entire region. It would seem that indeed they did, as part of the Israelite confederation, following their god El, who thus prevails. How else do we explain the rise of the eventual Israelites? The answer may be that some of the Hapiru became the Israelites, a number of whom in turn developed into fervent Yahwists.

Hebrews?

The position that the Hapiru/Habiru were specifically the Hebrews is based on both etymology and the acceptance of the biblical Israel foundation stories as "history." In one sense, the OT tales *are* history, as they describe people rampaging throughout the Levant, resembling the uncivilized and crude Hapiru/Habiru, considered robbers and sackers of cities.

---

[1] Syria is called *Sūriyā* in Arabic and was also *al-Sham(s)*, meaning "the sun."
[2] Finkelstein and Silberman, 321.
[3] See, e.g., Harrelson, van der Steen.
[4] Yarmuta/Yarmut/Jarmuth appears biblically at Jos 10:3, 5, 23; 12:11; 15:35; 21:29; Neh 11:29. Strong's (H3412) defines the word as "heights," referring to "a Canaanitish city in the lowlands of Judah with a king and located between Hebron and Lachish" and "a Levitical city of Issachar allocated to the Gershonite Levites."

WHO WERE THE ISRAELITES?

The term "Hebrew" (עברי *'Ibriy*), however, appears to derive from the town name of Eber or Heber[1] and to be unrelated etymologically to *'apiru*. Yet, based on a study of these terms' connotations, Near Eastern languages expert Rowton suggests that *'apiru* and *'ibri* "denote essentially the same social element."[2] He distinguishes the former as representing an uprooted social outcast from either a tribal or urban society, whereas the latter connotes the same element but *only* from the Israelite tribal society.[3] Interestingly, Philistine texts never use the term "Israelite" but only employ *'ibri* to connote the Hebrews,[4] indicating the former word was unknown or secondary to them.

Claiming there is "absolutely no relationship" between the Habiru and Hebrews, Rainey and others aver that the foundation of Israel stems from the Shasu instead. Although there are significant differences, both groups were composed of the nomadic *bedu*, the Egyptian term passed along as "bedouin," also part of the Amorite empire.

Bedu

Regarding the *bedu*, Redford remarks:

> The bedu in the Delta roused mixed feelings among the Egyptians. Elders, traditional in their outlook, despised these wanderers and their goats; the bedu were viewed as dirty and unkempt in their carriage and indifferent to the civilized ways of living. But to the young they embodied the ideal of a life of freedom from authority...[5]

The term Hapiru was used by the Egyptians to describe *bedu* brigands in the northern hill country of Israel,[6] while the Shasu of the southeastern region appear to be most influential in the southern sections of Israel, the area that came to be known as Judah/Judea.

Egyptian Campaigns

Like many other pharaohs had done and would continue to do, in the 15th century BCE Amenhotep II engaged in military campaigns against Canaan, a land called "Retenu" in Egyptian. Lists of prisoners of war include 3,600 Hapiru and 15,200 Shasu. In order to protect the residents from these marauders, Seti I also battled both the Hapiru and Shasu in Syro-Palestine: "Seti I (c. 1290 BCE) is said to have conquered the Shasu, Arabian nomads living just south and east of the Dead Sea, from the fortress of Taru in 'Ka-n-'-na.'"[7] This defeat too may have found its way into legend and myth about the

---

[1] Strong's H5677: "Eber or Heber ='the region beyond.'"
[2] Rowton, 18f.
[3] Rowton, 19.
[4] Rowton, 19.
[5] Redford (1992), 228-229.
[6] Redford (1992), 274.
[7] "Canaan," *New World Encyclopedia*.

hated enemy, Egypt. Seti's son was Ramesses II, the ruler most often considered to have been the pharaoh of Exodus. As suggested previously, these facts may explain in significant part the retooling of Canaanite and Amorite cosmological battles to represent Egypt and its ruler(s) as the enemy.

Seti also refers to the Shasu "from the fortress of Sile as far as Pa-Canaan," including "Upper Retenu."[1] Hence, it appears that "Shasu" here refers to an ethnicity also from *northern* Israel, rather than simply confined to the south, a confused identity resembling the Amorites.

Shasu of Yhw

As we have seen, the Hyksos have been said to represent the *hiq shasu/shosu*, connoting "rulers of nomad lands."[2] The troublesome š3sw/šʒśw/š3ś.w or Shasu are found in numerous Egyptian texts, including a list of Transjordanian peoples from the fifteenth century. In the time of Amenhotep III (c. 1400 BCE) a topographical list was created at the temple of Amon at Soleb that was copied "later by either Seti I or Ramesses II at Amarah-West" and that "mentions six groups of Shashu: the Shasu of S'rr, the Shasu of Lbn, the Shasu of Sm't, the Shasu of Wrbr, the Shasu of Yhw, and the Shasu of Pysps."[3]

Wanderers

The name "Shasu" is said to come from an Egyptian verb meaning "to move on foot," frequently employed to describe either journeys or the "daily motion of the sun."[4] It eventually was used to refer to "wandering groups whom we would call *bedu*, with the significant distinction that unlike their modern counterparts they lacked the camel."[5]

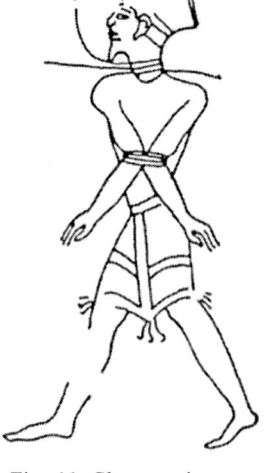

Fig. 41. Shasu prisoner bound around arms and neck, 12th cent. BCE. Line drawing of relief by Ramesses III at Madinat Habu, Egypt

An amalgam of these groups, the northern Hapiru and the southern Shasu, along with other Amorites and Semitic *bedu*, would explain many of the characteristics of the later Israelites, as depicted in the Old Testament and indicated by archaeological artifacts.

---

[1] Hasel, 41.
[2] "Hyksos," *Online Etymology Dictionary*.
[3] "Shasu," *Wikipedia*.
[4] Redford (1992), 271.
[5] Redford (1992), 271.

Plunderers

The word *shasu* may originate instead with the Ugaritic term *ṯš-* possibly meaning "plunder" and reflected in the Egyptian *š3ś.w*, denoting "plundering nomads."[1] Describing the Shasu, Redford states:

> Their lawlessness and their proclivity to make raids gave rise in Canaanite (and Hebrew) to the denominative verb *šasā(h)*, "to plunder."
>
> Shasu are found in Egyptian texts from the 18th Dynasty [c. 1550–c. 1292] through the Third Intermediate Period [1069–664].... lists from Soleb and Amarah, ultimately of fifteenth-century origin, suggest that an original concentration of Shasu settlements lay in southern Transjordan in the plains of Moab and northern Edom.[2]

Hence, for the most part the Shasu occupied lands settled by those later called "Moabites" and "Edomites," possibly as their ancestors. Historians Drs. Charles F. Aling and Clyde E. Billington surmise that the Egyptians lumped together under the name Shasu "all of the Edomites, Ammonites, Moabites, Amalekites, Midianites, Kenites, Hapiru and Israelites," a list that "should also probably include the Amorites and the Arameans."

Transjordan Origin

From the Egyptian sources, the Shasu seem to be "somewhat" different from the early Israelites in the book of Judges. Nevertheless, while the Hyksos evidently comprised Shasu possibly from the *western* region of Canaan, there is little doubt that the same "pastoral transhumants" occupied the lands from which the Israelites emerged, previously inhabiting the Transjordanian region in the 14th to 12th centuries BCE.

Concerning the Shasu and the settlement in the Late Bronze Age of the Israelite hill country, Rainey concludes:

> Today there is no reason to ignore Transjordan as the most probable source for the new immigrants who established the small villages on the heights of Mt. Ephraim (the Samaria hills). That their pottery and other artefacts show some continuity with Late Bronze material culture is no deterrent....
>
> The Egyptian records reveal that the *Shasu* pastoralists were becoming more numerous and troublesome during the thirteenth century B.C.E. The archaeological surveys in the central hill country indicate that the Iron I settlements initially sprang up in marginal areas where pastoralists could graze their flocks and engage in dry farming. Later they spread westward, cleared the forests and began building agricultural terraces. Nowadays there is no compelling

---

[1] Schniedewind, 209.
[2] Redford (1992), 272.

reason to doubt the general trend of the Biblical tradition that those pastoralists were mainly immigrants from Transjordan.[1]

The Transjordan origin would indicate the Amorite roots of these Shasu, speaking Babylonian and maintaining elements of that culture.

Westward Thrust

The Shasu of Moab and Edom evidently began making their push westward in earnest during the late 14th to mid-13th centuries BCE.[2] In response to this migration, the Egyptians beefed up their presence in the region, which means that any "Israelites" of the Exodus would have encountered Egyptian forces many times during their purported sojourn in the Sinai and into Canaan. Although an Amoritish people, at this point these Shasu were not literate,[3] which means they probably were not the Canaanitish Hyksos with sacred texts, although they may have been among them. Moreover, they likely possessed oral traditions, possibly hymns, songs and poetry, recording myths and legends.

Pithom

An Egyptian letter from around 1192 BCE discusses the "Shasu tribes of Edom" who "pass the fortress of Merneptah Hotep-hir-Maat...to the pools of Per Atum...which are in Tkeku."[4] The latter city, Per-Atum, is Pithom, where the Shasu evidently settled. Hence, the inclusion of Pithom in the OT may be based on Shasu traditions of having lived and worked there, although there were several "Houses of Atum" with which the Shasu could have been associated. The word "Shasu:Bedouin" in this passage has been translated as "Bedouin,"[5] reflecting the relationship between the two.

Goshen and Joseph

It is surmised that the general location where the Shasu settled in Egypt was that of Goshen, traditional home of the Hebrews, where the patriarch Joseph was said to have ended up, after fleeing a famine in Hebron (Gen 46:28-29). Goshen and Avaris, the Hyksos capital, lie within the Nile Delta, while Pithom lies just to the southeast of Avaris, the entire region of which, therefore, could have been inhabited by the Hyksos/Shasu, who appear to have come in waves, possibly represented in the different Hyksos stories previously discussed.

It is claimed that the "treatment of the Shasu Edomites by the officials of Pharaoh is reminiscent of Pharaoh's earlier treatment of

---

[1] Rainey (2001), 67-68.
[2] Redford (1992), 275.
[3] Redford (1992), 275.
[4] *Papyrus Anastasi* VI, 54-56; 4.16.
[5] See, e.g., Lemaire, 226.

the Israelites in Egypt during the time of Joseph,"[1] this latter story according to the Bible but not the historical record. Nor did they speak Hebrew, a later Semitic dialect evidently produced from the admixture of Canaanite, Amorite and Babylonian speakers of the Hapiru and Shasu tribes.

Even if the Shasu had among them proto-Israelites, and although they were taken captive in significant numbers, there is no historical record or archaeological evidence of two to three million of them living in an enclave as slaves in Egypt.

These Shasu may have comprised proto-Israelite Amorites who had lived in Egypt, some of whom were also descendants of the Hyksos expelled from the delta and subsequently settling in the Judean hill country. These Hyksos descendants may have been the western Shasu per the inscription by Seti I, as well as the Hapiru, while the later hill settlers were drawn from the southeastern *bedu* as well.

Aromatic Gum

Redford describes the Shasu thus:

> ...Already in the second half of the fifteenth century B.C. they comprised some 36 percent of the Palestinian captives brought back by Amenophis II... They are consistently described as being divided into "clans," each governed by a "chief"... Their proclivity for internecine strife drew expressions of contempt from Egypt. Their conflict with Pharaoh and, to a lesser extent, the latter's surrogates within the Canaanite principalities arose not out of objections to taxation or the draft...but in their well-deserved reputation as robbers and brigands whose code of conduct admitted little mercy on their victims. They lived in tents, in mountainous districts remote from towns, where woods and predators made travel risky. Their principal source of wealth was their cattle, and they were also renowned for an aromatic gum, which perhaps they found in the wild. But their life must have seemed to the Egyptians so Spartan that they contemptuously referred to them as "living like wild game."

> The Shasu settlement in the Palestinian highlands, or nascent Israel as we should undoubtedly call it, and whatever related group had begun to coalesce in the Judaean hills to the south, led a life of such rustic simplicity at the outset that it has scarcely left an imprint on the archaeological record.[2]

The "aromatic gum" for which the Shasu were known resembles manna, possibly explaining in part the latter motif's inclusion in the Exodus myth. As we can see, there was much interchange between the Shasu and Egyptians over a period of centuries, including many skirmishes, as well as ingresses into and exoduses out of Egypt.

---

[1] Aling and Billington
[2] Redford (1992), 279.

It is noteworthy that the vaunted frankincense and myrrh, presented along with gold to the newborn savior, Jesus, also are aromatic gums, demonstrating great reverence and demand for these substances. As we might expect, frankincense was "widely used by the ancient Egyptians in their religious rituals," evidently utilized in the mummification process, signifying that the Egyptian requirement would be great.

Hill Settlement

Around the start of the 12th century BCE, the Shasu began to emulate their Canaanite cousins in their settlements, by inhabiting the hill country. The Shasu settlement came during the destruction by the invading sea peoples, when both Canaan and Egypt essentially lost control of the region.[1]

Differences between these new "Israelites" and their Canaanite predecessors included the tendency towards a single cult site for several surrounding tribes, rather than the individual "high places" the later followers of Yahweh repeatedly destroy throughout the Old Testament, revealing the religious fanaticism of the southeastern Amoritish Yahwists/Judeans over the Canaanitish northern Israelites. The Israelite aversion to imagery of the deity is also more Arabian than Canaanite, reflecting not the "empty shrine" motif of the "solar theology," as Redford calls it, but, rather, the desert tribal proscription of idols.[2] Also, the lack of pig bones that distinguish Israelites from the Canaanites may reflect a taboo based on previous experiences with leprosy, which has been believed erroneously to be carried and transmitted by pigs, or with trichinosis.

Yhw is Yahweh?

As noted, one of the Transjordanian groups designated in Egyptian texts is the *t3 ssw yhw3* or "Shasu of Yhw," the latter term widely averred to refer to Yahweh. While most other examples of Shasu in conjunction with another name generally refer to place-names or toponyms, rather than god-names or theonyms, it is possible that these Shasu were known by the name of their deity. Instead of a flag representing their nation, therefore, the Shasu nomads may have carried a standard of their *god*, likewise a symbol of their people.

Regarding the term "Yhw," we read that the "hieroglyphic rendering corresponds very precisely to the Hebrew tetragrammaton YHWH, or Yahweh, and antedates the hitherto oldest occurrence of that Divine Name—on the Moabite Stone—by over five hundred years."[3] Redford also asserts that the Yhw of the Shasu undoubtedly

---

[1] Redford (1992), 280.
[2] Redford (1992), 280.
[3] "Shasu," *Wikipedia*.

refers to YHWH/Yahweh, which would mean that we have a pre-Israelite record from the late 15th century BCE of this tribal god.[1]

Seir

As concerns the apparent Transjordanian origin of Yhw/Yahweh, at Deuteronomy 33:2 we read a "blessing" from Moses in which Yahweh "rose up" or "dawned" from a place called Seir:

> The LORD came from Sinai, and dawned from Se'ir upon us; he shone forth from Mount Paran, he came from the ten thousands of holy ones, with flaming fire at his right hand...[2]

Seir is identified as "the land of Edom, south of the Dead Sea" and "a mountain range in Edom extending from the Dead Sea to the Elanitic Gulf."[3] Other biblical passages depict Yahweh as "going forth from Seir" and originating in Edom (Jdg 5:4).

The solar imagery here is noteworthy, describing Yahweh in terms of a fiery-handed sun god, shining forth from the mountain, here styled "Paran" (פארן *Pa'ran*), which means "place of caverns," an appropriate moniker for the location in the east where the sun god emerges from the nightly cave.

It is also noteworthy that the name "Seir" has been identified with Helios and Sirius,[4] the latter of which in antiquity heralded the arrival of the solar "messiah" Osiris.[5]

10,000 Holy Ones

The "ten thousands of holy ones" (קדש *qodeshim*)[6] at Deuteronomy 33:2 certainly does not refer to historical Israelites. Regarding this astrotheological motif, Massey comments:

> Under the name of Khabsu in Egyptian the stars are synonymous with souls. These in their nightly rising from Amenta were the images of souls becoming glorified. They came forth in their thousands and tens of thousands from the lower Egypt of the astronomical mythos, the earliest exodus being stellar. Thus we can realise the leader Shu, who stands upon the height of heaven, rod in hand, and who was imaged in the constellation Kepheus as the Regulus or law-giver at the pole.[7]

---

[1] Redford (1992), 273.
[2] The Hebrew verb for "to dawn" is זרח *zarach*, which also means to "come forth, break out, arise, rise up, shine" (H2224). The word is used at Genesis 32:31 to describe the rise of the sun over Jacob. This usage of זרח *zarach* in conjunction with the sun also occurs at Exodus 22:3 and Psalm 104:22.
[3] Strong's H8165.
[4] Per "Suidas," the hypothesized lexicographer of the Byzantine encyclopedia called the *Suda* (10th cent. AD/CE): Σείρ, σειρός: ὁ ἥλιος. Σείριος: ὁ ἀστρῷος κύων. Αἰλιανός: λοιμῶν δὲ ἐπιδημίαν ἔσβεσεν ὅδε ἀνὴρ καὶ τὴν ἀμφὶ τὸν κύνα Σείριον πρωτίστην ἐπιτολὴν καὶ τὴν ὁρμὴν τὴν ἔμπυρον ἡμερῶσαι τοῦ ἄστρου. καὶ Σείρ, σειρός, ὁ ἥλιος. This etymology is unattested elsewhere.
[5] See, e.g., *Christ in Egypt*.
[6] Strong's H6944.
[7] Massey (1907), 2.630.

In consideration of the fact that we know biblical scribes used ancient Egyptian and Babylonian solar hymns, poems and so on, whether directly or indirectly, it would not surprise us if in this verse in Deuteronomy they did likewise in borrowing their astrotheological mythology from Egypt.

Sin

In ancient Semitic lunar mythology, which preceded in many places solar mythology, the moon god is said to give birth to the sun, as Sin is the father of Shamash.[1] In this Deuteronomic verse, we can see that Yahweh emerging from Mt. Sinai reflects this myth, as well as the idea that the sun is "born" from the caverns of the night sky and the cave/womb of the earth, bringing with it the various stars visible in the dawn hours. Moreover, the suggestion is that Sinai was an area of moon worship for ancient Semites.[2] As Eckenstein remarks, "The monuments found in Sinai contain information which points to the existence of moon-worship there at a remote period of history."[3]

It has been asserted that the identity of the Shasu with the Israelites probably cannot be sustained, as the two were appointed differently, bearing dissimilar appearances. However, as the Israelites are a creation of subsequent centuries, it is possible that the Shasu descendants were part of the later amalgamated Israelite tribal confederacy, particularly as Yahwists/Judeans,[4] by this time adopting a different appearance, while maintaining the passionate worship of their god.

The end result is a "recognition that the Israelites emerged from unsettled, Late Bronze population groups known from written sources, such as the Shasu attested in the Egyptian sources."[5]

Early Israelite Religion

In addition to the religion of Yahweh, the Israelites—the northerners especially—were followers of El and other Canaanite deities, such as those of the Amoritish Babylonians. While the Shasus who settled the southern hill country may have been largely Yahwists, the northerners evidently were significantly Hapiru who were part of the Amoritish peoples, both Canaanite and Babylonian. Since the Bible claims the Amorites "dwell in the mountains" (Num 13:29), it would be sensible that they would follow El Shaddai, the "God of the mountain."

---

[1] Coulter and Turner, 423.
[2] See, e.g., Eckenstein (8ff), chapter 2: "Sinai a Centre of Moon-Cult."
[3] Eckenstein, 12.
[4] The Hebrew word for "Judea" or "Judah" is יהודה *Yĕhuwdah*, meaning "praised" (Strong's H3063), as in "praise Yahweh" (Gen 29:35). It should be noted that the Hebrew word "Yehudah" is essentially the same word as in the tetragrammaton יהוה YHWH, with the addition of the letter ד *daleth*.
[5] Finkelstein (2007), 94.

It should be kept in mind that the Semitic Hyksos and Canaanites were influenced by Egypt in religious matters, and vice versa. Dating to the 12th to 14th centuries BCE, the Ugaritic texts found at Ras Shamra reveal that various biblical tales, doctrines and terminology had their precedent in Canaanite religion. The texts demonstrate that the writers of the Pentateuch, for one, were well aware of these legends, traditions and practices, evidence proving that the biblical texts were written centuries later, proscribing behavior practiced by Israelites who remained part of their original Canaanite clan.

In order to maintain the purported historicity and literalism of the Bible, some apologists claim that Yahweh inspired the Bible writers such as Moses to know all about the Canaanite religion beforehand, in order to prevent the "chosen" from falling into a trap and being seduced by this allegedly evil people. Apologists also hold up the Ugaritic texts as evidence of why Yahweh needed to exterminate the evil Canaanites by brutally conquering their lands through Joshua and the Israelites.[1] As we know, however, there is no evidence that such a conquest ever occurred, and this apology rings not only hollow but also genocidal.

The facts all together indicate that the Israelites originally were practitioners of the Canaanite-Amorite religion and that the strongest proscriptions against their faith purportedly transpired during the reigns of the kings Hezekiah and Josiah, when Deuteronomy may have been composed.

Conclusion

While the words "Hebrew" and "Hapiru" may not be related etymologically, it seems that the tribes of Israel were drawn largely from the Semitic *bedu*, specifically the Shasu and Hapiru, along with others among the Amorites and Canaanites. The descriptions of the Hapiru and Shasu are similar to those of the Hyksos and Israelites, such as the supposedly historical material in the Bible that includes the rampaging through Canaan, slaughtering, pillaging and taking virgin girls as slaves. Of course, the scope to which these dastardly deeds has been inflated is not borne out by the archaeological or historical record, but in the Hapiru and Shasu portrayals we may find some of the historical material shaping the mythology in the Bible.

Eventually, the merged group moved into the southern part of Syria/Palestine, taking over Jerusalem. If the tribes who originally settled the north hill country were Canaanite followers of El, joined by Amoritish *bedu* and Babylonians, as well as Yahwists from the southeast, this fact would explain many characteristics of the Bible and Judaism.

---

[1] See, e.g., Jackson, 4.

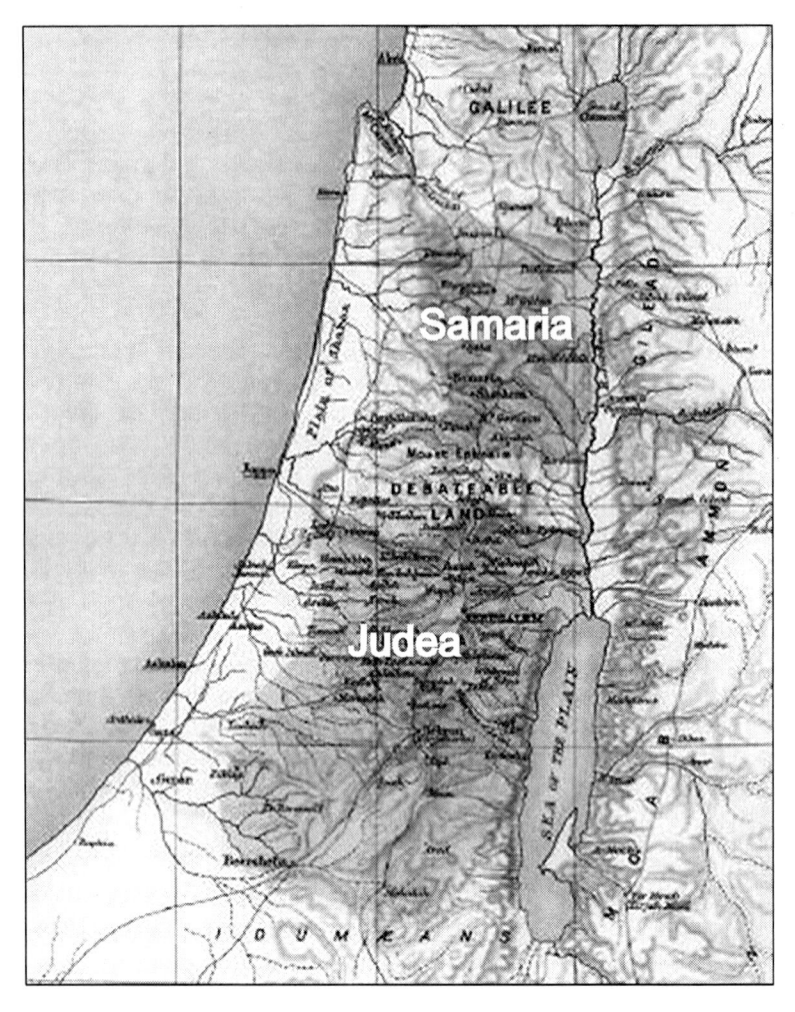

Fig. 42. Map with shaded areas showing hill settlements of Samaria and Judea, in between Jordan River/Dead Sea and Mediterranean coast (Smith, G.A.)

The Exodus as Myth

"...Moses, or the compiler of the Book of Genesis, whoever he may have been, manifests a familiar acquaintance with the religious epics of Babylonia, which go back to the twenty-third century B.C., to a date, i.e., about 800 years earlier than the reputed time of Moses. By being worked into these early Hebrew documents, Babylonian ideas were ensured persistence and obtained a world-wide currency."

Rev. Dr. A. Smythe Palmer, *Babylonian Influence on the Bible and Popular Beliefs* (3-4)

"The vanity of building up history out of myth by a process of rationalizing the primeval fables is indescribable!... The Hebrew miracles are Egyptian myths, and as such can be explained in accordance with nature....

"We have to face the fact, and it is well to do so in a manly fashion. We cannot wriggle out of it by squirming; we shall not avoid the collision by flinching. The light will not be shut out by blinking. The myths of Egypt supplied the mysteries of the world. The myths of Egypt are the miracles of the Hebrew writings, and a true explanation of the one must inevitably explode the false pretentions of the other. Half my labour has to be spent in reducing the Jewish mythology from the status of divine revelation and establishing its *relative* importance by the comparative method, which will be applied incessantly and remorselessly. The key of these writings was lost, and is found in Egypt.

"The original foundational matter of all the aptly named Mosaic writings is not, and was not, historical at all, but entirely mythical. The primordial Exodus, like the Genesis, belongs to the celestial allegory.

"...The myths of Egypt will be found to have been copied and reproduced, and declared to have been given directly from the hand and mouth of the Lord, whereas there was no revelation or divine origin in the matter. The Hebrews took them from the Egyptians..."

Gerald Massey, *A Book of the Beginnings* (2.176-178)

IT HAS BEEN SHOWN that Moses could not have written the Pentateuch, that he cannot be identified in the historical record, and that the biblical Exodus story ranks as implausible if not impossible as history, defying logic and physical laws, and having no external corroboration, such as artifacts or literary accounts. We have discussed also that there are a number of exoduses out of Egypt, the details of which could have been used to flesh out the biblical Exodus drama, which never happened as depicted. Moreover, we have discovered who the Israelites were, that their foundation was not like the story in the Bible, and that they practiced Egyptian-influenced Canaanite and Mesopotamian religion. In reality, there is little reason to pronounce the supernatural Exodus epic any more historical than the great dramas of the *Iliad* and *Odyssey*, as well as the *Epic of Gilgamesh*, the Baal myth, *Mahabharata*, *Ramayana*, *Beowulf*, *Eddas*, the *Popol Vuh* and other ancient writings.

Many of the major stories from the Old Testament are largely mythical, such as, most obviously, the supernatural tales full of magic and miracles. Although historical and geographical features may have been woven into the biblical tale to anchor it into history, the overall theme or core of the Exodus is likewise not a historical event but constitutes a motif found in other myths, including, evidently, that of Egypt, as well as Babylon and other areas.

Indeed, the Moses story as a whole reveals itself to be a mythical archetype from a remote era, wrapped in various more localized elements, attributes and additions in a setting of historicized fiction.

The Slaughter of Innocents

To begin with, at Exodus 1:22, in order to thwart his overthrow, the pharaoh orders the deaths of all male Hebrew children by drowning in the Nile. It is because of this decree that Moses's mother puts her baby into the river. However, the slaughter of innocent children or infants is yet another motif found in a number of mythologies, whereby the reigning monarch tries to prevent from being fulfilled a prophecy that a new king will be born who will depose him. As Walker says, "Innocents were slaughtered in the myths of Sargon, Nimrod, Moses, Jason, Krishna and Mordred as well as in that of Jesus."[1] Children are slain or menaced also in the stories of Oedipus, Perseus, Romulus and Remus, and Zeus, some of whose myths include being shut in chests and tossed into a body of water.[2]

It is surmised that this motif of infanticide has to do with the battle between day and night found in a number of myths, including the Egyptian story of Osiris, Seth and Horus. In this astrotheological interpretation, the "infants" are the stars blotted out by the serpent of night or "prince of darkness," in an attempt to destroy the sun as one of them, this latter perception of the solar orb as a star representing an astronomical insight that proves to be correct.

In Sumerian mythology, the stars were considered to be soldiers created by the heavenly god and great judge Anu to "destroy the wicked."[3] Hence, one can comprehend why the "prince of darkness" would wish to be rid of them. Here we also see that the idea of the high god as the creator of the stars and other celestial bodies does not originate with the biblical Yahweh. Associated with his son, Enlil, and the god Enki/Ea, Anu is part of a trinity, millennia prior to the biblical God the father, son and holy ghost.

---

[1] Walker (1983), 435.
[2] See, e.g., Hallet, 228-229, 233; Woodward, 5; Tichelaar, 43; Parker, et al., 203.
[3] *Larousse*, 55.

The Flight Archetype

Moses and the Exodus appears to be a Jewish emulation of an ancient mythical archetype found in several relevant areas, as noted. We have seen already that Tacitus discussed the "flight of Saturn" as the basis for the foundation of the city of Jerusalem. As had others since antiquity, in his *Hierozoicon* (34), influential French biblical scholar Rev. Samuel Bochart (1599-1667) also associated the Exodus with the Set/Typhon story, focusing on the plagues as aspects of the latter myth and declaring that "the flight of Typhon is the Exodus of Moses from Egypt."[1]

As also noted, Plutarch complained about the Judaization of the Egyptian myth of Seth-Typhon fleeing his battle with Horus.[2] In *De Iside et Osiride* or "Isis and Osiris" (31), found in his *Moralia*, the Greek mythographer remarks:

> But those who relate that Typhon's flight from the battle was made on the back of an ass and lasted for seven days, and that after he had made his escape, he became the father of sons, Hierosolymus and Judaeus, are manifestly, as the very names show, attempting to drag Jewish traditions into the legend.[3]

The original Greek of Plutarch's Typhon tale (363c-d) is:

οἱ δὲ λέγοντες ἐκ τῆς μάχης ἐπ' ὄνου τῷ Τυφῶνι τὴν φυγὴν ἑπτὰ ἡμέρας γενέσθαι καὶ σωθέντα γεννῆσαι παῖδας Ἱεροσόλυμον καὶ Ἰουδαῖον, αὐτόθεν εἰσὶ κατάδηλοι τὰ Ἰουδαϊκὰ παρέλκοντες εἰς τὸν μῦθον [*mython*].

Note that the last word in the Greek paragraph above is μῦθον *mython*, the accusative of μῦθος *mythos*, rendered here as "legend" but meaning also "myth," as well as "word, speech,"[4] hence "mouth."[5] Writing in the second century AD/CE, Plutarch is asserting basically that the Jewish tale is based on or woven into a myth: Thus, the flight or exodus motif serves as myth historicized, not literal history mythologized.

As we can see, in the typical ancient fashion of attributing a culture to legendary and eponymous heroes, such as Romulus and Remus founding Rome, some in antiquity averred there were two Jewish brothers named "Hierosolymus" and "Judaeus" or "Jerusalem" and "Judea," respectively. Moreover, these brothers were said to be the sons of the god Seth or Typhon, also known as Apophis and Baal, the Hyksos' main god, evidently serving as two tribal deities demoted to human status.

---

[1] Bochart's original Latin is: *Fuga Typhonis est Mosis ex Ægypto excessus*. (Bochart, 1712:341) The Latin word *excessus* means "departure," by which Bochart obviously intends the "Exodus"; hence the above rendering by Velikovsky (99).
[2] Massey (1881/2007), 2.181.
[3] Plutarch/Babbitt, 77.
[4] *OCGD*, 216.
[5] The Old English word for "mouth" is *mūth*, while μῦθος can be rendered *mūthos*.

Baal-Seth

Concerning the hybrid Egypto-Hyksos deity, Seth-Baal or Baal-Seth Swiss Catholic theologian and Egyptologist Dr. Othmar Keel and German religion professor Dr. Christoph Uehlinger state:

> The influence of the Egyptian deity Seth on the Canaanite Baal is certain.... *Seth-Baal*...is encountered regularly on the seal amulets that were mass-produced during the Ramesses Period... He appears occasionally already in the Late Bronze Age...[1]

Fig. 43. Seth-Baal (top), Baal-Seth and the sun god (bottom left two), and Seth with Amun name (bottom right), c. 16th-11th cents. BCE. Seal amulets (after Keel and Uehlinger, 115)

The Egyptian seal amulets of Seth-Baal in cruciform demonstrate a possible prototype for the famous "Alexamenos" graffito and for the story that the Jews worshipped an ass.

The syncretic Baal-Seth continued to hold prominence, especially as a war god and in association with a sun god. Both Baal and Seth are said to conquer sea serpents as well, while "at Lachish, Baal-Seth is shown adorned with two bull's horns" and in "one hand he has struck a horned snake on the back of the neck,"[2] elements similar to those within the Moses myth as well.

Keel and Uehlinger call Seth-Baal a "major deity," commenting:

> By means of the combination of Baal and Seth as serpent conquerors, the serpent, an Egyptian symbol of the danger in the dark of night and a Canaanite symbol of the stormy sea, became a symbol of danger in general. The god who could defeat such a creature is treated as a savior, pure and simple.[3]

Those promoting this legend may have been Jews laying claim to Set or Seth as their ancestor, as with the biblical Seth of Genesis (4:25), third child of Adam and Eve and the progenitor of the "good" humans. This story fits in with the Hyksos following Seth and, possibly, with the much later Sethian Gnostics.

The Great Mendes Stele

The flight of Typhon out of Egypt represents an archetypal theme within Egyptian or "Kamite" religion. An important interpretation of this idea follows along the lines of "as above, so below," with astrotheological connotation for the "coming out of Egypt":

---

[1] Keel and Uehlinger, 114.
[2] Keel and Uehlinger, 76.
[3] Keel and Uehlinger, 78, 96.

THE EXODUS AS MYTH

"*Coming out of Egypt*" is a Kamite expression for ascending from the lower to the upper heavens, which were divided in equinoctial signs.¹

The source of this contention is the Great Mendes Stele, as discussed in *Records of the Past* (8.91-92).

Found at Bulaq/Boulaq or Mendes/Tanen, the stele/stela was translated by Egyptologist Dr. Heinrich Karl Brugsch-Bey (1827-1894) and dated to the 32nd Dynasty (305-30 BCE). At the top of the stele is the typical solar winged-disk or *hut*, followed by an inscription:

> Hut, the great god, Lord of the heaven, the giver of beams, who comes out of the horizon on the side of Upper Egypt, and gives a pure life!²

Fig. 44. Great Mendes Stele, 3rd cent. BCE. Formerly in Bulaq Museum, Egypt

The other side refers to the "coming out of Lower Egypt,"³ the same region from which Moses and the Israelites likewise supposedly came out of that land. As we can see, the stele contains an emphasis on "coming out of Egypt," both the Upper (south) and Lower (north) sides, in this case representing the movement of the sun across the sky.

The Sun-Horus

Also depicted on the stele, as the "Great God of Mendes," is Horus in his form of Harpocrates, the Child, the morning sun, styled additionally Ra-Horakhti or "Horus of the Two Horizons." Like Hut, he is a solar deity, addressed on the stele thus:

> Long live the Sun-Horus, the strong youth, the Lord of the diadems, the glorious, the golden Horus, who has crowned his father, the King of Upper and Lower Egypt, the Lord of the country, the friend of Amen, to whom the Sun has granted victory, the Son of the Sun...⁴

Horus is called here the "Son of the Sun" and "Ptolemaios," reflecting the belief in the pharaoh Ptolemy II Philadelphius (309–246 BCE)⁵ as the living Horus. As such, he is also he "Who loves the Ram" and "whom the gods praise, whom the goddesses praise in his form of the Living Ram, who is rich in male power, who is the Prince of the Deities."⁶

---

¹ Massey (1883), 2.395.
² Birch, 8.91.
³ Birch, 8.92.
⁴ Birch, 8.95
⁵ Interestingly, Ptolemy II is the Egyptian ruler to whom the Indian emperor Ashoka purportedly sent his medical missionary Buddhist monks, according to the edicts. See my publication, *Michael Lockwood's Buddhism's Relation to Christianity Reviewed*.
⁶ Birch, 8.95

The Ram and Son of the Ram

In keeping with this ruminant theme, the Mendes stele contains a representation of a ram with a disk and horns, along with the inscription: "The sacred Ram-god, the Great God, the Life of Ra, the Generative Ram, the Prince of young women..." On this stele, we also read about the "holy Ram in the meadows of Mendes" who is the "Lord of the city of Mendes."[1]

On the other side is written, "The life, the Lord of the land, the Lord of might, Mer-Amen, the Son of Ra..." Brugsch-Bey notes that this part refers to Ptolemy II regarding the legend of the ram: "The King, the Ram, the Life of Ra, the Ram, the Life of Osiris, the Ram of Rams, the Prince of Princes..."[2]

The Horus-king is also called "This excellent god the image of the divine Ram," as well as the "divine efflux of the prolific Ram" and the "eldest son of the Ram, the creator of that which exists, who is enthroned in the seat of the Prince of the gods..."[3] Horus the Child is deemed the son of the ram god as well.[4]

As we can see, there is tremendous focus on the virile Ram, associated with divinity, the pharaoh and the sun. Throughout the Pentateuch too great emphasis is placed on the sacred ram, sacrificed on a variety of occasions in order to please and appease Yahweh, including all through the Exodus story.

In this regard, Orthodox Jewish rabbi Avraham Greenbaum recounts the tradition of the Exodus in the spring as occurring in the zodiacal sign of Aries:

> The Exodus from Egypt took place under the spring-time astrological sign of Aries, the Ram. In flagrant defiance of Egyptian worship of the Ram, the Children of Israel took their paschal lambs and slaughtered them as a sacrifice to *HaVaYaH*, showing that God alone rules in heaven and on earth.[5]

In this case, the Exodus would represent the movement of the sun out of the desolate winter signs into the promised land or meadows of spring.

The Exodus from Egypt of Osiris

As part of the "coming out of Egypt" tradition, Diodorus tells the story of Osiris leaving Egypt to travel to India, spreading viniculture along the way. The same tale of traveling to India is told of Osiris's Greek counterpart Dionysus or "Bacchus," said to have civilized a new land. Concerning Osiris's exodus from Egypt, Diodorus (1.17) remarks:

---

[1] Birch, 8.96.
[2] Birch, 8.92.
[3] Birch, 8.95.
[4] Hart, 44.
[5] Greenbaum, "From month to month."

THE EXODUS AS MYTH 201

It is moreover reported, that Osiris being a prince of a public spirit, and very ambitious of glory, raised a great army, with which he resolved to go through all parts of the world that were inhabited, and to teach men how to plant vines, and to sow wheat and barley. For he hoped that if he could civilize men, and take them off from their rude and beast-like course of lives, by such a public good and advantage, he should raise a foundation amongst all mankind...[1]

This evemeristic account of Osiris, whom Diodorus portrays at once as the sun and a historical person, may represent the garbling of astronomical myths. The notion of Osiris as a sort of "prince"[2] is noteworthy, since Moses has been styled a "prince of Egypt." In the Egyptian texts, Osiris, Horus and others are called by many divine epithets, including "Lord of lords," "King of kings" and "prince among princes."[3]

Like Dionysus, Osiris is associated with viniculture, and the two figures are identified clearly with each other in Diodorus's mind, who avers that the legendary Greek poet and prophet Orpheus brought Osiris worship to Greece and made the god into a Greek, Dionysus/Bacchus.[4]

In the Osiris-Dionysus myth, we see motifs similar to the Mosaic tale, including an origin in Egypt of a "prince" who leads an army of warriors on a civilizing journey, in the context of a divine mission.

Like Moses, Osiris is depicted as accompanied by his brother, according to Diodorus (1.17):

Then marching out of Egypt, he began his expedition, taking along with him his brother, whom the Greeks called Apollo....

It is said that two of his sons accompanied their father Osiris in this expedition, one called Anubis and the other Macedo, both valiant men...[5]

Light Bringer

Thus, as did Moses with Aaron, Osiris leaves Egypt with his brother Horus, the latter equated with Apollo, the sun, while Aaron

---

[1] Diodorus/Booth, 1.23-24. (See *The Study Guide* for the original Greek.) The word in Diodorus for "great army" is στρατόπεδον *stratopedon*, which means "army," as well as "camp," "encampment," associated with soldiers, as is the meaning of στρατός *stratos*, while πέδον *pedon* refers to "ground." Some form of στρατόπεδον *stratopedon* is used several times in the Septuagint (LXX Jos 4:3; Gen 12:7; Exod 13:20, 14:2, 10; Num 24:2; Deut 1:40; Pro 4:15), while *stratopedon* itself is employed at Jeremiah 48:12 (LXX 41:1).
[2] The word in Diodorus that Booth is rendering "prince of public spirit" is εὐεργετικὸν *euergetikon*, which means "a beneficent man," "benefactor" and "well-deserving man." (*OCGD*, 141) Here Osiris is a prince in the sense that he is an "outstanding member of a specified group," as in a "prince of a man."
[3] See, e.g., Murdock (2009), 320, etc.
[4] Diodorus/Booth, 1.29, 1.95. The epithet "Bacchus" has been asserted to designate the *resurrected* god. (See, e.g., "Dionysian mysteries" at *Wikipedia*.)
[5] Diodorus/Booth, 1.24. αὐτὸν δ᾽ ἐκ τῆς Αἰγύπτου μετὰ τῆς δυνάμεως ἀναζεῦξαι πρὸς τὴν στρατείαν, ἔχοντα μεθ᾽ αὑτοῦ καὶ τὸν ἀδελφόν, ὃν οἱ Ἕλληνες Ἀπόλλωνα καλοῦσιν.

(אהרון *'Aharown*) means "light bringer."[1] In this regard, the Latin word "Lucifer" and Hebrew הילל *heylel* likewise connote "light bearer,"[2] as does the Greek term "Phosphoros." This figure also was the Greek god Εωσφόρος Eosphoros—"dawn-bearer"—the morning aspect of the planet Venus, equated with the Canaanite god Shahar, whose twin brother, Shalim, was the evening aspect of Venus. It is noteworthy also that the term *'ar* or "light" "may be attested in texts from Ugarit as a component in personal names,"[3] predating the Bible by centuries.

Journey East

Osiris's exodus out of Egypt is even more impressive than that of Moses, in that the Egyptian god was said to have traveled also "through Ethiopia, all Arabia, India and Europe."[4]

Of Osiris we read further in Diodorus (1.19):

> Thence he passed through Arabia, bordering upon the Red sea as far as to India, and the utmost coasts that were inhabited; he built likewise many cities in India, one of which he called Nysa, willing to have a remembrance of that in Egypt where he was brought up....[5]

This account likewise sounds Mosaic, in that the route of the Exodus passes through the Red Sea along the southern coast, towards Arabia and India.

Along with the much larger scope of influence by the Osirian myth, another major difference is that, unlike Moses, who orders the slaughter of innocent men, women and children by the tens of thousands, Osiris "was not for war, nor came to fight battles, and to decide controversies by the sword, every country receiving him for his merits and virtues, as a god."[6]

The Exodus of Jesus

As we might expect in consideration of the numerous other parallels between Osiris and Jesus,[7] Jesus's pending death is described in the gospel of Luke (9:30-31) as an "exodus," rendered in the RSV as "departure":

---

[1] Strong's H175.
[2] Strong's H1966.
[3] Rahmouni, 125.
[4] Diodorus/Booth, 1.25.
[5] Diodorus/Booth, 1.26. Greek: ἔπειτα ποιήσασθαι τὴν πορείαν δι᾽ Ἀραβίας παρὰ τὴν Ἐρυθρὰν θάλατταν ἕως Ἰνδῶν καὶ τοῦ πέρατος τῆς οἰκουμένης. κτίσαι δὲ καὶ πόλεις οὐκ ὀλίγας ἐν Ἰνδοῖς, ἐν αἷς καὶ Νῦσαν ὀνομάσαι, βουλόμενον μνημεῖον ἀπολιπεῖν ἐκείνης καθ᾽ ἣν ἐτράφη κατ᾽ Αἴγυπτον. The "Red Sea" here is Ἐρυθρὰν θάλατταν *Erythran thalattan*, the accusative of ἐρυθρός *erythros* "red" (G2063) and θάλασσα *thalassa* (G2281), meaning "sea."
[6] Diodorus/Booth, 1.25.
[7] See, for example, my book *Christ in Egypt*.

THE EXODUS AS MYTH

And behold, two men talked with him, Moses and Eli'jah, who appeared in glory and spoke of his departure, which he was to accomplish at Jerusalem.

The pertinent pericope in the Greek is:

οἳ ὀφθέντες ἐν δόξῃ ἔλεγον τὴν ἔξοδον αὐτοῦ ἣν ἔμελλεν πληροῦν ἐν Ἰερουσαλήμ.

The relevant Greek term here is ἔξοδος *exodos/exodus*, which Strong's (G1841) defines as:

1) exit i.e. departure
2) the close of one's career, one's final fate
3) departure from life, decease

This word ἔξοδος *exodos* is used at Hebrews 11:22 to describe Moses's exodus as well, while at 2 Peter 1:15, the author speaks of his own coming demise as his exodos.

As concerns Jesus's exodus out of Egypt, the New Testament (1 Cor 10:4) identifies Christ as the supernatural "Rock" which accompanied the Israelites out of bondage into the wilderness and from which Moses drew the life-giving water. This motif is also reminiscent of Osiris's role as the water god.

Moreover, Yahweh is depicted as saying, "Out of Egypt have I called my son" (Hos 1:11), which refers to Jacob/Israel, but which Christian doctrine associates with Jesus (Mt 2:15). We are assured, therefore, that Christ led the Israelites out of Egypt. Hence, it is *his* Exodus in question as well. The Bible claims moreover that Jesus ended up in Egypt when his parents fled there during the massacre of the innocents by Herod. Hence, again he exits out of Egypt.

Pagan Exoduses

The term ἔξοδος *exodos* is translated also as "going out" and can be found in the ancient writings of Aristophanes, Aristides, Aristotle, Dionysius, Herodotus, Lucian, Pausanias, Plato, Plutarch, Strabo, Thucydides and Xenophon. In his *Clouds* (579), Greek playwright Aristophanes (c. 446-c. 386 BCE) uses ἔξοδος *exodos* in the sense of an "expedition." In *Lysistrata* (16), the playwright has one of his characters speak of women "getting away" from their daily labors and obligations,[1] conveying a sense of "fleeing."

In describing the scene of the Persian king Xerxes in the fifth century BCE following the Peneus River in Thessaly, Herodotus (7.130) says the ruler "asked his guides if there were any other outlet for the Peneus into the sea," the answer to which was no. The word here for "outlet" is ἔξοδος or exodus.

In the fourth century BCE, Plato (*Philebus* 33e) referred to forgetfulness as the "exodus of the memory,"[2] which he reiterated in

---

[1] Jack Lindsay translation.
[2] ἔστι γὰρ λήθη μνήμης ἔξοδος. (Plato, *Platonis Opera*, ed. John Burnet)

his *Symposium* (208a), remarking that "forgetfulness is an egress [exodus] of knowledge."[1] Other uses are rendered "way out," "exit" and "foray," as in the writings of Pausanias and Plutarch during the second century AD/CE. As we can see, the word "exodus" was common in antiquity, not limited to biblical myth.

The Exodus as Drama

Exodos has been used also to describe an element of a play, which seems appropriate for the unreal air of the biblical scenario. In his *Poetics* (12.1452b), the Greek sage Aristotle (384-322 BCE) defines *exodos* as part of a tragedy:

> We have already spoken of the constituent parts to be used as ingredients of tragedy. The separable members into which it is quantitatively divided are these: Prologue, Episode, Exode, Choral Song, the last being divided into Parode and Stasimon. These are common to all tragedies...[2]

It seems that Moses's Exodus is likewise part of a *play*, like the passion of Jesus and the rest of the gospel story, which is condensed into a short period and has many other elements indicative of a drama to be acted out. Similar ritual drama had been enacted in the stories of many divine figures before Jesus, including and especially Osiris and Dionysus.

Dionysian Drama

Indeed, Bacchus's myth would have been well known, as his proselytizing troops of devotees, styled "artists of Dionysus,"[3] traveled around the Mediterranean and beyond, putting on plays often in theaters especially constructed for the purpose.[4] Moreover, the priests and priestesses of other Greek cults, such as those of Zeus, Artemis and Apollo, would attend these religious plays, as part of sacred ritual.

In this way, Dionysian tradition and rituals became widespread and would have been known by Levantine peoples, including those who eventually became "Jews." The Bacchic artists' missionary acts

---

[1] λήθη γὰρ ἐπιστήμης ἔξοδος. (Plato/Burnet)
[2] The original Greek is: μέρη δὲ τραγῳδίας οἷς μὲν ὡς εἴδεσι δεῖ χρῆσθαι πρότερον εἴπομεν, κατὰ δὲ τὸ ποσὸν καὶ εἰς ἃ διαιρεῖται κεχωρισμένα τάδε ἐστίν, πρόλογος ἐπεισόδιον ἔξοδος χορικόν, καὶ τούτου τὸ μὲν πάροδος τὸ δὲ στάσιμον. (*Aristotle's Ars Poetica*, ed. R. Kassel) In the same passage, Aristotle explicates this element of a tragedy or play: "A prologue is the whole of that part of a tragedy which precedes the entrance of the chorus. An episode is the whole of that part of a tragedy which falls between whole choral songs. An exode is the whole of that part of a tragedy which is not followed by a song of the chorus. A parode is the whole of the first utterance of the chorus." ἔστιν δὲ πρόλογος μὲν μέρος ὅλον τραγῳδίας τὸ πρὸ χοροῦ παρόδου, ἐπεισόδιον δὲ μέρος ὅλον τραγῳδίας τὸ μεταξὺ ὅλων χορικῶν μελῶν, ἔξοδος δὲ μέρος ὅλον τραγῳδίας μεθ' ὃ οὐκ ἔστι χοροῦ μέλος· χορικοῦ δὲ πάροδος μὲν ἡ πρώτη λέξις ὅλη χοροῦ. (*Aristotle's Ars Poetica*, ed. R. Kassel)
[3] Easterling and Hall, 347.
[4] See, e.g., Meyer, M., 63.

resemble the later biblical "Great Commission" assigned to Jesus's disciples to spread the "good news" to much the same areas previously proselytized by the Dionysians (Mt 28:16-20).

Exodus as Midrash

In addition to emulating the myths of other cultures, as Jewish scribes had done in many other places of the Old Testament/Tanakh, the framers of the Exodus tale also may have utilized the pericope called "Second Isaiah" or "Deutero-Isaiah" for "the idea of an exodus from a land of oppression."[1] Deutero-Isaiah comprises the biblical passages of Isaiah 40-55, currently believed by scholarly consensus to have been written during and/or after the Babylonian period in the 6th century BCE. It appears that learned Jews who knew much of the Bible was allegory midrashically used Second Isaiah, among other texts, in order to create a mythical messiah, which is, in reality, Moses's role in saving the Israelites from bondage.

Other biblical texts possibly used to create the Exodus story include the Song of the Sea and Psalm 78, previously discussed, as well as Psalms 68 and 74, the latter at verses 13-15:

> Thou didst divide the sea by thy might; thou didst break the heads of the dragons on the waters. Thou didst crush the heads of Leviathan, thou didst give him as food for the creatures of the wilderness. Thou didst cleave open springs and brooks; thou didst dry up ever-flowing streams.

In this pericope alone we can see themes used by the creators of the Exodus myth, such as: the dividing of the sea; the "dragons/Leviathan" (Egyptians/pharaoh) destroyed; God-given food in the wilderness; cleaving open springs; and drying up streams, as in the conquest tale of Joshua crossing the Jordan dry-shod.

These and many other similar and relevant biblical passages do not represent a historical Exodus account but speak allegorically of the wonders of Yahweh, not Moses, in parting the sea and so on. It seems evident that such verses were used midrashically to create the Exodus tale and that the original villains of the story were the dragons and leviathans, discussed below.

Magical Rod

In producing assorted miracles, the prophet's rod is not unique but represents a magical stick used by a number of other mythical characters, such as the Greek god Mercury/Hermes:

> The caduceus or rod of Mercury is well known in poetic fables. It is another copy of the rod of Moses. He [Mercury/Hermes] is also reported to have wrought a multitude of miracles by this rod; and particularly he is said to kill and make alive, to send souls to the

---

[1] Wenham, 5. See also Van Seters (1994), 35-63. Dahoud points out that the author of Second Isaiah "firmly expresses his belief in the resurrection..." (Goedicke, 71)

invisible world and bring them back from thence. Homer represents Mercury taking his rod to work miracles, precisely in the same way as God commands Moses to take his.[1]

In this comparison, we see British theologian Rev. Dr. Adam Clarke (1760/2-1832) attempting to make the pagan account the copier of the Mosaic tale, when the opposite would be the case, or, perhaps, both drawing from the same, ancient mythical archetype.

The story of Hermes waking souls can be found in Homer's *Odyssey* (24.1):

> Now Cyllenian Hermes called forth from the halls the souls of the wooers, and he held in his hand his wand that is fair and golden, wherewith he lulls the eyes of men, of whomso he will, while others again he even wakens out of sleep.[2]

Fig. 45. Benjamin West, *The Brazen Serpent*, 1790. BJU Art Gallery and Museum, Greenville, SC

Thus, this motif existed in the literary record centuries before the Moses myth appears to have been composed. Again, if borrowing there be, it is from paganism to Judaism. Here the Greek word for "wand" is *rhabdos*, the same term used in the LXX to describe Moses's magical rod, to be discussed in detail later.

The 10 Plagues?

We have seen that the Exodus plagues could not have been historical. In his article "Redaction of the Plague Narrative in Exodus," biblical scholar and rabbi Dr. Moshe Greenberg (1928-2010) discusses the fact "there is considerable evidence that the present text is not of one piece."[3] Greenberg shows that the narrative was composed in stages, firstly with couplets totaling six plagues, to which were added the other four.[4] He also analyzes the fact that "some critics postulate three distinct narrative traditions in the plague story," citing P, J and E.[5] Greenberg concludes that the

---

[1] Clarke, 1.298.
[2] Butcher, 237. The original Greek is: Ἑρμῆς δὲ ψυχὰς Κυλλήνιος ἐξεκαλεῖτο ἀνδρῶν μνηστήρων· ἔχε δὲ ῥάβδον μετὰ χεροὶν καλὴν χρυσείην, τῇ τ' ἀνδρῶν ὄμματα θέλγει ὧν ἐθέλει, τοὺς δ'αὖτε καὶ ὑπνώοντας ἐγείρει. (Homer, *The Odyssey with an English Translation*)
[3] Goedicke, 245.
[4] Goedicke, 246, 250, etc.
[5] Goedicke, 247.

"plague narrative is the product of an elaborate growth of traditions..."[1]

The plaguing of humanity with some sort of disease or affliction is common throughout history, and such catastrophes frequently were attributed to divine intervention of one sort or another. If there is one or more omnipotent deity in charge of everything, it has been believed, it must be him (or them) causing the epidemic or disaster. Indeed, any number of gods or goddesses over the millennia have been blamed for natural disasters and diseases, including Seth/Baal, the god of the Hyksos and later Jewish sects. In this regard, we have seen already the suggestion that the plagues story emulates the pestilence of Typhon/Set.

Hence, the Exodus tale represents a literary device drawing upon the region's general worldview, via religious thinking. If one were trying to make an all-powerful God above the rest, one undoubtedly would ascribe a series of plagues to him or her alone, and if Yahweh is the god also of Seth-worshippers, it makes sense that the pestilence deity's attributes were attached to him and emphasized.

Pagan Divine Intervention

As in the Homeric epics, as well as so many other religious stories globally that involves divine intervention, the ancient gods were portrayed constantly as "messing around" with petty little humans. Again, the controlling of plagues by a deity is a relatively common motif in antiquity. For example, Pausanias (c. 110-180 AD/CE) repeatedly attributes either the staying or averting of plagues to various gods, including Apollo (1.3.4, 7.41.8, 8.41.8ff), Artemis (2.7.7ff), Hermes (9.22.1) and Pan (2.32.6).[2]

European historian Dr. Joseph P. Byrne summarizes this common motif:

> Epidemics were usually understood as having been let loose upon the world by supernatural forces: one or many gods, demons or spirits of the dead. In most cases, these heavenly beings were not seen as acting randomly but as responding to particular human actions that offended them.[3]

In this regard, we find several stories about plagues in Greece, especially one at Athens described by Thucydides, which allegedly killed the Athenian leader Pericles (c. 495-429 BCE). Byrne then names Latin writers Lucretius (99-55 BCE), Virgil (70-19 BCE) and Ovid (43 BCE-17 AD/CE) as utilizing the Athenian plague account in their own works. In this regard, Apollo in particular is highlighted, as the sun was considered to be the great healer against illness and

---
[1] Goedicke, 252.
[2] See *The Study Guide* for quotes by Pausanias in both English and Greek.
[3] Byrne, 594.

infirmity. Another famous episode of god-induced affliction occurs in the poem about Oedipus's patricide by the Greek writer Sophocles (496-406 BCE).[1]

Roman Pestilence

The Romans likewise kept records of pestilences, some of which were destroyed with the Celtic Gaul sacking of Rome in 390 BCE.[2] The later Roman writer Titus Livius or "Livy" (1.31) composed an account about one of Rome's early kings, Tullus Hostilius (fl. 673-641 BCE), who "brought a plague on the city and on himself because of his neglect of the gods, rendering both it [the city] and him afraid and ineffective."[3] Byrne further relates:

> A similar charge of bringing a plague on Rome as a result of religious impropriety was leveled at Scipio Aemelianus (censor in 142 BCE) by one of his rivals... As in many cultures, plague signaled to the Romans that their community was in some way out of favor with the gods, and that special consultation and communal action were required. Devastating plagues circa 436-33 BCE and circa 293 BCE induced the Romans to consult the Sibylline Books (a collection of mystic and prophetic writings attributed to oracular priestesses) and to take action through the dedications to Apollo the Healer in 433 BCE...and by bringing the cult of the healing god Asclepius to Rome and establishing it on Tibur island about 293 BCE... In both cases, these actions were said to have been immediately successful...
>
> Rome's story, however, is also one of nearly continual war, and numerous plagues and epidemic diseases played roles at different stages and at key moments in that story....
>
> In addition to accounts of historical plagues, plague became a kind of literary motif in Roman literature of the Golden Age (first century BCE...). Most authors...owe their descriptions and structure to the famous accounts of the Athenian plague (428-427 BCE) by the historian Thucydides (2.47-54)...[4]

As we can see, the blaming of plagues on gods and goddesses has been common, and religious propitiation is believed to be the remedy, which explains the establishment and installation of healing sects in various places. Such is the perspective also in the biblical accounts, which seek to appease Yahweh by means of mass sacrifices, by following the onerous law, as well as by numerous other measures.

The biblical composers of the fictional plagues story had much natural pestilence from which to draw as well, including locusts that continually swept through Egypt and Israel. Since plagues and epidemics often were recorded in antiquity, it is possible that there

---

[1] Byrne, 596-597.
[2] Byrne, 1.538.
[3] Byrne, 1.539.
[4] Byrne, 1.539-540.

were written texts of various pestilence accounts that the Bible writers utilized, perhaps during the Babylonian exile, if this part of the Exodus story was during that time.

Ra, Hathor and the Bloody Nile

In a myth similar to the biblical plague in which Egypt's water is turned to blood (Exod 7:14-25) but preceding the composition of that biblical myth by hundreds to thousands of years, the Egyptian sun god Ra sends his "divine eye" in the form of Hathor to punish the people for their treachery and rebellion against him. Hathor slaughters so many that their blood floods the Nile, turning it red. At this point, Ra repents and, in order to slake Hathor's bloodthirstiness, dyes a lake of beer blood red.[1] It is noteworthy that Hathor is a goddess of inebriation at whose festival the participants became intoxicated specifically with wine, in an act of "sacral drunkenness."[2]

Nergal the Pestilent

During the second millennium BCE, Mesopotamian scribes wrote about the Semitic underworld god Nergal, like the Greek deity of death Hades, "both benevolent and punitive," as a "protector of kings." He is also a "destroying flame" and "mighty storm," a "fearsome warrior god who looses war, pestilence and devastation upon the land."[3]

In a hymn from the Bronze Age entitled "An *adab* to Nergal for Šu-ilīšu" (39-53), we read:

> Lord of the underworld, who acts swiftly in everything, whose terrifying anger smites the wicked, Nergal, single-handed crusher, who tortures the disobedient, fearsome terror of the Land, respected lord and hero, Nergal, you pour their blood down the wadis [gullies] like rain. You afflict all the wicked peoples with woe, and deprive all of them of their lives.[4]

Nergal sounds very much like the later biblical Yahweh, as represented in many biblical verses.

Storm God of Hatti

We find other "plague prayers" in Hittite writings from the 14th century BCE, centuries before the Exodus story was written down, by this Indo-European ethnicity who thrived for centuries in the Levant. One of these prayers was spoken by a "priest of the gods," the Hittite king Mursilis II (fl. c. 1321-1295 BCE), who complained to the "stormgod of Hatti" that a pestilence had been causing "constant dying" for some 20 years. "Will the plague never be eliminated from

---

[1] Moret, 372; Armour, 88. (See also "Mythicist Milwaukee.")
[2] Bleeker, 91.
[3] Byrne, 594.
[4] Byrne, 595.

the land of Hatti?" he asks desperately.[1] It has been suggested that prisoners of war brought the plague to Mursilis's land.

Rešef of Canaan

An even more direct precedent for Yahweh as pestilence god is the Canaanite/Ugaritic underworld deity Rešef, as discussed in the Ras Shamra texts.[2] Rešef is portrayed wearing the horns of a gazelle, resembling depictions of Amun, Baal, Dionysus, Moses, Pan and others. In this regard, speaking of "bulls" and "gazelles" in a Ugaritic composition from Ras Shamra the *Krt Text* who may represent human officials, Gray remarks that they were likely "priests" and that they may represent Baal, "whose cult animal was the bull, and Rešef, who is represented with a head-dress mounted with gazelle-horns."[3]

Gray further states that the "bulls" were "seventy in number" and possibly reflect a priestly order of Baal, whose "cult animal was the bull and who is represented by bull's horns on his helmet."[4] The seventy (70) are prominent also in a text discussing the slaughter of oxen, sheep, goats, asses and other animals to Baal, as offerings at his funeral.[5] Seventy also is the number of the Canaanite Elohim, "gods" or "sons of El," discussed below.

Rešef was revered during the eighth century in the Aramaean states of Syria, also included in a Phoenician inscription that portrays him as "Reshef of the Bucks."[6] Hence, his worship extends from before the Bible was written and well into the time when the Jews first emerged as a separate tribe, constituting a direct cultural precedent.

As we can see, it was a common mythical religious theme to blame the actions of a people for a pestilence or disaster striking them. If one were to write a divine intervention story of deliverance, the plagues would fit in as a mythical or allegorical literary device. It is possible that the biblical composers drew from such sources as the Egyptian, Babylonian, Canaanite and Hittite plague and pestilence tales or a prevalent archetype that influenced them all.

Three Days of Darkness

One of the biblical plagues, the motif of three days of darkness, sounds as if it has been taken from a solar myth, in which the sun is deemed at the winter solstice both to "stand still" for three days and to be in the "womb of the night," as the days are the shortest of the

---

[1] Byrne, 595. See also Singer, It., 57ff.
[2] Gray, 133, 227.
[3] Gray, 147.
[4] Gray, 227.
[5] Gray, 301-302, citing Gordon *UH* 62, 18-29.
[6] Gray, 133.

THE EXODUS AS MYTH

year. In a similar vein, the theme of the sun standing still in the biblical story of Joshua (Jos 10:12-13), as well as Moses in the Talmud,[1] also represents the solstice, from the Latin words *sol* and *sistere*, meaning "sun stands still."

Rather than serving as a special instance of Yahweh's wrath, the Exodus plagues constitute but one such biblical episode, as the Good Book is full of such divine retribution, against both the enemies of the Israelites and the chosen themselves. Some of the historical plagues in the Levant during the centuries prior to the myth's composition could have been used in the text,[2] along with the observation of muddy, red waters in flooded rivers like the Adonis or Nile, but these facts still would not make the Exodus itself a "true story."

Fig. 46. Joshua commanding the sun to stand still. (*Treasures of the Bible*, 1894)

600,000 as a Mystical Number

We have seen that the Exodus itself could not have happened as described in the Old Testament and that the motif is mythical. As such, its elements are not literal history but, rather, allegorical, metaphorical, mythical and fictional. In this regard, there exists no credible, scientific evidence of the enslavement in Egypt of a massive number of Israelites, including the supposed 600,000 Israelite warriors.

In Numbers 1, Yahweh orders a painstaking census of all the Israelite males, a feat that would take a considerable amount of time and energy, in the midst of all the other chores assigned to the chosen. Since the number arrived upon (Num 1:46) was the exact figure as in the original Exodus, 603,550 men (Exod 38:26), it remains inexplicable why the all-knowing Yahweh would waste the time of his people in such a futile exercise.

The number appears to be symbolic, rather than actual, rounded off to represent 600,000, with sacred numerological significance. This understanding is common enough to appear in the article on "The Exodus" at *Wikipedia*:

---

[1] Babylonian Talmud, Tractate ʽAbodah Zarah Folio 25a: "A Tanna taught: Just as the sun stood still for Joshua, so did the sun stand still for Moses and for Nakdimon b. Gorion." (Epstein, 125)

[2] Sivertsen's speculative book proposing to demonstrate historicity behind Moses and the Exodus includes discussion of the bubonic plague as a "hitherto unsuspected factor in the fall of Canaanite cities and towns at the end of the Middle Bronze Age," along with malaria, which "played a role in the population increase of the Israelites relative to their lowland Canaanite neighbors in the Late Bronze Age." (Sivertsen, 150)

No evidence has been found that indicates Egypt ever suffered such a demographic and economic catastrophe or that the Sinai desert ever hosted (or could have hosted) these millions of people and their herds. Some scholars have rationalised these numbers into smaller figures, for example reading the Hebrew as "600 families" rather than 600,000 men, but all such solutions raise more problems than they solve. The view of mainstream modern biblical scholarship is that the improbability of the Exodus story originates because it was written not as history, but to demonstrate God's purpose and deeds with his Chosen People, Israel. Thus it seems probable that the 603,550 people delivered from Egypt (according to Numbers 1:46) is not simply a number, but a gematria (a code in which numbers represent letters or words) for *bnei yisra'el kol rosh*, "the children of Israel, every individual..."

Rather than representing an improbable amount of "real people," the biblical number 600,000 evidently constitutes a mystical figure, designed for magical purposes, such as a gematria or numerical code. This fact would negate also the argument, previously noted, that the Hebrew word אלף *'eleph*, usually translated as "thousand," connotes also "group" or "troops," indicating possibly a much smaller force. This apology is inconsistent with Jewish tradition and other writings, such as the Kabbalah.

The Kabbalah

In the Kabbalah, we find the 600,000 "letters," "aspects and meanings" and "interpretations" of the Torah. We also read about the "Six Hundred Thousand Souls," obviously an allegorical number of importance in mystical Judaism, ostensibly based on its significance in the Exodus.[1] As Rabbi Avraham Yaakov Finkel (b. 1926) states:

> There are 600,000 souls in the heavenly realm; these souls are the roots of all the souls of Israel. Each soul is made up of two parts, that is, each soul has an upper part that stays in heaven while its counterpart down below [in this world] inhabits the human body.... the souls of all the Jews are rooted in the 600,000 heavenly souls.[2]

The Kabbalah as a text is a later innovation; however, a significant portion of it, such as this concept, represents a continuation of ancient Judaic ideas, among others.

Jewish mysticism expert Dr. Gershom Gerhard Scholem (1897-1982) describes kabbalistic notions of the 600,000:

> They started from the old conception that the souls of Israel who went out of Egypt and received the Torah at Mount Sinai numbered 600,000. According to the laws of transmigration and the

---

[1] *Likutei Moharan* 119b: "The sum total of all Jewish souls in this world is 600,000. Of course, there are more than 600,000 souls, but the additional souls are offshoots of the 600,000 primary souls." (Finkel, 342-343.)
[2] Finkel, 255.

THE EXODUS AS MYTH

distribution of the sparks into which the soul disintegrates, these 600,000 primordial souls are present in every generation of Israel.[1]

To summarize this latter perspective of historicized allegory: "The 600,000 men who came up out of Egypt as Hebrew warriors in the Book of Exodus are 600,000 inhabitants of Israel in the heavens according to the Jewish *Kabalah...*"[2]

Thus, the number represents not simply one purportedly historical event but an ongoing aspect of mystical Judaism. The question remains, since the Exodus is clearly a mythical event, did the 600,000 exist as a mystical number deliberately utilized in the fictional account of Exodus because of its *prior* importance?

The Papyrus of Nebseni

Egyptian mythology is perhaps one source of the pre-biblical 600,000 "souls":

> In the Papyrus of Nebseni, the number of the Khus or spirits is reckoned as "four millions, six hundred thousand, and two hundred" (Rit., ch. 64, Papyrus of Nebseni).[3]

The Papyrus of Nebseni (BM EA 9900) is a version of the *Egyptian Book of the Dead* named for its scribe in the 18th Dynasty (c. 1587 BCE).

In the Papyrus of Ani version of the *Book of the Dead*, the numbers are not specified, as the "glorified" are simply "millions and hundreds of thousands." Egyptologist Sir Peter Renouf's translation of the Papyrus of Ani, chapter 64, includes an interesting sentence: "'I know the deep waters' is my name."[4] Thus, we see a reference to "deep waters," in Hebrew called תהום *tehom*, connoting "abyss." (Gen 1:2) This *Book of the Dead* chapter in general sounds biblical, reminiscent of parts of the much later book of Revelation.

British Egyptologist Dr. E.A. Wallis Budge (1857-1934) asserts that chapter/spell 64 is "probably one of the oldest of all..." In his edition of the Papyrus of Nebseni, we read:

> ..."I know the abysses" is thy name. I work for you, O ye *Khus*—four millions, six-hundred thousand, one thousand and two hundred are they... [I am] over their affairs working for hours and days in setting straight the shoulders of the twelve Saḥ gods and joining the hands of their company...[5]

---

[1] Scholem, 65.
[2] Massey (2007), 1.xi. See also Massey's extensive discussion of the Book of Enoch as a fictional text representing Jewish "history," including the Exodus, taking place allegorically. (Massey, 2007:2.216)
[3] Massey (1907), 2.720.
[4] Renouf, 119. Goelet (106) renders this passage: "I know the depths and I know your name."
[5] Budge (1898), 114.

Here we see familiar themes, such as "abysses" and a dozen gods, as well as the number 600,000 as a unit of *Khus* or "spirits."

The Khus or Spirits

The *khus* are mentioned throughout the *Book of the Dead*, especially as part of discussions about the Elysian or Elysium fields or heaven.[1] In the same passage of chapter 64, we read that the deceased, as the "Lord of Life," requests to "soar like a bird to see the companies(?) of the *Khus* in the presence of Rā day by day, who vivifieth every human being that walketh upon the regions which are upon the earth."[2] Thus, the *khus* are associated with the sun god; hence, Ra and the 600,000 could be identified with the solar Moses and the Israelites in the heavenly Promised Land.

Elsewhere the *khus* or "shining" parts of the "spiritual body" are "wards" who dwell with the gods in heaven, also the underworld or *tuat*.[3] American Egyptologist Dr. Ogden Goelet renders the *khus* as "bright expanses of gloriousness,"[4] evidently reflecting the heavens and/or their starry occupants. Also sounding stellar, they are additionally children of the gods, imperishable and indestructible.[5] The *khus* likewise resemble the "ten thousands of holy ones" that accompany the sun as it emerges from its nightly cavern. As we have seen, these "holy ones" apparently represent the stars.

In "A Hymn to the Setting Sun" from the Papyrus of Mut-ḥetep (BM No. 10,010), we read that every *khu* "shall come forth by day" and "shall gain power among the gods of the Tuat (underworld), and they shall recognize him as one of themselves; and he shall enter in at the hidden gate with power."[6] The setting sun in this hymn, Ra-Tem, is "adored by the gods and by the *Khus* in the underworld." Thus, it is to the *khus* in the heavenly fields that the "great god" appears,[7] much like Yahweh catering to Moses and his 600,000.

We also read in the Egyptian texts about the "maker of the gods," who "didst stretch out the heavens" and "make the earth to be a vast chamber for thy *Khus*..."[8] Again, we see various solar and stellar themes, including the heavens and the earth as a chamber, like the womb or underworld of the night. There are also references to "seven *Khus*," appointed by the underworld god Anubis as protectors of Osiris's corpse as it is being prepared for resurrection.[9]

---

[1] Budge (1898), cxxiii.
[2] Budge (1898), 114.
[3] Budge (1898), lxxxix, 40.
[4] Goelet, 106.
[5] Budge (1898), cxxvii, cxxix, cxxxii.
[6] Budge (1898), 40.
[7] Budge (1898), 43.
[8] Budge (1898), 44.
[9] Budge (1898), 47, 53.

Khu Cakes

The *khus* are offered cakes, which must not be stolen, as one must testify in the Hall of Maat not to have done so, in the famous spell 125 of the *Book of the Dead*:

> I have not purloined the cakes of the gods. I have not carried off the cakes offered to the *khus*.[1]

The cakes of the gods and glorified spirits sound similar to the manna from heaven for the chosen people.

Many of these themes are central to Egyptian religion, and it is likely that educated Jewish priests and scribes were aware of them. Indeed, these metaphysical and allegorical attributes fit in well with the kabbalistic interpretation of Israelite 600,000 as "heavenly souls."

It should also be noted that the *Book of the Dead* in one form or another was transmitted by copyists from its earliest appearance in the 16th century BCE to the Roman period, around 50 BCE, eventually widely available to priests and the common people alike of various cultures.

Cyrus the Christ

At Isaiah 45:1, the Persian king Cyrus (600/576-530 BCE) is celebrated as the "Lord's anointed" or *Christ*, as the word appears in the Septuagint:

οὕτως λέγει κύριος ὁ θεὸς τῷ χριστῷ μου Κύρῳ

Thus says the LORD God to his [my] Christ, to Cyrus[2]

The original Hebrew for "Christos" is מָשִׁיחַ *mashiyach*, "Messiah."

Cyrus was said to have employed 600,000 foot soldiers in his assault on Babylon that supposedly freed the Jews in Exile.[3] It could be that this number in the Exodus was struck upon also as a commemoration of that event of freedom from bondage, if its inclusion postdates the Cyrus story, or that the number in the Cyrus tale is likewise more of the same "sacred numerology" storytelling.

Either way, it is possible the Exodus account echoes in part or draws from this situation with the messiah Cyrus, who became a beloved figure in Jewish tradition for supposedly freeing the Jews from captivity. This purported escape from Babylon could also be construed as a divinely ordained exodus event.

There has been skepticism as to the historicity of the Cyrus tale as well, as some Jews may have resided voluntarily in Babylon, studying at the university and/or libraries there, while the "Lost Tribes" story seems to have been exaggerated in order to explain why

---

[1] Budge (1898), 191.
[2] My literal translation. The Greek word μου *mou* means "my," and, in the Vulgate, Jerome renders the passage thus: *haec dicit Dominus christo meo Cyro*. Here we see the word *meo*, connoting "my": "Thus says the Lord to my Christ Cyrus."
[3] Rollin, 1.315; Xenophon, *Cyropedia* (8.6.19; 6:419, 421).

the northern kingdom worshipped differently from the southern kingdom.

In any event, Cyrus the Christ, savior of the Jews, is depicted as wandering in the wilderness with 600,000 men. The Moses episode could have incorporated some of Cyrus's legend into it as well, or both could have drawn from the same mythical motif.

Like Cyrus before him, Alexander the Great was also said to have "six hundred thousand horsemen" during his campaign.[1] Rather than representing historical Hebrew forces, this number again appears to have significance on its own, including and especially when describing righteous warriors, heavenly armies or spiritual souls of some manner.

Mythical Pillars

It has been shown that the story of Yahweh's pillars of cloud and fire cannot be taken as literal history. Describing the appearance of the biblical pillar of fire and the subsequent routing of the Egyptians, in his *Miscellanies* (1.24) early Church father Clement of Alexandria (2nd-3rd cents. AD/CE) asserts that the Greeks borrowed this fiery military strategy:

> Perceiving this, Miltiades [c. 550-489 BCE], the Athenian general, who conquered the Persians in battle at Marathon, imitated it in the following fashion. Marching over a trackless desert, he led on the Athenians by night, and eluded the barbarians that were set to watch him....
>
> ...when Thrasybulus [d. 388 BCE] was bringing back the exiles from Phyla, and wished to elude observation, a pillar became his guide as he marched over a trackless region. To Thrasybulus by night, the sky being moonless and stormy, a fire appeared leading the way, which, having conducted them safely, left them near Munychia, where is now the altar of the light-bringer (Phosphorus) [Venus].
>
> From such an instance, therefore, let our accounts become credible for the Greeks, namely, that it was possible for the omnipotent God to make the pillar of fire, which was their guide on their march, go before the Hebrews by night. It is said also in a certain oracle, "A pillar to the Thebans is joy-inspiring Bacchus..."[2]

Clement contends that, on several occasions, the pagans adopted this pillar motif from the Hebrew scriptures, thus making a firm association between the two. In fact, the Church father essentially equates Yahweh's pillar with "Dionysus the pillar," to be discussed. We would do likewise, averring, however, that the biblical scribe(s) borrowed the more ancient *pagan* mythical motif and reworked it to revolve around the Israelites.

---

[1] Budge (2003), 397, 429.
[2] Roberts, 4.457-458. See also Snell, B., 77.

Parting and Crossing the Sea

The miraculous "parting of the Red Sea" and crossing it dryshod has mystified the credulous masses and sober scholars alike, who have put forth all sorts of speculation to explain it. However, as demonstrated, the parting of the waters and destruction of the pharaoh's hosts at the Red Sea are not recorded by any known historian, an understandable situation, since these themes are not historical but, again, are found in other cultures as *myth.*

This cosmological motif took on many forms in the Levant. As but one example, Moses's "miracle of drying up the waters to travel dry-shod was earlier performed by Isis, or Hathor, on her way to Byblos."[1] So too did Gilgamesh cross an impassable sea as he traveled along the path of the sun: "The hero stands at the entrance to the Waters of Death, which are supposed to surround the ocean. The 'Isle of the Blessed' is thought to be beyond these Waters of Death, just as in the case of the Netherworld."[2]

Ishtar and the Watery Gate

As another early example, in the legend of her descent into the underworld, appearing in the Sumero-Babylonian texts dating to at least the Late Bronze Age, the Babylonian goddess Ishtar is also portrayed as "parting the waters":

> Ishtar, on arriving at the gate of Hades,
> to the keeper of the gate addresses the word:
> "Opener (keeper) of the waters, open thy gate!
> Open thy gate that I may enter!..."[3]

The biblical tale may have been cobbled together from these tales as well as from Old Testament writings such as Isaiah 19:5, in which an "oracle" predicts Yahweh as saying, "And the waters of the Nile will be dried up, and the river will be parched and dry..." Much of Isaiah 19, in fact, appears to have been used by the writers of pentateuchal tales, as it repeats themes much like the Exodus without any indication of knowledge of Moses or the Exodus events as "history."

Sinuhe Crossing the Waterway

Yet another flight out of Egypt specifically across a waterway occurs in the popular Egyptian tale called, "The Story of Sinuhe," accepted by most scholars as a fictional account but nonetheless containing parallels to much later biblical narratives.

In this tale, the "son of the Sycamore," as the name Sinuhe means, flees King Amenemhet I (1991-1962 BCE) into Canaan, where he teams up with the local chief and fathers future chieftains. In his

---

[1] Walker (1983), 96.
[2] *Epic of Gilgamesh* 10.
[3] Sayce, 221.

elderhood, Sinuhe longs to return to Egypt and, after making a prayer, is invited back by the pharaoh of the time, Senwosret I, son of Amenemhet I. Sinuhe subsequently returns to Egypt, where he dies and is buried in a "beautiful tomb."

Like Moses, Sinuhe not only escapes Egypt across the waters but also is considered to be under divine providence: "On fleeing Egypt, Sinuhe crosses a waterway associated with the Goddess Maat, the Ancient Egyptian principle of truth, order and justice, in the vicinity of a sycamore tree."[1]

The Sinuhe narrative likewise has been compared to the biblical story of Joseph, who, after being forced into a strange land, was adopted into the royal class. Whether or not this story could have been used in the creation of comparable biblical tales might depend on its continual popularity for a thousand years or more, until the composition of the Bible.

The oldest extant manuscript of the Sinuhe tale dates from around 1800 BCE, preceding the purported time of Moses and the Exodus by hundreds of years and equivalent to the *Epic of Gilgamesh*. There are many other surviving fragments of this tale, demonstrating its ongoing appeal, and it is possible that elements of it ended up as folklore recorded in the later biblical texts.

While it may have been used in the creation of the Exodus myth, this account itself cannot be deemed historical. As German Egyptologist Dr. Hans-W. Fisher-Elfert states:

> Tales like those of "Sinuhe" or the "Eloquent Peasant" do not seem to have been connected to any single authentic or "historical" narrator.[2]

In any event, to reiterate, as is the Exodus theme in general, the biblical motif of parting and/or passing over water is not original.

Rama's Bridge

Another miraculous escape across a waterway occurs in the mythology of Ceylon/Sri Lanka, out of which the conquering shepherd kings from Rajputana or Afghanistan legendarily were driven across "Rama's Bridge," also known as "Adam's Bridge," and drowned.[3] In a similar vein, although it has been asserted as the meaning of "Hyksos," the phrase "shepherd king" would be more appropriate for the *pharaohs*,

Fig. 47. 'Rama's Bridge' between India (top) and Sri Lanka (bottom). (NASA)

---

[1] "Story of Sinuhe," *Wikipedia*.
[2] Tait, 120.
[3] Kapur, 217; de Silva, 291; Higgins, 2.634.

who were god-kings holding the shepherd's crook and serving as the "Good Shepherd."[1]

Coincidentally, the name of the island forming the first link in Rama/Adam's Bridge from the Indian mainland to Sri Lanka is "Rameswaram," which resembles Ramses or Ramesses, and derives from the name of the deity *Rama* and *iswar*, meaning "god."[2] Indian myth thus states that the god Rama crossed a sea via "Rama's Bridge," while Judeo-Christian tradition posits that the god-king Ramesses attempted to pass through the Red Sea by virtue of "Moses's Bridge," so to speak. The Egyptian name Ramesses or Ramses comes from the god Ra and *ms*, meaning "born of (the god) Ra," which is not much different from the moniker denoting "the god Rama." This comparison is not indicated etymologically, and there certainly was a series of historical Ramesses, but this coincidence remains intriguing.

Indian Jews

In a number of instances, it seems that very old mythical germs can be found in both the Indian and Egyptian cultures, which share many other attributes, as do the Indian and Jewish. Indeed, there are several reasons to aver that the "Abrahamites" represent a tribe of Semitic Brahma followers who migrated to what became Israel, via Ur, possibly from India. Not the least of these reasons is the comparison between Abraham and the god Brahma, particularly in consideration of the fact that the same name was found at Ebla in tablets from the 23rd century BCE.

Also highly suggestive is the remark by Aristotle, according to Josephus (*Ap.* 1.22/1.179), that the Jews were the remnants of ancient Indian philosophers styled Καλανοί *Kalanoi*, commonly rendered "Calami" or "Calani," and "Judaei" by the Syrians.[3] Moreover, we know that trading between Sumer and the Indus Valley occurred as early as the third millennium BCE,[4] with human

---

[1] See my book *Christ in Egypt* (310-312) for more information about the Egyptian role of the sun as the "unique shepherd, who protects his flock" (Assmann 1995:86), as well as the perception of the pharaoh as the "lord of the flocks" and "good shepherd."
[2] Eastwick, 716.
[3] Josephus/Whitson, 615. Josephus's original Greek is: κἀκεῖνος τοίνυν τὸ μὲν γένος ἦν Ἰουδαῖος ἐκ τῆς κοίλης Συρίας. οὗτοι δέ εἰσιν ἀπόγονοι τῶν ἐν Ἰνδοῖς φιλοσόφων, καλοῦνται δέ, ὥς φασιν, οἱ φιλόσοφοι παρὰ μὲν Ἰνδοῖς Καλανοί, παρὰ δὲ Σύροις Ἰουδαῖοι τοὔνομα λαβόντες ἀπὸ τοῦ τόπου: προσαγορεύεται γὰρ ὃν κατοικοῦσι τόπον Ἰουδαία. τὸ δὲ τῆς πόλεως αὐτῶν ὄνομα πάνυ σκολιόν ἐστιν: Ἱερουσαλήμην γὰρ αὐτὴν καλοῦσιν. (Josephus, Flavius. *Flavii Iosephi opera*. B. Niese. Berlin: Weidmann, 1892.)
[4] "There is extensive presence of Harappan seals and cubical weight measures in Mesopotamian urban sites.... A number of these Indus Valley seals have been found at Ur..." ("Meluhha") Since DNA testing indicates much of humanity emanated from India beginning tens of thousands of years ago and for millennia afterwards, including Indo-European culture and language, it is scientific to ask whether or not biblical religion is influenced by Indian philosophy. Many studies over the centuries have demonstrated numerous correspondences in Near Eastern and Indian religion and mythology.

settlement in the Indus possibly as early as 7,500 years ago.[1] There is little reason to insist that there were no shared, borrowed or exchanged religious beliefs in these regions during these many thousands of years.

It is also possible that, during this era, some Semites ended up in the Indus Valley along with any Sumerians, and that sometime later a tribe of them moved back into the Mesopotamian region to become "Abrahamites." These then may have moved into the Levant and mingled with other Semites there, acquiring attributes of other deities and having their tribal god Brahma demoted to a patriarch. This movement might explain Aristotle's Jewish Indian philosophers.

Moreover, Indo-European tribes such as the Hittites and Mitanni also thrived in the Levant for centuries, the latter of whom worshipping Indian deities.

Alexander and Cyprus

Josephus (*Ant.* 2.16.5/2.348) relates another sea crossing, when the Pamphylian Sea "retired" and afforded passage to Alexander and his troops, because it was the "will of God to destroy the monarchy of the Persians..."[2]

Strabo (14.6.3) tells a story also about the Pamphylian Sea and the island of Cyprus, recalling a scene similar to the crossing of a sea in the same region while chased by "arrows." The historian recounts that a poet, whom he surmises to be Hedylus (3rd cent. BCE), wrote about a voyage from the Cilician shore to the beach of Curias on Cyprus, across the "impassable sea," referring to the area of the Mediterranean between that island and the southern coast of Turkey:

> ...we hinds, sacred to Phoebus, racing across many billows, came hither in our swift course to escape the arrows of our pursuers...it is a matter of untold amazement to men to think how we ran across the impassable stream by the aid of a vernal west wind...[3]

The mythical passage across a body of water can be found in the Americas as well, as in the Maya story recorded in the *Popol Vuh* regarding the tribes that "crossed the sea, the waters having parted when they passed," reflecting the ancestral exodus from the homeland of Tulán.[4] This mythical motif, therefore, evidently reflects an archetype that dates back many thousands of years, possibly accompanying various peoples as they migrated out of Africa and into the Near, Middle and Far East.

---

[1] See Overdorf, "Archaeologists confirm Indian civilization is 2000 years older than previously believed."
[2] Josephus/Whiston, 64-65.
[3] Strabo/Jones.
[4] Hallet, 281; Goetz, 183.

The 12 Watery Divisions

Adding to the mythical notion of the parting of the Red Sea is the idea from antiquity that the waters were divided into 12 sections, representing the 12 tribes:

> The Targum of Jonathan says, the waters were divided into twelve parts, answerable to the twelve tribes of Israel, and the same is observed by other Jewish writers...grounded upon a passage in Psalm 136:13 and suppose that each tribe took its particular path.[1]

It should be recalled that the division of 12 in ancient mythology after the first millennium BCE often had to do with the zodiacal signs, to be discussed.

Controlling the Waters

As can be seen, the theme of sea/water crossing is not original or unique to the Exodus story, and there are many other ancient stories of legendary figures doing likewise,[2] reflecting the mythical motif of controlling "unruly waters." As part of these controlling-the-waters cycles, we find stories of battles between divine heroes and sea monsters around the Mediterranean.

Baal and Prince Sea/Judge River

In its description of the Exodus tale, *The Oxford Companion to the Bible* refers to the story as "embellished" and "mythological," using the ancient pre-Israelite core myth of the battle between the storm god and the sea:

> Embellishment, heightening and exaggeration can also be observed... in the Septuagint, the Hebrew phrase meaning "sea of reeds" is translated as "Red Sea," further enhancing the miracle. Likewise, the number of those escaping, according to Exodus 1.15 a small group whose obstetrical needs could be handled by only two midwives, becomes six hundred thousand men, as well as women and children (Exod. 12.37), an impossible population of several million.

> Another tendency is to mythologize. The escape of the Hebrews at the sea is recast as a historical enactment of an ancient cosmologonic myth of a battle between the storm god and the sea, found also in biblical texts having to do with creation (Job 26.12-13; Jer. 31.35; Pss. 74.12-17; 89.9-12; 93; 104...). This mythology is explicitly applied to the Exodus in Psalm 114, where the adversaries of the deity are the personified Sea and Jordan River, who flee at God's approach at the head of Israel...; Sea and Jordan are clearly related to Prince Sea and Judge River, the parallel titles of the adversary of the Canaanite storm god Baal in Ugaritic mythology (note the echoes of this motif in the New Testament, in such passages as Mark 4.35-41 par.; Rev. 21.1).[3]

---

[1] *Gill's Exposition*, citing "Pirke Eliezer, c. 42. Targum Jon. & Hieros. in Deut. i. 1. Jarchi, Kimchi, and Arama in Psal. cxxxvi. 13."
[2] See also Murdock (2009), 293ff.
[3] Metzger, 210.

Here we see the learned opinion that the Exodus, if originally a small historical event, has been embellished straight out of the myths of the Canaanites, specifically as concerns the battle between Baal and "Prince Sea" or "Judge River," personified natural elements.[1] From what has been demonstrated here, however, the Exodus is not a historical event with mythical additions but a pre-Israelite myth historicized. Gray suggests this myth represents the annual festival celebrating the "agricultural new year."[2]

As part of this literalization of myths, Psalm 114 states:

> When Israel went forth from Egypt, the house of Jacob from a people of strange language, Judah became his sanctuary, Israel his dominion. The sea looked and fled, Jordan turned back. The mountains skipped like rams, the hills like lambs. What ails you, O sea, that you flee? O Jordan, that you turn back? O mountains, that you skip like rams? O hills, like lambs? Tremble, O earth, at the presence of the LORD, at the presence of the God of Jacob, who turns the rock into a pool of water, the flint into a spring of water.

In this pericope appears the personified sea fleeing, as well as a rock-to-water miracle, both of which motifs are put in the context of the Exodus from Egypt. The word here for "sea" is ים *yam*, which a Semitic speaker might recognize also as the sea god Yamm, particularly if personified, as in this biblical verse. "Jordan" refers to the river, which is yet another body of water, one localized to Israel, across which the Israelites led by Joshua were said to walk dryshod,[3] a motif possibly based midrashically on Psalm 114.

In any event, we can see that Baal versus Yamm is equivalent to Yahweh/Moses controlling Yam. This psalm also contains the miracle of producing water from a rock, credited in antiquity not only to the god of Jacob and/or to Moses but also to deities of other cultures. Its presence in this psalm—attributed not to Moses but to Yahweh—underscores its allegorical or mythical nature.

Another example of Yahwistic control of the rivers and sea appears at Habakkuk 3:8:

> Was thy wrath against the rivers, O LORD? Was thy anger against the rivers, or thy indignation against the sea, when thou didst ride upon thy horses, upon thy chariot of victory?[4]

---

[1] See, e.g., Rahmouni, 123.
[2] Gray, 11.
[3] Joshua 3:13: "And when the soles of the feet of the priests who bear the ark of the LORD, the Lord of all the earth, shall rest in the waters of the Jordan, the waters of the Jordan shall be stopped from flowing, and the waters coming down from above shall stand in one heap."
[4] In this same Old Testament book (Hab 3:13), the prophet praises the Lord going "forth for the salvation of thy people, for the salvation of thy anointed." The Hebrew here for "salvation" is ישע *yesha*, essentially the same as ישוע *Yeshua* (H3443) or "Jesus," while "anointed" is משיח *mashiyach* or messiah, which is χριστός *christos* or "Christ" in the LXX. Hence, in this pre-Christian verse we have basically a "Jesus

Like Psalm 114 and many other biblical verses, this passage sounds much like a nonhistorical, mythical and astrotheological core struck upon by the Pentateuchal composers of the Exodus tale, who turned it into "history."

Heroes and Monsters

Thus, rather than serving as an "historical event," the Moses tale apparently represents in significant part the ancient motif of the sun and storm god battling the sea and/or controlling the waters, as found in the Sumero-Babylonian, Egyptian, Greek, Phoenician and Ugaritic/Canaanite myths of the eastern Mediterranean.

In antiquity, a number of cultures viewed the open sea as a diabolical menace full of monsters, including leviathans, serpents, dragons and demons of all manner. Moreover, the sea itself was perceived as a dangerous serpent, snake or dragon, and this primeval perception was projected in numerous derivations of an archetype.

This archetypal good-versus-evil conflict is represented in the myths of many cultures, such as:

- Apollo and Python
- Baal and Yamm
- Bel and Thamti[1]
- Beowulf and Grendel
- Byelobog and Chernobog
- Daniel and the Dragon
- Dionysus and Pentheus[2]
- Enki and the Dragon of Kur[3]
- Indra and Vritra[4]
- Kronos and Ophion
- Marduk and Tiamat
- Mithra and Ahriman
- Mordecai and Haman[5]
- Moses and Pharaoh

Christ." This pericope and many others evidently were used by the gospel writers as "messianic blueprints."

[1] Bel is Akkadian for "Lord," the same as the Canaanite "Baal."
[2] Euripides, *Ba*. 537-534.
[3] Baring and Cashford, 280.
[4] Berry, 20.
[5] Esther "10:7" or 10:3c-d, which can be found in the Septuagint only, is called "Addition F" to the Masoretic/Hebrew text: "Addition F gives the interpretation of Mordecai's dream, in which the two dragons are identified as Mordecai and Haman, and the stream as Esther." (Freedman, 427) The Greek for these passages is: ἡ μικρὰ πηγή ἣ ἐγένετο ποταμὸς καὶ ἦν φῶς καὶ ἥλιος καὶ ὕδωρ πολύ Εσθηρ ἐστὶν ὁ ποταμός ἣν ἐγάμησεν ὁ βασιλεὺς καὶ ἐποίησεν βασίλισσαν. οἱ δὲ δύο δράκοντες ἐγώ εἰμι καὶ Αμαν... Note that "Mordecai" in the LXX is Μαρδοχαῖος *Mardochaios*, the same as "Merodach" and "Marduk," two transliterations of the Babylonian god's name. Esther has been compared to Ishtar, Ashtar, Astarte, Astoreth, etc.

- Osiris/Horus and Seth
- Perseus and Gorgon
- St. George and the Dragon
- St. Patrick and the snakes
- Yahweh and Leviathan
- Zeus and Typhon

Tiamat, Monster of the Deep

This marine motif appears prominently in the Babylonian myth of the city god Marduk overthrowing the watery monster of the deep, Tiamat, a tale representing the god of light's control over the sea as well as the abyss of the night sky. In this regard, the discussion in Genesis (1:2-3) of "the deep" and "the waters" makes more sense with the background of Babylonian mythology:

> The earth was without form and void, and darkness was upon the face of the deep; and the Spirit of God was moving over the face of the waters. And God said, "Let there be light"; and there was light.

While evidently drawing from the Babylonian *Enuma Elish* cosmology,[1] the biblical scribes equated the main god therein, Marduk, with Yahweh. The Ugaritic for "primeval Ocean, deep" is *thmt*, while the Akkadian is *tiāmtu/tâmtu* and the biblical term תהום *tĕhowm/tehom*,[2] an Assyrian loanword cognate with Tiamat.[3] This term shares the same meaning with the *thalassa* or "sea" of the Greeks and later Gnostics, the latter of whom incorporated significant Sumero-Babylonian myths into their bizarre cosmology.

In this regard, the definition of *tehom* itself extends beyond the "mere" sea and is given as: "1) deep, depths, deep places, abyss, the deep, sea; a) deep (of subterranean waters); b) deep, sea, abysses (of sea); c) primeval ocean, deep; d) deep, depth (of river); e) abyss, the grave."[4] The Greek of the Old Testament for תהום *tĕhowm* is ἄβυσσος *abyssos*, whence "abyss," meaning "bottomless, unfathomable."

---

[1] See, e.g., Gray, 91.
[2] Schniedewind, 208; Strong's H8415.
[3] Shinan, 321. Earlier, Yahuda (128) had argued against this etymological connection, claiming that *tehom* is related to the Assyrian *tamtu*, which he dissociates from *tiamat* on the basis that the former term represents an inanimate "sea," while the latter is a living water monster. However, it is likely that the Bible writer(s) simply followed the trend of "taming the monster," so to speak, in rendering the sea as a mere mechanical creation of Yahweh, whom they were attempting to depict as *the* God of the universe and Creator of all: "That biblical writers dealt with figures of ancient Near Eastern mythology and modified them in keeping with their own concepts of cosmology is apparent in the manner in which Babylonian Tiâmat was demythologized in the Genesis Cosmology. Tiâmat of the *Enuma Elish*, dramatically personified in the Babylonian Creation-Conflict Cosmology, is demythologized and its personality annihilated as it is transformed into the material, impersonal Tehom of Genesis." (Shinan, 321)
[4] Strong's H8415.

THE EXODUS AS MYTH

The fall of mankind depicted also in Genesis is yet another pre-Hebraic Mesopotamian myth, represented in the Akkadian tradition as humanity's seduction by "the temptation of the dragon of the deep."[1]

Tannin and Leviathan

In the Bible, we read the tale at Isaiah 27:1 about Yahweh battling the "dragon" Tannin (Ugar. *Tnn*;[2] Heb. תנין *tanniyn)* and "sea monster" Leviathan (לויתן *livyathan)*[3]:

> In that day the LORD with his hard and great and strong sword will punish Leviathan the fleeing serpent, Leviathan the twisting serpent, and he will slay the dragon that is in the sea.

Regarding this theme, Lambert comments:

> It is now well known that Tannin and Leviathan (but not so far Rahab) are...borrowed [not] from Mesopotamian Marduk mythology, but from West Semitic traditions where Baal was the monster-slayer.[4]

Hence, while the Genesis story of the abyss draws from Babylonian myth, the Isaiah motif is Canaanite/Ugaritic, like the Baal cycle. This combination is precisely what we would expect to find as a result of the merger of Canaanite and Amorite peoples.

The plural of תנין *tanniyn* is the same word used to describe the "serpents" produced from the staffs of Aaron and the Egyptian magicians at Exodus 7:9-12, the Greek of which, δράκων *drakon* or "dragon," is the precise term employed to depict the snakes that crowned Dionysus at his birth.[5] Some form of *tannin* is used 28 times in the Bible to describe a dragon, serpent, venomous snake, sea monster and river monster.

Strong's (H8577) defines *tanniyn* as: "1) dragon, serpent, sea monster; a) dragon or dinosaur; b) sea or river monster; c) serpent, venomous snake."[6] The LXX uses the word κῆτος *ketos*, meaning "abyss, sea-monsters,"[7] as in "cetaceans," referring to whales. The same term κῆτος *ketos* is employed by Homer (*Il.* 20.147) to describe the "monster of the deep" pursuing the "dark-haired god" or Poseidon.

---

[1] Palmer, 30.
[2] Goedicke, 410.
[3] Strong's H8577 and H3882, respectively.
[4] Emerton, 138.
[5] See, e.g., Euripides, *Ba.* 88.101: στεφάνωσέν τε δρακόντων.
[6] *Tannin* also is rendered in several English editions of a number of biblical verses as "jackal." See, e.g., the NASB, RSV, NLT, NIV, etc., for Isaiah 43:20 and many other verses. Against this modern, rationalizing trend, the KJV translates *tannin* in these various verses as "dragons."
[7] *OCGD*, 184.

The word "leviathan" can be found in the Ugaritic as *ltn* or *lothan/lotan*, meaning "a sea dragon"[1] and representing a "personification" of the sea god Ym/Yamm/Yammu,[2] who is styled also "god of the immense (waters)."[3] An epithet of this Ugaritic monster from the sea is "the dominant one who has seven heads,"[4] reminiscent of the beast at Revelation 13:1: "And I saw a beast rising out of the sea, with ten horns and seven heads, with ten diadems upon its horns and a blasphemous name upon its heads." Ugaritic texts also describe Leviathan/Lothan as "the fleeing (?) serpent,"[5] using similar phraseology as in Isaiah 27.

Fig. 48. Doré, *Destruction of Leviathan*, 1865

It is noteworthy that the priestly name "Levite" too derives from a term meaning "serpent." The Hebrew word לוי *Leviy* is defined by Strong's (H3878) as "joined to" and by Gesenius as "adhesion," "garland" or "crown." The serpentine connotation can be found in the root word לוה *lavah*, as also in the term לויתן *livyathan* or Leviathan.

Rahab the Sea Monster

Considered to be a "demon," Tannin the dragon has been associated with not only Tiamat and Leviathan but also with the mysterious figure of Rahab. At Isaiah 51:9-10, the sea, dragon, deep and Rahab together are defeated by Yahweh:

> Awake, awake, put on strength, O arm of the LORD; awake, as in days of old, the generations of long ago. Was it not thou that didst cut Rahab in pieces, that didst pierce the dragon? Was it not thou that didst dry up the sea, the waters of the great deep; that didst make the depths of the sea a way for the redeemed to pass over?

Again, the Hebrew word for "sea" is ים *yam*, essentially the same as the sea god Yamm. The word for "deep" is תהום *tĕhowm*, the same as Tiamat, while "dragon" is תנין *tanniyn*. The reference to the "days of old" and "generations of long ago" indicates knowledge of these older myths, which obviously continued to affect Jewish thought and tradition. The "passing over" the sea by the "redeemed" indicates a mythical motif employed midrashically to flesh out the Moses tale.

---

[1] Schniedewind, 196.
[2] Rahmouni, 301.
[3] Rahmouni, 239.
[4] Rahmouni, 300ff.
[5] Rahmouni, 300, etc.

THE EXODUS AS MYTH

In Job 26:12, the word רהב *rahab* is used to describe the sea monster overcome by the book's hero. Strong's (H7293) defines *rahab* as: "1) pride, blusterer; a) storm, arrogance (but only as names); 1) mythical sea monster; 2) emblematic name of Egypt." The fact that Egypt was called by the same name as a mythical sea monster is significant and should be kept in mind, reflecting the dragon/sea monster archetype expressed in the Exodus myth.

It should be recalled that רחב Rachab or Rahab[1] is also the name of the "harlot" in the book of Joshua (2:1) who aided the Israelites in the destruction of the city of Jericho. Again, this "prostitute" is named in the New Testament as one of Jesus's four female ancestors listed in the genealogy of Matthew (1:5) but missing in that of Luke (3).

Pharaoh as Monster

To reiterate, this mythical monster motif evidently was used to create the Exodus myth, in which pharaoh and Egypt are cast in the role of the ancient and archetypical marine villain, with both Tannin and Rahab used in biblical texts as names for pharaoh and/or Egypt.[2] Further indicating the identification of the Red Sea tale as a pre-Israelite nature myth, Ezekiel (29:3) refers to "Pharaoh king of Egypt" as "the great dragon that lies in the midst of his streams," using the same term of תנין *tanniyn*, while the LXX employs the word δράκων *drakon*.[3]

At Ezekiel 32:2, Pharaoh is "like a dragon in the seas; you burst forth in your rivers, trouble the waters with your feet, and foul their rivers," the pertinent term here again is תנין *tanniyn*/δράκων *drakon*. Thus, the Bible identifies the pharaoh with the dragon, in turn associated with the sea monster and serpent.

Again, the fact that the kingdom of Amurru allegedly was destroyed by Ramesses III may account in part at least for the casting of "pharaoh" as the "dragon" in the Israelite version of this cosmological myth, as would be the chasing out of the Seth/Baal-worshipping Hyksos from Egypt by Ahmose I and other such friction over the centuries. In this regard, it is significant that the god Amurru has been identified with El, Marduk and Baal, all of whom battled the beast.

The Great Dragon

This "great dragon" and "ancient serpent" can be found in the biblical book of Revelation (12:9) as well, battled by the solar hero

---

[1] Strong's H7343.
[2] See also Ps 87:4, 89:10; Isa 51:9.
[3] This Greek term δράκων, meaning "dragon" or "serpent," is used numerous times in antiquity, such as by Aeschylus, Apollodorus, Aristophanes, Euripides, Hesiod, Homer and many others. The term *drakon* derives from the verb δέρκομαι *derkomai*, meaning "to see clearly."

Jesus Christ, and specially styled there as *drakon* and *ophis*: ὁ δράκων ὁ μέγας ὁ ὄφις ὁ ἀρχαῖος ὁ καλούμενος Διάβολος καὶ ὁ Σατανᾶς— "the great dragon, the ancient serpent called the Devil and [the] Satan," who is "thrown down."

This diabolical dragon/snake represents the same type of "monster of the deep" signified by the repeated biblical references to sea monsters, serpents, leviathans or "whales," as the KJV renders *tanniyn* (Gen 1:21).

Kronos, Ophion and Nachash

Another in this genre is the myth of the Greek titan Kronos/Cronus and Ophion, the former of whom is also Saturn, with whom Yahweh traditionally has been identified, as noted, and in a theme similar to Yahweh versus the serpent in the Garden of Eden. The moniker "Ophion" derives from the Greek term ὄφις *ophis*, meaning "serpent" or "snake," used in the Septuagint at Genesis 3:1:

> Now the serpent was more subtle than any other wild creature that the LORD God had made. He said to the woman, "Did God say, 'You shall not eat of any tree of the garden'?"

The Hebrew here for "serpent" is נחש *nachash*,[1] used 31 times in the Old Testament, including to describe the serpents magically created from the rods of the pharaoh's priests and Moses (Exod 4:3).

A deep- and snake-related theme occurs in the Greek poet Nonnus's *Dionysiaca* (8.158f), an epic poem dedicated to Bacchus, recited by the Greek goddess Hera:

Fig. 49. Mose's rod turned into a serpent, (*Holman Bible,* 1890)

> I will go to the uttermost bounds of Oceanos and share the hearth of primeval Tethys; thence I will pass to the house of Harmonia and abide with Ophion.[2]

Oceanos is the divine "World Ocean," while Tethys is a sea goddess, Harmonia the goddess of harmony, and Ophion the divine serpent. A possibly much older version and precedent of this hero-versus-monster myth appears in the Pygmy legends concerning the serpentine monster Lulu-Ngoogounogounmbar.[3]

Storm and Sun God

Controlling and battling the unruly waters and monstrous deep represent attributes of the storm god, who is often the sun as well. In

---

[1] Strong's H5175.
[2] Nonnos/Rouse, 2.285.
[3] Hallet, 165, 170, 173, etc.

THE EXODUS AS MYTH

the third-millennium texts found at Ebla, the most-often mentioned deity is the storm god Adda, the same as Hadad/Adad and Baal. Regarding the Levantine storm gods, in "YHWH as Storm-god and Sun-god," Dr. Paul E. Dion comments:

> During the last two millennia before the Christian era, the major religions of ancient Western Asia gave a central importance to a certain male deity, a lord of storm and rain, who controlled the most crucial factor in the agricultural economy of those cultures. This god was Tarkhunda to the Hittites, Teshup to the Hurrians, Haddu to the Amorites, Hadad, or simply Baal, "the Lord," to the Canaanites of the Syrian coast and to the Aramaeans. Even in the irrigation-based culture of Mesopotamia, storm-gods as Adad and Ninurta were also regarded as major deities.
>
> The nations of the ancient Near East were aware under all those names, further multiplied by their combinations with geographical designations (Teshup of Aleppo, Baal Zaphon, etc.), in actuality they were directing their devotion to a single Lord of weather and fertility. All those who worshipped a storm-god could use the Sumerogram ^{d}IM to write his name in the cuneiform script; the Egyptians called Baal all manifestations of the Asiatic storm-god, or identified them with their own indigenous Seth; and in Greco-Roman times, the storm-gods of all western Asia, whether from Anatolia or from Syria, became Zeus or Jupiter.[1]

This myth of the atmospheric, weather and fertility deity may be one of the oldest known cosmological themes devised by the human mind, possibly traceable to remote ages in Africa, tens of thousands of years ago. Considering their dramatic appearance and movements, it is understandable that storms would be perceived as alive, personified or animated by a godly force or controller.

The water-controlling storm deities are perceived often as solar, because the sun was deemed to create, manipulate and overcome storms, which sometimes were seen as pestilence by the adversary.

Concerning the water-subduing role of the sun god, Palmer comments:

> The mythologising faculty everywhere regarded the rising sun going forth to his daily conflict and victory as a warrior-god, whose spear and arrows were bright rays which he scattered around him; while the dark water, over which he mounted triumphant, and the clouds of night which he put to flight, were the vanquished monsters which he destroyed, either the devouring serpent of the deep or the flying dragons of the air.[2]

Here we see that the water-laden clouds too were serpentine and dragonlike monsters overcome by the sun's "spear and arrows" or rays.

---

[1] Dion, 49.
[2] Palmer, 19.

Marduk and the Sun

In this regard, the water-controlling Marduk/Merodach possesses a solar nature, as Oxford theologian and vicar Rev. Dr. Abram Smythe Palmer remarks:

> Merodach, the Vanquisher of the Chaos-Dragon, and so Creator of the ordered world, as being originally the Sun-God, occupied a place of supreme importance in the Babylonian religion, and by a reflex influence seems to have contributed shape to the theological conceptions of the Jews both as the Godhead and the Logos. In the prehistoric Accadian system his name was Amar-utuki, "The Brightness of the Sun," and inasmuch as that luminary appears to rise out of the sea, he was held to be the son of Ea, the god of the deep, "The first-born of the Deep.".... Among the Babylonians and Assyrians Amar-utuki or Amar-uduk became contracted into Maruduk and Marduk (and later Merodach)...[1]

The Amorites at Babylon beginning with Hammurabi favored Marduk, the various forms of whose name include the Sumerian AMAR.UTU and *Mar-Tu*. The discussion of "Amar-uduk" brings to mind the Amorite god Amurru, also said to be called "Mash." In this regard, American Assyriologist Rev. Dr. Albert T. Clay (1866-1925) states:

> Marduk has been regarded as being the contracted pronunciation of a syncretized name Amar-Utug, combining the West Semitic god Amar or Amur with Utug.... Mash was the name of a deity in Amurru as well as the name of a country and a mountain.[2]

Clay contends that the name "Marduk" is Babylonian and that its presence outside of that region reveals clear Babylonian influence. Marduk appears in the Bible, in a verse designed to subordinate him under Yahweh (Jer 50:2). His inclusion would not be necessary if there were not Marduk worshippers among the Israelites. The name "Mash" is of singular importance in our quest and will be discussed in depth below.

Marduk's "name, from the Sumerian *Amar-utuk* or *amar.UD*, seems to mean 'bull calf of the Sun.'"[3] While Utu is the Sumerian sun god, the Sumerian term *amr/amar* denotes "calf," "bull calf," "holy calf" and "calf of God."[4] Thus, "Marduk" is said to be the "solar calf," reminiscent of the Golden Calf, which could mean that the biblical story represents a swipe at the Marduk worship of the Amorites. In this regard, Jeremiah 50:2 refers to מרדך *Mĕrodak* or Marduk, who "has been shattered" (NASB) or "broken in pieces" (KJV).[5]

---

[1] Smith, M., 98-99.
[2] Clay, 179.
[3] Leviton, "Marduk."
[4] Human, 182; De Vito, 68;
[5] The Hebrew word is חתה *chathath*, which means "to be shattered, be dismayed, be broken, be abolished, be afraid." (Strong's H2865)

THE EXODUS AS MYTH

In this same regard, the Babylonian text of the second millennium the *Enuma Elish* attributes both solar and storm characteristics to Marduk:

> Enuma Elish 1:101-2, 157 and 11:128-20 apply solar qualities to Marduk, although storm language is more characteristic of him. The combination of solar and storm imagery and iconography in Mesopotamian sources and biblical texts raises an important issue.[1]

The most important issue here is the role of the sun and storm god in the Bible and Exodus myth.

Apollo and Python

We can see the solar connotation of this monster myth also in the story of Apollo fighting Typhon/Python, the pestilent and deadly serpent. Dating to centuries earlier, the battle between Apollo and Python was explained in the fifth century AD/CE by Roman writer Macrobius Ambrosius Theodosius (1.17.57-58) thus:

> The following is a natural-scientific explanation of the serpent's death, according to the Stoic Antipater... The emanation of the still-damp earth rose swiftly to the higher regions and, becoming warmed, rolled back down to the lower regions, like a deadly serpent, corrupting everything with the putrefying force to which dampness and warmth give rise, and it seemed to blot out the very sun with its thick murk and, in a sense, thinned out, dried out, and destroyed by the divine heat of the sun's rays, falling like a shower of arrows—hence the tale of the serpent slain by Apollo. There is also another interpretation of the serpent's destruction: though the sun's course never varies from the ecliptic, the shifting winds vary their course with a regular up and down movement, rolling along like a slithering serpent.[2]

Macrobius (1.17.59) continues discussing the solar serpent-slaying motif, remarking that the sun is named "Pythios" for its role in destroying the snake, as the solar orb "completed the proper course of its heavenly journey."[3] The Latin writer explains the relevant solar epithets of Apollo of "far-shooter" or "far-darter" as representing the longest solar "arrows" or rays at the summer solstice, when the sun is highest in the sky for the longest period of time.[4]

Apollo of Hierapolis is equated with the Babylonian god of wisdom and writing, Nebo or Nabu,[5] who was said to be a divine legislator, as was the Greek sun god himself. Macrobius (1.18.1) subsequently states that what was said of Apollo could be asserted of "Liber"—an epithet of another legislator, Dionysus/Bacchus, meaning "free"—

---

[1] Smith, M., 152.
[2] Macrobius/Kaster, 1.239.
[3] Macrobius/Kaster, 1.239.
[4] Macrobius/Kaster, 1.240-241.
[5] Macrobius/Kaster, 1.243.

remarking that "Aristotle, who wrote *Discourses on the Gods,* advances many proofs to support his claim that Apollo and father Liber are one and the same...."[1] Hence, the sun and wine god are the same, one intertwined with the other, like the grapevines themselves.

Since Bacchus is Apollo, he would possess the same solar attribute as dispensing with the dragon of the waters (Pentheus), as Moses also was said to have done in defeating pharaoh.

Horus and the Serpent/Crocodile

The myth of Horus spearing the serpent or crocodile (Seth), as at Edfu,[2] provides an Egyptian example of this archetypal solar myth. In addition to serving as a solar, dragon-cloud slaying ray, the spear is a symbol of the smith cult, popular at Edfu, possibly explaining the weapon's inclusion in the gospel story as well.

St. George and the Dragon

Like other "Christian" characters, the figure of St. George is an ancient god demoted to a saint, about whose myth Palmer remarks that "St. George vanquishing the Dragon was originally just the sun breaking through the obstructing clouds...and Horus spearing the infernal serpent bears the same meaning."[3]

Fig. 50. Horus of Edfu spearing the crocodile Set (Budge, 1920:16)

Indicating its antiquity, this solar monster-spearing myth can be found also in the Americas, for example in the story of Michabo, the god of light who "pierces with his dart the prince of serpents who lives in a lake and floods the earth with its waters."[4]

The story of Moses escaping into the waters, away from a pursuing villain who is then drowned, is reminiscent of the archetypal hero tale exemplified in the myths of the sun gods or solar heroes overcoming the "prince of darkness," or night/cloudy/stormy sky, conceived as a "watery abyss" or serpent/dragon that swallows up the light and goodness before being defeated.

Wandering the Wilderness

The motif of wandering in the desert is found in the stories of Dionysus, Gilgamesh, John the Baptist, Jesus, the Indian godman Buddha and others, representing a typical plotline to show the overcoming of hardships. Like Moses, Gilgamesh arrives at the mountain of the divine lawgiver after "wandering and roaming all over

---

[1] Macrobius/Kaster, 1.245.
[2] See, e.g., Apuleius/Griffiths, 174; Offord, 99.316.
[3] Palmer, 106.
[4] Palmer, 22.

THE EXODUS AS MYTH

the wilderness."[1] Although it may have other permutations and connotations, the myth essentially represents the journey of the sun, said to be desolate at various times of the year, depending on the location and era.

The same claim was made of the Persian king Cyrus, the beloved Christ of the Jews, who saved them from Babylon, according to the Bible: "Tradition said that Cyrus had once penetrated into Gedrosia on an expedition against the Indians, and had lost his entire army in the waterless and trackless desert..."[2]

The Greek word for "wilderness" in the LXX and New Testament is ἐρῆμος *erēmos*, connoting something or someone "desolate, lonely, solitary," a form of which was used hundreds of times in antiquity, including by the Greek playwright Aeschylus (525-456 BCE) to describe the mythical titan Prometheus on the "desolate and dreary crag" (*PB* 273).[3] Constantine Grethenbach was of the view that "Israel in the Mad-Debar or 'wilderness' has for its basis the popular myth of the hero's descent into Hades."[4] Certainly, Hades was considered to be a place of desolation; it is also the underworld, traditionally the place where the sun goes at night.

12 Wells and 70 Palms

Like the Moses myth overall, there is little reason to accept the 12 wells and 70 palms at Elim or Aileim as a historical detail. Explaining the mystical and astrological meaning of the 12 wells/fountains and 70 trees, in *On Flight and Finding* (*De Fuga* 33:184-186) Philo remarks:

> ...twelve is the perfect number, of which the circle of the zodiac in the heaven is a witness, studded as it is with such numbers of brilliant constellations. The periodical revolution of the sun is another witness, for he accomplishes his circle in twelve months, and men also reckon the hours of the day and of the night as equal in number to the months of the year, and the passages are not few in which Moses celebrates this number, describing the twelve tribes of his nation, appointing by law the offering of the twelve cakes of shewbread, and ordering twelve stones, on which inscriptions are engraved, to be woven into the sacred robe of the garment...
>
> He also celebrates the number seven, multiplied by the number ten; at one time speaking of the seventy palm-trees by the fountains, and in other passages he speaks of the elders, who were only seventy in number, to whom the divine and prophetical Spirit was vouchsafed.[5]

---

[1] Kovacs, M., 77.
[2] Rawlinson, 1881:3.383.
[3] Herbert Weir Smyth translation.
[4] Grethenbach, v. Hebrew: מדבר *midbar* (H4057), connoting "wilderness, pasture, uninhabited land."
[5] Philo/Yonge (2000), 337-338; (1894), 2.232.

Thus, it was the opinion of this Jewish philosopher 2,000 years ago that the number 12 was struck upon because of its zodiacal symbolism. In the same regard, while Philo sees the 70 as seven multiplied by 10, astrotheologically the number 70 represents the dodecans or 72 divisions of the zodiacal circle into five degrees each, a motif like the 12, which is found commonly in many mythologies, such as concerns the gods of Egypt, Greece and Rome.[1] It is possible that Philo wished to see "seven" because the number "exerts great influence upon the development of living beings and plants," as the Jewish philosopher Aristobulus of Paneas (c. 160 BCE) purportedly asserted.[2]

The 72 descendants of Jacob/Israel are said to have reproduced in Egypt in "rabbitlike rapidity," doubling their population every three or so decades, to the point where they purportedly had 600,000 men four centuries later.[3] This clearly mythical motif likely has to do with the 72 dodecans, a number frequently shortened to 70. The 72 descendants and 70 elders or disciples would symbolize the same mythical theme.

Manna and Heavenly Bread

The manna story is implausible as history, and, as previously noted, the mysterious "cakes" of the Egyptian gods and glorified spirits called *khus* sound similar to the biblical substance. It should be recalled that the apparently proto-Israelite Shasu was known for their aromatic gum, possibly included in the Moses myth in order to give a divine origin to their renowned product.

We have seen also that Exodus 16:15 associates the manna with bread, as does Exodus 16:29, 31:

> ...The LORD has given you the sabbath, therefore on the sixth day he gives you bread for two days... Now the house of Israel called its name manna; it was like coriander seed, white, and the taste of it was like wafers made with honey.

The idea of heavenly bread is abundant in Egyptian mythology too, and it would appear that the biblical motif is designed to compete with and subordinate the popular Egyptian theme as well.

Egypt

In addition to the *khu* cakes as a type of manna, the Egyptian concept of the "bread of life" can be found in the *Book of the Dead*, as in chapter/spell 53: "I eat bread from the house of the Lord of offerings."[4] This sacred bread was used by the Egyptians to propitiate the gods, miraculously provided also to the deceased in order to feed

---

[1] E.g., the twelve Saḥ gods, previously mentioned.
[2] Singer, Is. (1916), 2.98.
[3] Busenbark, 80.
[4] See Murdock (2009), 288ff.

THE EXODUS AS MYTH

him or her during the journey through the afterlife wilderness. As I relate in *Christ in Egypt*, bread is one of the main symbols of sustenance for the immortality of the dead in the Egyptian heaven, as in the Pyramid Texts as well.[1]

In the Pyramid Texts (c. fifth millennium BCE), we read:

...[Osiris] N. lives on the morning bread, which comes at its (appointed) time.

...The bread of your father is for you...[2]

Here it is morning bread, like the manna forming on the dew in the morn.

The Coffin Texts of the third millennium also discuss the sacred meal, including as the "bread of Osiris" likewise called the "daily bread."[3] The numerous references in Egyptian texts to this spiritual bread of life are reflected also in the gospel of John, in which Jesus is made to say, "I am the bread of life" (Jn 6:35) and so on.[4] Indeed, the manna story's *allegorical nature* and connection to Christ can be seen earlier at John 6:31-33, in which "the earthly manna eaten in the wilderness is a figure of the 'true' heavenly bread given by God in his Son."[5]

Sumer

In the Sumerian text *Inanna's Descent to the Underworld* (c. 1900-1600 BCE), we see reference to the "food of life" and "water of life" used by Father Enki to bring others back to life.[6] This ritual acts also like a baptism, as in the goddess Inanna's story of death and resurrection, after she is killed and hanged "from the nail":

One of you sprinkle upon her the "food of life," the other the "water of life." Then Inanna will arise.[7]

After Inanna is sprinkled, she resurrects out of the underworld, in a story evidently passed along in one form or another for many centuries and emulated in significant part in the Christ myth.

Ugarit

The motif of foodstuff from heaven and in the desert valleys can be found also in the Ugaritic texts, recalling the biblical claim that manna tasted like "oil": "The heavens rain down oil; the wadis run with honey..."[8] This passage has been likened to Hosea 6:1-3 and

---

[1] Murdock (2009), 289.
[2] PT 339:553b/T 149; W 13/PT 238:242a. Murdock (2009), 290.
[3] Murdock (2009), 290.
[4] For more information about the Egyptian influence on John, see my book *Christ in Egypt*.
[5] Mellor, 181.
[6] Kramer, 161, 165.
[7] Kramer, 165.
[8] Block (209), citing *CTA*, 6.3.6-7.

Psalms 65:9-13 and 68:9, reflecting not physical manna but the Baal cycle of vernal fertility, with its life-giving rains.[1]

India

Other texts, such as the Indian Atharvaveda (c. 1000 BCE), likewise depict ambrosia falling and "streams of honey" that flowed "upon the earth,"[2] resembling the Dionysian myth as well, to be discussed later.

Water from a Rock

Like that of the manna/honey, the miracle of producing water from a rock too must be considered as myth, concerning which Walker relates:

> Moses's flowering rod, river of blood, and tablets of the law were all symbols of the ancient Goddess. His miracle of drawing water from a rock was first performed by Mother Rhea after she gave birth to Zeus, and by Atalanta with the help of Artemis.[3]

In his *Hymn to Zeus* (28ff), Greek poet Callimachus (310/305–240 BCE) writes that the mother of the gods "Rhea causes the first waters to burst from the rocks of the sacred hill where Zeus was born."[4] Pausanias (3.24.2) tells us that the Greek maiden Atalanta "produced water from a stone in the wilds of Arcadia by striking the rock with her javelin."[5]

---

[1] Hosea 6:1-3: "Come, let us return to the LORD; for he has torn, that he may heal us; he has stricken, and he will bind us up. After two days he will revive us; on the third day he will raise us up, that we may live before him. Let us know, let us press on to know the LORD; his going forth is sure as the dawn; he will come to us as the showers, as the spring rains that water the earth." Here we can see themes that found their way into the New Testament, as well as the astrotheology or solar and nature worship of the older Semitic cultures such as the Canaanite and Mesopotamian. The "raising up" or resurrection after three days is also an astrotheological/solar motif, fallaciously presented as history in the NT. In reality, verses such as this one were used midrashically, as a "messianic blueprint," to create the Christ figure and gospel story.
[2] Velikovsky, 146.
[3] Walker (1983), 96.
[4] Stephens, 96. A.G. and G.R. Mair's translation: "And holden in distress the lady Rheia said, 'Dear Earth, give birth thou also! Thy birthpangs are light.' So spake the goddess, and lifting her great arm aloft she smote the mountain with her staff; and it was greatly rent in twain for her and poured forth a mighty flood." The last, relevant part (30) in the original Greek is: εἶπε καὶ ἀντανύσασα θεὴ μέγαν ὑψόθι πῆχυν πλῆξεν ὄρος σκήπτρῳ· τὸ δέ οἱ δίχα πουλὺ διέστη, ἐκ δ' ἔχεεν μέγα χεῦμα. (Callimachus, *Works*. Ed. A.W. Mair.) Here the word for "staff" is σκῆπτρον *skeptron*, the same as "scepter."
[5] Scanlon, 177. Pausanias/Jones (2.151): "The road from Zarax follows the coast for about a hundred stades, and there strikes inland. After an ascent of ten stades inland are the ruins of the so-called Cyphanta, among which is a cave sacred to Asclepius; the image is of stone. There is a fountain of cold water springing from the rock, where they say that Atalanta, distressed by thirst when hunting, struck the rock with her spear, so that the water gushed forth." The original of the relevant Greek is: ἔστι δὲ καὶ ὕδατος ψυχροῦ κρουνὸς ἐκβάλλων ἐκ πέτρας· Ἀταλάντην θηρεύουσαν ἐνταῦθα φασιν, ὡς ἠνιᾶτο ὑπὸ δίψης, παῖσαι τῇ λόγχῃ τὴν πέτραν καὶ οὕτω ῥυῆναι τὸ ὕδωρ.

THE EXODUS AS MYTH

Mithraic expert Dr. Maarten Jozef Vermaseren and Dutch archaeologist Dr. Carel Claudius van Essen also summarize a number of ancient water-producing miracles:

> Mithras is by no means alone in the performance of this miraculous deed, by which a spring is created. In the Veda it is Indra, who after drinking the potion of immortality, the soma, proceeds to subdue Vr̥ta, the snake which encircles the spring and watches over it and, thus makes the water accessible to mankind. Siva too in his turn opened up many springs and streams by a blow of his trident. In Greek mythology there is Poseidon who struck water from the rocks by means of his trident, and it is remarkable that, apart from the Acropolis, he also caused new springs to arise in Atlantis... In this respect Dionysus also was a miracle-worker, and according to Philostratus, *Imag.*, I,14 the Earth will even favour him in this... Atlanta, returning from hunting, also strikes a rock with her spear and creates a spring, and it would be easy to add a great many further examples of this phenomenon. Just as Prometheus provided mankind with fire, there are gods, heroes and saints, who have presented man with water, especially the wholesome liquid that is imbued with immortality.[1]

As we can see, this sacred act of miraculously producing water is common and not unique to Jewish myth. In this regard, an early instance of the sun god conjuring fresh water from the earth can be found in the Sumerian text "Enki and Ninhursag," which also discusses a fertile "promised land,"[2] thousands of years before the Exodus tale was composed.

Mithra

One of the more famous examples of miraculous water-production occurs with the Perso-Roman god Mithra "shooting at the rock," from which flowed water,[3] a scene similar to "Moses smiting the rock" (Num 20:11) in Christian iconography. Describing a particular Mithraic image of this scene, Vermaseren and van Essen further state:

> Mithras is seated on a rock with a bow in his hand, from which he shoots an arrow at another rock, thus producing an abundant flow of water. In front of this rock there kneels a person in Oriental dress and sometimes there are two, who immediately drink from the water... Whatever changes might have been introduced, the monuments clearly reveal that the *gemini*

Fig. 51. Mithra shooting an arrow into a rock to produce water, c. 2nd cent. AD/CE. Mithraeum at Neuenheim, Germany

---
[1] Vermaseren and van Essen, 194.
[2] See, e.g., Kramer, 144-145.
[3] Hinnells, 173; Walters, 47.

fratres [twin brothers] in the dipinto [painting] are not the two Dioscuri, but Cautes and Cautopates, who in the Mithras reliefs are usually represented as torchbearers. The two figures in Oriental dress are, according to some statements from antiquity, hypostases [supporting figures] of the Sun-god Mithras. These symbolize him in the morning and in the evening, and are respectively Sol Oriens ["Sun East"] and Sol Occidens ["Sun West"]. They are already present at Mithras' birth from the *petra genetrix* [generative rock] and sometimes they even act as assistants. Here, however, they enjoy the miracle by which Mithras with a shot from his bow releases the *fons concluse petris* ["rock-bound spring"]. In the same way as the *petra genetrix* symbolizes the vault of heaven from which the god is born, and the grotto (*antrum*), where Mithras slays the bull, is sometimes studded with stars, so the spring is here enclosed within the grotto, i.e., the vault of heaven.[1]

The sun is born each morning, out of the "cave," "grotto" or "rock," symbolizing not only the vault of heaven or tomb of the underworld but also the womb of the earth mother. In Greek, the noun for "rock," *petra*, is feminine, while in Latin, "mother" is *mater*, the root of "material" and "matter." The virgin-birth motif for Mithra is prominent in the Persian version of his myth, in which the virgin goddess Anahita is represented as the god's mother.[2]

The torchbearers on either side of the solar Mithra represent the sunrise or morning and sunset or evening, as well as the vernal and autumnal equinoxes. Thus, the motif of the godman between two others, as in the Jesus myth with the "thieves" crucified on either side, symbolizes the central sun surrounded by the morning and evening suns. In this regard, it is noteworthy to recognize that the cross has denoted the *sun* since remote antiquity.

Noting the connection between the Mithraic water-producing motive and not only the Moses but also the Jesus myth, mythicist Ken Humphreys comments:

> We have evidence that Mithras performed at least one miracle: the god released life-giving water from a rock by firing an arrow. Regurgitated in the story of Jesus, the god of the Christians claimed himself to offer, or even be, "living water":
>
> "All who drink once of the water that I will give them shall never thirst anymore." John 4.14[3]

As we have seen, controlling and producing water is a solar attribute, as the sun was seen to bring about the rains in their season.

---

[1] Vermaseren and van Essen, 194.
[2] See my article "Was the Persian Goddess Anahita the Pre-Christian Virgin Mother of Mithra?" Anahita may have been the Persian version of the Semitic virgin-mother goddess Anat, possibly "blended" in antiquity during the reign of Artaxerxes Longimanus (fl. 464-424 BCE). (See, e.g., Müller, 4.lv)
[3] Humphreys, "The Gospel of Mithras."

Spiritual Rock

In a statement against the literal interpretation of the biblical motif, the apostle Paul (1 Cor 10:4) tells us that Moses's rock was not "real" but spiritual, symbolic of Christ:

> ...and all drank the same supernatural drink. For they drank from the supernatural Rock which followed them, and the Rock was Christ.

As we can see, there are a number of parallels and precedents for this spiritual or mythical "miracle" in religions and mythologies of different cultures. There seems little scientific reason to accept one supernatural rendition as myth and another as history.

Krishna

In the Hindu myths, in addition to Indra and Shiva as openers of springs and wells we also find the story of Krishna smiting a rock with his *chakra* or discus, causing a "spring of sweet water to bubble up,"[1] reminiscent also of Exodus 15:25, in which Moses magically changes brackish water to "sweet water."

Poseidon

In his contest with the goddess Athena over the city subsequently styled "Athens" for the winner, the Greek god Poseidon also "smote the rock," striking the Acropolis with his trident to create a salt-water stream, pool or sea, a myth related by Herodotus and fleshed out by later writers.[2] One of these later authors, Apollodorus (2nd cent. BCE), remarks (3.14.1):

> So Poseidon came to Attica first and struck his trident on the Acropolis producing a sea, now called Erechtheis.[3]

One might suggest that the creation of an entire sea rates as a more impressive miracle than simply bringing forth a relatively small spring. It appears to be a matter of bias which supernatural tale we choose to believe as "history," reflecting "real" divine miracles.

Dionysus

The text *Imagines* traditionally attributed to Greek sophist Philostratus of Lemnos (b. c. 190 AD/CE) is part of a corpus composed

---

[1] Tod (2.1204-1205): "While Krishna thus prophesied, it was observed to him by Arjun that the water was bad, when Krishna smote the rock with his chakra (discus), whereupon a sweet spring bubbled up..."

[2] Herodotus (8.55): "In that acropolis is a shrine of Erechtheus, called the 'Earthborn,' and in the shrine are an olive tree and a pool of salt water. The story among the Athenians is that they were set there by Poseidon and Athena as tokens when they contended for the land." ἔστι ἐν τῇ ἀκροπόλι ταύτῃ Ἐρεχθέος τοῦ γηγενέος λεγομένου εἶναι νηός, ἐν τῷ ἐλαίη τε καὶ θάλασσα ἔνι, τὰ λόγος παρὰ Ἀθηναίων Ποσειδέωνά τε καὶ Ἀθηναίην ἐρίσαντας περὶ τῆς χώρης μαρτύρια θέσθαι. (Herodotus/A. D. Godley)

[3] Palagia, 41. Apollodorus's original Greek is: ἧκεν οὖν πρῶτος Ποσειδῶν ἐπὶ τὴν Ἀττικήν, καὶ πλήξας τῇ τριαίνῃ κατὰ μέσην τὴν ἀκρόπολιν ἀπέφηνε θάλασσαν, ἣν νῦν Ἐρεχθηίδα καλοῦσι. (Apollodorus/Frazer)

evidently by two or three individuals of the same name, dating to the second and third centuries AD/CE. In this text (1.14), we read:

> We must not be surprised if in honour of Dionysus the Fire is crowned by the Earth, for the Earth will take part with the Fire in the Bacchic reveal and will make it possible for the revelers to take wine from springs and to draw milk from clods of earth or from a rock as from living breasts.... Megaera causes a fir to shoot up beside him and brings to light a spring of water, in token, I fancy, of the blood of Actaeon and of Pentheus.[1]

Centuries earlier, Athenian playwright Euripides (480-406 BCE) told a similar Dionysian tale of miraculously produced wine, milk and honey, as will be discussed below.

Forty Days, Nights and Years

At Exodus 24:18, Moses is depicted as spending 40 days and nights on Mt. Sinai/Horeb:

> And Moses entered the cloud, and went up on the mountain. And Moses was on the mountain forty days and forty nights.

The story of Moses's 40 days on the mountain is reiterated in Deuteronomy 9 and 10, with the same behavior depicted of Elijah at 1 Kings 19:8, as the latter prophet is portrayed fasting for 40 days and nights upon Mt. Horeb, the alternate or twin of Sinai.

The period of 40 days/nights can be found elsewhere in the Bible, in the story of Noah and the ark (Gen 7), as well as in the tale of Joseph's father, Jacob/Israel, being embalmed (Gen 50:2-3). The 40-day motif also appears in the story of spying on Canaan (Num 13:25) and in that of Jesus and his temptation in the desert by Satan (Mt 4:2; Mk 1:13; Lk 4:2), as well as his 40-day post-resurrection appearance to his disciples (Acts 1:3).

This theme appears in Semitic mythology centuries before the time of Moses or Jesus, in the story of the Babylonian hero Enkidu[2] battling his evil alter ego, Gilgamesh, for 40 days and nights.

There is also the 40-day period of "Lent" and fasting celebrated each year by Christians as a time of the spring blooming. This 40-day period in ancient myth apparently represents the time it takes for certain seeds to germinate after they have been planted in the spring.[3] Moreover, the 40 *years* of the Exodus seems to be a reiteration of this mythical and sacred number. In this scenario we have a period of 40 from the barren soil of the desert germinating into the land of "milk and honey."

---

[1] Philostratus/Fairbanks, 61.
[2] Older scholarship transliterates the name Enkidu as "Eabani," "Enkimdu" and "Enkita."
[3] See, e.g., Massey (2007), 1.271

Mishnah

The sacred number 40 likewise appears prominently in the origin myth about the Mishnah, the "second law" of the Talmud, said to have been transmitted to Moses on Mount Sinai but in reality representing scriptural analysis and commentary by rabbis from the first century BCE to the second AD/CE. According to this tradition, the Mishnah was passed along orally from Moses by 40 "receivers," who were "qualified by ordination to hand it on from generation to generation," until the time of Rabbi Judah "the Holy."[1]

The Many Arks

We have seen that the tale of the magical ark of the covenant is implausible as "history." It is further noteworthy that the ark's importance is emphasized in the southern kingdom Yahwistic source text or "J," while the northern Israelite Elohist or "E" never mentions this artifact supposedly vital to Israel's existence.[2]

Even if the artifact were real—and its omission in E indicates otherwise—it would not have been unique or original, as there were many such divine arks in antiquity, a ritualistic object continuing in use to this day in places like India and Tibet. In this regard, Exodus 25:40 depicts the Lord as telling Moses to build the ark, "after the pattern for them":

> And see that you make them after the pattern for them, which is being shown you on the mountain.

About this verse, the churchman Clarke notes that there are many "imitations" of the ark of the covenant "among several heathen nations." He cites the Latin writer of the second century AD/CE Apuleius (*De Aur. Asin.* 2) as "describing a solemn idolatrous procession, after the Egyptian mode" in which the author says: "A chest, or ark, was carried by another, containing their secret things, entirely concealing the mysteries of religion."[3] The

Fig. 52. The ark, bark, barque or boat of Amun, carried in procession at the Opet Festival

"Egyptian mode," apparently, has to do with an "ark that carried the Egyptian god Amun during the Opet Festivals." Since these processions date back far earlier than the biblical ark stories, it can

---

[1] Barclay, 1.
[2] Friedman (2003), 19.
[3] Clarke, 1.448. Apuleius's original Latin in *The Golden Ass/Metamorphoses* (11.11) is: *Ferebatur ab alio cista secretorum capax penitus celans operta magnificae religionis.* A different rendering of this passage is: "Another bore an ark full of secret things, holding in its depths the mysteries of the glorious faith." (Apuleius/Butler, 2.136.)

be surmised that the "imitation" occurred from Egypt by the later Israelites.

The Latin word for "chest" or "ark" in Apuleius is *cista*, which can also be rendered "box" and "woven or wicket basket." Jerome's Latin Vulgate Bible uses the word *arca* to describe the biblical ark, both of Noah and Moses.

Aaron and Horus

The Hebrew word for "chest/ark" is ארון *'arown*, which is not much different from the name "Aaron," אהרון *'Aharown*, Moses's brother (Exod 4:14) and head priest of the ark cult and Mosaic law. It is possible that, rather than representing a real person, this mythical character was specifically named for his ark-keeping duty.

Aaron also could be taking the place of Horus, the name of not only Osiris's son but also his brother, whose moniker in Greek is Ὧρος or Ὧρον in the accusative, which could be pronounced "Horon" or "Oron," without the initial aspirant "h." The name "Aaron" also has an aspirant and is pronounced "a·har·ōn'." While etymology does not indicate a relationship, it is possible that speakers of Hebrew and Greek in antiquity likewise noticed the similarity between the names. Moreover, Aaron in Arabic is هارون Harun, similar to the Semitic god-name Horon, identified with Horus.[1]

As noted, the name Aaron means "light bringer," while Horus is significantly a solar deity, also the bringer of light, as is his Greek counterpart, Apollo. Horus too had his own ark, a beautiful example of which was discovered at Edfu.

In addition, the Egyptian baby sun god Sokar, an alter ego of Horus, was brought out in an ark annually at the winter solstice.[2] Again, to this day, gods and goddesses in Hindu and Buddhist ceremonies likewise are paraded in such arks, as they have been since antiquity.

Kibotos

At Numbers 10:33, the Greek of the LXX for the "ark of the covenant" is ἡ κιβωτὸς τῆς διαθήκης, the first noun, κιβωτός *kibotos*, meaning "box, chest, coffer" and διαθήκης *diathekes* denoting "disposition," as well as "arrangement; will; treaty; covenant."[3]

This same term κιβωτός *kibotos* can be found in Pausanias (1.18.2), for example, concerning the Samothracian gods called Dioscuri, in a story similar to one in the Bible at 1 Samuel 6:19:

> The sanctuary of the Dioscuri is ancient.... Above the sanctuary of the Dioscuri is a sacred enclosure of Aglaurus. It was to Aglaurus and her sisters, Herse and Pandrosus, that they say Athena gave

---

[1] See *The Study Guide*.
[2] See my book *Christ in Egypt* for more on the baby Sokar, who was carried out of the temple each year at "Christmas."
[3] *OCGD*, 79.

THE EXODUS AS MYTH

Erichthonius, whom she had hidden in a chest, forbidding them to pry curiously into what was entrusted to their charge. Pandrosus, they say, obeyed, but the other two (for they opened the chest) went mad when they saw Erichthonius, and threw themselves down the steepest part of the Acropolis.[1]

Here the word "chest" is the preferred translation for *kibotos*. As discussed, in the Bible we are informed that it is deadly to look into the ark, as in this Greek story.

Erichthonius was a mythical early king of Athens said to be born of would-be rapist Hephaistos's semen, as Athena wiped it from her thigh and threw it to the ground. Although she thus remained a virgin, Athena raised the child as her own, brought to her through miraculous intercession. Essentially, in this tale we have a virgin-mother goddess placing another deity into an ark/chest, which drives the beholder to fatal madness when opened. This myth of a baby secreted in a box or "ark," invoking a boat, fits into the genre also of the infant cast away in a reed boat or chest.

Treasure Chest

The Greek orator Lysias (c. 445-c. 380 BCE) in *Against Eratosthenes* (12.10) uses the term *kibotos* to describe what has been rendered as a "money-chest," like a treasure chest or temple treasury, of which in Jerusalem the golden and jewel-encrusted ark of the covenant was the centerpiece.

Pelops and Cleomedes

Also according to Pausanias (6.22.1), a *kibotos* or chest/ark was used to hold the bones of the mythical Greek king Pelops near the sanctuary at the Greek city of Pisa, founded by Pisus.[2] Both Pausanias (6.9.7)[3] and Plutarch (*Rom.* 28.4-5)[4] recount the tale of the "mad man" Cleomedes of Astypaleia, who, after destroying a pillar holding up the roof of a children's school, bringing it down upon them, hides in a large *kibotos* that no one subsequently can open. When finally the lid is removed, the chest is discovered to be miraculously empty. Afterwards, it was claimed this disappearing

---

[1] Pausanias/Jones, 1.87. The Greek translated as "for they opened the chest" is ἀνοῖξαι γὰρ σφᾶς τὴν κιβωτόν.

[2] ὀστᾶ τὰ Πέλοπος ἐν τῇ κιβωτῷ φυλάσσουσι.

[3] ἐμπεσόντος δὲ τοῦ ὀρόφου τοῖς παισί, καταλιθούμενος ὑπὸ τῶν ἀστῶν κατέφυγεν ἐς Ἀθηνᾶς ἱερόν· ἐσβάντος δὲ ἐς κιβωτὸν κειμένην ἐν τῷ ἱερῷ καὶ ἐφελκυσαμένου τὸ ἐπίθημα, κάματον ἐς ἀνωφελὲς οἱ Ἀστυπαλαιεῖς ἔκαμνον ἀνοίγειν τὴν κιβωτὸν πειρώμενοι· τέλος δὲ τὰ ξύλα τῆς κιβωτοῦ καταρρήξαντες, ὡς οὔτε ζῶντα Κλεομήδην οὔτε τεθνεῶτα εὕρισκον, ἀποστέλλουσιν ἄνδρας ἐς Δελφοὺς ἐρησομένους ὁποῖα ἐς Κλεομήδην τὰ συμβάντα ἦν.

[4] ἀπολομένων δὲ τῶν παίδων διωκόμενον, εἰς κιβωτὸν καταφυγεῖν μεγάλην καὶ τὸ πῶμα κατακλείσαντα συνέχειν ἐντός, ὥστ᾽ ἀποσπάσαι μὴ δύνασθαι πολλοὺς ὁμοῦ βιαζομένους· κατασχίσαντας δὲ τὴν κιβωτόν, οὔτε ζῶντα τὸν ἄνθρωπον εὑρεῖν οὔτε νεκρόν. ἐκπλαγέντας οὖν ἀποστεῖλαι θεοπρόπους εἰς Δελφούς, οἷς τὴν Πυθίαν εἰπεῖν.

child-killer was a "hero" and "immortal," yet again associating a divinity with an ark.

Ark of Osiris

To reiterate, the same basic concept and word, *kibotos*, were used to describe the biblical ark of Noah (Gen 7:7). Like Noah, Osiris too was "shut up in his ark," as related by Plutarch (*De Iside* 39):

> The story told of the shutting up of Osiris in the chest seems to mean nothing else than the vanishing and disappearance of water. Consequently they say that the disappearance of Osiris occurred in the month of Athyr, at the time when, owing to the complete cessation of the Etesian winds, the Nile recedes to its low level and the land becomes denuded. As the nights grow longer, the darkness increases, and the potency of the light is abated and subdued.[1]

Although the Egyptian calendar wandered, Athyr in this myth apparently refers to November, a dry month and the same time of the year when Noah was said to enter his ark, just before the rains (Gen 7). As we can see, this ancient source provides a naturalistic explanation for this motif: The annual vanishing and reappearance of water in the region.

Also in the same section of *De Iside* (39), Plutarch uses the term *kibotos* to describe the sacred rites of Osiris:

> On the nineteenth day they go down to the sea at nighttime; and the keepers of the robes [stolists] and the priests bring forth the sacred chest containing a small golden coffer, into which they pour some potable water which they have taken up, and a great shout arises from the company for joy that Osiris is found.[2]

Dionysus's Ark

Osiris's counterpart Dionysus also was placed in an ark, as in a tale recounted by Pausanias (7.19.6-9) about the Trojan Greeks who "found an ark sacred to Liber [Dionysus], which when Eurypilus opened it and saw the image of Bacchus hidden within, he was immediately insane."[3] This Eurypilus or Eurupulos (Εὐρύπυλος) was a suitor of Helen of Troy and a hero from the Trojan War, as found in Homer.

As Pausanias states (7.19.6), this ark/chest story is credited with the cessation of human sacrifice to the goddess Artemis.[4] Note that

---

[1] Here Plutarch uses the term σορός *soros* for "chest," which could also mean "urn," "coffin," "vessel" or "ark." This same word σορός *soros* is used at Gen 50:26, to describe Joseph's coffin, and at Job 21:32 to depict a "tomb."
[2] καὶ τὴν ἱερὰν κίστην, οἱ στολισταὶ καὶ οἱ ἱερεῖς ἐκφέρουσι χρυσοῦν ἐντὸς ἔχουσαν κιβώτιον, εἰς ὃ ποτίμου λαβόντες ὕδατος ἐγχέουσι, καὶ γίγνεται κραυγὴ τῶν παρόντων ὡς εὑρημένου τοῦ Ὀσίριδος.
[3] Allen, D., 238.
[4] "The sacrifice to Artemis of human beings is said to have ceased in this way. An oracle had been given from Delphi to the Patraeans even before this, to the effect that a strange king would come to the land, bringing with him a strange divinity, and this

Christianity too evidently was created in significant part in order to end widespread human sacrifice; hence, in this Greek tale we have a precedent for the later Christian effort.

We read further in Clarke about the sacred ark of the Trojans, which contained Dionysus's image:

> Pausanias likewise testifies [7.19.6] that the ancient Trojans had a sacred ark, wherein was the image of Bacchus, made by Vulcan, which had been given to Dardanus by Jupiter. As the ark was deposited in the Holy of Holies, so the heathens had in the inmost part of their temples an *adytum* or *penetrale,* to which none had access but the priests. And it is remarkable that among the Mexicans, Vitzliputzli, their supreme god, was represented under a human shape, sitting on a throne, supported by an azure globe which they called heaven; four poles or sticks came out from two sides of this globe, at the end of which serpents' heads were carved, the whole make a litter which the priests carried on their shoulders whenever the idol was shown in public.[1]

The Greek word in the pertinent Pausanias passage for "ark" or "chest" is λάρναξ *larnax,* meaning "coffer, box, chest." Regardless of the preferred word, the concept is basically the same as in the story of Aglaurus, using the term *kibotos.* Moreover, here we learn about not only the ark of Dionysus but also that of the Mesoamericans, who share many rites, traditions and myths in common with the "Old World."[2]

As part of the Bacchic spring feast, a "sacred ship, steered by the priest of Dionysus, was carried aloft in procession round the marketplace."[3] During this annual festival also, an image of Bacchus himself was borne as part of the procession through the streets, heralding the god.[4]

Again, if we are going to depict the incredible fairytales of one culture as "history," then we must be prepared to include the stories of other cultures in this category as well. Or, we could choose to accept them as mythical, allegorical, fictional and symbolic.

---

king would put an end to the sacrifice to Triclaria. When Troy was captured, and the Greeks divided the spoils, Eurypylus the son of Euaemon got a chest. In it was an image of Dionysus, the work, so they say, of Hephaestus, and given as a gift by Zeus to Dardanus." παύσασθαι δὲ οὕτω λέγονται θύοντες τῇ Ἀρτέμιδι ἀνθρώπους. ἐκέχρητο δὲ αὐτοῖς πρότερον ἔτι ἐκ Δελφῶν ὡς βασιλεὺς ξένος παραγενόμενος σφίσιν ἐπὶ τὴν γῆν, ξενικὸν ἅμα ἀγόμενος δαίμονα, τὰ ἐς τὴν θυσίαν τῆς Τρικλαρίας παύσει. Ἰλίου δὲ ἁλούσης καὶ νεμομένων τὰ λάφυρα τῶν Ἑλλήνων, Εὐρύπυλος ὁ Εὐαίμονος λαμβάνει λάρνακα· Διονύσου δὲ ἄγαλμα ἦν ἐν τῇ λάρνακι, ἔργον μὲν ὥς φασιν Ἡφαίστου, δῶρον δὲ ὑπὸ Διὸς ἐδόθη Δαρδάνῳ.

[1] Clarke, 1.448.
[2] See my essay "Parallels between Mesoamerican and Middle Eastern/Egyptian Religion and Mythology."
[3] Pausanias/Frazer, 2.374.
[4] Pausanias/Frazer, 2.379-380.

Rather than serving as historical events in which God sanctified the ark, the magical-chest story represents a literary device and motif found in other religions and myths.

Covenants and Testaments

As noted, the Greek word for "covenant" or "testament," διαθήκη *diatheke*,[1] can also be found in God's covenant with Noah, as well as in the New Testament in Matthew (26:28), Mark (14:24), Luke (1:72; 22:20), Acts (3:25; 7:8), Revelation (11:29) and various epistles.

Pagan Covenants

As concerns non-biblical usage, the word διαθήκη *diatheke* appears in the works of numerous pagan writers in antiquity, such as Appian, Aristophanes, Demosthenes, Diodorus, Isocrates, Josephus, Lucian, Plato and Plutarch. Aristophanes (*Birds*, 440) employs the term to convey "to arrange an arrangement," in the name of Apollo.[2] In *Wasps* (584), the playwright uses *diatheke* to denote a will, as in "last will and testament," a connotation likewise intended by the Greek orator Demosthenes (384-322 BCE)[3] and by Plato, as in his *Laws* 11.923-924. Plato's *Laws* (11.926b) also uses the term *diatheke* to refer to "ordained laws concerning testaments,"[4] and it has been surmised that the Bible drew upon Plato as well, which would be possible if parts of the Pentateuch were composed or redacted as late as the third century BCE.

Diodorus (*Lib.* 12.12.4) uses the term specifically to convey "covenants," in discussing Charondas, a "celebrated lawgiver of Catania, in Sicily," identified as having lived during the sixth century BCE, possibly as a student of the great sage Pythagoras (c. 580-504 BCE). After discussing the legislator's "unique law on evil association," the Sicilian historian remarks:

> Charondas also wrote another law which is far superior to the one just mentioned and had also been overlooked by lawgivers before his time. He framed the law that all the sons of citizens should learn to read and write, the city providing the salaries of the teachers; for he assumed that men of no means and unable to provide the fees from their own resources would be cut off from the noblest pursuits.
>
> In fact the lawgiver rated reading and writing above every other kind of learning, and with right good reason; for it is by means of them that most of the affairs of life and such as are most useful are concluded, like votes, letters, covenants, laws, and all other things which make the greatest contribution to orderly life...[5]

---

[1] Strong's G1242.
[2] μὰ τὸν Ἀπόλλω 'γὼ μὲν οὔ, ἢν μὴ διάθωνταί γ᾽ οἵδε διαθήκην ἐμοί.
[3] E.g., *Against Aphobus 1, Against Macartatus*, etc.
[4] Plato/Fowler, 11.433
[5] Diodorus/Oldfeather, 4.399.

It was related of Charondas that he committed suicide in accordance with his own laws, after he perpetrated the capital offense of entering the public assembly wearing his sword.

As we can see, there is nothing singularly special or sacred about the usage of this covenant terminology in a lawgiver tale.

The Golden Calf Redux

The Golden Calf which so irritated the Yahweh-obsessed Moses that he smashed the tablets with the 10 Commandments is declared to have been transmitted with the Israelites from Egypt, as in Exodus (32:4, 8): "These are your gods, O Israel, who brought you up out of the land of Egypt!"

Philo of Alexandria and various Church fathers also claimed that the Golden Calf came from Egypt, following the Bible. We have seen already how Egypt adopted various Semitic deities; this cultural exchange occurred in the other direction as well. Regarding Egyptian religious influence on the Levant, including its deities, Dr. Tryggve N.D. Mettinger, a professor of Old Testament Studies at the University of Lund, comments:

> Egyptian gods must have been known in the Levant during the Late Bronze Age, the time of the Egyptian empire, and probably already during the latter part of the Early Bronze Age. During later periods, names of Egyptian deities even occur as theophoric elements in Phoenician and Punic personal names. This testifies to the continued importance of cultural contacts between Egypt and the rest of the Mediterranean world. Thus, Isis occurs as an onomastic element from the eighth century and onwards and Osiris as early.[1]

This exchange included a temple of Osiris at pre-Israelite Jerusalem, previously noted. In this regard, the solar deity Horus was portrayed as the son of Hathor, "the cow." Hence, he would be a "golden calf," while, as discussed, Marduk too was the "solar calf" who was "broken into pieces." (Jer 50:2)

Molech

The Golden Calf has been identified also with the Semitic god Molech, whom, according to the Bible (Hos 8), the Israelites had been worshipping for years, even though they supposedly were in Egypt during that time.

Since the Bible depicts the Israelites isolated in the wilderness as spontaneously worshipping the Golden Calf, it is inferred that they had known this worship well, such that it was familiar to them naturally. This idea seems strange considering that the Israelites purportedly had been in Egypt for some 600 years, since the time of Joseph. How then did they become so acquainted with Molech?

---

[1] Mettinger, 175.

Baal, El and Atak

Another candidate for the Golden Calf is Baal, depicted as horned and representing the bull.[1] The Canaanite "father of the gods" is also "El the Bull" or "Bull El" (*tr 'il*).[2] As Mark Smith remarks:

> Many scholars are inclined to see El's rather than Baal's iconography behind the famous "gold calf" of Exodus 32 and the bull images erected by Jeroboam I at Bethel and Dan (1 Kings 12), but this iconography has been traced back to Baal as well. Here we might include not only the depiction of Baal in the Ugaritic texts but also the "fierce young bull" (symbol) of the storm-god Adad. Nonetheless, the tradition in ancient Israel favors Bethel originally as an old cult-site of the god El (secondarily overlaid—if not identified—with the cult of Yahweh), perhaps as the place-name Bethel (literally, "house of El") would suggest (Genesis 28:10-22).[3]

The confusion that the Golden Calf is both Semitic and Egyptian may result in part from the fact of Baal syncretized with the Egyptian Seth, the result of which, Baal-Seth, is depicted with horns.

The biblical *destruction* of the golden calf also appears to be a mythical motif in itself, found in Ugaritic texts such as KTU 1.3:III:46, which recites acts by Baal, including the smiting of Yamm and the annihilation of the god of "immense waters." At one point, the speaker says: "I destroyed the calf of 'Ilu, 'tk..."[4] The calf of the Canaanite high god El—one of the major deities in the Old Testament—is the god *'tk* or Atk/Atak/Atik/Atiku/Ataku, the "divine bull-calf" or "divine bullock."[5]

In any event, it is possible that any one or all of these gods could have been in the mind of the biblical writers attempting to outlaw the worship of all but Yahweh. This suggestion is especially true in consideration of how popular was the calf-god motif in the region, reflecting the significance of the bull and cow in the sustenance of life in antiquity.

Mythical Giants

Although some of the taller local tribes such as the Amalekites have been lighted upon in order to bring realism to the story, the Exodus "giants" or *nephilim* tale represents not "history" but an astral or astrotheological motif. In Aramaic, the word *nephila* refers to the constellation of Orion,[6] the giant hunter in the sky who plays an important role in Egyptian religion, among many others. *Gesenius*

---

[1] See, e.g., Niditch, 15.
[2] Day, 34.
[3] Smith, M. (2001), 32.
[4] Rahmouni, 118, 212.
[5] Rahmouni, 256, etc. Atak is also rendered "El's rebellious calf" or "Rebel, the Calf of El."
[6] See, e.g., Job 38:31 in the Aramaic Targums.

cites the "Chaldean"[1] (Akkadian) of this term as נפלא *nephla*, meaning "the giant in the sky, i.e. the constellation Orion, plur. the greater constellations."[2] The plural term *nephilim*, therefore, represents constellations or *stars*, like the *khus* of Egypt.

Another Semitic term used for Orion, גבור *gibbowr*, means "strong man" or "giant"[3] and was "taken from ancient Near Eastern mythology."[4] Orion is called "the giant" also in Arabic, as *al-jabbar*, likewise employed to describe the constellation in the Peshitta or Syriac translation of Amos 8, Job 9:9 and Job 38:31.[5] At Psalm 19:5, it is the *sun* that is called גבור *gibbowr* or "giant."

Sons of God

Again, at Genesis 6:1-4, these Nephilim are said to have been the products of the "sons of God" mating with the "daughters of men." Gray surmises that these verses describing the "amours of the 'sons of God' with the daughters of men" reflect the Canaanite myth of El, "father of the divine family," begetting first the stars of dawn and dusk. This motif appears also at Job 38:7, in which the "sons of God" are mentioned "in parallel" with the "morning-stars."[6] In the myth, El is depicted as seducing two women and begetting the "twin-gods *Šḥr* and *Šlm*, 'Dawn' and 'Evening.'"[7] These twins, Shahar and Shalim, are called *'elm*, "gods,"[8] basically the same word as *elohim* in the biblical Hebrew.

This motif is similar to the Mithraic theme of the god between the two torchbearers or "dadophoroi," representing dawn and dusk, as well as to Christian iconography, in which the two thieves surrounding Christ symbolize heaven and hell. The Canaanite name for the star-god of dusk is essentially *salem*, denoting "peace" in later Hebrew, as in Jeru-*salem*, and in the Arabic greeting, سلام *salaam*.[9] Gray notes that the word Salem's meaning of "peace" is secondary,

---

[1] The term "Chaldean" has been used to describe Assyro-Babylonian priests who originated in Mesopotamia but who eventually became wandering mendicants teaching astronomy/astrology, the Mesopotamian religions in general also known as "Chaldean." The designation "Chaldean" also came to be employed in classical antiquity to describe Aramaic. The Bible uses the term *Kasidim* almost 70 times to describe these southern Mesopotamian people and "wise men," rendered in the LXX as Χαλδαῖος *Chaldaios*, in the singular.
[2] *Gesenius*, DLVI.
[3] Strong's H1368.
[4] Kraus, 272.
[5] The Hebrew for Job 9:9 and 38:31, for example, employs the term כסיל *Kĕciyl* for Orion (H3685).
[6] Gray (1965), 158-159.
[7] Gray (1965), 14.
[8] Gray (1965), 185.
[9] Gray (1965), 185ff.

while "completion" is the root, and here it must connote the completion of a day, which could be perceived as a peaceful time.[1]

In any event, Van Seters avers that the biblical scribes borrowed from Greek mythology "the idea that the gods cohabited with human women and begat superhuman, gigantic offspring."[2]

Battle

Representing not a unique "historical" event, the myth of a battle with giants is found in a number of cultures globally. As but one example, Pausanias (1.25.2) tells us about a "legendary war with the giants who once dwelt about Thrace and on the isthmus of Pallene."[3] This mythical event is recorded in stone at the theater dedicated to Attalus I (269-197 BCE), king of Pergamon,[4] called Σωτὴρ Soter or "Savior" centuries before Christ's purported advent.

Describing the stories of battles between gods, Canaanite mythologist Dr. Ulf Oldenburg remarks:

> The close similarity between the Hurrian, Phoenician and Greek theogonies shows that we have to do with one mythological pattern and...the Greeks must have received this from the Orient, probably via Phoenicia.[5]

Apparently dating back thousands of years, the Pygmies/Ituri/Efé have a story of the triumph of their first man, Efé, over "giant monsters of heaven."[6] In the Egyptian archetype, the conflict is said to represent the victory of the sun over the darkness, as in the story of Osiris/Horus versus Set/Seth.

Conclusion

The Exodus story constitutes not history but myths, stories and traditions of various cultures that served as important reflections of humanity's observations of its natural environment over a period of many thousands of years.

So blatant were the similarities between the Bible and "heathen" traditions that earlier scholars such as Sir Raleigh asserted the Mosaic books to be "stolen almost word for word" by Homer, for one.[7] Evidence to the contrary reveals that these "stolen" elements were combined in a distinctive manner to produce the Moses myth, in order to provide a foundational tradition equal to or better than the epics of other cultures.

---

[1] Gray (1965), 14.
[2] Gmirkin, 6; Van Seters (1992), 80, 155-156.
[3] Pausanias/Frazer, 1.36.
[4] Paus. 1.25: πρὸς δὲ τῷ τείχει τῷ Νοτίῳ γιγάντων, οἳ περὶ Θρᾴκην ποτὲ καὶ τὸν ἰσθμὸν τῆς Παλλήνης ᾤκησαν.
[5] Oldenburg, 9.
[6] Hallet, 120.
[7] Raleigh, 1.195.

The epic's main character, Moses, is significantly not a historical individual but a mythical one with solar attributes, among others, as we shall see. Other elements of the Exodus myth not covered in the current chapter, such as the 10 Commandments, will be discussed in detail below.

Fig. 53. Ass-headed man crucified, with inscription "Alexamenos worships his god," c. 3rd cent. AD/CE. Graffito found at Rome

Fig. 54. Chaos ocean monster battled by Semitic sun god, c. 7th cent. BCE? (Layard, plate 19/83)

The Lawgiver Archetype

"But we must make mention of the lawgivers who arose in Egypt and who ordained some strange and marvelous customs. For in primitive Egypt, after life had become settled (which according to myth took place in the era of gods and heroes), they say that the first person who convinced the people to use written laws was Mneves, a man both lofty in spirit and the most altruistic in his way of life of any lawgiver in memory. He claimed that Hermes had given these laws to him as a source of many substantial benefits; and this, they say, is just what Minos of Crete did among the Greeks and Lycurgos among the Lacedaemonians, the former asserting that he had received his revelations from Zeus, the latter from Apollo. And it is a tradition as well among most other nations that this kind of inspiration was the case, being the cause of many blessings to those who believed. Among the Aryans, they record, Zathraustes [Zarathustra/Zoroaster] pretended that the Good Spirit gave him the laws; and among those called the Getae, who aspire to immortality, Zalmoxis in like manner credited the familiar Hestia with the revelation; and among the Judaeans, Moyses attributed them to the God called by the name of Iao. For all of them believed either that their intent was wonderfully and thoroughly divine if the result would be of benefit to the mass of men, or else they knew that the common people would obey more readily if they were faced with the majesty and might of the beings said to have devised the laws."[1]

Diodorus Siculus, *The Antiquities of Egypt* (1.94)

WE HAVE SEEN that there exists no scientific evidence for a historical Moses or Exodus as depicted in the Bible, and that Israelites were founded as a confederation of hill tribes, rather than through a dramatic exodus out of Egypt. We have concluded that attempts at associating or identifying various purported historical characters and events with Moses and the Exodus have been unsuccessful, often constituting convoluted efforts to fit the purported history to the biblical tales and vice versa. Also demonstrated is the fact that many of these biblical themes are clearly mythical, including the exodus itself, desert/wilderness sojourn, sea parting, heavenly bread, plagues, godly arks, covenants and battles with giants.

With such facts, the figure of Moses resolves not to a historical but to a mythical character, evidently created not only to give divine legitimacy to the biblical law but also to incorporate the worshippers of other religions, such as the followers of Shamash, El, Baal, Dionysus, Horus and numerous other deities popular in the eastern Mediterranean and beyond.

---

[1] Diodorus/Murphy, 119. See *The Study Guide* for the relevant Greek.

As previously mentioned, there have been various prophets and lawgivers in a number of cultures globally, often representing not real people but a tribal or ethnic expression of an archetype that dates back many millennia. This era occurred long before the purported time of the allegedly historical Moses during the 13th century BCE, and many centuries before the Jewish tale was written down. Indeed, this concept of a divinely inspired or appointed leader may date back tens of thousands of years, to the earliest human communities.

The Hero's Birth

One motif common among lawgivers, kings, heroes and deities of old is a miraculous or unusual birth. In the Mosaic nativity story at Exodus 2:1-10, the newborn prophet is placed in a reed basket and set afloat in a river, to be discovered and raised by another family. This story has been compared frequently to the birth tales of other legendary individuals, such as the Akkadian king Sargon the Great (fl. c. 2334–2279 BCE) and the Indian virgin-born hero Karna, both of whom were portrayed as placed by their mothers in reed boats on a river, to be discovered by others.[1] As noted, "Moses" is said to connote "drawn," as from water, a title that could be applied to various heroes saved from the water. Moreover, the fact that Moses's "biography"—supposedly written by the patriarch himself—completely skips his childhood indicates the story's fictional and mythical nature.

Sargon the Great

Regarding these various nativity myths, American professor Dr. David Leeming remarks that the "leaving of the baby in a basket on a river ties Moses to the unusual beginnings of several mythological or legendary heroes, including, for instance, Sargon of Akkad and Siegfried in Germany."[2] Both Sargon and Siegfried go on to become rulers, as does Moses.

Concerning the "Babylonian Moses," Sargon, British Assyriologist Dr. George Smith (1840-1876) states:

> In the palace of Sennacherib at Kouyunjik [Kuyunjik], I found another fragment of the curious history of Sargon... This text relates that Sargon, an early Babylonian monarch, was born of royal parents, but concealed by his mother, who placed him on the Euphrates in an ark of rushes, coated with bitumen, like that in which the mother of Moses hid her child (see Exodus ii). Sargon was discovered by a man named Akki, a water-carrier, who adopted him

---

[1] It has been reported erroneously (including in the first edition of my book *The Christ Conspiracy*) that the Indian river-borne hero was Krishna. However, the story in the *Mahabharata* (8) involves the birth of *Karna*, via the impregnation of the young virgin Kunti by the sun god Surya, after which the new mother is promised her virginity will remain intact. The virgin mother Kunti gives birth immediately to a "shining bright" child, whom she places in the river.
[2] Leeming (2006), 270.

as his son, and he afterwards became king of Babylonia.... The date of Sargon, who may be termed the Babylonian Moses, was in the sixteenth century B.C. or perhaps earlier.[1]

Since Smith's era, Sargon I has been placed in the 23rd-24th centuries BCE, long before the purported time of Moses. As we can see, this scholar of a past era was knowledgeable and scientific about his subject matter; indeed, Smith was an archaeologist on the important excavation at Nineveh, capital of the Assyrians, where he himself unearthed the legend of Sargon.

Moreover, Smith is the discoverer and translator of the *Epic of Gilgamesh*, one of the most famous and important ancient texts of all time. The British scholar's work was pioneering and exemplary, and his conclusions were substantially correct, not "outdated" merely by the fact that he came to them during the 19th century. The greatest adjustment during the century and a half since Smith's time, perhaps, is the dating, which has been fine-tuned due to subsequent discoveries.

Many other such conclusions from earlier scholars have been verified or accepted in the past century, including the doubting of Moses and the Exodus as historical entities, comparing, for example, Moses's birth with that of Sargon's to demonstrate the mythicality of this motif, as Smith had done shortly after discovering the Sargon myth.

Because the Moses story contains Egyptian words, it is argued that it could not have been based directly on the Sargon tale.[2] However, the Babylonian story still could have been in the minds of the Moses myth's composers, using Egyptian archaicisms and terms added for realism, as fiction writers often do.

Ra-Horakhti

The biblical mythmakers may have drawn as well from the Egyptian birth narratives of Ra-Horakhti and others to create an amalgam. Ra-Horakhti is the combined Ra and Horus, both solar deities, representing "Ra, who is Horus of the Two Horizons," the sun at sunrise and sunset. Regarding the biblical mythmaking, religious studies professor Dr. Robert K. Gnuse states, "In my opinion the biblical author has used both the Sargon legend and the Horus myth."[3]

Walker likewise elaborates on this theme, mentioning various similar hero births, including that of the syncretized Ra-Horakhti:

> The Moses tale was originally that of an Egyptian hero, Ra-Harakhti, the reborn sun god of Canopus, whose life story was copied by biblical scholars. The same story was told of the sun hero [Ion]

---

[1] Smith, G., 224-225.
[2] See, e.g., Kitchen, 564.
[3] Gnuse (2011), 52.

fathered by Apollo on the virgin Creusa; of Sargon, king of Akkad in 2242 BC; and of the mythological twin founders of Rome, among many other baby heroes set adrift in rush baskets. It was a common theme. Another Egyptian version of the bulrush basket made it a dense mass of papyrus plants growing out of the water, where Isis placed the infant Horus. In India, the Goddess Cunti gave birth to a hero-child and set him adrift in a similar basket of rushes on the river Ganges.[1]

In the Moses motif, we have what appears also to be a Jewish rendering of the fleeing Isis giving birth to Horus secretly in the swamp, afterwards drawing the child out of the water and resuscitating him when Seth kills him, as in Diodorus (1.25.6).

Dionysus

The solar Dionysus's association with marshes[2] is reminiscent also of this tale of Horus in a swamp or marsh endangered by the prince of darkness Seth.[3] The story appears to be a depiction of the sun being drawn out of the "marshy dawn" or a sunrise over a "reed sea," saved from the water by the virgin-mother dawn goddess.

Apollo and Creusa

As we can see, the miraculous birth motif extends to numerous figures, including solar heroes such as Horus and Apollo. Regarding the myth of Apollo and Creusa, theologian Dr. Marguerite Rigoglioso remarks:

> Creusa, the daughter of the legendary Athenian king Erectheus (grandson of the miraculously born Erichthonius), was impregnated by Apollo and gave birth to her child in a cave, where she left him to die. Interestingly, it was a Delphic Pythia who found and raised the infant (Euripides, *Ion* 12-28, 1334-69), which suggests an intimate connection among Creusa, Apollo, the cave, virgin birth, and the priestesshood of Delphi.[4]

Again, Apollo was invoked as Dionysus, who in turn is identified with the Egyptian god Osiris, all of whom possess prominent solar attributes. In this regard, the Egyptian temple was considered "the place of the birth of the sun,"[5] recalling of the "tent of the sun" in the solar hymns of Egypt, Babylon and Israel, to be discussed below.

Again, the birth of the sun-engendered child in a cave is a common solar motif representing the day star's entry into the night sky or tomb/cave, where it is perceived as dying and resurrecting or being reborn.

---

[1] Walker (1988), 441. "Horakhti" is also transliterated as "Horakhty," "Herakhti," "Harakhti" and "Harakhty," among others.
[2] Pausanias/Frazer, 2.212ff.
[3] See, e.g., Ruether, 66.
[4] Rigoglioso (2009), 198.
[5] *Orientalia Lovaniensia periodica*, 12-13.170.

Shamash

Continuing this nativity theme, German religious historian Dr. Claudia Bergmann notes the similarity between the Moses birth motif and one involving the solar Shamash, when the Hebrew infant in the basket is "seen by the pharaoh's daughter, just as the newborn of the ancient Near Eastern Boat Motif is described as being seen by the god Šamaš [Shamash]."[1]

Adonis

The Greco-Syrian god Adonis was "born in Arabia where Moses dwelt, and was, in his myth, hidden in an ark entrusted to Proserpine [Persephone/Kore]....."[2]

Tyro's Twins

As another example of a water-drawn hero, in a note explicating Aristotle's "The Tyro" (*Poet.* 1454b), named for the Greek princess impregnated by Poseidon, editor Dr. W.H. Fyfe remarks that "Tyro's twins by Poseidon, who appeared to her in the guise of the river Enipeus, were exposed in a little boat or ark, like Moses in the bulrushes, and this led to their identification."[3]

Noah's Basket?

The same Hebrew word for "basket" at Exodus 2:5 to depict Moses's vessel of abandonment, תבה *tebah*, is employed also to describe Noah's "ark."[4] This ark theme in the Noah myth has been said to represent the phases of the moon, a motif likewise associated with Osiris, who, again, was said to be shut in his ark on the same day as tradition holds of the biblical patriarch.

Philo

Reflecting the mythical nature of the Moses tales, in his strikingly misogynistic allegorizing of this birth myth, Philo (*Moses*, 39/27) puts forth the "gnostic" idea of Moses having *no* mother, "born of the father alone":

> ...in accordance with the honour due to the Creator of the universe, the prophet hallowed the sacred seventh day, beholding with eyes of more acute sight than those of mortals its pre-eminent beauty, which had already been deeply impressed on the heaven and the whole universal world, and had been borne about as an image by nature itself in her own bosom; for first of all Moses found that day destitute of any mother, and devoid of all participation in the female generation, being born of the Father alone without any propagation by means of seed, and being born without any conception on the part

---

[1] Bergmann, 66.
[2] Allen, D., 80-81.
[3] Aristotle, vol. 23.
[4] Strong's H8392; Gen 6:14, etc.

of any mother. And then he beheld not only this, that it was very beautiful and destitute of any mother, neither being born of corruption nor liable to corruption...[1]

As we can see, Philo evidently believed it a wonderful thing to be born without any "participation in the female generation," "destitute of any mother" and therefore "neither born of corruption nor liable to corruption." In other words, "mother" and "female" equal "corruption," according to the Jewish philosopher.

In any event, the mythical divine-birth motif has been very common and often represents a solar, lunar or other astrotheological or nature-worshiping concept.

Divine Legislators

Like the divine birth, another ubiquitous tradition was that of civilizing laws and texts passed from a deity to a prophet or holy man, as demonstrated in the quote by Diodorus at the head of this chapter. The common divine lawgiver myth is summarized likewise by Dr. Henricus Oort, a Dutch theologian and professor of Hebrew Antiquities at the University of Leiden:

> No one who has any knowledge of antiquity will be surprised at this [attribution of civilization] to one or more great men, all of whom, without exception, were supposed to have received their knowledge from some deity. Whence did Zarathustra (Zoroaster), the prophet of the Persians, derive his religion? According to the belief of his followers, and the doctrines of their sacred writings, it was from Ahuramazda (Ormuzd) the god of light. Why did the Egyptians represent the god Thoth with a writing tablet and a pencil in his hand, and honor him especially as the god of the priests? Because he was "the lord of the divine word," from whose inspiration the priests, who were the scholars, the lawgivers, and the religious teachers of the people, derived all their wisdom. Was not Minos, the law-giver of the Cretans, the friend of Zeus, the highest of the gods? Nay, was he not even his son, and did he not ascend to the sacred cave on Mount Dicte to bring down the laws which his god had placed there for him?[2]

Referring in the first century BCE to the "dual law," as in *deuteronomy*, Strabo (*Geo.* 16.38-40) discussed various lawgivers of antiquity, among them Moses:

> Law is twofold, divine and human. The ancients regarded and respected divine, in preference to human, law; in those times, therefore, the number of persons was very great who consulted oracles, and, being desirous of obtaining the advice of Jupiter, hurried to Dodona, "to hear the answer of Jove from the lofty oak." The parent went to Delphi, "anxious to learn whether the child which had been exposed (to die) was still living;" while the child itself "was gone to the temple of Apollo, with the hope of discovering its

---

[1] Philo/Yonge (1855), 3.117-118.
[2] Oort, et al., 1.103.

parents." And Minos among the Cretans, "the king who in the ninth year enjoyed converse with Great Jupiter," every nine years, as Plato says, ascended to the cave of Jupiter, received ordinances from him, and conveyed them to men. Lycurgus, his imitator, acted in a similar manner; for he was often accustomed, as it seemed, to leave his own country to inquire of the Pythian goddess what ordinances he was to promulgate to the Lacedæmonians.

What truth there may be in these things I cannot say; they have at least been regarded and believed as true by mankind. Hence prophets received so much honour as to be thought worthy even of thrones, because they were supposed to communicate ordinances and precepts from the gods, both during their lifetime and after their death; as for example Teiresias, "to whom alone Proserpine gave wisdom and understanding after death: the others flit about as shadows."...

Such were Amphiaraus, Trophonius, Orpheus, and Musæus: in former times there was Zamolxis, a Pythagorean, who was accounted a god among the Getæ; and in our time, Decæneus, the diviner of Byrebistas. Among the Bosporani, there was Achaicarus; among the Indians, were the Gymnosophists; among the Persians, the Magi and Necyomanteis, and besides these the Lecanomanteis and Hydromanteis; among the Assyrians, were the Chaldæans; and among the Romans, the Tyrrhenian diviners of dreams.

Such was Moses and his successors; their beginning was good, but they degenerated.[1]

Thus, the ancient world was well aware of the divine lawgivers and their two-fold law. Here we see an ancient comparison from 2,000 years ago between Moses and numerous other lawgivers, such legislators often said to be born of a mortal and a god.[2]

Philo too (*Moses* 2.3.12) revealed he was aware of legislators of other nations but insisted that Moses was the "most admirable of all the lawgivers who ever have lived in any country either among the Greeks or among the barbarians, and that his are the "most admirable of all laws and truly divine."[3] Such efforts constitute obvious propaganda designed for legal hegemony and cultural supremacy.

The following list includes lawgivers around the Mediterranean, Africa, Europe and Asia over the last several thousand years. This roster of the renowned represents not only godly prophets and supposedly mortal heroes but also deities themselves said to be imbued with the power of legislating. The list is not exhaustive, as there are many more such sacred figures purported to have founded numerous civilizations, cultures or ethnicities, including, for example, in the Americas.

---

[1] Strabo/Hamilton, 3.180.
[2] *Journal of the North China Branch of the Royal Asiatic Society*, 8-9:24; Waddell, 35.
[3] Philo/Yonge (2000), 492.

1. Achaicarus/Ahiqar/Ahika of Assyria[1]
2. Adar/Ninib of Nippur[2]
3. Amasis of Egypt[3]
4. Amphiaraus of Argos[4]
5. Apollo of Greece
6. Baal Berith of Canaan
7. Boccharis/Bocchoris/Bakenranef of Egypt[5]
8. Buddha of India/Asia
9. Charondas of Sicily
10. Decæneus of the Byrebistas[6]
11. Demeter and Kore of Greece
12. Dionysus of Greece
13. El/Ilu of Canaan/Ugarit
14. Enki/Enlil of Mesopotamia
15. Gilgamesh of Mesopotamia
16. Hammurabi of Babylon
17. Hermes of Egypt/Greece
18. Inana/Inanna of Sumer[7]
19. Isis of Egypt[8]
20. Lawspeaker of Scandinavia
21. Lycurgus of Sparta[9]
22. Manes of Maeonia/Lydia[10]
23. Manis of Phrygia[11]
24. Mannus of Germany
25. Manu of India
26. Mercury of Rome
27. Minos of Crete
28. Mneves/Menes/Menas of Egypt[12]
29. Monius of Egypt[13]
30. Moses of Israel

---

[1] Strabo (*Geo.* 16.39) mentions Achaicarus, whose story is found also in an Aramaic papyrus from around 500 BCE.
[2] Clay, 179-180.
[3] Diodorus 1.95; Diodorus/Murphy, 120.
[4] Strabo, *Geo.* 16.39.
[5] Diodorus 1.94.5: τέταρτον δὲ νομοθέτην φασὶ γενέσθαι Βόκχοριν τὸν βασιλέα, σοφόν τινα καὶ πανουργίᾳ διαφέροντα. Sherman (19): "Diodorus mentions five Egyptian monarchs as great legislators: Menes, Sasychis, Sesostris, Boccharis (called the Wise), and Amasis."
[6] Strabo (*Geo.* 16.39).
[7] Kramer, 159-160, citing *Inanna's Descent*.
[8] Diodorus 1.14; Diodorus/Murphy, 15.
[9] Diodorus 1.94.1-2; Strabo, *Geo.* 16:39; Josephus, *Ap.* 2.220.
[10] Plutarch, *Iside* 24; cf. Herodotus, 1.94; 4.45.
[11] Upton, 16.
[12] Diodorus 1.94; Diodorus/Murphy, 119.
[13] This figure, Monius, was equated with Moses by the Jewish rabbi Aben Ezra or Abraham ibn Izra, with both names said to derive from Mὼ *Mo*, meaning "water." (Veil, 161)

31. Moso of Israel[1]
32. Musaeus of Greece[2]
33. Neba or Nebo of Babylon, Borsippa and Sumeria[3]
34. Nimrod of Babylon
35. Orpheus of Greece
36. Osiris of Egypt
37. Plato of Greece
38. Pygmy lawgiver of the Congo
39. Romulus of Rome
40. Sasychis of Egypt[4]
41. Sesoösis of Egypt[5]
42. Shamash of Babylon
43. Shapash of Ugarit
44. Shu of Egypt[6]
45. Solon of Greece
46. Thoth of Egypt
47. Trophonius of Boetia[7]
48. Ur-Nammu of Sumeria
49. Þorgnýr of Iceland
50. Zalmoxis of the Getae[8]
51. Zarathustra/Zoroaster of Persia
52. Zeus of Greece[9]

To reiterate, some of these divine lawgivers were gods, while others were said to be heroes or prophets who allegedly received the laws from a god or goddess. In certain instances, both occur, such as with Apollo, who himself is a divine lawgiver but who was claimed also to use human agents such as Lycurgus of the Lacedaemonians/Spartans. The same development occurred with Ahura Mazda,

---

[1] A Byzantine text relates that the ancient Greek scholar Lucius Cornelius Alexander Polyhistor (fl. 1st cent. BCE) described a Hebrew *woman*, Moso (Μωσώ), "whose composition is the laws of the Hebrews." (Cook, 15)
[2] Eusebius, *Prep. Evang.* 9.27.
[3] Isaiah 46:1. Strong's (H5015) defines נבו *Nēbow* as a "prophet" as well as "a Babylonian deity who presided over learning and letters; corresponds to Greek Hermes, Latin Mercury and Egyptian Thoth." Hence, he shares the same role as Hermes, the civilizer and lawgiver. *Gesenius* comments that Nebo is the planet Mercury, "worshipped as the celestial scribe by the Chaldeans (Isa. 46:1) and the ancient Arabians." The popularity of Nebo/Mercury worship among the Chaldeans/Babylonians and Assyrians is evident from names such as Nebuchadnezzar and Nabonedus.
[4] Diodorus 1.94.3; Diodorus/Murphy, 119.
[5] Diodorus 1.94; Diodorus/Murphy, 120.
[6] Massey (1907), 2.630. Shu was identified frequently with Thoth or Hermes/Mercury, while his son Seb/Geb was said to be equivalent to Kronos/Saturn. (Boylan, 171; Brugsch, 13, 20)
[7] Strabo, *Geo.* 16.39.
[8] Diodorus 1.94; Diodorus/Murphy, 119. The Getae constituted various tribes who lived in Thrace.
[9] Strabo, *Geo.* 16.39.

Shamash, Zeus and Hermes/Thoth, said to be the civilizing entities themselves but also to employ human intermediaries to convey the legislation. Traditionally, it is the sun who gives the law to mankind; thus, Apollo, Shamash, and so on.

Ur-Nammu

As part of lawgiver literature extending back thousands of years, the Sumerian legislator myths were recorded on cuneiform tablets from the late third to early second millennia BCE, centuries before the purportedly historical Moses allegedly climbed Mt. Sinai and served as the prophet for the Jewish heavenly ruler of the universe, Yahweh.

Citing the Sumerian figure of Ur-Nammu (fl. c. 2112–2095), in *History Begins at Sumer* Dr. Samuel N. Kramer included an entire chapter entitled, "The First 'Moses,'" in which he remarks, "There are indications that there were lawgivers in Sumer long before Ur-Nammu was born."[1] He also states that the literature of the Sumerians "left its deep impress on Hebrews," clarifying that the influence was indirect, through the Canaanites, Babylonians and others subsequent to the Sumerian culture.[2]

Fig. 55. Sumerian king Ur-Nammu approaches the god Enlil, c. 21st cent. BCE. Stele from Mesopotamia

Ur-Nammu was the builder of the Great Ziggurat at Ur, the best preserved and most famous of these striking Mesopotamian edifices, which was dedicated to the city's patron deity, the moon god Nanna. Ur-Nammu is known also for descending into the underworld in a myth 2,000 years older than the same tradition regarding Jesus Christ. His legal code is the oldest surviving and contains several laws very similar to those in Hammurabi's code and the much later Mosaic law.

Menes/Manes, Manis and Mannus

Even earlier than Ur-Nammu was the Egyptian king Μήνης Menes, as Herodotus and Manetho style him, thought to have lived at some point between 5867 and 3000 BCE, this latter date representing the First Dynasty's founding, as accepted by modern consensus. Menes, also known as Hor-Aha Men and Tusu-Menna, is said to have founded the city of Memphis, as well as uniting Upper and Lower Egypt. Egyptologists surmise that this "name," Menes, may be in reality a *title* for the pharaoh known as Narmer, historical founder of the First Dynasty, as well as for other individuals.

---

[1] Kramer, 55.
[2] Kramer, 143-144.

THE LAWGIVER ARCHETYPE

In his quest, Menes led his army "across the frontier and won great glory."[1] Menes's tale sounds like a basic archetypal framework upon which the Moses/Promised Land and other such lawgiver/prophet stories were woven, some of these with similar names or titles.

For example, there is also Manes the first king of Maeonia/Lydia,[2] as well as Manis, first king of Sumeria and Phrygia, and Mannus, divine lawgiver of the Germans. Although he seems to drop out of sight afterwards, Mannus was discussed by Tacitus (*Germania* 2), speaking firstly of the Germans:

> In their ancient songs, their only way of remembering or recording the past, they celebrate an earth-born god, Tuisco, and his son Mannus, as the origin of their race, as their founders. To Mannus they assign three sons, from whose names, they say, the coast tribes are called Ingævones; those of the interior, Herminones; all the rest, Istævones. Some, with the freedom of conjecture permitted by antiquity, assert that the god had several descendants, and the nation several appellations, as Marsi, Gambrivii, Suevi, Vandilii, and that these are genuine old names.[3]

The genealogy assigned to Mannus and his three sons is reminiscent of Noah and his three sons, possibly representing a very ancient legendary archetype that predates both cultures by thousands of years. The native Teutonic tribal word for "Germans," *Alemanni*, appears to derive from Mannus, as does the German *alle Männer*, meaning "all men."[4] In this regard, Mannus was considered to be the "first man," a common role for a lawgiver, such as Menu in the Indian mythology.

Menu/Manu

The original Moses has been traced also to Menu or Manu, the Sanskrit word मनु *manu* meaning not only "man" but also "wise," "intelligent" and "thinking," as in the Latin-derived "*men*tation." Like Menes, apparently, *manu* is not necessarily a name of a particular person but a title signifying the "Man par excellence or the representative man and father of the human race,"[5] also the "legislator" or "lawgiver." This title denoting lawgiver, we are told, was "aspired to by all the leaders of antiquity."[6]

---

[1] Verbrugghe, 131.
[2] Faber, 2.195.
[3] See, e.g., Kelley, Donald, 95.
[4] Peck, 1.726.
[5] *Sanskrit Dictionary for Spoken Sanskrit*, spokensanskrit.de
[6] Jacolliot, 75.

Minos

Another of the aforementioned versions of this archetype is the Cretan king Minos, a title said to derive from Menes.[1] Regarding this "Cretan Moses," famed archaeologist Sir Dr. Arthur J. Evans, excavator of the site of Knossos on Crete, remarked:

> ...it is as the first lawgiver of Greece that [Minos] achieved his greatest renown, and the code of Minos became the source of all later legislation. As the wise ruler and inspired lawgiver there is something altogether biblical in his legendary character. He is the Cretan Moses, who every nine years repaired to the cave of Zeus, whether on the Cretan [Mount] Ida or on [Mount] Dicta, and received from the god of the mountain the laws for his people. Like Abraham, he is described as the "friend of God."[2]

Various important attributes of both Moses and Abraham thus are not original or unique to them, as can be said of many other Mosaic and Abrahamic motifs and characteristics.

Law Code/Tablets of Law

The lawgiver archetype usually includes a law code or codes, comprising commandments of one sort or another. To reiterate, the Ten Commandments evidently represent a modified version of various ancient writings, such as in Egyptian, Babylonian and other texts. In addition to the 10 Commandments are the numerous laws in the books of Leviticus, Deuteronomy and elsewhere, such as at Exodus 20:22-23:23. In this regard, this biblical "Book of the Covenant" reflects the "Canaanite variation" of the various civil codes of the second millennium BCE, such as the laws of the Babylonians, Hittites and Assyrians.[3]

Ebla and Baal-Berith

In the Ebla texts from the third millennium BCE can be found numerous Semitic religious and social practices that predate similar Hebrew doctrines, rituals and traditions by many centuries. These analogous practices include a complex legal code and scapegoat rituals, preceding not only the Hebrew but also the Canaanite/Ugaritic cultural equivalents. There is little reason to suppose that the Israelite law truly was handed down supernaturally by Yahweh to a historical Moses, rather than representing a continuation of this very old code.

Walker relates that the "stone tablets of law supposedly given to Moses were copied from the Canaanite god Baal-Berith [Jdg 8:33], 'God of the Covenant.'"[4] She then adds that the Canaanite Ten

---

[1] See, e.g., Wunderlich, 196-198.
[2] Evans, 426.
[3] Gray (1965), 8.
[4] Walker (1983), 677.

THE LAWGIVER ARCHETYPE

Commandments were "similar to the commandments of the Buddhist Decalogue" and that, in the ancient world, "laws generally came from a deity on a mountaintop," such as in the story the Persian god Ahura Mazda giving the tablets of the law to the prophet Zoroaster or others discussed here, including Gilgamesh, Hammurabi and Minos.

Egyptian Book of the Dead

The basic sentiment of various biblical commandments can be found in the *Egyptian Book of the Dead*, particularly the 125th chapter or spell, which existed by at least the 19th century BCE. This spell contains much else beyond the 10 Commandments, however, resembling some of the numerous other commandments, ordinances and instructions of Exodus, Leviticus and Deuteronomy.

The *Book of the Dead* likewise depicts the "Hall of the Double Law or Truth where the divine lawgiver Osiris presided as Judge of the Dead."[1] It is before Osiris in this hall that the deceased must appear to state the 42 affirmations and denials or "negative confessions" about behaviors during the life of the deceased.

Because these are "negative confessions," instead of the commandment, "You shall not steal," the deceased, hoping for eternal life in heaven, states, "I have not stolen."[2]

Enki, Enlil and the Tablets of Me

Another code "divinely handed down" can be found in *Inanna's Descent* (2nd millennium BCE) in the story of the "seven divine laws," which the goddess Inanna "fastened at the side," while placing in her hand "all the divine laws," as she descended into the underworld.[3] In a similar vein are the decrees or *mes* initially collected by Enlil, eventually given to his brother and Inanna's father, Enki, god of wisdom and magic.

The lawgiver, "king of the gods" and "ruler of the universe," Enlil was also called "mountain" (*kurgal*), and his temple was the "House of the Mountain." He was likewise the "prophet" or mouthpiece for the heavenly Anu or An, centuries before Moses on Mt. Sinai with Yahweh. Like Yahweh, Enlil both created mankind and destroyed it with a flood.

Fig. 56. Enki, Sumerian god of wisdom and fresh water, c. 2200 BCE. Cylinder seal, British Museum

---

[1] Hallet/Pelle, 108-109.
[2] See *The Study Guide* for the full chapter 125.
[3] Kramer, 159-160.

The "biblical" counterpart is therefore archetypical and mythical, not reflective of "history."

Tablets of Destiny

This Mesopotamian myth about civilizing foundational decrees and godly gifts is reiterated in the *Enuma Elish*, in the Babylonian tale of Tiamat and the "tablets of destiny" After a fierce battle between Tiamat and Marduk reenacted during the spring's New Year festival, these powerful artifacts ended up in the hands of Marduk, conferring upon their holder(s) the "supreme authority as ruler of the universe."[1]

The Code of Hammurabi

Detailed legal pronouncements for numerous situations can be found also in the Code of Hammurabi, which dates to the 18th century BCE and in which four of the 10 biblical commandments appear repeatedly.

For example, the ninth of the Ten Commandments or Decalogue is, "You shall not bear false witness against your neighbor," whereas in the Code of Hammurabi, we read: "1. If a man bring an accusation against a man, and charge him with a (capital) crime, but cannot prove it, he, the accuser, shall be put to death.... 3. If a man, in a case (pending judgment), bear false (threatening) witness, or do not establish the testimony that he has given, if that case be a case involving life, that man shall be put to death."[2]

As another example, the familiar eighth commandment, "You shall not steal," is similar to Hammurabi's sixth commandment: "If a man steal the property of a god (temple) or palace, that man shall be put to death; and he who receives from his hand the stolen (property) shall also be put to death." The punishment for breaking the biblical commandments likewise is death.

Roman Tables of Law

In addition, it was the "custom among the ancients to [engrave] their laws on tables of brass, and fix them in some conspicuous places, that they might be open to the view of all."[3] In this regard, in his *History of Rome* (3.34-37), Livy refers to the "Laws of the Ten Tables" that were "passed by the Assembly of Centuries," a legislative body called "Comitia Centuriata."[4] These were created around 451-449 BCE by 10 men or a decemvirate, who initially made 10 tables and then added two more. These 12 contained the Roman law code,

---

[1] Rosen, 283.
[2] Harper, 11.
[3] Davidson and Clarke, v. 89-139, note on Ovid (*Metamorphoses* 1.92): *Nec verba minacia fixo aere legebantur*. Speaking of the Golden Age, Ovid says: "No harsh decrees were fixed on brazen plates." Arthur Golding's translation from 1567 renders this passage as: "there was no threatning lawe [i]n brazen tables nayled up" (sic).
[4] ...*centuriatis comitiis decem tabularum leges perlatae sunt*...

called "Law of the Twelve Tables" or *Lex XII Tabularum*,[1] which formed the core of the Roman Constitution, inscribed on 12 tablets or either ivory or bronze and hung in the Forum.

Plato's Laws

A number of commentators in antiquity—including Aristobulus of Paneas (2nd cent. BCE) and Church fathers Justin Martyr,[2] Clement of Alexandria (*Strom.* 1.22), Origen (182-254 AD/CE) and Eusebius (263-339 AD/CE)[3]—pointed out the correspondences between Moses and Plato, attempting to make the latter the plagiarist of the former, to suit biblical doctrine and precedence. However, chronology tells another story, and there are recent scholarly efforts to demonstrate that the Mosaic law in the Pentateuch draws from Plato.[4]

Aristobulus of Paneas supposedly was a wandering Hellenistic Jewish philosopher who studied in Alexandria during the second century BCE. It has been surmised that he is the Aristobulus to whom the Jewish apocryphal text 2 Maccabees (c. 124 BCE) is addressed, which indicates he may have known about the Jewish Dionysus worship discussed therein.

Aristobulus purportedly referred to a flawed earlier Greek translation of the Pentateuch that was replaced by the Septuagint. Interestingly, his account appears to be devoid of any indication of the events in Genesis, leading some scholars to conclude that the book was not in this earlier edition.[5] The existence of this purported earlier Greek text, however, has been questioned.

In a fragment of his writings preserved by Church historian Eusebius (*Praep. ev.* 13.12), Aristobulus "deduces from certain previous discussions (no longer extant) that both Plato and Pythagoras drew upon a translation of the Mosaic Law before the time of Demetrius of Phalerus (and this before the Septuagint...)."[6]

However, the editors of *The Jewish Encyclopedia* assert that "further examination of the works attributed to Aristobulus confirms the suspicion as to their genuineness aroused by their eclectic character" and that the quotes attributed to him are "probably

---

[1] See *The Study Guide* for selections of the code.
[2] Ciholas (223): "The most extensive and somewhat unexpected accusation of Plato's plagiarism of Moses appears in the writings of Justin."
[3] Eusebius (*Praep. ev.* 11.10) claimed to be quoting the philosopher Numenius of Apamea essentially as saying: "Plato derived his idea of God from the Pentateuch. Plato is Moses translated into the language of the Athenians." (Velikovsky, 109) There, the Church father cites Numenius as remarking, "What else is Plato but Moses speaking Attic Greek?" As Eusebius was a fervent Christian apologist, his citation has been questioned; however, Numenius's alleged observation would not be uncharacteristic for the era, as we can see here.
[4] For an analysis of the comparisons, see Sinks's "The Laws of Plato Compared with the Laws of Moses." As of the writing of this book, Gmirkin was working on a relevant monograph possibly to be titled *Plato and the Creation of the Hebrew Bible*.
[5] See, e.g., Gmirkin, 8.
[6] Singer, Is. (1916), 2.98.

spurious," drawing upon the later Philo, for example.[1] In any event, these quotes, which may date from the second century of the common era instead, demonstrate once more that in ancient times Moses and Plato were being compared.

Philo too was fascinated by Platonic philosophy, and "at many points we have the impression that he considered Plato as the Attic Moses."[2] The fact that Philo spends so much time on Plato, his "philosophical master" whom he calls "the most holy Plato" (*Prob.*13),[3] demonstrates that Jews had been interested in the Greek philosopher for some time.

In *Preparation for the Gospel* (11.10.14ff), Eusebius spends considerable time on this subject of Plato "stealing" Mosaic ideas; however, modern scholarship recognizing the late dating of much of the Pentateuch may prove the opposite.

Concerning St. Augustine's Platonic esteem and need nevertheless to subordinate the Greek philosopher to the Bible, Dr. Paul Ciholas remarks:

> Plato's influence on Christianity is discussed mostly in Books VIII and X of *The City of God*. There Plato is considered as one of the greatest minds of antiquity, superior to many gods. The task of Augustine is to vindicate the greatness of Plato while proclaiming him inferior to prophets and apostles.
>
> The debt of Christianity to the Platonic system is only reluctantly conceded by Augustine...[4]

Parallels between biblical and platonic ideology were so obvious in antiquity that it was surmised, as by Ambrose of Milan, that Plato had traveled to Egypt and the Levant, meeting with the prophet Jeremiah (655-586 BCE), son of Hilkiah the priest, who purportedly "found" the Pentateuch.

This anachronistic notion has been rebutted, and there is little evidence that pre-Christian Greek philosophy was influenced by Jewish texts, rather than the other way around. The fact that the Jewish scriptures needed to be translated into Greek demonstrates how popular, esteemed and entrenched was the Hellenization of the Mediterranean of the time.

Rather than assuming Plato had a copy of a text that does not appear in the historical record until centuries later—a text sacred to one of the most secretive sects, who thought it blasphemy for outsiders to read—it would seem that both Greeks and Jews had access to far older legal codes, as discussed here.

---

[1] Singer, Is. (1916), 2.98.
[2] Ciholas, 221.
[3] κατά τον ἱερώτατον Πλάτωνα. See Philo/Winston, 2.
[4] Ciholas, 220.

The Lawgiver Archetype

Hecataeus of Abdera

The Mosaic law is not original and was not given to the Hebrew lawgiver by Yahweh via a miraculous event on Mt. Sinai. Regarding the Greek historian Hecataeus of Abdera, who was known in antiquity to have drawn up a foundational story for Moses and the Israelites, Gmirkin remarks:

> Plato's *Laws*—which Jaeger considered a major source on Hecataeus's foundation story—recommended twelve tribes as the ideal number. Twelve-tribe alliances were a common feature in Greek tradition.[1]

Contra the apologists of yore who thought Plato plagiarized Moses, Gmirkin theorizes that the creators of the Mosaic law had before them a copy of Plato's Laws, at Alexandria during the third century BCE, when they drafted the Pentateuch as we know it.

While the Bible's composition certainly dates to a later period, the Iron Age hill settlements who emerged as Israelites apparently already had a legal code of some sort, and we may surmise that Jewish priests and scribes accessed the libraries of Ashurbanipal and Babylon during the seventh and sixth centuries BCE. These facts do not preclude continuously reworking of oral traditions and texts for centuries until they took the shape in the Pentateuch, possibly influenced by Plato.

Pygmy Lawgiver

The idea of a divine lawgiver dates back millennia, possibly to the earliest human communities. Among these groups would be the Pygmies of Central and South Africa, whose legends were recorded in modern times by Belgian anthropologist Dr. Jean-Pierre Hallet (1927-2004). For decades, Hallet lived on and off among the peaceful Pygmy people of the Congo named Efé, recording their traditions as pristinely as possible and demonstrating they had not been influenced by biblical tales at that point.

In this regard, Hallet's entire book *Pygmy Kitabu* is dedicated not only to recording these stories but also to showing that there is no reason to attribute them to the Bible and any possible missionary activity. On the contrary, these myths seem to represent far older archetypal germs of biblical, Egyptian and Near Eastern stories, among others.

As concerns the antiquity of the legislator and law motif, regarding the *Book of the Dead* and Mosaic law Hallet and his assistant Alex Pelle remark:

> Osiris's legal code rather strikingly resembles the Pygmies' Sinai-style commandments. The legendary history of Osiris echoes the Pygmy stories of the ancestral lawgiver. The Efe legends tell of how

---

[1] Gmirkin, 50.

this civilizing hero ascended to heaven and assumed his role as the patron saint or angel of the moon. A similar ascent was attributed to Osiris and to another Egyptian divinity, Thoth, who may represent Osiris in the specific role of moon-god, since he was portrayed like Osiris as the civilizing hero and the "begetter of law."[1]

As noted, Philo wrote about Moses's ascension, as an immortal to sit with God, and the New Testament represents the Hebrew lawgiver appearing at Jesus's transfiguration as an immortal in heaven. (Mt 17:3) As we can see, the divine legislator appears to be pre-historic and initially reflective of archaic lunar mythology possibly dating to many thousands of years ago.

Hallet and Pelle devote considerable space to the lawgiver legends, remarking:

...The Egyptian founders of man's oldest historic civilization identified the Pygmies with their great ancestral gods.

The God of these beautiful Pygmy "gods" is represented as the Giver of the Law. "In the beginning," say the Pygmies, "God lived with men and gave them his commandments." The religion of the gods is practiced by every person who observes the Pygmies' Sinai-style commandments. About their legal code, [anthropologist] Schebesta says, "The commandments and prohibitions of the Supreme Legislator are another thing from taboo, and are not merely economic or social precepts: they are of an ethical nature."...

...God is usually represented as the original source of the commandments, the lunar angel as the intermediary who transmits the deity's laws to the primordial Pygmy nation.[2]

Hallet and Pelle go on to explain that the first man is the lunar angel who receives the law and commandments from God. They also say: "Like Thoth and Osiris, the ancestral Efé lawgiver is represented as the inventor of all the arts and sciences."[3] These arts and sciences included astronomy, botany, medicine, music and zoology, remnants of which possibly were passed along from remote ages and carried with migrations out of Africa. These observations would change, of course, based on the natural environment as peoples migrated. Since these origin stories are incorporated into religion in countless ways, religious ideas too accompanied peoples migrating for thousands of years, likewise mutating according to environment and era.

Mountains of the Moon

As stated by Hallet and Pelle, the Pygmies claimed that "in ancient times their lawgiving father-god-king reigned near Ruwenzori, the Mountains of the Moon."[4] The scholars further remark:

---

[1] Hallet and Pelle, 109.
[2] Hallet and Pelle, 106.
[3] Hallet and Pelle, 110.
[4] Hallet and Pelle, 111.

In this neighborhood, according to the Pygmies, they received the deity's laws and commandments. Moses' book of Exodus locates the lawgiving scene at a mountain called Sinai. Its name has well-known connections with Babylonian Sin, the god of the moon. The *Britannica* article on this god says that "in Arabia and throughout the Semitic races of Western Asia the moon god was from the beginning the most important deity." By placing the lawgiving scene at Sinai, the mountain of Sin, the Bible seems to confirm that the commandments were handed down from the Mountain of the Moon.[1]

Hence, we have a lawgiver associated with mountains. Indeed, the mountain of the moon would be called "Sin" in Semitic, the name of the moon god, said to be related to the Sinai of biblical myth. Hallet and Pelle further point out that the volcanic scenes in the biblical tale are inappropriate for the region of the Levant and Arabia; these very ancient stories likely come from elsewhere, therefore, possibly the "still-active Virunga volcanoes...located within easy reach of the Pygmy-populated forest near the Mountains of the Moon."[2]

When factored in with all the other research by Hallet, Pelle and others regarding the Pygmies, along with what we know about comparative religion elsewhere, it is reasonable to see in these myths evidently very ancient germs of stories handed down to us in literature from other locations and later epochs.

Conclusion

The archetypal lawgiver myth as discussed throughout the current chapter takes the following basic framework:

1. The hero goes on an arduous journey.
2. He must cross an impassable body of water.
3. He climbs a mountain.
4. There he speaks with the great or most high god.
5. He receives a law or civilizing code.
6. He proceeds into the "promised land," where he teaches the people.

Not all lawgivers possess all of these attributes, while some have more. Many details differ, as does order, based on location, era, ethnicity, language and so on.

Nevertheless, it is clear that the idea of a man, woman or deity transmitting a divine law code to humanity ranks as very ancient and pre-Mosaic, resolving to a mythical archetype expressed in many places. Moreover, several of these figures have a great deal in common with Moses in numerous details but precede his appearance in the historical record, which occurs centuries after his purported era.

---

[1] Hallet and Pelle, 111.
[2] Hallet and Pelle, 116.

Fig. 57. Sunrise over Luxor, Egypt, as the baby sun god Horus emerges from the reeds of the Nile. (RaniaHelmy)

Fig. 58. Mary A. Lathbury, *Pharaoh's Daughter Finding Moses*, drawing the baby from the reeds of the Nile, 1898. (*Child's Story of the Bible*)

The Dionysus Connection

"The only gods the Arabs recognize are Dionysus and Urania; the way they cut their hair—all round in a circle, with the temples shaved—is, they say, in imitation of Dionysus. Dionysus in their language is Orotalt, and Urania Alilat."[1]

Herodotus, *The Histories* (3.8.3)

"...the time and manner of the greatest and most holy solemnity of the Jews is exactly agreeable to the holy rites of Bacchus; for that which they call the Fast they celebrate in the midst of the vintage..."

Plutarch, *Symposiacs* (4.6.2)

"In Bacchus we evidently have Moses. Herodotus says [Bacchus] was an Egyptian... The Orphic verses relate that he was preserved from the waters, in a little box or chest, that he was called *Misem* in commemoration of the event; that he was instructed in all the secrets of the Gods; and that he had a rod, which he changed into a serpent at his pleasure; that he passed through the Red Sea dry-shod, *as Hercules subsequently did*...and that when he went to India, he and his army enjoyed the light of the Sun during the night: moreover, it is said, that he touched with his magic rod the waters of the great rivers Orontes and Hydaspes; upon which those waters flowed back and left him a free passage. It is even said that he arrested the course of the sun and moon. He wrote his laws on two tablets of stone. He was anciently represented with horns or rays on his head."[2]

Sir Godfrey Higgins, *Anacalypsis* (2.19)

"That the god Bacchus was the archetype of Moses seems to have been the opinion of many learned men, particularly the celebrated Bishop Huet, and...Vossius, who agree that the Arabian name of Bacchus is *Meses*."

Logan Mitchell, *Christian Mythology Unveiled* (13)

ONE OF THE renowned ancient legislators was the Greek god Dionysus, said to have traveled widely and to have civilized many lands with his laws. Over the centuries, many scholars have noticed correspondences between Dionysus/Bacchus and Moses, such as we have already noted, including the ark and the wilderness sojourn. There are many other such parallels, as we shall also see, detailed in numerous accounts from antiquity which demonstrate

---

[1] Herodotus/de Selincourt, 156. Διόνυσον δὲ θεῶν μοῦνον καὶ τὴν Οὐρανίην ἡγέονται εἶναι, καὶ τῶν τριχῶν τὴν κουρὴν κείρεσθαι φασὶ κατά περ αὐτὸν τὸν Διόνυσον κεκάρθαι· κείρονται δὲ περιτρόχαλα, ὑποξυρῶντες τοὺς κροτάφους. ὀνομάζουσι δὲ τὸν μὲν Διόνυσον Ὀροτάλτ, τὴν δὲ Οὐρανίην Ἀλιλάτ.

[2] "Dionysos threatens the River Hydaspes when the god attempts to drown his troops." ("Phaethon," *Theoi.com*, citing Nonnos, *Dionysiaca* 23.236 ff, tr. Rouse.)

that correlations between the Dionysian and Jewish religions were noticed thousands of years ago.

Early History

The earliest extant reference to Dionysus by that name appears on a stele from the 13th century BCE found at the ancient city of Pylos on the Greek Peloponnesus, traditional home of King Nestor from Homer's *Iliad*. Written DI-WO-NI-SO-JO in the Mycenaean script called Linear B, "Dionysus" may be the pre-Greek Pelasgian name for the vine and wine god. In this regard, linguist Dr. Carl J. Becker comments that "**Deiw*...is also the root of Dionis, the epithet of Sabasius, the beer god...."[1] He further remarks:

> Dionis was the epithet for and then the priest or acolyte of the tradition of Hermes whose earlier affiliation was with Sabazius, a beer god. According to Antonije Skokljeve and Ivan Skokljeve, Dionis, a Pelasgian god, was the son of Zevs from Nissa, a forested hill in Thrace. The Hellenic Greeks would come to know Dionis as Dionysus, a wine god in the Age of Iron.[2]

The Pelasgian proto-Dionysus could date to the middle of the second century or perhaps earlier.

The Pelasgians

A possible source of proto-Greek wine myths, the Pelasgian natives of Greece have been surmised to come originally from Egypt,[3] as was asserted anciently of Dionysus as well. It has been said that their name means "sea men," and their description in the *Odyssey* as existing "among the tribes in the ninety cities of Crete, 'language mixing with language side by side,'"[4] sounds like they were part of the sea peoples, as does their notoriously warlike nature.

Crete

Like Moses's lawgiver counterpart Minos, Dionysus has a long history with the island of Crete, where these prominent figures may have shared mythical attributes. In this regard, Dionysian scholar Dr. Carl Kerenyi (1897-1973) examined the evidence of a proto-Dionysus character on Crete centuries to millennia prior to the god's clear emergence under that name, as the deity of mead, the fermented honey popular on the island before the cultivation of the grapevine and wine-making.

---

[1] Becker, 223. Hastings (3.36) says that *sabaia* means "beer" in Illyrian, the language of Indo-European peoples by the same name who thrived in the western Balkans and southeastern Italian peninsula in antiquity. The Illyrian ethnicity emerged around 1000 BCE, while the Illyrian language became extinct by the fifth century BCE.
[2] Becker, 247.
[3] Hugh Johnson, "Story of Wine."
[4] Homer, *Odyssey*, 19.175–19.177 (Fagles translation).

THE DIONYSUS CONNECTION

The reverence of a wine deity likely dates back many thousands of years, based on the antiquity of wine-making, which extends to at least 7,000 years ago in what is now the country of Georgia. Iran and Armenia are also sites of early viniculture, dating to around 4,500 and 4,100 BCE, respectively.

Dionysus as a Cretan wine god seems to have accompanied the spread of viniculture from Egypt, where wine-making can be traced to pre-dynastic times 5,200 years ago or more.[1] This introduction of the grapevine on Crete, along with the development of viticulture and viniculture,[2] may have been facilitated by the people later known as the Phoenicians, whose major city, Byblos, was occupied beginning around 8800 to 7000 BCE.[3]

Moving even farther back, Oxford scholar Robert Graves (1895-1985) sees the god of intoxicated revelry in a cave painting dating to possibly 10,000 or more years ago, obviously not labeled by the Greek moniker "Dionysus" but possessing related archaic attributes. In *The White Goddess*, Graves first describes a popular Dionysian festival celebrated for centuries before the common era:

> At Athens, the [Bacchic] festival, called the Lenaea, ("Festival of the Wild Women") was held at the winter solstice, and the death and rebirth of the harvest infant Dionysus were similarly dramatized. In the original myth it was not the Titans but the wild women, the nine representatives of the Moon-goddess Hera, who tore the child in pieces and ate him. And at the Lenaea it was a yearling kid, not a bull, that was eaten; ...Apollodorus says that Dionysus was transformed into a kid...[4]

Here we see that Dionysus dies and is reborn at the winter solstice or "Christmas," the traditional time of Jesus's birth.[5] The Passion of Osiris too was celebrated at that time around the turn of the common era, per the Egyptian wandering calendar, and the births of several other solar deities traditionally occurred throughout the month of December as well.[6] It is further noteworthy that, whereas Jesus is the Lamb, Dionysus is the Kid or baby goat.

Lunar Observations

As another astrotheological theme, Graves's nine "wild women" serving as satellites of the lunar goddess are said to represent phases of the moon, which "eats" the light of the weak winter sun as it wanes, tearing the solar orb to pieces. A similar motif can be found in

---

[1] Kerenyi, 56-57.
[2] "Viticulture" is the cultivation of grapevines, while "viniculture" is "the process or business of growing grapes and making wine." "Vinification" is also the process of wine-making, and the study of wine and winemaking is called "oenology."
[3] Peltenburg and Wasse, 182.
[4] Graves, R., 399.
[5] See my article "Dionysus: Born of a Virgin on December 25th, Killed and Resurrected after Three Days."
[6] See my *2010 Astrotheology Calendar*, 35.

the tale of Bacchus's alter ego Osiris, who is rent into 14 pieces—the days of the waning lunar fortnight—by the serpent of the night, Seth. The interplay in this Egyptian myth reflects that of the sun and moon, a natural cycle that seemed sacred and divine to the ancients, the reverence for which was taken quite seriously.

It is because of this mythical and astrotheological configuration that Graves next identified the ancient cave painting as relating the same "Bacchic" scene:

> The most ancient surviving record of European religious practices is an Aurignacian cave-painting at Cogul in North-Eastern Spain of the Old Stone Age Lenaea. A young Dionysus with huge genitals stands un-armed, alone and exhausted in the middle of a crescent of nine dancing women, who face him. He is naked, except for what appear to be a pair of close-fitting boots laced at the knee; they are fully clothed and wear small cone-shaped hats. These wild women, differentiated by their figures and details of their dress, grow progressively older as one looks clock-wise around the crescent...[1]

Again, by using the term "Dionysus," Graves is not asserting that it was written on the walls of the cave; rather, he is employing it to describe a very ancient archetype. The Aurignacian period extended from 34,000 to 23,000 years ago, and, while this particular set of cave paintings has been placed by more recent scholars into later times within the past 10,000 years—also an uncertain date—it remains possible that the primeval cult of the wild nature god existed farther back, perhaps in once-fertile areas now submerged, desertified or otherwise destroyed.

Many ancient cave paintings are found in now-submerged places around the Mediterranean, which may have had some sort of primitive viticulture and viniculture using wild grapes many thousands of years ago. The beauty and grace of these paintings demonstrate a cultured people, as well as one in which certain individuals—here artists who were possibly also priests—possessed enough leisure time to create works of art that have stood the test of time.

Sumerian Dionysus?

We have seen already that the epithet "Dionis" evidently represents a Pelasgian god affiliated with the beer deity. As concerns a possible non-Greek, early origin of Dionysus, Becker posits a Sumerian root for the theonyms Diony, Dionis, Dionigi and Dionizy:

> It was Diony...that would travel to the Near East and pick up the suffix *sus*, meaning "healing" in Sumer. In Sumer he was known as *IA-U-NU-ShUSh* that meant "seed of semen of life giving, healing." Upon his return to Europe he became known as Dionysus.[2]

---

[1] Graves, R., 399.
[2] Becker, 352.

THE DIONYSUS CONNECTION

Some have noted the similarity of this Sumerian healing god's name IAUNuShUSh to "Yehoshua" ("Yah saves"), essentially the same as "Joshua," which is "Jesus" or "Iesous" in the Ionic Greek.[1] This name "Iesous" in turn is related to the Attic form "Iaso" and "Iasios" or "Jason," which connote "healer."[2]

Becker also says:

> In ancient Danubian tradition Dionis was associated with the beer god and with the horse; Dionysus is associated with the grape and goat.[3]

In this regard, possibly the oldest known script was discovered at the Danubian site of Tărtăria, Romania, on tablets thought to date to 5500-5300 BCE. The three small tablets of clay inscribed with "proto-writing" called "Vinča symbols" or "Vinča signs" have not been deciphered yet.

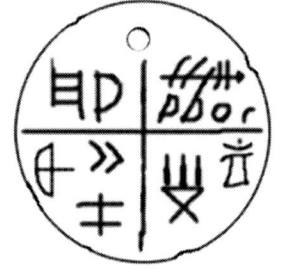

Fig. 59. Vinča symbols, c. 5300 BCE. Clay amulet from Tărtăria, Romania

Dionysus in Literature

As concerns the extant historical record, Dionysus is mentioned or featured by many ancient writers, some of whom wrote entire tracts, histories or plays about him, these latter performed in numerous theaters throughout the region, as noted. A wildly popular god around the Mediterranean wherever the grapevine has grown, Dionysus's name is raised up hundreds of times in literature, and his image is featured on thousands of artifacts.

Therefore, we will concentrate only on those writers and myths relevant to this current comparative-religion study. Also, in places where there is repetition, the full testimony of these various individuals both from antiquity and in more modern times, has been included in *The Study Guide*.

Summarizing the works by some of these ancient writers, Israeli scholar Dr. Abraham Schalit (1898-1979) remarks:

> The non-Jews of Alexandria and Rome alleged that the cult of Dionysus was widespread among Jews. Plutarch gives a Bacchanalian interpretation to the Feast of Tabernacles... According to Plutarch the subject of the connection between the Dionysian and Jewish cults was raised during a symposium held at Aidepsos in Euboea, with a certain Moiragenes linking the Jewish Sabbath with the cult of Bacchus, because "even now many people call the Bacchi 'Sabboi' and call out that word when they perform the orgies of Bacchus." Tacitus too thought that Jews served the god Liber, i.e., Bacchus-Dionysus, but "whereas the festival of Liber is joyful, the Jewish festival of Liber is sordid and absurd." According to Pliny,

---

[1] See, e.g., Allegro, 35.
[2] See., e.g., Ruck (2001), 146.
[3] Becker, 354.

Beth-Shean was founded by Dionysus after he had buried his wet nurse Nysa in its soil. His intention was to enlarge the area of the grave, which he surrounded with a city wall, although there were as yet no inhabitants. Then the god chose the Scythians from among his companions, and in order to encourage them, honored them by calling the new city Scythopolis after them (Pliny, *Natural History* 5:18, 74).

An inscription found at Beth-Shean dating from the time of Marcus Aurelius [121-180 AD/CE] mentions that Dionysus was honored there as *ktistes* [founder]. Stephen of Byzantium reports a legend that connects the founding of the city of Rafa also with Dionysus (for the Dionysian foundation legends of cities in the region, see Lichtenberger's study). It is wrong to assume as some do that Plutarch took his account of the festival of Tabernacles from an antisemitic source, for despite all the woeful ignorance in his account it contains no accusation against, or abuse of, the Jews.

It is more likely that Plutarch described the festival of Tabernacles from observation, interpreting it in accordance with his own philosophical outlook, which does not prevent him, however, from introducing into it features of the cult of the famous Temple of Jerusalem gleaned by him in his wide reading. The description as a whole, however, is of Tabernacles as it was celebrated in the Greek diaspora at the end of the first and the beginning of the second century C.E., and not as it was celebrated in the Temple, which had already been destroyed for more than a generation. The festival undoubtedly absorbed influences from the environment, so that Plutarch could indeed have witnessed what he recognized as customs of the Dionysian feast.[1]

In view of what we have seen and will continue to see here, we submit that Plutarch's account is not "woefully ignorant" and that the influence of Dionysianism on Jewish religion began before the First Temple period, including among the Amoritish proto-Israelites who eventually settled the hill country.

Beth Shean

The important ancient town of Beth Shean or Beit She'an (Bethshan, Βαιθσάν, Βεθσάνη)—meaning "house of tranquility"—was called "Scythopolis" in Greek and supposedly was founded by Dionysus. Beth Shean is referred to several times in the biblical books of 1 and 2 Samuel, as well as in

Fig. 60. Beth Shean, here called by Greek name, Scythopolis (Nichalp)

---

[1] *Encyclopedia Judaica* (2008).

Judges and others, and is located strategically in the fertile Jordan Valley, south of the Sea of Galilee and east of the Samarian hill country. Situated at the juncture between the Jordan and Jezreel Valleys, this region is also deemed the "West Bank" of the Jordan River. It is noteworthy that one of the area's largest winepresses was found at Jezreel, one of many such devices in ancient Israel.[1]

The Scythopolis/Beth Shean region began to be occupied from at least the fourth millennium BCE, with settlements in the third millennium onward, until an earthquake destroyed it in the Early Arab period (749 AD/CE).

In the Late Bronze Age (15th-12th cents. BCE), Beth Shean was an Egyptian administrative center, followed by a Canaanite city (12th-11th cents. BCE) and then an Israelite settlement (10th cent.-732 BCE). During this time, the people worshipped many different gods, including those of the Canaanites, Egyptians, Greeks and Philistines. A stele from the era of pharaoh Seti I mentions Egypt's victory over the neighboring hill tribes, among whom were the Hapiru.[2]

Grapevine cultivation in the Beth Shean area apparently began during the fourth millennium BCE,[3] and it may be suggested that the vine and wine cult existed in the region long before the Israelites arrived or emerged. As noted, Greek occupation of Asia Minor to the northwest began by 1200 BCE, leaving several centuries between that time and when the Pentateuch emerges clearly in the historical record.

Therefore, it is probable that the rituals of the Jews during the time of Diodorus and Plutarch derived from many centuries before, with influence from other cultures over the centuries that the area was occupied. This influence, of course, would extend to peculiarities of the Dionysian cultus as developed hellenically. So entrenched was the city's association with Bacchus, in fact, that Pliny the Elder (23-79 AD/CE) equated Beth Shean/Scythopolis with Nysa, "so named of Father Liber, because his nurse was buried there."[4]

Thus, it should not surprise us if the town was "founded" by the archaic wine god and if the Jewish fertility and harvest festival comprised many elements of Bacchic religion, possibly absorbed during the occupation of Beth Shean by Israelites. Other cities, such as Rafa, Rafah or Raphia (Egyptian *Rph*) in southern Israel/Palestine on the border of Egypt, were claimed also, as by Stephanus of Byzantium (fl. 6th cent. AD/CE), to have been founded by the wine god.

---

[1] Govier, "Biblical Archaeology's Top Ten Discoveries of 2013."
[2] "Beit She'an," *Jewish Virtual Library*.
[3] McGovern, et al., 26.
[4] Pliny, *Nat. Hist.* 5.18; Pliny/Holland, 1.71.

Homer

Centuries prior to the appearance of Moses in the literary record, Dionysus is included around 900 BCE in *The Iliad* and *The Odyssey*. In *The Iliad* (6.130-141), Homer depicts the Trojan War hero Diomedes—expressing trepidation at battling the gods—as describing the Spartan king and lawgiver Lycurgus's encounter with Dionysus:

> ...for even the son of Dryas, mighty Lycurgus, lived not long, seeing that he strove with heavenly gods—he that on a time [drove] down over the sacred mount of Nysa the nursing mothers of mad Dionysus; and they all let fall to the ground their wands, smitten with an ox-goad by man-slaying Lycurgus. But Dionysus fled, and plunged beneath the wave of the sea, and Thetis received him in her bosom, filled with dread, for mighty terror gat hold of him at the man's threatenings. Then against Lycurgus did the gods that live at ease wax wroth, and the son of Cronos made him blind; and he lived not for long, seeing that he was hated of all the immortal gods. So would not I be minded to fight against the blessed gods.[1]

Here we find mention of Dionysus on Mt. Nysa, born of two mothers, and fleeing into the sea from a tyrant who is killed, indicating these motifs date back to at least the 10th century BCE. This subduing of Lycurgus under Dionysus may reflect a political change or desire, such as raising the "Dionysian" city of Thebes above Sparta.

In *The Odyssey* (11.321-325), the myth of Ariadne, Theseus and Dionysus is briefly mentioned, relevant especially because Bacchus's wife, Ariadne, is the Cretan lawgiver Minos's daughter. This "marriage" possibly reflects a merger between peoples, one of whose lawgivers was Minos and the other Bacchus.

In consideration of how the Greek poet treats his subject matter, as if such well-developed stories were common knowledge, we can evince that various of these mythical themes in some form may be centuries to millennia older than the period of Homer.

Hesiod

The grape and wine are ever-present in the Homeric epics,[2] while around 750 to 650 BCE the Greek poet Hesiod (*Op.* 614, *Theog.* 914) also related that the sacred beverage was a gift from Dionysus. In his *Theogony* (940-949), Hesiod describes the birth of Dionysus to the mortal woman Semele, subsequently deified, as well as his marriage to Ariadne.[3] The poet styles Bacchus as the "golden-haired," representing an obvious solar epithet; so too was Apollo "golden-haired."[4]

---

[1] Homer/Murray (1965), 271.
[2] See, e.g., Unwin, 86.
[3] Hesiod/Evelyn-White, 149.
[4] Aristotle, *Rhetoric* 3.8.6.

THE DIONYSUS CONNECTION

In his *Shield of Hercules* (394-401), Hesiod speaks of the noisy locust in the heat of summer:

> And when the dark-winged whirring grasshopper, perched on a green shoot, begins to sing of summer to men—his food and drink is the dainty dew—and all day long from dawn pours forth his voice in the deadliest heat, when Sirius scorches the flesh (then the beard grows upon the millet which men sow in summer), when the crude grapes which Dionysus gave to men—a joy and a sorrow both—begin to colour, in that season they fought and loud rose the clamour.[1]

Here we see a description of the ripening of the "crude grapes," which are likewise a gift from Bacchus. Dionysus's association with Sirius is noteworthy, as Osiris has a close connection to Sirius, including being identified with the "sharp star," as well as its husband, when it is deemed to be Isis. Indeed, Sirius rising heliacally in the summer signifies the birth of Osiris, as well as the Nile overflowing its banks (Isis) to produce the wheat and other foliage, such as the popular and sacred grapevine.

In *Works and Days* (609-614), Hesiod recounts the process for wine-making, also using astronomical details for the timing:

> But when Orion and Sirius are come into midheaven, and rosy-fingered Dawn sees Arcturus, then cut off all the grape-clusters, Perses, and bring them home. Show them to the sun ten days and ten nights: then cover them over for five, and on the sixth day draw off into vessels the gifts of joyful Dionysus.[2]

Hesiod translator Dr. Hugh G. Evelyn-White notes that the time when "rosy-fingered Dawn sees Arcturus" is September, the full harvest of the grapes. The fruits are then turned into the divine elixir of the god of revelry and truth, as in the saying, *In vino veritas* or "In wine, truth," referring to the reduction of inhibition after one has imbibed alcohol.

Hesiod wrote during the era when the Jewish reformer kings Hezekiah and Josiah may have been composing or commissioning parts of the Pentateuch. However, elements of the Mosaic epic apparently come from the following decades to centuries, after Homer and Hesiod wrote about Dionysus.

Homeric Hymns

We turn next to the hymns ascribed pseudepigraphically to Homer that date from around the seventh to sixth centuries BCE. *Homeric Hymn 1 to Dionysus* describes the birth of the god, addressed as "heaven-born" and "insewn," born to Zeus by "pregnant Semele" near the "deep-eddying river Alpheus."[3] The hymn explains that there are several versions of the god's birth, which is to be

---

[1] Hesiod/Evelyn-White, 247, 249.
[2] Hesiod/Evelyn-White, 49.
[3] Homer/Evelyn-White, 287.

expected for the deity of the grapevine, a plant spread far and wide in antiquity, among numerous cultures around the Mediterranean and beyond, into India and many other regions.

One of these other accounts of the god's nativity is described thus: "The Father of men and gods gave you birth remote from men and secretly from white-armed Hera."[1] Hera, of course, is the wife of Zeus, the latter of whom we can see here addressed as "Father of men and gods," displaying the concept of God the Father several centuries before the common era and the rise of Christianity.[2] In this regard, Hera is depicted in myths as bathing once a year in order to renew her virginity; hence, she is a virgin mother.[3]

In this Homeric hymn (1), we also read about Mt. Nisa or Nysa: "There is a certain Nysa, a mountain most high and richly grown with woods, far off in Phoenice, near the streams of Aegyptus [Egypt]."[4]

In language that sounds biblical, the god's mother, Semele, is described in this hymn as "Thyone" or Θυώνη, meaning "portion of sacrifice," from the Greek verb θύω *thyo*, to "offer burnt-sacrifice," referring to her incineration by Zeus upon Bacchus's birth. Hence, she sacrifices herself to give birth to the messiah, as Dionysus is styled "savior,"[5] using the same term employed in the Bible to describe Yahweh and Jesus.[6] The scapegoat sacrifice of a sacred personage for the benefit of humanity, as we find in the later Christianity, was common centuries before Jesus's purported advent, exemplified also in the stories of Prometheus and Persephone.

In *Homeric Hymn 26 to Dionysus*, we read more about the "loud-crying god, splendid son of Zeus and glorious Semele" who grew up "in the dells of Nysa" in a "sweet-smelling cave."[7] In this hymn, Bacchus is also styled "god of abundant clusters," referring to the all-important grape.

Anacreon

The Greek lyric poet Anacreon (582-485 BCE) composed a number of odes to Bacchus and wine. The poet (*Ode 6 on Bacchus*) also emphasizes the god as "young and fair"[8] and "youthful," conveying his symbolizing indestructible life, immortality and regeneration. *Ode 18* praises Dionysus as "the god of wine and joy."[9] Anacreon also has

---

[1] Homer/Evelyn-White, 287.
[2] The nominative and genitive of Ζεύς Zeus are Δῖος Dios, while the Laconic or Boeotian form is Δεύς Deus, cognate with the Latin *deus*, whence the Italian *dio*, French *dieu*, Spanish *dios*, etc.
[3] James, E.O, 196; Rigoglioso (2010), 65ff; (2009), 121, etc.
[4] Homer/Evelyn-White, 287.
[5] Pausanias (2.37.2) calls Dionysus Σαώτης *Saotes*, meaning "Savior" and deriving from σαόω *saoo*, the same root as σωτήρ *soter*. (Liddell, 724)
[6] LXX Deut 32:15; Lk 1:47; Jn 4:42.
[7] Homer/Evelyn-White, 451.
[8] Pindar/West, 176.
[9] Pindar/West, 185.

an ode (26), "In Praise of Wine," in which he extols the virtues of this ancient medicine and intoxicant that helps people forget their woes.[1] *Ode 27* again praises Bacchus as the god of wine and joy.[2] In *Ode 50*, Anacreon exalts Bacchus's medicinal contribution of wine and grapes, which prove to be the "best physician."[3]

Pindar

Like Anacreon, the Greek poet Pindar (522–443 BCE) composed a dithyrambic or "wildly enthusiastic" hymn to Bacchus in the *Seventh Isthmian Ode*, including attributes such as the solar epithet "fair-haired" or "flowing-haired" (εὐρυχαίτης). Both Anacreon and Pindar serve to demonstrate how important and hoary was the worship of the god of wine. Indeed, the proliferation of the Dionysian cult by this time, demonstrated in the widespread observance and literature concerning the god, serves as evidence of its antiquity.

Herodotus

In the fifth century BCE, in discussing the Ethiopian city of Meroe, Herodotus (2.29) commented, "The inhabitants worship Zeus and Dionysus alone of the gods, holding them in great honour."[4] At 2.42, the Greek historian relates that Dionysus is the same as Osiris:

> ...not all Egyptians worship the same gods—the only two to be universally worshipped are Isis and Osiris, who, they say, is Dionysus.[5]

Among a number of other parallels with Osiris, Dionysus is hacked to pieces, by giants, after which his mother, the nature and grain goddess Demeter/Ceres, puts him back together and restores him to life, a myth similar to elements of the deaths and resurrections of both Osiris and Horus.

Pig Sacrifice

Herodotus (2.47-49) further recounts that, in Egypt, the "unclean" pig was sacrificed only to Dionysus and the moon, swineherds serving as an "untouchable" class:

> Pigs are considered unclean. If anyone touches a pig accidentally in passing, he will at once plunge into the river, clothes and all, to wash himself; and swineherds, though of pure Egyptian blood, are the only people in the country who never enter a temple, nor is there any intermarriage between them and the rest of the community...
>
> The only deities to whom the Egyptians consider it proper to sacrifice pigs are Dionysus and the Moon. To both of these they offer pigs at the same time, at the same full moon, and afterwards eat the flesh...

---

[1] Pindar/West, 190.
[2] Pindar/West, 190; Pindar/Greene, 37.
[3] Pindar/Wheelwright, 56.
[4] Herodotus/de Selincourt, 96.
[5] Herodotus/de Selincourt, 101.

> Everyone, on the eve of the festival of Dionysus, sacrifices a hog before the door of his house.... In other ways the Egyptian method of celebrating the festival of Dionysus is much the same as the Greek...
>
> Now I have an idea that Melampus the son of Amythaon knew all about this ceremony; for it was he who introduced the name of Dionysus into Greece... The names of nearly all the gods came to Greece from Egypt.[1]

As is evident, the taboo against pigs is not confined to the Jewish culture but existed in Egypt as well, demonstrating that it was not a result of a commandment from Yahweh exclusively to his chosen. The plunging into water related to swine-herding reminds one of the destruction by Jesus of Satan's minions by casting them into pigs and drowning them (Mk 5:13).

Appropriately, the legendary Pylos ruler and seer Melampus is asserted traditionally to have introduced Dionysus to the Greek mainland. Pylos, as noted, is where the earliest known reference in Greek to the god was discovered.

Reincarnation

At 2.123, Herodotus relates that Dionysus and his grandmother Demeter, goddess of earth and grain, introduced the concept of transmigration of the soul, also known as reincarnation or metempsychosis:

> The Egyptians say that Demeter and Dionysus are the chief powers in the underworld; and they were also the first people to put forward the doctrine of immortality of the soul, and to maintain that after death it enters another creature at the moment of that creature's birth. It then makes the round of all living things—animals, birds and fish—until it finally passes once again, at birth, into the body of a man. The whole period of transmigration occupies three thousand years. This theory has been adopted by certain Greek writers, some earlier, some later, who have put it forward as their own....[2]

The word for "transmigration" here is περιήλυσις *perielysis*, which means "coming around" or "revolution." As we can see, the idea of rebirth or revivification in a new body was well known nearly 500 years before the common era, undoubtedly extending back much farther and possibly having its origin in India or even earlier in Africa. The introduction of this type of resurrection is attributed to Dionysus, one of the chief gods of the underworld, like Osiris, Lord of Resurrection.[3]

Orotalt

As we saw, Herodotus (3.8) described the popular wine god's presence among the Arabs, saying that Bacchus and his wife,

---

[1] Herodotus/de Selincourt, 104-105.
[2] Herodotus/de Selincourt, 131.
[3] See, e.g., my book *Christ in Egypt* for a discussion of Egyptian resurrection.

"Urania" (Venus/Aphrodite), were the only deities recognized by them, the god's Arabian name rendered "Orotalt."[1] Appropriate for this comparison to Dionysus, the Arabian/Nabatean god Orotalt was known by the epithet Ḏū Shará, Dushara or Dusares, meaning "Lord of the Mountain." Here again is the theme of a lawgiver associated with a mountain and its deity, in this case Mt. Seir,[2] whence Yahweh was said to emanate as well (Deut 33:2), revealing an important parallel between "Dionysus" and the Jewish god.

Orotalt may be identified with the deity *A'arrā*, equivalent to Dusares, "the most important Nabatean deity, himself identified with Dionysus..."[3] Others suggest that "Orotalt" represents a corruption or "phonetic transcription" of the name Ruḍā or Ruldaw/RḌW/Y, an Arabian sun god[4] "identical with one of the deities from Dumah."[5] Dumah evidently refers to the ancient Akkadian city of Adummatu, in what is now northwestern Saudi Arabia, near Jordan.

Nifty Nabateans

This solar deity was worshipped by the famous Arab merchants, the Nabateans, who traded in spices, such as frankincense and myrrh, as well as medicine, among other products. Although at some point they abstained from alcohol consumption, their abstinence eventually adopted into Islam, it appears that among the "medicine" they traded was wine: According to Diodorus (19.94.3), Hieronymus of Cardia (4th cent. BCE) recounted the Nabateans as teetalers; however, following "a certain Athenodorus," writing around 60 BCE, the Nabateans "held magnificent drinking-bouts."[6]

Concerning Hieronymus's statements, we read: "In the course of time the Nabateans changed their way of life to become excellent wine-growers, both in the Negev and in Transjordan."[7] In this regard, the industrious Nabateans had planted extensive vineyards and other vegetation in the desert.[8] Coins dating to the third century AD/CE from the region of Bostra, where viticulture had been practiced for centuries to millennia, depict a wine-press and inscription to "Dousaria"[9] (Orotalt/Dionysus), revealing that the practice continued in the region into the common era.

---

[1] Herodotus/de Selincourt, 156.
[2] Hare and Kressel, 57.
[3] Asheri, 407.
[4] Doniger, 70.
[5] Restö, 604.
[6] Retsö, 285.
[7] *Israel Museum Journal*, 3.32.
[8] Langfur, "Nabateans."
[9] Lutz, 152.

The Arabian Bacchic-devotee haircut mentioned by Herodotus (3.8.3) may be a form of tonsure, a pre-Christian rite adopted by monks of certain Christian sects, with the bulk of the head shaved, leaving a ring above the ears.

Mysteries of Dionysus

We learn further from Herodotus (4.79) about the Scythian impression of the "mysteries of Dionysus," which drove their participants into a "Bacchic frenzy."[1] The Greek historian (4.65) discusses "the *Iacchus* song, which is sung at the Dionysiac mysteries," familiar from the "religious ceremonial at Eleusis."[2] Herodotus (8.65) also relates that "Iacchus" is the "cry of the mysteries."[3] The term Iacchus or Iakkhos (Gk: Ἴακχος) means "song," applied to Dionysus as an epithet and associated with other deities, such as his wife, the love goddess Aphrodite.[4] Thus, the highly popular god was a major figure in the mysteries, particularly those of the famed Eleusis. Moreover, Iakkhos has been equated with "Iao" and the Jewish tetragrammaton YHWH.[5] Hence, again, it would not be surprising if Jews were involved in Bacchus worship.

Fig. 61. Celtic head with tonsure, c. 3rd century BCE. Stone carving from Czech Republic (CeStu)

Orphic Hymns

The Greek figure of Orpheus is not a single "historical" individual but a combination of characters, real and mythical, along with the multiple people who wrote the hymns pseudepigraphically attributed to him. This fictional composite is depicted in antiquity as the "St. Paul" of his purported time, travelling in nearly the same areas as the later Christian apostle, while preaching the god known as "Savior" (Bacchus), centuries before Jesus Christ supposedly lived.

The Orphic Hymns are dated by mainstream scholarship to between the sixth century BCE and the fourth century AD/CE, while remaining devoid of any significant Christian influence. There are those, furthermore, who see in these hymns very ancient ideas

---

[1] Herodotus/de Selincourt, 240-241.
[2] Herodotus/de Selincourt, 469.
[3] καὶ οἱ φαίνεσθαι τὴν φωνὴν εἶναι τὸν μυστικὸν ἴακχον.... τὴν δὲ ὀρτὴν ταύτην ἄγουσι Ἀθηναῖοι ἀνὰ πάντα ἔτεα τῇ Μητρὶ καὶ τῇ Κούρῃ, καὶ αὐτῶν τε ὁ βουλόμενος καὶ τῶν ἄλλων Ἑλλήνων μυεῖται· καὶ τὴν φωνὴν ἧς ἀκούεις ἐν ταύτῃ τῇ ὀρτῇ ἰακχάζουσι. Here we see τὸν μυστικὸν ἴακχον or "the Iacchon mystery," from the "mysteries verb" Ἰακχάζω *Iakkhazo*, meaning "to shout."
[4] Euripides, *Cyclops* 69.
[5] Colenso, 3.310. See discussion below.

possibly emanating from pre-Greek Pelasgian culture,[1] which in turn was associated in antiquity with both mainland Greece and Crete.[2] Diodorus (3.67.5) tells us that traditionally Orpheus was said to have written in the Pelasgian alphabet, which would make him an archaic figure.

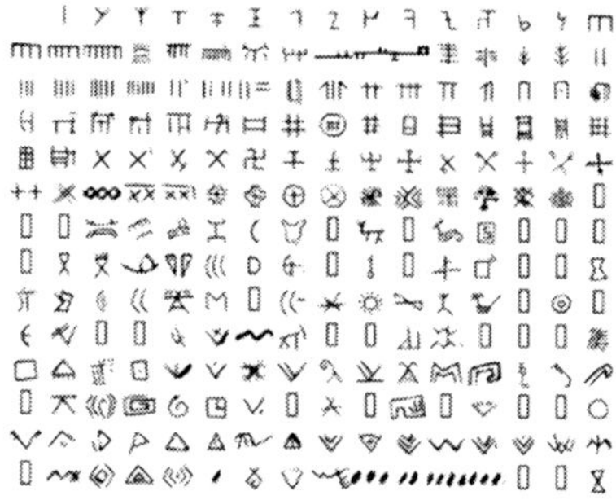

Arguing for the latest dating of the Orphic Hymns to the third or fourth centuries AD/CE, New Testament professor Dr. Matthew E. Gordley nevertheless remarks that they contain much older ideas:

Fig. 62. Possibly proto-Pelasgian Vinča script, c. 5th millennium BCE, Romania

> First, though composed later than the Colossian hymn, the Orphic Hymns contain within them elements derived from Orphic worship, and Greek religion in general, that most certainly originated centuries before the birth of Christ. The position that a majority of scholars favor holds that the hymns were not simply composed out of thin air by a third or fourth century poet with a long list of divine epithets ready at hand. Rather, in the third century, revered literary sources already in existence were tapped for the creation of an appropriate cult literature for the newly popularized religious movement associated with Orpheus.[3]

Whether or not the hymns are late, Orphic religious elements predate Christianity by centuries. These include characteristics of Dionysus's "life," as well as rituals, traditions and doctrines, in common with the Mosaic tale and religion.

---

[1] See, e.g., Pausanias (3.20.5), who claimed that Orpheus was especial to the Pelasgians, as well as Herodotus (2.51), who recounted that the Orphic/Bacchic/Samothracian mysteries gods, the Cabeiri, originally were Pelasgian: "Whoever has been initiated into the rites of the Cabeiri, which the Samothracians learned from the Pelasgians and now practice, understands what my meaning is. Samothrace was formerly inhabited by those Pelasgians who came to live among the Athenians, and it is from them that the Samothracians take their rites." The Pelasgians may have worshipped the god Ares as their sun god, representing the warrior aspect of the solar deity. Robert Graves (*Greek Myths* 1.27) asserts that the principal Pelasgian deity was a parthenogenetic female named Eurynome who gave birth to all creation without male consort.

[2] Strabo, *Geography*, 5.2.4: "Almost every one is agreed that the Pelasgi were an ancient race spread throughout the whole of Greece, but especially in the country of the Æolians near to Thessaly.... Homer informs us that there were colonies of them in Crete... Likewise Æschylus in his Suppliants, or Danaids, makes their race to be of Argos near Mycenæ." τοὺς δὲ Πελασγούς, ὅτι μὲν ἀρχαῖόν τι φῦλον κατὰ τὴν Ἑλλάδα πᾶσαν ἐπιπολάσαν καὶ μάλιστα παρὰ τοῖς Αἰολεῦσι τοῖς κατὰ Θετταλίαν... παρ᾽ ὅσους ποτὲ ἀφιγμένοι τετυχήκασι. καὶ γὰρ τῆς Κρήτης ἔποικοι γεγόνασιν, ὥς φησιν Ὅμηρος... Αἰσχύλος δ᾽ ἐκ τοῦ περὶ Μυκήνας Ἄργους φησὶν ἐν Ἱκέτισι καὶ Δαναΐσι τὸ γένος αὐτῶν...

[3] Gordley, 164.

Pergamon and Tenedos

Gordley also suggests that the "likely place of composition of these hymns was Pergamum [Pergamon] in Asia Minor."[1] As such, they may reflect originally the attributes of an ancient wine god of that region in what is now Turkey, where grapes had been grown and wine made for thousands of years. To this day and despite the land's Islamic status, this northwestern region of Turkey produces popular wines, such as on the island of Bozcaada or Tenedos, famed for its grapes since antiquity, with 80 percent of its arable land used for grapevines.

Nile-Born Musaeus

According to Eusebius (*Praep. ev.* 13.12), citing Aristobulus of Paneas (fl. c. 160 BCE?), the Orphic hymns contained the following sentiments about the legendary Athenian lawgiver Musaeus (c. 450 BCE), whom the Church father surmises is Moses:

> ...So men of old, so tells the Nile-born sage,
>
> Taught by the twofold tablet of God's law...[2]

While this poem overall is addressed ostensibly to Musaeus, this part of it apparently refers not to the historical philosopher by that name, or to the Hebrew Moses, but, rather, to Dionysus.

Illustrating Dionysus's solar nature, in the Orphic hymns Apollo frequently is invoked as Bacchus.[3]

Euripides

The ancient Athenian playwright Euripides (5th cent. BCE) wrote a lengthy narrative about Dionysus and his female followers called *The Bacchae*, starting the account with the god speaking about himself, as the son of Zeus/God (Διὸς παῖς *dios pais*) and Semele.

Euripides next depicts Dionysus at Thebes describing his various travels, evidently reflecting the spread of viticulture or vine-growing:

> I have left the wealthy lands of the Lydians and Phrygians, the sun-parched plains of the Persians, and the Bactrian walls, and have passed over the wintry land of the Medes, and blessed Arabia, and all of Asia which lies along the coast of the salt sea with its beautifully towered cities full of Hellenes and barbarians mingled together; and I have come to this Hellene city first, having already set those other lands to dance and established my mysteries there, so that I might be a deity manifest among men.
>
> In this land of Hellas, I have first excited Thebes to my cry, fitting a fawn-skin to my body and taking a thyrsos in my hand, a weapon of

---

[1] Gordley, 165.
[2] Eusebius/Gifford, 15.720. Jonathan Edwards's translation renders the pertinent lines thus: "So was it said of old, so he commands, Who's born of water, who received from God... The two great tables of the Law."
[3] Taylor, T., 178.

ivy. For my mother's sisters, the ones who least should, claimed that I, Dionysus, was not the child of Zeus, but that Semele had conceived a child from a mortal father and then ascribed the sin of her bed to Zeus, a trick of Kadmos', for which they boasted that Zeus killed her, because she had told a false tale about her marriage. Therefore I have goaded them from the house in frenzy, and they dwell in the mountains, out of their wits; and I have compelled them to wear the outfit of my mysteries. And all the female offspring of Thebes, as many as are women, I have driven maddened from the house, and they, mingled with the daughters of Kadmos, sit on roofless rocks beneath green pines. For this city must learn, even if it is unwilling, that it is not initiated into my Bacchic rites, and that I plead the case of my mother, Semele, in appearing manifest to mortals as a divinity whom she bore to Zeus.[1]

Here we see a description of Bacchanal rites that likely date back much earlier, in vine-growing regions from thousands of years previously, possibly exemplified in the archaic cave drawing from Spain, for example. In this tale, the Theban king, Pentheus, objects to "this new deity," whom he calls "a sorcerer, a conjuror from the Lydian land," and is subsequently destroyed for his blasphemy.[2]

Euripides (*Ba*. 75-79) speaks of "a deity manifest among men," an important theme reiterated five centuries later in the Christ myth. He also describes the revelry with which the god is served, "dancing in inspired frenzy over the mountains with holy purifications." The poet (*Ba*. 100-102) further calls Dionysus the "bull-horned god,"[3] who is "crowned with a crown of snakes"[4] or dragons, making of him an ophite deity/serpent god as well.

Moreover, we read in Euripides (*Ba*. 142-143) that when Bacchus is "sweet in the mountains"—possibly referring to both honey and ripened grapes in hillside vineyards—the "plain flows with milk, it flows with wine, it flows with the nectar of bees."[5] The playwright (*Ba*. 704-711) also tells the story of wine, water, milk and honey "flowing miraculously from the earth."

Euripides (*Hec*. 1252) has his character Polymestor call Dionysus "our Thracian prophet."[6] In another work, *Antiope*, Euripides refers to

---

[1] Euripides/Buckley.
[2] Eur. *Ba*. 219, 234. "This new deity" is τὸν νεωστὶ δαίμονα, the latter word "daimon" meaning "divine being," as well as "evil spirit," latched upon by Christianity as a "demon." The Greek word for "sorcerer, conjurer" is γόης *goēs*, this latter term found on a pre-Christian magical cup discovered at Alexandria, Egypt, that also includes the term *chrēstos*, rather than *christos*.
[3] ταυρόκερων θεόν.
[4] ἐστεφάνωσέν τε δρακόντων στεφάνοις.
[5] ῥεῖ δὲ γάλακτι πέδον, ῥεῖ δ᾽ οἴνῳ, ῥεῖ δὲ μελισσᾶν νέκταρι.
[6] The complete line is ὁ Θρῃξὶ μάντις εἶπε Διόνυσος τάδε. The word for "prophet" here is μάντις *mantis*, meaning "diviner, seer, prophet," used hundreds of times in antiquity by Aeschylus, Aristophanes, Aristotle, Demosthenes, Diodorus, Euripides and many others. The translators of the Septuagint also used this term μάντις *mantis* to describe "soothsayer" and "diviner," as at Joshua 13:22 and 1 Samuel 6:2. The original Hebrew

"the pillar of the Evoean God,"[1] connoting Bacchus, a motif comparable to Yahweh's "pillars" in the desert, both words the same in Greek.

Horns

Concerning Dionysus's horns, Euripides (*Ba.* 918-922) depicts the character Pentheus as remarking to the god:

> Oh look! I think I see two suns, and twin Thebes, the seven-gated city. And you seem to lead me, being like a bull and horns seem to grow on your head. But were you ever before a beast? For you have certainly now become a bull.[2]

Much of Dionysus's myth is contained in Euripides's texts, having a centuries-long tradition, rather than having been fabricated by the poet. Indeed, if the germ story reflects the introduction into the Theban region of vine-growing and wine-making, it could be several thousand years old, since viticulture in the areas to the east of the Black Sea such as Armenia and Georgia dates to some 6,000 or 7,000 years ago.

Pentheus the Serpent

Euripides (*Ba.* 537-544) describes Dionysus's adversary Pentheus as "descended from a serpent":

> What rage, what rage does the earth-born race show, and Pentheus, once descended from a serpent—Pentheus, whom earth-born Echion bore, a fierce monster, not a mortal man, but like a bloody giant, hostile to the gods.
>
> οἵαν οἵαν ὀργὰν ἀναφαίνει χθόνιον γένος ἐκφύς τε δράκοντός ποτε Πενθεύς, ὃν Ἐχίων ἐφύτευσε χθόνιος, ἀγριωπὸν τέρας, οὐ φῶτα βρότειον, φόνιον δ᾽ ὥστε γίγαντ᾽ ἀντίπαλον θεοῖς...

Here we also see the word δράκοντος *drakontos* the singular genitive of δράκων

Fig. 63. Bacchus and serpent, 1ˢᵗ cent. AD/CE. Fresco from Pompei, National Archaeological Museum, Naples, Italy

---

term in these verses is קָם *qacam* (H7080), which Strong's defines also as "false prophets of Israel."

[1] *Antiope* is a lost work estimated to date to 411-408 BCE, fragments of which are found in other texts. The relevant Greek from Euripides (*Ant.* fr. 263) is στῦλον εὐίου θεοῦ *stulon euiou theou*, where *euiou* is an epithet of Bacchus, reflecting the cry of his maenads. (Snell, 77) The Greek word στῦλος *stulos/stylos* is used also in the Old Testament to describe the pillar of cloud and of fire in Exodus (e.g., 13:21). The relevant Hebrew word, עַמּוּד *'ammuwd* (H5982), is employed to portray a "pillar of heaven" or "very high mountain" as well. (See *Gesenius*.)

[2] Euripides/Buckley. The original Greek: καὶ μὴν ὁρᾶν μοι δύο μὲν ἡλίους δοκῶ, δισσὰς δὲ Θήβας καὶ πόλισμ᾽ ἑπτάστομον· καὶ ταῦρος ἡμῖν πρόσθεν ἡγεῖσθαι δοκεῖς καὶ σῷ κέρατα κρατὶ προσπεφυκέναι. ἀλλ᾽ ἦ ποτ᾽ ἦσθα θήρ; τεταύρωσαι γὰρ οὖν.

or "dragon," rendered as "serpent" and so on, a term previously discussed as part of the ancient drama of a deity battling a monster or dragon.

In this regard, Pentheus is also described in this paragraph as a "fierce monster" (ἀγριωπὸν τέρας) and "like a bloody giant," reflected in the Greek φόνιον δ'ὥστε γίγαντ', this latter word from γίγας *gigas* meaning "giant."

Proselytizing Play

It appears that Euripides's *Bacchae* was to Dionysus what the Pentateuch was to Yahweh, in the sense that both texts sought to establish their gods as centrally important to humanity or, at the very least, to their immediate followers. It would be plays such as *The Bacchae* that were acted out by wandering proselytizers in the theaters especially designated for Dionysus, with audiences that included local priests and priestesses of other deities,[1] as noted. Such proselytizing plays, therefore, would have been witnessed by many people around Greece and beyond, spreading the Dionysian religion and viniculture in numerous places.

Aristophanes

In 411 BCE, Athenian playwright Aristophanes (*Thes.* 990) composed a chorus with Dionysian epithets: "Oh, Evius, oh, Bromius, oh, thou son of Semele, oh, Bacchus, who delightest to mingle with the dear choruses of the nymphs upon the mountains, and who repeatest, while dancing with them, the sacred hymn, Euios, Euios, Euoi!"[2] These shouts are comparable to the divine tetragrammaton יהוה *Yēhovah* or YHWH, which can be transliterated in Greek as ιευε *ieue*.[3] This scenario is reminiscent of the prehistoric imagery described by Graves, indicating a possibly very archaic origin of the cult of revelry.

Plato

In his work *Ion* (534a), Plato (5th-4th cents. BCE) likewise discussed various aspects of the Dionysus myth, including referring to the god's female followers styled "maenads" or "bacchantes" drawing "milk and honey from the rivers."[4] Plato explicates this theme, likening the songs of the lyric poets to "the sweets they cull from honey-dropping founts."[5]

---

[1] *The Bacchae* was performed first at the Theater of Dionysus Eleuthereus in Athens in 405 BCE.
[2] Aristophanes/O'Neill, vol. 2.
[3] See, e.g., Piepkorn, 3.50; Higgins, 1.327.
[4] Plato/Jowett, 1.223.
[5] Plato/Fowler, 423. ὥσπερ αἱ βάκχαι ἀρύονται ἐκ τῶν ποταμῶν μέλι καὶ γάλα κατεχόμεναι, ἔμφρονες δὲ οὖσαι οὔ, καὶ τῶν μελοποιῶν ἡ ψυχὴ τοῦτο ἐργάζεται, ὅπερ αὐτοὶ λέγουσι. λέγουσι γὰρ δήπουθεν πρὸς ἡμᾶς οἱ ποιηταὶ ὅτι.

Megasthenes

A Greek ethnographer and ambassador to India, Megasthenes (c. 350-290 BCE) composed a book called *Indica*, which discusses Indian gods who have been supposed to be equivalents of Hercules and Dionysus, generally taken to be Krishna and Shiva or Indra, respectively.[1] Only fragments of Megasthenes's work survive, in the writings of others such as the Greco-Roman historian Arrian (86-c. 160 AD/CE) and Strabo.

Regarding Dionysus/Bacchus in India, Megasthenes is recorded as stating:

> On such grounds they called a particular race of people Nyssaians, and their city Nyssa, which Dionysos had founded, and the mountain which rose above the city Mêron, assigning as their reason for bestowing these names that ivy grows there, and also the vine, although its fruit does not come to perfection, as the clusters on account of the heaviness of the rains fall off the trees before ripening. They further call the Oxydrakai descendants of Dionysos, because the vine grew in their country, and their processions were conducted with great pomp, and their kings on going forth to war and on other occasions marched in Bacchic fashion, with drums beating, while they were dressed in gay-coloured robes, which is also a custom among other Indians....[2]

Strabo recounts Megasthenes as relating that the Indian philosophers who "live on the mountains are worshippers of Dionysos, showing as proofs that he had come among them the wild vine, which grows in their country only, and the ivy, and the laurel, and the myrtle..."[3] He further states that they "observe also certain customs which are Bacchanalian."

In his *Natural History*, Pliny relates Megasthenes as commenting:

> For the Indians stand almost alone among the nations in never having migrated from their own country. From the days of Father Bacchus to Alexander the Great their kings are reckoned at 154, whose reigns extend over 6451 years and 3 months....
>
> Father Bacchus was the first who invaded India, and was the first of all who triumphed over the vanquished Indians....[4]

In reality, Indians did migrate from their own land in remote antiquity and many times since then, as the Indo-European family tree and DNA studies indicate. The point is also well taken, however, that the subcontinent has been occupied continually by the same ethnicities for many thousands of years, since migrating out of Africa

---

[1] Because Megasthenes does not mention Buddhism, and due to a dearth of archaeological and literary evidence, this latter belief system is thought not to have taken a noticeably distinct form until the reign of emperor Ashoka in the decades that followed.
[2] McCrindle, 110.
[3] McCrindle, 97.
[4] McCrindle, 115.

13,000 or more years ago, according to one mainstream genetics theory.

Nysa in India

It was common in antiquity to have many villages or cities of the same name, such as the numerous Alexandrias, named for the Greek conqueror. In this regard, Megasthenes recounts:

> Many writers further include in India even the city Nysa and Mount Merus, sacred to Father Bacchus, whence the origin of the fable that he sprang from the thigh of Jupiter. They include also the Astacani, in whose country the vine grows abundantly...[1]

The Astacani evidently were a Bactrian people, occupying the land northwest of India that is now Afghanistan.

Speaking of the "Pandaean nation," Megasthenes states:

> The city of Nysa is assigned to this region, as is also the mountain sacred to Jupiter, Mêros by name, in a cave on which the ancient Indians affirm Father Bacchus was well nourished...[2]

He next repeats the story of Dionysus born from Zeus's thigh. In his *Indica*, he recounts the same tales about Dionysus in India, with his descendants as the "Nysaioi."[3] The Greek ambassador historian is skeptical and states that these stories are "but fictions of the poets."[4]

Meros

In his *Anabasis* (5.1.6), Arrian depicts Acuphis, the "president" of the Indian city of Nysa, sent out to meet with Alexander the Great during his incursion into India:

> The god [Dionysus] indeed called the city Nysa, and the land Nysaea after his nurse Nysa. The mountain also which is near the city he named Meros (*i.e.*, thigh), because, according to the legend, he grew in the thigh of Zeus. From that time we inhabit Nysa, a free city, and we ourselves are independent, conducting our government with constitutional order. And let this be to thee proof that our city owes its foundation to Dionysus; for ivy, which does not grow in the rest of the country of India, grows among us.[5]

The "thigh" birth motif in the Bacchus myth has been compared to Genesis 46:26, which refers to Jacob's progeny emanating from his "loins." In the Septuagint, the Greek for "loins" in this Genesis verse is the plural genitive μηρῶν *meron*, the same term as "thigh" in the

---

[1] McCrindle, 152-153.
[2] McCrindle, 156.
[3] McCrindle, 179.
[4] McCrindle, 180.
[5] Arrian, 266. Νῦσάν τε οὖν ἐκάλεσε τὴν πόλιν Διόνυσος ἐπὶ τῆς τροφοῦ τῆς Νύσης καὶ τὴν χώραν Νυσαίαν· τὸ δὲ ὄρος ὅ τι περ πλησίον ἐστὶ τῆς πόλεως καὶ τοῦτο Μηρὸν ἐπωνόμασε Διόνυσος, ὅτι δὴ κατὰ τὸν μῦθον ἐν μηρῷ τῷ τοῦ Διὸς ηὐξήθη. καὶ ἐκ τούτου ἐλευθέραν τε οἰκοῦμεν τὴν Νῦσαν καὶ αὐτοὶ αὐτόνομοι καὶ ἐν κόσμῳ πολιτεύοντες· τῆς δὲ ἐκ Διονύσου οἰκίσεως καὶ τόδε σοι γενέσθω τεκμήριον· κιττὸς γὰρ οὐκ ἄλλῃ τῆς Ἰνδῶν γῆς φυόμενος παρ᾽ ἡμῖν φύεται. καὶ ταῦτα πάντα Ἀλεξάνδρῳ πρὸς θυμοῦ ἐγίγνετο.

Dionysus myth. In antiquity, as in the Bible (e.g., Gen 24:2), the word "thigh" was a code word for "penis."[1] The removal of Dionysus from the womb of a woman to become an emission from a god's penis could be interpreted as recording in myth the intrusion and dominance of the patriarchy.[2]

Conquest and Wine

According to Arrian, Megasthenes further says:

> Dionysos, however, when he came and had conquered the people, founded cities and gave law to these cities, and introduced the use of wine among the Indians, as he had done among the Greeks, and taught them how to sow the land, himself supplying seeds for the purpose... ...he instructed the Indians to let their hair grow long in honour of the god, and to wear the turban; and that he taught them to anoint themselves with unguents...[3]

Grape-growing or viticulture in India dates back to at least the main Indus Valley era (3300–1300 BCE),[4] believed to have been introduced to the region from Persia during the fourth millennium. It is likely that the reverence on the subcontinent for the wine deity, by whatever name, dates back to that era.

During his Indian expedition, Megasthenes relates, Bacchus "disguised the arms with which he had equipped his troops, and made them wear soft raiment and fawn-skins." We read that the spears were "wrapped round with ivy, and the thyrsus [staff] had a sharp point." The troops carried cymbals and drums, and used wine to "divert" the Indians' thoughts "from war to dancing." Employing these techniques, including "Bacchic orgies," the god was able to subjugate the Indians "and all the rest of Asia."[5]

Fig. 64. Bacchic staff or thyrsus

Artapanus

If we factor in the writings of Jewish historian Artapanus of Alexandria (c. 3rd or 2nd cent. BCE) about Moses, we will find even more comparisons to Dionysus, such as in Eusebius's account (*Prep. evang.* 9, 27.12) in which the Israelite patriarch consecrates a cow, because it is useful in ploughing the earth. In turn, Diodorus (1.87.2; 3.64.1) relates that the cow is sacred for ploughing the earth and that Dionysus was the "first man to yoke cows to the plough."[6]

---

[1] Walker (1983), 143.
[2] See, e.g., Rigoglioso for analysis of this male-dominant transition.
[3] McCrindle, 199-200.
[4] The date for initial human occupation of the Indus Valley has been pushed back possibly to 7,500 BCE. See Overdorf.
[5] McCrindle, 157.
[6] Gardner, et al., 40.

Artapanus (27.15f) also states that Moses "names another city and river Meroe," while in Diodorus (2.38.4) Dionysus "leads his army to a place called Meros."[1]

According to the Alexandrian (27.22), while in Arabian exile Moses sends his army to battle Egypt, while Diodorus (3.73.4) recounts that Dionysus "grows up in Arabia and fights against Egypt."[2]

Artapanus (27.40) also makes of Moses the inventor of "many useful machines," while Diodorus asserts that Bacchus invented "many things useful."[3] It is further noteworthy that Artapanus (27.6) identifies Moses with Hermes or Thoth, the Greco-Egyptian divine messenger and mythical lawgiver.[4]

Moses as Orphic Teacher

Essentially equating the Hebrew prophet and Greek wine god, Artapanus makes Moses the teacher of Orpheus, calling the biblical figure Μουσαῖος *Mousaios.* This same moniker is employed by Diodorus (1.96.2) in a story about Orpheus's visit to Egypt, with his companion Mousaios/Musaeus.[5] This association appears to be an attempt at establishing priority and dominance, extending to the Dionysian cultus itself, since Orpheus was the major proselytizer thereof.[6]

Regarding Artapanus's account about Moses, Near Eastern and Jewish studies professor Dr. Holger M. Zellentin remarks:

> Carl Hollady suggested that Moses's miraculous escape from prison is a reference to Dionysus's escape from prison.... Furthermore, the association of Jews with the Dionysus cult may be implicit in 2 and 3 Maccabees....[7]

The apocryphal texts 2 Maccabees was composed in Greek, likely at Alexandria around 124 BCE, while 3 Maccabees apparently dates to the first century BCE or AD/CE.

Interestingly, Artapanus appears to be oblivious to the existence of the Pentateuch or other biblical scriptures, as if they had not been written or circulated by his time. In any event, it is surmised that Artapanus used Dionysus's myth to pad out his "biography" of Moses, and it is evident from the Alexandrian's writing that Jews were aware of the correspondences between Moses and Dionysus centuries before the common era.

---

[1] Gardner, et al., 41.
[2] Gardner, et al., 42.
[3] Gardner, et al., 37.
[4] Gardner, et al., 34.
[5] Gardner, et al., 37.
[6] See, e.g., Matthews, 8, citing Holladay.
[7] Gardner, et al., 49.

Apollodorus

Continuing the discussion of Orpheus and his master, Athenian historian and mythographer Apollodorus (c. 180-c. 120 BCE) related (*Lib.* 1.3) that the legendary poet "invented the mysteries of Dionysus, and, having been torn in pieces by the Maenads, he is buried in Pieria."[1]

Apollodorus (1.6.2) also recounts Dionysus's battle with the giant using the magic wand: "Eurytus was killed by Dionysus with a thyrsus,"[2] which is a fennel stalk covered with ivy vines and leaves. He further speaks of the repeated theme of killing giants, reciting not only the demise of Eurytus by Dionysus with his thyrsus but also other giant-killing, including Ephialtes shot by Apollo, and Mimas attacked with red-hot metal missiles by Hephaestus/Hephaistos. Thus, Dionysus kills one of the earth goddess Gaia's giant sons, Eurytus, during a battle between the gods and these giants, reminiscent of the biblical battles with giants, including between David and Goliath. Obviously, this theme in the Bible is not original or "historical."

Apollodorus (3.4.2) also relates the birth of Dionysus and death of his mother Semele, during which time Zeus hid the child from Hera by turning him into a kid and giving him to Hermes to take to "Nysa in Asia." Thus, again, Dionysus possessed the epithet of "Kid," like Jesus the "Lamb."

Maccabees

In the apocryphal book of the second century BCE 1 Maccabees (1:41ff), we are told that Antiochus Epiphanes introduced pagan worship into the temple at Jerusalem: "Many even from Israel gladly adopted his religion; they sacrificed to idols and profaned the sabbath" (1:43).[3] We read at 2 Maccabees 6:7 that the Jews were compelled by the Seleucid king to "wear wreaths of ivy and walk in the procession in honor of Dionysus" during a Bacchic festival.[4] 3 Maccabees (2:29) states that the Egyptian ruler purportedly had the Jews "marked with an ivy leaf, the sign of Dionysus."[5] It is claimed that Antiochus also introduced the orgiastic Bacchic rites, but this story may serve as a cover for practices that had already been occurring for centuries, such as the temple cult prostitutes mentioned in the Bible.

---

[1] "Orpheus," *Wikipedia*.
[2] Εὔρυτον δὲ θύρσῳ Διόνυσος ἔκτεινε, rendered literally as "Eurytus thus with thyrsus Dionysus killed."
[3] *NRSV Bible*, 539.
[4] Gardner, et al., 42.
[5] Gardner, et al., 42.

Bacchus and Yahweh

Regarding 2 Maccabees and the ancient association of Yahweh with the gods of other cultures such as Zeus or Jupiter, American New Testament professor Dr. Sean M. McDonough remarks:

> An even more common identification, however, was Dionysus. Tacitus (*Hist.* 5.5:5), Lydus (*De Mensibus* 4:53), and Cornelius Labeo (ap. Macrobius, *Saturnalia* 1:18:18-21) all make this association, and a coin from 55 BCE of the curule aedile A. Plautius shows a kneeling king who is labeled BACCHIVS IVDAEVS. E. Babelon argues that this must be the high priest, "the priest of the Jewish Bacchus." This identification may have been based on more than mere speculation. According to 2 Macc. 6:7, the Jews "were compelled to walk in the procession in honor of Dionysus, wearing wreaths of ivy"...[1]

Bacchius Iudaeus

The coin discussed by McDonough was minted by the Roman moneyer A. Plautius, possibly in commemoration of the Hasmonean Jewish king and high priest Judah Aristobulus II (fl. 67-63 BCE) or his successor John Hyrcanus II (fl. c. 63-40 BCE).[2]

The coin's reverse with the Latin inscription *BACCHIUS IUDAEUS* shows what may be a ruler kneeling before a camel, appropriate for a Near or Middle Eastern monarch.[3] The figure is holding what is identified as an olive or palm branch, perhaps offering peace or supplication, after the Jews had been battling Rome in Judea for many years.

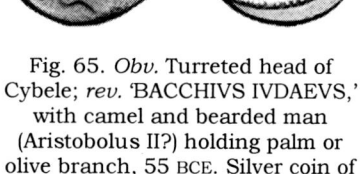

Fig. 65. *Obv.* Turreted head of Cybele; *rev.* 'BACCHIVS IVDAEVS,' with camel and bearded man (Aristobolus II?) holding palm or olive branch, 55 BCE. Silver coin of A. Plautius, Babelon Plautia 13

It is suggested likewise that the inscription may refer not (only) to Aristobulus but (also) to Judea as a whole, with the apparent image of Cybele on the obverse possibly symbolizing her curing of "Bacchus's" madness, perhaps reflecting that Judea sanely had entered into the empire.[4]

In a similar vein as the observation by French numismatist Dr. Ernest Babelon (1854-1924), the inscription—interpreted by some experts as "Bacchius the Jew"[5]—also may reflect Aristobulus II as another "New Dionysus" (discussed below), indicating his initiation

---

[1] McDonough, 88.
[2] See, e.g., the work of numismatist David B. Hendin.
[3] The word *Bacchius* may be a convention indicating a "priest of Bacchus." Debate about the coin includes whether or not the camel would be appropriate for Judea or only for Arabia. A Nabatean meaning is suggested, which may represent a prominent merchant connection to Judea via the wine trade of the time. (See "Reconsidering BACCHIVS IVDAEVS," *Forum Ancient Coins*.)
[4] "Reconsidering BACCHIVS IVDAEVS," *Forum Ancient Coins*.
[5] Per Hendin.

into the Bacchic cultus. In any event, the possible link here between Bacchus and Judea is intriguing.

Lydus

In the sixth century AD/CE, Byzantine historian Ioannis Lydus or "John the Lydian" (4.53) remarked of Yahweh:

> ...the Greeks say that he is the Dionysus of Orpheus, because, as they themselves say, at the holy place of the temple in Jerusalem, from both pillars vines fashioned from gold used to hold up the curtains that were variegated with purple and scarlet: On the basis of this, they supposed that it was a temple of Dionysus.[1]

Moreover, Lydus (4.51) relates: "Liber, the name for Dionysus among the Romans, meaning 'free'—that is, the Sun."[2] Thus, Dionysus was identified commonly with Yahweh and was the sun. This equation was acknowledged in pre-Christian Maccabean texts discussing Jewish Bacchus worship.

Varro

In the first century BCE, Publius Vergilius Maro or "Virgil/Vergil" (*Georgics* 1.7-9) cited Roman statesman Marcus Terentius Varro (116-27 BCE) as relating that Bacchus and Ceres's "gifts" were used to mix wine with "drinks" of the river god Achelous, Homer's origin of the world's fresh water.[3] This myth is similar to Yahweh's miracle via Moses of creating "sweet" water.

In Varro, various disciplines come together, as this celebrated scholar wrote about the seemingly disparate subjects of the Latin language, the Roman gods and agriculture. However, when we realize how closely the ancient deities were perceived as intertwined with, and responsible for, the growth of plants, we can understand why these topics are related. Moreover, various gods were claimed to be responsible for language, serving as the "Divine Word."

Varro's oft-cited volumes on the Roman religion were destroyed during the Christian era, but because of this crossover, some of his information about the gods is retained in his texts on Latin and agriculture/husbandry.

For example, we read in Varro's agricultural text (1.2) that it was Father Bacchus to whom goats were sacrificed, "that they might make expiation with their lives..."[4] In other words, Dionysus's followers engaged in scapegoat rituals, abundantly present around

---

[1] Andrew Eastbourne translation.
[2] Eastbourne translation.
[3] Varro's original Latin is: *Liber et alma Ceres, vestro si munere tellus Chaoniam pingui glandem mutavit arista, poculaque inventis Acheloia miscuit uvis...* Greenough renders this relevant last part: "And mingled with the grape, your new-found gift, The draughts of Achelous..." Without using the god's name, but substituting instead "man," Owen renders the Varro passage thus: "Bacchus and Ceres, by whole gifts divine, Man chang'd the crystal stream for purple wine..." (Varro/Owen, 12)
[4] Varro/Owen, 39.

the Mediterranean, including in the Levant, as reflected repeatedly in the biblical sacrifice and as the basis of the gospel story.

Cicero

Regarding Dionysus, in *Of the Nature of the Gods* (3.58), Roman statesman Marcus Tullius ("Tully") Cicero (106-43 BCE) comments:

> There are many also of the Dionysi. The first was the son of Jupiter and Proserpine. The second, who is said to have killed Nysa, was the son of Nilus. The third, who reigned in Asia, and for whom the Sabazia were instituted, was the son of Caprius. The fourth, for whom they celebrate the Orphic festivals, sprung from Jupiter and Luna, the first, who is supposed to have instituted the Trieterides, was the son of Nysus and Thyone.[1]

Thus, Cicero speaks of multiple Dionysuses, as do other ancient writers, including Diodorus.

While some attributes from "real people" may have been attached to the Dionysus myth, what we are seeing is the typical syncretism and assimilation of attributes concerning a god and his cult, in this case the popular grapevine and wine cult/god moving around the world. The syncretism explains the many different and sometimes contradictory themes in the Dionysian myth, as it was eventually passed down to us.

Diodorus

We have already examined numerous quotes from Diodorus (1st cent. BCE), including about the relationship between Osiris and Dionysus. The Greek historian (1.23) asserts further that the Dionysian mysteries were founded upon those of Osiris.

Referring to some of the "most learned of the Indians," Diodorus (2.38) describes Dionysus's mythical journey to India, reflecting the spread of viticulture and viniculture:

> They say that, in ancient time, when men lived scattered and dispersed here and there, Bacchus, with a great army from the west, overran all India, which at that time had no considerable city in it able to make any resistance; and that a plague (through the violent and parching heat) destroying many of his [Bacchus's] soldiers, they say, that prudent general drew his army out of the plains to the tops of the mountains, where (by means of the cool blasts of the refreshing air, and drinking of the spring-waters there at hand) they were restored to their former health; and that the place where his army was thus recovered, was called the Thigh; hence the Grecians frame a story of this god to this day, that Bacchus was bred in the Thigh.

---

[1] Cicero/Francklin, 189. *Dionysos multos habemus, primum Iove et Proserpina natum, secundum Nilo, qui Nysam dicitur interemisse, tertium Cabiro patre, eumque regem Asiae praefuisse dicunt, cui Sabazia sunt instituta, quartum Iove et Luna, cui sacra Orphica putantur confici, quintum Nyso natum et Thyone, a quo trieterides constitutae putantur.*

Afterwards (they say) he diligently employed himself in sowing and planting divers fruit-trees, and imparted the art to the Indians, and found out the use of wine, and other things conducing to the comfort of man's life. He built likewise stately cities, and removed the villages to more commodious situations; and instituted the manner of divine worship, and made laws, and set up courts of justice; and at last, for the many excellent inventions imparted to the Indians, he was esteemed as a god, and obtained immortal honours.

They report that he had a regiment of women in his army, and that in the heat of battle he made use of timbrels and cymbals, the trumpet being not at that time found out: and that after he reigned over all India for the space of two-and-fifty years, he died of extreme old age, leaving the kingdom of his sons, who enjoy it, and their posterity after them, successively, till many ages after the regal authority was abrogated, and the cities were governed by a democracy. These are the things related of Bacchus and his posterity by the inhabitants of the mountain parts of India.[1]

As we can see, in these pithy paragraphs appear many correspondences between the tales of Bacchus/Dionysus and Moses, which will be delineated and discussed below. As an example here, Diodorus relates the tale of Dionysus's army being saved from the "plague" of the burning desert heat by finding spring water in the mountains.

In chapter 3, Diodorus spends more time discussing Dionysus's army spreading all the way to India, bringing with it knowledge of the grapevine. The historian (3.62) gives the god the Greek epithet διμήτωρ *dimetor*, meaning "two mothers" and "twice born,"[2] the Latin form of which is *bimater* or *bimeter*.

Crucifixion

At 3.65.5, Diodorus discusses the pre-Christian crucifixion of Dionysus's enemy, Lycurgus,[3] using the same term, ἀνασταυρόω *anastauróo*, employed in the gospel tale. Hence, we have the theme of suffering and crucifixion in the Dionysian mythos, in which the god himself is said to be hung from a tree.[4] Bacchus's association with trees, earning him the epithets of "Dendreus," "Endendros" and "Dendrites," apparently reflects early intoxicants created from the sap of pine and fir trees.[5]

---

[1] Diodorus/Booth, 1.132-133. See *The Study Guide* for Diodorus's original Greek.
[2] διμήτορα δὲ τὸν Διόνυσον ὑπὸ τῶν παλαιῶν ὠνομάσθαι. (Diodorus/Dindorf, 1.290) My literal rendering of this passage is: "'Two-mothered Dionysus' by the ancients he is named."
[3] καὶ τὸν Λυκοῦργον ζωγρήσαντα τυφλῶσαί τε καὶ πᾶσαν αἰκίαν εἰσενεγκάμενον ἀνασταυρῶσαι.
[4] Carotta, 4.
[5] Ruck, 187.

Army

Diodorus (4.2.6) further states that Bacchus "also led about with himself an army composed not only of men but of women as well, and punished such men as were unjust and impious."[1]

Osiris

A similar travel tale is told of Osiris, who was said to have marched from Egypt to India—specifically across the "Red" or "Erythraean sea"[2]—spreading viniculture along the way. Again, Diodorus relates: "Some of the early Greek mythologists call Osiris 'Dionysus,'" reflecting that the "Greek" god was considered to be Egyptian, one with Osiris.

The Sun

Diodorus (11) also equated Bacchus with Osiris and with the sun:

Now when the ancient Egyptians, awestruck and wondering, turned their eyes to the heavens, they concluded that two gods, the sun and the moon, were primeval and eternal; and they called the former Osiris, the latter Isis, assigning each of these names according to some relevant characteristic. For, translating these appellations into the Greek idiom, Osiris is the "many-eyed," and quite properly so; for he spreads everywhere his rays, as if to observe with many eyes all the land and sea. Even the poet [Homer] expresses his agreement with this conceit:

The Sun, who sees and hears all things.

Some of the early Greek mythologists call Osiris "Dionysus" and also, changing the word slightly, "Sirius;" of these, Eumolpos in his Bacchanalian verse says:

Dionysus shining like a star, eye aflame with rays.

And writes Orpheus;

For that reason they call him "Bright" and "Dionysus."[3]

This identification of Dionysus and Osiris with the sun rates as highly noteworthy.

Horace

In his *Ode* to Bacchus (2.19), Latin poet Horace (65-8 BCE) repeats a number of Dionysian themes:

The stream of wine, the sparkling rills
That run with milk, and honey-dew
That from the hollow trunk distils;
And I may sing thy consort's crown,
New set in heaven, and Pentheus' hall

---

[1] περιάγεσθαι δ' αὐτὸν καὶ στρατόπεδον οὐ μόνον ἀνδρῶν, ἀλλὰ καὶ γυναικῶν, καὶ τοὺς ἀδίκους καὶ ἀσεβεῖς τῶν ἀνθρώπων κολάζειν.
[2] Diodorus 1.19.
[3] Diodorus/Murphy, 14.

With ruthless ruin thundering down,
And proud Lycurgus' funeral.
Thou turn'st the rivers, thou the sea;
Thou, on far summits, moist with wine,
Thy Bacchants' tresses harmlessly
Dost knot with living serpent-twine.
Thou, when the giants, threatening wrack...[1]

Among other motifs in this same ode, Horace also refers to the "bending" or bowing of rivers by the god, an indication of Dionysus's crossing dryshod the rivers Orontes and Hydaspes.[2]

Ovid

In his *Metamorphoses* (3.315), Roman writer Publius Ovidius Naso or "Ovid" (43 BCE-17/18 AD/CE) relates that Bacchus is "twice born."[3] Ovid (*Met.* 3.509ff) also recounts the story of Pentheus and Bacchus, as found in Euripides's *Bacchae* but with differences and embellishments. Regarding Dionysus's horned appearance, the Latin poet remarked: "Adorn your head with horns, and Bacchus you will be."[4]

Seneca

In his *Hercules Furens* (899-900), Roman dignitary Seneca (4 BCE-65 AD/CE) sums up Bacchus as "the tamer of Lycurgus and the ruddy sea, who bears a spear-point hidden beneath his vine-wreathed staff."[5]

Seneca translator Dr. Frank Justus Miller notes that the "ruddy sea" refers to the body of water that Dionysus "crossed when he conquered India."[6] Seneca's original Latin for "ruddy sea" is *rubri maris*,[7] the word *rubri* or "ruddy" connoting redness, as in the Red Sea. In the Vulgate, "Red sea" is *mare Rubrum*. Again, if Dionysus was "born" in Egypt, then he could be said to cross the Red Sea when his viniculture cult found its way east.

Pliny the Elder

In his *Natural History* (6.21), Roman dignitary and philosopher Gaius Plinius Secundus or "Pliny the Elder" (23-79 AD/CE) speaks of "Father Liber" and his conquest of India, referring to the "city Nysa"

---

[1] Conington translation.
[2] Horace/Lytton, 231: *Tu flectis amnes...*
[3] *bis geniti.*
[4] Ovid (*Ep. Sapph.* 15.24): *Accedant capiti cornua—Bacchus eris!* One translation favors "wreaths of ivy" for *cornua*, indicating a symbolic meaning of the word vis-à-vis the Dionysian myth. *Cornua*, however, literally means "horns."
[5] Seneca/Miller, 1.79.
[6] Seneca/Miller, 1.79.
[7] Seneca/Miller, 1.78: *adsit Lycurgi domitor et rubri maris, tectam virente cuspidem thyrso gerens...*

and "Mountain Merus" consecrated to the god, the latter mountain "from which arose the fable that he sprung from the seed of Jupiter."[1]

Speaking of the Greek island of Andros, Pliny (2.103) also refers to a "fountain in the temple of Father Bacchus, which upon the Nones of January always runneth with water that tasteth like wine..."[2] Here we see the water-to-wine miracle on the 5th of January (Nones), while the 6th represents the birthday of Osiris, Dionysus and Jesus, discussed below.

Plutarch

Throughout this work, we have read repeated remarks regarding Dionysus, as well as Osiris, by the Greek writer and priest Plutarch, during the second century AD/CE. From Plutarch we also learn that Dionysus is "counted a physician for finding wine, the most pleasing and most potent remedy," as well as for "bringing ivy, the greatest opposite imaginable to wine, into reputation..."[3]

Plutarch reiterates that "the ancients of all the creeping beasts consecrate the snake to Bacchus, and of all the plants the ivy..."[4] The emphasis on ivy in the Bacchic mythos occurs because the plant was used to counter the effects of alcohol, preventing drunkenness and "hangovers."[5]

Jewish Dionysus Worship

In his *Moralia* (*Quaes. Conv.* 4.6), in a section discussing what god the Jews worshipped, Plutarch relates that Bacchus was "one of the gods worshiped by the Hebrews," reflecting the Dionysus-Yahweh connection. In this regard, the Greek historian states that "Adonis is supposed to be the same with Bacchus; and there are a great many rites in both their sacrifices which confirm this opinion."[6]

Plutarch includes the Dionysian follower Symmachus's question to grandfather Lamprias about the identity of Adonis with Bacchus, "to be inscribed and enrolled in the mysteries of the Jews?"[7] He next relates the Athenian Moiragenes as averring that the two gods "are the very same."

When questioned about the proofs for this equation of Bacchus with "Adonis," Plutarch (*Quaes. Conv.* 4.6.2) again cites Moiragenes's monologue about the Jewish god, equating Adonis with Adon, as well as claiming that the Jews followed Bacchic rites:

...the time and manner of the greatest and most holy solemnity of the Jews is exactly agreeable to the holy rites of Bacchus; for that which

---

[1] Pliny/Holland, 1.127.
[2] Pliny/Holland, 1.104.
[3] *Symposiacs* 3.1.3. Plutarch/Goodwin, 3.263.
[4] *Symposiacs* 3.5.2. Plutarch/Goodwin, 3.274.
[5] Yang, 36.
[6] *Symposiacs* 4.5.3. Plutarch/Goodwin, 3.310.
[7] Plutarch/Goodwin, 3.310.

they call the Fast [Day of Atonement] they celebrate in the midst of the vintage, furnishing their tables with all sorts of fruits, while they sit under tabernacles made of vines and ivy; and the day which immediately goes before this they call the day of Tabernacles [Sukkah (σκηνή)]. Within a few days after they celebrate another feast, not darkly but openly, dedicated to Bacchus, for they have a feast among them called Kradephoria, from carrying palm-trees, and Thyrsophoria, when they enter into the temple carrying thyrsi. What they do within I know not; but it is very probable that they perform the rites of Bacchus. First they have little trumpets, such as the Grecians used to have at their Bacchanalia to call upon their Gods withal. Others go before them playing upon harps, which they call Levites, whether so named from Lusius or Evius—either word agrees with Bacchus. And I suppose that their Sabbaths have some relation to Bacchus; for even at this day many call the Bacchi by the name of Sabbi, and they make use of that word at the celebration of Bacchus's orgies...

Nor would it be absurd, were any one to say that the name Sabbath was imposed upon this feast from the agitation and excitement (σόβησις [sobesis]) which the priests of Bacchus indulged in. The Jews themselves testify no less; for when they keep the Sabbath, they invite one another to drink till they are drunk; or if they chance to be hindered by some more weighty business, it is the fashion at least to taste the wine...

...But there are other arguments which will clearly evince the truth of what I assert. The first may be drawn from their High-priest, who on holidays enters their temple with his mitre on, arrayed in a skin of a hind embroidered with gold, wearing buskins, and a coat hanging down to his ankles; besides he has a great many little bells hanging at his garment which make a noise when he walks the streets. So in the nightly ceremonies of Bacchus (as the fashion is among us), they make use of musical instruments, and call the God's nurses χαλκοδρυσταί [khalkodrustai]. High up on the wall of their temple is a representation of the thyrsus and timbrels, which surely can belong to no other God than Bacchus. Moreover they are forbidden the use of honey in their sacrifices, because they suppose that a mixture of honey corrupts and deads the wine.[1]

From Plutarch, we can see that in antiquity several Dionysian practices of the Jews were surmised, with proofs for this observation. Plutarch further tells us that the ancients called Bacchus "good counsellor," as the wisest god, similar to Jewish notions about Yahweh.

---

[1] *Symposiacs* 4.6.2. Plutarch/Goodwin, 3.310-312. For the Greek, see *The Study Guide*. As concerns the word "Sabbath," we know since Plutarch's time that there existed a Babylonian term *shabbatu* or *shabattu*. For a discussion of this passage, see Whittaker, 6.126ff.

THE DIONYSUS CONNECTION

Feast of the Booths

Oxford scholar Rev. Dr. Edward Hayes Plumptre (1821-1892) summarizes Plutarch's identification of the Jews as Dionysus followers:

> The resemblance between the Feast of the Tabernacle and the Greek festivals in honour of Bacchus, or Dionysos, is noticed at some length by Plutarch [*Sympos.* 4]. He describes the booths of palm-branches and ivy, and the Levites playing on their cithems; the mitre, the tunic, the bells of the high priests' vestments. He, for his part, had no doubt that the festival was at the *Thyrsophoria* of the Greeks, and that the Jews were worshippers of Bacchus.[1]

The Jewish Feast of the Tabernacle or Booths, also called Sukkoth (סכה cukkah*)*, is mentioned several times in the Bible, purportedly representing "a reminiscence of the type of fragile dwellings in which the Israelites dwelt during their 40 years of travel."[2]

Vintage

The tabernacles/booths festival occurs at a very auspicious time of the year, from late September to late October, a period Plutarch points out coincides with the vintage, or wine produced from the grape harvest. This association occurs at Deuteronomy 16:13:

> You shall keep the feast of booths [Sukkoth] seven days, when you make your ingathering from your threshing floor and your wine press...

Interestingly, it was during this vinicultural festival that, according to the Bible, Moses ordered his followers to read the entire Torah out loud once every seven years (Deut 31:10-11). Moreover, Solomon was said to have dedicated his temple at this important time (1 Ki 8; 2 Chr 7).

It should be recalled also that El Elyon, the Most High sun and wine god of both Canaanites and Israelites, was celebrated during the *marzeah* drinking banquet, which likely was held during the time of the vintage as well. Hence, it would not be much of a step to move from El Elyon worship to that of Bacchus.

In addition to the eye-opening exposition about Jewish Bacchic worship, we also learn from Plutarch that the pine tree is dedicated to Dionysus, because "it gives a pleasant seasoning to wine, for among pines they say the sweetest and most delicious grapes grow."[3] This seasoning reflects the Greek practice of putting pine into their wine, as in the infamously bitter retsina.

---

[1] Plumptre, 249.
[2] "Sukkot," *Wikipedia*.
[3] Plutarch/Goodwin, 319.

Pausanias

The numerous references in the second century AD/CE by Pausanias to monuments and other artifacts associated with Bacchus in various locations demonstrate the continued popularity and importance of the god. While Dionysus is associated with Osiris, Pausanias (2.13) tells us also that, as one might expect, the Egyptian god's sister-wife, Isis, was worshipped alongside Bacchus at a place called Omphalos/Umbilicus,¹ the "navel of the world."

At 2.20, 23, the Greek writer discusses "Bacchus when he led his army to Argos" and mentions also the "army of Dionysus."²

Referring to the inhabitants of Brasiae, Greece, and contending that the story is found nowhere else in the country, Pausanias (3.24.3) remarks that "Semele, after giving birth to her son by Zeus, was discovered by Cadmus and put with Dionysus into a chest, which was washed up by the waves in their country..."³ At 3.24.4, he states:

> The people of Brasiae add that [the queen of Thebes/goddess] Ino in the course of her wanderings came to the country, and agreed to become the nurse of Dionysus. They show the cave where Ino nursed him, and call the plain the garden of Dionysus.⁴

Pausanias (4.36.7) also states that "there is a spring below the city near the sea, the water of which they say gushed forth for Dionysus when he struck he ground with a thyrsus." He continues: "For this reason they call the spring Dionysias."⁵ Here we see several germane elements included in the Moses myth.

Arrian

Like Varro, Cicero, Diodorus and others, in the second century AD/CE Arrian too spoke of different Dionysi, one Athenian Iacchus as the son of Zeus and Kore/Persephone, and the other the Theban.⁶

Arrian also mentions a "Dionysopolis," where a statue of the god washed ashore, a city formerly called Κρυνος Krunos, reflecting its nearby springs.

---

¹ ἀπὸ δὲ τοῦ Ὀμφαλοῦ προελθοῦσι Διονύσου σφίσιν ἱερόν ἐστιν ἀρχαῖον, ἔστι δὲ καὶ Ἀπόλλωνος καὶ ἄλλο Ἴσιδος. τὸ μὲν δὴ ἄγαλμα τοῦ Διονύσου δῆλον πᾶσιν, ὡσαύτως δὲ καὶ τὸ τοῦ Ἀπόλλωνος· τὸ δὲ τῆς Ἴσιδος τοῖς ἱερεῦσι θεάσασθαι μόνον ἔστι. (*Pausaniae Graeciae Descriptio*)
² Pausanias/Taylor, 1.178.
³ Pausanias/Wycherley, 2.153.
⁴ Βρασιᾶται δὲ καὶ τάδε ἐπιλέγουσιν, Ἰνὼ σφίσιν ἐς τὴν χώραν ἀφικέσθαι πλανωμένην, ἐλθοῦσαν δὲ ἐθελῆσαι τοῦ Διονύσου γενέσθαι τροφόν· καὶ ἀποφαίνουσι μὲν τὸ ἄντρον ἔνθα τὸν Διόνυσον ἔθρεψεν Ἰνώ, καλοῦσι δὲ καὶ τὸ πεδίον Διονύσου κῆπον.
⁵ Pausanias (4.36.7): ἀφικομένων δὲ ἐς Κυπαρισσιὰς ἐκ Πύλου σφίσι πηγὴ ὑπὸ τῇ πόλει πλησίον θαλάσσης ἐστί· ῥυῆναι δὲ Διονύσῳ τὸ ὕδωρ λέγουσι θύρσῳ πλήξαντι ἐς τὴν γῆν, καὶ ἐπὶ τούτῳ Διονυσιάδα ὀνομάζουσι τὴν πηγήν.
⁶ *Anabasis of Alexander* 2.16; Arrian/Chinnock, 118. πολλαῖς γὰρ γενεαῖς πρότερον τιμᾶται ἐν Τύρῳ Ἡρακλῆς ἢ Κάδμον ἐκ Φοινίκης ὁρμηθέντα Θήβας κατασχεῖν καὶ τὴν παῖδα Κάδμῳ τὴν Σεμέλην γενέσθαι, ἐξ ἧς καὶ ὁ τοῦ Διὸς Διόνυσος γίγνεται.

Justin Martyr

In the middle of the second century AD/CE, Justin Martyr and several other early Church fathers discussed Dionysus/Bacchus/Liber, basically repeating the themes previously analyzed.

Justin relates that, in an Orphic hymn equating the Greek gods Zeus, Helios, Hades and Dionysus, the composer also invokes Orpheus's friend Musaeus and the "Word divine," the "one and universal king," as well as the "self-begotten" and "only One, of whom all things and we ourselves are sprung."[1] This writing sounds so Judeo-Christian that Justin raises up this poem as an example of monotheism.[2]

Justin also claims that several other Greek luminaries, such as Homer, Plato, Aristotle, Diodorus and others, had borrowed heavily from the Pentateuch, demonstrating that even in antiquity and among Christian apologists the parallels between pagan and biblical stories and traditions were noticed and remarked upon. Many of these similarities, however, existed hundreds to thousands of years earlier, before Hebrew emerged as a separate language and the Bible was composed.

Lucian of Samosata

In his essay "Dionysus, an Introductory Lecture" (1), famed satirist Lucian (c. 125-c. 180? AD/CE) also discusses Bacchus, recounting the god's triumph in India and relating it to his own "foibles" from incessant criticism of his works. Lucian's commentary includes mention of the wild and serpent-girded maenads, the ivy, tambourines and "horns like a new-born kid's."[3]

Lucian (3) writes that the Bacchantes and their god used fire to conquer the Indians, "for fire is the Bacchic instrument, Dionysus's very birthright,"[4] referring to the ancient myth in which Bacchus's mother, Semele, is consumed by Zeus's lightning. This motif is reminiscent of the pillar of fire leading the Israelites through the desert, and, indeed, we read that fiery Bacchus himself is a "pillar." The association of Bacchus with or as fire is also suggestive of Yahweh's burning bush, a solar attribute.

Clement of Alexandria

Writing in the second to third centuries, theologian Clement Alexandrinus appears to have known that already in antiquity people were making comparisons between Moses and Dionysus. We have seen that decades earlier Plutarch had equated the Jewish Feast of the Tabernacles with the Bacchic fall ritual and centuries before

---

[1] Roberts, 2.302.
[2] Justin, *Hortatory Address to the Greeks* 15; Roberts, 2.303.
[3] Lucian/Fowler, 252-253.
[4] Lucian/Fowler, 253.

Diodorus had compared the two lawgivers. It is reasonable to assert that others in antiquity did likewise, and it is useful to remind here of the massive amount of cultural destruction since ancient times, including various relevant writings.

In *Miscellanies* (1.16), Clement remarks that the Greek god "on whose account the Dionysian spectacles are celebrated, will be shown to be later than Moses."[1] In his calculations, the Church father (*Misc.* 1.21) concludes that Moses was "shown to have preceded the deification of Dionysus six hundred and four years..."[2] This contention is demonstrated in the present work to be erroneous, as the wine god precedes the Hebrew lawgiver by hundreds to thousands of years, including in the pertinent region as El Elyon among many other forms.

Also in chapter 21, Clement attempts to show that Mosaic law is older than the "philosophy of the Greeks," with the latter the plagiarists of the former. As we have seen, however, the Mosaic law and lawgiver evidently are remakes of older archetypes found in numerous places, centuries to millennia before the Israelite myth was composed.

In order to convince his audience to accept as "historical fact" the supposed appearance of God as a pillar of fire in the desert, the Alexandrian raises pagan parallels for this divine intervention, including as concerns Dionysus. We have seen also that Clement (*Misc.* 1.24) describes a Bacchic or Orphic oracle comparable to the pillars of Yahweh in Exodus.[3]

In any event, Clement evidently was under pressure to establish Moses as the original legislator, a reflection of the fact that the Hebrew patriarch was being compared to other lawgivers, as by Diodorus, whom the Alexandrian father specifically mentions in this discussion.[4]

Polyaenus

Another discussion of Dionysus occurs in a text from the second century AD/CE, the Macedonian rhetorician Polyaenus's *Strategems in War* or Στρατηγήματα *Strategemata* (1.1-2), in which we read about the wine god's "expedition against the Indians." Most of the details of Polyaenus's account can be found in earlier writings about Dionysus. The Macedonian mythographer provides a fairly complete summary of the Dionysian myth.

---

[1] Roberts, 4.404.
[2] Roberts, 4.423.
[3] Roberts, 4.457-458. See also Snell, B., 77.
[4] Roberts, 4.404.

Philostratus

In *Imagines* (1.14ff), Philostratus (2nd-3rd cents. AD/CE) reiterates the story of Dionysus's birth from Semele, with the god's bright light shining "like a radiant star" as he is born in a "charming" cave filled with foliage, including Bacchus's signatory ivy and grapevine. Philostratus next states that the earth "will take part with the fire in the Bacchic reveal and will make it possible for the revelers to take wine from springs and to draw milk from clods of earth or from a rock as from living breasts."[1]

At *Imagines* 1.18, the Greek philosopher discusses Dionysus's followers, referring to painted scenes from Mt. Cithaeron of "choruses of Bacchantes, and rocks flowing with wine, and nectar dripping from clusters of grapes, and the earth enriching the broken soil with milk."[2] He also refers to serpents standing erect and thyrsus "trees" dripping with honey. There follows a reminder of the terrible story of Pentheus's slaughter.

In the next section (1.19), Philostratus discusses Tyrrhenian pirates and their ship, saying that "the thyrsus here has grown in the midst of the ship and serves as a mast, and sails dyed purple are attached to it, gleaming as they belly out in the wind, and woven in them are golden Bacchantes on Mount Tmolus and Dionysiac scenes from Lydia."[3]

The philosopher then states: "That the ship seems to be embowered with vine and ivy and that clusters of grapes swing above it is indeed a marvel, but more marvelous is the fountain of wine, for the hollow ship pours forth the wine and lets it drain away." Here is yet another depiction of a wine miracle.

Catholic scholar Pierre Danet (18th cent.) says that Philostratus "assures us that the Indians held that their Bacchus came to them out of Assyria," which the Frenchman avers demonstrates that Dionysus is Noah.

Porphyry

In describing the abolition by one Amosis of the "law of sacrificing men in the Egyptian city of Heliopolis," ancient Greek historian Porphyry (c. 234-c. 305 AD/CE) tells us in *Animal Food* (2.55) about a man on the island of Chios, Greece, torn to pieces as a sacrifice to Bacchus.[4] Porphyry (*A.F.* 3.16) iterates that the Greeks "united a ram to the statue of Jupiter, but the horns of a bull to that of Bacchus."[5]

---

[1] Philostratus/Fairbanks, 60-61.
[2] Philostratus/Fairbanks, 73.
[3] Philostratus/Fairbanks, 79.
[4] Porphyry/Taylor, 87.
[5] Porphyry/Taylor, 111.

The historian (*A.F.* 3.17) also confirms Dionysus's epithet of "kid," *hinnuleius* in the Greek.[1]

In *On the Cave of the Nymphs* (6), referring to bowls and amphorae traditionally used to hold wine, Porphyry remarks that they are symbols of Bacchus, "friendly to the vine, the gift of God; since the fruit of the vine is brought to a proper maturity by the celestial fire of the sun."[2] Here we see the correlation between the grapevine and the fiery sun, which ripens the fruit and ferments the wine.

Eusebius

Citing others such as Diodorus, Eusebius (3rd-4th cents. AD/CE) recounted numerous aspects of the Dionysus myth, including the god as "brought from Egypt by Orpheus" (*Praep. ev.* 10:8),[3] as well as serving as the "twin brother" of Osiris and the inventor of wine and beer. Eusebius also mentions Bacchus's *bimater* or "two-mothered" status, his wands used as clubs, his allegorization by Porphyry, his rending by the Titans, and his being horned and identified with the sun.

According to Jerome, Eusebius related that Dionysus had arrived in Attica in 1497 BCE, while the god was reborn of Semele at Thebes around 1387 BCE.[4] This anachronism evidently reflects the movement of the Bacchic wine cult.

At *Preparation for the Gospel* 9.27, Eusebius mentions Artapanus's book *Concerning the Jews*, in which the author equates "Mouses" (Moses) with Musaeus.[5]

Human Sacrifice

We also learn from Eusebius about human sacrifice associated with Bacchus,[6] in his *Theophania* (2.58), where he recounts evidently the same story as Porphyry of a sacrifice of a man to the "Omadian Bacchus in Chios, when they had torn him (to pieces)!"[7]

Like numerous other cultures in antiquity, the Hebrews were known to practice human sacrifice, such as the sacred-king scapegoat ritual. It is this practice encountered in the Bible when Abraham is about to sacrifice his son and when God completes the ritual with his own son. Indeed, the latter once-for-all sacrifice of Jesus Christ was designed to put an end to what was obviously a

---

[1] Porphyry/Taylor, 111.
[2] Porphyry/Taylor, 179-180.
[3] Eusebius/Gifford, 15.514.
[4] Ruck, 180.
[5] Eusebius/Gifford, 15.462.
[6] Eusebius/Gifford, 15.924.
[7] Eusebius/Lee, 115.

problem around the Mediterranean.¹ Hence, this ritual too connects the Dionysian and Jewish religions.

Sepphoris Mosaics

It is obvious not only that Jews were well aware of Bacchus but also that they revered his cult enough to feature him prominently, according to Maccabees, as well as Plutarch's statements and the depiction of Dionysus's life-cycle in ancient mosaics in Israel.

Indeed, the presence of Dionysus on mosaics from the third to fourth centuries AD/CE in the finely appointed home of the apparent Jewish patriarch at Sepphoris or Tzippori, a village in Galilee, lends weight to Plutarch's commentary.² Significantly, this imagery depicts Bacchus and Herakles in a wine-drinking contest, which Dionysus wins, a theme flagrantly featured in the prominent Jewish citizen's home. Since Herakles was a favorite of the Phoenicians, this symbolism could reflect the defeat of that faction commercially, in the wine trade. This central place for Bacchus indicates the wealth of the community depended significantly on the blessings of the grape.

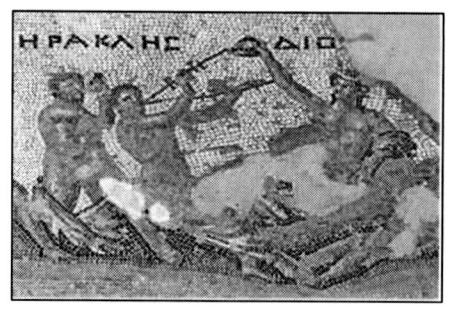

Fig. 66. Herakles and Dionysus, 3rd-4th cents. AD/CE. Mosaic at Sepphoris/Tzippori, Israel

If these later Jews were aware of Dionysus and unflinchingly revered him, it is reasonable to suggest that Israelites knew about his worship and myth in more remote antiquity, particularly as they became wine connoisseurs, a trade that dates back 3,000 years in the hill country where they emerged.

It is very significant that this site of Bacchus worship, Sepphoris, was deemed the Cana of the New Testament, where Jesus was said to have produced his water-to-wine miracle.³ It is clear that the gospel writers were imitating the popular Dionysus worship with the newly created Christ character.

---

[1] See Acharya (2004).
[2] Bowersock (39) describes the mosaic found in a "luxurious villa" at Sepphoris, which has images of an infant Dionysus and a drunken Heracles around its sides, among others featuring the wine god in particular. Bowersock avers that only a wealthy Jew could have owned such a villa in Sepphoris, populated largely by Jews, and he repeats the proposition that such an individual may have been the patriarch. See also Schlesier, 7.
[3] "The village [Sepphoris] is identified with the Second Temple-period Cana of John 2. Here Jesus reluctantly performed His first miracle of turning water to wine at a wedding feast, and thus emerged from His 'hidden years' to begin His three-year ministry in the Galilee." (*Fodor's Israel*, 239).

Macrobius

In the fifth century AD/CE, Macrobius published a book called *Saturnalia*, which discusses numerous deities of the Roman Empire at that time, including various Greek gods who are identified with each other and possess many solar attributes. In this regard, Macrobius treats virtually all such deities as sun gods, including and especially Dionysus/Bacchus/Father Liber.

Bacchus as Apollo

As we have seen, the Roman writer also equated Bacchus with Apollo, whose battle with the serpent or water monster he identified as a solar myth. In his comparisons, Macrobius (1.18.7) further remarked:

> But given the earlier proof that Apollo and the sun are the same, and the subsequent demonstration that father Liber is the same as Apollo, there can be no doubt but that the sun and father Liber must be considered aspects of the same godhead... They observe the holy mystery in the rites by calling the sun Apollo when it is in the upper (that is, daytime) hemisphere; when it is in the lower (that is, nighttime) hemisphere, it is considered Dionysus, who is Liber.[1]

Thus, again, Bacchus possesses the same role as Osiris, the sun of the night or "underworld."

Solar Dionysus

Macrobius (1.18.9-10) also cites depictions of Dionysus, including as symbolically representing the winter solstice, "like the image the Egyptians bring out from its shrine on a fixed date, with the appearance of a small infant, since it's the shortest day."[2] Other Bacchic images represent the equinoxes and summer solstice, the latter sporting a long beard indicating the length of the day.

More proofs of Dionysus's solar nature can be found in Macrobius, including citations of older texts such as the Orphic hymns. The name Sabazius or Sebazius is explained (1.18.11) as denoting the Thracian sun god, equated with Dionysus and previously mentioned as an archaic beer god. Moreover, the "physical scientists" explain that Dionysus is the "mind of Zeus," because "the sun is the mind of the cosmic order..."[3]

As is appropriate for a legislator, the sun, "whom they call with the surname Dionysus," is the "god of good counsel,"[4] similar to a title ascribed to Bacchus by Plutarch.

---

[1] Macrobius/Kaster, 1.249.
[2] Macrobius/Kaster, 1.249, 251. For further discussion of this Egyptian "Christmas" ritual involving a baby sun god born of a virgin goddess, see my book *Christ in Egypt*.
[3] Macrobius, 1.18.15; Kaster, 1.253.
[4] Macrobius/Kaster, 1.255.

THE DIONYSUS CONNECTION

Macrobius is insistent on Dionysus's solar nature, as in the Orphic hymns: "The sun, whom they call with the surname Dionysus."[1]

We learn also from the Roman (1.18.18) the neat solar summation ascribed to Orpheus, previously mentioned:

εἷς Ζεύς, εἷς Ἀίδης, εἷς Ἥλιος, εἷς Διόνυσος.

One Zeus, one Hades, one Helios, one Dionysus.

Iao

In addition, we discover that, by the authority of the "sacred verses" of the oracle of Apollo of Claros, another name given to the sun is "Iao." Says Macrobius (1.18.19-20):

> For when Apollo of Claros was asked, concerning the god called Iaô, which of the gods he should be considered, Apollo replied as follows:
> Those who know the mysteries should conceal things not to be sought.
> But if your understanding is slight, your mind feeble, say that the greatest god of all is Iaô:
> Hades in winter, Zeus at the start of spring, the sun in summer, delicate Iacchos [=Dionysos] in the fall.[2]

Macrobius (1.18.21) cites earlier writer Cornelius Labeo (c. 3rd cent. AD/CE?) as identifying "father Liber and the sun as Iaô."[3]

As concerns this name Iao, Macrobius editor Dr. Robert A. Kaster remarks:

> Derived from *Yahu*, a form of the sacred name of the Jewish God, "Iaô" appears in syncretizing contexts, as here, in Gnostic texts, and as a name to conjure with in the magical papyri.[4]

Thus, again, Yahu or Yahweh, the Jewish tribal war god, is equated with Iao and is therefore solar as well. Moreover, if Iao is also Dionysus, then so too is Yahweh.

Also, Macrobius (1.19.16) identifies Dionysus's thyrsus/wand as a solar artifact, as is Mercury's caduceus, the staff with intertwined snakes,[5] essentially the same as Moses's rod.

Hermias

In his scholia or commentary on Plato's *Phaedrus*, Neoplatonist philosopher Hermias or Hermeias of Alexandria (c. 410-c. 450 AD/CE), in speaking of the renewing nature of Bacchus's nymphs, remarks that "this Dionysus or Bacchus

Fig. 67. Hermes's winged caduceus with two snakes

---
[1] Macrobius/Kaster, 1.225.
[2] Macrobius/Kaster, 1.257. ...φράζεο τὸν πάντων ὕπατον θεὸν ἔμμεν Ἰαώ, χείματι μέν τ' ἀΐδην, Δία δ' εἴαρος ἀρχομένοιο, Ἠέλιον δὲ θέρευς, μετοπώρου δ' ἀβρὸν Ἰαώ.
[3] Labeo, *On the Oracle of Apollos of Clarus*; Stern, no. 445. Macrobius/Kaster, 1.257.
[4] Macrobius/Kaster, 1.255.
[5] Macrobius/Kaster, 1.267.

supplies the regeneration of every sensible nature."[1] In this regard, Kerenyi likewise writes about Dionysus as the "archetypal image of indestructible life," representing eternal life, like his Christian imitator.

Nonnus

In the late fifth or early sixth century AD/CE, Greek poet Nonnus/Nonnos composed an epic poem entitled *Dionysiaca*, the longest such work that has survived from antiquity. The poem uses Homeric language and hexameter in describing Dionysus's life, expedition to India, and his "triumphant return to the west."

As we know, this tale of Dionysus's journey to India is a millennium or more older than the time of Nonnus's writing, and it is believed that the poet obtained much of his information from more ancient texts that predated the common era by centuries. While drawing on Homer, Nonnus was influenced also by Hesiod, Euripides, the Theban poet Pindar (522-443 BCE) and Callimachus. He may allude as well to the lost poems of Euphorion of Chalcis (b. c. 275 BCE), Peisander of Laranda (fl. c. 3rd cent. AD/CE) and the Libyan epicist Soteirichus (3rd-4th cents. AD/CE). In this regard, Nonnus is considered a chronicler of "lost Hellenistic poetry and mythic traditions," reflecting his reliance upon older sources.

Read widely in late antiquity and into the Byzantine era (330-1453 AD/CE) and Renaissance (14th-17th centuries AD/CE), Nonnus's massive work includes 48 books containing different episodes in the mythical life of Dionysus/Bacchus. We read in book 2, for example, about the battle of the gods and giants, reminiscent of other great epics such as the *Mahabharata* and *Iliad*.

Book 4 (260ff) speaks of Kadmos/Cadmus's knowledge of Egyptian secrets and wisdom. A Phoenician prince whose sister was Europa and who traditionally founded the Greek city of Thebes, Cadmus was given credit for bringing the "Phoenician" alphabet to Greece. Per Herodotus's reckoning, Cadmus's era was about 2000 BCE, long before the Phoenician invention of the alphabet, so this story may reflect the proto-Greek Pelasgian alphabet instead.[2] Nevertheless, it is important to note that aspects of Greek culture have been attributed since antiquity to the Egyptians and Phoenicians, these two ethnicities themselves sharing a cultural exchange for centuries, at least as early as 4,600 years ago.[3]

---

[1] Porphyry/Thomas, 1.248.
[2] The Pelasgian alphabet has been surmised since antiquity to be equivalent to the Phoenician. Robert Graves (225) cites Diodorus (3.67; 5.56-74) as stating that 13 consonants in the Greek alphabet constituted the Pelasgian alphabet, increased to 16 by Cadmus. Graves (228) also relates that Pliny "states positively in his *Natural History* that the first Latin alphabet was a Pelasgian one."
[3] Redford (1992), 22.

THE DIONYSUS CONNECTION

Book 7 of Nonnus describes the birth of Dionysus to the mortal Semele, impregnated by Zeus/God at the bidding of Aion, a god of Time. Book 8 depicts Semele's fiery death because of trickery by Zeus's jealous wife, Hera. Dionysus is snatched up by Zeus and, in book 9, reborn, given to Hermes and handed off to the Theban queen-goddess "Ino of the Waters," an appropriate designation for one drawing a god from the waters. Hence, the god is "twice-born."

The Sun, Wine and Grapevine Paramours

As do the earlier sections, Nonnus's books 10 through 12 contain nature-worshipping themes, including the discovery of wine and a tale about the young Bacchus "falling in love" with a boy, Ampelos/Ampelus, who in reality represents the vine. In this regard, we can see that what appears to be a homoerotic and pederastic myth in fact has nature-worshipping significance, as Ampelus is changed into the grapevine, which the solar Dionysus adopts as his plant, subsequently discovering the magical elixir of wine.

After this story, in book 13 we find Zeus ordering Dionysus to take his human army to India, where he was said to have spread viniculture and viticulture. Because of his skills in wine-making, Bacchus is able to defeat the Indians by making them drunk.

Staphylus and the Grape Bunch

Another nature-worshipping theme occurs in Nonnus's book 18, in which an Assyrian man named "Staphylus" (Στάφυλος) and his family become drunk with Dionysus at a banquet. The following morning, Staphylus/Staphylos "talks about the gods and giants, as well as the origin of the Indians, and then dies." The Greek word *staphylos* or *staphyle* refers to a bunch of grapes, a theme to be discussed below.

The Ruddy Sea

In books 20 and 21 of his *Dionysiaca*, Nonnos/Nonnus sets his tale in Phoenicia and/or Arabia, which is relevant for the reason that it demonstrates an association of Bacchus with the Near and Middle East, the area in which the Moses myth was formulated. Book 20 recounts the driving of Dionysus and his followers into the "ruddy sea" in "Arabia" by the king Lycurgus, a motif also related by Seneca.[1]

In book 22, we are treated to Bacchus's performance of miracles, including turning water to milk and compelling rocks to spout wine. The Indians are not impressed and nonetheless attack his army. Books 23 and 24 recount this war, verse 23.18 discussing Dionysus's

---

[1] In describing the Erythraean Sea into which Dionysus plunges, Nonnus uses the Greek word Ἐρυθραίης, the same as ἐρυθραῖος *erythraios*, from the root ἐρυθρός *erythros*, which means "red." (Liddell & Scott) Herodotus (1.180; 2.11; 4.42) uses the phrase Ἐρυθρὴν θάλασσαν *Erythrēn thalassan* to describe the "Red Sea" into which the Euphrates empties, not far from Egypt, and from which the Phoenicians sailed.

crossing of the Hydaspes river with his army, during which time he drowns his foes.[1] In book 25, Dionysus finally causes the Indians to become drunk and incapacitated, so he can sack their city.

In book 25 too (380ff), we read about Dionysus's shield, covered by constellations and various scenes from Greek mythology. Numerous other adventures follow that resemble depictions of various characters in the Old Testament, engaging in episodes of sex scandals, more fighting, battles with giants, divine interventions, trickery and so on.

Along the way, the Indians manage to kill many of Dionysus's followers or Bacchantes (35), while in book 36 the gods step in to take sides, much like in the Homeric and Indian epics, as well as in the various biblical battles between the Yahwists and devotees of other gods around the region.

The war ends in book 40 with the defeat of the Indians and triumph of Dionysus, like his biblical counterparts conquering the natives of Midian and Canaan. In this same book, Dionysus is depicted as traveling to the Phoenician city of Tyre, where he learns about the city's mythical founding by the demigod and son of Zeus, Hercules/Herakles.

Another epic clash occurs between the armies of Poseidon's sea gods and those of Dionysus in book 43, in "a war of the waters and a battle of the vine." In book 44 of the Dionysiaca appears the tale of the god's arrest and imprisonment at the hands of Pentheus, for which act the latter is torn to pieces by the maenads, who include his own mother.

Book 47 recounts the motif of Bacchus introducing viticulture to the Thebans, who, when drunk, kill the first farmer who produces wine, an elderly tiller who himself previously had gotten intoxicated, in a tale reminiscent of the biblical tiller Noah's drinking binge in Genesis 9. The farmer's daughter, Erigone, subsequently commits suicide and is made by Zeus into the constellation of the same name. Hence, again we are looking not at "history" of "real people" but at mythical motifs designed to explain how various phenomena and traditions came to be. In specific, this motif is astronomical or astrotheological in nature.

Finally, book 48 recounts the myth about Hera provoking giants to attack Dionysus, who kills them. In this book also, Bacchus travels to Asia Minor. At this point, the god is placed among the Olympians.

To reiterate, Nonnus's epic poem, which recounted several myths of Dionysus that had been around for 1,000 or more years, was popular from the time of its composition (5th-6 cents. AD/CE), all the way through the Renaissance, which ended in the 16th century AD/CE.

---

[1] Nonnos/Rouse, 2.201.

Sanford

Starting in at least the early 17th century in Western scholarship, European theologians and others began noticing the parallels between Dionysus and Moses. One of the theologians around this time who made a case for a Moses-Dionysus connection was English scholar Hugh Sanford (d. 1607). Published in 1611 but completed several years earlier, Sanford's Latin opus *De Descensu Domini Nostri Iesu Christi ad Inferos* was built upon for decades afterwards and presented significant comparisons between the two figures.

Sanford's work is summarized by Don Allen:

> Following the evidence of ancient history and his three linguistic laws, Sanford discovers that Isis is the mother of Moses and that Moses was also known as Misen, Mises and Moso. Sanford finds it more reasonable to identify Moses with Bacchus of Nysa, a place-name which is an anagram of "Syna" or Sinai. Reading Nonnos' epic about Bacchus, Sanford noticed the name Maira, the dog-star, a distorted form of the name of Moses' sister Miriam. Orus is Aaron; and Caleb, which means "dog" in Hebrew, is Bacchus' companionable pet...[1]

In consideration of what we know about Osiris, Horus and Isis, it is reasonable to find in Moses, Aaron and Miriam their traces,[2] especially since Osiris is equated with Dionysus, who in turn has been identified with Moses. We have seen also that Aaron and Horus possess intriguing commonalities, and it is noteworthy that Isis was styled with the Egyptian epithet "Meri," meaning "beloved,"[3] while מרים *Miryam* is Semitic for "Maria" and "Mary."

Nysa-Sinai Connection

Sanford also thus averred that Nysa was an anagram of Sinai. The Greek word for Nysa is Νῦσα, which could be pronounced "Neesah," while the LXX for Sinai is Σινα, the pronunciation of which is "Seenah."

Summarizing these correlations popularized centuries earlier by Sanford, English Egyptologist Dr. Samuel Sharpe (1799-1881) added: "Nysa was an Egyptian method of spelling Sinai backward; and...Mount Sinai had been for untold ages, before the reputed period of Moses, a 'holy hill,' the fabled resort of the gods."[4]

Vossius

Another scholar of the 17th century who made the Moses-Dionysus connection was Dutch theologian and humanist professor

---

[1] Allen, D., 65.
[2] See, e.g., my book *Christ in Egypt*.
[3] See Murdock (2009), 120ff.
[4] Wilder, 50.

Dr. Gerhard Johannes Vossius (1577-1649), also known as Gerhard Johan Voss, whose real name was Gerrit Janszoon Vos.

In his massive Latin work *De theologia gentili et physiologia Christiana*, initially published around 1641 and never translated into English, the devout Christian Vossius contended that humanity had made the "mistake of looking to Nature rather than to the God of Nature," which led to the proliferation of nature gods and goddesses such as "Joves and Junos, found in every sacred acre of the world."[1] These nature-based pagan deities, Vossius averred, were biblical figures erroneously perceived: "Great patches of Vos's book are devoted to the borrowed Hebrew theologies and sacred histories of the ethnics."[2] Vossius makes many equations between these various Jewish and Gentile characters, including that "Moses is Liber, Osiris, Monius, Mises, Moso and Milichus."[3]

Regarding Vossius, Don Allen remarks:

> Picking up Sanford's Nysa-Sinai intimation, Vos develops the Moses-Bacchus relationship still further. Both heroes spent a good deal of time in the Arabian desert, and the Dionysian laureate Nonnos probably had the crossing of the Red Sea in mind when he wrote of his hero that "he took to his heels and ran in fear too fast to be pursued/until he leaped into the gray waters of the Erythraian Sea."[4]

Allen next comments: "There is little doubt that Vos knew more about world religion than almost anyone else in his generation..."[5]

As it turns out, where there is smoke, there is fire, and these learned individuals were not mistaken in noticing and explicating this comparative-religion theme of Moses and Dionysus. Since they were largely clergy with a vested interest and, probably, sincere beliefs, they could not or would not admit that the Jewish supernatural stories were unoriginal and had borrowed from the pagan myths, rather than the other way around. Nor could they afford to look closely at the guarded meanings or "mysteries" behind these myths so commonly held.

Bochart

The Moses-Bacchus correlation appeared so obvious (and fascinating) to the European educated elite, the majority of whom were Christian authorities, that they spent centuries engaged in its analysis. One conclusion as to how this strange development had occurred was proffered by Samuel Bochart in the 17th century.

Bochart surmised that, after Moses's story became known throughout the Levant, Phoenician sailors led by Cadmus, a supposed contemporary of Joshua, adopted the tale and spread it

---

[1] Allen, D., 68.
[2] Allen, D., 68.
[3] Allen, D., 68.
[4] Allen, D., 69.
[5] Allen, D., 69.

wherever they went. This conclusion of Phoenicians spreading religion via their many sea voyages is highly valuable,[1] but the facts indicate the opposite transmission, as the Bible writers composed myths largely revolving around the deities of the Phoenicians, Canaanites and Ugaritians, as well as the Sumero-Babylonians, Akkadians, Assyrians, Egyptians, Greeks, Persians, Indians and so on.

Moreover, Cadmus's era was almost a thousand years earlier than Joshua, per Herodotus, so they could not have been contemporaries, even if these figures both were historical.

Bochart associated Bacchus with the biblical character of Nimrod as well, an identification built upon by other writers who followed.

Gale

So close were these correspondences in the Dionysus myth that certain devout believers wrote long treatises presenting the parallels' purported biblical originals. One such individual was British theologian and vicar Rev. Theophilus Gales (1628-1678), who cited biblical chapter and verse whence the Greek poets allegedly had plagiarized their Bacchic tales.

In his book *The Court of the Gentiles*, in the chapter "The Theogonie of Bacchus from Sacred, or Hebrew, Names and Traditions," Gale lists 17 parallels between the Moses and Dionysus stories and tries to trace them to the Bible, providing various scriptures as their basis. He begins by attempting to show how several of Dionysus's names were "of Hebrew extract," stating that "in prosecution of our undertaking, we shall endeavor to demonstrate that the many fabulous narrations of Bacchus, his names and attributes, were but corrupt and broken imitations of Jewish names and traditions."[2]

Building upon the work of Sanford and Bochart, Gale cites Dionysian epithets purportedly lifted from the Bible, including Bacchus, Jacchus, Euvius, Adonis and Sabus. He also discusses the connection between Yah/Iah, Iao and Iacchus, while Adonis is equated by him with Adonai.[3]

---

[1] See, e.g., Sanford Holst, *Phoenicians*. The Phoenicians were expert sea travelers and traders who circled the Mediterranean and beyond for centuries, eons before their recognition as a people of that name. Holst presents the case that the people inhabiting the very ancient city of Byblos, beginning about 5,200 years ago, became excellent sailors early on and plied their trade around the sea for some 2,000 years before the common date for the emergence of the "Phoenicians" around 1200 BCE. The Phoenicians thus were "diffusionists extraordinaire," spreading culture, including religious ideas, for thousands of years. Holst provides reasons to suggest that the Minoan culture was influenced by these early Phoenicians, whose ancient city is also intertwined with the Egyptian myth of Osiris, showing a relationship between those two lands as well. This Phoenician relationship can be seen in the presence of wood from the famed "cedars of Lebanon" in Egyptian tombs.

[2] Gale, 24.

[3] Gale, 27.

Jehovahnissi

As concerns the name "Dionysus," Gale insists it comes from Exodus 17:15, in which, after the slaughter of the Amalekites, Moses is claimed to have set up an altar at Rephidim with the unusual name "Jehovahnissi." The churchman speculates that, since Dionysus was from Arabia, basically where Mt. Sinai was situated, he or the Greek poets must have seen the altar and copied the name. There exists no evidence that such an altar was ever visible for anyone to see or copy, but this name indeed may reflect the ancient Bacchus cult among the Semites, including the Israelites, as we shall see.

Included in Gale's analysis is the Nysa-Syna transposition. Gale also equates with Canaan the "land of honey" through which Dionysus was said to travel.[1] He further discusses the comparison between Bacchus or Boachus and Noachus or Noah, including that the latter was said to have introduced the grapevine (Gen 9:20).

We have seen already the bulk of these comparisons in the ancient writings previously examined. Those who followed Gale and others of this era—and there were many—repeated many or most of these same parallels. (For the rest of Gale's list, see *The Study Guide*.)

Thomassin

In 1682, French Catholic priest Louis Thomassin (1619-1695) also addressed the comparisons between Moses and Dionysus, recounting Vossius's work and summarizing the main parallels, including:

> Moses was born in Egypt, and Orpheus, in the hymns attributed to him, renders the same testimony to Liber, or to Bacchus; making him son of the goddess Isis, and making him born from the waters of the Nile, where Moses was exposed....[2]

Thomassin also discusses the name of Moses, which "comes from that which was pulled from the waters." He calls the lawgiver by the Latin moniker *Masa extraxit* ("Moses extracted") and says that "Orpheus in the Hymns or in the Mysteries gives to Bacchus the name of *Mises*, and names him born from the waters..."

As parallels between the Greek and Hebrew figures, the French priest raises up the two mothers, Nysa, the flight across the Red Sea, the presence of women in the army, the horns, the smiting of a rock for water, the serpent, the "dog," the "milk and honey," the role of lawgiver, the "double law" and the miraclemaking.

Thomassin cites many of the ancient sources for these comparisons, including Clement, Diodorus, Euripides, Nonnus, Orpheus, Plutarch, Sophocles and Strabo.

---

[1] Gale, 27.
[2] Thomassin, 24.

Patrick

Around the same time, English bishop and theologian Dr. Simon/Symon Patrick (1626-1707) continued the analysis, remarking that, "in Orpheus's hymns, Bacchus is called Mises, which seems to be the same with Moses; out of whose story all that the Greeks and others say of Bacchus seems to have been framed."[1]

Thus, yet another Christian authority of a past era was aware of the numerous striking and important parallels between Moses and Dionysus, but, as also a believer in the Bible, he too attempted to trace the Dionysian myth to the Hebrew lawgiver. Nevertheless, it is apparent that these stories are mythical, and the evidence indicates the myth existed first in other cultures, including the Egyptian, Greek, Asian Minor and Levantine.

Patrick also believed Justin Martyr had demonstrated that the major Bacchic proselytizer, Orpheus, learned a number of his doctrines from Moses's books.[2] However, there is little evidence of detailed knowledge by Gentiles of the biblical stories before these latter were rendered into Greek during the third or second centuries BCE. Justin's attempts would reveal nevertheless that early Christians were aware of the parallels between the Dionysian/Orphic religion and that of Moses.

Danet

In 1700, French scholar and philologist Pierre Danet published *A Complete Dictionary of the Greek and Roman Antiquities*, in which he included a lengthy entry for Bacchus/Dionysus, recounting his myth and relating Vossius's comparisons between him and the Israelite lawgiver. Danet translates a long passage from Vossius's Latin, asserting Moses as Bacchus and detailing the numerous correlations such as the "dog" companion and emphasis on grapes:

> One of the most faithful servants of Moses is Celeb, who gave such illustrious proofs of his courage and fidelity when he went to observe and discover the promised Land, and brought back with the other spies the famous bunch of grapes. In like manner, the poets make a dog to have been the companion of Bacchus, the Hebrew word *Celeb* signifying a dog. Nonnus relates the discourse of Bacchus, when he translated his dog to the stars and

Fig. 68. Michiel van der Borch, *Spies return from Canaan with grapes*, 1332. Vellum, National Library of The Netherlands, The Hague

---

[1] Patrick (1738), 255.
[2] Patrick (1695), 8.

made a constellation of it, called *Maera* or "Little Dog," which contributes to the ripening of the grapes.

Orpheus gives Bacchus the title of a lawgiver..., attributing to him a double Law, as if he alluded to the Two Tables of the Law of Moses or to Deuteronomy...[1]

In his entry on "Bacchus," Danet states that ancient Egyptians and Greeks confounded Dionysus with "Phoebus, Apollo, Pluto, Apis, Anubis and Osiris," as well as Janus and Noah. Says he: "Plutarch undertakes to prove that Bacchus is the God of the Hebrews and that all the observations of the Jews are nothing else but the ceremonies of Bacchus."[2]

Huet

Following Bochart was his pupil, the bishop of Avranches Dr. Pierre Daniel Huet (1630-1721), an esteemed scholar in his own right who continued the Moses-Dionysus discussion. Huet suggested, as a related aside, that the famed Greek poet Homer "may have been an Egyptian and not a Greek; further [Homer] read all of Moses' writings and took over his sacred history and his theology."[3] Huet averred that "Moses was converted by the Phoenicians into the gods Taautus [Thoth] and Adonis."[4]

Concerning this contention, Don Allen remarks:

> The second metamorphosis fits very snugly, because Adonis was born in Arabia where Moses dwelt, and was, in his myth, hidden in an ark entrusted to Proserpine [Persephone/Kore].... [According to Huet,] Adonis is, of course, the same as Bacchus, Mercury, Osiris, Apollo and Helios; hence, since Moses is Adonis, he is also these other gods. ...by looking about, Huet discovers Moses in the pantheons of Persia, China, Japan, Mexico and the primitive religions of the Germans, French and English. He is, of course, best found in Greece and Rome, and in the latter country he was worshiped as Romulus.[5]

As writers in antiquity had discussed a number of Dionysuses, so too does Huet bring up various Bacchi as originating with the Pelasgians, referring to one such Dionysus as "Moses."[6] From all the evidence presented here, this Dionysus would be centuries older than the Moses character, however, the latter evidently created largely in the seventh to third centuries BCE.

The one conclusion we surely can make about this centuries-long continuity of scholarship is that the parallels between Dionysus and Moses are real and highly conspicuous. Furthermore, what Huet's

---

[1] Danet, "Bacchus."
[2] Danet, "Bacchus."
[3] Allen, D., 80.
[4] Allen, D., 80.
[5] Allen, D., 80-81.
[6] Huet, 221: *Atqui Dionysus ille fuit Moses.*

THE DIONYSUS CONNECTION 323

"monomania" actually reflects are stories of lawgivers and founders of nations similar in many aspects to Moses.

Hence, this learned Christian authority is perceiving a genuine phenomenon, but there is a more universal reason behind this coincidence, as it has to do significantly with the sun, the object of worship for thousands of years that ancient writers such as Macrobius found as the basis of many deities, including the bulk of those discussed by Huet.

Thus, the equation of these gods and heroes is also sensible, although none of their myths is exactly the same, obviously. In reality, universal myths and archetypes are changed according to the era and location of a particular culture or ethnicity, its environment, emphases and mores, traditions and rituals.

Voltaire

So striking and well known were these correspondences between Moses and Bacchus that famed French scholar Voltaire (1694-1778) expounded upon them as well:

> The ancient poets have placed the birth of Bacchus in Egypt; he is exposed on the Nile and it is from that event that he is named Mises by the first Orpheus, which, in Egyptian, signifies "saved from the waters"... He is brought up near a mountain of Arabia called Nisa [Nysa], which is believed to be Mount Sinai. It is pretended that a goddess ordered him to go and destroy a barbarous nation and that he passed through the Red Sea on foot, with a multitude of men, women, and children. Another time the river Orontes suspended its waters right and left to let him pass, and the Hydaspes did the same. He commanded the sun to stand still; two luminous rays proceeded from his head. He made a fountain of wine spout up by striking the ground with his thyrsus, and engraved his laws on two tables of marble. He wanted only to have afflicted Egypt with ten plagues, to be the perfect copy of Moses.[1]

The connection to the Orontes river is interesting, in light of its location, near Ugarit, where the Semitic wine god was revered in antiquity. During the fifteenth and fourteenth centuries BCE, the "territory west of the Orontes, as far as the Mediterranean coast, belonged to Egypt."[2] Hence, crossing the river to the east would constitute "fleeing from Egypt."

Sun Standing Still

Here we see correlations between not only Dionysus and Moses but also Bacchus and Joshua, such as the sun standing still. Rather than serving as an impossible "historical fact," the tale of the day star arrested in its course reflects the solstice. This motif is clearly part of

---

[1] Voltaire (1824), 1.374-375.
[2] Redford (1992), 167.

a solar *myth*, not history, unless we are to allow that Dionysus's story too is "real."

Alas, even the great Voltaire writes here as if he believed the Dionysian myth was a copy of a historical Israelite lawgiver, rather than both representing a mythical founder archetype.

Edwards

The Moses-Bacchus connection became so well known by the time of American theologian Rev. Jonathan Edwards (1703-1758) that he composed notes about it in his renowned *Blank Bible*, explaining that the "blind heathen" had heard of Moses's biblical adventures and had imitated them in "whom they called Bacchus."[1]

In this regard, American religion professor Dr. Gerald R. McDermott states:

> Edwards noted in his Blank Bible that heathen stories about gods and goddesses were actually distortions of Hebrew counterparts. Saturn, for example, is a transmutation of Adam, Noah and Abraham; Hercules is a Greek rendition of Joshua, Bacchus of Nimrod, Moses and the Hebrew deity; Apis and Serapis are Egyptian retellings of the story of Joseph.[2]

While the churchman Edwards objected to the "blind heathen" supposing that the ancient gods were the same as biblical figures, he himself was compelled to admit the similarities and derive one from the other, the Bible taking precedence based on his conditioning and vocation.

Bell

In *Bell's New Pantheon*, published in 1790, John Bell presented the Moses-Dionysus arguments in detail, with a long list incorporating many of the aspects we have already seen. He began his analysis with a comparison of Bacchus and Nimrod, a study worth examining, as the latter thus may serve as another legislator and wine-god archetype.

Among other parallels, Bell noted the similarity between Bacchus and "Barchus," "son of Chus," referring to Nimrod, son of Cush (Gen 10:8; 1 Chr 1:10). Both are "hunters," and, as the first king of the wine-making region of Babylon, Nimrod is associated with the grapevine.

Dupuis

In his opus *Origine de tous les Cultes, ou la Réligion Universelle* or *Origin of All Religious Worship*, French professor Charles Dupuis (1742-1809) built upon this scholarship and laid out the universal syncretism in all its glory. Dupuis's multivolume opus influenced

---

[1] McDermott, 127-128, etc.
[2] McDermott, 94.

many people during his time and for decades after, including Napoleon Bonaparte and possibly various American Founding Fathers,[1] remaining relevant to this day.

Dupuis compares Dionysus's miracles with those of Moses and Jesus. He also discusses in detail the astrotheological or solar connotations of the archetypal myth.

Dupuis is one of the first voices raised in this debate who did not automatically default to biblical priority and who suggested that biblical figures are copies of ancient myths, not the other way around. In this mythicist view, these biblical characters are as mythical as their archetypal predecessors, who possess astrotheological significance.

Hort

By the early 19th century, the devout continued to highlight the numerous striking parallels between Moses and Dionysus, including English scholar Rev. William Jillard Hort, who essentially repeated the same list as Gale.

Even though the Moses-Dionysus connection had been made for centuries by some of Europe's best scholars, the bulk of whom were erudite clergy, Hort's treatise was subjected to ridicule by those who, thinking in terms of Moses as a historical individual, could not fathom how the two characters could be comparable.[2]

Le Brun

In spite of the attempts over the centuries that made the pagans the borrowers of biblical tales, the perspective continued to shift, and the less devout and non-bibliolatrous evinced that Moses was based on Dionysus. One such commentator was French novelist Charles-Antoine-Guillaume Pigault-Lebrun or "Le Brun" (1753-1835), who in his *Doubts of Infidels* (1803) remarked:

> The history of Moses is copied from the history of Bacchus, who was called Mises by the Egyptians, instead of Moses. Bacchus was born in Egypt; so was Moses... Bacchus passed through the Red Sea on dry ground; so did Moses. Bacchus was a lawgiver; so was Moses. Bacchus was picked up in a box that floated on the water; so was Moses.... Bacchus by striking a rock made wine gush forth... Bacchus was worshipped...in Egypt, Phoenicia, Syria, Arabia, Asia and Greece, before Abraham's day.[3]

---

[1] See my article "Did George Washington and Thomas Jefferson Believe Jesus was a Myth?"
[2] See *The Study Guide* for more information.
[3] Draper, 514; Pigault-Lebrun, 19-20. The original of this work was in French and was called *Le Citateur*. An English translation was included in a volume with the peculiar title: *An Eye-Opener, "Citateur, par Pigault." Le Brun, Doubts of Infidels*, by someone named "Zepa."

Here we see the logical conclusion made in the early 19th century that Moses's account is mythical, copied *from* paganism *to* Judaism, rather than the other way around, as centuries of clergy had averred, thereby continually acknowledging the parallels.

"Abraham's day" is estimated to be sometime between the 20th and 17th centuries BCE, depending on the source. However, skeptical scholarship contends that the Abraham stories were created much later and that Abraham too is not a historical person.

Bellamy

Taking the perspective that there was a "historical" Bacchus, John Bellamy (fl. c. 1818) identified him as the "same person whom Herodotus calls Sesostris." His reasons are primarily that "Sesostris came out of Egypt with a great army, and invaded the east in the same manner, and with every circumstance as is recorded of the true Bacchus, who, on account of his conquest, was celebrated in various nations by different names."[1]

Bellamy then lists several names or epithets by which Bacchus/Dionysus has been known, including "Sheshac" by the Arabs and "Belus" by the Chaldeans, "Mars" or "Valiant" by the Phrygians and Thracians, and, of course, "Osiris" in Egypt.[2] "Belus" is the Latin for Bel, Akkadian for Baal, the Canaanite god and epithet of Yahweh. Here we would have a Semitic prototype from which the Hebrews could have drawn to flesh out both Yahweh and Moses.

Bellamy continues with his list of attributes common to both Bacchus and Sesostris, again concluding that Dionysus *is* Sesostris, the latter of whom in turn is thought to be the king Shishak mentioned at 2 Chronicles 12:2-3. This Shishak, it should be noted, has been equated by numerous Egyptologists with the pharaoh Shoshenk or Sheshonk I (c. 943-922 BCE). As we know, the mythical Bacchus precedes Sheshonk by centuries.

Demonstrating the confusion that comes with trying to fit mythical characters into history, Bellamy next says that "whoever attentively examines the theology of Bacchus as recorded in the mythology of the heathens, and compares it with the books of Moses, will conclude that the true Bacchus was Moses himself, and that the true Jupiter, the father of Bacchus, was Jehovah the father of all mankind."[3]

We could not agree more, except that none of these figures in the paragraph above is historical or *the* god of the universe. That these characters are mythical explains why they are treated so confusedly in both ancient and modern times. For, how could Moses be Bacchus be Sesostris/Shishak, if these are all historical individuals?

---

[1] Bellamy (1820), 150.
[2] Bellamy (1820), 150.
[3] Bellamy (1820), 152.

Bellamy traces the word "Jupiter" or, rather, "Jao Pater" to Jehovah/Yahweh, an association over 2,000 years old, with Diodorus equating "Iao" with Jupiter.

Bellamy touches on the parallels already seen, naming the rivers that Dionysus was said to cross dryshod as Orontes and Hydaspes, as Horace and Voltaire had done. Bellamy also points out that Diodorus and Strabo "affirm that the sepulcher of Osiris (Bacchus) was unknown to the Egyptians," comparing this motif with the biblical account of no one knowing Moses's "sepulcher unto this day" (Deut 34:6).

Jehovah Nisi

In his comparisons to show that the "heathen" Bacchus was borrowed from Moses, Bellamy too addressed the epithet "Jehovah Nisi," to be discussed in detail below:

> I shall have occasion to show, when at the end of the Pentaeuch I prove the heathen mythology to be taken from the ancient Scriptures, that the Bacchus of the heathens was Moses. Bacchus, from the place where he resided, and obtained a knowledge of all the learning of Arabia as well as of Egypt, was called Dionysius [sic], i.e., *Dio* and *Nisi*. Plutarch mentions the flight Διονύσου, of *Dio-nysius*—Homer speaks of the city *Nisa*, sacred to Bacchus. *Nisi* [sic] was a city close to a mountain in Arabia. At Nisi Moses resided forty years, and was instructed in mount Sinai respecting the rites and ceremonies of divine worship. For this reason it was that he built an altar there, which he called *Jehovah Nisi*: Exod. [17:15]. The same is said of Bacchus by Ovid, "Bacchus was instructed in the highest wisdom in a mount of Arabia called Nisi." Diodorus Siculus informs us that the ancient Brahmans acknowledge the whole system of their civil and religious polity to have been derived from Dionysius [sic]. It is also worthy of remark that *Nisi* and *Sini* have a corresponding significance...[1]

Again, the Hebrew for Sinai is סיני *Ciynay*, which is essentially a transposition of נסי *nissi*. Considering that both sites have been said to be near Egypt and/or in Arabia, among other locales, this analysis linking them is not farfetched, especially in view of the rest of the correspondences between Moses and Dionysus.

Clarke

Continuing this scholarship, in his commentary on Exodus 4:17 published in 1836, Rev. Clarke likewise engaged in the Bacchus-Moses comparison, taking the view, as we would expect from a clergyman, that Moses existed first.

In Clarke's work, we see the same themes, admitted against interest by another theologian, who surely took the time to verify these correspondences, discovering whence they came, as they had

---

[1] Bellamy (1813), 194.

been scrutinized for at least 200 years by numerous European and American scholars, representing possibly unparalleled peer review.

Higgins

Also in the early 19th century, British magistrate Godfrey Higgins (1772-1833) repeated these various Mosaic and Bacchic correlations given currency by so many previous authorities, in his book *Anacalypsis*.

Darlington

Published in 1832, *A Catechism of Mythology* by American writer William Darlington likewise highlighted the various parallels between Bacchus and Moses, concluding that the pagans copied the Bible.

Taylor

All of this research over a period of centuries led to the conclusion by some that various biblical characters rank as allegorical figures, a view expounded upon in the works of English minister Rev. Dr. Robert Taylor (1784–1844). Labeled "the Devil's Chaplain" by his detractors, Taylor composed mythicist works asserting that certain biblical figures were *mythical*, not historical. Preaching this mythicism from his popular pulpit, the reverend was charged with "blasphemy" and imprisoned on two occasions for a year or more each, during which time he languished but put his thoughts into writing. In his book *The Diegesis*, Taylor likewise recited various Moses-Dionysus parallels, such as already provided in the present work.

Since Taylor's time, many others have written about these correspondences, not a few from the perspective that Moses is a mythical copy of Dionysus and not the other way around.

Massey

Gerald Massey too listed the various parallels between Moses and Dionysus, connecting them to Egyptian myth, especially as concerns the wind and atmospheric god Shu, mediator between heaven and earth. In the Egyptian texts, Shu is addressed as "the god dwelling in the divine Sekt," this latter term designating an "ark or cabin."[1]

The British scholar also explains the significance of the moniker Jehovahnissi or Jehovah-Nisi, as part of the Shu myth:

> Bacchus and Moses are but two forms of Shu-Anhar. Shu is modified into Khu, meaning to govern—a lawgiver. Shu is god of the vine and standard or pedestal. The altar raised by Moses to Jehovah-Nissi is called the lord of my standard.[2]

---

[1] Massey (2007), 2.265-266.
[2] Massey (1974), 264-265.

Massey adds to the lengthy list an overlooked parallel:

> Bacchus is said to have married Zipporah, a name of Venus, one of the seven planets. The priest of Midian had seven daughters; Moses married one of these, whose name was Zipporah.[1]

Hence, both legislators were married to one of a group of seven, an astrotheological motif to be discussed.

Conclusion

The Greek god Dionysus's worship extends back at least 3,200 years, but the reverence for a wine deity in general is much older. Extant ancient texts describing Bacchus's myth date from the 10th century BCE to the fifth century AD/CE. For many centuries since antiquity, scholars, theologians and others have noted numerous parallels between Dionysus and Moses, most attempting to establish biblical priority but some declaring that the former post-dated and was derived from the latter.

We have seen that important aspects of Bacchus's life, described consistently for centuries dating back to the 10th century BCE at the latest, correspond to that of the Israelite lawgiver. Also discussed is the contention by Plutarch that the Jews practiced Bacchic rituals and that Diodorus equated the Jewish god with Dionysus, a reverence evident from Dionysian artifacts such as mosaics in at least one house of a wealthy and powerful Jew.

Since it appears that the Moses character was not created until sometime during or after the Babylonian exile, possibly with his myth in the Pentateuch not taking its final biblical form until the third century BCE, it is conceivable that Bacchic ideas from the Greek historians and poets prior to that time, such as Homer, Hesiod, Herodotus, Euripides and many others, were incorporated directly in the biblical myth. It is also possible that the framers of the Moses myth were aware of the Dionysian myths because they had been written into plays performed around the Mediterranean for centuries. The story of Bacchus in particular would have been well known enough not to need to rely on the texts directly; hence, the Dionysus-Moses connection could have been made early.

---

[1] Massey (2007), 2.264.

Fig. 69. *The Dance of Cogul*: Small black 'Dionysus' with enormous genitals appears at center right; of 45 dancers, nine are women, c. 10,000 BP? Rock drawing, Lleida, Spain (Henri Breuil)

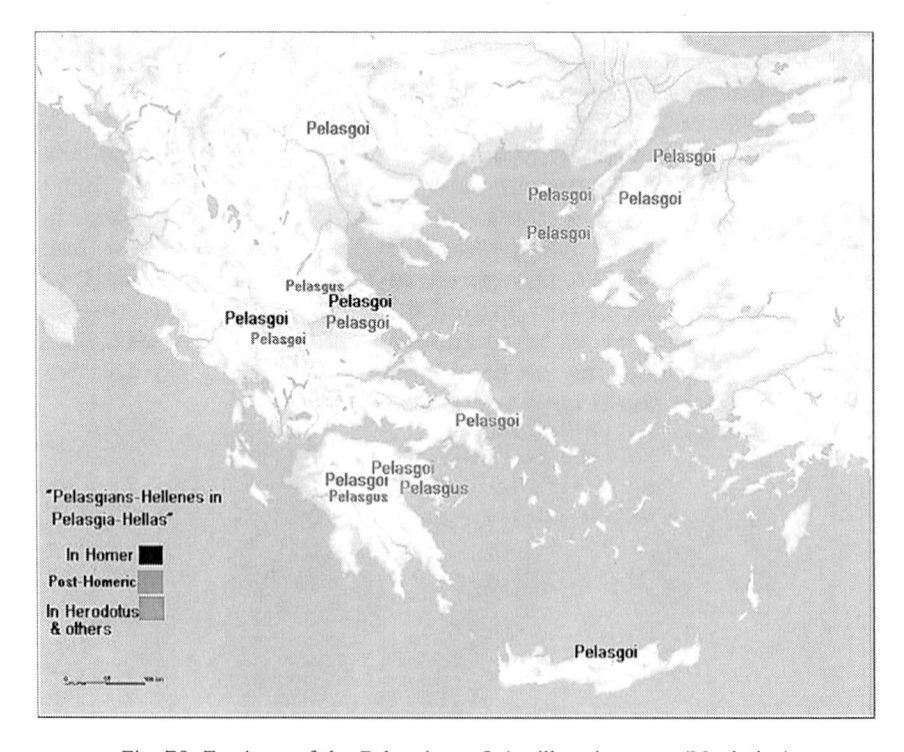

Fig. 70. Territory of the Pelasgians, 2nd millennium BCE (Megistias)

The Life of Dionysus

"The Bacchus story also contained remarkable similarities to Mosaic attributes and legends. For, as Bochart pointed out, both Bacchus and Moses were born in Egypt, shut up in an 'ark,' and put on the waters. Both fled from Egypt toward the Red Sea and had serpents (in Moses' case, a bronze serpent). For both, water flowed from a rock and milk and honey were provided. Both were called legislators, turned sticks into snakes, saw light in the darkness, and had unknown tombs..."

Dr. Gerald R. McDermott, *Jonathan Edwards Confronts the Gods* (91)

THIS CHAPTER analyzes in depth the characteristics that Dionysus/Bacchus shares with Moses, gathered together from ancient primary sources, as reiterated by many writers over the past several centuries. Because we are dealing with a god whose reverence is so archaic and widespread, there exist numerous traditions associated with his worship not strictly from Greek mythology but representing elements from other, older cultures as well. Like other mythical figures in antiquity, this multifaceted god was said to symbolize multiple characters, some of whom ancient writers and worshippers believed were historical.

As noted in the discussion of syncretism, the merger of gods with each other and with real people is quite common in the development of myth, as was understood in antiquity, in the analyses of various ancient writers concerning the different Dionysuses, for example. Here we will treat the composite figure as one myth for ease of reference, as, again, it is clear that such "confusion" or syncretism was recognized anciently as well.

Bacchic Attributes

The following list highlights some of the attributes of the Dionysian myth in common with that of Moses:

1. Like the Hebrew prophet, Dionysus was said to be born in or near Egypt,[1] reflected in the epithet Nilus or "of the Nile."[2]
2. Dionysus was "saved from the waters" in a small box or chest.[3]
3. Bacchus's epithet was "Mises,"[4] similar to "Moses."
4. The Greek god was said to be "Bimater" or to have two mothers,[5] like Moses with his birth and adoptive mothers.

---

[1] See, e.g., the *Homeric Hymn 1 to Dionysus*.
[2] Cicero, *N.D.* 3.58.
[3] Pausanias 3.24.3.
[4] For a discussion of *Orphic Hymn 42*, see below.
[5] Diodorus 3.62; Homer, *Il.* 6.130; Pausanias 3.24.4.

5. Dionysus was "brought up near a mountain of Arabia called Nisa,"[1] comparable to Mt. Sinai, where Moses spent many years.
6. Like Moses exiled to "Arabia," Bacchus grew up in Arabia and battled Egypt.[2]
7. Bacchus married Venus, one of the seven "planets," while Moses's wife, Zipporah, is one of seven sisters.
8. Like Moses (Exod 2:22), Dionysus fathered children.[3]
9. Like Yahweh's burning bush, Dionysus was "the fire," appropriate for a solar hero.[4]
10. Dionysus was instructed in the "secrets of the gods,"[5] serving as a prophet.[6]
11. Wherever Bacchus marched, the "land flowed with wine, milk, and honey."[7]
12. Bacchus carried a magical rod that he could change into a serpent[8] and that was wrapped with snakes like a caduceus,[8] similar to Moses's staff and brazen serpent pole.
13. Like the biblical pestilences, Dionysus caused a "plague of insanity" to befall the women of Athens, who killed themselves, a curse ended by creating a new religious festival to propitiate the gods.[9]
14. Disbelievers in Bacchus's religion were "smote with disease in their private parts,"[10] much like the hemorrhoids of Yahweh (1 Sam 5:9, 6:4-5).
15. Dionysus's army included both men and women,[11] as did the Israelites fleeing Egypt.
16. Like Yahweh's pillar of fire leading the way, the solar "joy-inspiring" Bacchus himself was considered to be a "pillar to the Thebans."[12]
17. Again like the biblical fire column, Dionysus used fire to lead his army through India.[13]
18. As Moses battled Pharaoh the "dragon," Dionysus smote Pentheus the "serpent."[1]

---

[1] Homer, *Il.* 6.130. Diodorus (4.2.4) quotes *Homeric Hymn* 1.8-9 (Diodorus/Murphy, 20).
[2] Artapanus, 27.15f; Diodorus 2.38.4, 3.73.4.
[3] Apollodorus, *Epit.* E.1.9.
[4] Philostratus, *Imag.* 1.14; Philostratus/Fairbanks, 61.
[5] Voltaire (1829), 483.
[6] Euripides, *Hec.* 1252.
[7] Euripides, *Ba.* 142-143, etc.
[8] Macrobius 1.19.16.
[9] Callimachus/Mair, 189, citing: "Athen. xiv. 618 E, Poll. iv. 55. *Cf.* Apollod. iii. 14. 7 and Hesych s.vv., Aelian, *N.A.* vii. 28."
[10] *Scholia* on the *Acharnians* (243). See discussion in text.
[11] Diodorus 4.2.6.
[12] Euripides, *Ant.* fragment 263; Clement/Ferguson, 85.143.
[13] Euripide, *Ant./Hec.* 1252; Lucian/Fowler, 253. Lucian, *Bacch.* 3: ὅπλον γάρ τι Διονυσιακὸν τὸ πῦρ, πατρῷον αὐτῷ κἄκ τοῦ κεραυνοῦ.

19. Bacchus fled to the "ruddy sea,"[2] escaping from a tyrant, who was killed.[3]
20. The Greek god used his magic wand to divide the waters of the rivers Orontes and Hydaspes, in order to cross dryshod.[4]
21. As did Moses, Dionysus drowned his enemies while crossing a river.[5]
22. Both lawgivers introduced sacred music.[6]
23. Dionysus had a "Maira,"[7] comparable to Moses's "Miriam" or "Maria."
24. Both Bacchus and Moses's female followers sang and danced with glee at the vanquishing of their enemies.[8]
25. In order to refresh his army, Bacchus brought forth miraculously a spring of water[9] (and "fountain of wine"[10]) by striking the ground with his magic rod or thyrsus.
26. Dionysus slew a giant during a battle using his sacred wand/thyrsus,[11] comparable to Moses using his magical rod to slay the Amalekites.
27. Like Moses, Bacchus was ordered by a deity to "destroy an impious nation."[12]
28. Like the Hebrew prophet, Dionysus was the great civilizing force who created a government according to a "constitutional order."[13]
29. Bacchus was the legislator,[14] bearing the title θεσμοφόρος *thesmophoros* or the "lawbearer," who "engraved his laws on two tables of marble."[15]

---

[1] Euripides, *Ba.* 537-544.
[2] Seneca, *Herc. Furens* 899-900; Nonnus 20.
[3] Homer, *Il.* 6.130, etc.
[4] Higgins, 2.19. See, e.g., Horace 2.19.17: *Tu flectis amnes...* "You bend the rivers..."
[5] Nonnus 23.
[6] Strabo 10.3.17; Exod 1.
[7] Gale, 1-2:30; Nonnos 5.212ff.
[8] Euripides, *Ba.* 75-79.
[9] Diodorus 2.38; Pausanias 4.36.7, etc.
[10] Diodorus 3.66.2.
[11] Apollodorus 1.6.2; Pausanias/Frazer, 2.322; Nonnus 48, etc.
[12] "Jupiter sends Iris to Bacchus to order him to go and destroy an impious nation in the Indies; God ordered Moses to go into Palestine to abolish the abomination of an idolatrous people." (Mayo, 3.203)
[13] Arrian, *An.* 5.1.6: ἐν κόσμῳ πολιτεύοντες (lit. "in world/order/government/constitution being a citizen"), where κόσμος *kosmos* means "order, arrangement," as well as "decency, good behavior," "good government, constitution" and "world, universe." The root verb πολιτεύω *politeuo* denotes "to be a citizen" and "live in a free state, have a certain form of government," etc.
[14] Diodorus (2.38) and others relate that Dionysus made laws in India and elsewhere.
[15] Houston, 1.213. See also Ovid (*Tristia* 5.3.25-26): *scilicet hanc legem nentes fatalia Parcae stamina bis genito bis cecinere tibi.* Summarizing this passage, professor Dr. Ned Lukacher (38) relates that, per Ovid, Bacchus is the "god whose double birth means that the Parcae have spun for him a double law."

30. One of Bacchus's festivals was the Sabazia,[1] while Moses instituted the Sabbath.[2]
31. Bacchus had a sacred ark in which his image was placed, the sight of which drove its beholders insane.[3]
32. As did the Hebrew lawgiver, Dionysus had two horns or rays on his head, associated with the bull.[4]
33. Like Moses and his law, Bacchus learned the "rites of sacrifice," which he taught to his people.[5]
34. Like that of Moses, Dionysus's religion had detailed instructions on how to sacrifice various animals, such as oxen, goats, sheep and bulls.[6]
35. A principal Dionysian celebration was the "vintage Feast of Bowers," following the autumnal equinox, while the Jewish fall festival of the Feast of the Tabernacles was said to have been instituted by Moses and to represent the time of the vintage.[7]
36. Dionysus had a dog for a companion,[8] while Moses had a companion named "Dog" in Hebrew (Caleb).[9]
37. Like Moses's Caleb, Bacchus's dog leads to the "promised land" full of juicy grapes.[10]
38. Dionysus's major festival was held at the vernal equinox,[11] the time of Israel's mythical entrance into the Promised Land, establishing the Jewish New Year[12] and annual Passover celebration, as well as the time of Christ's passion.
39. Bacchus was associated with books and literacy,[13] another appropriate attribute for a lawgiver said to have written books.
40. Like Moses, whose sepulcher is unknown "unto this day," no one knew where Bacchus was buried.[14]
41. As the Hebrew lawgiver was said to ascend to heaven, so too did Dionysus rise into heaven.[15]

---

[1] Cicero, *N.D.* 3.58.
[2] LXX: σάββατα; Vulgate: *sabbati*.
[3] Pausanias 7.19.6-9; Allen, D., 238.
[4] Euripides, *Ba.* 88.100, 919-22, etc.
[5] Ovid, *Fast.* 3.727: *Ante tuos ortus arae sine honore fuerunt*.
[6] Schlesier, 47ff.
[7] See, e.g., Wright, 62.
[8] Nonnos 5.212ff.
[9] The original Hebrew is כלב *Kaleb*, as at Numbers 13:6, defined as "dog" (Strong's H3612).
[10] Danet, "Bacchus."
[11] Pausanias 3.22.2; Aeschylus, *Prom.* 455.
[12] Philo (*Moses* 2.39.222) asserts that Moses set the new year at the vernal equinox. See, e.g., Philo/Yonge (2000), 510.
[13] See, e.g., Obbink, "Dionysos in and out of the Papyri" in Schlesier, 281ff.
[14] McDermott, 91; Bellamy (1820:152) equates Osiris with Dionysus and cites Diodorus and Strabo referring to Osiris's unknown tomb.
[15] *Assumption of Moses*; Talmud (*Yoma* 4a); Pausanias 3.18.11: "Here are Dionysus, too, and Heracles; Hermes is bearing the infant Dionysus to heaven..."

42. As Moses was the deliverer of Israel out of Egypt, called σωτήρ *soter* at Acts 7:35, one of Bacchus's epithets is *Soter* or "savior, deliverer."[1]
43. Like Joshua, Moses's successor, Dionysus used treachery and deceit to subdue a barbarous nation and sack its cities.[2]
44. Also like Joshua, Dionysus made treaties with those through whose lands he and his followers passed.[3]
45. As did Moses[4] and Joshua, Bacchus commanded the sun to stand still.[5]
46. Like that of the Bible, Dionysus's religion was a proselytizing faith.

As concerns the priority of these attributes, whether associated first with Dionysus or Moses, we need to disentangle the various periods when these figures and characteristics emerge initially in the literary and archaeological record. Dionysus's name appears first in the extant historical record, and the proto-Bacchic solar, fertility, mead and wine god predates Moses the prophet by millennia, as do numerous lawgivers and myths of law codes, exoduses, unusual births, sea-controlling and water-producing miracles, and so on.

Bacchus's most archaic form may be the Thracian, Sumerian or Egyptian wine deity, reflected in the latter culture in the very ancient god Osiris, whose myth contains several relevant "Bacchic" motifs and began to be formulated over 5,000 years ago. Meanwhile, the evidence points to the Moses character as syncretized and his story written between the seventh and third centuries BCE, using some older germ myths and core texts.

In any event, in discussing Dionysus/Bacchus we can be assured that we are dealing with a *myth*, even if some person or persons contributed a detail or saying here and there. Hence, there is little reason to insist that these supernatural stories revolving around a mythical god are actually "historical," taken from the "true" story of Moses and attached to the mythological tale of Dionysus. The more logical conclusion is that the attributes are mythical, regardless of whose "biography" they first padded out, although the evidence does suggest that parts of the Moses myth were based directly on the ancient and well-developed Greek myth. As myths with meaning, these tales likely originate in a remote age, possibly attached to the vine/wine deity several thousand years ago.

---

[1] Taylor, B., 528.
[2] Nonnus (25) and others recount that Bacchus tricked the Indians into becoming drunk so that he could vanquish them.
[3] Jos 9:15; Pausanias 2.20, 23; Diodorus 3.
[4] Babylonian Talmud, Tractate *'Abodah Zarah* Folio 25a; Epstein, 125.
[5] Several sources cite this motif as appearing in the Orphic hymns. See, e.g., Doane, 91; Voltaire (1901), 191; Higgins, 2.19. I have been unable to find the original source of this contention, but it would not be surprising if the solar Dionysus, like other deities of the sun, was depicted as controlling the solar orb in this manner.

God of Nysa

Dionysus's birthplace was said to have been in numerous places, as is fitting for a mythical character based on the spread of the vine and wine: "Everywhere we seem to have discerned the birthplace of the god; yet everywhere we learn that he was no native..."[1]

As noted, in his identification of Osiris with Dionysus, Diodorus (1.15.6) related an ancient etymology for the Greek god's name:

> Osiris was also a proponent of agriculture. A son of Zeus, he was raised at Nysa, in Arabia Felix not far from Egypt; in fact, the name Dionysus, which he bears among the Greeks, derives from both his father and the locale.[2]

At 4.2.4, Diodorus explains further the commonly held etymology for the name "Dionysus": "Dio- (from Dios, the genitive form of the nominative Zeus) and -nysus (Nysa)."[3] The pronunciation of the name "Dionysos" to an ancient Greek sounded like "the god of Nysa," which is why in antiquity we find that very etymology being posited. As Classics professor Dr. Carl A.P. Ruck states:

> The name of Dionysus himself contains the Indo-Europeans' word for their chief god, Zeus/Dios, and testifies to an attempt to incorporate the alien deity into Indo-European mythology as a son of Zeus, the so-called "Nysian Zeus."[4]

Whether or not this etymology is accepted by modern scholars, many ancients perceived it to be so, and sacred sites called Nysa sprang up in a variety of places. Regarding the location of Nysa, Apollodorus editor Sir James G. Frazer (1854-1941) relates:

> According to Diodorus Siculus [3.59.2; 3.64.5; 3.65.7; 3.66.3], Nysa, the place where the nymphs reared Dionysus, was in Arabia, which is certainly not a rainy country; but he admits [3.66.4; 3.67.5] that others placed Nysa in Africa, or as he calls it, Libya away in the west beside the great ocean. Herodotus speaks of Nysa as "in Ethiopia above Egypt" [2.146], and he mentions "the Ethiopians who dwell about sacred Nysa and hold the festivals in honour of Dionysus" [3.97] But in fact Nysa was sought by the ancients in many different and distant lands and was probably mythical, perhaps invented to explain the name of Dionysus.[5]

---

[1] Wilder, 50.
[2] Diodorus/Murphy, 20. Diodorus/Booth (1.23): "They say that Osiris was given to husbandry, that he was the son of Jupiter, brought up in Nysa, a town of Arabia the happy, near to Egypt, called by the Greeks Dionysus, from this father, and the place of his education." γενέσθαι δὲ καὶ φιλογέωργον τὸν Ὄσιριν, καὶ τραφῆναι μὲν τῆς εὐδαίμονος Ἀραβίας ἐν Νύσῃ πλησίον Αἰγύπτου Διὸς ὄντα παῖδα, καὶ τὴν προσηγορίαν ἔχειν παρὰ τοῖς Ἕλλησιν ἀπό τε τοῦ πατρὸς καὶ τοῦ τόπου Διόνυσον ὀνομασθέντα.
[3] διὸ καὶ τραφέντα τὸν Διόνυσον ἐν τῇ Νύσῃ τυχεῖν τῆς προσηγορίας ταύτης ἀπὸ Διὸς καὶ Νύσης.
[4] Ruck, 181.
[5] Apollodorus/Frazer, 1.321.

THE LIFE OF DIONYSUS 337

In addition to Herodotus's "Ethiopian" Nysa, Diodorus (1.15; 3.63) and Arrian (*Ind.* 100.v.; *Q. Curt.* 8.10) cite various locales by that name in Arabia and India. Greek grammarian Hesychius of Alexandria (c. 4th-5th cents. AD/CE) mentions numerous Nysas and Nysaean mountains in Arabia, Babylon, Cilicia, Egypt, Erythea, Ethiopia, India, Libya, Lydia, Macedonia, Naxus, Syria, Thessaly and Thrace.[1]

It is important to note that ancient writers called lands east of the Mediterranean "India," as exemplified by Ovid (*Ars Amatoria* 1.53) when he conflates Joppa with "India."[2] The terms "India" and "Arabia" often refer to a similar region. The Nysa in "India" could refer also to the Bactrian kingdom.

The confusion of Nysas stems from the facts that the story is mythical, that these areas are in the same general location, and that in antiquity borders were frequently blurred.

Thus, the 20 or more Nysas or Nisas in Africa, Arabia and India evidently were named for a location in ancient myth, as they surely do not represent sites where the Greek god actually was born or lived. The naming of locations after places in myths is common and should be kept in mind when looking for Exodus sites as well, including the original Mt. Sinai.

Alexander the Great

It has been suggested that the tale of Dionysus in India reflects the Indian incursions of Alexander the Great, which might have been so, if the latter actually had made it into India and spread the Dionysian cultus there. However, the Bacchic tale echoes a possibly much earlier time, during which the grapevine and wine god initially made their way to India. Naturally, it is possible that wherever Alexander *did* journey, and there was no grapevine or wine already present, he indeed introduced it.

Moreover, Euripides already had told the story of Dionysus in India during the century prior to Alexander's birth.[3] If there were an influence, it would be likely that the Greek general and Bacchus devotee was attempting to emulate his favored god by making the excursion in the first place. In consideration of his devotion to the wine god, it is also possible that Alexander was inspired to make his journey at least in part by the accounts of Dionysus in India, not the other way around.

---

[1] Rawlinson, 224.
[2] Although the mythical Greek figure Andromeda traditionally comes from Joppa, Ovid (*Ars* 1.53) sings: *Andromedan Perseus nigris portarit ab Indis*—"Perseus carried Andromeda from blackest India."
[3] "Certainly the idea of the god's wanderings cannot have been suggested, as appears to be sometimes imagined, by the expedition of Alexander the Great to India (see F. A. Voigt, in W. H. Roscher's *Lexikon der griech. und röm. Mythologie*, i.1087), since they are described with geographical precision by Euripides, who died before Alexander the Great was born."

Drawn from the Nile

As noted, in *Of the Nature of the Gods* (3.58), Cicero speaks of Dionysus as "Nilo," in the ablative, designating origin; hence, the god is "of the Nile." The epithet "Nilus" was also used, as by Plutarch (*De Iside* 363d),[1] to describe Osiris, the Egyptian "Lord of the Vine," so to speak, serving as the Nile itself and viewed as "drawn from the waters" in the daily Egyptian behavior (Diod. 1.97.2).[2] Hence, Osiris was "drawn from the Nile," and, as Dionysus was equated with Osiris, the ancient writers told the same tale of Bacchus, both also said to be born on January 5th or 6th.

January 5/6th

As related by early Church father Epiphanius (*Pan.* 29.7-30.3), the Egyptians celebrated an annual festival of drawing out Nile water, on the 11th day of the month of Tybi (January 5/6th), believing that "the water was magically transformed into wine, or that special healing power, magical virtue, was to be attributed to it."[3] As Hungarian anthropologist Dr. Geza Roheim (1891-1954) states:

> It is the birth of Osiris, who like Moses (The Child) comes from the water. The Greek equivalent of Osiris is Dionysus. The water-miracle is equally performed by Dionysus, and what is more, exactly at the same date (5/6th of January = 11th Tybi) as in Egypt.[4]

Like these Egyptian and Greek gods, Christ too was said to have been born on January 5th or 6th, a celebration marked in the Armenian Orthodox and Coptic Churches to this day.[5] All three of these gods' births have been placed also at the winter solstice, appropriate for solar deities. Osiris's birth has been celebrated traditionally at the summer solstice as well.

As noted, Pliny (2.103) recounted that a Bacchus temple on Andros had a fountain where the water tasted like wine during the Nones of January (5th), another important source of this water-to-wine miracle associated also with both Osiris and Dionysus, a fitting attribute for a sun and vine god. In the Bible (Jn 2:1-11), the later Jewish version, Jesus, was said to do this same miracle, at the wedding feast of Cana, an absurd tale if taken literally, depicting Christ's miraculous production of 130 to 190 *gallons* of wine for an already besotted gathering.[6]

---

[1] οὕτω παρ' Αἰγυπτίοις Νεῖλον εἶναι τὸν Ὄσιριν; 364a: οἱ δὲ σοφώτεροι τῶν ἱερέων οὐ μόνον τὸν Νεῖλον Ὄσιριν καλοῦσιν.
[2] ἐν μὲν γὰρ Ἀκανθῶν πόλει, πέραν τοῦ Νείλου κατὰ τὴν Λιβύην ἀπὸ σταδίων ἑκατὸν καὶ εἴκοσι τῆς Μέμφεως, πίθον εἶναι τετρημένον, εἰς ὃν τῶν ἱερέων ἑξήκοντα καὶ τριακοσίους καθ' ἑκάστην ἡμέραν ὕδωρ φέρειν εἰς αὐτὸν ἐκ τοῦ Νείλου.
[3] Epiphanius/Williams, 2.61.
[4] Roheim, 360.
[5] See my *2010 Astrotheology Calendar*, 36.
[6] At John 2:6, we read that Christ had changed the contents of "six waterpots of stone" that held "two or three firkins apiece." The Greek word for "firkins" is μετρητής *metrētēs*

Mises

We have seen the assertion that the name "Moses" means "drawn out" in Hebrew and "born of" in Egyptian.¹ Indeed, the Egyptian term for "birth" is basically *ms* or *mes*,² while in Coptic it is *mise*.³ Moreover, the epithet "Mises" or Μίσης, a Bacchic title found in *Orphic Hymn 42*, is similar to the Greek Μωυσῆς or "Moyses" of the Septuagint.⁴

Since Bacchus was deemed an Egyptian god in ancient times,⁵ it is understandable he would share a title such as "Mises," also said to connote "saved from the waters" in Egyptian.⁶ In the "Hymn to Mises" (*O.H. 42*), Dionysus is said to be the offspring of the "Good Counselor of a hundred names, and the pure and holy Mise..."⁷ Using the same basic Greek term, the biblical Yahweh too is the "Wonderful Counselor" (Isa 9:6),⁸ of whom Moses was claimed to be a holy prophet.

Mentioned additionally by the Greek poet Herodas in the third century BCE,⁹ Mises is androgynous or "two-natured," associated with the goddess Kore or Persephone.¹⁰ In this regard, we also find

---

(G3355), defined as "a measurer, the name of a utensil known as a amphora, which is a species of measure used for liquids and containing somewhat less the nine English gallons or about (40 l)." The lowest figure, if we use the amount of 40 liters multiplied by 12, is around 127 gallons of wine; multiplied by 18, the number climbs to 190 gallons.
¹ Nohrnberg, 135.
² Collier, 155;
³ Allen, J.P. (2000), 9.
⁴ E.g., Exod 2:11.
⁵ Herodotus 2.47; Herodotus/Waterfield, 114.
⁶ Voltaire (1824), 1.374. In consideration of the mystical focus on birth and assorted other such allegorical comparisons, such as the ritual of the aqueous Osiris being "born" as he is drawn from the Nile, it appears that being born (Egypt. *ms*) may have been viewed as "drawn from the waters," as in the waters of the womb.
⁷ Halperin, 100.
⁸ Hebrew: יעץ *ya`ats*; Greek: βουλῆς *boules*. This passage in Isaiah is rendered in English as a future "prediction": "For a child will be born to us, a son will be given to us; And the government will rest upon his shoulders. And His name shall be called Wonderful Counsellor," etc. In reality, the Greek makes it clear that this verse is *past* tense: For example, the word here rendered "will be born," ἐγεννήθη, is a past tense, the aorist indicative passive of the verb γεννάω, meaning "beget" or "give birth to." The same word is used at Acts 7:20: "At this time, Moses *was* born..." Matthew (1:16), Mark (14:21) and John (9:2, 19, 20) also use this word, always rendered in the past. The same assertion of past tense can be made for the other verbs in the Isaiah passage, such as ἐδόθη, aorist indicative passive of δίδωμι, meaning "was given," etc. The Isaiah scripture is therefore not a "messianic prophecy," but it apparently *was* used via midrash to create the Christ character.
⁹ Herodas, 10. Herodas editor Nairn remarks that Mise is "one of the deities associated with Demeter" a female "assistant/companion" to Dionysus, as he interprets *Orphic Hymn 42*, who "dwells in Eleusis" and is a "goddess of the underworld like Kore." All of these roles would be held by the bi-natured Dionysus as well.
¹⁰ Halperin, 100, 103.

reference to "the *Mises* or Bacchus *Diphues*,"[1] this latter term meaning "twice-grown" or "two-natured." In another translation of the same Orphic hymn, Dionysus/Iacchus is addressed as "Mises, ineffable, pure..."[2] My very literal translation of the original Greek is as follows:

Orphic Hymn 42
Mises, incense from a storax tree

Thesmophoros, I call thyrsus-bearer Dionysus,
Seed much-courted, many-named Good Counselor,
Pure and good-holy Mises, ineffable queen,
Male female, two-formed, delivering Iakkhos.
Either in Eleusis delighting in the temple incense,
Or also in Phrygia with Mother mysteries-turning,
In Cyprus delighting with well-crowned Kytherea,[3]
And in pure, wheat-bearing fields exult
With your Mother Goddess, dark-bearer Isis majestic,
Of Egypt, beside a stream with attending nurses.
Goodwill from coming noble-finish labors.[4]

XLII. ΜΙΣΗΣ, θυμίαμα στύρακα.

Θεσμοφόρον καλέω ναρθηκοφόρον Διόνυσον,
σπέρμα πολύμνηστον, πολυώνυμον Εὐβουλῆος,
ἁγνήν τ' εὐίερόν τε Μίσην, ἄρρητον ἄνασσαν,
ἄρσενα καὶ θῆλυν, διφυῆ, λύσειον Ἴακχον·
εἴτ' ἐν Ἐλευσῖνος τέρπῃ νηῷ θυόεντι, 5
εἴτε καὶ ἐν Φρυγίῃ σὺν μητέρι μυστιπολεύεις,
ἢ Κύπρῳ τέρπῃ σὺν ἐυστεφάνῳ Κυθερείῃ,
ἢ καὶ πυροφόροις πεδίοις ἐπαγάλλεαι ἁγνοῖς
σὺν σῇ μητρὶ θεᾷ μελανηφόρῳ Ἴσιδι σεμνῇ,
Αἰγύπτου παρὰ χεῦμα σὺν ἀμφιπόλοισι τιθήναις· 10
εὐμενέουσ' ἔλθοις ἀγαθ' ἐκτελέουσ' ἐπ' ἀέθλοις.

The epithet θεσμοφόρος *thesmophoros* or "lawbearing" is a title likewise applied to the Greek goddess Demeter (Herodotus, *Hist.* 6.91), who also shares the moniker "Thesmophorae" with her daughter, Persephone/Kore, as in Aristophanes's book *Women at the Thesmophoria* (283-285). As we can see from the Orphic poem, Mises/Dionysus/Iacchus is bigendered, both male and female, equated with Persephone/Kore, who is also the god's virgin mother.[5] All three figures of Demeter, Kore and Dionysus served as lawgivers,

---

[1] Knight, 90.
[2] Orpheus/Taylor, T., 141. Taylor lists the pertinent hymn as "XLI" or 41, whereas more modern sources cite it as 42.
[3] Or "fair Aphrodite."
[4] Original Greek from Abel, *Orphica*, 81.
[5] Rigoglioso (2010), 119-122.

associated with the mysteries of Eleusis, as well as those of Isis, as this hymn demonstrates.

Twice-Born Grapevines

We have seen the story of Dionysus being "bimater" or having two mothers. Diodorus (3.62) explains the "twice-born" epithet as having to do with grapevines, which are first born as they sprout from the ground and born again as they put forth leaves and ripe fruit. This "two-mothered" attribute is expressed in myths of Bacchus being born of one woman and set adrift in either the Nile or the Aegean, as well as the tale of the babe sewn up in Zeus's thigh, when his mother, Semele, is immolated by the sky god's lightning bolt.

The connection here to nature is important, as Dionysus's alter ego Osiris in significant part represents the Nile River overflowing its banks, fertilizing the soil of Isis and bringing forth the sprouted plants upon which all Egypt depended. In this regard, Osiris is often painted green, in imitation of foliage and photosynthesis, as noted.

Marriage to Zipporah

At Exodus 2:21, Moses was said to have married one of the Midianite priest Jethro's seven daughters, named Zipporah or צפרה *Tsipporah.* It is claimed that "Zipporah" is an epithet of Venus,[1] Bacchus's wife and one of the seven "planets" known to the ancients, who included the sun and moon among the five planets visible with the naked eye.

In Strong's (H6855), צפרה *Tsipporah* is defined as a "little bird." In the Septuagint, the Greek equivalent, Σεπφώρα *Sepphora,* is used also to translate שפרה *Shiphrah,*[2] a name of one of the Hebrew midwives at Exodus 1:15 (KJV). As we can see, only the initial letters differ between Zipporah and Shiphrah in the Hebrew, both of which connote a sibilant sound, "ts," "z," "s" or "sh." In this regard, Massey asserts that "Zipporah and Shiphrah

Fig. 71. Venus (?), dubbed the "Mona Lisa of Galilee," c. 4th cent. AD/CE. Mosaic from Sepphoris, Israel

---

[1] Diodorus (4.6) states that Dionysus married Aphrodite, the Greek name for Venus, a union that produced the fertility god Priapus. Bacchus is also named as Aphrodite's *son,* in a typical Goddess consort-son myth. Venus is assimilated to Dionysus's traditional wife, as Ariadne Aphrodite. (Kerenyi, 106) Plutarch (*Theseus* 20.34) states that the forest on Cyprus where Ariadne was said to be buried was called the "grove of Ariadne Aphrodite" (Ἀριάδνης Ἀφροδίτης).
[2] H8236 or H8235, which Strong's states are the same.

are identical," and that Zipporah is "Venus above the horizon."[1]

As would be appropriate for the planet or "star" Venus—as well as for Aphrodite, goddess of love—*Shiphrah* also means "brightness, beauty," and, possibly, "to adorn with stars and constellations" (*Gesenius*) as in Job 26:13: "By his spirit he hath garnished the heavens; his hand hath formed the crooked serpent" (KJV).

In this regard, it is intriguing that in the famous Jewish city of Tzippori or Sepphoris appears an ancient mosaic from the third century AD/CE believed to be a depiction of Venus and styled the "Mona Lisa of the Galilee." The correspondence between Sepphora and Sepphoris ranks as noteworthy as well.

Genital Mutilation

In the biblical tale, after removing her son's foreskin with a sharp rock (Exod 4:25), Zipporah throws the organ at Moses's feet and says, "Surely you are a bridegroom of blood to me!"[2] This bizarre episode resembles stories of castration in the name of the Goddess, such as the Syrian Cybele cult, with the theme of her son-consort castrating himself. Additionally, it should be recalled that the *bride* of Bacchus, Aphrodite or Venus, is created out of the bloody foam after Ouranos's testicles are severed and thrown into the sea.

Regarding Zipporah, Judaic studies professor Dr. Marc A. Krell comments that "in *Counter-traditions in the Bible*, Ilana Pardes has uncovered Ugaritic, Sumerian and Egyptian Goddess-centered texts that parallels biblical myths of Eve, Zipporah, Miriam, Yocheved, Shifra, Puah and Pharaoh's daughter."[3]

Concerning this marriage motif, Israeli professor Dr. Ilana Pardes relates:

> What most biblical scholars have overlooked is that the representation of Zipporah comes strikingly close to representations of guardian goddesses in polytheistic texts. Such goddesses are frequently the primary caretakers of striving young heroes. Thus Babylonian rulers are designated as the protected "bridegrooms" of Ishtar; ...in Sumerian mythology the goddess Inanna ensures the prosperity of King Dumuzi; and even in the *Odyssey* and the *Aeneid*, it is Athena and Venus who are the primary guardians and instructors of their respective protégés, Odysseus and Aeneas.[4]

In Zipporah and Moses, we evidently have another example of the mother-protector and consort-son sacred marriage, such as Inanna/Inana and Dumuzi or Aphrodite/Venus and Aeneas.

---

[1] Massey (2007), 2.277.
[2] The New Living Translation notes here: "The Hebrew word for 'feet' may refer here to the male sex organ." The LXX differs from the Hebrew and Latin: ἔστη τὸ αἷμα τῆς περιτομῆς τοῦ παιδίου μου, which can be rendered literally as: "You are the blood of the circumcision of my child."
[3] Krell, 94.
[4] Pardes, 89.

THE LIFE OF DIONYSUS

Burning 'Bush'

The discussion of the Bacchae/maenads in Euripides (*Ba.* 757-758) with their burning locks resembles Yahweh's burning bush,[1] and, indeed, "the Fire" is a central feature in one Dionysian myth lends credence to this notion. In this regard, we have seen several instances in which Dionysus is associated with fire, such as "the fire in the Bacchic reveal" by Philostratus of Lemnos. This solar motif represents Porphyry's "celestial fire of the sun" ripening the grapes, among other functions.

Land Flowing with Milk and Honey

As seen above, in his commentary on Exodus 3.8, Clarke remarks: "*A land flowing with milk and honey...* The poets feign that Bacchus, the fable of whom they have taken from the history of Moses, produced rivers of milk and honey, of water and wine..."[2] He then reproduces the Greek of Euripides ("*Bacch.*, Επoδ., ver. 8"), after which he further comments:

> "The land flows with milk; it flows also with wine; it flows also with the nectar of bees (honey)." This seems to be a mere poetical copy from the Pentateuch, where the sameness of metaphor and the correspondence of the description are obvious.[3]

We have mentioned already a number of sources for this motif, including Euripides (*Ba.* 142-143). If copying there be, it is *from* pagan myth *to* the Bible, not the other way around, but the parallel is clear enough that clergy have been compelled to address it.

Smiting Unbelievers

We have seen previous instances in which people were struck down for looking into a sacred chest, box or ark, including the story of Athena and Aglaurus. In the Bacchic myth of Pentheus in Euripides also appears an example where mockery and rejection of the god can be fatal. In discussing 1 Samuel 6:19 about the stricken men of Beth Shemesh, Bishop Patrick recounts:

> Out of this story, as *Bocharius* [Samuel Bochart] ingeniously conjectures, the *Greeks* forged the Fable of *Bacchus*, who was very angry with the *Athenians*, because they did not receive his Mysteries with Pomp, when they were brought out of *Boeotia* into *Attica*, and smote them with a sore Disease in their Secret Parts.[4]

As previously mentioned, this last bit also sounds like Yahweh smiting the men of Ashdod with hemorrhoids.

Both Patrick and Bochart noticed the parallels but, as is typical of clergymen, tried to attribute them to copying by the Greeks, rather

---

[1] ἐπὶ δὲ βοστρύχοις πῦρ ἔφερον, οὐδ᾽ ἔκαιεν.
[2] Clarke, 1.314.
[3] Clarke, 1.292.
[4] Patrick, 70.

than the other way around. As we know, however, the Greek myths are not dependent on the Bible, and the similarities at times exist because both versions share a common mythical archetype, as well as probable direct borrowing in parts of the Pentateuch from well-known Dionysian mythology. These instances of syncretism would include deity-ordained pestilence, plagues and other divine retribution throughout the Bible.

Athenian Plagues

Subsequent to the actual plagues of 432, 429 and 427/6 BCE that killed the Athenian leader, Pericles, Aristophanes's play *The Acharnians* was presented at the Dionysian festival of Lenaea/Lenaia. In this drama, the Acharnians detest their enemies for destroying their vineyards, as part of the Bacchic cultus central to the story. At one point (501ff), the protagonist calls on Poseidon to bring about earthquakes to destroy the houses of the Lacedaemonians, who have cut down the vines.

The ancient commentary ("scholia") on *Acharnians* explains in the following manner the references to the "upright" and "erect" phalluses carried by the "basket-bearer" in the Bacchic procession:

> Statues of Dionysus were brought to Athens by one Pegasus, a native of Cleutheris in Boeotia, but were treated with ridicule. The deity, in revenge for this insult, sent a terrible disease which attacked them in the private organs, and the oracle said the only way to get rid of this disease was by adopting Dionysus as their god, and the phallus as a symbol of his worship, in memory of the organ affected.[1]

Regarding this annotation on the verse in Aristophanes, British classicists and ancient history professors Drs. David Braund and John Wilkins state:

> The Aristophanic scholia on the *Acharnians* (243) relate a tradition according to which the Athenians did not accept with appropriate honour the statue of the god which Pegasus had brought from Eleutherae. In retribution the god sent them some sort of venereal disease...[2]

As noted earlier, a number of myths from the Greeks and others frequently depict gods and goddesses exacting brutal punishment for hubris, blasphemy and assorted other "crimes" against them. The biblical story of supernatural retribution ranks as no more plausible than these other myths.

---

[1] Stone, L., 41.
[2] Braund, 470. The commentary on *Acharnians* appears in *Scholia in Aristophanem* Pars 1, *Prolegomena de comoedia. Scholia in Acharnenses*, Equites, Nubes; ed. Nigel G. Wilson. Groningen: Bouma's Boekhuis, 1975. It should be noted that the "council" gathering on the Pnyx hill near the Athenian Acropolis, as in this play, is designated by the Greek word *ecclesia*, which in the Christian era came to be rendered "church."

Passover, Vernal Equinox and Wilderness

The setting of the year's start and Passover in the spring or at the vernal equinox can be found at Exodus 12:2:

> This month shall be for you the beginning of months; it shall be the first month of the year for you.

The first month of the year is named at Exodus 13:4 as "Abib," later called "Nisan" and running from March to April. The Hebrew word אביב *'abiyb* means:

> 1) fresh, young barley ears, barley
>
> 2) month of ear-forming, of greening of crop, of growing green Abib, month of exodus and passover (March or April)[1]

As we can see, the month of Abib or Aviv is named for its vernal fertility, the reawakening of life after the death of winter.

Concerning this Exodus scripture, English bible scholar and minister Rev. Dr. Matthew Henry (1662-1714) comments:

> They had hitherto begun their year from the middle of September, but henceforward they were to begin it from the middle of March, at least in all their ecclesiastical computations. Note it is good to begin the day, and begin the year, and especially to begin our lives, with God. This new calculation began the year with the spring, which *reneweth the face of the earth*, and was used as a figure of the coming of Christ...[2]

The Babylonian-named Nisan or Nissan is the month in which the "Passover lamb" Christ—here equated with the spring—was said to be "crucified" and "resurrected," essentially also at the vernal equinox, representing the old myth of dying and rising spring deities. The "cross" of the equinox represents the time of the year when the day and night are equal. There are thus two crosses, spring and fall or autumnal, explaining the different crucifixion scenes in the biblical myth.[3] The autumnal equinox also clarifies why the Israelites were said to start their year previously in the middle of September, the time of the fall harvest and new wine.

As concerns the mythical nature of the Passover, we read:

> Despite the Exodus story, scholars believe that the passover festival originated not in the biblical story but as a magic ritual to turn away demons from the household by painting the doorframe with the blood of a slaughtered sheep.[4]

This bloody magic ritual was part of the Babylonian *mašmašu* priesthood, discussed below.

---

[1] Strong's H24.
[2] Henry, 1.267.
[3] The synoptics depict the crucifixion as occurring on the 15th of Nisan, while in John it is the 14th, the first a solar date and the second lunar. Moreover, the scenes are portrayed diversely, with different people appearing at Jesus's cross, as Massey states that the diverse depictions represent the sun at the vernal and autumnal equinoxes.
[4] "The Exodus," *Wikipedia*, summarizing Levinson, 58.

Dionysian Spring Festival

Emphasis on the vernal equinox occurs in the Dionysian religion as well, previously mentioned, during which time the god and his ark were carried in procession. Regarding Bacchus's association with the vernal equinox, Pausanias (3.22.2) states:

> Above Migonium is a mountain called Larysiumi sacred to Dionysus, and *at the beginning of spring they hold a festival in honor of Dionysus*, and among the things they say about the ritual is that they find here a ripe bunch of grapes.[1]

This story is reminiscent of the biblical tale of the spies entering the Promised Land and discovering grapes.

The Bacchic spring theme thus also involves the wilderness sojourn, along with the emphasis on the Ram or Lamb:

> The Legislator of the Jews fixed the commencement of their year in the month Nisan, at the Vernal Equinox, at which season the Israelites marched out of Egypt and were relieved of their long bondage; in commemoration of which Exodus, they ate the Paschal Lamb at the Equinox. And when Bacchus and his army had long marched in burning deserts, they were led by a Lamb or Ram into beautiful meadows, and to the Springs that watered the Temple of Jupiter Ammon.[2]

The story of escaping bondage commemorated at the vernal equinox, when a new year begins, represents a solar myth based on winter's transition to spring.

Possibly reflecting the same motif as on the Mendes stela with its "holy ram in the meadows of Mendes," in the Dionysian myth the "burning meadows" and "desolated wilderness" are metaphors for the winter months, traditionally dry in the relevant regions during that time. The entry into the "promised land" and "beautiful meadows" is the renewal of spring, with the watery temple of the father god's ram aspect symbolizing the new year rains.

Lamb of the Desert

As noted, Dionysus "the Kid" provides water to his army in the middle of the desert, a water-producing miracle also found in the Moses myth, which likewise revolves significantly around sacred rams and lambs. Ruminants constitute a major focus throughout the Pentateuch, in which Moses sacrifices the "ram of the burnt offering," using its blood to consecrate the newly built altar for Israel (Lev 8:18). Lambs too are offered as sacrifices, as at Genesis 22:7 and Numbers 28:11. Leviticus 4:32 and 5:6 discuss a lamb for a sin offering, while elsewhere the lamb serves as a burnt offering (Lev 9:3)

---

[1] Emph. added. Greek of the italics: καὶ ἦρος ἀρχομένου Διονύσῳ τὴν ἑορτὴν ἄγουσιν... The word here for "spring" is ἦρος *eros* from ἔαρ *ear*, meaning "spring, prime." (*OCGD*, 94)

[2] Pike, 466.

and guilt offering (Lev 14:24-25). Exodus 29 gives detailed instructions on how to sacrifice the ram, serving as a burnt offering also at Leviticus 16:3, a guilt offering at Leviticus 19:21, and a "ram of atonement" at Numbers 5:8. We also hear about the "goat of the sin offering," as at Leviticus 10:16 and 16:10, which describe the scapegoat ritual to remove sins, the same concept represented in the gospel story with the "Lamb of God" sacrificed for the sins of mankind.

These biblical beasts were sacrificed during the "feast of the lamb" or Passover (Exod 12) on the 14th day of the first month, equivalent to the vernal equinox. These elements represent aspects of "astronomical fables,"[1] as, in astrology, the ram is equivalent to Aries, representing the precessional age of the era as well as the month in which spring transitions from winter.

Exodus into the Sea

As early as Homer, we read that, like Moses, Dionysus and his devotees were pursued into a ruddy sea by an angry king. While Moses and his crew are chased towards the holy mountain of Sinai, Bacchus and his followers are driven down the sacred mount of Nysa. Like Moses's kingly pursuer, the Greek god's persecutor, the tyrannical Spartan ruler Lycurgus/Lykourgos, dies a horrible death. Other writers of antiquity who refer to the battle between Lycurgus and Dionysus include Aeschylus, Ovid, Seneca, Pausanias, Pseudo-Hyginus (3rd cent. AD/CE) and Nonnus.

In *The Iliad* (6.129-143), composed around 900 BCE, the character of Diomedes describes the homicidal king driving the god and his followers down the Nysean hill:

> ...all of them shed and scattered their wands on the ground, stricken with an ox-goad by murderous Lykourgos, while Dionysos in terror dived into the salt surf, and Thetis took him to her bosom, frightened, with the strong shivers upon him at the man's blustering. But the gods who live at their ease were angered with Lykourgos, and the son of Kronos struck him to blindness, nor did he live long afterwards, since he was hated by all the immortals.[2]

Lycurgus's punishment for dishonoring the gods was firstly to murder his own wife and daughter in a fit of madness, "in the belief that they were spreading vines," and secondly to die horribly by being eaten by wild animals.

---

[1] Dupuis, 174.
[2] Hadas and Smith, 18. εἰ δέ τις ἀθανάτων γε κατ' οὐρανοῦ εἰλήλουθας, οὐκ ἂν ἔγωγε θεοῖσιν ἐπουρανίοισι μαχοίμην. οὐδὲ γὰρ οὐδὲ Δρύαντος υἱὸς κρατερὸς Λυκόοργος δὴν ἦν, ὅς ῥα θεοῖσιν ἐπουρανίοισιν ἔριζεν: ὅς ποτε μαινομένοιο Διωνύσοιο τιθήνας σεῦε κατ' ἠγάθεον Νυσήϊον: αἱ δ' ἅμα πᾶσαι θύσθλα χαμαὶ κατέχευαν ὑπ' ἀνδροφόνοιο Λυκούργου θεινόμεναι βουπλῆγι: Διώνυσος δὲ φοβηθεὶς δύσεθ' ἁλὸς κατὰ κῦμα, Θέτις δ' ὑπεδέξατο κόλπῳ δειδιότα: κρατερὸς γὰρ ἔχε τρόμος ἀνδρὸς ὁμοκλῇ. τῷ μὲν ἔπειτ' ὀδύσαντο θεοὶ ῥεῖα ζώοντες, καί μιν τυφλὸν ἔθηκε Κρόνου πάϊς: οὐδ' ἄρ' ἔτι δὴν.

The Ruddy Sea

As we have seen, in his *Hercules Furens* (899-900), Seneca calls Bacchus "the tamer of Lycurgus and the ruddy sea..."[1] Seneca translator Miller notes that the "ruddy sea" refers to the body of water that Dionysus "crossed when he conquered India."[2] Seneca's original Latin for "ruddy sea" is *rubri maris*,[3] the word *rubri* or "ruddy" connoting redness, as in the *Red* Sea. If Dionysus was "born" in Egypt, then he could be said to cross the Red Sea when his viniculture cult found its way to India. Here is one possible meaning of the motif of crossing the Red Sea; there are others, apparently.

Don Allen avers that Nonnus "probably had the crossing of the Red Sea in mind when he wrote of his hero that 'he took to his heels and ran in fear too fast to be pursued/until he leaped into the gray waters of the Erythraian Sea.'"[4]

It should be noted that the phrases "Erythraian Sea" and *Rubrum Mare* are used in antiquity to describe the Red Sea, the Indian Ocean or the Persian Gulf.[5]

Since antiquity, comparisons have been made between the Spartans and Jews, including their legislators, about which subjects Dr. Louis H. Feldman notes:

> In the first place, there is the parallel...between their respective lawgivers, Moses and Lycurgus, both of whom (Diodorus 1.94.1-2) claimed a divine origin for their laws... Moreover, both Lycurgus and Moses (according to Hecateus, *apud* Diodorus 40.3.6) instituted a rigorous training program for their youth.[6]

Diodorus related that there were those who claimed Lycurgus, Solon and Plato "borrowed from Egypt many of those laws which they established in their several commonwealths."[7]

Pro-Wine Propaganda

The Lycurgus myth and the several others concerning Dionysus's mockers appear to represent objections to the proliferation of the grapevine and wine, which was the meaning behind the tale of Bacchus traveling widely around the Mediterranean and beyond. One could see how those who benefited from viticulture and viniculture

---

[1] Seneca/Miller, 1.79.
[2] Seneca/Miller, 1.79.
[3] Seneca/Miller, 1.78: *Te te laborum socia et adiutrix precor, belligera Pallas, cuius in laeva ciet aegis feroces ore saxifico minas; adsit Lycurgi domitor et rubri maris, tectam virente cuspidem thyrso gerens, geminumque numen Phoebus et Phoebi soror, soror sagittis aptior, Phoebus lyrae, fraterque quisquis incolit caelum meus non ex noverca frater.*
[4] Allen, D., 69.
[5] Sidebotham, 182.
[6] Feldman, 196.
[7] Diodorus/Booth, 1.97. Diodorus (1.98): καὶ Λυκοῦργον δὲ καὶ Πλάτωνα καὶ Σόλωνα πολλὰ τῶν ἐξ Αἰγύπτου νομίμων εἰς τὰς ἑαυτῶν κατατάξαι νομοθεσίας.

might devise deadly myths of this sort to prevent others from likewise imposing a ban on the vine and wine. In this regard, we find the same sort of wrathful behaviors by the gods of both the Old and New Testaments.

The situation would be similar to the bans on alcohol and cannabis in various places today, some of which carry with them the death penalty for illicit drug trade. In this Bacchic myth, we see punishment imposed for the opposite reason, as the grapevine and wine were highly valued as gifts of the gods, and to oppose them was sacrilegious. Such blasphemy was seen as directed at the sun as well, since it was "he" who grew the vine and ripened the grapes, the sun represented by various gods, such as Helios, Apollo, Dionysus and numerous others of antiquity, explicated by Macrobius and others.

Food of the Gods

Previously discussed was the mythical nature of manna, with various parallels in pagan mythology, including the Dionysian. The concept of the "manna from heaven" extends to "divine honey," a motif commonly associated with Bacchus, as the god of honey and mead on Crete.[1] Indeed, honey has been deemed the "food of the gods" in not a few civilizations, including the Cretan, in which the culture of bees, honey and mead were deeply entrenched, at such an archaic age as to predate the cultivation of the vine and wine-making on that island. Rather than representing a "historical event," the biblical "honey from heaven" could symbolize yet another rehashed Dionysian motif.

Women Celebrating

Another parallel between the Moses and Dionysus myths occurs in Exodus 15, when Miriam and all the Israelite women dance in a celebratory frenzy praising Yahweh, much like the Bacchae or Dionysian priestesses and maenads in their ecstatic rapture.

Timbrels

At Exodus 15:20, Miriam and the other rapturous Hebrew dancers are depicted as using "drums" or "timbrels" in their victory celebration:

> Then Miriam, the prophetess, the sister of Aaron, took a timbrel in her hand; and all the women went out after her with timbrels and dancing.
>
> λαβοῦσα δὲ Μαριαμ ἡ προφῆτις ἡ ἀδελφὴ Ααρων τὸ τύμπανον ἐν τῇ χειρὶ αὐτῆς καὶ ἐξήλθοσαν πᾶσαι αἱ γυναῖκες ὀπίσω αὐτῆς μετὰ τυμπάνων καὶ χορῶν

---

[1] Kerenyi, 31.

The Greek word here for "timbrels," τύμπανα *tympana*, is employed also by Euripides in his *Bacchae* (59) to describe the drums of Dionysus's "sacred band" of women. While discussing what he would do to the doubting Pentheus, Bacchus remarks:

> But, you women who have left Tmolus, the bulwark of Lydia, my sacred band, whom I have brought from among the barbarians as assistants and companions to me, take your drums, native instruments of the city of the Phrygians, the invention of mother Rhea and myself, and going about this palace of Pentheus beat them...[1]

Euripides also refers in his *Cyclops* (65), to the *tympana* or drums of the Bacchae.

The Hebrew word for "timbrel," "tambourine" and *tympana* is תֹף *toph*,[2] whence comes the place-name תפת Topheth or Tophet,[3] where the Israelites burned their children to the Ammonite, Canaanite and Phoenician fire and solar god Molech/Moloch or Baal.[4] During these sacrifices, the תפים *tophim* would be beaten in order to drown out the cries of the perishing children.

Relating an appalling account of the Carthaginian child sacrifice to Kronos or Saturn, Plutarch (*De Superstitione* 13) uses the same term, τύμπανα *tympana*:

> ...with full knowledge and understanding they themselves offered up their own children, and those who had no children would buy little ones from poor people and cut their throats as if they were so many lambs or young birds; meanwhile the mother stood by without a tear or moan; but should she utter a single moan or let fall a single tear, she had to forfeit the money, and her child was sacrificed nevertheless; and the whole area before the statue was filled with a loud noise of flutes and drums took the cries of wailing should not reach the ears of the people.[5]

Both Mosaic and Bacchic instances of drum use revolve around the vanquishing of the divine prophet's enemies, with the maenads also rejoicing in the god himself at *Bacchae* 156: "...sing of Dionysus, beneath the heavy beat of drums, celebrating in delight the god of delight..."[6] Russell points out that this concept of the timbrel drum has precedent in Ugaritic and Sumerian texts as well.[7]

---

[1] Euripides/Buckley
[2] Strong's H8596.
[3] Strong's H8612.
[4] Jer 7:31-32, 19:4-6; 2 Ki 23:10.
[5] Plutarch/Babbitt, 493-494. The original Greek uses the form τυμπανιζόντων *tympanizonton*: ἀλλ' εἰδότες καὶ γιγνώσκοντες αὐτοὶ τὰ αὑτῶν τέκνα καθιέρευον, οἱ δ' ἄτεκνοι παρὰ τῶν πενήτων ὠνούμενοι παιδία κατέσφαζον καθάπερ ἄρνας ἢ νεοσσούς, παρειστήκει δ' ἡ μήτηρ ἄτεγκτος καὶ ἀστένακτος. εἰ δὲ στενάξειεν ἢ δακρύσειεν, ἔδει τῆς τιμῆς στέρεσθαι, τὸ δὲ παιδίον οὐδὲν ἧττον ἐθύετο· κρότου τε κατεπίμπλατο πάντα πρὸ τοῦ ἀγάλματος ἐπαυλούντων καὶ τυμπανιζόντων ἕνεκα τοῦ μὴ γενέσθαι τὴν βοὴν τῶν θρήνων ἐξάκουστον.
[6] Euripides/Buckley.
[7] Russell, 17.

Water Manifestation

There exist in Dionysian myth multiple instances of miraculous manifestation of water, as well as wine, milk and honey, some of which we have seen already.[1] Describing an area in the Peloponnesus not far from where the earliest extant mention of Dionysus was discovered, Pausanias (4.36.7) remarks:

> When Cyparissiae is reached from Pylos, there is a spring below the city near the sea, the water of which they say gushed forth for Dionysus when he struck the ground with a thyrsus. For this reason they call the spring Dionysias.[2]

It is possible that this aqueous miracle itself dates to the second millennium BCE or earlier, as applied to other gods such as Osiris.

In a chapter entitled Ἄγγελος or "Angel/Messenger" in Euripides's *Bacchae* (704-710), it is Dionysus's followers who bring forth water, as well as wine, milk and honey, by striking the ground with their staff:

> They put on garlands of ivy, and oak, and flowering yew. One took her thyrsos and struck it against a rock, from which a dewy stream of water sprang forth. Another let her thyrsos strike the ground, and there the god sent forth a fountain of wine. All who desired the white drink scratched the earth with the tips of their fingers and obtained streams of milk; and a sweet flow of honey dripped from their ivy thyrsoi....[3]

As we can see, the miracles of the Bacchae are even more impressive than those of Moses.

Jehovahnissi

To reiterate, in antiquity Yahweh was identified with and as Dionysus. Also noted was the verse at Exodus 17:15, which has been raised as an example of the Yahweh-Dionysus connection:

> And Moses built an altar, and called the name of it Jehovahnissi.

The original Hebrew of this passage is:

ויבן משה מזבח ויקרא שמו יהוה נסי

Here we see again the peculiar god-name יהוה נסי *Yĕhovah nicciy*, rendered in the King James Bible and elsewhere as "Jehovahnissi." Other versions transliterate the epithet as "Jehovah-nissi," "YHWH Nissi" and "Yahweh-Nissi." The LXX renders the term as κύριός μου

---

[1] See, e.g., Philostratus, *Imag.* 1.18 and Nonnus, 22.
[2] Pausanias/Jones, 2.377. ἀφικομένων δὲ ἐς Κυπαρισσιὰς ἐκ Πύλου σφίσι πηγὴ ὑπὸ τῇ πόλει πλησίον θαλάσσης ἐστί: ῥυῆναι δὲ Διονύσῳ τὸ ὕδωρ λέγουσι θύρσῳ πλήξαντι ἐς τὴν γῆν, καὶ ἐπὶ τούτῳ Διονυσιάδα ὀνομάζουσι τὴν πηγήν.
[3] Euripides/Buckley: θύρσον δέ τις λαβοῦσ᾽ ἔπαισεν ἐς πέτραν, ὅθεν δροσώδης ὕδατος ἐκπηδᾷ νοτίς: ἄλλη δὲ νάρθηκ᾽ ἐς πέδον καθῆκε γῆς, καὶ τῇδε κρήνην ἐξανῆκ᾽ οἴνου θεός: ὅσαις δὲ λευκοῦ πώματος πόθος παρῆν, ἄκροισι δακτύλοισι διαμῶσαι χθόνα γάλακτος ἑσμοὺς εἶχον: ἐκ δὲ κισσίνων θύρσων γλυκεῖαι μέλιτος ἔσταζον ῥοαί. ὥστ᾽, εἰ παρῆσθα, τὸν θεὸν τὸν νῦν ψέγεις εὐχαῖσιν ἂν μετῆλθες εἰσιδὼν τάδε.

καταφυγή or "Lord [of] my refuge," while the Vulgate prefers *Dominus exaltatio mea* or "Lord [of] my exaltation."

Yĕhovah nicciy appears only this once in the Bible and is defined by Strong's (H3071) as:

> Jehovah-nissi = "Jehovah is my banner"
>
> the name given by Moses to the altar which he built in commemoration of the discomfiture of the Amalekites

The root of נסי *nicciy* is נס *nec*, meaning:

> 1) something lifted up, standard, signal, signal pole, ensign, banner, sign, sail
> a) standard (as rallying point), signal
> b) standard (pole)
> c) ensign, signal[1]

This same Hebrew root נס *nec* is employed at Numbers 21:8-9 to describe the pole upon which Moses placed his magical serpent of brass, while Dionysus is famed for carrying his magical thyrsus or pole, which he turned into a snake. Dionysus also is associated with snakes by way of his serpentine crown.

Yahweh Hisses

The term *niccy/nissi* ("ensign") is used also at Isaiah 5:26, in which Yahweh is described as stretching forth his hand upon the nations:

> And he will lift up an ensign to the nations from far, and will hiss unto them from the end of the earth...

This verse resembles the tale of Moses establishing the altar and battling the Amalekites, lifting his hand to make the "sign of the cross," as later Church fathers depicted his act, and raising up the serpent of brass on the pole, with its "hiss." The Hebrew word rendered "hiss" is שרק *sharaq*, denoting "to hiss, whistle, pipe," a possible indication of Yahweh's serpentine nature at this point,[2] sensible also in consideration of the god's apparent role as the goddess Jahi's serpent, previously discussed. It has been surmised that this passage is part of a redaction in Isaiah (5-12) that occurred during Josiah's reign.[3]

Parable of the Vineyard

Significantly, Isaiah 5 is called the "Parable of the Vineyard" and continually invokes the metaphor of a vineyard and wine, strongly recalling the myth of Dionysus, with its heavy emphasis on viniculture and wine-besotting. This same parable appears to be the

---

[1] Strong's H5251.
[2] Strong's H8319. The Greek verb in the LXX is συρίζω *surizo*, meaning "to hiss," as well as "to whistle" and "to play the pipe." (*OCGD*, 311) The Vulgate uses a form of the verb *sībilāre*, also connoting "to hiss at" and "to whistle."
[3] Russell, 109.

basis for the lengthy vineyard invocations in the synoptic gospels.[1] These Bible verses demonstrate the great reverence with which the grape and vine were held by the Israelites and Jews.

Dian-nisi, Great Judge of Heaven and Earth

The term "Jehovahnissi" is similar to "Dionysus," with the name of the god (Dio=Zeus), along with "nissa" or "nissi" and so on. This latter word resembles the ending of the name "Dionysus" in other languages, such as Basque, which calls the Greek god "Dunixi."[2] Another of these monikers may be Dian-nisi, as discussed in Transactions of the Society of Biblical Archaeology by Assyriologist Dr. William Henry Fox Talbot (1800-1877):

> The great name of the sun in Assyrian theology was *Daian-nisi* or *Dian-nisi*, which means "the Judge of Men." Some years ago I ventured to affirm that this name is the same with the *Dionysus* of the Greeks. All know that the worship of Dionysus was *derived from the* East—in very ancient times, for he is mentioned by Homer. In the early mythologies the name of Dionysus signified the sun, for Herodotus [3.8] says that the only god worshipped by the Arabians was Dionysus; now it is certain that the Arabians worshipped the sun, and the Assyrian records confirm this by saying that tribute was brought by the Queen of the Arabians, who used to worship the sun. Osiris and Dionysus were the same, according to the judgment of Plutarch (Isis et Osiris, cap. 28). And he quotes from Heraclitus that Dionysus was Hades. But Hades, or Pluto, was fabled to be the judge of departed souls.[3]

Talbot next cites an inscription of Babylonian king Nebuchadnezzar II (4.29):

> *Ana Shems Dainu tsiri Bit Dian-nisi bit-zu in Babilim in kupri u agurri shakish ebus.*
>
> To the Sun the Judge supreme the temple of Dianisi, his temple, in Babylon in bitumen and bricks grandly I built.[4]

Talbot states that this inscription represents a record of the Babylonian king constructing a temple to Dionysus,[5] a proposition that would not be surprising, in consideration of the centuries-long viniculture and presence of the (solar) wine god in the region, under a variety of names and epithets, as he was assimilated into a region.

---

[1] Mt 21:33-43; Mk 12:1-14; Lk 20:9-19.
[2] Aulestia, a28.
[3] Talbot, 2.33. Talbot was one of the first decipherers of the cuneiform inscriptions from the important Assyrian site of Nineveh, excavated by Sir Henry Rawlinson.
[4] Talbot, 2.33. Rev. J. M. Rodwell provided a different translation, rendering the term "Dian-nisi" as "guide of men," rather than leaving it as a divine epithet of the sun: "To the sun, the judge supreme who perfects good in my body, *a house for that guide of men,* even his house, in Babylon, of cement and brick, skilfully did I make." (Emph. added.) If the epithet is left untranslated, the relevant phrase (italics) reads: "House of Dian-nisi."
[5] Talbot, 8.306.

Since the Assyriologist's time, the inscription was discovered at Pylos identifying Dionysus, extending this god-name's appearance back to the 13th century at the latest. The Greeks themselves were in Asia Minor by this time as well. Hence, this name could have been known in the Levant for centuries by the time of the Nebuchadnezzar inscription, adapted to give it a Babylonian connotation.

Divine Judge of Men

According to Talbot, the Assyrian cuneiform for *Dian-nisi*, a solar epithet denoting "judge of men," is as follows:[1]

𒀭 𒐊 𒐊 𒌑 . 𒉎 𒐊 *Daian-nisi* or *Dian-nisi*

In this regard, the Akkadian noun for "judge" is *dayānnu*,[2] while "to judge" legally is *diānu*, cognate with the Hebrew דין *diyn*, also meaning "to judge."[3] The Akkadian word $^{d}dayānnū$ with a superscript "d" indicates a "divine" judge,[4] basically a god-name or theonym. Deities such as Marduk and Enlil were called *madānu* or "Divine Judge."[5]

In Akkadian, *nišē* or *nišū* connotes "mankind," "humanity" or "people,"[6] while the Assyrian word *nisi* means "men" or "people."[7] The Ugaritic cognate is *inš*, and in Arabic the word is *'ins* أِنْس.

Osiris

The epithet *dian-nisi* is found also in a passage in the "Annals of Ashurakhbal,"[8] "where the sun has the title, *Shemesh dian-nisi zalul-su khiga*, meaning the deity 'whose flail is good.'"[9] At this point, Talbot comments:

> Now this almost identifies the Assyrian Dian-nisi with the Egyptian Osiris: for, it is well known that Osiris usually holds in his hand an emblem of authority, which some consider to be a flail, and others a whip.[10]

Osiris is the great judge in the Hall of Truth, identified for at least 2,500 years with Bacchus. The association with Shamash or Shemesh, the Mesopotamian sun god, is noteworthy as well, since Dionysus was a solar deity.

---

[1] Talbot, 2.33.
[2] Rahmouni, 314.
[3] Strong's H1777.
[4] Rahmouni, 65, 351.
[5] *Akkadian Dictionary.*
[6] *Akkadian Dictionary.*
[7] Norris, 2.401.
[8] *Proceedings of the Society of Antiquaries of Scotland*, 6.199.
[9] Talbot, 8.306, citing British Museum 18, 44.
[10] Talbot, 8.306.

In addition, the fact that the cruel and vicious Assyrian warrior-king Ashurakhbal or Aššur-nāṣir-pal II[1] (883-859 BCE) is depicted on an inscribed "sculptured slab" holding a cup of wine as a libation to the gods is significant and adds to the contention that Dian-nisi refers to Dionysus.[2]

Although the etymology may not be acceptable to mainstream scholarship, it is possible that anciently this god-name took on different connotations to the various ethnicities as they rendered it into their own languages. In this regard, puns and general word-play were popular pastimes in antiquity, particularly as deities were seen to represent the hidden hand behind creation and to imbue it with mystical and magical meaning, including and especially words.

Fig. 72. Ashurnasirpal II holding a wine cup, 9th cent. BCE

'Dog' as Companion

We have seen that both Bacchus and Moses had "dog" companions, as is the meaning of the Hebrew name "Caleb" or "Kaleb." It is interesting also that the "Dog of Orion" or "Dog of the Giant" (Canis Major) in Arabic is called Al Kalb al Jabbār.[3] The suggestion here is that the "dog" companion of the solar hero is Canis Major or Orion in general, as was the case with the solar Osiris, whose brother was Anubis, the jackal-headed god. It is noteworthy that this term *kaleb* is utilized in the OT to indicate "of a male cult prostitute" (Deut 23:18), also called קדש *qadesh*[4] or "holy," as noted.

Dionysus's companion Maira was the faithful dog of Erigone, daughter of Ikarios, the first Greek vintner, who was killed because, when they became drunk, his customers thought he had poisoned them. According to the myth, previously mentioned, a distraught Erigone committed suicide and was placed among the stars, where too ends up her canine companion who guarded her body.

Maira thus symbolizes Canis Minor, the lesser dog star. The vicious heat of the summer days over which Maira reigns is her vindication for Erigone's death. This time of the dog star leads to the harvest of the grapes and the vintage, a fact that appears to be the symbolism behind the biblical spies story leading to the promised land to find the enormous bunch of ripened grapes.

---

[1] Holloway, 31.
[2] *PSAS*, 6.199.
[3] Allen, R., 117, 119.
[4] Strong's H6945.

Joshua's appearance in the Caleb story may signify that the Israelite savior represents the summer sun, while Moses is the winter sun of the wilderness.

Sun Standing Still

As noted, both Moses and Joshua are depicted as arresting the course of the sun, the same theme evidently found in the Dionysian myth as well as in Hindu, Buddhist, Chinese and Mexican myths, to name a few. As also mentioned, the word "solstice" comes from the Latin meaning "sun stands still," and this motif is yet another solar *myth*, not an impossible "historical" event based on bad science. In this regard, Joshua's miracle is depicted in Jewish literature as occurring at the summer solstice.[1]

In *On the Latin Language* (6.8), Varro (1st cent. BCE) explains:

> There is a second motion of the sun, differing from that of the sky, in that the motion is from *bruma* "winter's day" to *solstitium* "solstice." *Bruma* is so named, because then the day is *brevissimus* "shortest": the *solstitium*, because on that day the *sol* "sun" seems *sistere* "to halt," on which it is nearest to us. When the sun has arrived midway between the *bruma* and the *solstitium*, it is called the *aequinoctium* "equinox," because the day becomes *aequus* "equal" to the *nox* "night." The time from the *bruma* until the sun returns to the *bruma*, is called an *annus* "year," because just as little circles are *anuli* "rings," so big circuits were called *ani*, whence comes *annus* "year."[2]

Thus, the Roman scholar demonstrates scientific knowledge two millennia ago, including the definition of solstice as "sun halts."

Also, rather than reflecting a "historical" event, the biblical story may have incorporated scriptures such as Habakkuk 3:11: "The sun and moon stood still in their habitation at the light of thine arrows as they sped, at the flash of thy glittering spear."

Conclusion

As we can see, there exist numerous correspondences between the Greek and Israelite lawgivers, so much so that it appears either one myth was copied from the other or both shared the same basic archetype. In consideration of Dionysus's appearance in the historical record by name by the 13th century BCE, whereas Moses cannot be found in the literature until many centuries later, it would seem that the latter is a remake of the former. With a number of significant

---

[1] van Goudoever, 74, citing the early rabbinical text *Seder Olam* xi: "...the summer solstice, being the day at which the sun stood still for Joshua (the 92nd day from 1 Nisan, which in that year coincided with the spring equinox)."

[2] Varro/Kent, 2.181. *Alter motus solis est, [alter caeli] quod movetur a bruma ad solstitium. Dicta Bruma quod brevissimus tunc dies est; Solstitium quod sol eo die sistere videbatur, [aut] quod ad nos versum proximum est. Sol[stitium] cum venit in medium spatium inter brumam et solstitium, quod dies aequus fit ac nox, Aequinoctium dictum. Tempus a bruma ad brumam dum sol redit, vocatur Annus, quod ut parvi circuli Anuli, sic magni dicebantur circites Ani, unde Annus.* (Varro/Spengel, 75)

parallels in Homer's description of the Greek god dating to the 9th or 10th centuries BCE at the latest, we can suggest that Moses is a later version of the highly popular and widespread sun and wine god, called Dionysus at some point but stretching back in archetypal form to an unrecorded and primeval deity. In this same regard, there are many similarities between Dionysus and Jesus as well, as also demonstrated here.

Again, there are differences between these tales, some of them profound, but such is always the case when myths and archetypes are shared by different cultures, to be cherry-picked and added to according to themes relevant to the particular ethnicities.

Additionally, a significant portion of Bacchus's tale was played out in theaters across the Greek-speaking world, which included much of the Mediterranean during the centuries when Greek was the *lingua franca* of the region. The Dionysus cult, with its widespread viticulture and traveling proselytizers, was an important factor in the known world for hundreds of years.

The archetypal story expressed in the Moses myth clearly has its origins in polytheistic culture, whether Assyrian, Babylonian, Canaanite, Egyptian, Greek or much older. It was not adapted *from* a monotheistic culture but could have been adapted easily *to* a monotheistic culture by demoting or syncretizing the various sacred figures. Dionysus was a mythical character, largely a solar-mead-wine god, and the archetypal story repeated here revolves around him, originally created for him and his lawgiver archetype; hence, if copying there be, it is in the direction of Bacchus to Moses.

Fig. 73. Dionysian maenads or women with thyrsi and drums dancing around an idol of Bacchus as a pillar with branches (not shown), c. 420 BCE. Red figure stamnos by Dinos painter, Museo Nazionale Archeologico, Naples, Italy

Fig. 74. Moses's sister, Miriam, dancing with a timbrel. (André, 1884)

The Vine and Wine

"From being relatively unimportant, the deities of wine and the vine gradually came to the forefront of religious consciousness, as symbols concerned with rebirth and the life hereafter....

"...Jewish ritual reflects a number of symbolic themes connected with wine and the vine that are similar to those of other religions in south-west Asia during the first and second millennia BC. The Old Testament thus provides us with much evidence concerning both the general distribution of viticulture within the lands neighbouring Israel and Judah, and also the symbolic significance of wine and the vine, much of which was later to be incorporated into Christian religion....

"...when men are sent by Moses at God's command to explore Canaan in the Book of Numbers [13:23, 26] they specifically cut off a vine branch bearing a cluster of grapes which they bring back to the Israelites together with pomegranates and figs."

Dr. Tim Unwin, *Wine & the Vine* (79, 82)

"Wine was from early times a proverbial part of the richness of the promised land, and it naturally appears to have been an important aspect of the life of Jews at all periods after they came into Canaan. So it was one of the first fruits and tithes which must be offered, and it was used with a great many of the sacrifices of the Temple."

Dr. Erwin R. Goodenough, *Jewish Symbols in the Greco-Roman Period* (129)

"The Old and New Testaments use the words *wine* 280 times, *vine* 49 times, *vineyard* 72 times, *cup* 49 times and *winepress* at least 15 times... The Old Testament commonly uses words like *tirosh* (new wine) and *yayin* (fermented wine) respectively to describe wine."

Dr. Randall Heskett and Joel Butler, *Divine Vintage* (17)

IN THE MYTH of Dionysus there exists heavy emphasis on the grapevine, viticulture, viniculture and wine. One of the reasons the god's cult extended so thoroughly around the known world of the time is precisely because of the popularity of grapes and wine, which spread widely east and west, taking with them the cult of the wine deity, by whatever name. Included in this vast viticultural and vinicultural heritage were the Israelites and Jews.

The grapevine's hardiness and ability to sprout shoots that intertwine with objects have made it a very popular plant and motif in literature and art. The plant's fruits have been praised as gifts from the gods, particularly the intoxicating fermented product, which gladdens the human heart and reduces sorrow. The sun as the glorious grower of the vine and righteous ripener of the grape was extolled as the godhead behind the divine plant, and Dionysus was the embodiment of both solar power and foliage, while his blood was the juice and wine.

In numerous places in antiquity, the vine and its products were considered sacred, and wine was viewed as a "potent medicine" that renews youth, deemed so by Plato (*Laws* 2.666b):

> ...when a man has reached the age of forty, he may join in the convivial gatherings and invoke Dionysus, above all other gods, inviting his presence at the rite (which is also the recreation) of the elders, which he bestowed on mankind as a medicine potent against the crabbedness of old age, that thereby we men may renew our youth, and that, through forgetfulness of care, the temper of our souls.[1]

The grape and wine have been so important to life in the Mediterranean that Plato devoted considerably more space to these subjects in his *Laws*.[2]

A wine cult of this manner and magnitude would have instant devotees and would connect far-flung peoples all around the Mediterranean and beyond, as we know in reality did occur.

Early History

To reiterate, viticulture and viniculture date back thousands of years in various places, such as Armenia, Georgia, Persia and Turkey. At Çatalhöyük in Turkey, as another example, evidence of grape seeds and possible wine-making has been found from a civilization dating to 7500-5700 BCE.[3] Wine expert Dr. Robert E. McGovern calls the libation the "sine qua non of any Anatolian beverage," discussing its usage among the Sumerians, Hittites and others in the Near East.[4]

Regarding the origin of wine-making, Dr. Michael Poe states:

> There is still considerable speculation about where "vitis vinifera" or the wine grape first originated. Some think it started south of the Caucasus and south of the Caspian sea; others believe [it originated] in Egypt and traveled into the Middle East. According to William Younger in his book, *Gods, Men and Wine*, "It is in Egypt where we must go for our fullest knowledge of man's early and deliberate growing of wine." Plutarch said that he was told that Osiris was the first to drink wine and to teach men how to plant the vine.[5]

As indicated by his Egyptian equivalent as the god of wine, the notion that Dionysus was "born" in Egypt suggests that it was believed organized wine-making originated in that nation, which in

---

[1] Plato/Bury, vols. 10 and 11. In the previous section (*Laws* 2.666a), Plato's Athenian advocates making it illegal for children under the age of 18 to drink wine, demonstrating the antiquity of that legal debate.
[2] E.g., *Laws* 844-845.
[3] "History of the wine press," *Wikipedia*.
[4] McGovern, 186.
[5] Poe, "Wine in Ancient Egypt."

THE VINE AND WINE

fact does have a long history of viniculture, again dating to at least pre-dynastic times, around 3200 BCE.[1]

While beer was the beverage for commoners in Egypt and elsewhere, the elite preferred wine, a status symbol.[2] Hence, we can see that viniculture and wealth go hand in hand and that the wine god would be of special importance to the rulers, whose views would influence the masses extensively, including and especially about religion.

Egypt's Vineyards

Ancient Egyptian vineyards possessed fascinating names, such as "Vineyard Ways of Horus" and "Horus on the Height of Heaven," this latter designation evidently dating to at least the First Dynasty, some 5,000 years ago.[3] This heavenly Horus vineyard remained in production into the common era, until 300 AD/CE.[4] Wine thus stayed very popular in Egypt for thousands of years, treated as an important spiritual and physical medicine, as well as a central focus in parties with dancing and music.[5]

Wine's religious significance and prominence in Egypt are indicated by the fact that "Rameses III lists 513 vineyards belonging to the temple of Amon-Ra."[6] Such skilled wine production was a significant economic factor as well, and entire communities depended upon it.

Fig. 75. Egyptian grape cultivation and wine production, c. 1500 BCE. Tomb painting from Thebes, Egypt

Oenological Osiris

Summarizing the Egyptian wine cultus, Iain Gately states:

> The annual rise of the Nile was associated with Osiris, god of the dead, of life, of vegetable regeneration, and of wine. In the dynastic era, Egypt had become a producer as well as an importer of *irp* [wine]. It remained an elite beverage; hence its protection by the most important deity in the Egyptian pantheon. After a fashion, Osiris and wine were made for one another. According to legend, he had died and been reborn, and the vine was a natural example of renewal—

---

[1] Kerenyi, 56-57; Poe.
[2] Gately.
[3] Poe.
[4] Poe.
[5] Dalby, 129.
[6] Poe.

every winter it withered back to its roots, every spring it put forth new shoots. The end and resurrection of Osiris were celebrated over the Oag festival, immediately preceding that of the Drunkenness of Hathor. For the duration of its festivities, Osiris was known as "the lord of *irp* through the inundation," and the hieroglyphics [sic] that constitute the event's name show three wine jars on a table, with a fourth being offered by a human hand. In the latter stages of the dynastic era, the worship of Osiris, and consumption of wine, became even more closely intertwined. His devotees, after prayers and rituals, would eat bread and drink wine in the belief that these were the transubstantiated flesh and blood of their divinity.

Wine, as befits its status as a luxury with divine associations, was manufactured with much more sophisticated methods and with a great deal more care than any other agricultural product.

As can be seen, there are several mythical motifs and traditions in the Osirian religion that were reproduced within Christianity, including death and resurrection, as the "true vine" (Jn 15:1) and "root of Jesse" (Rom 15:12). Also striking here is that the wine and bread serve as a sacrament and a sacred communion representing the blood and body of the god, as in the later Christian tradition.

Sacred Chalice

Wine was so important that pharaohs were buried with their favorite wine chalices, as evidenced by the grave goods of Tutankhamun, which also included "twenty-six wine jars, containing vintages up to thirty-six years old, produced by fifteen different winemakers."[1] Many other tombs contained numerous wine amphorae and, possibly, sacred chalices, these latter likely stolen long ago. Here could be one source of the *mythical* "Holy Grail" stories.[2]

Near Eastern Trade

Much of the wine imported into Egypt came from the Levant, as far back as the days of the first Egyptian king, called "Scorpion" (c. 3150 BCE?).[3] This commerce continued for millennia, as "Phoenician kings of Ugarit and Tyre organized trading ventures to Egypt in which oil, wine and copper figured prominently."[4]

Thus, Semitic regions of the time also were engaged in viticulture and viniculture, along with their attendant sacred cult. Indeed, the Ugaritic writings discuss wine many times, including as a libation of

---

[1] Gately.
[2] The Holy Grail or sacred chalice theme derives not from the story of a historical Jesus passing along a cup made supernatural by his use but existed for eons prior to the common era, revolving around not only wine but also menstrual blood, with the cup symbolizing the womb. For more information, see the works of Barbara G. Walker, including her book *Man Made God*.
[3] McGovern, 91.
[4] Redford (1992), 227.

the gods, as in the texts *El's Divine Feast* and the *Epic of Kirta* or *Legend of Keret/Krt*, previously discussed.[1] The Ugaritic wine rituals included what Canadian theologian Dr. Daniel Timmer calls "the Rites of the Vintage," discovered in a library at the home of the high priest and "the fullest Ugaritic ritual found to date."[2]

Says Timmer:

> The importance of the rite is evident from the number of deities (nearly thirty) and sacrifices (about 180) that it involves.
>
> The festival takes place in the month of *Rišyn*...meaning "first" or "best" wine [*riš yn*]), "roughly the last lunar month before the fall equinox... The beginning of the text dictates that a representative cluster of grapes be cut from its vine to serve as, or alongside, a peace offering for El. Subsequently the king is ritually purified, proclaims the festival from his throne, then goes to the temple where he sets up booths for various deities on the roof.[3]

As we can see, there are several themes here that sound very biblical, including the fall festival like the Feast of Tabernacles, which features both the tabernacles/booths and vintage. It is also evident that wine and the grape harvest were highly important to the Ugaritians, whose high god El was the same as that of the Israelites. Indeed, the peace offering of the grape cluster to El reminds one again of the spies carrying Canaan's grapes to Moses.

Wine Goddesses

Centuries before the male Dionysus dominated the Mediterranean, the wine *goddess* was a feature of ancient religion, including in Egypt:

> Wine was considered a particularly special offering to any of the ancient Egyptian gods and goddesses. But it was Renentet (also called Ernutet or Renen-utet) the goddess of plenty and harvests who invariably had a small shrine near the wine press and vat, as well as on the spout where the juice flows from the vat to the receiving tank.... The goddess Hathor (Het-hor) was, among other things, the goddess of wine and intoxication.[4]

Here we see that Hathor is joined by the goddess Renenutet as symbolizing wine and its effects.

Another vine and wine goddess was the Sumerian Geštinanna/ Geštinana or Ngeshtin-ana. Her name means "heavenly grapevine," "vine of heaven" or, literally, "wine/vine of the heavens/the god An," demonstrating the sacredness of this plant thousands of years ago.

The daughter of Enki and the Sumerian mountain-mother goddess Ninhursag, Ngeshtin-ana was the sister of Dumuzi, the revivifying solar and fertility god who is rescued out of the

---

[1] See, e.g., Timmer, 19-21.
[2] Timmer, 20.
[3] Timmer, 21.
[4] Poe.

underworld by Inanna/Inana, the Sumerian equivalent of Aphrodite/Venus. As the later Semitic god Tammuz, Dumuzi took over the role of his Sumerian sister, Geshtinanna, to become the fall harvest deity associated with the vine and wine. Possibly identified with Ngeshtinana was another Sumerian wine goddess called Ama-geštin or "Mother Wine/Vine."

Vine as Tree of Life

Depictions of grapevines from antiquity indicate the plant was perceived also as the Tree of Life:

> The Tree of Life was probably originally the grapevine; the two syllables of the Sumerian word for "grapevine," GESHTIN, mean "tree" and "life." For the grapevine as the Tree of Life in religious imagery, we may also recall Christ's words, "I am the vine, ye are the branches" (St John 15:5).[1]

Tree of Life traditions can be found around the world, including in the Americas, and this mythical motif has been fundamental to humanity for many thousands of years. The portrayal of the mythical Christ as the "vine," as was said previously of Bacchus, is noteworthy also.

Greek Viniculture

The spread of wine from Egypt's fertile regions such as the Nile Delta to other places, including nearby Crete, may explain in part the Dionysian "out of Egypt" motif. The cultivation of wine in northern Greece possibly dates to at least 4500 BCE,[2] an indication that the wine god/dess, by whatever name, may have been revered in that region by that time. Many of the Dionysian myths take place in the area, such as the tale of Bacchus and the Thracians. Because of viniculture's long history near the Black Sea, it has been surmised also that the Thracians introduced viniculture into Egypt initially, from where it may have proliferated afterwards to other regions, including southern Greece, as on Crete.

Because of his longevity and the diffusion of Greek culture, religion and language, it is to Bacchus's myth that we will turn again for characteristics of the wine cultus. It is likely that many of these attributes and traditions could be found scattered around the eastern Mediterranean for hundreds to thousands of years before the wine deity became known by the Dionysian monikers and peculiarities.

Dionysian Cult Extensions

Wherever cultivation of the grapevine spread, so too did the worship of the vine and wine deity, from remotest times by names unknown to us but accompanying the deification of this fruitful and

---

[1] Mooney, "The Tree of Life and Ancient Tree Worship."
[2] Sparks, K., 203.

utile plant. From Egypt, the Levant, Mesopotamia, Sumeria, Arabia and India to Macedonia and Greece as well as into the other parts of Europe, including the mysterious and secluded region of the Basques in the heart of European wine country, we find the worship of Osiris, Tammuz, Geshtinanna, IAUNuShUSh, Orotalt, Dusares, DI-WO-NI-SO-JO, Iacchos, Bacchus, Dionysus, Dian-nisi or Dunixi, dating back thousands of years. Anywhere the grapevine yielded its fruits, there would reside the god or goddess of revelry and intoxication, a religious cult to inspire endless devotees.

By whichever gender or name, this nature deity's reverence was one of the most extensive in antiquity, as well as one of the most primordial. With this massive cultus there was a tremendous amount of wealth as well, including and especially in property, with temple estates, theaters, vineyards and wineries around the Mediterranean.[1] As a major part of this bounty, temples of many different deities were used in antiquity as treasuries for large sums, considered to be safely under divine protection.

Blood and Resurrection

Since antiquity, grape juice and wine have been perceived as the "blood" of both the fruit itself and of the vine and wine deity.[2] After it was pressed, the grape juice would flow into underground pots, depicted as the god "cultivated in the underworld."[3] Out of this tomb, Dionysus was said to reemerge during the festival of Anthesteria, in February, when "the urns were opened, and the god's spirit was reborn as an infant."[4] The "graves of the dead released their spirits as well at this time, and for the three days of the festival, ghosts roamed abroad in Athens."[5]

This spooky theme is reminiscent of the oft-ignored gospel tale of saints rising out of their graves at Jesus's crucifixion (Mt 27:50-52):

> And Jesus cried again with a loud voice and yielded up his spirit. And behold, the curtain of the temple was torn in two, from top to bottom; and the earth shook, and the rocks were split; the tombs also were opened, and many bodies of the saints who had fallen asleep were raised, and coming out of the tombs after his resurrection they went into the holy city and appeared to many.

Jesus is depicted as resurrecting after three days (Mt 12:38-40), a type of rebirth, and the three-day period or *triduum* is noteworthy in the Bacchic tale as well. The triduum's existence as a mythical solar and vinicultural motif, not as "history," explains its presence in the gospel story.

---

[1] For a discussion of Dionysian cult economics, see Holster, "Cults of Dionysos: Economic Aspects" in Schlieser, 61ff.
[2] Ruck, 194.
[3] Ruck, 194.
[4] Ruck, 194.
[5] Ruck, 194.

Regarding this scenario of Bacchus in the underworld, Ruck remarks that "Dionysus is identical with the 'liquid portion of the clustered grape' which he 'discovered'..., and it is only by sacrifice of himself that he can offer his gift of wine."[1]

In this same type of sacrifice, Matthew 26:27-28 refers to Jesus offering wine as his "blood of the new testament" (KJV):

> And he took the cup, and gave thanks, and gave [it] to them, saying, Drink ye all of it; For this is my blood of the new testament, which is shed for many for the remission of sins.[2]

This atonement includes the god's "death," as his "body" is crushed through the wine press, rended into numerous pieces, producing his life-giving "blood."

New Dionysus

Concerning the sacredness of this act, Ruck further comments: "In the making of wine, the god's experience was analogous to mankind's journey toward redemption through the mouldering tomb."[3] The importance of these notions is reflected by their presence in the New Testament, with its "new Dionysus," Jesus Christ.

In this regard, by the time of the common era, the Eleusinian mysteries and Bacchus worship were so important that Roman emperors such as Julius Caesar and other elite themselves were considered to be a "New Dionysus," generally as a result of their initiation into the Bacchic mystical rites.[4] This divine role, however, appears to be centuries older, as Alexander the Great too allegedly was an initiated "New Dionysus," according to one ancient story, now considered by some to be "thoroughly discredited"[5] but nonetheless related in antiquity by Greek philosopher Diogenes Laertius (c. 200-c. 250 AD/CE), for one.[6]

Wine Epithets and Roles

Several of Dionysus's many epithets revolve around the vine and wine, including, among others: Liber or "Free," for the exhilarating freedom of wine; Sabasius ("Intoxication?"[7]) and Torcularius ("Presser of Wine or Oil"), for his invention of the wine press.[8] Mithra too was

---

[1] Ruck, 202.
[2] καὶ λαβὼν τὸ ποτήριον καὶ εὐχαριστήσας ἔδωκεν αὐτοῖς λέγων, Πίετε ἐξ αὐτοῦ πάντες τοῦτο γάρ ἐστιν τὸ αἷμά μου τὸ τῆς καινῆς διαθήκης τὸ περὶ πολλῶν ἐκχυνόμενον εἰς ἄφεσιν ἁμαρτιῶν. Emphasis: "my blood of the new testament."
[3] Ruck, 194.
[4] See Murdock, *A Pre-Christian 'God' on a Cross?*
[5] Tarn, 2.56.
[6] Diogenes (6.2.63): "When the Athenians gave Alexander the title of Dionysus, he said, 'Me too you might make Sarapis.' Some one having reproached him for going into dirty places, his reply was that the sun too visits cesspools without being defiled." (R.D. Hicks translation)
[7] Jones, B.C., 69; Bochart, 441: *Nec male jungitur Saboe cum סבא [Cěba'] sit inebriari.*
[8] Mayo, 205.

called Sabasius,[1] as was Zeus.[2] In *Agamemnon* (970), Aeschylus depicts Zeus, Dionysus's father, as making wine from the "bitter grape";[3] thus, he too is a vintner god.

Father Bacchus

We have seen that the figure of Staphylus the grapevine or bunch of grapes is considered another of Dionysus's lovers, as on the Greek island of Thasos, while in another myth he is the son of Bacchus and Ariadne, a nature-worshipping theme, rather than a homoerotic and/or incestuous account concerning real people.

When we factor in Dionysus's solar nature, as the ripener of the grape and fermenter of the wine, these mythical motifs take on an astrotheological aspect: The sun "loves" and "nurtures" the grapevine, in order to produce ripe grapes, grape juice and wine.

In this regard, other characters by the name of Staphylus figure into other myths regarding Dionysus, as his cult spread around the Mediterranean and beyond. Other of Dionysus's children possess oenophilic names, such as Oenopion or "wine drinker" and Euanthes or "well blooming."[4]

Elixir of Love

Euripides's description of Dionysus includes that "he gives to mortals the vine that puts an end to grief," stating that, without wine, "there is no longer Aphrodite or any other pleasant thing for man."[5] Appropriately one of Dionysus's consorts, Venus or Aphrodite is the goddess of love, and the popular perception apparently was that it was wine which imbued the capacity for love, a gift from the gods as potent as any other.

Hence, we can see a major reason for the intense devotion to such a cult not only of revelry but also of love. Moreover, a medicine that drowns out sorrow is likewise powerful, especially in times and places when tragedy and misery have reigned for eons or strike on a regular basis.

---

[1] Shaw, 192. This name "Sabasius" may emanate from the Middle Eastern Sabians, the pre-Islamic Arab star observers and worshippers whose astrotheological religion is called "Sabaism." (Craig, 2.603-604) The moniker may also be related to the term "Sabaoth," the biblical צבא *tsaba'* or "host of heavens" (Gen 2:1), as well as "Sabazeus," "Sabazios," etc.
[2] Shaw, 193.
[3] Aeschylus/Capps, 83.
[4] See also Apollodorus (*Epit.* E.1.9), who refers to the story of Dionysus and Ariadne, whose marriage produced Thoas, Staphylus, Oenopion and Peparethus. Plutarch (*Thes.* 20) ascribes the paternity of Staphylus and Oenopion to Theseus.
[5] Euripides, *Ba.* 772-774: τὴν παυσίλυπον ἄμπελον δοῦναι βροτοῖς. οἴνου δὲ μηκέτ᾽ ὄντος οὐκ ἔστιν Κύπρις οὐδ᾽ ἄλλο τερπνὸν οὐδὲν ἀνθρώποις ἔτι. Here Aphrodite is referred to as Κύπρις Kypris, meaning "Venus" and the same as "Cyprus." Hence, the Greek island by that name serves as the location of Aphrodite's most prominent cult center, turned into a site for the worship of the Virgin Mary.

Wedding Feasts

The influence and importance of the vine and wine cult cannot be overemphasized, and anyone creating a competing religion would be compelled to deal with it, helping to explain the Mosaic connection, as well as the focus on wine in the New Testament. The NT wedding feast of Cana in John's gospel, with its massive amounts of wine, sounds very Dionysian, and Bacchus's myth also includes a sacred marriage or hierogamy, to his wife, Ariadne, a scene popularly depicted on vases.[1] Since Dionysus is "the Kid," this famous marital science may be reflected in the "wedding feast of the lamb" at Revelation 19:9.[2] All that is wanting in the Cana story is an account of the guests reclining and flinging wine at the walls, as was a popular Greek custom.[3]

Baal's Cup

This elixir of love needs a fitting container, and the concept of the "holy grail" or "sacred chalice" dates back thousands of years, long before the story was incorporated into the Christ myth. We have mentioned already the sacred wine chalices of Egyptian royalty. As a comparable example in Canaanite literature, in the text "Baal's Drink" the Canaanite god is depicted as possessing a magnificent goblet or "holy cup" for wine, like the Holy Grail.

Baal also provides the other deities with "jars of wine,"[4] a "thousand jars he drew of the wine,"[5] a motif reflective also of the god's gargantuan size.[6] This myth resembles the much later Cana myth, with Jesus producing the absurd amount of some 130 to 180 gallons of wine miraculously produced from water, to serve an already half-drunk wedding party.

In the Baal Cycle, the captive "Judge River" is depicted as honoring Baal the Conqueror by giving him food and drink:

> ...he put a cup in his hand,
> a goblet in both his hands,
> a large beaker, manifestly great,
> a jar to astound a mortal,
> a holy cup that women should not see,
> a goblet that Asherah must not set her eye on;
> he took a thousand jugs of wine,
> he mixed ten thousand in the mixing bowl.

---

[1] See, e.g., the discussion by Victoria Sabetai, "Eros Reigns Supreme: Dionysos' Wedding on a New Krater by the Dinos Painter," in Schlesier.
[2] NLT: "And the angel said to me, 'Write this: Blessed are those who are invited to the wedding feast of the Lamb.' And he added, 'These are true words that come from God.'"
[3] Several ancient depictions portray a game called κότταβος kottabos/cottabus, in which the participants attempt to hit targets with wine dregs using drinking cups. Alas, by Christ's purported time, this fascinating pastime had all but vanished.
[4] Smith, M. (1994), 1.83.
[5] Smith, M. (1994), 1.95-96.
[6] Smith, M. (1994), 1.110.

He arose, he sang a song;
there were cymbals in the minstrel's hands...[1]

Here we see an emphasis on a "holy chalice" and large amounts of wine, as well as a minstrel singing and playing cymbals, similar to the Bacchic, Mosaic and Christian myths. This myth has to do with natural cycles, not with the biographies of real people.

Sacred Drinking Banquet

These holy chalices would have been used in drinking banquets like those of Dionysus:

> The *marzēaḥ* represents a type of drinking banquet dedicated to the gods, and it crossed many cultures throughout the Fertile Crescent; evidence of its celebration has been found in ancient Israel, Ugarit, Phoenicia and Babylonia, and it is featured in rabbinic literature. It originated in Ugarit, which was famous for its wine and supported a wine-god cult, and it was associated with Ugarit's chief god, El, aspects of whom would later migrate west to Greece as Dionysus.[2]

Here we see that Ugarit was an important wine center with a wine cult, over a millennium before the common era, and that Dionysus picked up elements of El worship, the latter god evidently as El Elyon, the wine deity.[3] This Semitic drinking banquet called *mrzḥ*, *marziḫḫu*, *marzēaḥ* or *marzeah* appears to be a very ancient religious festival that began possibly in Eblaite times or long before and continued into the first century BCE,[4] revolving around the vine and wine deity or deities, including El, Shamash and Baal.[5] In the text "El's Divine Feast" (KTU 1.114) about his *marzeah/marziḥ*, the gods are depicted as becoming intoxicated with wine.[6]

In his study *Phoenician Solar Theology*, Australian professor Dr. Joseph Azize contends that the *marzeah* or divine feast provides evidence of Semitic sun worship,[7] sensible since the various deities to whom the festival and cult were dedicated are largely solar.[8] An "institution known throughout the ancient Near East,"[9] the *marzeah* also appears to be related to funeral celebrations and underworld mythology. Azize points out that the *mrzḥ* is associated especially with Shamash and must have possessed "some serious wealth."[10] He further states, "If traditional understandings of the *mrzḥ* are correct,

---

[1] Arnold and Beyer, 52.
[2] Heskett and Butler, 71.
[3] Heskett and Butler, 28.
[4] Azize, 180ff; Smith, M. (1994), 1.140.
[5] Smith, M. (1994), 1.142.
[6] See, e.g., Goedicke, 393.
[7] Azize, 3, 165, etc.
[8] Schniedewind (199) defines *mrzḥ* as both a "men's drinking club" and "cultic/funerary feast."
[9] Schniedewind, 20.
[10] Azize, 182.

this sodality would provide indirect evidence for an association between the sun (and the sun deity) with the realm of the dead."[1]

Biblical scriptures at Amos 6:4-7 describe these wine banquets, which were held also among Jews:

> Woe to those who lie upon beds of ivory, and stretch themselves upon their couches, and eat lambs from the flock, and calves from the midst of the stall; who sing idle songs to the sound of the harp, and like David invent for themselves instruments of music; who drink wine in bowls, and anoint themselves with the finest oils, but are not grieved over the ruin of Joseph! Therefore they shall now be the first of those to go into exile, and the revelry of those who stretch themselves shall pass away.

The Hebrew word here for "bowls" or "sacrificial bowls" is מזרק *mizraq*, defined also as a container specifically for wine, used to toss this liquid.[2] Frequently employed in the Pentateuch and other OT texts to denote "pots" and "bowls," this term *mizraq* in Amos 6 is surmised to be related to *mrzḥ*,[3] which "revelry" is specifically mentioned at Amos 6:7 using the Hebrew term מרזח *marzeach*.

Strong's defines מרזח *marzeach* as "cry, cry of joy, revelry" and "mourning cry...perhaps, feast cry."[4] This festival cry resembles the "Evoe!" of the Bacchantes, and the Jewish wine celebration appears to have been influenced by Greek customs and Orphic themes, including the reclining on beds while feasting, as well as harp-playing. In this regard, this verse in Amos 6 reflects the ancient portrayal of King David as Orpheus, as we discover in artwork as well.

Fig. 76. King David as Orpheus with harp and snake, 508 AD/CE. Synagogue mosaic from Gaza, Israel Museum

Isaiah 24:7-9 speaks of Yahweh's desolation in which the "wine mourns, the vine languishes, all the merry-hearted sigh," in an apparent description of a Bacchic-type *marzeah* destroyed.[5]

Tel Kabri

The importance of wine to the Canaanites was underscored by the discovery in 2013 of Israel's oldest and largest known wine cellar, in

---

[1] Azize, 263.
[2] Strong's H4219.
[3] See, e.g., Greer's *The Use of MZRQ in Amos 6:6: Amos 6:4-7 in Light of the MRZḤ Banquet.*
[4] Strong's H4798.
[5] See, e.g., Brown, J.P., 154.

The Vine and Wine

a Canaanite palace dating to around 1700 BCE, at the site of Tel Kabri, near Akko.[1] The palace itself contained "spectacular frescoes from the Aegean Islands," demonstrating the connection to the winebibbing Minoan civilization. In the palace's cellar were 40 wine jars that would have held about 500 gallons of the libation, enough to fill some 3,000 bottles.[2] This site is surmised to be one of the locations where Canaanite rulers engaged in a *marzeah* banquet, while the wine may have tasted like the Greek retsina,[3] following wine recipes like those discovered on cuneiform tablets at Mari.

By the time the Moses story was composed, wine and vine reverence, ritual and myth were pervasive, and it appears that the Israelites were aware of Dionysus in specific, perhaps reflected in the epithet YHWH-nisi, as well as the later reverence for Bacchus depicted in 2 Maccabees and by Plutarch, evidenced by at least one Dionysian mosaic in the house of prominent Jews, possibly vintners or wine distributors.

This indication is given further credence by the fact that wine continued to be valued well into the common era by pious Jews, such as famed Rabbi Maimonides (1135-1204 AD/CE), who compared the Mishnah to wine, demonstrating ongoing Jewish reverence for this libation. In this regard, wine is discussed numerous times throughout the Talmud, as possessing sacred attributes.

Biblical Grape Reverence

We have seen that the Bible is full of grape and wine references, indicating the plant and beverage's importance to Jews and others of the region. The vineyard and winepress were valuable parts of Israelite culture, especially in the rest of the Tanakh beyond the Torah. The Hebrew word for "wine," יין *yayin*, appears 140 times in the Old Testament, while תירוש *tiyrowsh* or *tirosh*, representing "new wine," can be found in 38 instances.[4] The New Testament uses the Greek word for "wine," οἶνος *oinos*, 33 times, while "wineskins" or ἀσκός *askos* appears in a dozen instances.[5]

The NT also contains 23 references to "vineyard," ἀμπελών *ampelōn*, while "vine" (ἄμπελος *ampelos*) occurs nine times, the same word used to describe both Jesus (Jn 15:1, 5) and Bacchus's love interest Ampelos.[6] This term ἄμπελος *ampelos* is employed for "vine" in the Septuagint of Deuteronomy 8:8, which lists the "seven species" (שבעת המינים *Shiv'at HaMinim*) of "sacred fruits and grains" abundant in the Promised Land:

---

[1] Wilford, "Wine Cellar, Well Aged, Is Revealed in Israel."
[2] Govier, "Biblical Archaeology's Top Ten Discoveries of 2013."
[3] Wilford.
[4] Strong's H3196 and H8492.
[5] Strong's G3631 and G779.
[6] Strong's G290 and G288.

...a land of wheat and barley, of vines and fig trees and pomegranates, a land of olive trees and honey...

The Hebrew word here for "vine" is גֶפֶן *gephen*.

Israel as Vine

Gephen also refers figuratively to the "vine of Israel,"[1] including at Psalm 80:9 to describe the nation itself, as the "vine out of Egypt."[2] This psalm demonstrates Yahweh's role as a "vineyarder" or "vinedresser," as he is called in the NT (Jn 15:1); in other words, a vine god like Dionysus. *Gephen* is used metaphorically likewise at Isaiah 34:4 to describe the "stars fading at Jehovah's judgment" as "leaves [that] fall from the vine." At Hosea 10:1, we read that "Israel is a luxuriant vine that yields its fruit," using *gephen* in the Hebrew and *ampelos* in the LXX.

As part of this ancient Jewish vine/wine reverence, Judges 9:13 names the libation as the drink that "cheers gods and men." In a list of divine gifts provided by Yahweh, Psalm 104:15 praises the "wine to gladden the heart of man."

Noah, the Vintner

In Genesis 9:20-27, the biblical patriarch Noah is deemed "the first tiller of the soil" and depicted as enjoying his wine, thus serving as the legendary original cultivator and vintner.[3] In an episode that sounds very Bacchic, Noah becomes drunk and naked, exposing himself to his sons. This myth is used to explain the tradition of black slavery, as the patriarch curses his son Ham, father of Canaan and progenitor of the Hamite race, for informing his brothers about Noah's indiscretion.

This biblical story involving Noah disinheriting his grandson Canaan "seems to represent an origin legend concerning the ancient discovery of the cultivation of grapes around 4000 BCE in the area of Ararat, which is associated with Noah."[4] Hence, in the Bible the Israelite wine god is raised above that of the Canaanites.

Fig. 77. Cornelis Cort, *The Mocking of Noah*, c. 1560. Engraving (*The Story of Noah*, pl. 6)

---

[1] Strong's H1612.
[2] At Psalm 80:14, the vine of Israel is ravaged by "the boar from the forest," a menace to grapegrowing that likewise may explain in part the taboo against pigs.
[3] The notion of Noah as the "first tiller" appears to contradict the earlier biblical claim of Adam and Eve's son Cain as the first "tiller of the ground." (Gen 4:2).
[4] "Canaan," *New World Encyclopedia*.

THE VINE AND WINE

To reiterate, the earlier Ugaritic wine cult is evidenced in KTU 1.114, in which the gods are said to eat and drink, consuming wine "until sate, vintage until inebriated."[1] The Ugaritic text "Tale of Aqhat" (KTU 1.17-19) may provide a precedent for the Noah-Ham curse, in that it highlights the behavior of a *loyal* son as "taking my hand when I am drunk, supporting me when sated with wine."[2]

The parallels between Bacchus and Noah have been obvious enough that the two have been identified with each other over the ages. In this regard, Vossius posited a possible lineage from Noah to Dionysus, when referring to *homines eruditi* or certain "erudite men," discussing the origin of the name Bacchus:

> Volunt enim ex נח, *Noach*, esse *Noachus*, hinc *Nachus*, inde *Bachus*, tum *Bacchus*.[3]
>
> They wish for out of [Noah], *Noach*, to be *Noachus*, hence *Nachus*, from there *Bachus*, and *Bacchus*.

Again, the drunkenness and lewd impression of the Noah story resemble the popular Bacchic orgies, outlawed in Roman times. This Dionysian celebration is evident also in the drunken revelry during the Jewish festival of Purim, during which a "drinking party" or *mishteh*,[4] reminiscent of a *marzeah*, is held to commemorate the deliverance of the Jews from the Persian Empire.

Eshcol

As was the case with the personified Staphylos, Semites evidently also anthropomorphized the grape bunch, as a figure biblically called "Eshcol" (אשכל *'Eshkol* or "cluster"):

> In pre-Israelite traditions Eshcol (Grape Cluster) appears to be the god of grapes or wine (Gen. 14:13). Eshcol in later Biblical testament was absorbed into El elyon, the chief Canaanite/Israelite deity who becomes in one manifestation a wine god.[5]

Although overtly the verses in Genesis 14 appear to represent historical Amorites, combined with Numbers 13:23-24, as follows, the figure of Eshcol seems to have been originally an Amorite wine god:

> And they came to the Valley of Eshcol, and cut down from there a branch with a single cluster of grapes, and they carried it on a pole between

Fig. 78. Israelite spies bringing back huge grape cluster from Canaan. (*Treasures of the Bible*)

---

[1] Schniedewind, 25.
[2] Fawkes and Allan, 7.
[3] Vossius, 1.144.
[4] Strong's H4960; e.g., Esther 1:3-7; 2:18; 5:4-5, etc.
[5] Heskett and Butler, 95.

two of them; they brought also some pomegranates and figs. That place was called the Valley of Eshcol, because of the cluster which the men of Israel cut down from there.

Concerning Eshcol/Eshkol, Lemche remarks that this term is "generally reckoned a personification of the valley of Eshkol close to Hebron, and visited by Moses' spies (Numb 13:23) who brought back a cluster of grapes from the Valley of Eshkol that could only be transported by two grown-up men."[1]

The bearing of the grape clusters on a pole in procession sounds very Dionysian, and, as noted, the theme of retrieving grapes from a "promised land" can be found in the Bacchic myth, representing the fertility of spring.

Here we see how important the grapevine was to the early Israelites, as well as the existence of several Semitic wine gods in the relevant region. In this regard, Heskett and Butler surmise that Eshcol was absorbed into the El Elyon wine cult,[2] significant because the Israelites also worshipped this latter god, as their "Most High."

Fig. 79. *Rev.* grape bunch between two grape leaves; *obv.* head of Dionysus (not shown), c. 530 BCE. Silver coin, Naxos, Greece

Melchizedek or 'Righteous Molech'

At Genesis 14:18 appears the story of Melchizedek, biblical king of Salem and high priest of El Elohim, known for his communion of bread and wine. It is after the order of Melchizedek that Jesus is made to be a high priest forever repeatedly in the epistle to the Hebrews.[3] Like his disciple Christ at the Last Supper, Melchizedek brings out bread and wine, this time in order to bless Abram/Abraham (Gen 14:19). Here it should be recalled that "Abram" appears to be an anthropomorphization of the Indian god Brahm or Brahma, thus subordinated under Melchizedek and El Elohim.

"Melchizedek" often is rendered "my king is Sedek," but it could also be translated "Righteous Molech,"

Fig. 80. Charles Foster, *Offering to Molech*, 1897. (*Bible Pictures and What They Teach*)

---

[1] Lemche (2004), 122.
[2] Heskett and Butler, 28.
[3] E.g., Heb 5:6; 6:20; 7:17, 21.

THE VINE AND WINE

a remnant, perhaps, of Israelite adherence to the Ammonite god Molech.[1] In this instance, the "ruler" of Salem would be Molech, now dominated by El Elohim. This suggestion of the theonym "Molech" as intended in various verses, rather than the noun "king," is validated by Acts 7:43, which renders the "king" at Amos 5:25-27 as the god's name, Μολὸx *Moloch*, instead of the noun connoting a monarch.

Wine-Drenched Messiah

Demonstrating the intensity of biblical respect for wine, at Genesis 49:11, purportedly written by Moses, we find the following bizarre scripture regarding the coming messiah:

> Binding his foal to the vine and his ass's colt to the choice vine, he washes his garments in wine and his vesture in the blood of grapes; his eyes shall be red with wine, and his teeth white with milk.

This verse concerns the expected ruler of Israel, the savior who will take the scepter from Judah, the reigning tribe of the time. This passage is viewed as one of the many "messianic scriptures" supposedly predicting Jesus Christ but in reality serving as "blueprints," used midrashically or *allegorically* by Jewish scribes to create the Christ character. But, why would Israel be ruled by a besotted winebibber? In Genesis 49, the grape and wine are so important that this attribute is listed first in the characteristics of the anticipated messiah in this passage.

Blood of the Grape/Messiah

In this Genesis passage and at Deuteronomy 32:14, wine is called the "blood of the grape," while, as we have seen, it is also the blood of Jesus (Mt 26:28), who is viewed as the "stem/sprout/shoot/root of Jesse" (Rom 15:12), evidently referring to the grapevine. Hence, we can see that wine is central to both messianic Judaism and Christianity, and that, in significant part, Jesus is a rehash of the vine and wine god Dionysus, whose blood also was that of the grape. In this same regard, we find the typical solar-fertility significance of wine in Egypt, including as the "blood of Osiris."[2]

Tammuz

One of the earlier deities possibly perceived as this oenophilic savior was the solar-fertility god Tammuz, originally the Sumerian Dumuzi. Like Dionysus, Tammuz was a "dying and rising" solar-fertility figure whose resurrection was celebrated in spring.[3] This Semitic deity also appears to be a form of the vine/wine god in significant part, having taken the role of his sister, as noted, celebrated in later times also as the god of fall harvest.

---

[1] 2 Chr 28:3, 33:6; Jer 7:31, 19:2–6; Lev 18:21.
[2] See, e.g., Murdock (2009), 291-292.
[3] Shoham, 170.

So popular was Tammuz that a Hebrew summer month remains named after him,[1] from the Babylonian god-name for June and July, corresponding to the zodiacal sign of Cancer. This summer month is appropriate for a solar deity and a perfect time for the growth of the grapevine and the ripening of the fruit. Following the summer solstice, the month Tammuz was a traditional time of mourning in the Babylonian culture because of the decline towards winter, with the increasingly intense summer heat, which kills flora and fauna, and causes drought.

The god's death and lamentation recorded in the biblical book of Ezekiel (8:14) occurred in the fall with the harvest, per Rabbi Pinchas Frankel:

> The "Tammuz" cult involved the symbolic death of Tammuz. The death of this god was initially symbolic of the grain being turned into wine or beer for the new wineskins. The wine was put into jars and stored underground... When the tanks ran dry, the gods of wine and beer failed, and they had to be aroused or resurrected with wine and music, to restore the harvest. This religion began in Babylonia, was adopted throughout the world, and even by the Jews...[2]

Here once more is a theme found within the Dionysian religion at Athens, with an evident origin elsewhere. The reverence of and familiarity with a wine god and vintage ritual by the Jews in Ezekiel's era (c. 622-570 BCE) is apparent from this Tammuz worship.

The Law and Wine

The other books of the Torah/Pentateuch—again, all supposedly written by Moses—have a very different perspective of wine than the giddy, messianic drunkenness of Genesis, indicating these texts were composed by diverse hands. Leviticus, Numbers and Deuteronomy take a much dimmer view of wine than does Genesis, exhorting followers to abstain from its consumption, including and especially the "separated" priests called Nazarites (Num 6:3).

One would think that if the coming messiah were to be wine-drenched, there would be more focus on this sacred beverage in the rest of the Pentateuch, particularly if one person, Moses, wrote it. Yet, Exodus mentions wine by name only once (29:40), as a libation for the sacred lamb sacrificed morning and evening, in the instructions to Moses (and Aaron) on how to commit the massive slaughter of bulls, sheep and other animals for which the Jewish ritual is known.

---

[1] van Goudoever, 73. See also Wiki ("Tammuz"): "The name of the month was adopted from the Babylonian calendar, in which the month was named after one of the main Babylonian gods, Tammuz." See also Bienkowski (97): "In Early Dynastic Lagash the sixth month of the year was named after the festival of Dumuzi, and in a later north Mesopotamian calendar one of the months is called Dumuzi. The fourth month of the Standard Babylonian calendar was called *D'uzu* or *Dûzu*, and *Tammuz* is still used in Arabic and Hebrew as the name for July."

[2] Frankel, "The Month of 'Tammuz' and Jewish Feminism."

These sacrifice directions represent a mere pittance of the enormous amount of detailed instructions from Yahweh to these patriarchs that were simply "lost," to be found centuries later by Josiah's priest Hilkiah, the possible author of them in the first place. Again, since these rituals were so important to Yahweh, in all their tedious and bloody details, compelled upon the chosen over a period of 40 years in the harsh desert, one wonders where the Lord was during these several centuries when his painstaking instructions were carelessly "lost" and his sacrifices were not being done properly.

Uzziah and Hezekiah

Despite the supposed importance of the law and its restrictions regarding wine, we find evidence of the libation's continued significance in Israelite life. Regarding the so-called LMLK jar-handle seals from Judea, discussed below, Rainey evinces that they are stamps indicating "special brands of produce from royal farms," the produce in question here being wine.[1] In specific, these wine jar seals would belong to the vineyards of the Judean king Uzziah (8th cent. BCE), which Rainey concludes were in the hill country.[2]

Along with these vineyards are Uzziah's great-grandson Hezekiah's wineries, whence in the late seventh to early sixth centuries BCE the king sent shipments of wine, apparently, to Arad in Israel.[3] If these vineyards were part of the "house of Jesse," we can fathom what the "shoot" or "sprout" of Jesse predicted at Isaiah 11:1—said to be the expected, wine-soaked messiah—would represent, giving the savior a viticultural significance.

Wine Chambers and Banqueting House/Temple

In an apparent religious ritual also indicating the drink's sacredness to the Israelites, the "house of Yahweh" or Jerusalem temple contained chambers into which people were led in order to be given wine (Jer 35:2). This same "banqueting house" may be referred to in the erotic biblical book Song of Songs/Solomon (2:4): "He brought me to the banqueting house, and his banner over me was love." The relevant phrase here is בית יין *bayith yayin*, this latter word generally denoting "wine." The LXX styles this chamber οἶκος τοῦ οἴνου *oikos tou oinou* or "house of wine," the word *oikos* also connoting "temple," as does the Hebrew *bayith*. Thus, the lover is brought into the "temple of wine," in a text held sacred by hundreds of millions worldwide.

It is clear that wine remained central to Jewish religion, which means that its producers were important, wealthy and influential, intertwined with a powerful priesthood.

---

[1] Rainey (1982), 57.
[2] Rainey (1982), 58.
[3] Rainey (1982), 59.

New Testament

As mentioned and as was the case with the Greek son of God and the Egyptian savior, the blood of the grapes is also that of Jesus (Mt 26:27-29), and wine metaphors continue in the New Testament. Indeed, the Jewish competition with Babylon is evident from Revelation 14:8-11, which contrasts Babylon's wine with the "wine of the wrath of God, which is poured out without mixture into the cup of his indignation." Regarding this passage, theologian Dr. Gregory K. Beale comments:

> While the intoxicating effect of Babylon's wine seemed strong, it is nothing in comparison to God's wine. Babylon's wine made the nations submissive to her will only temporarily. The effect will wear off at the end of time. Then the ungodly will become drunk with God's wine, the effect of which will not be temporary. God's wine will make the nations submissive to his judicial will forever...[1]

Beyond the Bible, Jews to this day recite a *berakhot* or benediction for food and wine before meals: "Bless art Thou, O Lord our God, King of the Universe, who hast created the fruit of the vine."[2] On the eve of the Jewish Sabbath and other holidays, a sanctification called *kiddush/qiddush*—the same word as *qadesh*, meaning "holy"—is said over a cup of wine before the meal.[3] The cup used is a special chalice, often an engraved silver goblet, resembling the Holy Grail in significance. It is evident that wine has been very important within Judaism, as it had been in paganism, its bounty attributed to God.

Moreover, as one of the seven species of sacred fruits, the grape cluster carried by the two "spies" is a symbol for Israel itself, stylized in art as the logo of Israeli Ministry of Tourism (left), for example, or offered as bumper stickers and so on.

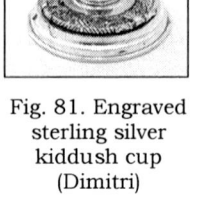

Fig. 81. Engraved sterling silver kiddush cup (Dimitri)

Summarizing the Jewish reverence for the grape, Dr. Tim Unwin states:

> Considerable emphasis has been given here to the symbolism of wine and the vine in the Old Testament for two main reasons: first, it can be seen as reflecting several of the broader symbolic representations of wine and the vine in the ideologies of most of the religions in south-west Asia in the first and second millennia BC, and secondly, and more importantly, much of this symbolism was then taken over

---

[1] Beale, 759.
[2] Doniger, 123.
[3] Doniger, 639.

THE VINE AND WINE 379

and developed in Christianity, which in time became the dominant ideology of societies in which wine was to be the most important alcoholic beverage. A second crucial ideological influence on these societies was that of Greece, and it is therefore to a discussion of the symbolism of the Greek god Dionysus, that this chapter now turns.[1]

Indeed, and in this book as a whole, we have covered already the issue of Dionysus in significant detail. As it turns out, one could say that Moses is the Old Testament Dionysus, while Jesus is the NT version, adapted for the needs of the time.

Water to Wine

As another example, the water-to-wine miracle in the gospel story is not historical but mythical, found in the myths of other cultures. We have seen already several instances of Baal, Dionysus or the latter's followers miraculously producing wine, often in great quantities. In another instance, Diodorus (3.66.2) says that "the Teians produced, as a proof of the birth of Dionysus among them, [the fact] that even to his time at a stated period there was in their city a fountain of wine, spontaneously flowing from the earth and of excellent fragrancy."[2]

One version of the miracle of "wine" from water can be found in Egypt, regarding the Nile flood, thousands of years before the common era:

> The water to wine motif goes...at least as far back as the Old Kingdom of Egypt, and is related to myths about the inundation. Much like Lucian's explanation of the Adonis river in Lebanon turning into "blood" every year, likewise the ancient Egyptians saw the reddish waters of the annual floods (caused by mountain sediment from melting snow)...as the gods turning its water into wine.[3]

Again, this idea of bloody waters also resembles one of the 10 plagues of the Exodus. The river-flooding connotation evidently arose from the observations of the water-to-wine process of nature.

As stated in *Christ in Egypt* (292-293), at Pyramid Text 442:820a, Osiris—who was the "first to drink wine" and who taught mankind about the vine, according to Plutarch—is referred to as the "Lord of Wine in the...festival," again evoking the wedding feast of Cana.

Concerning the water-to-wine miracle at John 2:3-9, Dr. Erich Neumann reminds us that Osiris was a wine god and that January 6th—one of Christ's several birthdays, as well as the "Feast of

---

[1] Unwin, 85.
[2] Jodrell, 404. καὶ Τήιοι μὲν τεκμήριον φέρουσι τῆς παρ᾽ αὐτοῖς γενέσεως τοῦ θεοῦ τὸ μέχρι τοῦ νῦν τεταγμένοις χρόνοις ἐν τῇ πόλει πηγὴν αὐτομάτως ἐκ τῆς γῆς οἴνου ῥεῖν εὐωδίᾳ διαφέροντος· τῶν δ᾽ ἄλλων οἱ μὲν ἱερὰν Διονύσου δεικνύουσι τὴν χώραν, οἱ δὲ ναοὺς καὶ τεμένη διαφερόντως ἐκ παλαιῶν χρόνων αὐτῷ καθιδρυμένα.
[3] "God Almighty," *Freethought Nation*.

Epiphany," commemorating Jesus turning water into wine—"is also the anniversary of the water-wine transformation performed by Osiris."[1]

A relevant utterance occurs in the Pyramid Text of Unas/Unis/Wenis (W 143/PT 210:130c): "...the water of Unis is wine, like the Sun." This last verse hints at the most obvious meaning behind the miracle of turning water into wine: To wit, the sun's ripening of the grape on the vine and fermenting of the grape juice.

Thus, this motif represents significantly the natural process of water being turned into wine, as the vine draws in the former and creates the latter. The perceived orchestrator of this natural "miracle" has been the sun, which brings the life-giving rains, causes the seeds to germinate, creates photosynthesis, grows the vine, ripens the grapes and ferments the wine. In this regard, the deities who turn water to wine are significantly solar.

Temple Sluice

It is noteworthy that at the temple of Apollo at Corinth, Greece, there exists a hidden sluice used in antiquity by pagan priests to change water poured in one end to wine coming out the other. Concerning this device, Loeb's Diodorus editor notes, "Archaeological evidence that a miraculous flow of wine was caused by the priests of a temple (of Dionysus?) of the fifth century B.C. in Corinth is presented by Campbell Bonner, 'A Dionysiac Miracle at Corinth,' *Am. Journal of Archaeology*, 33 (1929), 368-75."[2] I was fortunate enough to see this sluice up close while participating in the American School of Classical Studies' excavation at the site.

Ass and Foal

Another Bacchic connection occurs in the theme of the wine-drenched messiah riding an ass at Genesis 49:11, as Dionysus too is depicted as sitting on an ass, drunk. In consideration of all the parallels in this present work between Bacchus and Moses (and Jesus), it would be logical to suggest that the Genesis passage concerning the drunken messiah on an ass is straight out of Dionysian myth/literature.

Fig. 82. Dionysus with kantharos or cup reclining on ass, c. 460-423 BCE. Coin from Macedonia, Schonwalter Collection

Hephaistos

In one myth, Dionysus leads the inebriated Hephaistos on an ass back to Mt. Olympus, the heavenly city, after the smith god had been tossed out by the goddess Hera. As we read in *Pausanias* (*Guide to Greece* 1.20.3):

---

[1] Neumann, 239.
[2] Diodorus/Oldfeather, 2.302.

THE VINE AND WINE

One of the Greek legends is that Hephaestus, when he was born, was thrown down by Hera. In revenge he sent a gift of a golden chair with invisible fetters. When Hera sat down she was held fast, and Hephaestus refused to listen to any other of the gods save Dionysus—in him he reposed the fullest trust—and after making him drunk Dionysus brought him to heaven.[1]

Here is a triumphal entry upon an ass into the heavenly city, much like that of Jesus entering Jerusalem upon "an ass and her foal," a bizarre verse that makes sense as midrash of Genesis 49:11, which in turn appears to have been borrowed from Dionysian myth.

Significantly, an Ugaritic mug has a scene of El holding a cup, with an attendant about to pour the wine, behind whom is an "equid having the appearance or carriage of a colt or foal."[2]

Of course, in antiquity the ass would be a favored vehicle for drunken guests to return home after a sacred banquet. Hence, the hero or deity riding an ass might symbolize especially a wine cult.

Little Asses

This ass-and-foal motif may represent also the progression towards the fall ripening and harvest of the grapes, portended by the prominence in the constellation of Cancer of the two "autumnal stars" called by the Romans the Aselli or "Little Asses."[3] These Little Asses were said to "feed at the manger" of two other stars of the Crab constellation called the "Crib" or "Manger."[4] The sun in Cancer at the summer solstice, therefore, could be said to "ride in triumph into the city of peace on an ass and her foal." This time of the year is the season when the grapes are ripening on the vine, approaching the triumphal harvest and vintage in the fall. This motif may explain the comparison of Jacob's son Issachar to an ass as well.[5]

As concerns when these motifs may have come into currency, certain constellations appear to have been devised several thousand years before the common era.[6]

---

[1] Pausanias/Jones, 1.99.
[2] Goedicke, 395.
[3] Pliny, *Nat. Hist.* 18.353/18.121: *sunt in signo cancri duae stellae parvae aselli appellatae, exiguum inter illas spatium obtinente nubecula, quam praesepia appellant.* Bostock and Riley (4.121) number this passage as 18.80 and render it: "In the constellation of Cancer, there are two small stars to be seen, known as the Aselli, the small space that lies between them being occupied by a cloudy appearance, which is known as the Manger..." Pliny's Latin for "manger" is *praesaepe*, which can also mean "stable, stall, fold, pen," and which is the same word Jerome uses in the Vulgate (Lk 2:7) to describe the "manger" in which the baby Jesus was placed.
[4] Willis, 101.
[5] The 12 tribes likely are named after *gods* subordinated under Yahweh, the number based on the zodiac. In this regard, each has been assigned a classical zodiac sign, in the case of Issachar, Cancer. It is surmised that the name Issachar may derive from *ish Sokar*, or "man of Sokar," reflecting tribal worship of the Egyptian deity by that name, a form of Osiris and Horus. (See, e.g., "Issachar," *Wikipedia*.)
[6] See Pellar for more information.

The Shoot of Jesse

A major aspect of the vine imagery occurs in the biblical emphasis upon the "shoot of Jesse," previously noted, which has been interpreted to refer to the coming messiah and which clearly was used as a scriptural "blueprint" in the creation of the Christ character. The relevant messianic verse at Isaiah 11:1 states:

> There shall come forth a shoot from the stump of Jesse, and a branch shall grow out of his roots.

In the Bible, Jesse is the father of King David, from whose house it was claimed the messiah would come; hence, the (conflicting) genealogies in Matthew and Luke. The Hebrew equivalent of "shoot" in this verse is חטר *choter*, defined by Strong's (H2415) as "branch, twig, rod." The Hebrew word translated here as "branch" is נצר *netser*, sharing the same root as "Nazarite" or "Nazarene."

In the Hebrew of Isaiah 11:10, we read that the "root of Jesse" is also a "signal" or "ensign" to the people, using the same term נס *nec* or *nissi*,[1] as in "Jehovahnissi."

The LXX of Isaiah 11:1 is as follows:

καὶ ἐξελεύσεται ῥάβδος ἐκ τῆς ῥίζης Ιεσσαι καὶ ἄνθος ἐκ τῆς ῥίζης ἀναβήσεται

The pertinent word here for "shoot," "rod" or "sprout" is ῥάβδος *rhabdos*, while ῥίζα *rhiza* appears twice in this verse, rendered "stump" and "root."

To reiterate, the New Testament epistle to the Romans (15:12) cites this passage from Isaiah referring to the "shoot," "branch" and "root" of Jesse, which is Jesus:

> and further Isaiah says, "The root of Jesse shall come, he who rises to rule the Gentiles; in him shall the Gentiles hope."

In the NT Greek, the word for "root" is ῥίζα *rhiza*, the same term used in Isaiah.

The Magic Rod

Denoting "shoot, branch, rod, stick, wand, staff, scepter," ῥάβδος *rhabdos* is employed at Exodus 4:20 as well, to describe what has been translated as the "rod of God." As is evident, this imagery concerns foliage, especially that of the vine. The Hebrew equivalent for Aaron and Moses's "rod," "staff" or "wand" (Exod 7:9) is מטה *matteh*. Strong's (H4294) defines *matteh* also as "tribe" and "branch," the latter similar to the wand carried by Dionysus, the thyrsus. The Vulgate uses the Latin term *virga*, defined as "rod," "wand," "green stick," "twig," "stalk" and "sprout," representing also a "branch of the ancestral tree."[2]

---

[1] Strong's H5251.
[2] Andrews and Freund, 1636.

THE VINE AND WINE

The word *rhabdos* is used a dozen times in the New Testament, defined as "rod, staff, scepter" and "stave."[1] Like the "thyrsos staves" of the wandering Bacchic maenads, this same object, the *rhabdos*, is the staff/stave each disciple may or may not take with him on his mission, in the contradictory biblical verses at Mark 6:8 and Luke 9:3.

Tirosh and Lulav

In this regard, Hesychius defined θύρσος *thyrsos* using the term *rhabdos*, thus equating the two. Theologian Rev. Dr. John P. Brown also sees a cognate of *thyrsos* in the Hebrew word for "(new?) wine," תירוש *tiyrowsh/tirosh*, both possibly related to the name of the Asian Minor god "Tarhui of the vine."[2]

In addition, during the viticultural Feast of the Tabernacles the rabbis hold a green date palm branch called a לולב *lulav*, which was rendered *thyrsos* in Jewish writings in Greek.[3] Hence, the Jewish *lulav* could be designated also as a *rhabdos*.

Hermes

We have seen already the tale in *The Odyssey* where Hermes lulls and awakens with his rod. In *The Iliad* (24.343) too, Homer speaks of this son of God and messenger, who with his wand (ῥάβδος *rhabdos*) "lulls to sleep the eyes of whom he will."[4] The same basic story is told once more in *The Odyssey* (5.47), this time with the "Argus-slayer" flying to the nymph Calypso, while bearing "the wand with which he seals men's eyes in sleep or wakes them just as he pleases..."[5]

Homer uses the term several more times, in describing the magic wands of both Hermes and the witch Circe. In the Homeric *Hymn 4 to Hermes*, much is also made of the messenger god's golden wand of riches, which Apollodorus (3.10.2) tells us was offered by the sun god to Hermes in exchange for the latter's shepherd's pipe.[6]

Fig. 83. Hermes with winged boots and caduceus, c. 480 BCE. Red figure lekythos, Metropolitan Museum, New York (David Liam Moran)

---

[1] Strong's G4464.
[2] Brown, J.P., 156.
[3] E.g., 2 Macc 10:7; Brown, J.P., 157.
[4] εἵλετο δὲ ῥάβδον, τῇ τ'ἀνδρῶν ὄμματα θέλγει ὧν ἐθέλει.
[5] εἵλετο δὲ ῥάβδον, τῇ τ'ἀνδρῶν ὄμματα θέλγει, ὧν ἐθέλει, τοὺς δ'αὖτε καὶ ὑπνώοντας ἐγείρει.
[6] Apollodorus/Frazer, 2.10-11.

Circe

Like Homer, Apollodorus (*Epit.* E.7.15) employs the word *rhabdos* to describe the wand used by Circe to transform Odysseus's men into animals: "And when they had drunk, she touched them with a wand and changed their shapes, and some she made wolves, and some swine, and some asses, and some lions."[1]

Apollo's Oath

In the *Hymn 4 to Hermes* (4.528-540), Apollo—deemed in other texts to be the "savior"—vows an oath to the messenger god that sounds not unlike Yahweh establishing Moses's divine mission:

> And Apollo swear also: "Verily I will make you only to be an omen for the immortals and all alike, trusted and honored by my heart. Moreover, I will give you a splendid staff of riches and wealth: it is of gold, with three branches, and will keep you scatheless, accomplishing every task, whether of words or deeds that are good, which I claim to know through the utterance of Zeus. But as for sooth-saying, noble, heaven-born child, of which you ask, it is not lawful for you to learn it, nor for any other of the deathless gods: only the mind of Zeus knows that. I am pledged and have vowed and sworn a strong oath that no other of the eternal gods save I should know the wise-hearted counsel of Zeus. And do not you, my brother, bearer of the golden wand, bid me tell those decrees which all-seeing Zeus intends.[2]

As we can see, Hermes carries Apollo's magical staff, composed of gold with three branches, like a tree or vine. The Greek word for "staff" here is, appropriately, ῥάβδος *rhabdos*.

Athena

Athena also carries a *rhabdos*, as at *Odyssey* 13.429, in which the goddess magically turns the arriving hero into an old man, changing him back with the same wand later in the story (16.172), before returning him to a state of decrepitude (16.456).

These transformations are similar to the changing of staffs into serpents by Aaron, Moses and the pharaoh's priests. If we are to allow Moses and his magic wand as "historical," why should we not do likewise with Hermes, Circe, Apollo and Athena?

Diviners and Herbalists

The word *rhabdos* is used repeatedly also by Herodotus (4.67), to describe the "wands" or "rods" of "diviners":

> There are many diviners among the Scythians, who divine by means of many willow wands as I will show. They bring great bundles of wands, which they lay on the ground and unfasten, and utter their

---

[1] Apollodorus/Frazer, 2.287. πόντων δὲ αὐτῶν, ἐφαπτομένη ῥάβδῳ τὰς μορφὰς ἠλλοίου, καὶ τοὺς μὲν ἐποίει λύκους, τοὺς δὲ σῦς, τοὺς δὲ ὄνους, τοὺς δὲ λέοντας.
[2] Homer/Hesiod/Evelyn-White (1920), 403.

divinations as they lay the rods down one by one; and while still speaking, they gather up the rods once more and place them together again.¹

The laying of rods as a divining tool resembles the throwing of I Ching sticks, as done in China for thousands of years. The *rhabdos* as a willow wand is thus a tree branch or stick, like the thyrsus.

The thyrsus possesses medicinal properties as well, as explained by Ruck:

> As I have shown in a recent study of the Eleusinian Mysteries, this sceptre of Dionysus takes on a particular meaning when we consider that such hollow stalks were customarily employed by herbalists in Greece to preserve the freshness of the wild plants they gathered...and that "ivy" or *kissos* (κίσσος), a plant sacred to Dionysus, was the sort of magical wild plant that would have been gathered in this manner, for it was reputed to be poisonous, with a deranging effect upon the mind.²

Although it too was an intoxicant, ivy was used also in antiquity as a cure for hangover, as noted, explaining in significant part the herb's importance to the Dionysian cult.

While the preferred wood for the staff or pole of the thyrsus carried by Dionysus and his Bacchantes appears to have been fennel, the cultic artifact at times was draped with not only ivy but also grape leaves, vines and grapes themselves.³ Ovid (*Met.* 3.662-664) calls the thyrsus "a spear enveloped in vine-leaves,"⁴ and theologian John Brown claims *thyrsos* as another name for "vine."⁵ We are told by Nonnus (12.330ff) that the god also would turn his staff into a sickle in order to reap the grapes.⁶

Sprouting Bacchus

Moreover, in archaic vase paintings, the god is depicted as holding not only the thyrsus but also a sprouting grapevine, which entwines itself around the image. Here we can see a depiction of the all-important shoot or sprout, explaining its biblical significance as

---

¹ Herodotus/Godley (2.265): μάντιες δὲ Σκυθέων εἰσὶ πολλοί, οἳ μαντεύονται ῥάβδοισι ἰτεΐνῃσι πολλῇσι ὧδε: ἐπεὰν φακέλους ῥάβδων μεγάλους ἐνείκωνται, θέντες χαμαὶ διεξειλίσσουσι αὐτούς, καὶ ἐπὶ μίαν ἑκάστην ῥάβδον τιθέντες θεσπίζουσι, ἅμα τε λέγοντες ταῦτα συνειλέουσι τὰς ῥάβδους ὀπίσω καὶ αὖτις κατὰ μίαν συντιθεῖσι. (Note that *rhabdos* in one form or another is used four times in this sentence.)
² Ruck, 183.
³ Bolton, 188.
⁴ *Ipse racemiferis frontem circumdatus uvis pampineis agitat velatam frondibus hastam*: "Bacchus [Dionysos] himself, grape-bunches garlanding his brow, brandished a spear that vine-leaves twined." Brookes More (1.111) renders the full passage thus: "And Bacchus in the midst of all stood crowned with chaplets of grape-leaves, and shook a lance covered with twisted fronds of leafy vines." These vines could be ivy, but some images show the distinct grape leaf.
⁵ Brown, J.P., 136.
⁶ "...he made his sharp thyrsus into the cunning shape of the later sickle with curved edge, and reaped the newgrown grapes." (Nonnos/Rouse, 2.421)

the coming messiah. In this regard, Aaron's staff is depicted also as budding or sprouting (Num 17:8).

Older depictions show Dionysus without the thyrsus but still holding a fruiting grapevine. The god's birth is represented by a sprouting grapevine as well, always an indication that Bacchus is nearby. Hence, the sprout or shoot is a clear symbol of Dionysus, evidently adopted into Jewish and Christian theology for the purpose of incorporating this popular pagan motif.

Sacred Serpents

Fig. 84. Bacchus, born from Zeus's thigh, holds a sprouting grapevine, c. 460 BCE. Museo Nazionale di Spina, Ferrara, Italy

The magical wand, staff or rod of Hermes, the famous winged caduceus (Gk: κηρύκειον *kērukeion*), has two snakes intertwined around it, like the sprouting shoot.

The Egyptians are depicted in the Bible as themselves possessing magical serpent staffs, and indeed we see that such rods were popular in the land of the Nile as well. In this regard, we find a staff dedicated to Osiris topped with a pine cone, much like the thyrsus, and wrapped with two snakes like the caduceus.

The snake theme occurs on the staffs of other deities, lawgivers, healers and heroes, such as that of the Greek healing god Asclepius, which has a single snake wrapped around its central pole. This pagan motif can be found at Numbers 21:9, reflected in the Hebrew veneration of the ancient serpent god: "Moses made a serpent of brass, and put it upon a pole, and it came to pass that if a serpent had bitten any man, when he beheld the serpent of brass he lived."

Fig. 85. Pinecone staff of Osiris, 1224 BCE. Egyptian Museum, Turin, Italy

Fig. 86. Rod of Asclepius

Regarding this magical fetish, Merlin Stone says, "And in Jerusalem itself was the serpent of bronze, said to date back to the time of Moses and treasured as a sacred idol in the temple there until about 700 BC."[1]

Metatron's Rod

Concerning Moses's rod and the snake-entwined caduceus, Dr. Frederick Turner from the University of Texas remarks:

---

[1] Stone, M., 209.

The staff of Moses is said in ancient Jewish folk tradition to have been given to him by the angel Metatron, who is the messenger spirit between God and human beings. The staff was originally a branch of the Tree of Life, from which Metatron plucked it when the world was young. Sometimes the staff itself is called Metatron; like Ningizzida, the Mesopotamian messenger god, who is depicted alternatively as a caduceus or in human form with two snakes coming out of his shoulders, the god and his symbol are confused. Metatron's rod is thus one version of the magic staff shared by many circum-Mediterranean and Asian religions, and is a direct analogue of the caduceus of Hermes/Mercury.[1]

As we can see, the motif of a snake-entwined staff/rod goes back at least to the Mesopotamian messenger god, Ningizzida/Ningishzida, a forerunner of the Greek Hermes and Roman Mercury, who in turn are syncretized with the Egyptian Thoth and replicated in Metatron.

Metatron himself is equated with Yahweh in the apocryphal text 3 Enoch 13,[2] in a sense placing his rod in the Jewish tribal god's hands. In this regard, Moses and Yahweh are also equivalent, as they are in intertestamental literature making the "patriarch" a *god*.

Moreover, Moses and Aaron's rods—essentially the same as the magical staffs of other deities and heroes—was a "branch of the Tree of Life,"[3] which we have seen to be also the grapevine. This branch/rod was specified in antiquity likewise to have served as the "Life-giving Cross of Christ."[4]

Ugaritic and Egyptian Divine Staffs

The Ugaritic texts speak of a "*gamlu*-staff" in one divine epithet, "possessor of the *gamlu*-staff," a motif often associated with gods and royalty.[5] The Amorite god Amurru in particular was associated with the *gamlu*,[6] significant in that Moses evidently is a remake of Amurru/Masu in part. Dr. Aicha Rahmouni states that there are "ample precedents for wooden staffs that serve as divine (or royal) symbols and also function as weapons."[7] She gives as an example the wooden shepherd's staff "well attested as a divine and royal symbol" and which "serves as a magical weapon of the exorcist against witches..."[8]

Serpents and vines are connected apparently for a number of reasons, including their shared ability to intertwine with objects, the snake in effect a "living vine." Both the vine and serpent have the capacity to push through spaces where others cannot go, such as

---

[1] Turner, 119.
[2] Baker, 99.
[3] Stewart, 4.104.
[4] Stewart, 4.104.
[5] Rahmouni, viii, 102ff.
[6] Rahmouni, 104.
[7] Rahmouni, 105.
[8] Rahmouni, 105.

into mysterious "inner sanctums," as witnesses of the mysteries. Moreover, the snake appears to be guarding the sacred plant's roots as it thrives underground. The ancients also may have surmised that through their burrowing the serpents brought life to the soil, providing aeration and drainage.[1]

Conclusion

The various mythical attributes discussed here have to do with nature worship, including and especially the reverence for the grapevine, the sun and fertility, the cult of which proliferated widely in remote antiquity. A further study of the spread of the grapevine, viticulture and viniculture would reveal much about the antiquity of the "Dionysian" cult in any given place, by whatever name.

It is evident that numerous religious and spiritual ideas have been diffused through viticulture and viniculture. These concepts include motifs found within both the Old and New Testaments. As we know, in the New Testament, wine is so important that it serves as Jesus's blood and the holy communion libation.

With all this emphasis on wine, the Israelites could not have missed the cult and god that came with the grapevine, as they assuredly did not live in a vacuum and in fact were notorious for "whoring after" many other gods besides Yahweh for centuries. Indeed, the Jews' anticipated messiah was to be wine-drenched, proving there were wine cultists among them—wealthy as they likely were—who decided to follow suit with their neighbors in having a vine and sun lawgiver as a national founder, evidently commissioning the composition of the Moses myth.

---

[1] See, e.g., Steila and Pond, 35.

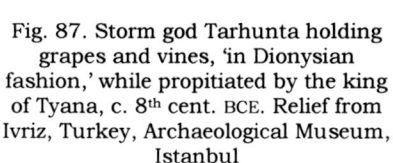

Fig. 87. Storm god Tarhunta holding grapes and vines, 'in Dionysian fashion,' while propitiated by the king of Tyana, c. 8th cent. BCE. Relief from Ivriz, Turkey, Archaeological Museum, Istanbul

Fig. 88. Bacchus holds a fruiting grapevine in his left hand and a wine jar in his right, facing his wife, Ariadne, or a nymph, c. 520-510 BCE. Amphora by the Andokides and Lysippides painters, Louvre Museum, Paris

Fig. 89. Dionysus holding a thyrsus and sprouting grapevine, c. 490-480 BCE. Kylix by Makron, Antikenmuseen, Berlin

Fig. 90. Giovanni Lanfranco, *Moses and the Messengers from Canaan*, carrying grapes, 1621-1624. Getty Center, Los Angeles, CA

Fig. 91. Hephaistos led back to heaven by Dionysos, riding an ass, c. 430 BCE. Attic Red Figure oinochoe, Metropolitan Museum, New York

The Great God Sun

"The evidence for the sun cult manifests itself in Europe from as long ago as the fourth millennium BC, when Neolithic farmers recognized the divine power of the solar disc...

"...Solar religion manifested itself not only in acknowledgement of the overt functions of the sun—as a provider of heat and light—but also in recognition of influences that were more wide-ranging...

"To early communities, the sun was an enigma, with its nightly disappearance from the sky and the withdrawal of its heat for half the year. The sun's value as a life-force was revered...."[1]

Dr. Miranda J. Aldhouse-Green, *The Sun: Symbol of Power and Life*

"As the bestower of light and life, ancient cultures generally identified the sun as the symbol of Truth, the all-seeing 'one eye' of justice and equality, the fountainhead of wisdom, compassion, and enlightenment, the healer of physical and spiritual maladies, and, above all, the fundamental source of fecundity, growth, and fruition, as well as of death and the renewal of life."[2]

Dr. Federico Mayor, *The Sun: Symbol of Power and Life*

"To the ancients...heaven was the land of gods and mystery. The sky...was itself living. The stars were the abode of the gods. The shining stars were indeed themselves luminous gods. Astronomy was the knowledge not of heavenly bodies, but of heavenly beings: It was the heavenly, celestial cosmic or divine knowledge—knowledge of devas—the bright luminous gods."

Dr. S.B. Roy, *Prehistoric Lunar Astronomy* (1)

ONE OF THE principal objects of adoration over the course of human history has been the sun, worshipped in countless cultures globally for thousands of years. Solar worship has been particularly popular in areas plagued with cold, darkness or cloudiness, as well as in fertile agricultural lands dependent on knowledge of the sun's movements across the sky. These sun-worshipping locales extend from the farthest reaches north, through the equator and into the southern hemisphere. Not only gods but also many goddesses were said to possess solar attributes, and, by the process of syncretism, numerous deities of the Mediterranean and beyond were perceived to be solar. Desert regions too displayed reverence for the sun, although less so because the unbearable heat also made the solar orb an enemy and pestilence. Even though like other desert religions it was significantly lunar in nature,[3] Judaism too has been part of this great global solar tradition.

---

[1] Singh, 295.
[2] Singh, 7.
[3] See, e.g., Theodor Reik, *Pagan Rites in Judaism*.

The epithets for the "God Sun" have included virtually all the names and titles held to be holy by thousands of cultures for millennia, such as "Almighty," "Healer," "King of kings," "Lord of lords," "Prince of princes," "Savior" and so on.[1] Hence, these divine epithets in the Bible are not original or unique to Yahweh or his son, Jesus.

Shamash, Lord of the World

As indicated, the Sumero-Babylonian sun god and divine lawgiver Šamaš/Shamash has been identified with El, Baal and Yahweh, three designations for God in the Old Testament. Shamash's worship extends back some 5,000 years to the kings of Ur, as related by University of Pennsylvania Assyriologist Dr. Morris Jastrow (1861-1921):

> In Ur itself, Shamash was also worshipped in early days by the side of the moon-god. Eannatum, of the dynasty of Isin (c. 2800 B.C.), tells of two temples erected to him at that place; and still a third edifice, sacred to both Nannar (the moon-god) and Shamash at Ur, is referred to by a king of the Larsa dynasty, Rim-Sin (c. 2300 B.C.).[2]

Shamash's Sumerian equivalent is UD, or "Utu" in Akkadian, the solar son of the moon god and "lord of truth" dating back thousands of years and depicted as wearing a horned helmet, reflecting the solar-rays theme.[3] University of Cambridge professor Dr. John H. Rogers describes a scene with the "sun-god, Shamash...shown as a bearded man with rays flaring from his shoulders, cutting his way through the eastern horizon with his characteristic serrated knife."[4]

With his worship extending into the Neo-Babylonian period (626-539 BCE), Shamash was a dominant force for millennia in the very area where the proto-Israelite Amorites thrived and merged with various peoples, absorbing, adopting and demoting their deities.

שמש Shemesh

As also discussed, the Semitic solar god-name "Shamash" has been passed along in Hebrew, denoting "sun." *Gesenius* notes that שמש *shemesh* or *shamash* is a "primitive word, found under the radical letters *sm, sr, sn, sl,* in very many languages, compare the old Germ. *Summi* (whence *Summer, Sommer*), Sanscr. *sura, surja,* Germ. *Sunne, Sonne,* Eng. *sun,* Lat. *sol*..."[5]

When one considers the assertion that the radical *sm* serves as a very ancient root signifying "sun," as also in "summer," the relationship between שם *shem*—signifying "name" and often used to

---

[1] See, e.g., *Christ in Egypt* and *Suns of God*.
[2] Jastrow, 70-72.
[3] See, e.g., Mellinkoff, 4.
[4] Rogers, J.,11.
[5] *Gesenius*, 174.

designate Yahweh—and שמש *shemesh,* meaning "sun," ranks as noteworthy.

Shamash's name itself derives from the Babylonian word for "sun," *shamshu,*[1] which indicates that the later Hebrew word for "sun," שמש *sh.m.sh,* actually reflects the Babylonian sun *god,* not just a term for the solar orb. In this regard, then, we are justified in reading "Shamash Yahweh" at Psalm 84:11 as a *theophoric title,* rather than a designation of Yahweh "merely" as the sun. In other words, the Hebrew appears to state: "Shamash is Yahweh" or vice versa.

It is interesting that שמש *shemesh/shamash* also means "officiant, minister, attendant, helper,"[2] since these roles too were those of the sun, as well as of various (solar) priesthoods.

God of My Father

As we have seen, in the Amarna letters discovered in Egypt, written mostly in Akkadian cuneiform and dating to the 14th century BCE, there appear solar hymns invoking "the King my lord, my sun, my god." Another text found at Amarna includes a poem (138) to Shamash in which he is referred to repeatedly as "the god of my father."[3] This designation is not unique to the Bible, therefore, but preceded the Jewish texts by centuries to millennia.

Semitic Sun Goddess

Shamash is related to the name of the sun *goddess* of the Ugaritic/Canaanite pantheon, Shapsh, Shapash or Šapšu, transliterations of the Ugarit word for "sun," *špš.*[4] In his index entry for "*špš* sun," Schniedewind notes: "cp. Akka *šamšu*; Heb. שמש," in other words *shemesh.*[5] The transition from *shapash* to *shamash* evidently reflects the Babylonian/Amorite origin of, or influence on, the southern Israelites, as opposed to the Canaanitish northern tribes.

Archaeologist and linguist Dr. Cyrus Gordon explicates this relationship:

špš שמש—The p in *špš* "sun" originated

Fig. 92. Shapash/Shipish, sun goddess of Ugarit and Ebla, winged and in cruciform or cross shape, 2nd millennium BCE

---

[1] "Shamash," *New International Encyclopedia,* 20.786.
[2] Rabbi Bahir Davis: "Shamash (שמש) means officiant, minister, attendant, in other words, helper. And it also is the word for sun."
[3] Winckler, 257. See *The Study Guide* for the present volume.
[4] Schniedewind, 19, 86; Rahmouni, 252, etc.
[5] Schniedewind, 207.

as a transitional intrusion between -m and -š:šampš- > šapš-; cf. Eng. "Sampson" for "Samson."[1]

Hence, the sun goddess's name is comparable to "Sampson" or "Samson," the moniker of another solar biblical hero.

As is logical for a solar deity, Shapash was involved in dividing the seasons of the year: "In Ugaritic myth and ritual, the Sun goddess played a crucial role at the transition of the seasons, marking off the time of the festivals."[2] The sun goddess's epithets included "the luminary, the lady," "the lamp of the gods," "the scorcher, the power of the sky" and "the eternal Šapšu."[3]

Shapash/Shamash the Lightbringer and Lawgiver

The role of the sun god/dess includes that of the "upholder of the law" and "deity of justice":

> The Akkadian/Babylonian sun god Shamash or Shemesh, also a bringer of light, upholder of law and order, and prophetic oracle, was originally an eagle-shaped Sun-goddess, as seen in an Sumerian artifact, and as demonstrated in personal names Ummi-Shamash, which means "My Mother is Shamash." Phoenicians called her Shapash, and [She] was the goddess of the Sun. Called the Luminary of the Deities, the Torch of the Gods, She sees all that transpires on Earth by day and guards the souls of the dead in the underworld by night. Like the Akkadian Shamash, She is a deity of justice, often serving to mediate for the deities in disputes. She is related to Shamsh, Chems, an Arabic Sun-goddess worshipped at sunrise, noon, and sunset.[4]

Shapash is mother, luminary, torch, bringer of light, all-seeing by day and guardian by night. In essence, she is the omniscient light of the world that every eye can see.[5]

Whether female or male, Shapash/Shamash is the just and righteous upholder of the law, therefore the lawgiver or legislator. As noted, in ancient mythology, the Code of Hammurabi was provided to the Babylonian lawgiver by Shamash, in a similar manner in which Moses/Mosheh was said to receive the 10 Commandments from the solar Yahweh.

Thus, for eons, the divine legislator or lawgiver role was traditionally held by the sun, in numerous manifestations globally. This legislative role can be found in Babylonian sun hymns that sound much like the Egyptian and biblical solar hymns previously discussed, such as:

> The law of mankind dost thou direct,
> Eternally just in the heavens art thou,

---

[1] Gordon (1998), 33.
[2] Becking, 106.
[3] Rahmouni, 241, 252, 271.
[4] "Shapash, Shapshu."
[5] Cf. John 8:12, Rev 1:7.

Of faithful judgment towards all the world are thou.
Thou knowest what is right, thou knowest what is wrong...
O Shamash! Supreme judge of heaven and earth are thou...
O Shamash! Supreme judge, great lord of all the world art thou;
Lord of creation, merciful one of the world art thou...
O Shamash! on this day purify and cleanse the king, the son of his god.
Whatever is evil within him, let it be taken out....[1]

In another hymn, Shamash is called "judge of the world" and "director of its laws."[2] We have seen already the epithet of "judge of man" or Dian-nisi.

In these Babylonian hymns, as in the Akkadian, Assyrian, Egyptian, Phoenician and Ugaritic/Canaanite, we can find many correspondences with the depiction of the biblical "LORD God," whether Yahweh, El, Elohim, Baal, Adonai or a combination thereof. Hence, there appear many "biblical" themes, such as the "law of mankind," justice in heaven, divine righteousness, the concept of a supreme judge, the "lord of all the world," the "lord of creation," the "merciful," God as purifier, and the idea of the son of God, as well as the divine king.

These solar poems sound very monotheistic, with the high god in his heaven; here we can see whence our traditional concepts of God come. These numinous notions are repeated in the Bible and are clearly related to, if not derived from, Babylonian, Canaanite, Egyptian and other sources, not arising as a result of unique "divine revelation" to the "chosen people."

Samson the Sun

As a blatant example of how a sun god has been turned into a biblical hero, we can cite the story of Sampson or Samson (Jdg 13-16), written שמשון *Shimshown*, meaning "like the sun."[3] The first three letters of Samson are שמש *sh.m.sh*, and we noted previously the relationship also to the Semitic sun goddess Shapash.

Samson's story possesses a number of solar and lunar elements, such as the tearing down of the two pillars of the temple, a solar motif likewise found in the myth of Hercules/Herakles. In this myth, the Greek son of Zeus/God legendarily erects the two "columns" or mountains on either side of the Strait of Gibraltar, the western edge of the world and opening to the underworld, where the sun sets.[4] This same theme can be seen in the images of Ur-Nammu, Shamash and other figures between two mountains and/or columns.

---

[1] Jastrow, 300-301, citing IV R. 28, no. 1.
[2] Jastrow, 302.
[3] Strong's H8123.
[4] See, e.g., Strabo (3.5.5) referring to "the pillars which Pindar calls the 'gates of Gades' when he asserts that they are the farthermost limits reached by Heracles." (Strabo/Jones, 2.137)

Another soli-lunar theme is the loss of strength when the sun god or solar hero's "hair" or rays are cut by the moon goddess, the significance of the story of Samson and Delilah (Jdg 16:19).

King, Shepherd and Raiser of the Dead

In the Ugaritic texts, the king is called "the sun" or "my Sun," as was the case traditionally in Egypt and other places, where the king and sun deity or deities frequently were intertwined, syncretized, identified and equated with each other.

As seen, so too is the Amorite/Babylonian Shamash the ruler or king, among other divine attributes, recounted by Jastrow:

> The titles given to Shamash by the early rulers are sufficiently definite to show in what relation he stood to his worshippers, and what the conceptions were that were formed of him. He is, alternately, the *king* and the *shepherd*... In the incantations, Shamash is frequently appealed to, either alone, or when an entire group of spirits and deities are enumerated. He is called upon to *give life to the sick man*. To him the body of the one who is smitten with disease is confided. As the *god of light*, he is appropriately called upon to *banish "darkness"* from the house, darkness being synonymous with misfortune; and the appeal is made to him more particularly as the *"king of judgment."*
>
> From this, it is evident that the beneficent action of the sun, was the phase associated with Shamash. He was hailed as the *god that gives light and life to all things*, upon whose favor the prosperity of the fields and the well-being of man depend. He *creates the light and secures its blessings for mankind*. His favor produces *order and stability*; his *wrath brings discomfiture and ruin* to the state and the individual. But his power was, perhaps, best expressed by the title of *"judge"*—the favorite one in the numerous hymns that were composed in his honor....
>
> He *loosens the bonds of the imprisoned, grants health to the sick*, and even *revivifies the dead*. On the other hand, he puts an end to wickedness and destroys enemies. He makes the weak strong, and prevents the strong from crushing the weak. From being the judge, and, moreover, the supreme judge of the world, it was but natural that the conception of justice was bound up with him. His light became symbolic of righteousness, and the absence of it, or darkness, was viewed as wickedness. Men and gods look expectantly for his light. He is the guide of the gods, as well as the ruler of men.[1]

Italicized here are numerous attributes of Shamash that are expressed later of Yahweh, as well as many other deities around the Middle East and beyond. A number of these traits also feature prominently in the Christ myth, such as the king, shepherd, light of the world, dispeller of darkness, beneficent judge and wrathful avenger, healer of the sick, raiser of the dead, and ruler of men. It could not be clearer where the numerous divine attributes come from

---

[1] Jastrow, 70-72. (Emph. added.)

that are used to describe the biblical god and his son: Very ancient mythology and religion, especially sun worship or heliolatry.

Jesus as Shamash

In consideration of how many of the same characteristics the two figures share, it may come as no surprise that King Jesus is identified with Shamash biblically. In the book of Malachi (4:2)—which precedes directly the first New Testament text, generally the gospel of Matthew—the prophet writes of the coming "Sun of Righteousness" who will arise with "healing in its wings." This solar symbolism ranks as highly ancient, long predating the composition of the Old Testament, as shown, with the sun viewed since remote antiquity as the righteous judge and guardian of the world, as well as the savior and healer, frequently depicted as winged because of the fact that birds fly high, towards the solar orb.

Fig. 93. Egyptian winged sun disk, like the biblical 'Sun of Righteousness' (Mal 4:2), surrounded by two serpents, like the caduceus or symbol of healing

The "Sun of Righteousness" in Malachi is considered to be the coming messiah, Jesus Christ, whose solar attributes rate as extensive. Malachi's original Hebrew uses the word שמש sh.m.sh or shemesh/shamash to describe the savior, serving as a divine title, not just the physical sun. Hence, Jesus basically is Shamash.

The Greek translation of Malachi 4:2 renders "sun" as ἥλιος helios, the same as the Greek sun god's name. Thus, Jesus is Helios, an identification demonstrated throughout the ages since Christianity's inception, including in Christ's replacement of the sun god's central position in zodiacs.[1] Jerome's Latin rendering of שמש shemesh is "sol," as at Malachi 4:2, connoting that Jesus is Sol, the Roman sun god.[2]

El the Canaanite High God

Another Semitic solar deity was El, whose Eblaite predecessor probably can be found in "personal names written *il, i-lum...*"[3] One of the gods of the Israelite fathers, El was depicted as worshipped by the Hebrews at a variety of locations, including Jerusalem, Beerlahai roi, Bethel, Penuel and Shechem, according to the Bible.[4] Referring to the relevant biblical verses, Gray comments: "Such instances definitely relate the worship of the patriarchs and their contemporaries in

---

[1] As J. Glen Taylor (1994:90) remarks, "Christ too was sometimes pictured as a sun-god."
[2] For more information, see *Suns of God* and my ebook *Jesus as the Sun throughout History*.
[3] Emerton, 131.
[4] Genesis 14:18, 16:7-14, 28, 32:23-33 and 33; see also Gray (1965), 168.

Palestine to the particular deity El, whom we now know as the supreme god of the pantheon of ancient Ugarit."[1]

In the Ugaritic pantheon, as expressed in the Ras Shamra texts from the 13th or 14th century BCE, El is the "senior god" among the Elohim. In Canaanite writings, El is the "Creator" and "Builder of Built Things,"[2] precisely the same role as played by the later Yahweh. As he does in the Jewish scriptures, in the earlier Ugaritic texts El bears many epithets, one of which, *ab šnm*, appears to mean "father of the years," which, Gray points out, resembles the "Ancient of Days" of Daniel 7.13.[3] As did many other places, pre-Israelite Jerusalem possessed a shrine to El,[4] in later centuries syncretized to Yahweh.

The word אל *'el* meaning "God" or "god" appears 238 times in the Old Testament,[5] demonstrating its importance. The plural אלהים *'elohiym* or "gods" is used in many more instances, 2606 times.[6] Other examples of Hebrews worshipping multiple gods include the verses at Genesis 31:19, where Rachel is said to have stolen her father's "household gods" or "idols," תרפים *teraphim*, a word used 15 times in the Old Testament, eventually meaning "disgraceful things" in rabbinical Judaism.

Yahweh and Saturn

Like Yahweh constantly meddling in the Israelites' lives, El was the "paramount authority in social affairs."[7] Also like Yahweh, El has been surmised to be both a solar and lunar deity,[8] identified as well with the planet Saturn,[9] one of the gods of the Israelites as well, as at Amos 5:26:

> You shall take up Sakkuth your king, and Kaiwan your star-god, your images, which you made for yourselves...

The "Sakkuth" or "Sikkuth" is both a "Babylonian deity" and the word used to describe the Jewish "tent," "booth" and "tabernacle,"[10] explaining the latter's sacredness, as they were associated evidently with a god or goddess of nature. The term "Kaiwan," "Kiyuwn," "Chiun" and so on means "pillar"[11] and represents the Babylonian version of Saturn or Kronos/Cronus, as well as the Syrian god Adar/Ninib.[12] Since this verse indicates Jews were worshipping

---

[1] Gray (1965), 161.
[2] Oldenburg, 16.
[3] Gray (1965), 155.
[4] Cross, 99.
[5] Strong's H410.
[6] Strong's H430.
[7] Gray (1965), 155.
[8] Gray (1965), 156.
[9] Duncker, 1.357.
[10] Strong's H5522.
[11] Strong's H3594.
[12] The *Catholic Encyclopedia* remarks: "The same word [*Kaiwan*] (interpreted to mean 'steadfast') frequently designates, in the Babylonian inscriptions, the slowest-moving

Kaiwan, we may say they were worshipping also Saturn and Adar, the latter of whom was called "Masu," the same spelling as "Moses," to be discussed.

The Amos passage (LXX) is reflected at Acts 7:43 as well:

> And you took up the tent of Moloch, and the star of the god Rephan, the figures which you made to worship; and I will remove you beyond Babylon.

Again, the New Testament writers rendered the word at Amos 5:26 not as "king" but as *Molech*, validating that some of the mentions of "king" in the OT in reality are references to the Semitic *god*, a number of whose attributes Yahweh absorbed. According to the Bible, Molech/Moloch is equivalent with Sakkuth, also worshipped by Jews. Rephan or Ῥαιφάν *Rhaiphan* is surmised to be an incorrect transliteration of Kiyuwn and representative also, therefore, of Saturn.[1]

Israelite Saturn worship is reflected in the fact that the Jewish weekly holy day occurs on the god's traditional day, called "Saturday" in English, the end of which is heralded by the "appearance of three stars in the sky."[2]

Israelite Syncretism

Regarding the syncretism of Israelite polytheism, Mark Smith remarks:

> ...Israelite religion apparently included worship of Yahweh, El, Asherah and Baal.... El and Yahweh were identified... Features belonging to deities such as El, Asherah and Baal were absorbed into the Yahwistic religion of Israel.[3]

At Joshua 22:22, we read אל אלהים יהוה אל אלהים יהוה or "El Elohim Yahweh," invoked twice. The same phrase, אל אלהים יהוה, is used at Psalm 50:1, again "El Elohim Yahweh."

A Handy Concordance of the Septuagint lists Greek epithets for Yahweh, such as *theos theos* ("god god") and *theos theos kurios*, ("god god lord") both of which are used to render the biblical phrase "El Elohim Yahweh." Under its entry for θεός *theos*, the LXX concordance cites numerous instances of several gods or god-names associated,

---

planet; while Sakkuth, the divinity associated with the star by the prophet, is an alternative appellation for Ninib [Adar], who, as a Babylonian planet-god, was merged with Saturn. The ancient Syrians and Arabs, too, called Saturn Kaiwan, the corresponding terms in the Zoroastrian Bundahish being Kevan. The other planets are individualized in the Bible only by implication. The worship of gods connected with them is denounced, but without any manifest intention of referring to the heavenly bodies. Thus, Gad and Meni (Isaias, [65:11]) are, no doubt, the 'greater and the lesser Fortune' typified throughout the East by Jupiter and Venus; Neba, the tutelary deity of Borsippa (Isaias [46:1]), shone in the sky as Mercury, and Nergal, transplanted from Assyria to Kutha (2 Kings 17:30), as Mars." (Herbermann, 2.30)

[1] Strong's G4481.
[2] "Shabbat," *Wikipedia*.
[3] Smith, M. (2002), 7-8.

identified or syncretized with Yahweh in the Bible. These gods/epithets include:

> Adonai; El; El Elohim; El Jehovah; El Shaddai; Elah; Eloah; Elohim; Jah Jah; Jah Jehovah; Jehovah; Jehovah Elohim; Shaddai, Trooz, etc.[1]

Genesis 46:3 speaks of El as the "God of thy father," the word for "God" here being the plural Elohim, as it is also at Genesis 33:20, shortened to אלהי *elohey*.

Majestic Plural

The usage of Elohim in the Old Testament as referring to "God" in the singular is styled the "majestic plural," also known as the "royal we." The comparable Ugaritic/Canaanite term *'l-h-m* likewise was used to designate both a singular "God" and plural "gods." Hence, the concept of Elohim as "God" would remain unoriginal to the Jewish religion and would constitute not "divine revelation" but a continuation of pre-Judaic Semitic religion.

The God of Exodus?

Further indicating that there exists an Ugaritic/Canaanite myth at the core of the Exodus tale, Mark Smith explores the question, "Was El the Original God of the Exodus?" Says he:

> ...C.F.A. Schaeffer has written, followed by N. Wyatt and me, that El may have been the original god connected with the Exodus from Egypt and that this event was secondarily associated with Yahweh when the two gods coalesced. Numbers 23:22 and 24:8 (cf. 23:8) associate the Exodus not with Yahweh but with the name of El: "El who freed them from Egypt has horns like a wild ox." (This description also evokes El's attribute animal at Ugarit, the ox, reflected in his title "Bull El.") The poems in Numbers 23:24 contain the name of Yahweh (23:8, 21; 24:6), but it is considerably rarer than the name of El (23:8, 19, 22, 23; 24:4, 8, 16, 23). Indeed, El is attested almost three times as often as Yahweh. Accordingly, B.A. Levine seems correct in suggesting that these poems preserve an old repertoire of El tradition, now synthesized with references to Yahweh. If so, these texts contain a valuable witness to El as the god of the Exodus, at least in one of the Israelite traditions.[2]

The Exodus story evidently represents largely a reworking of an Egyptian and Canaanite cosmological themes, including among the latter one that originally had as its god, El, not Yahweh. The Yahwist tribal deity was intruded into the tale with his purported introduction on Mt. Sinai, even though he was introduced already to Abraham, who built a shrine to him at Shechem. Both tales are mythical devices used to demote pre-Yahwist gods under the Judean tribal deity.

---

[1] *A Handy Concordance*, 113-114.
[2] Smith, M. (2001), 146-147.

The Bull

As we can see, among the Canaanite divine epithets appears "Bull El" or *ṯr 'el*, interestingly similar to the much later *el toro* in Spanish, although the Ugaritic apparently would be pronounced more like "Thor." We are also reminded of *tauros* and *taurus*, meaning "bull" in Greek and Latin, respectively. In this regard, J. Brown comments that "names of wine...and the bull...are in the oldest stratum of the vocabulary common to Semitic and Indo-European."[1]

Concerning this title "the Bull," Gray comments:

> However we may explain this title *ṯr 'el*, it is remarkable that the God of Jacob is spoken of as אביר ['*abiyr*, "the Strong"], which also means "a bull." Since we find the fertility-god Baal in the Ras Shamra texts mating with a heifer, presumably as a bull, this may be a point at which El and Baal were assimilated, as Jahweh and Baal were at Dan in the time of Jeroboam and possibly earlier....[2]

At Genesis 49:24, in which Yahweh is called by the epithet meaning "Strong/Mighty" or "Bull," אביר *'abiyr*,[3] he is labeled also "the Shepherd" (רעה *ra'ah*), a title likewise held by the Egyptian pharaohs and various gods and godmen, including Jesus.

Any gods revealing themselves to humanity in the industrialized world today likely would not go by the epithet of "the Bull" or "the Shepherd." Indeed, these sacred names for divinity are appropriate mostly for a certain time and locale, and would not be perceived by, say, Alaskan natives, who traditionally had no bulls or sheep. Hence, we can see that the Bible is a cultural artifact, a product of its era and location.

Ram

The word אל *el* or *al*, meaning "strong" or "mighty," is part of the name "Israel," as in אל אלהי ישראל *'El 'elohey Yisra'el* (Gen 33:20), "the mighty God of Israel" a "name given to an altar, a location, by Jacob."[4] The term אל *el/al* is said to derive from the root איל *'ayil*, meaning "ram."[5]

As is evident, the Hebrew words for אל *el* "mighty" and אל *'El*, referring to the god or god-name, are the same. Thus, the Hebraized El was identified as or with the Ram, appropriate for a cult created or promulgated widely during the precessional age of Aries (c. 2300-c. 150 BCE).[6]

---

[1] Brown, J.P., 136.
[2] Gray (1965), 158.
[3] Strong's H46.
[4] Strong's (H415) defines this single word *Eleloheisrael*, broken down as *'El 'elohey Yisra'el* or *El-elohe-Israel*, as "the mighty God of Israel" and the "name given to an altar, a location, by Jacob."
[5] Strong's H352.
[6] The knowledge of the precession of the equinoxes is claimed to have been discovered only by the Greek astronomer Hipparchus during the second century BCE. However,

El the Merciful

Unlike the fire-snorting and intolerant later god of the Bible, who lays waste to countless cities and villages, slaughtering millions, El is depicted in the Ras Shamra texts as tolerant and kindly.[1] It may be that, as the environment around the Jews became more hostile both naturally and manmade, so too did their combined El-Yahweh become less kindly and tolerant, eventually losing his Canaanite roots.

In the earlier, Ugaritic texts, El is called "the Kindly One, El, the Merciful," which is almost verbatim with a much later Quranic text in Arabic.[2] As Gray says, "Here we are very close to the God of the patriarchs who called Abraham to be his friend."[3] The pericope at Isaiah 41:8 about "Abraham the friend"[4] may be part of the changeover from when Aristotle/Josephus's Kalanoi or "Syrian Jews" from India demoted their god "Father Brahma" and accepted the Canaanite "Father of All," El.

Holy Mount of Elohim

At Ezekiel 28:14, we find a reference to the "holy mountain of Elohim," again, the latter term denoting "the gods." This "mountain of the gods" evokes the myths of Mount Olympus with the 12 Greek gods and the Scandinavian assembly of the 12 in Asgard,[5] among many others. The mountain home of the Ugaritic pantheon was said to be Mt. Zaphon, known modernly as Jebel al-Aqra and in the Bible at Isaiah 14:13,[6] which refers to the "mount of assembly...of the north" (צפון *tsaphown*),[7] indicating the heavens and stars.[8]

70 Sons of El

In Genesis 6 and at Deuteronomy 32:8, we read about the "sons of God" or bene Elohim, which epithet has its counterpart in Ugaritic (*b'n il* or "sons of El") and in Phoenician writings, in reference to the Western Semitic "council of the gods."[9] The Elohim are shown by the

---

there are many indications that the precession had been known for centuries if not millennia to some extent by the Babylonians at least, if not also by advanced and ancient cultures such as the Egyptian and Indian. (See, e.g., *Hamlet's Mill*, as well as the works of astronomer Dr. Edwin C. Krupp, Brian Pellar, et al.) The precise dating range for the precessional ages varies from source to source.

[1] Gray (1965), 160.
[2] Gray (1965), 160.
[3] Gray (1965), 160.
[4] Isaiah 41:8: "But you, Israel, my servant, Jacob, whom I have chosen, the offspring of Abraham, my friend..."
[5] Gray (1965), 24.
[6] Schniedewind, 7, 18.
[7] Strong's H6828, meaning "north" and derived from *tsaphan*, denoting "to hide, treasure, treasure or store up" (H6845).
[8] See also Psalm 48:2.
[9] Heiser ("Deuteronomy 32:8 and the Sons of God," 3) remarks: "Literary and conceptual parallels discovered in the literature of Ugarit...have provided a more

Ugaritic tablets to be the 70 sons of the Ugaritic deities Ilu (El) and Athiratu (Asherat), also the 70 brothers of Baal.[1]

Regarding El's sons, Oldenburg remarks:

> In Job 38:7, we read that at the foundation of the earth "the morning stars sang together, even all the sons of Elohim shouted for joy." Thus the morning stars are the sons of El...[2]

Hence, El is the sun, while his offspring represent the stars, as well as Venus and other elements.

Genesis 10 depicts around 70 nations, each of which would have its own deity, one of whom was Yahweh.[3] Biblical verses starting at Numbers 29:13 describe sacrifices "offered on each of the days of Sukkot."[4] Adding together the number of bullocks sacrificed, on the seventh day the total number reaches 70, "one for each of the Gentile nations." Interestingly, the sacrifice of 70 bulls occurs in the myth of Baal, the "mighty one,"[5] centuries before the Bible was composed.

As we have seen, there are also 70 Jewish elders, like Jesus with his 70 disciples in the New. In this regard, John Day remarks:

> It is in connection with the Canaanite god El and his pantheon of gods, known as "the sons of El," that a direct relationship with the Old Testament is to be found. That this is certain can be established from the fact that both were seventy in number.[6]

Thus, as have many other gods, El/Ilu had a son;[7] hence, the "son of God" motif is not unique to the much later Christianity. El is also styled *'ab 'adm* or "father of men,"[8] the latter word being *adam*. In this "Father of Adam" epithet, again we can see whence biblical tradition derives.

---

coherent explanation for the number 70 in Deuteronomy 32:8—and have furnished powerful ammunition to textual scholars who argued against the 'sons of Israel' reading in MT [Hebrew Masoretic Text]. Ugaritic mythology plainly states that the head of its pantheon, El (who, like the God of the Bible, is also referred to as El Elyon, the 'Most High') fathered 70 sons, thereby setting the number of the 'sons of El' (Ugaritic, *bn'il*). An unmistakable linguistic parallel with the Hebrew text underlying the LXX reading was thus discovered, one which prompted many scholars to accept the LXX reading on logical and philological grounds: God (El Elyon in Deut. 32:8) divided the earth according to the number of heavenly beings who already existed from the time of creation. The coherence of this explanation notwithstanding, some commentators resist the LXX reading, at least in part because they fear that an acceptance of the בני אלים/אלהים (*bny 'lym/'lhym*) readings (both of which may be translated 'sons of gods') somehow requires assent to the notion that Yahweh is the author of polytheism."

[1] Gray (1965), 78.
[2] Oldenburg, 18.
[3] See Sanders (77ff) for a thorough discussion of Genesis 10.
[4] Kantor, 1.
[5] Rahmouni, 58.
[6] Day, 23.
[7] Rahmouni, 207.
[8] Gray (1965), 159. See also Rahmouni (e.g., 331) for instances in which El is called "father."

Yahweh as El's Son

In *The Origins of Biblical Monotheism: Israel's Polytheistic Background and the Ugaritic Texts*, Mark Smith evinces that Yahweh is one of the "sons of the Elohim," as at Deuteronomy 32:8-9, part of the "Song of Moses":

> When the Most High gave to the nations their inheritance, when he separated the sons of men, he fixed the bounds of the peoples according to the number of the sons of God. For the LORD's portion is his people, Jacob his allotted heritage.

The "bounds of the peoples" refers to the numbering of 70 nations, after the 70 Canaanite gods. As one of El's sons, Yahweh would be the "son of the sun," a solar attribute.

Sons of the Most High

The verse at Deuteronomy 32:8 may be related to Psalm 82:6, in which the "sons of the Most High" (עליון *'elyown*) are discussed, appearing as bene Elyon in the Hebrew. After analyzing this passage in Psalms, Smith remarks: "If this supposition is correct, Psalm 82 preserves a tradition that casts the god of Israel in the role not of the presiding god of the pantheon but as one of his sons."[1] Moreover, biblical and Semitic languages scholar Dr. Michael S. Heiser notes that Psalms 82 and 89 reflect the "council of Elohim" in the clouds,[2] as is appropriate for astrotheological entities.

In the next verse in Deuteronomy (32:9), in which El assigns "the bounds of the peoples" (ethnoi), the tribal Lord to whom Jacob/Israel is allotted is יהוה *Yĕhovah*. In this pericope, then, Yahweh is evidently designated a "divine son" of El Elyon, the high god of the Canaanite pantheon given dominion over a "chosen people," much as El's sons were allotted lands or tribes in Canaanite mythology. This passage was written possibly during the time of Amos in the eighth century BCE, when Yahweh begins to dominate at Jerusalem.

In describing the "royal figure" of King El, "Father of the Exalted Ones," Gray remarks that "we may recognize 'El Elyon, called the Most High,' who, according to Eusebius' citation from Philo of Byblos was senior god in the Canaanite pantheon, or El Elyon, El the Most High, Creator of Heaven and Earth...locally worshipped in Jerusalem before David occupied the city."[3] Thus, El Elyon was the high god of Jerusalem before Jews took it over, adopting and adapting the deity by absorbing his characteristics into Yahweh, his "son."

In this regard, Gray states further of El Elyon that "many of his attributes were inherited by Yahweh through local association, the

---

[1] Smith, M. (2001), 48.
[2] Heiser, "Should the Plural אלהים of Psalm 82 Be Understood as Men or Divine Beings?," 3.1, 4.0.
[3] Gray (1965), 157.

phraseology and imagery of many of the old hymns finding new expression in the liturgy of the cult of Yahweh."[1] It should be recalled that El Elyon was a solar god of wine in particular, syncretized with other Semitic wine gods such as Eshkol, and the "most high" part of the mythology generally relates to the sun at its zenith. Hence, Yahweh too takes on solar and vinicultural attributes.

Several texts entitled the "Enthronement Psalms"[2] are "enriched" by Canaanite liturgies, and Gray also cites Psalm 72:8 as reflecting "the Canaanite conception of El reigning,"[3] establishing divine dominion: "May he have dominion from sea to sea, and from the River to the ends of the earth!" Thus, El prevails, as is the meaning of "Israel."

Yw, son of El

A northern Canaanite or Ugaritic text (KTU 2.4.13-14) includes the word "Yw," juxtaposed with the god-name Ym or Yamm,[4] suggesting Yw too is a theonym.[5] The Ugaritic text in question is titled "El's Proclamation of Yamm," which reads:

And Latipan El the Benefi[cient] speaks:

The name of my son (is?) Yw, O Elat. And he pronounces the name Yamm....[6]

Here it appears that Yw is one of El's sons or *bene Elohim*, previously discussed.

In a Canaanite myth, we read about the "building of a 'house' for a certain god." Concerning this god, Gray comments: "This favoured deity is apparently the son of El named Yw, the Beloved of El."[7] The resemblance between YHWH and YW is suggestive, and, again, it is contended that the subordinate Yahweh was considered originally the son of El, like Yw. The epithet "beloved of El" is also noteworthy in that much later we find in Christianity the "beloved son of God," Jesus Christ.

El's Wives Asherat and Anat

Like Abraham and Moses, El lived in the desert with two wives, Asherah and Anat, the latter of whom is called "virgin" yet bears El a son, as does Asherah. In Canaanite, Asherah is aṯrt, transliterated also as Aṯerat, Atherat or Asherat, serving as the mother goddess and

---

[1] Gray (1965), 157.
[2] E.g., Psalms 24, 29, 46, 95, 96, 97, 99, etc.
[3] Gray (1965), 158.
[4] Yamm is a Semitic sea god comparable to Poseidon/Neptune. As Mark Smith (151) remarks: "The cult of Yamm may have continued in the first millennium Phoenician cities, to judge from late classical sources. Third century coins attest to Poseidon as the sea-god of Beirut."
[5] Smith, M. (1994), 1.149.
[6] Smith, M. (1994), 1.132. The relevant Ugaritic is šm bny yw 'elat. (Gray, 1957:134)
[7] Gray (1965), 23.

"lady of the sea" who appears in later times as Astarte and Ishtar. Biblically, she is both Asherah[1] and Astoreth, also called Elat in Ugarit, cognate with the Arabic Allat. Aterat/Asherat/Asherah is depicted in Canaanite texts as prostrating herself before El and, like the Virgin Mary with God the Father, bearing him sons,[2] as noted.

Sons and Venus

One of Asherah and El's sons, Attar or Athtar/Ashtar, was styled "king" and identified with Venus as the morning star,[3] the same as Shahar in the Ugaritic texts. Ashtar is pre-Ugaritic, however, appearing in the Ebla texts centuries earlier.[4]

The two "sons" thus are aspects of Venus, equivalent to the son of Yahweh, King Jesus, called the "morning star" in the biblical book of Revelation (2:28, 22:16). Thus, we have a God the Father of the Morning Star over 1000 years before Jesus supposedly walked the earth.

In the Ugaritic texts, the morning and evening stars are also named "the cutter twins, sons of one day, the most beautiful sons of the Sun, who suck the nipple of Asherah's breasts."[5] Here these two are specifically named as sons of the sun, which is El.

These twin faces of Venus also marked the seasons within archaeoastronomy.[6] Similarly, in Isaiah 14 Venus is deemed "Lucifer" or Helel,[7] representing both Eosphoros and Phosphoros, the morning and evening aspects of Venus. At Isaiah 14:12, this figure is called "Hêlēl ben Šaḥar," the latter phrase denoting "son of Shahar," the morning aspect of Venus.

This situation is similar to that of Jesus's biblical father, Yahweh, who, unbeknownst to his many faithful, was also the consort of Asherah, as evidenced by a number of artifacts, including biblical inferences. For example, at 2 Kings 23:7, we learn that Yahweh and Asherah had been paired in the temple, much like the hierogamy or sacred marriage of Asherah and El or, later, Baal.[8] This inference is validated by inscriptions from the site of Kuntillet Ajrud in the northeastern Sinai (9th-8th cents. BCE), saying, "Yahweh of Samaria and his Asherah" and "Yahweh of Teman and his Asherah."[9] Here we

---

[1] Strong's H842.
[2] Arnold and Beyer, 54, 56.
[3] Gray (1965), 157, 76, 169, 177.
[4] Snell, 133.
[5] Dijkstra, 107.
[6] Dijkstra, 107.
[7] Strong's H1966.
[8] Oldenburg, 30ff. Schniedewind (19): "In the well-known Hebrew inscriptions from Kuntillet 'Arjrud and Khirbet el-Qom, Asherah seems to be the consort of the Israelite patron deity, Yahweh."
[9] "Asherah," *Wikipedia*: "Some biblical scholars believe that Asherah at one time was worshiped as the consort of Yahweh, the national God of Israel. There are references to the worship of numerous Gods throughout Kings, Solomon builds temples to many

also see Yahweh's reign from northern Israel, the capital of which was Samaria, to Teman, in the southeastern kingdom of Edom.

This switchover from El to Baal represents one of many instances of "jockeying for position" by various gods and goddesses that indicate mergers of different tribes and peoples, with their various tribal or familial deities demoted or raised according to social status. In such mergers, dominant cultures usually will receive the honor of "top god," so to speak. If we see, for example, the intrusion of a "father" or "son" in myths about gods, we can infer that, at that point, a new tribe or culture has been incorporated into the demographics. The same can be said with the prostration of gods or goddesses to each other, as a sign of respecting a higher authority under whose dominion the other deities must now fall.

Wine

When Asherah, the "mother of the gods," arrives at El's door and prostrates herself at his feet, he offers her food and drink:

Are you hungry...
or thirsty...?
Have something to eat or drink:
eat some food from the table,
drink some wine from the goblet,
blood of the vine from the golden cup.[1]

Here we can see the focus on wine, as the "blood of the vine" to be drunk from a "golden cup," another holy chalice/grail. These ideas obviously maintained currency for thousands of years before they were adopted into Christianity.

King

Biblically (1 Sa 12:12) and elsewhere, El (or Elohim) is called *melek*, denoting "king" but also serving as the name of the dreaded Molech and a title of Yahweh. Gray remarks that it is "now recognized by an increasing number of responsible scholars that Yahweh, the god of a militant tribal group, was first subordinated to El the Canaanite high god before he took over his attributes and functions as King and Creator."[2]

Gods during his reign and Josiah is reported as cutting down the statues of Asherah in the temple Solomon built for Yahweh. (Josiah's grandfather, Manasseh, had erected this statue. 2 Kings 21:7) Further evidence includes, for example, an 8th-century combination of iconography and inscriptions discovered at Kuntillet Ajrud in the northern Sinai desert where a storage jar shows three anthropomorphic figures and an inscription that refers to 'Yahweh ... and his Asherah.' Further evidence includes the many female figurines unearthed in ancient Israel, supporting the view that Asherah functioned as a goddess and consort of Yahweh, worshiped as the Queen of Heaven." Scholars continue to debate whether the term "Asherah" refers here to the goddess herself or merely to her groves or cult symbols, which would represent nevertheless a nod to goddess worship. See, e.g., Taylor, J.G. (1994), 54.

[1] Arnold and Beyer, 56.
[2] Gray (1965), 161.

Yahweh's ultimate supremacy ranks not as a divinely revealed reality but as a *cultural development* asserting that the Jewish tribal deity represents *the* God of the universe. This fact of El's initial supremacy over Yahweh had been surmised by many earlier scholars, confirmed later by more modern discoveries such as the Ras Shamra texts.

One verse in which Yahweh is called "king" appears at Psalm 95:3:

> For the LORD is a great God, and a great King above all gods.

כי **אל** גדול **יהוה ומלך** גדול על־כל־**אלהים**:

Here we see the words "El Yahweh Melek Elohim," in that order, reading only the bolded text right to left. The term מלך *melek* is utilized 2523 times in the Hebrew Bible, most of which are translated as "king" (2518).[1] Other renderings include "royal," "Hammelech," "Malcham," "Molech" and "Moloch."

As another example, Psalm 10:16 begins with יהוה מלך or "Yahweh melek." As we might expect with the emphasis of divine kingship, Yahweh receives this epithet of מלך *melek* many times in the Old Testament,[2] as noted. Since biblically we are told that the Israelites in fact did worship Molech, some of the uses of מלך *melek* to describe Yahweh may represent in reality an epithet reflecting the god's reverence, rather than simply denoting "king," as at Amos 5:26, previously noted.

Molech represented the brutal and fierce, burning aspect of the sun, reflected in the cruel and harsh nature of his worship.

El Shaddai

As seen, at Exodus 6:3 the god of Abraham was "God Almighty," אל שדי *'el Shadday* in the Hebrew, the name of a Mesopotamian tribal deity. Again, this epithet appears several times also in Genesis,[3] while the divine name שדי *Shadday* alone is used four dozen times in the OT/Tanakh to describe Yahweh. Cross notes that "Shaddai" is used as an epithet of God in the book of Job some 30 times, while "Yahweh" only appears in Job at the beginning and end of the book, as well as "in rubrics of the Yahweh speeches where it probably is secondary."[4] In reality, Shaddai serves as the name of a West Semitic god, another of the many Canaanite Elohim, possibly one of El's sons.

---

[1] Strong's H4428.
[2] See, e.g., Psalms 5:3, 44:5, 47:2, 68:25, 74:12, 84:4, etc.
[3] See, e.g., Genesis 17:1, 28:3, 35:11, 43:14, 48:3.
[4] Cross, 59-60.

Mountain God?

The word *shaddai* not only connotes "almighty" but also appears to be related to the Akkadian term *šadû*, meaning "mountain."[1] Concerning El Shaddai, Meissner remarks:

> The Shaddai element seems to mean "the mountain one" and to be related to other Western Semitic divine epithets known from Ugaritic sources. It also seems to refer to the cosmic mountain. Shaddai may be an epithet of Ba'al-Hadad... It cannot be established whether Shaddai was an old Amorite deity, brought to Palestine by the patriarchs and early identified by them with the Canaanite 'El, or whether Shaddai was originally a cultic epithet for the Canaanite 'El.[2]

El Shaddai seems to serve as a bridge between the Amorites and Canaanites, a perfect combination for his later Israelite followers. Meissner summarizes the Hebrew worship of El Shaddai thus:

> In the pre-Mosaic religion of the Hebrews, the chief god of the patriarchs was Shaddai.... The evidence suggests, first, that the principal deity of the pre-Mosaic patriarchs was a mountain god or a god cloaked with mountain imagery. 'El Shaddai was "the god of the mountain." Second, the Hebrews, like their Semitic ancestors, had a keen sense of relationship between a patriarchal group and its deity. The deity was actually a member of the clan and could be addressed as "father" or "brother." Albright (1957) has rejected the notion of an El monotheism among early Western Semites. El was probably a father-god in early Hebrew popular tradition. A son, Shaddai, appears in the form of a storm god.[3]

The inference that the early Hebrews were followers of El of the mountain seems logical for hill settlers. Mountains frequently create their own stormy weather, which explains that connection, while they also often are associated with the sun.

The Archer

Shaddai also may have been the name of an archer god or epithet of Yahweh as an archer. At Job 6:4, we read about Shaddai's poisonous arrows, as in the myth of the Syro-Palestinian god Resheph, whose menacing bow full of troubles and pestilence was stopped by Baal.[4] The "archer" is also a solar epithet, as in Apollo's title of "far-shooter" or "far-darter,"[5] signifying the sun's rays penetrating the atmosphere and earth, especially as piercing through

---

[1] Smith, M. (1994), 1.187.
[2] Meissner, 117.
[3] Meissner, 116.
[4] Walton (2009), 5.260. Job 6:4: "For the arrows of the Almighty are in me; my spirit drinks their poison; the terrors of God are arrayed against me."
[5] See, e.g., Aristotle's *Rhetoric* 3.8.6, in which the solar Apollo, the "Delos-born," is addressed as: "Golden-haired far-darter, son of Zeus." The original Greek is ἕκατος *hekatos*, translated also as "far-shooting" and "archer."

the black, dragonlike storm clouds. The "darts" or flashes of lightning are also dangerous solar aspects cited in the myth of Dionysus.[1]

Enlil and Ellil

Another storm god evidently connected to El is the Sumero-Babylonian lawgiver Enlil, whose name evidently was rendered "Ellil" in later Akkadian, Assyrian, Canaanite and Hittite texts. Ellil first appears in Assyrian writing during the reign of Amorite king Shamshi-Adad I in the 19th to 18th centuries BCE.[2] Ellil is surmised also to be the same as the Helel of Isaiah 14:12-15, in other words, Lucifer/Venus.[3]

Like Moses and Jesus, Enlil/Ellil was the mediator between the heavenly God (Anu) and man, and was the "king of kings."[4] Other epithets for Enlil/Ellil include "king of lands," "king of heaven and earth" and "father of the gods."[5] Like Yahweh, Enlil sends a flood to kill all of humanity, with one hero, Utnapishtim or Ziusudra/Xisuthros—clearly a Noah precursor—surviving with the help of the god Ea. Concerning the Utnapishtim-Noah connection, scholars such as Dr. Ben Foster, an Assyriologist at Yale University, assert unequivocally that "the details of the two stories are unmistakably the same story."[6] It is noteworthy that in the original Sumerian myth it is the *sun god*, Utu, who rescues humanity,[7] revealing Yahweh's solar nature in the same role as well.

Lord of the Storm

Enlil/Ellil means "Lord of the Storm," equivalent to Hadad/Adad. Enlil's role is also similar to that of the Egyptian atmospheric god Shu, who shares some basic symbolism with the Christian savior, called "Ye*shua*" in Hebrew.

As seen, it is probable that some of the Moses story was adapted from the storm-god mythos, such as the drowning of the prophet's enemies by conjuring the waters with his magic rod, which causes the Red Sea to part and then close upon the "dragon" pharaoh and his legions.

---

[1] See, e.g., Plutarch, *Symp. Quaes. Conv.* 1.6.2, in which a story about the Persian king Mithridates VI of Pontus (fl. 120–63 BCE) recounts that he was supposedly marked as an infant with lightning, ostensibly from Bacchus, which left a mark on his forehead. As an adult, he was purportedly hit by lightning again, which strikes appeared to make him a favorite of the gods, and "in those many dangers by lightning he bore some resemblance to the Theban Bacchus." (Plutarch/Goodwin, 3.220)
[2] Boardman, 223.
[3] See, e.g., Gallagher, "On the Identity of Hêlēl ben Šaḥar of Is. 14:12-15."
[4] West, 184.
[5] "Enlil," *Wikipedia*.
[6] "The Epic of Gilgamesh," *Annenberg Learner*.
[7] See, e.g., Kramer, 153.

Adad/Hadad

Depicted as mounting a bull in a similar way as the Persian god Mithra was portrayed later in Roman art, Adad is "the deity who became Baal *par excellence* in Canaan," originally "the god manifest in the violent rain- and thunder-storms of autumn and late winter."[1] Concerning Adad as storm god, Gray states:

> This is the role he seems to play in the Execration Texts, as indeed also in the Ras Shamra myth of the conflict with the Unruly Waters. It was only later that he was identified with the vegetation which was stimulated by the winter rains and he became a dying and rising god, as in the Ras Shamra myth of his conflict with Mot....[2]

The Egyptian "Execration Texts" are inscribed sherds and other artifacts from the second and third millennia BCE[3] that name enemies and alien disturbers of Egypt, used for magical purposes to end such troubles. It is in an execration text from around the 20th century BCE that we discover the first mention of "Jerusalem," then a proto-Israelite enclave, predating the purported time of David by 1,000 years.[4]

Gray specifically deems Adad/Hadad a "dying and rising god," as were many deities in antiquity, both male and female.[5] Again, the Ras Shamra texts with the related Adad-Mot myth date from the 13th or 14th century BCE.[6] Thus, the prophet, savior or god controlling and calming the "unruly waters" is a very ancient motif that predates Moses and Jesus's purported similar miracle by many centuries. This storm-calming is naturally an attribute of the sun and storm god, again often the same entity.

Baal

Adad was the quintessential Baal, "the thunderer who mounts the clouds"[7] and "rider of the clouds"[8] who fertilized the earth with his life-giving rain. In the Ras Shamra texts, Baal is depicted as dying and rising out of the underworld in his victory over the drought and

---

[1] Gray (1965), 153.
[2] Gray (1965), 153.
[3] Redford (1992:87) remarks: "The most precious source bearing on Egypt's relations with Asia in the late Middle Kingdom, the so-called Execration Texts, must be dated from about 1850 to 1750 B.C."
[4] Freedman, et al., 694–695.
[5] Although apologists claim otherwise, the scientific evidence remains clear concerning this mythical death-resurrection motif in many cultures in antiquity. See, e.g., *The Riddle of the Resurrection* by Mettinger. The resurrection of the god was popular also in Mesoamerica, based on observations of nature, not Christian influence.
[6] The Ugaritic word *mt* or *mōtu* means "death" and is cognate with the Hebrew מות *maveth* (H4194). (Schniedewind, 198)
[7] Frank, 80.
[8] Rahmouni, 288–291, etc.

pestilence god Mot.[1] He also appears with the "Virgin Anat,"[2] again, a goddess who is portrayed also as a mother.

Again, in the OT, Baal is equated with Yahweh, and Yahweh was assimilated to to the Canaanite god at the village of Dan in northern Israel during the sixth century BCE at the latest. It is important to note that in "many regions of the ancient Near East, not least in Upper Mesopotamia, Syria and Anatolia where agriculture relied mainly on rainfall, storm-gods ranked among the most prominent gods in the local panthea or were even regarded as divine kings, ruling over the gods and bestowing kingship on the human ruler."[3]

Conclusion

As part of the great solar tradition that can be found in many places globally, the peoples of the ancient Near and Middle East revered a wide variety of sun deities, including the Babylonian Shamash and "god of the fathers," as well as the Canaanite goddess Shapash. These deities possessed numerous divine epithets and attributes adopted by biblical figures such as Yahweh, Samson and Jesus.

Among these solar deities was the Semitic high god El, identified with Yahweh and Saturn, and appearing in the Bible numerous times as part of Israelite syncretism. Indeed, El may be the god of Exodus, associated with the bull and ram. El and the 70 Canaanite gods and "sons of El" thrived mythically on a holy mount, again part of ancient solar mythology signifying the sun and dodecans.

One of these "sons of God" appears to be the Jewish tribal god Yahweh, while others are the two aspects of Venus, dawn and dusk, born to El's dual wives. Another biblical god is El Shaddai, a mountain and solar deity as well, while storm gods such as Enlil and Adad often possess solar attributes as well, since it was believed in antiquity that the sun had a part in creating and controlling storms of various types.

El as the "Most High" or El Elyon was especially sacred to the Israelites and is not only solar but also a wine god, revealing the significance of that sacred libation as well.

---

[1] See, e.g., Russell (41), who refers to Baal's "return from the dead" as symbolizing the "return to life and fecundity." In the Ugaritic texts, the "prince, lord of the earth" Baal is represented clearly as dead, "lifted up" by Shapash, the "lamp of the gods." (Rahmouni, 57-58)

[2] Gray (1965), 159. The idea of the virgin mother who nevertheless has a consort and is depicted as engaging in "sex" appears to be difficult to grasp, but this parthenogenetic motif is well represented in mythology in many places globally. (See, e.g., *Virgin Mother Goddess of Antiquity* by Rigoglioso.) In very ancient myths, the goddess is portrayed as bringing forth without consort. She may be "raped" in later myths, in order to impose male dominance; however, she remains the virgin creatrix, because she is a *myth*, not a real person with genitalia. Hence, the debate about "maiden" and "virgin" is moot, as "virgin" is generally intended when dealing with creation myths, regardless of the deity's gender.

[3] Schwemer, "Abstract."

Fig. 94. Shamash between Mashu's Twin Peaks, wearing a horned helmet and with solar rays from shoulders and arms, 3rd millennium BCE. Akkadian, British Museum

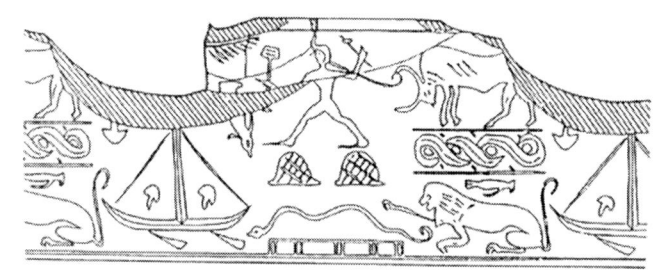

Fig. 95. Storm god Baal-Zephon holds a thunderbolt and stands on two mountains, with a serpent below, c. 16th cent. BCE. Cylinder seal from Tell el Daba/Avaris

Fig. 96. Mount Sinai (right), with St. Catherine's monastery at foot of Horeb (left), 1570-2. Oil painting by El Greco, Historical Museum of Crete, Iraklion

Yahweh and the Sun

"And he brought me into the inner court of the house of the LORD; and behold, at the door of the temple of the LORD, between the porch and the altar, were about twenty-five men, with their backs to the temple of the LORD, and their faces toward the east, worshiping the sun toward the east."

Ezekiel 8:16

"And he put down the idolatrous priests, whom the kings of Judah had ordained to burn incense in the high places in the cities of Judah, and in the places round about Jerusalem; them also that burned incense unto Baal, to the sun, and to the moon, and to the planets, and to all the host of heaven.... And he took away the horses that the kings of Judah had given to the sun, at the entering in of the house of the LORD...and burned the chariots of the sun with fire."

2 Kings 23:5, 11

"And he removed out of all the cities of Judah the high places and the sun-images...

"...And they broke down the altars of the Baals in his presence; and the sun-pillars that were on high above them he cut down... and he broke down the altars, and beat the Asherahs and the graven images into powder, and cut down all the sun-pillars throughout the land of Israel, and returned to Jerusalem."

1 Chronicles 14:5, 34:4, 34:6 (Darby)

"Archaeological findings also testify to the existence of a cult of sun worship in ancient Israel. Archaeological findings and biblical evidence confirm close relations between God and the sun, and the heavenly body is seen as similar to God. In many cases, the sun symbolizes God as a kind of portrait. However, the sun was apparently not conceived as an image, but rather as part of divine revelation."

Dr. Pnina Galpaz-Feller, Samson: The Hero and the Man (33)

BIBLICAL AND JUDEO-CHRISTIAN tradition asserts that the Jewish tribal god was transcendent, beyond all visible phenomena such as the sun, moon, planets, stars and so on, thus making him superior to and creator of these entities. Using circular reasoning, it is averred that, since the Bible is "God's Word," Yahweh must be the one true divine power of the cosmos. This vaunted impression, however, is a late theological development, and it is known from scriptures such as Ezekiel 8:16 and 2 Kings 23:5-11 that the Jews indeed worshipped the sun, as well as the moon, stars and so on, sharing the polytheistic astral religion of their neighbors and predecessors.

In several ancient traditions, the patriarch Abraham is depicted as a renowned astronomer who taught that science to the Phoenicians, after having learned it from the star-gazing Chaldeans, identified by Hecataeus as the priests of the Babylonians.[1] Concerning Jewish sky-watching, Baker comments:

> The Jews were famous as astronomers, although this is rarely noted. Theophrastus, a Greek writing at the end of the fourth century BCE, said: "The Jews converse with each other about the deity, and at night time they make observations of the stars, gazing at them and calling on God in prayer." Little is known of their ancient astronomy, although it is interesting to note that most of the evidence for names of stars and constellations is found in Job, which is either old or consciously archaising and depicts the older ways: Aldebaran and the Hyades, known as "the Moth," the Pleiades, known as "the Cluster"; Orion, known as "the Stupid One"; and the Chambers of the South (Job 9.9); Ursa Major, known as "the Winnowing Fan," an unidentified "Chamber"; Canis Major and Sirius, known as "the Hairy Ones" or "the Evil Ones" (Job 38:13...); and the *mazzārôt* (Job 38:32)...[2]

These celestial bodies are depicted in the Bible as sentient beings, as at Job 38:7, which speaks of "when the morning stars sang together, and all the sons of God shouted for joy..."[3] The "sons of God" in this verse are the bene Elohim, the sons of the solar El previously discussed, who symbolize the stars and of whom Yahweh evidently was one.

Again, Yahweh possesses numerous attributes of other, often older gods, seemingly as many as the Jewish scribes and mythmakers could find, rolled into one, in order to assert superiority and dominance over all other deities. Included among these many characteristics are solar aspects that link this tribal god to other deities of the Mediterranean, such as those whom Macrobius deemed solar in nature.

As stated, in other, older religious and mythological systems such as the Egyptian and Indian we also find a transcendent creator God or Goddess "above" the sun, moon, stars and so on. Hence, even this sublime god-concept is not new and unique to Judaism, and does not represent evidence that the Bible is indeed God's word.

Origins and History

How far back the god Yahweh can be traced remains inconclusive, but we do have some indications. In this regard, Delitzsch discusses the appearance of personal names among the

---

[1] Diodorus 1.28.1. See, e.g., Gmirkin, 35.
[2] Baker (2012), vol. 1.
[3] See, e.g., Isaiah 14:12; Jude 1:13.

North Semitic tribes who "settled in Babylonia about 2500 B.C.,"¹ including "God has given," "God with me," "Belonging to God" and so on. As evidence, the German theologian presents three small clay tablets from the Department of Assyrian and Egyptian Antiquities at the British Museum that date to the reign of Hammurabi's father, Sin-Muballit (fl. c. 1792 BCE). On these tablets from the 18th century BCE appear variations of cuneiform rendered by Delitzsch as *"Yahwè is God."*

Fig. 97. Cuneiform 'Yahwè is god' tablets from Babylon, 18th cent. BCE. (Rogers, R.W., 91)

Ia - a' - ve - ilu
Ia - ve - ilu
Ia - 'ú - um - ilu

Fig. 98. Cuneiform of North Semitic 'Jau is God,' 18th cent. BCE. (Rogers, R.W., 91)

Concerning Delitzsch's reading of these texts, Rev. Dr. Robert W. Rogers (1893-1929), professor of biblical exegesis at Drew University, remarks: "There can be no doubt that Ja-u-um-li is to be read 'Jau is god'; it is exactly the equivalent of the biblical name Joel."² While this purported evidence of early theophoric YHWH names remains debated, this god-name could have been part of pre-Israelite Semitic tradition, such as the "use of *ya-wi* in Amorite personal names."³

The Amorites comprised the North Semitic tribes who settled in Babylon around 2500 BCE and whose Canaanite pantheon may have included not only El or *ilu* but also at some point Iave or YHWH, apparently as El's son. The evident fact that the proto-Israelite nomads called Shasu of Yhw were part of the Amorites would explain how North Semitic language and YHWH ended up in Judea, dawning from Seir. It should be recalled that the Arab version of the solar Dionysus, Orotalt, likewise reigned in Seir.

As shown, YHWH as the dominant god appears to be a later development out of the Semitic tradition, and Yahweh or "Jehovah" was but one of many variations of this Semitic theonym, with other forms transliterated thus:

> Jehovah *Jehova* (Hebrew)
>
> Also known as: Ahiah, Hehuah, Iah, Iaw, Ie, Ieu, Ieui, Jah, Jahve, Jahweh, Jaldabaoth, Jao, Jhvh, Jhwh, Jod-heh-vav-heh', Yahowah, Yahu, Yahveh, Yahweh, Yaw, Yehoveh, Yhwh.⁴

The sacred name or tetragrammaton יהוה YHWH has been found in paleo-Hebrew on the Mesha stele (c. 840 BCE) and on ostraka or

---

¹ Waardenburg, 169.
² Rogers, R., 93. יואל *Yow'el*, meaning "Yahweh is God" (H3100).
³ Goedicke, 289.
⁴ Coulter and Turner, 250.

potsherds from Israel dating to the ninth century BCE. Although the exact etymology and pronunciation of YHWH remain unknown, "some scholars trace it through the Phoenicians, as an appellation for the sun."[1]

To Be or Create?

As concerns the etymology of YHWH, Cross remarks that the "accumulated evidence...strongly supports the view that the name *Yahweh* is a causative imperfect of the Canaanite-Proto-Hebrew verb *hwy*, 'to be.'"[2] Elsewhere, we read:

> The original pronunciation of YHWH was lost many centuries ago, but the available evidence indicates that it was in all likelihood Yahweh, meaning approximately "he causes to be" or "he creates." The origins of the god are unclear: One influential suggestion, although not universally accepted, is that the name originally formed part of a title of the Canaanite supreme deity El, *el dū yahwī ṣaba'ôt*: "El who creates the hosts," meaning the heavenly army accompanying El as he marched out beside the earthly armies of Israel. The alternative proposal connects it with a place-name south of Canaan mentioned in Egyptian records from the Late Bronze Age.[3]

Yahweh thus may have begun as a "creator" epithet of the god El, while the *place-name* Yahu "appears to be associated with Asiatic nomads in the 14th to 13th centuries BCE." The same word, Yahu, as a Jewish *god-name* can be found also in the Aramaic papyri from Elephantine (5th cent. BCE).[4]

El Yah

An inscription dating to the Late Bronze Age (c. 1220 BCE) from a temple at Lachish, southwest of Jerusalem, contains the phrase "El Yah," providing evidence of these two gods' syncretic nature at that time. During that era, the area was occupied by Jebusites, Hittites and Amorites: "The Jebusites were of mixed Amorite and Hittite blood,"[5] the same mixture as the later Israelites according to Ezekiel 16:3, previously noted.

Baker points out that the god-name El is older than Yahweh and that it should have faded away by the time of the Exile centuries later, if the Pentateuch represents "history." However, El continues to be popular in biblical writings, increasingly so, as "the writings from the exilic period and later use El more frequently than the earlier texts."[6] This fact appears to be at odds with the biblical Yahwist henotheism.

---

[1] Houghton, 265.
[2] Cross, 65.
[3] Adapted from *Wikipedia*'s "Yahweh" article.
[4] Parke-Taylor, 80.
[5] "Ancient Jerusalem."
[6] Baker (1992), 20.

Solar Yahwism

We have seen already how Yahweh is identified with or possesses the attributes of several pre-Israelite, Semitic solar, storm and fertility deities such as Shamash, Baal, El and Adad. Along with his tabernacle and numerous other elements with astronomical or astrotheological meaning, Yahweh himself has many solar characteristics, previously discussed and delineated further by biblical scholar Rev. Dr. J. Glen Taylor in *Yahweh and the Sun: Biblical and Archaeological Evidence for Sun Worship in Ancient Israel.* Indicating its pervasiveness, Taylor calls this Jewish sun worship "solar Yahwism," remarking:

> Several lines of evidence, both archaeological and biblical, bear witness to a close relationship between Yahweh and the sun. The nature of that association is such that often a "solar" character was presumed for Yahweh. Indeed, at many points the sun actually represented Yahweh as a kind of "icon." Thus, in at least the vast majority of cases, biblical passages which refer to sun worship in Israel do not refer to a foreign phenomenon borrowed by idolatrous Israelites, but to a Yahwistic phenomenon which Deuteronomistic theology came to look upon as idolatrous.... an association between Yahweh and the sun was not limited to one or two obscure contexts, but was remarkably well integrated into the religion of ancient Israel.[1]

Yahweh's solar nature was suppressed in later centuries, when the Deuteronomist theology began to be developed, evidently during the eighth to sixth centuries BCE.

Nevertheless, the solar Yahwist mythology continued into the common era with the second book of Enoch (1st cent. AD/CE?), among other writings and artifacts. In 2 Enoch, the pseudepigraphic author purporting to be the patriarch himself describes his vision of God in solar terms: "I have seen the Lord's eyes shining like the sun's rays and filling the eyes of man with wonder."[2] This description reminds one of Moses's shining face (Exod 34:29, 35) and Jesus during his transfiguration (Mt 17:2).

Pseudo-Enoch continues with his depiction of Yahweh, including storm-god attributes: "...I heard the words of the Lord, like incessant great thunder and hurling clouds."[3]

Dating the previous century or two, the first book of Enoch has a distinct "sun angel," Shamshiel or שמשיאל in the Aramaic and Σεμιήλ in Greek, also transliterated as Samsâpêêl, Shamshel, Shamsiel or Shashiel. Shamshiel is one of the "Watchers" in that mysterious book, called by a name that means "sun of God."

---

[1] Taylor, J.G. (1993), 257.
[2] Barnstone, 7.
[3] Barnstone, 7.

Sun Artifacts

In his book *The Early History of God: Yahweh and the Other Deities in Ancient Israel*, Mark Smith includes a chapter entitled, "Yahweh and the Sun." In this chapter, Smith provides a subsection, "The Assimilation of Solar Imagery," commenting upon the biblical "chariots of the sun" and several other solar artifacts and biblical verses:

> In its denunciation of various temple practices, 2 Kings 23:11 includes "the chariots of the sun" (*markĕbôt haššemeš*). The picture is apparently one of chariots carrying the sun on its course, being pulled by horses. Archaeological findings may add to this picture. Horse figurines with a sun disk above their heads have been discovered at Iron Age levels at Lachish, Hazor and Jerusalem. The uppermost register of the tenth-century stand from Taanach likewise bears a sun disk above the body of a young bull. At Ramat Rahel, two seals dating to the Persian period (ca. 587-333) depict bulls with solar disks between their heads. Finally, the imagery of divine wings, as in Psalms 17:18, 36:7, 57:1, 61:64 and 63:7, invites comparison with the winged sun disk represented on pre-exilic seals (although the imagery could have coalesced with the iconography of the cherubim in the Judean temple). It would appear from Ezekiel 8:16 and 2 Kings 23:11 that either solar worship or worship of a solarized Yahweh took place in the temple during the waning years of the Judean monarchy.[1]

As can be seen, the sun was associated with the chariot, horse and bull, the latter as in the "golden calf." Included in Smith and Taylor's analysis is an artifact called the Taanach cult stand (10th cent. BCE), which uses a depiction of a sun disk above a bull to represent YHWH.[2]

Several scriptures refer to חמנים *chammanim*, often translated as "incense altars," serving as part of the polytheistic Semitic worship.[3] These artifacts are mentioned in 1 Chronicles 14 and 34, for example, rendered by various translations as "sun images," "sun pillars" or "sun idols."[4] The apparent sun pillars or statues were to be destroyed along with the *asherim* and other cult objects, and are surmised to have been dedicated particularly to the solar Baal.[5]

There are many other artifacts and scriptures in which solar imagery is applied to Yahweh, including Deuteronomy 33:2, previously discussed as depicting the god's dawning from the east and shining forth over the mountain, with his fiery flame. Another solar scripture appears at 2 Samuel 23:4, concerning the God/Rock of Israel, about whom we read that "he dawns on [men] like the

---

[1] Smith, M. (2002), 151-152.
[2] Taylor, J.G. (1994), 55ff.
[3] Lev 26:30; 2 Chr 14:5, 34:4, 34:7; Isa 17:8, 27:9; Eze 6:4, 6:6.
[4] Strong's H2553.
[5] See, e.g., McClintock and Strong, 4.469-470.

morning light, like the sun shining forth upon a cloudless morning, like rain that makes grass to sprout from the earth."

LMLK Seals

We have discussed already the biblical association of Jesus with the "sun of righteousness" with "healing on its wings," invoking very old solar symbolism and a winged sun disk. As another example, "pottery found throughout Judea dated to the end of the 8th century BC has seals resembling a winged sun disk burned on their handles...argued to be the royal seal of the Judean Kingdom."[1] The pre-exile seals are called "LMLK," referring to the Hebrew letters *lamedh mem lamedh kaph*, which connote "belongs to" or ownership, specifically of clay jars during Hezekiah's reign. This fact is ironic, since Hezekiah is depicted as a violent reformer king and reputed destroyer of idols.

Fig. 99. Winged sun disk, c. 700 BCE. LMLK seal, Judea

Demonstrating the solar symbol's ongoing importance, another Judean pottery sherd from the seventh century BCE owned by the "king of Zph" depicts the two-winged sun disk.[2]

It is significant that the archaeological site at Lachish has produced more of these LMLK seals than any other location and that paleo-Hebrew ostraca have been discovered there as well, with its long history of El Yah worship and mixture of proto-Israelite Amoritish peoples.

Yah, Jah, Yahh

In the Bible, another name for the Lord is יה *Yahh*, *Yah* or *Jah*, as at Psalm 14:35.[3] As noted, יה *Yahh* is used 49 times in the Old Testament and is considered an "abbreviation," "contraction" or "shortened form" of Yahweh, although some have submitted that *Yah* is an older, more primitive usage.

As an example of Yah, at Psalm 68:4 the singer says:

שירו לאלהים זמרו שמו סלו לרכב בערבות ביה שמו ועלזו לפניו:

> Sing to God [Elohim], sing praises to his name [Shem]; lift up a song to him who rides upon the clouds; his name [Shem] is the LORD [Yah], exult before him!

---

[1] "Akhenaten," *Wikipedia*. More information about this subject of the solar nature of Yahweh and his son, Jesus, can be found in *Suns of God* and *Jesus as the Sun throughout History*.
[2] See, e.g., "The LMLK Research Website," which discusses some 1,000 pottery handles with royal inscriptions on them, many of which have two- or four-winged representations.
[3] Strong's H3050.

The solar imagery of Elohim Yah riding upon the clouds, like Helios/Apollo in his chariot, is evident in this verse, especially when one considers the apparent *shem-shemesh* connection. In the same psalm (68:4, 8-9), as well as at Psalm 104:3 and Deuteronomy 33:26, Yahweh is depicted as riding through the skies upon clouds and creating rain.

Sun and Shield

Another solar scripture is Psalm 84:11:

For the LORD God is a sun and shield.

The relevant Hebrew is:

שמש ומגן יהוה אלהים

Shemesh magen Yahweh Elohim

Again, *shemesh* or *shamash* means "sun" and is the name of the Babylonian sun god. *Magen* denotes "shield," as in the "Magen David" or "Star of David" of the modern era, giving it also a stellar connotation. A possible intention of this verse would be to identify "Yahweh Elohim" as or with Shamash.

To reiterate, there are many such biblical verses and other extrabiblical proofs of Yahweh's solar nature,[1] another of which is his mythical appearance at Exodus 3:2 as an "eternally burning bush," resembling a sun with a corona of rays.

Psalm 104

Biblical sun worship thus is evident in numerous texts, including Psalm 104, previously discussed. Scholars have continued to debate how the parallels between Psalm 104 and Akhenaten's "Hymn to the Sun" came about, whether there is direct influence or derivation through the Phoenicians or Canaanites, but a relationship is evident.

In this regard, John Day remarks:

> It is clear enough that Psalm 104 has some elements reflecting Canaanite mythology, such as the storm god and conflict with the waters motifs and the bringing of rain attested in vv. 1-18 (and the use of the name Leviathan in v. 26). Dion has rightly argued that Psalm 104 constitutes an amalgamation of Canaanite storm god and Egyptian Sun god motifs to Yahweh—vv. 1-18 and 20-30 respectively. ...
>
> ....Eventually an Israelite author combined motifs from Akhenaten's Sun hymn with other motifs originating in the Canaanite storm god (vv. 1-18), thus producing the psalm we now have.[2]

The full title of Dion's article is entitled: "YHWH as Storm-God and Sun-God: The Double Legacy of Egypt and Canaan as reflected in

---

[1] See also *Suns of God* and *Jesus as the Sun*.
[2] Gillingham, 223-224.

Psalm 104." In any event, the inclusion of this solar hymn reveals Israelite sun worship.

Tempestuous Yahweh

Like other sun gods, Yahweh had a tempestuous side, in which he served as a storm god, controlling the weather. Yahweh's storm-god and/or weather-controlling aspects are exemplified at Job 38:1, 9, 25-29, 34-37; Psalm 18:10-14; Isaiah 19:1; and Ezekiel 1:4, 28. His apparent Ugaritic predecessor Yw, son of El, may have been a storm deity as well, like Hadad/Adad, also identified with Baal and Yahweh.

Yahweh's stormy attributes are laid plain in these various biblical books, equating him with Baal, Adad, Marduk and Seth, among others. As another example, one word for "storm" or "storm-wind" in Hebrew is סופה *cuwphah*,[1] used at Numbers 21:14 to describe the miracle at the Red Sea.

Yahweh's meteorological attributes are exemplified also in the cloud by which he leads the Israelites through the desert, where, upon Mt. Sinai and in the tabernacle, Yahweh likewise appears to Moses from the middle of a cloud.[2]

In the Pentateuch, the word "cloud" (ענן *'anan)* is employed some 42 times in relationship to Yahweh. For example, Exodus 16:10 reads:

> And as Aaron spoke to the whole congregation of the people of Israel, they looked toward the wilderness, and behold, the glory of the LORD appeared in the cloud.

In reality, it is the radiant glory of the *sun* that appears in or through the clouds.

Mazzaroth/Mazzaloth

In addition to blatant and hidden sun worship, Israelite astronomical or astrotheological knowledge is demonstrated by numerous other elements in the Bible, including what is called the מזרה *mazzarah*. This latter term appears at Job 38:32) and usually is transliterated as "Mazzaroth" or "Mazzaloth." Strong's defines מזרה *mazzarah* as "the 12 signs of the Zodiac and their 36 associated constellations."[3] The LXX renders the term μαζουρωθ *mazouroth*, while the Vulgate translates *mazzarah* as *luciferum*, meaning "light-

---

[1] Strong's H5492.
[2] Exodus 24:16: "The glory of the LORD settled on Mount Sinai, and the cloud covered it six days; and on the seventh day he called to Moses out of the midst of the cloud."
[3] Strong's H4216. It is significant that the apparent root of *mazzarah* is *nazar*, also the root of Nazarite and Nazareth (Strong's H5144); hence, instead of "Jesus of Nazareth," the mythical New Testament figure might be labeled "the sun of the Mazzaroth." Thus, the "inn" where Jesus is "born" could represent one of the lodging places or inns of the sun.

bearer" and referring also to the morning/day star or dawn aspect of Venus.

At 2 Kings 23:5, we find the related word מַזָּלוֹת *mazzalah*, defined as "constellations" and "signs of zodiac (maybe),"[1] also rendered "planets" in English translations, μαζουρωθ *mazouroth* in the LXX and *duodecim signis* or "twelve signs" in the Vulgate.

Regarding מַזָּרָה *mazzarah*, Gesenius says:

> מַזָּרָה...lodging places, inns...of the sun. The Hebrews gave this name to the twelve signs of the Zodiac, called in [Arabic] the circle of palaces; these were imagined to be the lodging-places of the sun during the twelve months...[2]

Here we see that the 12 zodiacal signs represent "lodging places," "inns of the sun" and "palaces," in which the sun abides.

Stations and Mansions of the Sun

Analyzing the biblical use of the term "Mazzaroth," Rev. Dr. Edward Greswell (1797-1869) comments that the zodiac is "divided out into twelve equal parts, each of which is visited by the sun, and each is occupied by the sun, in its turn; and therefore so long as the sun is passing through it, and is as yet confined within its limits, each may be regarded as the house or chamber of the sun for the time being."[3]

Hence, the ancients viewed the sun as visiting, residing in and passing through the signs, stations, mansions and houses of the zodiac, the primitive origin of which may date back 5,000 or more years,[4] while its classical Babylonian/Chaldean rendition has been dated to the early first millennium BCE.[5] Moreover, various individual constellations may have been devised many thousands of years before that, such as recounted by Brian R. Pellar, who cites

---

[1] Strong's H4208.
[2] *Gesenius*, cccclxi.
[3] Greswell, 3.251.
[4] In his book *The Astronomy of the Bible* (161), Christian royal astronomer Dr. E. Walter Maunder traces the roots of the Babylonian zodiac to some 5,000 years ago. Richard D. Flavin has made the case that the "Karanovo stamp seal," a Chalcolithic Bulgarian artifact, contains a rudimentary form of the zodiac dating to between 5,000 and 7,000 years ago. The Egyptians also may have possessed a crude type of zodiac predating the classical Babylonian. (See Murdock 2009:266ff) Indian Brahmanic astronomers lay claim to a zodiac from thousands of years ago as well. John Rogers (10-11) thinks the Dendera zodiac "seems to be a complete copy of the Mesopotamian zodiac," as it is nearly identical to the Seleucid zodiac. Rogers suggests investigating whether or not the zodiac originated in Elam, east of Sumer, rather than Sumer itself.
[5] In an article representing current mainstream consensus, *Wikipedia* states: "The classical zodiac is a modification of the [Sumero-Babylonian] MUL.APIN catalogue, which was compiled around 1000 BC. Some of the constellations can be traced even further back, to Bronze Age (Old Babylonian) sources." Another article states that the MUL.APIN was created between the 14th and 12th centuries BCE ("History of constellations," *Wikipedia*).

scholarship that some were mapped possibly up to 100,000 years ago.¹

Manzaltu/Manzazu

The Catholic Encyclopedia also discusses these "stations" or "abodes of the gods," asserting that the zodiacal signs long predate the purported period of the biblical Exodus:

> Long before the Exodus the Twelve Signs were established in Euphratean regions much as we know them now. Although never worshipped in a primary sense, they may have been held sacred as the abode of deities. The Assyrian *manzaltu* (sometimes written *manzazu*), "station," occurs in the Babylonian Creation tablets with the import "mansions of the gods"; and the word appears to be etymologically akin to *Mazzaloth*, which in rabbinical Hebrew signifies primarily the Signs of the Zodiac. The lunar Zodiac, too, suggests itself in this connection. The twenty-eight "mansions of the moon" (*menazil al-kamar*) were the leading feature of Arabic sky-lore, and they served astrological purposes among many Oriental peoples.²

This Semitic term for "stations" or "mansions of the gods," *manzaltu/manzazu*, may predate the Hebrew *mazzaroth* by centuries.

Thus, the Semitic reverence for the zodiac extends back thousands of years and represents "stations," a possible precedent for the "stations of the cross" in the Christ myth as well. We also possess in this motif a likely explanation for the enigmatic scripture at John 14:2, in which Jesus is made to say, "In my father's house are many mansions."³

The book of Job, in which the mazzaroth appears, has been considered traditionally to be among the oldest writings in the Bible, but modern scholarship suggests it was composed between the sixth and fourth centuries BCE.⁴ This dating would allow for Neo-Babylonian astral mythology to have been incorporated into the text, acquired during the so-called exile of the sixth century and afterwards. It is also likely, however, that the Israelites prior to that time were somewhat knowledgeable about astronomy and astrology, since their deities were astrotheological in significant part.

---

¹ Pellar, "The Foundation of Myth: A Unified Theory on the Link Between Seasonal/Celestial Cycles, the Precession, Theology, and the Alphabet/Zodiac."
² Herbermann, 2.31.
³ The original Greek for "mansion" is μονή *monē* (G3438), which also means "abode" and which connotes "monastery" in current parlance.
⁴ This motif of "righteous suffering man and his god" has been found in older Sumerian, Babylonian and Egyptians texts, and appears to be a fictional genre, rather than a literal history. (See "The 'Job motif' in earlier literature.") As such, the book of Job may include oral tradition and give the appearance of a text more archaic than when it was written down or composed initially, drawing upon older writings.

Jewish Zodiacs

The Israelite reverence for sun worship extends from the ethnicity's inception into the common era, during the late Classical and Byzantine periods, when zodiacs appear in synagogues and include imagery of the Greek sun god Helios. Zodiac panels have been discovered at the synagogues of Hammath Tiberias, Sepphoris, Beth Alpha, Naaran, Susiya, Ussefiyeh and Ein Gedi,[1] dating back to as early as the fourth century AD/CE and for centuries afterwards.

Regarding the Jewish zodiac, in "Mosaics as Midrash: The Zodiacs of the Ancient Synagogues and the Conflict between Judaism and Christianity," art historian Yaffa England remarks:

> The zodiac, with Helios at the center, found in five synagogues from the fourth to sixth century is a riddle to this day. It has been suggested that it may be a consequence of pagan influence on non-Rabbinic, "Hellenistic" Jews or evidence of belief in evil spirits, black magic and astrology among the Jews of Israel. Alternatively, it is even seen as evidence that some Jews worshipped Helios as a minor deity.[2]

In this regard, J. Glen Taylor remarks that "in Jewish incantations and prayers of the Graeco-Roman period we find such prayers as 'Hail Helios, thou God in the heavens, your name is mighty...'"[3]

Based also on the statements by Philo and Josephus equating the 12 tribes of Israel with the signs of the zodiac,[4] along with various biblical verses, it is evident that Jewish regard for the zodiac and its divisions of 12 dates back centuries before the common era. Furthermore, the reverence for Helios dovetails with the Semitic worship of the solar Yahweh, El, Baal and Shamash.

Ezekiel's Godly Visions

Knowing these facts of Jewish astrolatry, the enigmatic imagery in the biblical book of Ezekiel (c. 6th cent. BCE) can be analyzed as depicting many aspects of astral religion/astrotheology. In this regard, Ezekiel's mysterious vision in chapter 1 has been said for centuries to have occurred at the summer solstice, the same as the 17th day of the fourth month, as represented in the Slavonic version of *The Book of Enoch*.[5] Summer solstice myths hold that the solar hero attains to his or her full glory at this time of year, when the days are the longest and are victorious over the night or "prince of darkness."

---

[1] See, e.g., Rachel Hachlili's *Ancient Mosaic Pavements*.
[2] Avery-Peck, 11.
[3] Taylor, J.G. (1994), 61.
[4] Philo, *Moses* 3.12; Philo/Yonge (1855), 3.99; Josephus *Ant.* 3.8; Josephus/Whiston, 75. See discussion in text below.
[5] van Goudoever, 74.

Four Living Creatures

In his account, the heavens open, and Ezekiel sees "visions of God." The word and hand of the Lord are upon the prophet, who recounts at 1:4-6:

> As I looked, behold, a stormy wind came out of the north, and a great cloud, with brightness round about it, and fire flashing forth continually, and in the midst of the fire, as it were gleaming bronze.
>
> And from the midst of it came the likeness of four living creatures. And this was their appearance: they had the form of men, but each had four faces, and each of them had four wings.

In this tempestuous vision portraying storm mythology, these four living creatures are called "cherubim" (Ezek 11:22), who, along with the seraphim or "burning ones" on the ark of the covenant, represent "personifications respectively of the dragonlike storm clouds and the serpentine lightnings."[1]

Ezekiel's "four living creatures" are described as having the faces of a man, lion, ox and eagle (1:10ff):

> As for the likeness of their faces, each had the face of a man in front; the four had the face of a lion on the right side, the four had the face of an ox on the left side, and the four had the face of an eagle at the back.[2]

Fig. 100. Anonymous, *Ezekiel's Vision*, 1670. Copy from *Iconum Biblicarum* by Matthaeus Merian the Elder

The four in Ezekiel could be equated with the faces of Baal Tetramorphos, who "had four visages—those of lion, bull, dragon and human—and reported to have been erected centuries earlier in a temple in Jerusalem."[3]

In the *Egyptian Book of the Dead*, we read about the "four *Khus*" or eternal spirits "who are in the train of the lord of the universe,"[4] evoking similar imagery, especially in consideration of the role of *khus* in adoring the setting sun and possessing other solar and stellar aspects, previously discussed.

Another related quartet would be Macrobius's four solar aspects of Hades, Zeus, Helios and Dionysus, which likely represents an earlier configuration.

---

[1] Palmer, 93. "Cherubim" (Heb. כרובים *kĕruwbim*) is the plural of "cherub," meaning "angel." (Strong's H3742)

[2] See also Ezekiel 10:14: "And every one had four faces: the first face was the face of the cherub, and the second face was the face of a man, and the third the face of a lion, and the fourth the face of an eagle."

[3] Tomlinson, 270.

[4] Budge (1898), 156, rendering chapters/spells 96 and 97 in the Papyrus of Nu.

Fixed Signs

Ezekiel's vision has been linked to the synagogue zodiacs with Helios and his quadriga chariot in the center:

> Here is the sun, indeed at the center of the universe, in a chariot controlled by a charioteer, in a vision recalling Ezekiel's vision of the divine chariot (Ezekiel 1). The charioteer is God, in control of the four horses, over and above the stars and the constellations, that is, over fate and destiny.[1]

Ezekiel's four beasts evidently symbolize the fixed points of the zodiac, the man equated with Aquarius, the ox or cherub with Taurus, the lion with Leo and the eagle with Scorpio. These points represent the signs immediately after the winter solstice, vernal equinox, summer solstice and autumnal equinox, respectively.

The association of these biblical four with the solstices and equinoxes or seasons may be indicated by the presence of the seasons in the corners of the synagogue zodiacs, serving as the four "living creatures" pulling the solar chariot.[2]

Concerning this equation, van Goudoever comments:

> The Glory of the Lord, which was seen by Ezekiel, is elsewhere called "Chariot of the Cherubim" and can easily be recognised as a kind of "sun-chariot." The four "living creatures" are supposed to correspond to four signs of the Zodiac.... In agreement herewith the future city is described as having 12 gates, three gates for each direction.... And in his vision of the future Temple, Ezekiel saw the Glory of the Lord returning through the eastern gate.[3]

Thus, Ezekiel's chariot is that of the sun and zodiac, with the 12 "gates" or signs and an eastern entrance where the sun god rises.

The Chariot or Merkabah of the Sun

The coglike "wheel within a wheel" of Ezekiel 1:16 thus could describe not only a sun chariot but also a zodiacal configuration. Concerning Ezekiel's cherubim, wings and wheels, Jamieson, Fausset and Brown mention the "symbolical figures, somewhat similar" of the Chaldeans/Assyrians that "symbolize the astronomical zodiac, or the sun and celestial sphere, by a circle of wings or irradiations."[4]

These "wheels" or *ophanim*, a word referring also to an order of angels,[5] make up the sapphire-like "throne" or "chariot"[1] (*merkabah*)

---

[1] Zanger, "Jewish Worship, Pagan Symbols," *Bible History Daily*.
[2] van Goudoever, 74.
[3] van Goudoever (72-72) subsequently attempts to assert that this situation in Ezekiel had "nothing to do with sun worship." As it assuredly *did* have to do with sun worship, it is possible that here it is Ezekiel's own bias being repeated, as he tried to dissociate the true Israel from such "false worship." In order to do so, the prophet pretended that the glory of the sun and that of Yahweh were separate attributes.
[4] Jamieson, et al., 1.568.
[5] See Dead Sea Scroll 4Q405. See also Nitzan, 12.313.

of conveyance in which, Ezekiel 1:26-28 claims, rides the Lord, as we have seen in the "Yahu" coin from Gaza, for example.

Again, a common portrayal of the sun god can be found at 2 Kings (23:11), in the "chariots of the sun," essentially Helios and his quadriga chariot.[2] Other solar charioteers include Apollo, Surya and Krishna. In this same regard, Ezekiel (1:27-28) uses solar imagery to describe Yahweh's arrival:

> And upward from what had the appearance of his loins I saw as it were gleaming bronze, like the appearance of fire enclosed round about; and downward from what had the appearance of his loins I saw as it were the appearance of fire, and there was brightness round about him.

Fig. 101. Apollo/Helios in his quadriga chariot with four horses. Roman mosaic

> Like the appearance of the bow that is in the cloud on the day of rain, so was the appearance of the brightness round about. Such was the appearance of the likeness of the glory of the LORD. And when I saw it, I fell upon my face, and I heard the voice of one speaking.

Here the bright, fiery and brazen glory of the Lord appears like a rainbow in the clouds, solar imagery that could not be more obvious.

The Beasts on the Temple Wall

Guided by Yahweh himself, Ezekiel next has a vision of the temple at Jerusalem, in which the prophet digs into a hole in the wall to discover a door. Behind this aperture lies the sight of "vile abominations" being committed by the 70 Jewish elders. At Ezekiel 8:10-11, the biblical prophet writes:

> So I went in and saw; and there, portrayed upon the wall round about, were all kinds of creeping things, and loathsome beasts, and all the idols of the house of Israel. And before them stood seventy men of the elders of the house of Israel, with Ja-azani'ah the son of Shaphan standing among them. Each had his censer in his hand, and the smoke of the cloud of incense went up.

Here we see a discussion of the elders in the temple's inner sanctum blasphemously worshipping "creeping things and loathsome beasts on the walls," which may be a reference to the zodiac.[3] The

---

[1] This throne with living beasts is styled also a "chariot," as at Ezek 43:4 in the LXX, which adds ἅρμα *arma* or "chariot" to "the vision [of the chariot] which I had seen by the river Chebar."
[2] The Greek is τὸ ἅρμα τοῦ ἡλίου *to harma tou heliou*, this latter word the same as the sun god's name.
[3] See, e.g., Ankerberg and Weldon.

imagery could represent also the polytheistic iconography of the Assyrians, Babylonians, Canaanites and Egyptians, which would indicate that, by Ezekiel's time (7th-6th cents. BCE), the Jews were maintaining their ancient polytheistic worship, despite the alleged reforms by Hezekiah and Josiah. Indeed, it surmised that the push for monotheism did not begin in earnest until Ezekiel's time, during the Babylonian exile and for centuries afterwards.

Tammuz and the Sun

It is also in this biblical book (Ezek 8:14) that the author bemoans the wailing of the Jewish women for Tammuz, the dying and rising solar-wine god annually lost on the autumnal equinox and found again at the vernal equinox. This Tammuz pericope is followed by Ezekiel's commentary (8:16) on the 25 men with their backs to the temple facing east in sun worship.

Concerning this tradition of Tammuz mourned, Dutch professor Dr. Meindert Dijkstra points out that Ezekiel 8:16 represents a clear break from the solar cult, with the Yahwists rejecting the connection to the sun god, whose worship obviously had existed for centuries in Israel.[1]

Feast of the Tabernacles

During the time of Tammuz's lamentation, following on the heels of the droughty summer months comes the welcome rain of the fall. As mentioned, one Jewish autumnal celebration is the Feast of the Tabernacles or Booths, earlier called the "Festival of the Fruit Harvest"[2] or *Bikkurim*. Concerning this festival, Dijkstra says that it was "celebrated at the end of the year close to the autumnal equinox and later known as חג הסכות [*chag cukkah*] 'the Feast of Tabernacles'" and that "the rite was abandoned in the Second Temple Period as too offensive to YHWH."[3]

Dijkstra also states that, nevertheless, the ritual "may have been a genuine part of the Jerusalem cult of YHWH, which show either features of solar worship or, in any case, worship of a solarized Yahweh."[4]

These tabernacles or booths possess a solar nature, as does Yahweh/Moses's tabernacle or "tent of the sun," to be discussed. As we can see, the festival is considered both solar and early Yahwistic, a fall equinox celebration occurring for thousands of years, as part of the harvest.[5]

---

[1] Becking, 88.
[2] Exod 23:16, 34:22; Num 28:26; 1 Kings 8:2, 8:65.
[3] Becking, 104.
[4] Becking, 104.
[5] For a listing of various fall celebrations in the months of September and October, see my *2010 Astrotheology Calendar*.

Lunar Deity

In addition to the solar Yawi/Yahweh/Yah is a Canaanite moon god named *yrḥ* Yerach or Yarih, appearing in El's *marzeah*,[1] whose Akkadian cognate is *(w)arḫu*. In the Ugaritic texts, Yarih or Yariḫu is involved as the "luminary of the heavens,"[2] an indication of the lunar cult. The Hebrew equivalent is ירח *yareach*,[3] a term used more than two dozen times in the Old Testament and possibly recognizable to its ancient readers as referring not simply to the lunar orb but also to this ancient Semitic moon god. In this regard, we are reminded of the scholarship of Dr. Theodor Reik (1888-1969) concerning the Jewish god's lunar nature as well, evident in the Jewish religious calendar, based significantly on the phases of the moon. As Lina Eckenstein remarks, "The Hebrews came from a stock of moon-worshippers."[4]

Iah

Another lunar theonym belongs to the Egyptian moon god "Iah," also transliterated as Yah, Jah, Jah(w), Joh or Aah, a moniker of the luni-solar Jewish tribal god and resembling the Sumero-Babylonian Ea as well.[5] Budge equates Iah or Aah with the Hebrew ירח *yareach*.[6] Since Iah was eventually syncretized with Osiris, whom Budge calls "Asar-Aah"[7] and who is equated with Yahweh, it is reasonable to compare Iah with Yah/Yahu/Yahweh/YHWH.

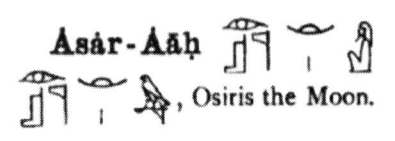

Fig. 102. Soli-lunar Osiris syncretized to Aah or Iah, the moon god. (Budge, 2010:1.83)

This notion of soli-lunar significance is reflected also in the fact that Iah/Aah/Ah was known as "Aa" or "Aos" in Mesopotamia, where *she* was the consort of Shamash and mother of Tammuz, while in Egypt "Aa" was another name for Ra, the sun god.[8]

Ieuo

In discussing the origin of Yahweh, many writers since antiquity have pointed to the Phoenician god Ἰευώ or Ieuo of Byblos, where Baal also reigned. For example, according to Eusebius and Porphyry,

---

[1] Schniedewind, 19, 119.
[2] Rahmouni, 232, 244.
[3] Schniedewind, 162; Strong's H3394. This Semitic word also means "month" (Schniedewind, 194) and is employed 11 times in the Old Testament in that capacity and twice more as "moon" (H3391).
[4] Eckenstein, 10, citing Artapanus in Alexander Polyhistor.
[5] Eckenstein, 10.
[6] Budge (1920/2010), 1.29.
[7] Budge (1920/210), 1.83.
[8] Coulter and Turner, 3, 230, 250.

the Phoenician chronicler Philo of Byblos (c. 64-141 AD/CE) recounted that the legendary Babylonian priest Sanchoniathon of Beirut purportedly equated Ieuo with Yahweh.[1]

In this same regard, Ieuo has been identified with the Yw in Ugaritic text KTU II IV.13-14, as related by Mark Smith:

> The background of the name *yw* in line 14 has been debated. Eissfeldt...identified this name with the god Ieuo attested in Philo of Byblos' *Phoenician History*. In this passage, this figure is said to be the god of the priest named Hierombalos who dedicated his work to the king of Beirut... If the correlation were correct, it would provide additional evidence for the cult of Yamm in the first millennium. A number of scholars have identified either *yw* or Ieuo with the name of Yahweh, however. Albright...and Barr...accept the identification of Ieuo with Yahweh....[2]

Concerning the identification of Yahweh with Yw and Ieuo, Gray remarks: "If we accept *Yw* as a Canaanite deity he is more likely to be the Syrian deity Ιευω...mentioned by Eusebius as the god of Byblos, whose priest Hierombalos is cited as an authority behind Sanchuniathon, whom Philo of Byblos quotes."[3]

According to Philo, Sanchoniathon deemed Ieuo "the Most High God," written in Greek Ἐλιοῦν *Elioun*,[4] the same as El Elyon, the Canaanite/Israelite sun and wine god.

The Gnostic First and Second Books of Ieu/Jeu/Jeou/Ieou[5] bear a name of the divine creator that resembles both Ieuo and the French word *Jeudi*, meaning "Thursday," or *Iovis Dies* in Latin—the "day of Jove" (Jupiter/Zeus, etc). In turn, "Jove" is similar to "Jehovah" or "Jahveh," and the Jewish god was associated in antiquity also with the Greco-Roman father god. Moreover, both Ieu and YHWH are associated with the theonym Iao or Jao.[6]

Iao

In ancient times, the god-name Ἰαώ Iao was identified as representing both a solar deity and Yahweh.[7] As noted, in a discussion of various lawgivers and gods of the known world,

---

[1] Baumgarten, 41; Sale, 17.275.
[2] Smith, M. (1994), 1.151-152.
[3] Gray (1965), 180.
[4] Colenso, 5.308.
[5] Doresse, 105; Murdock (2009), 277.
[6] See, e.g., Baker (1992), 81.
[7] As we have seen, in describing an oracle of Apollo of Claros, Macrobius (1.18.19) related that Iaô was another name for the sun. (Macrobius/Kaster, 1.255) Interestingly, a similar name, Ιαως *Iaos*, is used in the LXX at 1 Chronicles 8:10 to render the Hebrew word יעוץ *Y@'uwts*, generally transliterated as "Jeuz," meaning "counsellor" and the name of the head of the tribe of Benjamin. In the Latin, Jerome renders the word as "Iehus."

Diodorus (1.94.2) remarked that "among the Jews Moses referred his laws to the god who is invoked as Iao."[1]

Also in the first century BCE, Iao was equated with Yahweh by Roman statesman Marcus Terentius Varro (116-27 BCE), per Christian historian Lydus (c. 490–554 AD/CE) in *De Mensibus* (4.53). Also associated by Varro with Iao is the "Iu" in Iupiter or Jupiter,[2] the same as Zeus Pater, the Greek "God the Father," and Dyaus Pitar of Indian religion. There are many instances in which Zeus is identified with Yahweh, including by the Jewish author of the Letter of Aristeas (*Ep. Arist.* 16), as well as through the efforts of Antiochus IV, who forced the Jews to accept Zeus in their temple at Jerusalem, as described in the first and second books of the Maccabees.

Regarding the god of the Jews, Lydus relates:

> There has been and still is much disagreement among the theologians regarding the god who is worshipped by the Hebrews. For the Egyptians—and Hermes [Trismegistus] first of all—theologize that he is Osiris, "the one who exists," ...the Roman Varro, when discussing him, says that among the Chaldaeans, in their mystical [writings], he is called "Iaô," meaning "mentally perceived light" in the language of the Phoenicians, as Herennius [Philo] says.[3]

It is noteworthy that Egyptians prior to Lydus's time identified Yahweh with Osiris, as we are justified in doing likewise. Hermes Trismegistus is not a historical personage but a tradition comprising thousands of texts in the name of this mythical compilation of characters, evidently including the Greek Hermes and Egyptian Thoth. The assessment that "Hermes" equated Yahweh with Osiris probably reflects ideas in one or more Hermetic texts composed in the first centuries of the common era or earlier.

Chaldeans and Judith

We read further in Lydus (4:38) that the "Chaldeans call the god (Dionysus or Bacchus) Iao in the Phoenician language" and that "he is often called Sabaoth..."

The Jews themselves were deemed the descendants of the Chaldeans in at least one pre-Christian text, the apocryphal Jewish book of Judith (5:6).[4] Possibly composed around 100 BCE, Judith recounts the tale that the Jews were delivered "by the hand of a female." Judith's commentary focuses upon the periods of Nebuchadnezzar, the Persians and Antiochus Epiphanes. In any

---

[1] παρὰ δὲ τοῖς Ἰουδαίοις Μωυσῆν τὸν Ἰαὼ ἐπικαλούμενον θεόν.
[2] Fahlbusch (4:733): "In his speculations regarding the pure and imageless origins of Roman religion, Varro refers to the pure religion of Israel and its God (Yahweh), whom he equates with Iovis Pater (Father Jove, i.e., Jupiter). The God of the Jews, he said, is Iovis, for it does not matter by what name he is called so long as what is meant is the same..."
[3] Translation Andrew Eastbourne.
[4] McDonough, 92.

event, the solar Iao of the Chaldeans is the Yahweh of the Jews, as well as Dionysus.

Dead Sea Leviticus and LXX

The term ΙΑΩ IAO as a transliteration of יהוה YHWH can be found in a Greek papyrus fragment of Leviticus from the Dead Sea (4Q120), possibly dating to the first century BCE or so.[1] The use of Iao in the Greek Bible is attested by Tertullian (*Ad Valent.* 14.4), relating that the Valentinian Gnostics discussed the *cry* "Iao!" to explain how "the name Iao comes to be found in the Scriptures."[2]

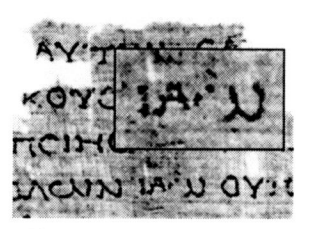

Fig. 103. Yahweh written as IAO (inset), c. 1st cent. BCE. Dead Sea Scroll fragment 4Q120, Rockefeller Museum, Jerusalem

Alpha and Omega

The Gnostic reference to Iao in the scriptures may concern the verse at Revelation 1:8, in which the writer makes God/Christ say, "I am the Alpha and Omega," reflecting the letters alpha (A) and omega (Ω), the beginning and end respectively of the Greek alphabet[3]:

ἐγώ εἰμι τὸ Ἄλφα καὶ τὸ Ὦ

When ancient writers depicted Yahweh as Iao and associated or identified the latter with numerous other deities, including various sun gods, they recorded an actual perception from their time and probably much earlier.

Gnostics

Speaking of the Gnostic IAO,[4] Canadian archaeologist and linguist Dr. David H. Kelley avers that "Iao seems to be a syncretism of Hebrew Yahweh with Egyptian ideas of a supreme creator, himself a syncretism of ancient Egyptian concepts with Hellenized Greek ideas."[5] We have seen one Egyptian equivalent, Iahu/Iah/Aoh, which may have been identified with Yahu/Yahweh/Ieuo/Iao.[6]

A Coptic-Gnostic text of the late second century AD/CE called *The Apocryphon of John* (2.11.29–31) names Iao or Yao as one of the Gnostic otherworldly rulers styled "archons," about whom the author states that "the fourth is Yao, he has a serpent's face with seven

---

[1] See, e.g., Bromiley, 4.158; Parke-Taylor, 84. According to Vermes, fragment 20 of 4Q120 from the DSS Leviticus (4QLXX Lev^b) represents the biblical verse Lev 4:27.
[2] Roberts, 15.140. The relevant Latin is: *Inde invenitur Iao in scripturis.*
[3] McDonough, 53.
[4] For a lengthy discussion of Iao and the Gnostics, see Bishop Colenso's translation of F.C. Mover's essay, in *The Pentateuch and Book of Joshua Critically Examined* (Appendix III, 5.305ff).
[5] Kelley, David, 477.
[6] See, e.g., Grethenbach, 119.

heads; the fifth is Sabaoth, he has a dragon's face..."[1] The equation here of Iao with the serpent and of Sabaoth with the dragon is noteworthy, as similar terminology is used to describe the serpent, dragon of the deep, pharaoh and so on.

Sabaoth

The theonym Iao was used popularly in the magical papyri and other artifacts of the first centuries surrounding the common era: "The name Iao also appears on a number of magical texts, inscriptions and amulets from the ancient world."[2] These artifacts include an amulet from the first century BCE that reads: "IAO IAO SABAOTH ADONAI."[3] This sort of invocation indicates a Semitic origin but passes seamlessly into the formalized Gnosticism of the second century AD/CE onwards.

In the New Testament, the word Σαβαώθ *Sabaoth* is used twice, at Romans 9:29 and James 5:4. Strong's defines the term as: "Lord of the armies of Israel, as those who are under the leadership and protection of Jehovah maintain his cause in war."[4] The title "Sabaoth" derives from the Hebrew root צבא *tsaba'*, which is defined as "hosts," as in both warfare and heaven. In its astral connotation, צבא *tsaba'* means "host (of angels)...of sun, moon, and stars...of whole creation."[5] Hence, we see an astrotheological theme in the "host of heavens."

Concerning the amulets and the YHWH-Iao connection, Classics professor Dr. Campbell Bonner relates:

> As to the meaning of Iao, there can be no doubt, especially since the subject was thoroughly investigated by Graf von Baudissin; and, in fact, the combination of Ιαω Σαβαωθ Αδωναι [Iao Sabaoth Adonai] "JHVH of hosts, Lord," which is common on both amulets and papyri, is convincing in itself.[6]

As noted, "Sabaoth" may be related to "Sabeus," which in turn is an epithet of Dionysus, who is also equated with Iao by Macrobius. Thus, Yahweh is Iao is Bacchus, and all are the sun.

---

[1] Frederik Wisse translation. Stevan Davies renders the relevant passage thus: "Fourth, Yao with the face of a seven headed snake; Fifth, Sabaoth who has the face of a dragon..." Barnstone (56) translates the pericope as "the fourth Iao, with the face of a seven-headed snake; the fifth Adonaios, with the face of a dragon..."
[2] McDonough, 93.
[3] McDonough, 94.
[4] Strong's G4519.
[5] Strong's H6635. Several scholars in the past have suggested that צבא *tsaba'* is the Semitic root of "Sabeans," the name of a widespread pre-Islamic Arab ethnic group noted for the worship of stars or the "host of heavens."
[6] Bonner, 30. von Baudissin's book is *Kyrios als Gottesname in Judentum*.

The Sun

To reiterate, Iao was identified with the sun, as in the mysteries and the oracle of Apollo at Claros. Macrobius (1.18.20) relates that Iao was "supreme god among all," represented by the wintry Hades, the vernal Zeus, the summery Helios and the autumnal Iao,[1] also noted as Iacchus or Dionysus, the latter's role as the sun in the fall appropriate for a wine god.

As can be seen from ancient testimony, and as related by Dr. Roelof van den Broek, a professor of Christian History at the University of Utrecht: "Iao stood for the Sun."[2]

Adon-Adonai-Adonis

Once again, both Plutarch (*Quaest. Conv.*) and Macrobius (4th cent. AD/CE) identified the solar Iao with Bacchus, who in turn was equated by Diodorus with Yahweh. Plutarch (*Symp.* 5.3) also associates Bacchus with Adonis.[3]

As noted, Adon or its plural Adonai is yet another epithet of "God," used 335 times in the Old Testament to connote "Lord"[4] and evidently related to "Adonis," the name of the Greco-Syrian god. In this regard, a number of scholars in the past such as Freud and Frazer likewise discussed "Adonis" as meaning "Lord" and demonstrated its relationship to "Adonai." Regarding Adonis, Frazer remarks:

> The true name of the deity was Tammuz: the appellation of Adonis is merely the Semitic *Adon*, "lord," a title of honour by which his worshippers addressed him. In the Hebrew text of the Old Testament the same name Adonai, originally perhaps Adoni, "my lord," is often applied to Jehovah.[5]

Having translated the works of various ancient writers and knowing them well, Frazer also relates that the association of Adonis with Tammuz was made in antiquity, including by Christian writers Origen, Jerome, Theodoretus (393-457 AD/CE), the Paschal Chronicle author (7th cent. AD/CE) and Melito (d. 180 AD/CE).

The word Adon/*'adn* as in Adonai can be found in the Ugaritic, for instance, in the title *adn ilm rbm* or "Lord of the Great Gods," preceding its usage within Judaism by centuries.[6] An even older rendering of "Lord" in the context of divinity may be found, perhaps, in the Eblaite god *Adānu*, the possible head along with *Bēlatu* of the Eblaite pantheon, whose "Mesopotamian counterparts would be Enlil

---

[1] See also McDonough, 92.
[2] Quispel, 39.
[3] Plutarch/Goodwin (3.310): "Now Adonis is supposed to be the same with Bacchus." Original Greek: τὸν δ'Ἀδωνιν οὐχ ἕτερον ἀλλὰ Διόνυσον εἶναι νομίζουσι.
[4] Strong's H113.
[5] Frazer, 5.6.
[6] See, e.g., Smith, M. (1994), 1.112; Rahmouni, 25ff.

and Ninlil, while in Canaan of the Late Bronze Age their equivalents would be El and Asherah."[1]

Hence, we can surmise the passing down of this very ancient god-name in the Greco-Syrian form of Adonis, especially in consideration of the influence of the Phoenicians, who worshipped Adon and who originated the alphabet as we know it, possibly adapted from the Pelasgians, leading to Greek literacy.

Regarding the Adonis-Adonai connection, Leeming states:

> Adonis was a Greco-Roman version of a Semitic god of Mesopotamia who at various times was identified with Osiris and Tammuz as well as with Jesus. Adonis' Semitic name, Adonai, means "the Lord." In some versions of his story he was born of a virgin (Myrrha), and some versions say that at his death he was castrated. After his death the red anemone sprang in symbolic resurrection from the earth.[2]

Since Tammuz was one of the Semitic deities associated with the grape harvest, in the same role as Osiris and Dionysus, these latter gods therefore also would be identified with Adonis/Adon/Adonai.

Because both Yahweh and Adonis were associated with the solar Iao, again it is logical to equate Adonis with Adon, as the ancient themselves likely did.[3] Iao is "the title of the autumnal Sun," and his title "tender Iao" may reflect the Greco-Syrian god, labeled "tender Adonis."[4] We read also from Colenso that "Adonis was actually named in Byblus and Lebanon 'the Most high God,' exactly as here IAO is styled in the oracle."[5]

If Iao, Adonis and Dionysus are the sun, yet they are also identified with Yahweh, we can conclude that the Jewish tribal god too is a typical solar deity, as found in numerous cultures dating back to remote antiquity, in the very eras and areas in which he flourished as a tribal god.

Conclusion

Regarding how Yahweh eventually ended up as the dominant god of the Israelites in Judea, one popular theory holds that he was a favored deity of certain Amorites, part of the pre-Judaic Semitic multi-tribal ethnicities who occupied southern Syria/Palestine and eventually in part came to dominate the northern Israelites as well. Egyptian Execration Texts (c. 1850-1800 BCE) "trace the social and religious development of the Amorites...in Palestine and Southern Syria from a stage when they retained a political organization and religion characteristic of a tribal state to the stage when they had

---

[1] Gordon (2002), 4.211.
[2] Leeming (1990), 153.
[3] Colenso (1865) 5.279; 5.299, 5.307 citing Lucian's *de Dea Syria*, 6.
[4] Macrobius 1.18.20. See, also Bion of Phlossa/Smyrna, *Idyl.* 1.79. Banks (169) renders the relevant Greek ἁβρὸς Ἄδωνις as "delicate Adonis." See also Proclus, *Ad Solem*/"To the Sun," v. 26. (*Sallust*, 120)
[5] Colenso, 5.307.

finally settled down to the sedentary life of farmers."[1] From the subsequent mingling of peoples, some Amorites, including the Shasu of Yhw, eventually became Yahwists, Judeans and Jews.

Originally, these peoples were followers of multiple deities around the eastern Mediterranean and Levant, including El, Baal, Tammuz and other Semitic gods, many of whom were significantly solar and atmospheric in nature. At some point during the first millennium BCE, this ancient community struck upon the tribal war god Yahweh above all others, carrying his standard in their battles.

The reality is that the ancient world flourished with a plethora of deities, many of whom possessed numerous solar attributes, including those discussed in the present work. Yahweh represents another of the same type, building on the ancient solar mythology and astral religion, demonstrated abundantly in texts and artifacts reflecting his solar nature and syncretized attributes from a number of sun gods and goddesses from antiquity.

---

[1] Gray (1965), 152.

Fig. 104. Sun god Helios surrounded by 12 zodiacal signs, with four solstices and equinoxes in corners, 6th cent. AD/CE. Synagogue mosaic from Beit Alpha, Israel (NASA)

Fig. 105. Zodiac with Helios in center, 6th cent. AD/CE. Synagogue mosaic, Tzippori/Sepphoris, Israel. (G.dallorto)

Moses as Solar Hero

"This deity [Adar] represented the sun god primitively worshipped at Nipur (now Niffer) in Babylonia, who afterwards came to be regarded as a sort of Chaldean Herakles.... he was called Uras in Akkadian, and also in Semitic, when regarded as 'the god of light.' But he was further known in Assyrian as Baru, 'the revealer,' though we learn from a Babylonian text...discovered in Upper Egypt that his more usual title was Masu, 'the hero,' a word which is, letter for letter, the same as the Hebrew Mosheh, 'Moses.' Masu is defined as being 'the sun god who rises from the divine day.'"

> Rev. Dr. Archibald H. Sayce, *Records of the Past* (1.90-91)

"Many of the stories concerning Moses, Joshua, Jonah and other Bible characters are solar myths."

> John E. Remsburg, *The Christ: A Critical Review and Analysis of the Evidence of His Existence*

"Who was Moses the lawgiver, originally?... He was, I venture, another sun god.... The basic Moses mytheme is that of the sun (god) which emerges from the tent of concealment, the night, and bestows commandments upon a king. Like many other mythical sun-characters (still reflected in Elijah, Esau, Samson and Enoch), and other gods, too (Gad, Miriam, Jubal, Joshua), Moses must have begun as a god pure and simple, but as Hebrew religion evolved toward monotheism, the stories could only be retained by making the gods into human heroes."

> Dr. Robert M. Price, "Of Myth and Men"

IT HAS BEEN shown that the story of Moses and the Exodus can be understood not as literal history or history mythologized but as *myth historicized*. The lawgiver motif ranks as solar and allegorical, reflecting an ancient archetype extant also in the myth of Dionysus, god of vine and wine, who shares numerous significant attributes with Moses. Likewise demonstrated in the present work is the solar nature of many ancient gods, including Yahweh, biblically presented as the source of the patriarch's revelation and legislation. Who, then, is Moses?

Based on evidence from comparative religion and mythology studies, as well as agriculture, anthropology, archaeoastronomy, archaeology, art history, economics, etymology, history, linguistics, philosophy, psychology, sociology, viniculture, viticulture and other disciplines, many people over the centuries have concluded that Moses is a solar hero, as is his successor, Joshua.[1] In this regard, in

---

[1] An analysis of his myth reveals Joshua to be a typical solar hero as well: For example, the Bible (Jos 10:12-13) depicts him as working with the sunrise to blind his enemies by making the sun (and moon) stand still, attributes of the sun god. Again, see *Suns of God* for more information on Joshua.

Christian Mythology mythicist scholar John M. Robertson remarked: "That Joshua is a purely mythical personage was long ago decided by the historical criticism of the school of Colenso and Kuenen; that he was originally a solar deity can be established at least as satisfactorily as the solar character of Moses, if not as that of Samson."[1]

Like Samson, Yahweh and Dionysus, in many essentials Moses also ranks as a solar hero or sun god, said to be Masu, Mashu, Mash or Shamash. As Yahweh became increasingly powerful, the "pure and simple god" Moses was demoted to the status of patriarch, who nonetheless remained the central figure in the foundational myth of the Israelite nation.

Moses as God

In a possible confirmation centuries later that Moses was at one point a god, the *Exodus* of Ezekiel the Dramatist (2nd cent. BCE), labels the patriarch as "God and King," as well as the "faithful servant and son" of Yahweh.[2] We have seen that Yahweh mythically appears to have been the son of El. In turn, it seems that the *god* Masu/Mashu was styled a "son of Yahweh," possibly as one of the Elohim.

Ezekiel's *Exodus* may have served as one of the sources for Philo of Alexandria, who builds upon this mythology by presenting the Jewish prophet as an immortal god and son of God.[3] Philo asserts that Moses was given dominion over the whole world by Yahweh, as his heir and "partaker with himself" in portions of creation reserved for God.[4] As such, the elements obeyed the commands of Moses, their master.

Regarding the lawgiver, Philo remarks further:

> ...Has he not also enjoyed an even greater communion with the Father and Creator of the universe, being thought unworthy of being called by the same appellation? For he also was called the god and king of the whole nation, and he is said to have entered into the darkness where God was; that is to say, into the invisible, and shapeless, and incorporeal world, the essence... he established himself as a most beautiful and Godlike work, to be a model for all those who were inclined to imitate him.[5]

---

[1] Robertson, 99. Colenso wrote a series of controversial volumes entitled *The Pentateuch and Book of Joshua Critically Examined*, in which he argued against the literal and historical accuracy of certain parts of the biblical texts. His work was popularized significantly through the writings of Dutch theologian Rev. Dr. Abraham Kuenen (1829-1891). Assorted theologians and bibliolaters spilled considerable ink to silence this dissent from biblical inerrancy. The damage was done, however, and today there appears to be a higher percentage of Bible skeptics in the educated Western world than at any time in history.
[2] Baker (1992), 42.
[3] Philo, *Moses* 251.288; 1.28.155-158
[4] Philo/Yonge (2000), 473.
[5] Philo/Yonge (2000), 474.

Hence, Moses is the pre-Christian son of God running the world precisely as was said later of Jesus Christ. As is fitting for a god, in the Talmud and Quran, Moses is depicted as a king, the monarch of Ethiopia;[1] thus, he would bear the epithet *mlk/melek/molech* in Hebrew.

Assumption of Moses

The Moses mythmaking literature continued for centuries after the Pentateuch was composed. Another text in this genre assigning divine and supernatural attributes and roles to the patriarch is the *Assumption of Moses*, possibly composed beginning in the time of Antiochus Epiphanes, also in the second century BCE,[2] and continuing into the first century AD/CE.

In this text, Moses is "assumed" into heaven, leaving Joshua in charge, while the lawgiver remains alive in heaven as the supernatural mediator between Yahweh and his priests, possessing immortality and preexistence.[3] This heavenly assumption is reflected also in the gospel story of Jesus transfiguring on the mount between Moses and Elijah (Mt 17:1-9).

The motif of Moses's assumption is similar to the ascension of Dionysus and other solar deities, and it would be a necessary attribute for those wishing to create a competing religion. In this text too (11.5-8), Moses's "sepulcher is from the rising of the sun to the setting thereof, and from the south to the confines of the north; all the world is his sepulcher,"[4] another concept with solar mythological relevance.

The ideas in this text also were built upon by Philo, apparently, when he discussed the patriarch's assumption (*Moses* 2.51.288):

> ...he was about to depart from hence to heaven, to take up his abode there, and leaving this mortal life to become immortal, having been summoned by the Father, who now changed him, having previously been a double being, composed of soul and body, into the nature of a single body, transforming him wholly and entirely into a most sun-like mind...[5]

Here we see again the suggestion of Moses as the son of the Father, as Philo repeatedly calls God, years before Christ's purported ministry as the "only begotten son of God."

A Samaritan text from the fourth century AD/CE continues the idea of Moses *as* Yahweh,[6] a suitable identification in consideration of the fact that both are apparently tribal gods and significantly solar in nature.

---

[1] Talmud/Polano, 130-131.
[2] Baker (1992), 44.
[3] *Assumption of Moses* 1.12-14; Singer, Is., 9.57.
[4] Singer, Is., 9.57.
[5] Philo/Yonge (2000), 517.
[6] Baker (1992), 99.

Solar Aspects

The solar aspects and attributes of the Moses story are numerous, and we have reviewed many of them already, including his heavenly assumption, which produces a "sun-like mind." The motif of Moses leaving Joshua as his successor is another solar element, as the lawgiver appears to represent the fall and winter sun, while Joshua is the spring and summer sun. As such, Moses leads the chosen to the Promised Land, where he turns them over to Joshua, who rises in triumph to the summer solstice, when he makes the solar orb stand still. Moses's similar trick would occur, therefore, at the winter solstice. Thus, these twin sun gods rule from equinox to equinox, while other solar personifications mark the periods from solstice to soltice, as is the case with Jesus and John the Baptist, said traditionally from antiquity to be born six months apart, on December 25th and June 24th, respectively.

Another prominent example of the patriarch's solar nature is his nativity tale, similar to that of a number of solar heroes such as Apollo, Dionysus, Horus and other deities and lawgivers. So proliferate around the Mediterranean were solar attributes in general that, again, Macrobius spent considerable time making the case that the majority of these figures resolve to sun gods.

Price summarizes some of the more striking solar characteristics in the Moses myth:

> ...The basic Moses mytheme is that of the sun (god) which emerges from the tent of concealment, the night, and bestows commandments upon a king. The sun is also the source of both death (by sunstroke) and healing. Psalm 19, as Old Testament scholars uniformly admit, comes from Akhenaten's Hymn to the Sun. It speaks of the sun's glorious emergence from his tent, then extols the glory of the commandments, as if there were some connection between the two—which, of course, there was, since the sun was the origin of the law. We also see this atop the famous stone table of Hammurabi's Code which shows the emperor receiving the law from the hand of Shamash the sun god. Moses was originally the law-giving sun, as we can still glimpse in Exodus 34:29-35, where Moses emerges from the tent of a meeting with new commandments, and with his face shining, not coincidentally, like the sun! And like Apollo, he can inflict flaming doom or heal it (Numbers 21:4-9) and even bears the caduceus like Apollo...[1]

The usual biblical comparison with Akhenaten's "Hymn to the Sun" is Psalm 104, which Gray calls a "Hebrew adaptation" of the Egyptian hymn.[2] Such solar hymns were fairly common in antiquity in a variety of cultures, including the Sumerian and Semitic, and Psalm 19 also serves to illustrate the solar nature of much Judaic

---

[1] Price, "Of Myth and Men."
[2] Gray, 5.207.

tradition and ritual, as another writing within this astrotheological genre.

The Tent of the Sun

It is fitting for a solar hero to be housed in a sun tent, a common motif in solar mythology. In this regard, the true nature of Moses's "covenant with the Lord" is reflected by the esoteric or mystical meaning of the patriarch's tabernacle or house of worship as the "tent of the sun." In the OT description of how Moses is to build the tabernacle (Exod 15, 26), there appears several times the word אהל *'ohel*,[1] meaning "tent" or "tabernacle," "tent of the Lord" and "sacred tent of Jehovah."[2] The root of *'ohel* is אהל *'ahal*, which, appropriately, means "to shine."[3] Concerning this motif, theologian Dr. William P. Brown states that "the metaphorical background of the sun's tent (*'ōhel*) or canopy...is likely a vestige of the Mesopotamian myth of the sun-god's repose with his spouse."[4]

The word *'ohel* is used also in the mundane sense, referring to the tents of nomads, while another word, משכן *mishkan*, is likewise translated as "tabernacle."[5] The Greek equivalent of *'ohel* is σκηνή *skēnē*, defined as "a tent, booth, tabernacle, abode, dwelling, mansion, habitation,"[6] employed in the Septuagint to describe the Israelite religious "booths" or *sukkoth* (e.g., Lev 23:42).

The Israelite tabernacle is oriented to the east (Num 3:38), to the rising sun, and takes the basic shape of an Egyptian temple,[7] which in turn is said to be the place of the sun's birth, as noted. Like Yahweh, the solar El too had his "tent of meeting,"[8] a possibly portable shrine that may have served as a "regular feature of his cult in the Amarna age."[9] Thus, the sacred tent is not original or unique to Judaism.

Hero Who Goes Out

The word אהל *'ohel* is employed at Psalm 19:4 to describe the personified heavens extolling Yahweh's glory, in which the Almighty has set the "tent for the sun," rendered in the Hebrew as אהל שמש *'ohel shemesh*.

---

[1] Strong's H168.
[2] The tabernacle is emphasized particularly by the Priestly source text or "P." (Friedman, 2003:22) Its emphasis, Friedman argues (2003:23), requires that the text was composed before the Jerusalem tabernacle was destroyed in the sixth century.
[3] Strong's H166.
[4] Brown, W., 97.
[5] Strong's H4908. E.g., Exod 26:7.
[6] Strong's G4633. The word σκηνή *skēnē* also appears many times in ancient, nonbiblical writings, including of Aeschylus, Apollodorus, Aristotle, Demosthenes, Diodorus and so on. For example, in Diodorus (11.10), we read about the Persian king Xerxes's "royal pavilion," in the form βασιλικῆς σκηνῆς *basilikēs skēnēs*.
[7] Houghton, 266.
[8] Smith, M. (1994), 1.189.
[9] Harrison, 404.

Also at Psalm 19:4, the "tent of the sun" is considered to be the "night quarters of the שמש"[1] this latter word, again, *shemesh* or "sun," a mere letter different from the name משה *mshh* or "Moses." In the morning, "the sun then leaves its chamber..."[2]

In this regard, biblical scholar Dr. Hans-Joachim Kraus comments: "In a Sumerian hymn the sun god is called the 'hero who goes out'..."[3] Moses too is the "hero who goes out," in his exodus or "going out" of Egypt, a prominent aspect of his story.

Great Judge

Continuing the imagery about the sun, Psalm 19:6 reads:

Its rising is from the end of the heavens, and its circuit to the end of them; and there is nothing hid from its heat.

Regarding this latter part, Kraus observes that the last verse (Ps 19:6c) "is derived from the Shamash-tradition of the Babylonian hymns, for the sun god is considered the highest judge, the one who has insight into all the deeds of men."[4]

Here we can see the ancient tradition of perceiving the sun as the "great judge," previously discussed as concerns the Neo-Babylonian solar epithet *Dian-nisi*, associated with Shamash and possibly Osiris,[5] therefore plausibly representing "Dionysus."

From the Bible, we also learn that nothing can be hidden from the sun's sight and that all things are exposed before it. Oaths also are taken in the sight of the sun, and the sun's judgeship throughout thousands of years across a wide spectrum of cultures should not be underestimated in importance, from antiquity to the present.[6]

In the end, it is the *sun* who is the ultimate judge and lawgiver, and who has his tent of meeting, where his mysteries and laws are revealed.

12 and 70 Redux

We have discussed already the magical number configuration of 12 and 70 at Exodus 15:27, in which there are twelve springs and seventy palms, representing the 12 tribes and 70 elders. The seventy "elders of God" apparently are symbolic of the Canaanite pantheon, in which the high god El is depicted as having 70 sons.

In this same regard, Josephus (*Ant.* 3.7) elucidates the mystical and astrotheological meaning of Moses's tabernacle:

---

[1] Kraus, 272.
[2] Kraus, 272.
[3] Kraus, 272.
[4] Kraus, 272.
[5] Talbot, 8.306.
[6] For further information on solar worship and astrotheology in general, see *Suns of God* for many more details concerning the sun's role in human religion dating back thousands of years.

> And when [Moses] ordered twelve loaves to be set on the table, he denoted the year, as distinguished into so many months. By branching out the candlestick into seventy parts he secretly intimated the *Decani*, or seventy divisions of the planets; and as to the seven lamps upon the candlesticks, they referred to the course of the planets, of which that is the number... Now the vestment of the high priest being made of linen, signified the earth; the blue denoted the sky, being like lightning in its pomegranates, and in the noise of the bells resembling thunder... Each of the sardonyxes declares to us the sun and the moon; those, I mean, that were in the nature of buttons on the high priest's shoulders. And for the twelve stones, whether we understand by them the months, or whether we understand the like number of the signs of that circle which the Greeks call the Zodiac, we shall not be mistaken in their meaning.[1]

The nature worship in the Mosaic tradition could not be clearer, incorporating solar symbolism and astrolatry. For example, the 12 stones symbolize the tribes or "sons" of Jacob, a number that Josephus firmly establishes as the months of the year and zodiacal constellations.

Earlier in the same century as Josephus, Philo (*Moses* 1.34.188-189) had associated the 12 wells at Aileem with the twelve Israelite tribes and the 70 palms with the Jewish elders,[2] which in turn symbolized the 12 zodiacal signs and 70 dodecans, as discussed. Again, Philo relates that the 12 tribes were equated with the signs of the zodiac, remarking:

> Then the twelve stones on the breast, which are not like one another in colour, and which are divided into four rows of three stones in each, what else can they be emblems of, except of the circle of the zodiac?[3]

Philo thus demonstrates that the allegorical and astrotheological nature of various biblical themes has been understood for a long time:

> ...the Mosaic account...is allowed by all philosophers, as well as most of the early Jews and Christian fathers, to contain a mythos or allegory—by Philo, Josephus, Papias, Pantaenus, Irenaeus, Clemens Alex., Origen, the two Gregories of Nyssa and Nazianzen, Jerome, Ambrose...[4]

As concerns the 12 tribes, Redford concludes: "The division of Israel into twelve tribes is, even on the basis of Biblical record, a somewhat artificial arrangement, and may owe more to a calendrical criterion employed by the later monarchy than to historical origins."[5]

---

[1] Josephus/Whiston, 91.
[2] Philo/Yonge (2000), 476-477.
[3] Philo/Yonge (1855), 3.99, cited as *Moses* 3.12.
[4] Higgins, 1.34.
[5] Redford (1992), 295.

This astrological symbolism evidently was devised significantly from the Babylonians, possibly when the Jewish priest-astronomers were in exile there. As the dodecans, the 70 sons or elders of El too would be part of this great Semitic astrotheological tradition.

The Menorah

Josephus (*Ant.* 3.6.7/3.145) is explicit also in relating other aspects of Jewish tradition as possessing astrological or astrotheological significance, including the menorah or seven-branched candlestick, which denotes the sun in the middle, surrounded by the moon and five planets: Mars, Mercury, Jupiter, Venus and Saturn.[1]

Like many other "Jewish" religious accoutrements and traditions, the menorah too is not unique, appearing in the dedications to many gods in antiquity, and cannot be considered scientifically to represent "divine revelation" to the "chosen people."[2]

Regarding such candelabras in antiquity, Benedictine monk Dom Augustin Calmet (1672-1757) "remarks that the ancients used to dedicate candlesticks in the temples of their gods, bearing a great number of lamps."[3]

In this regard, Clarke states:

> Pliny, *Hist. Nat.* [34.8], mentions one made in the form of a tree, with lamps in the likeness of apples, which Alexander the Great consecrated in the temple of Apollo.
>
> And Athenaeus [15.19, 20] mentions one that supported three hundred and sixty-five lamps, which Dionysius the younger, king of Syracuse, dedicated in the Prytanaeum at Athens.[4]

Obviously, this pagan candelabra with 365 branches symbolizes the days of the year, yet more astronomical or astrotheological significance in this genre. In any event, we can see how the Mosaic tabernacle and associated accoutrements, rituals and traditions themselves are astrotheological in nature.

Moses's Shining Face

Adding to the solar imagery associated with the Jewish legislator, Exodus 34:29 describes the solarized Moses coming down the mountain after speaking with Yahweh, not realizing that the "skin of his face shone":

---

[1] Josephus/Whiston, 73.
[2] Clarke, 1.448.
[3] Clarke, 1.433.
[4] Clarke, 1.448-449. In his chapter on "Couches of Brass," Pliny remarks: "The tripods, which were called Delphian, because they were devoted more particularly to receiving the offerings that were presented to the Delphian Apollo, were usually made of brass: also the pendant lamps, so much admired, which were placed in the temples, or gave their light in the form of trees loaded with fruit [*mala*]; such as the one, for instance, in the Temple of the Palatine Apollo, which Alexander the Great, at the sacking of Thebes, brought to Cyme, and dedicated to that god." (Pliny/Bostock, 6.154)

When Moses came down from Mount Sinai, with the two tables of the testimony in his hand as he came down from the mountain, Moses did not know that the skin of his face shone because he had been talking with God. And when Aaron and all the people of Israel saw Moses, behold, the skin of his face shone, and they were afraid to come near him. But Moses called to them; and Aaron and all the leaders of the congregation returned to him, and Moses talked with them. And afterward all the people of Israel came near, and he gave them in commandment all that the LORD had spoken with him in Mount Sinai.

In this passage, the Hebrew word rendered "shone" is קרן *qaran*, which means "to shine," "to send out rays" and "to display or grow horns, be horned."[1] *Gesenius* defines *qaran* also as "to radiate, to emit beams." In his Latin Bible, Jerome renders *qaran* as *cornuta* or "horned," which could also be translated "radiant."

Horned Hero

This motif of radiant solar beams represents the source of Moses portrayed with horns, as is the case of other solar heroes or sun gods, including the Sumerian UD/Utu and Semitic Shamash. As stated, the myth of the Greek lawgiver with the horns is found in the Bacchus tale by at least the fifth century BCE, when Euripides wrote, but it likely dates much farther back, as is the case with these others.

The feature of Moses with horns was well known in Christian tradition, as famously depicted by Michelangelo in his marble statue of the patriarch. As noted, these horns have multiple meanings, including evidently serving to indicate Moses as "son of the cow,"[2] part of the "bull" tradition associated with various gods and other figures antiquity that includes the Golden Calf.

Fig. 106. Michelangelo, *Moses* with horns, c. 1513-1515. Marble, San Pietro in Vincoli, Rome

It should be recalled that the words "wine" and "bull" are part of the oldest linguistical layer shared by both Semitic and Indo-European.[3] In consideration of this fact, it would be logical to suggest that the horned wine god is a very ancient concept.

---

[1] Strong's H7160.
[2] In the Bible (Num 18:2), Aaron and Moses are said to descend from Levi, their great-grandfather, whose mother is Leah, meaning "the cow." Meyers (108) states: "Hebrew *lē'â*, 'cow,' possibly meaning 'strength,' as Akkadian *littu*, 'cow,' is related to *lē'ûtu*, 'strength, power.'" Another highly esoteric meaning possibly syncretized to these others could be the horns as representing the psychedelic or entheogenic ergot fungus on rye, said to resemble "spurs." Certainly, this symbolism would be appropriate as well for the god of intoxicated revelry, such as the horned Bacchus or any of his counterparts.
[3] Brown, J.P. , 136.

Solar Rays

In his explanation of the verse at Exodus 34:29, Philo (*Moses* 2.14.69-70) essentially depicts the lawgiver as a solar hero, also portraying Moses's 40-day Sinai experience in terms much like the later gospel motif, with various tests of his mind, body and soul, such that he would grow in strength. Next, the Jewish writer comments:

> Then, after the said forty days had passed, he descended with a countenance far more beautiful than when he ascended, so that those who saw him were filled with awe and amazement; nor even could their eyes continue to stand the dazzling brightness that flashed from him like the rays of the sun.[1]

Hence, Moses's mountain mission made him "dazzlingly bright," flashing "like the rays of the sun."

Veil of the Sun

It is for this reason of blinding bedazzlement that Moses was said to wear a veil (Exod 34:33-35):

> And when Moses had finished speaking with them, he put a veil on his face; but whenever Moses went in before the LORD to speak with him, he took the veil off, until he came out; and when he came out, and told the people of Israel what he was commanded, the people of Israel saw the face of Moses, that the skin of Moses' face shone; and Moses would put the veil upon his face again, until he went in to speak with him.

The Hebrew word here for "veil" or "vail," is מסוה *macveh*, pronounced "mas·veh'" and used in the Bible only in these three verses.[2] The word describing Moses's face as having "shone" in this verse also is קרן *qaran*.

At Psalm 104:29, we read the similar theme of Yahweh hiding *his* face, in one of the verses traceable to Akhenaten's solar hymn:

> When you hide your face, they [living things] are terrified.... (NIV)

As part of the Akhenaten literature, the Amarna letter 147.5-10 from the Phoenician king Abi-milku "seems to appropriate the language of Aten hymns when addressing the pharaoh: 'My lord is the Sun god, who rises over the lands day after day, as ordained by the Sun god, who gives life by his sweet breath and diminishes when he is hidden.'"[3] The hiding of the shining face represents a solar motif, reflecting clouds, nighttime, winter or an eclipse, the latter of which in particular instilled fear in the ancients.

---

[1] Philo/Colson, 4.485. See also Philo/Yonge (2000), 497.
[2] The Greek of the LXX is κάλυμμα *kalumma* (G2571), meaning "covering, veil." Numerous Greek writers in antiquity used this same term or a form thereof, such as Aeschylus, Aristophanes, Diodorus, Euripides, Homer, Pausanias, Sophocles and Strabo.
[3] Gillingham, 222.

As another example in Egyptian religion, Massey mentions also the Egyptian savior god Shu, best known for his (solar) role as the wind and air between heaven and earth: "Moses under the veil is Shu in the shade; Moses wearing the glory of God upon his face is Shu who 'sits in his father's eye,' the eye of the sun..."[1]

As we can see, the veil motif belongs to ancient, pre-Israelite solar mythology, including as applied to the god Shu, whose name resembles the Sumero-Semitic term *mashu*.

Etymology of Moses Revisited

We have seen it contended that the name "Moses" (מֹשֶׁה *Mosheh*) is derived from both Hebrew, מָשָׁה *mashah* or "to draw," and the Egyptian root word *ms* or *mes*, meaning "born."[2] As has been demonstrated throughout this book, between the Semitic and Egyptian cultures there exists a longstanding and profound connection, including exchange of language and religion. Regarding the name "Moses," however, British Egyptologist Dr. Kenneth A. Kitchen asserts that the moniker may not possess an Egyptian derivation and that the Semitic pronunciation is "mashu":

> ...The name of Moses is most likely *not* Egyptian in the first place!... It is better to admit the child was named (Exod. 2:10b) by his own mother, in a form originally vocalized *Mashu*, "one drawn out" (which became *Moshe*, "he who draws out," i.e., his people from slavery, when he led them forth). In fourteenth/thirteenth-century Egypt, "Mose" was actually pronounced *Masu*, and so it is perfectly possible that a young Hebrew Mashu was nicknamed Masu by his Egyptian companions; but this is a verbal pun, not a borrowing either way.[3]

Thus, "mose" would be rendered *masu*,[4] which could serve as a "nickname" for Mashu or "Moses."

Obviously, we do not concur that Moses was a historical personage who actually led his people out of Egypt or who had companions to give him a nickname. The point is well taken, nevertheless, that there exist various names by which this figure could be deemed, including Mashu or Masu, terms that go beyond the Hebrew or Egyptian connotations and possess solar associations.

Moses-El

The moniker "Moses" can be found in what amounts to either a theophoric name or a theonym, Misheal, as at Joshua 19:26. The relevant word in a list of Levitical cities and villages allotted to the tribe of Asher is מִשְׁאָל *Mish'al*,[5] which Oxford Assyriologist Dr. Archibald H. Sayce (1846-1933) asserts is a combination of "Mash" or

---

[1] Massey (1907), 2.662.
[2] Budge (2003a), 1.321.
[3] Kitchen, 297.
[4] See also Maspero, 8.450.
[5] Strong's H4861.

"Moses" and "El." Speaking of a text called the "City List of Thuthmose III," compiled by the pharaoh who died around 1425 BCE, Sayce states:

> Jacob-el and Joseph-el are not the only names in the List of Thothmes in which the name of a biblical personage has been combined with the title of a divinity. We find among them also the name of Mash-el, the Misheal of Joshua [19:26], where the title of *el* is attached to a name which, philologically, is the same as that of Moses.[1]

British royal physician Dr. Thomas Inman (1820-1876) evinced that the "Mash" in Mash-el represents Shamash.[2] Hence, the sun god's abbreviated name would be מש *mash*, similar to משה *mashah*, whence "Moses."

Messiah

It is also noteworthy that these same letters begin the word "messiah" or משיח *mashiyach*,[3] the primitive root of which is משח *mashach*,[4] the same as the root of "Moses" and denoting "to anoint" or "to consecrate." Hence, "Moses" could be perceived as a messiah, the savior who brought the Israelites to the Promised Land; indeed, Christ is called the "second Moses."[5]

Additionally, the Ugaritic term for "anoint" is *mšḥ*,[6] while an Egyptian term for "anoint" is *mas*, *mâsu* or *mesu*, sharing a common meaning with "messiah."[7] In consideration of their fascination with Hebrew letters, puns and word play, as well as the religious rituals and traditions of other cultures, it is likely that Hebrew priests and scribes of antiquity were conscious of these various congruences.

Mesore, the 'Birth of the Sun'

As an illustration of this type of syncretism, the remote origin of "Moses" may not have Egyptian significance, but in later times the name was associated with the Egyptian "born" or "child." In this regard, the Egyptian moniker *mesore*, meaning "birth of the sun," may have been in the minds of the Moses mythographers as well at some point.

In reference to the Egyptian winter-solstice celebration as related by Church father Epiphanius (c. 310/20-403 AD/CE), religious historian Dr. Raffaele Pettazzoni remarks:

---

[1] Sayce (1894), 339. See also Orr, 3.2066.
[2] Inman, 96.
[3] Strong's H4899
[4] Strong's H4886.
[5] See, e.g., Bromiley, et al (1985:621) discussing "Moses as a Type of the Messiah" and the "Messiah as the Second Moses."
[6] Schniedewind, 198.
[7] See Murdock (2009), 334.

The Egyptian for "birth of the sun" was *mesorê*, and Mesore in Egyptian usage was the name of the last month of the year, the fourth of the third *tetramenia*, i.e., of the last of the three seasons, which had four months each. This referred precisely to the feast of *mesorê*, with which the new year began.[1]

Logically, the New Year begins with the "birth of the sun," generally the winter solstice but also the vernal equinox, when the Israelites celebrated the New Year and Passover, a commemoration said biblically to have been initiated by Moses. This motif evidently also symbolizes the passing of the torch from the fall/winter sun (Moses) to the spring/summer sun (Joshua).

As concerns Moses and the epithet *mesore*, Massey comments:

> Musu, Moshé or Messu would be named after the child of the waters, who was the Mes-ar or Mes-ur of the month of Mesore; the first-born, the elder-born, the water-born; the new-birth coinciding with that of the inundation.[2]

Again, myths and traditions often have multiple meanings, which suits their nature as expressions of the sacred and supernatural, as such "coincidences" have appeared to humanity since antiquity to be part of the divine plan of the "Great Architect."

Masu the Hero

Yet another of these possible multiple meanings lies in the assertion by Sayce that Mashu or Masu, as found in Babylonian tablets, was the same word as Mosheh/Moses. Elsewhere, Sayce reiterates that, in Hebrew, Moses/Mosheh "is most easily explained by the Babylonian Masu, 'hero.'"[3]

The Assyriologist further elucidates:

> Masu, hero, an epithet of several deities, specially Adar, Merodach and the Sun-god; also "a scribe," or "librarian," and in astrology connected with Taurus.[4]

Thus, in Babylon "Masu" would be a title of Shamash, evidently associated with Moses. Speaking of the Assyrian solar warrior god, legislator and son of Bel, Adar or Atar, also known as Uras among other names, Sayce also comments:

> In the inscriptions of Nineveh, the title of "hero-god" (*masu*) is applied to him with peculiar frequency; this was the characteristic upon which the Assyrian kings more particularly loved to dwell. In Babylonia, on the other hand, Adar was by no means so favourite a divinity. Here it was the milder and less warlike Merodach that took

---

[1] Pettazzoni, 172.
[2] Massey (2007), 2.420.
[3] Sayce (1894), 339.
[4] Sayce (1887), 553.

his place. The arts of peace, rather than those of war, found favour among the Semitic population of the southern kingdom.¹

The British scholar notes that Merodach/Marduk is styled also by the Sumerian title "MAS-MAS"² or *maš-maš*, pronounced "mash-mash" and denoting "conjurer," "charmer," "sorcerer," "incantation priest" and "wonderworker."³ This designation *maš-maš* or *mašmašu* was held by the gods El, Ninib, Nergal, Ningizzida and Dumuzi as well.⁴

Mash

Reminiscent of Misheal or Mash-el, Clay asserts that the name of the Amorite deity "Mash" can be found in the "Mash-mannah" of 1 Chronicles 12:10 (משמנה *Mishmannah*),⁵ in the *Mish`am* at 1 Chronicles 8:12 (מעשם)⁶ and in the "gentilic name Mishraites" at 1 Chronicles 2:53 (משרעים).⁷ Referring to his book, *Amurru*, Clay also discusses the relationship between Mash and Shamash:

> In *Amurru* it was conjectured that perhaps in the absence of any etymological explanation of Shamash, it may have been from *Ša Mash* "(the god) of Mash," like the Arabic *Dhu'l Sharâ* etc., in other words that the mountain Mashu was his habitat....
>
> The consort of Mash was Mashtu. They are called the children of the god Sin... Mash is also a name of the god ᵈNin-IB; the sign MASH is used interchangeably with ᵈNin-IB....
>
> It was also contended in *Amurru*...that the deity Mash was carried by the Semites to Babylonia at a very early time. In the first three dynasties, Kesh, Erech and Ur, names compounded with the deity Mash or Mesh predominate. Especially at Erech in the early period do we find evidence of the worship of this deity. Some have translated this element as meaning "hero"...⁸

Here Clay is identifying Mash with Sayce's "hero" epithet, insisting it is a theonym and equating the deity Mash with not only Adar/Ninib but also Amurru: "The last two names of the Kish Dynasty, as well as three in the following two dynasties, are compounded with the name of Mesh (or Mash)."⁹

Clay also states that "Mash was a deity similar to the mountain or storm-deity Uru" and that "Mash, Mesh and Mish are also elements that figure prominently in the temple names of Nineveh, Cutha and

---

¹ Sayce (1887), 152.
² Sayce (1887), 153.
³ Geller, 45.
⁴ Muss-Arnolt, 607; "Mašmaš [SORCERER]," *The Pennsylvania Sumerian Dictionary*. See also "A balbale to Ningiszida (Ningiszida B)," lines 8-15; Rahmouni, 177.
⁵ Strong's H4925.
⁶ Strong's H4936.
⁷ Strong's H4954.
⁸ Clay, 179-180.
⁹ Clay, 67.

Akkad."[1] He further surmises that the city of Damascus originally was named Ki-Mash.[2]

The Babylonian god Mashu is described by Charles Coulter and Patricia Turner as follows:

> Moon god. Brother of Mashtu the goddess of the moon. Both are children of Nannar....[3]

In consideration of the fact of much Babylonian influence on the Bible and Israelites, it is reasonable to suggest that Moses was a rehash in significant part of this deity.

Library of Ashurbanipal

At Nineveh in what is now Iraq, Assyrian king Ashurbanipal (fl. 669-631 BCE) collected a royal library of 20,000 or so tablets, including the popular *Epic of Gilgamesh* and the cosmological *Enuma Elish*. Most of these tablets and writing boards were inscribed in Akkadian, using cuneiform; others are written in Neo-Babylonian script and in Assyrian.[4]

It is said that, despite its destruction centuries earlier, the enduringly famous Royal Library of Ashurbanipal inspired Alexander the Great to create his own. While the Greek commander died before doing so, his wish was begun by Ptolemy I (367-c. 283 BCE), called *Soter* or "Savior," whose effort led to the establishment of the famous Library of Alexandria. As it is to the Alexandrian library that we may look for much of Christian theology, it is to the Ashurbanipal library, among others, that perhaps we may turn to find the origins of significant Old Testament mythology and tradition.

The city of Nineveh was "sacked by an unusual coalition of Medes, Persians, Babylonians, Scythians and Cimmerians in 612 BCE." Ashurbanipal had made enemies in his aggressions to build his city and library, but one wonders who could have put together this "unusual coalition" and what was its purpose. It is possible that many of the texts, including more portable papyri and leather scrolls, were removed elsewhere, perhaps ending up in the city of Babylon, which itself was destroyed less than a century later (539 BCE) by the Persian king Cyrus, the "savior" and "christ" of the Jews (Is 45:1).

Before the Babylonian destruction, it may be that Jewish priests and scribes accessed one or more of the region's libraries, which may

---

[1] Clay, 180.
[2] Clay, 123, etc.
[3] Coulter and Turner, 311.
[4] The bulk of the discovered tablets, which are fragmented into some 30,000 pieces, are in the British Museum, in a collection now undergoing modern analysis, through the Library of Ashurbanipal Project. The texts' original handling after their discovery in the 19th century has confounded many of them inextricably, compounding the problems with their cataloguing.

have included texts from Ashurbanipal, such as those recounting the various tales of Adar, Marduk, Shamash, Mash, Mashu or others.

Amarna

The Babylonian tablet Sayce earlier refers to that came from Upper Egypt and mentions Adar as *masu* or *massû* was discovered in 1887 among the Amarna letters. In his report on the discovery of the Amarna documents, Rev. Dr. Angus Crawford remarks that it is "curious" that "we find the name 'Moses' on these tablets a century before the date of the Exodus. Masu or Moses is apparently identified with the sun god."[1]

One of the main correspondents in the letters, Amenhotep III, had married a Mitanni princess, who brought her Indo-European and Semitic gods with her to Egypt. His son, Akhenaten, also married a Mitanni woman, syncretizing her god Baal, the winged sun disc, with Aten worship.[2] It is possible that among these deities from the "Asiatics" was Mash, Adar, Marduk, Shamash or other sun god with the Masu epithet.

On one of the Amarna tablets, we read the initial prayer by a "Pu-Addi," who addresses his deity as "the sun god who rises from the divine day."[3] Concerning this text, Sayce comments:

...In a despatch from Zinarpi to the Egyptian king the Pharaoh is called, as usual, "the Sun-god rising from the Divine Day"; and it is then added, in a parenthesis, "whose name is Masu [or Masi]." This proves not only that the term "Masu" was applied to the Sun-god, but was actually used of the Egyptian Pharaoh in the century before Moses was born.[4]

16 ki-i-ma Samsi   is-tum
Like the sun-god(rising) from

17 D.P. yumi :   sa sumu
the divine day: whose name (is)

ma-si
Masi:

Fig. 107. Amarna tablet no. 6. (Sayce, 1888:10.500)

At this point, Sayce comments:

Masi is letter for letter the same as the Hebrew משה, "Moses"...[5]

Elsewhere, Sayce explicates:

Now, the Assyrian equivalent of the Hebrew *Mosheh*, "Moses," would be *maŝu*, and, as it happens, *maŝu* is a word which occurs not infrequently in the inscriptions. It was a word of Akkadian origin, but since the days of Sargon of Akkad had made itself so thoroughly at

---

[1] Crawford, 5.177.
[2] Crawford, 5.169.
[3] Crawford, 5.171.
[4] Sayce (1890), 24.26. French Egyptologist Urbain Bouriant (1849-1903), the discoverer at Amarna of Akhenaten's "Hymn to the Sun," gave copies of several Akkadian tablets from Amarna to Sayce to translate, including the one in question, a "small dark tablet of coarse clay" that the Assyriologist labels "No. VI" (6). (Sayce 1888:10.488, 499).
[5] Sayce (1888), 10.500.

home in the language of the Semitic Babylonians as to count henceforth as a genuinely Semitic term.[1]

The Assyriologist also asserts that *maṣu* or "hero" has no connection with its homophone *māšu* or *maashu*, meaning "double" and serving as the name of the twin mountain, Masu/Mashu, in the *Epic of Gilgamesh*.

Hero or Twin?

The Akkadian *māšu* or *maashu* is derived from the Sumerian *maš*, denoting not only "twin" but also "brother/sister," "young man" and "man, husband, male, grown-up."[2] *Māšu* can also mean "child," which ties it into the Egyptian *ms*, *mes* or *mas*.[3]

Using the same initial cuneiform symbol as *māšu* or "twins," a relevant Sumerian term is MAŠ.SU, in Akkadian *massû*, meaning "leader, expert."[4]

massu [LEADER] (24x: Ur III, Old Babylonian) wr. mas-su "leader, expert" Akk. *massû*

[1]   mas-su

The Akkadian *massû* may have been confounded with the Sumerian *mes*, meaning "hero; (to be) manly; young man."[5] Although etymologically these terms *maṣu* and *māšu* are said to be unrelated, it is possible that ancient priests and commoners alike interchanged them, whether by mistake or deliberately, as was the case with other relevant terms such as *maš* and *muš*, discussed below. The common mythical theme of the "hero twins" also may be reflected in any possible confounding of these various terms. As an example of this popular motif of twin heroes in connection with the sun, in Native American mythology the sun was "broken in two and became culture hero twins."[6]

The Leader

The epithet *maṣu/massû* meaning "leader" becomes even more germane to our analysis in that it was "said exclusively of gods and rulers..."[7] In one pre-Sargonic Sumerian text using this term, we read

---

[1] Sayce (1887), 46.
[2] "Maš [TWIN] wr. maš 'twin' Akk. *māšu*," *PSD*.
[3] The etymological database compiled by G. Bronnikov and Phil Krylov at Starling.rinet.ru includes a proto-Afroasiatic root *ma/ič-* for the proto-Semitic *ma/it* and the Egyptian *ms*, both meaning "child."
[4] "Massu [LEADER]," *PSD*.
[5] *ePSD Sumerian Sign-name Index*.
[6] Leeming (2010), 1.358-359.
[7] Kleinerman, 164.

the phrase *lugal-mas-su* or "the lord is leader."[1] The famous Mesopotamian king Urnamma or Ur-Nammu (3rd millennium BCE) too was called *mas-su ki-en-gi-ra* or "leader of Sumer."[2] Another apparent leading citizen was styled Enlil-massu,[3] which would mean "Enlil is leader." In a Sumero-Babylonian text entitled "The Seven Evil Spirits," the figure Enkidu is "exalted Massu of the gods."[4] Dumuzi/Tammuz is also called *mas-si-e*,[5] which sounds like the *masi* of the Amarna text.

It is obvious that Assyriologists of the past were startled to see these "Moses" epithets of gods and kings, *mashu, masu* or *massû*, staring at them. Their enthusiastic conclusions linking Mashu/Masu/Massu to Moses were ignored, however, as this mythological line of thought was swept back under the literalizing carpet by biblical scholars and theologians. This point of contention represents one of many with Assyriologists who, with an onslaught of eye-opening texts, suddenly found their faith and that of their colleagues to be challenged.

Nevertheless, the work of these Assyriologists in translating and disseminating the Utnapishtim flood myth as found in the *Epic of Gilgamesh* has led to the conclusion by many mainstream scholars that the biblical Noah account is dependent on the much older Mesopotamian version. Many discoveries since that time, including the Eblaite and Ugaritic texts, have led to further enlightenment as concerns biblical origins in pre-Israelite Near Eastern religion and mythology. It is time for the same type of scrutiny to be applied to the origin of the Moses and Exodus myth.

Gilgamesh and Mt. Mašu

A major factor in this quest for the origins of the Moses account is the *Epic of Gilgamesh*, which was extremely famous around the Near East for thousands of years, with copies of it found in Turkey, Syria, Mesopotamia and the Levant,[6] as at Megiddo, in Israel, thus connecting the two cultures. Since the earliest parts of this epic date to at least 1800 BCE, with the era of a possible "historical" king by that name around 2600 BCE,[7] this myth predates the composition of the Moses tale by over a thousand years.

The continuity of the epic's popularity can be seen in the fact that it was included in the Ashurbanipal library, around 650 BCE. Thus, the text likely would have been present in one or more Babylonian libraries during the exile in the sixth century and could not have

---

[1] Di Vito, 66, 110, 303.
[2] Flückiger-Hawker, 60, 107, 336.
[3] Kleinerman, 47.
[4] Horne, 231, 232.
[5] Langdon, 28.145.
[6] Snell, 88.
[7] See, e.g., Snodgrass, 107.

been unknown to the Jews, especially those literate individuals in Babylon. This fact is especially true since the Israelites appear to have come significantly from the same stock as the Chaldeans/ Amorites, whose hero was Gilgamesh, considered to be semidivine or a demigod.

The combination of texts and traditions from Western Semites such as the Canaanites, Ugaritians and Phoenicians, reflecting the northern kingdom, with those of the Babylonian-influenced Amoritish tribes of the southern hill country or Judea, explains very well the mixture we find in the Bible. If we add in the Egyptian and Indo-European influence through the Hittites and Mitanni, as well as Greeks during the late second to first millennia, numerous biblical elements are laid plain.

Moreover, the fact that there are Sumero-Babylonian, Akkadian and Hittite editions of the *Epic of Gilgamesh*[1] reflects a perfect match for the mixed beliefs of the hill settlement tribes as well. As demonstrated by its usage at Ugarit, the epic was a school text, which again indicates it was known widely by numerous individuals around the Levant for a very long time. Jewish scribes and other literate persons could not have been ignorant of its existence or contents.

Historicity?

As noted, it is believed that there is a historical core to Gilgamesh:

> Gilgamesh apparently was a historical person, the king of the city-state of Uruk (biblical Erech) sometime between 2700 and 2500 B.C.E. There is little historical kernel, however, to the epic by that name. Some traditions even identified Gilgamesh with one of the traditional Mesopotamian gods: with Dumuzi (Tammuz), the annual dying and rising god; with Ningishzida, a tree god; or with Nergal, the supreme god of the underworld.[2]

While there may have been a king by this name, the epic itself clearly represents not a "biography" but a solar-fertility myth in significant part. Among many other redactions, Gilgamesh's legend evidently was accreted with details from real people, such as King Gudea of Lagash (2144-2124 BCE), the end result of which is a composite character.

In this regard, University of Pennsylvania professor of Hebrew and Semitic languages and literature Dr. Jeffrey H. Tigay details the epic's construction over a period of 1,500 years in his monograph "The Evolution of the Pentateuchal Narratives in Light of the Evolution of the *Gilgamesh Epic.*" Again, a story with such longevity must have been known by millions across several relevant ethnicities and civilizations.

---

[1] See, e.g., Tigay, 37.
[2] Batto, 17-18.

Although the tale's germ could represent typical mythmaking associated with a ruler, including ascribing his right to rule to the sun god's authority, as occurred with Hammurabi, Gilgamesh's role in the epic is one of a solar hero, not a real person. It is his *myth* that has been copied, evidently, in the stories of many later heroes and lawgivers, including the Judaized Moses.

Moreover, it is noteworthy that the Babylonian hero has been identified with various deities of the region, including Tammuz, the solar harvest/wine god, and Ningishzida, the tree god. This latter deity, as we shall see, is also a solar serpent god, representing the constellation of Hydra as well.[1] The connection to Nergal is also interesting, in that Gilgamesh's journey appears to be an underworld myth resembling that of Osiris. Moreover, all three of these gods were styled with the epithet *maš-maš* or "mash-mash."

A priesthood attempting to syncretize all of these deities would naturally latch onto a moniker they had in common; hence, eventually one would speak of the god "Mash" or "Mashu" to connote this syncretic entity, later demoted to a "patriarch" styled "Mashah" or "Mosheh."

Etymology of Gilgamesh

In the oldest Sumerian texts, the name of the hero is *Bilgames* ($^d bil_3$-*ga-mes*), while in Old Babylonian it is GIŠ-gim-maš or "Gishgimmash." The cuneiform for this name is ⌞𒄑𒂆𒈧⌟ (*Gilgameš*), the last part of which name is the symbol 𒈧, representing *maš* and

^dGIŠ-gím-maš :

Fig. 108. Old Babylonian for 'Gilgamesh' (*Epic* 11.322)

connoting a number of different concepts, including: "border, boundary," "to be pure" and "goat; sacrificial animal for omens."[2]

The term is also the suffix of the word Ša-maš or Shamash, the sun, and, therefore, one could suggest again that the sun god was called *maš* or "Mash." As we have seen, Assyriologist Clay surmised Mash and Shamash to be the same as the term meaning "hero" or "leader."

The Hebrew word for "Gilgamesh" is גילגמש, the suffix of which contains the first two letters of the name משה Mosheh and last two of *shemesh*. Although it is said not to derive from the Semitic term גלגל gilgal, meaning "wheel" or "circle,"[3] a Semitic speaker might hear in the word "gilga-mesh" a connotation of "wheel of Moses" or "circle of Mash." This misconception, whether deliberate or accidental—keeping in mind that few ancients were professional etymologists and that many intellectuals, bards and poets in antiquity enjoyed wordplay and fanciful etymologies[4]—may have led to the change in

---

[1] Rogers, J., 13, 14, 15, etc.
[2] ePSD Akkadian Index.
[3] Strong's H1536.
[4] See, e.g., Porphyry's writing on the origin of various godnames, as in *Suns of God*, 64.

the hero's name over a period of centuries. It is significant that *gilgal* or *galgal* is defined in the Talmud as referring also to the zodiacal circle.[1]

In *Amurru*, Clay "endeavored to show that *Giš-bil-ga-Meš* (Gilgamesh) was a West Semitic name, which contains that of the god Mesh or Mash..."[2] Hence, he would be another "Mash" to be syncretized with his godly counterparts to produce "Moses."

Twin Mountains

In the Gilgamesh epic, Mašu or Mashu is the name of the sacred mountain guarded by the scorpion men from which the sun god, Shamash, comes riding in a chariot each morning and to which he returns every night.[3] To summarize:

> After reaching Mount Mašu in Tablet 9, Gilgamesh travels along the "road of the sun" on which he encounters dense darkness. Gilgamesh begins the journey into the twelve leagues of darkness at Mount Mašu, which guards the rising and setting of the sun.[4]

Sharing this symbolism, an Akkadian sun hymn reads:

> Sun-god, when you rise from the Great Mountain, when you rise from the Great Mountain, the "Mountain of the Spring," when you rise from Duku, the place where the destinies are determined, when you rise at the place where heaven and earth embrace, at the horizon.[5]

This scene reminds one also of Moses's striking of the rock at the foot of Mt. Sinai to produce a spring (Exod 17:6).

Gemini

The *māšu* or *maashu* epithet was applied also to the constellation of Gemini, the "twins," signifying that the term was well known in antiquity, designated by *māšu/maš* and connoting also "star."[6]

māšu [MAŠ.TAB.BA : ►╋ ╠═ ►╤┐] (also : ma(š)šû feminine : māštu)

1) Ė : twin (brother, sister) 2) İ : a) divine name b) Gemini constellation : [MUL.MAŠ.TAB.BA] 3) plant name : [Ú.MAŠ.TAB.BA]

Mashu denoting "twins" is used in the names of the ninth, 10th, 11th and 12th ecliptic constellations of the Babylonians as well.[7]

A list of deities from the text "Prayer to the Gods of the Night," dating to the Old Babylonian period (c. 1830-1530 BCE), reveals the theonym "Mash," apparently as Gemini:

---

[1] Pellar (2009), 12.
[2] Clay, 84.
[3] Littleton, 1.1343; Horowitz, 96ff.
[4] Bautch, 54.
[5] Horowitz, 316.
[6] Miller and Shipp, 89.
[7] Allen, R., 231, 233-4, 236.

Ahati [unidentified]; Gaga [unidentified]; ᵈDumuzi [Aries]; ᵈNingizzida [Hydra]; E-pa-e [Square of Pegasus? Jupiter?]; mul.Mul [Pleiades]; Is-li-e [the Bull's Jaw = Hyades]; Sipa.zi.an.na [Orion]; Kak.si.sa [Sirius]; Ban [the Bow = Canis Major]; Gir.tab [Scorpius]; A-mushen [Aquila]; Ku₆ [Piscis Austrinus]; Shim.mah [the Swallow]; Ud.ka.duha [the Panther]; Mash [Gemini?]; Mar.tu [unidentified; means the country of Amurru].

The suggestion is that the god Mash is identified with Gemini.[1]

Horned Peaks

The Akkadian word *māšu* or *mashu/maashu* thus is used to describe the "Twin Mountains" of the Gilgamesh myth, reflecting the symbolism of the two peaks through which the sun rises and sets.[2] The twin or horned peaks could represent another connotation of the "horns" in the Moses and Dionysus myths as well.

Again, the symbolism of the sun between two pointed mountains is widespread in antiquity, including in Mesopotamia and Egypt, as well as in the Americas. The twin-peaked mountain motif is comparable to Horus of the Two Horizons, and these twins have been identified also as the "two breasts" of Mother Earth.[3]

In this regard, Mt. Sinai and Mt. Horeb have been conceived since antiquity as "twin peaks" in a similar fashion. At the traditional site for Mt. Sinai in the Sinai, St. Catherine's Monastery is set at the foot of twin peaks, one of which is taken to be Mt. Horeb and the other Sinai.[4]

A similar sacred-mountain tale can be found also in the Indian story of the cosmic Mount Mandara, used to churn the "Ocean of Milk" by the Indian sun god Vishnu, in order to create the precession of the equinoxes.[5] Another popular Indian myth concerns the sacred Mt. Meru, the latter name similar to Dionysus's Merus/Meros and apparently related etymologically to Mašu.[6]

The Gilgamesh-Mashu imagery has been compared also to that of the much later Jewish book of 1 Enoch,[7] which may have acquired this theme from Babylon.

---

[1] Rogers, J., 15.
[2] Horowitz, 97.
[3] Bautch, 139.
[4] See, e.g., *The Bible Cyclopaedia*, 1. 599; *The Holy Bible: According to the Authorized Version*, 1.188; Conder, 4.190. The peaks behind the monastery are frequently styled Mts. St. Catherine and Sinai, but the former is locally known also as Horeb.
[5] See Murdock and Barker (2012), 7.
[6] Richter-Ushanas, 170.
[7] See, e.g., Bautch.

The Moses Connection

Considering the facts discussed here, it should come as no surprise if the Moses myth were based significantly upon the Gilgamesh legend. This connection has been proposed in the past, including by German Assyriologist and Semitic philologist at University of Marbug Dr. Peter Jensen, in his book *Gilgamesch-Epos und Odyssee*. Concerning Jensen's work, American philologist Dr. Theodore Ziolkowski states:

> After an exhaustive exposition of the epic of Gilgamesh, Jensen sets out to demonstrate that Moses is the Gilgamesh of Exodus who saves the children of Israel from precisely the same situation faced by the inhabitants of Erech at the beginning of the Babylonian epic (125-58). He goes on for a thousand pages to depict parallels between Gilgamesh and Abraham, Isaac, Samson, David and various other biblical figures and arrives inevitably at Jesus, who turns out to be "nothing but an Israelite Gilgamesh...."[1]

In addition to the many other commonalities, the Babylonian epic's manner of composition itself reveals a process evidently similar to that by which the later Exodus drama likewise was composed.[2] As Tigay remarks:

> A typical current view would summarize the evolution of the Pentateuch more or less as follows. The original literary units underlying the Pentateuch were single narratives about the early Hebrew tribes and their leaders. Such narratives were for the most part created, and at first transmitted, orally, some think in poetic form. In the course of time, some of them were gather together into cycles dealing with various individuals (e.g., Abraham, Jacob) or other common subjects (e.g., the Egyptian bondage, the exodus, the conquest); the cycles were later linked together into lengthier narratives series...[3]

We would clarify, however, that these "leaders" were largely the *gods* of these various tribes, demoted to "patriarchs," "prophets" and "judges," and syncretized with one another over the centuries.

Tigay also remarks that "the stages and processes through which the [Gilgamesh] epic *demonstrably* passed are similar to some of those through which the Pentateuch narratives are *presumed* to have passed."[4]

---

[1] Ziolkowski, 26. Although other Assyriologists agreed with him, Jensen was widely assailed by theologians and biblical scholars, who attacked his methodology because they did not like his conclusions that the Bible did not represent literal history. Jensen apparently believed that the future would recognize his effort as possessing merit.
[2] See, e.g., Batto, 18-19.
[3] Tigay, 22-23.
[4] Tigay, 27.

Arabian Tales

Islamic scholars in antiquity likewise recognized the relationship between Moses and Gilgamesh when they used more of the latter's characteristics to flesh out the Islamic Moses, known as Musa/Mūsā or Mushas (موسى) in Arabic. Hence, in a thorough analysis we are justified also in acknowledging this comparison.

In this regard, professor of Islamic Studies and Comparative Religion at the University of Washington Dr. Brannon M. Wheeler states, "The Muslim exegetical image of Moses in the Quran is linked with ancient Sumerian stories of Gilgamesh..."[1]

Wheeler further says:

> In Muslim exegesis on the episode of Moses at the well of Midian there are several allusions to elements from the Epic of Gilgamesh....
>
> It does not appear that Muslim exegetes were familiar with the name of Gilgamesh; but that they were familiar with certain key elements of the Gilgamesh story, especially his journey to Utnapishtim, is evident.[2]

Although there is insufficient space for such a study here, if we look to Arabian stories of Moses, including in the Quran, we will find additional comparisons with the Gilgamesh epic.[3] The Arabs may have known the ancient Mesopotamian hero by the name of Musa, rather than Gilgamesh, lending credence to our conclusions that Gilgamesh is Masu/Mashu/Mash and Mashah/Mosheh/Moses.

Commonalities with the Bible

The parallels between Gilgamesh and Moses are many, and there are differences as well. Some of these variant details, such as the Utnapishtim flood story, found their way into other biblical myths, including those purported to have been written by Moses himself. The commonalities include the following, in the order of the Moses myth as in the Bible. For the exact book or tablet in which these themes appear, please consult the epic itself.[4]

1. Like Moses, Gilgamesh is considered wise and learned in the mysteries.
2. As do the Israelites in Egypt, a people labors to build a city.[5]
3. Gilgamesh is known for killing men, like Moses with the Egyptian and later the Amalekites, Midianites and so on.[6]
4. Like Moses, a hero wanders in the wilderness and thrives in the desert with animals.

---

[1] Wheeler, B., i.
[2] Wheeler, B., 30.
[3] See, e.g., Wheeler, B., 28, 30ff.
[4] One translation of the Epic of Gilgamesh is included in *The Study Guide*.
[5] Exod 1:1.
[6] Exod 2:12.

5. The Babylonian hero speaks to the bright sun god, and his face is lit up, like the burning bush and Moses's shining countenance.[1]
6. A man (Enkidu) is sent to act as a savior or messiah.
7. The hero has a brother with whom he goes on his quest, to "travel an unknown road and fight a strange battle."
8. Gilgamesh's destiny is ordained by Enlil, the "father of the gods," like Moses's fate determined by Yahweh.
9. A magical serpent features prominently, like Moses's rod and bronze snake.[2]
10. As in the Exodus, the common people lament abuses by a king.[3]
11. Gilgamesh petitions the high god on behalf of the suffering people, and the deity responds by sending "strong allies," including "great winds," such as the "north wind, the stone and icy wind, the tempest and the scorching wind," comparable to the biblical plagues.
12. The high god's allies are compared to vipers, dragons and serpents, resembling the biblical controlling of snakes and monsters, as well as to a "destroying flood and the lightning's fork."
13. Gilgamesh goes on an arduous journey to the "garden of the gods" and the "garden of the sun," comparable to the Exodus into the Promised Land.
14. Gilgamesh miraculously crosses an impassable sea with "waters of death."
15. The number 12 is significant in both myths.
16. A magical plant/flower provides everlasting life, like the manna miraculously giving life to the chosen people.
17. Gilgamesh provides fresh water on a mountain, like Moses striking the rock.
18. Two brothers fight a giant, like the biblical battles against the Amalekites.
19. The Babylonian hero prays to the moon god, Sin,[4] a name from which comes "Sinai," where Moses prays to the soli-lunar god Yahweh.
20. The hero climbs a sacred mountain where he finds the high god, whom he reveres with animal sacrifice and offering.
21. As Moses was 40 days in the wilderness of Mt. Sinai,[5] the Babylonian struggle between good and evil lasts 40 days and

---

[1] Exod 3:2.
[2] Cunningham (91): "...in the Epic of Gilgameš, Enkidu and the Underworld, the earliest copies of which date to the Old Babylonian period, Gilgameš defeats a snake..."
[3] Exod 5:1.
[4] See, e.g., Kovacs, M., 75.
[5] Exod 24:18.

nights, representing the battle between Gilgamesh and his "alter ego" Enkidu.
22. Gilgamesh kills the Bull of Heaven, while Moses destroys the sacred or heavenly Golden Calf.
23. Like Aaron and his priestly sacrament,[1] a brother receives the drink of the gods and royalty, the best wine, which serves as a civilizing or salvific force, indulged in like a communion food.
24. Gilgamesh was a "despoiler of women," while Moses gave the Midianite virgin girls to his warriors as their booty.[2]
25. As happened to Moses with Aaron, Gilgamesh's beloved brother, Enkidu, dies.[3]
26. Gilgamesh writes down his adventures, like Moses with the Pentateuch.[4]
27. Like that of the Hebrew lawgiver in the Bible, Gilgamesh's death is recorded in the epic.[5]

The variances between the Gilgamesh and Moses stories are explained by the era and location, reflecting also the values of the people, as well as the agendas of the wealthy elite and ruling class of the time. These differences are germane in establishing the various influences, mores and other important aspects of a particular culture. As we can see, however, there are many details in common that indicate a shared archetype, some of which we will examine further.

The Quest

As in the myths of Herakles, Dionysus, Moses and others, the Mesopotamian leader/hero sets out on a laborious journey to paradise:

> Gilgamesh...travels through twelve leagues of darkness along the "path of the sun." He emerges from that leg of the journey at the place where the sun rises. There he finds trees with precious stones that serve as fruit and foliage... After an encounter with the ale-wife Siduri near the cluster of trees, he must cross the sea as well as the waters of death (Hubur) to arrive at Utnapishtim's home...

> ...in Epic of Gilgamesh 9 the scorpion beings warn that no people can cross through the peaks of Mašu; later the ale-wife informs Gilgamesh that crossing the sea, a feat performed only by the sun-god, would be difficult (Epic of Gilgamesh 10). Yet Gilgamesh accomplishes both tasks impossible for ordinary humans.[6]

The gem-filled, sunrise paradise has been called the "garden of God," and the parallels to various biblical themes are obvious, such

---

[1] Num 18:12.
[2] Num 31.
[3] Num 33:33.
[4] Deut 31:9.
[5] Deut 34:5.
[6] Bautch, 232-234.

as the Garden of Eden, as well as Moses crossing the sea, finding miraculous "fruit and foliage" and a promised "land of milk and honey."

Shining Face and Burning Bush

Along his journey, Gilgamesh speaks to Shamash, requesting to "behold the sun that I may be saturated with light,"[1] reminiscent of Yahweh's burning bush and solar appearance, as well as Moses's shining face after his *tête-à-tête* with the Jewish god.

Wandering the Wilderness

Gilgamesh's ordeal passing through the 12 "leagues of darkness" represents the sun moving through the hours of night, found in Egyptian mythology concerning the passage of the deceased via the 12 gates, as in the New Kingdom *Book of the Amduat*.[2] This movement through the darkness reminds one of Osiris's role as the sun of the night sky, re-emerging via the "jeweled gate" of sunrise, as the newborn Harpocrates or Horus the Child.

In later times such as during the first millennium BCE, the dozen gates, as well as the 12 tablets of the epic itself, also may have come to symbolize the months of the year or signs of the zodiac, again like the 12 "tasks" of Herakles or the many examples of "the 12" in the Bible and other ancient mythology.[3]

Moreover, the god of night is considered frequently to be the deity of desert pestilence as well, as with Set/Seth. Hence, we can see how the expedition would constitute "wandering in the desert" or desolation. It would also reflect the similar Greek motif of Hades and the desolate underworld.

Crossing the Sea, Waters of Death and Promised Land

The epic includes a warning to Gilgamesh about crossing the sea and waters of death:

> Gilgamesh, never has there been a passage
> And no one since all eternity could cross the sea—
> Samas the hero has crossed the sea,
> But who besides Samas can cross it?
> Difficult is the passage and troublesome the way,
> Impassable are the waters of death...[4]

On the other side of the sea is the "Isle of the Blessed," sounding much like the "Promised Land." Here we have an episode of a divinely inspired lawgiver miraculously crossing an impassable sea, in order to reach paradise.

---

[1] Kovacs, M., 77.
[2] See, e.g., Murdock (2009), 269ff, etc.
[3] See my article, "The Twelve in the Bible and Ancient Mythology."
[4] Carus (1901), 15.363.

It is noteworthy that the miraculous "crossing of the sea" was previously accomplished *only* by the *sun god* and that, in his journey across the mountains, Gilgamesh is consciously *imitating* Shamash.[1]

The crossing of the sea by the solar deity symbolizes the sun's reflection on water, especially at dawn, after battling the mighty "waters of death" or "unruly waters," again a highly popular myth around the Mediterranean.

Bull of Heaven

In the epic, Gilgamesh defeats the "Bull of Heaven," a motif reminiscent of the Mithraic bull-slaying theme and the biblical destruction of the Golden Calf. The "bull of heaven" was also an epithet of Adad,[2] depicted as standing on a bull, reminding us again of the Mithraic tauroctony. The overcoming of the bull is said to represent the ending of drought, signifying the arrival in the spring by the solar hero, who brings with him the rains. It is evidently in part at least because of the role of the bull in spring fertility, as well as plowing and planting, that the powerful animal was settled upon to symbolize the vernal equinox as the zodiacal sign of Taurus, representing April-May.

Concerning the biblical book of Hosea, which is a "prophecy" or warning to the northern kingdom of Israel by the Judean prophet about the continued worship of the Golden Calf, Rabbi Greenbaum comments:

> One of the underlying metaphors of the entire prophecy is of Ephraim as a calf that was intended to learn to bear the yoke and plow the field of Torah and mitzvos ["commandments"], but which rebelled. The metaphor is bound up with the fact that Joseph (father of Ephraim, corresponding to the constellation of Shor, Taurus, the "Ox") was blessed by Moses as a "first-born ox" (Deut. 33:17).[3]

It is noteworthy that the Greek word in the Septuagint verse at Deuteronomy 33:17 used to describe the "glory" of Joseph as a "bull" is ταῦρος *tauros* or Taurus. Thus, Joseph corresponds to Taurus, having been "blessed by Moses," the latter supposedly the author of Deuteronomy, in which Joseph is compared to a "firstling bull" or "firstborn bull," and so on.

Greenbaum clearly associates the Hebrew word שׁור *showr*, meaning "ox, bull, cow, bullock,"[4] with the constellation of Taurus, in turn implying the intention by the prophecy's author to indicate the metaphor of this zodiacal sign assigned to Joseph and his son Ephraim.

---

[1] Bautch, 237.
[2] Rahmouni, 319.
[3] Greenbaum, "Hosea Chapter 11," *Know Your Bible.*
[4] Strong's H7794.

Precession of the Equinoxes

This theme may reflect also the transition between the *equinoctial ages* of Taurus and Aries, during a later era but preceding Hipparchus (c. 190-c. 120 BCE), traditional discoverer of the precession of the equinoxes. Evidence indicates knowledge of the precession to a certain extent centuries earlier than the Greek astronomer.[1] It may be simply that Hipparchus was the first to summarize in writing the ideas of the precession that had been formulated over a period of hundreds to thousands of years.

In his study of the zodiac and constellations, *The Foundation of Myth*, Pellar relates that "the image of a bull, as Taurus, the 'bull of heaven,' was probably first set down as a quartet (along with Leo, Scorpio, and Aquarius) in either Sumer or Elam as a cardinal point between 4400 and 2200 BCE (Rogers 1998: 24)."[2]

Cambridge scholar John Rogers thus avers that the constellation of Taurus, represented as a bull, was devised as a cardinal point two to four thousand years before Hipparchus. This fact would explain to some extent the commonality of the divine bull motif dating back millennia. The timeframe also follows roughly the precessional era in which Taurus was said to rule.

Indeed, Taurus—called in the Babylonian star catalogues $GU_4.AN.NA$ or "the Steer of Heaven"—has been used to mark the vernal equinox since at least the Middle Bronze Age (c. 2100 to 1550 BCE).[3] It is noteworthy that the motif of the heavenly bull did not appear in the Old Babylonian editions of the Gilgamesh epic, but it *can* be found in the Akkadian and Hittite versions during the Middle Babylonian period (c. 14th cent. BCE).[4] This development that would suggest the later writers became aware of Taurus during their time.

Battling a Giant

Gilgamesh's battle against the "storm-roaring" giant of the cedar forest, Huwawa/Humbaba, reminds one of Moses's fight not only with Amalekites but also with the pharaoh, as in the ancient archetype previously discussed, concerning the storm and sun god versus the monster/serpent of the deep.

Speaking of Humbaba, Assyriologists Jastrow and Clay remark:

> ...we encounter in the Yale tablet for the first time the writing of Ḫu-wa-wa as the name of the guardian of the cedar forest, as against Ḫum-ba-ba in the Assyrian version... The name would thus present a complete parallel to the Hebrew name Ḥowawa (or Ḥobab) who

---

[1] See, e.g., *Hamlet's Mill* and Krupp, as in Murdock (2009), 265ff.
[2] Pellar (2012), 3, citing: Rogers, John H. 1998. "Origins of the Ancient Constellations: I. The Mediterranean Traditions," *Journal of the British Astronomical Association* 108: 9–28.
[3] "Babylonian star catalogues," *Wikipedia*.
[4] Tigay, 25, 37.

appears as the brother-in-law of Moses in the P document, Numbers 10, 29.[1]

Numbers 10:29 names the son of Moses's Midianite father-in-law as חבב *Chobab*, a West Semitic or Amoritish name meaning "beloved" and "cherished."[2] Judges 4:11 appears to name Hobab erroneously as Moses's father-in-law himself. In either case, the biblical character may have been based on the Babylonian giant, at least nominally.

Cedar Mountain

The attempt in the epic to take over the cedars of Lebanon is interesting, as it may reflect the desire of the Amoritish Babylonians of the time when this passage was altered from its original Sumerian version. In the original Sumerian, the "Cedar Mountain" that Gilgamesh must approach is located to the east of Sumer, towards the rising sun, whereas in the later Old Babylonian redaction of the epic, the mountain has been changed to the west, in Lebanon, whence the famed cedars,[3] which the Amorites wanted to acquire. It is possible that the original location to the east was purely symbolic as the place of the rising sun; or, this part of the epic originally may have referred to cedars to the east, in Iran, India or what is now Afghanistan and so on.

Winemaker

According to the myth, Gilgamesh is an "arrogant ruler who kills men and despoils women,"[4] while, again, Moses too was known to kill men and give virgin slave girls as war booty to his followers. Gilgamesh's civilizing comes not only from the laws given to him by Shamash but also from the advice of the wine goddess, revealing the importance of that libation in this myth as well. This oenological deity is the "ale-wife" Siduri, also a "winemaker," "woman of the vine, the maker of wine."[5]

Hence, the wine goddess guides the solar hero. As Mary Ellen Snodgrass comments:

> The winemaker Siduri, like the Greek wine god Dionysus, offers pragmatic wisdom: She advises Gilgamesh to delight in the everyday joys of feasting, good company, cleanliness and family life."[6]

Unwin explains this motif as a fertility tale:

> The imagery connecting fertility with wine and the vine is also illustrated by the Sumerian *Epic of Gilgamesh*, dating from the first centuries of the second millennium BC, but probably existing in much the same form many centuries earlier.... Gilgamesh encounters

---

[1] Jastrow and Clay, 23.
[2] Strong's H2246.
[3] Tigay, 41.
[4] Snodgrass, 107.
[5] Gilgamesh (1960), 97; Unwin, 79.
[6] Snodgrass, 108.

Siduri by the garden of the gods where "there was fruit of carnelian with the vine hanging from it..."[1]

Further demonstrating wine's ritual and magical importance in Babylonian religion, in the epic's conclusion with Gilgamesh's death (117-118), "bread offerings are made and libations of wine are poured out..."[2] In Babylonian incantations and potions, such as to the goddess Ishtar, wine is one of the magical substances used to produce supernatural results, including to combat witchcraft itself.[3]

This tale is comparable also to the Noah myth: "Noah's experience with viticulture, enology and wine drinking find a parallel in the Gilgamesh epic, which dates from the fourth millennium BCE."[4] The central focus on the sun and wine reveals that the Gilgamesh tale is a solar and vegetation/fertility archetype, evidently utilized in the creation of the Moses story and possibly influencing the Dionysus myth as well.

Wine and Bread Communion

In a related theme, the transformation of Gilgamesh's adopted brother,[5] the wild man Enkidu, comes through a tradition and ritual that likewise sound very biblical:

> Enkidu is seduced by a "harlot from the temple of love" (Epic of Gilgamesh, 1960:99), who later also introduces him to the pleasure of wine, saying to him:
>
> "Enkidu, eat bread, it is the staff of life; drink the wine, it is the custom of the land." So he ate till he was full and drank strong wine, seven goblets. He became merry, his heart exulted, and his face shone. He rubbed down the matted hair of his body and anointed himself with oil. Enkidu had become a man. (Epic of Gilgamesh, 1960-65-6)
>
> Enkidu thus becomes a man by eating bread and drinking wine, symbolising the development of agriculture which raised humanity above nature.[6]

The "harlot from the temple of love" resembles a priestess of Aphrodite/Venus, whom we have seen is comparable to Zipporah, Moses's wife.

Moreover, the civilizing or salvational effect thus is produced mystically through bread and wine, as well as by anointing, as in the Bible. Enkidu's transformation of having his eyes opened has been

---

[1] Unwin, 79-80.
[2] Unwin, 81.
[3] Abusch and Schwemer, 368, etc.
[4] Heskett and Butler, 10.
[5] In the earlier Sumerian texts, Enkidu is depicted as Gilgamesh's "servant." (Tigay, 33)
[6] Unwin, 81.

compared to Genesis 3:5, in which the magical fruit is said to impart knowledge that will make humans like gods.[1]

From what we currently know, the transition from wild to civilized, raising mankind above nature, evidently began to occur in Turkey, at Gobekli Tepe, starting possibly 15,000 years ago. It may be that some of these spiritual ideas were germinated in the minds of these prehistoric, apparent Natufians that long ago.

In his analysis of the themes from Gilgamesh paralleled in the Bible, Swedish theologian Dr. Helmer Ringgren (1917-2012) points out that these various motifs were not present in the Sumerian version of the epic and that "they belong to a stratum of the Gilgamesh tradition which is definitely Semitic, perhaps even influenced by West Semitic ideas."[2] He further asks whether or not counterparts in the epic to biblical stories can be "interpreted as borrowings from the Western Semites (Amorites, etc.)?"[3]

Despite the epic's enduring popularity, we do not possess a complete story with all the details of the Gilgamesh epic, and it is possible that some of the missing parts contain even more parallels to various biblical legends and myths. In any event, mainstream scholars are convinced that the Utnapishtim myth serves as the root of the Noah and Flood story, and it is reasonable to propose that the epic also contributed to many other biblical tales, such as that of Moses and other patriarchs. Important scholarship has been done in this regard on comparisons between Gilgamesh and Jesus as well.[4]

To summarize, in the Gilgamesh tale, we have a hero or leader (*mašu?*) climbing the holy mountain (Mashu) in order to emulate the path of the solar legislator (Shamash), much like the Moses (Mosheh) myth.

Mŝ the Sacred Serpent

Adding to the Mosaic syncretism, in the Ugaritic mythology appears a figure called Mŝ or Mush, son of Baal and Anath, possibly equivalent to Adar as "Mash," son of Bel. Mŝ/Mush was propitiated to prevent poisonous animals like scorpions and serpents from attacking, in essence making of him a snake god.[5] Mŝ's name is asserted to be not Semitic or Egyptian but Sumerian, such as by Brandeis University linguist Dr. Michael C. Astour (1916-2004), who states that there is no Egyptian linguistic borrowing in the Ugaritic texts and who demonstrates instead an abundance of Sumerian religious ideas in Canaanite mythology.[6] He avers that both Mŝ or

---

[1] See, e.g., Ringgren in Goedicke, 408. The rendered "God" in Gen 3:5 is *elohim*, which, as we have seen, is plural.
[2] Goedicke, 408-409.
[3] Goedicke, 411.
[4] See, e.g., Jensen's *Das Gilgamesch Epos in der Welt-literatur*.
[5] Sayce 1887:479.
[6] Astour, 231.

Mŝi and Moses are Sumerian, remarking, "It is therefore preferable to detach Môše from Egyptian loan-names."[1]

Snake God

According to Astour, the term Mŝ reflects a Sumerian deity, the source of numerous Ugaritic references to a snake god,[2] equivalent to Muš, meaning "serpent."[3] This moniker "Mush" thus would be appropriate for a serpent-cult founder, "Moses," "Mosheh" or "Musa," as in Arabic. In the Sumero-Babylonian mythology, there appears also a constellation Muš, which "loosely corresponds" to the hydra or multiheaded snake/serpent.[4] Hence, this Sumerian word and concept were passed along in the Babylonian tradition, as shown additionally in this periodical entry:

Fig. 109. Cuneiform *muš*, Sumerian for 'snake' or 'serpent'

> muš [SNAKE] (192x: ED IIIa, ED IIIb, Old Akkadian, Ur III, Old Babylonian, Middle Babylonian) wr. muš "snake" Akk. ṣēru[5]

This word can be found almost 200 times in extant writings, including tablets from Uruk, Lagash, Nippur, Ebla and Ugarit.[6] The term *muš* occurs in the Gilgamesh epic (10.305), while in another tablet we find the phrase *gal muš*, which means "big snake."[7] A common form is *muš-a*, used in the texts *Inanna's Descent* and *Dumuzi's Dream*, for example.[8]

In *Inanna's Descent to the Underworld* (376-383), Dumuzi begs Utu to change his extremities into a serpent's "hands and feet" in order to "escape my demons": Thus, "Utu turned Dumuzid's hands into snake's hands. He turned his feet into snake's feet."[9] Here we see the theme of the sun god controlling the serpent, as well as giving magical serpentine attributes to the goddess's consort-son in order to protect him from demons.

Serpent Monsters

In the Neo-Babylonian era, Inanna's Semitic counterpart, Ishtar, was symbolized by the *mušḫuššu*, a monstrous creature with a

---

[1] Astour, 230.
[2] Astour, 231.
[3] Astour, 229; Rahmouni, xxiv. Astour (230) asserts that the Sumerian homonyms *muš*, meaning "serpent," and *mûšu*, meaning "night," are not related. The fact remains remarkable that in a number of religious systems, including the Egyptian and Christian, the night sky or "prince of darkness" is identified as or with a serpent.
[4] See, e.g., the Mesopotamian text called the "MUL.APIN," c. 14th-11th cent. BCE.
[5] Etymology by Steve Tinney and Philip Jones, "Muš [SNAKE]," *PSD*.
[6] "Muš [SNAKE]," *PSD*.
[7] "Early Dynastic Officials."
[8] "Muš [SNAKE]," *PSD*.
[9] "Inana's descent to the nether world: translation," *The Electronic Text Corpus of Sumerian Literature*.

snakelike tongue, depicted on the goddess's famous gate at Babylon (6ᵗʰ cent. BCE). Marduk too is associated with the *mušḫuššu*, a word derived from the Sumerian MUŠ, and the creature may also be the dragon in the apocryphal Jewish tale of "Bel and the Dragon." Another term is *mušnammiru*, which means "who illuminates" and is an epithet of Shamash.¹

An Akkadian cognate of the Sumerian *muš* is *bašmu*,² used in the *Enuma Elish* to describe the offspring of the serpent monster of the deep, Tiamat, and "presumably cognate" also with the Semitic term *bṯn*, as in the Ugaritic texts.³ As Cambridge University fellow Dr. Graham Cunningham remarks, "Snakes can also be regarded as similar to chaos-monsters..."⁴

Fig. 110. *Mušḫuššu* or "reddish/fierce snake," originally 6ᵗʰ cent. BCE. Reconstructed Ishtar Gate from Babylon, Pergamon Museum, Berlin

Archaic Serpent Cult

We have seen numerous examples of snake worship, including and especially the serpent motifs in the Bible, particularly in the Moses account. In this same regard, serpent worship may be among the oldest known religious reverence, possibly dating back some 70,000 or more years. This contention is evidenced possibly by the discovery in the 1990s by archaeologists in a remote cave in Botswana, Africa, of what could be a giant carved python which may date from that remote era and indicate a ritualistic purpose.⁵

Although the cave-python thesis remains unproved, archaic serpent reverence can be found among the local San or Khoisan people, also known as Bushmen, among whom the python is one of their top three most important animals.⁶ Another very archaic ethnos, the Pygmies of the Congo, also had important myths about serpents/snakes and dragons, possibly dating back many thousands of years.⁷

As mythologists Patricia Ann Lynch and Jeremy Roberts state:

> Snakes, particularly the python, play prominent roles in African mythology. A serpent named Aido-Hwedo carried the Fon Creator,

---

¹ Rahmouni, 243.
² Rahmouni, 143.
³ Smith and Pitard, 2.249.
⁴ Cunningham, 91.
⁵ Handwerk, "'Python Cave' Reveals Oldest Human Ritual, Scientists Suggest."
⁶ Britt, "Scientists find first known human ritual." The San have a myth in which the daughter of the creator/supreme being styled "Mantis" marries a snake. (Leeming, 2010:1.75)
⁷ Hallet and Pelle, 55-56, etc.

Mawu-Lisa, in his mouth as she created the world. Chinawezi, the cosmic serpent of the Lunda people, governed the earth and its waters. Snakes were commonly associated with rain and the rainbow.[1]

It should also be noted that one currently mainstream DNA theory contends that the San constitute the world's oldest known ethnicity, the most direct descendants of the proposed "Genetic Eve," from whom it is hypothesized come all *Homo sapiens sapiens*.[2]

Incantation Texts

Venomous snakes have the seemingly godly ability of inflicting near-instant death, like the lightning strikes of the sky god but much more frequently fatal to humans and other animals. Hence, in the Mesopotamian incantation texts, poisonous creatures like snakes and scorpions understandably were of special concern. Therefore, the gods and goddesses who potentially controlled them were to be appeased and revered above many others.[3]

If one is religious and believes in an all-powerful god or gods, one naturally will suppose that the divine is controlling and sending snakes to do his/her bidding, including and especially exacting capital punishment for some grievous offense. Thus, we can understand the intense fear, respect and reverence that would lead to a serpent cult, evidenced by the popularity of such beliefs in many places globally for thousands of years.

Snake-Charmers

Snake-controlling spells appear in the Babylonian "Exorcist's Handbook," while the Sumerian-derived Akkadian designations for "exorcist" include *maš-maš* and *muš-la-la-ah-hu*, meaning "snake-charmer."[4] Semitic languages professor Dr. Markham J. Geller asserts that these latter two words are synonyms.[5] These facts tie snakes into the *mašmašu* priesthood, to be discussed below.

In the Ugaritic texts, it is the god *ḥrn* or Horon/Ḥôrānu who "plays an important role casting spells against snakes..."[6] It is noteworthy also the Semitic word for "snake," *nḥš* (Heb. נחש *nachash*), is "perhaps related to the Babylonian serpent god Šaḫan."[7]

Snake of Enki

Since snakes live underground, including beneath temples, it has been believed that underworld deities in particular control and send

---

[1] Lynch and Roberts, 10.
[2] See, e.g., "Mitochondrial Eve," *Wikipedia*.
[3] See, e.g., Cunningham, 105.
[4] Geller, 45.
[5] Geller, 45.
[6] Rahmouni, 343. See *The Study Guide* for more on Horon.
[7] Schniedewind, 199-200; Strong's H5175.

serpents out for various purposes, principally as a punishment.¹ It is significant that the earliest incantation texts indicate a time when Enki, another god linked to the underworld,² was "especially associated with illness-bringing snakes." In this regard, the epithet *muš ᵈen-ki* or "snake of Enki"³ indicates his status as a serpent deity in significant part.

Moreover, Cunningham states that in the "Epic of Gilgameš, Enkidu and the Underworld, the earliest copies of which date to the Old Babylonian period, Gilgameš defeats a snake..."⁴ The defeat of an opponent generally conveys control over that adversary, suggesting that, like Enki, Gilgamesh here is given the status of a snake god as well. In turn, Gilgamesh has been associated with Moses since antiquity, and it is significant that the biblical lawgiver too possesses important serpent-deity attributes.

Ningishzida the Mush

Another underworld and serpent deity is the Mesopotamian agricultural and fertility god Ningishzida, who was understandably the subject of magical incantations by priests, including one text invoking his "mouth" as that of a "magician" and a "snake":

> Lord, your mouth is that of {a pure magician} {(*1 ms. has instead:*) a snake with a great tongue, a magician} {(*1 ms. has instead:*) a poisonous snake}, Lord Ninĝišzida, ...! Ninĝišzida, your mouth is that of a pure magician...⁵

The original Sumerian of this text repeats the terms *maš-maš*, *maš* and *muš*:

8. lugal ka-zu {maš-maš maš} {(*1 ms. has instead:*) muš /eme\ mah maš-maš mah} {(*1 ms. has instead:*) muš uš₁₁} en

   ᵈnin-ĝiš-zid-da ki /ra\ [ki ra-ra]

9. ᵈnin-ĝiš-zid-da **ka-zu maš-maš maš en** ᵈnin-ĝiš-zid-da **ki [ra ki ra-ra]**

Here *maš-maš* is rendered "magician," while *maš* is "pure," and *muš* is "snake." One manuscript ("ms.") reads "snake" (*muš*), rather than "magician" (*maš*), indicating that these terms were considered interchangeable to some extent. The alliteration in this passage suggests what must have appeared to be a very magical incantation, pregnant with meaning and power. Hence, we might surmise that

---

¹ See, e.g., Cunningham, 78.
² In one myth, Enki battles a dragon of *Kur*, the abyss or underworld. (Baring and Cashford, 280.)
³ Mesopotamian incantation text 26; Cunningham, 37.
⁴ Cunningham, 91.
⁵ "A balbale to Ninĝišzida (Ninĝišzida B)," lines 8-9.

MOSES AS SOLAR HERO

"Mash" and "Mush" were considered highly powerful sacred epithets, apparently rolled into one in "Moses."

Like Ishtar and Marduk, Ningishzida is also styled with the epithet *muš-huš* ("mush-hush") or *mušhuššu/mušḫuššu* (Akk.), meaning "fierce serpent," "serpent-dragon" or "monster."[1] Ningishzida's son, Dumuzi/Tammuz called "Damu" ("child"), is also known as *muš-a* and *muš-huš*.[2]

Like the apocryphal Moses, son of Yahweh, Ningishzida is the son of the heavenly god, Anu. He was also believed to be an ancestor of Gilgamesh, indicating again that the latter heroic compilation incorporates the serpent-underworld god's attributes in his myth. The snake god's connection with the king Gudea is significant—Gudea is called the "son of Ningishzida"[3]—in that it seems some of the latter's biographical details were interwoven into the Gilgamesh myth.

Solar Aspects

Ningishzida is also called the "god of dawn and dusk," reminding us of the twin aspects of Venus, as embodied in Ugaritic mythology by Shahar and Shalim. As we have seen, this attribute is also significantly solar, representing the sun in the morning and evening. The Mesopotamian solar-serpent god's status as the underworld deity resembles the role of Osiris and other deities symbolizing the sun's nightly passage.

In this regard, the text "Ningishzida's Journey to the Netherworld" contains much solar mythology, with its calls to "arise" and "sail" in a "boat." It also resembles various Egyptian hymns and spells for the passage of the deceased king into the underworld. As we might expect, this sacred passage includes the consumption of "choice wine," part of the medicine chest of antiquity.

Medicine Deity

It is significant too that this god is the patron of medicine, with his snake-entwined imagery reproduced as a symbol of modern medicine. The iconography of Ningishzida includes depictions of the god with a snake head, as well as an image that resembles the later caduceus of Hermes, the staff of Asclepius and the serpent rod and brazen fetish of Moses.

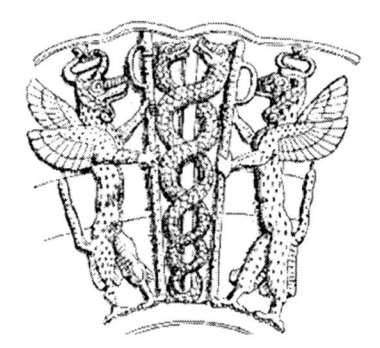

Fig. 111. Libation vase of Gudea with dragon Mušḫuššu, 21st cent. BCE. Louvre

---

[1] "A balbale to Ninĝišzida," line 5.
[2] Astour, 174; Mundkur, 67; "Mušhuš [MONSTER]," *PSD*.
[3] Hallo, 433.

The oldest of its kind extant, this Mesopotamian artifact dates to the 21st century BCE, long before the purported historical Moses. This god, therefore, is extremely old, and it is clear that he was addressed by essentially the same title as "Moses" many centuries before the Jewish bible was written.

Beer and Wine

As beer itself, Ningishzida's son Dumuzi/Tammuz descends into underground containers, while the same fate is destined for his "sister," Geshtinanna, whose name means "leafy grapevine,"[1] much like serpents, which go underground and then appear alive again on the surface. Thus, the two siblings symbolize grain and vine, harvested at six-month intervals from each other, grain in the spring and grapes in the fall. Hence, they are underground for six months at opposite times from one another.[2] As we have seen, in the Jewish era Tammuz came to signify the wine harvest as well, reflecting the omission of female divinities in biblical texts.

Significantly, Geshtinanna is depicted in another myth as Ningishzida's wife,[3] once against demonstrating the intimate connection between wine and snakes.

Mosheh and the Serpent

There exists good reason to suggest that the mythical and syncretic Moses is based significantly on not only the sun and wine god but also the serpent deity, including and especially Ningishzida as Muš, *muš-huš* or Mŝ, as he appears to have been passed along in the Ugaritic texts.

In this regard, Astour summarizes his case that the name Mosheh/Moses seems to be derived from the serpent god, rather than the Egyptian term for "born":

> For the Hebrew Môše, too, the association with the Canaaneo-Sumerian serpent-god seems to be much more convincing than with the pale banal Egyptian hypocoristic [diminutive] from some name composed with ms(w) "born." The ophic features of Moses are very pronounced: his sacred emblems are the serpent-wand and the bronze serpent on a pole; his tribe is Levi, whose name signifies "serpent" and who was the son of Leah, the "cow"...; he is a healer in the full sense

Fig. 112. Mór Than, *Moses and the Nehushtan*, 1879. Plan for stained glass window, Ferencváros Church, Hungarian National Gallery

---

[1] Shushan, 77.
[2] Shushan, 77.
[3] Johansen, 51, 54.

of this word, knowing both how to cause and to heal diseases.[1]

We have seen how Moses and Aaron's staffs turn into snakes (Exod 4:3, 7:10), how Yahweh sent "fiery serpents" against the Israelites (Num 21:6), and how the patriarch raised up a magical bronze serpent, נחשתן *Nĕchushtan* (2 Ki 18:4),[2] as a talisman against death by snake bite (Num 21:9). We have noted too that the entwined snakes symbolizing the healing deity date to at least the third millennium BCE, with the magical and healing serpent-controlling spells part of an ancient priesthood.

We also have discussed that the Levitical priesthood is named from the same root as "Leviathan," connoting sea monster. Noteworthy too is Yahweh's "hissing," previously mentioned. Additionally, some of the *muš* terms, such as *bašmu*, are used to designate a horned serpent, providing yet another reason for that motif in the Moses myth.

Important also is the suggestion that the biblical term נחש *nachash* denoting "serpent" could represent the Babylonian snake god Šaḫan, cast in Genesis 3 in the role of bringer of knowledge and wisdom.

Bi-gendered

Concerning the sacred serpent, Walker relates:

> The biblical Nehushtan was a deliberate masculinization of a similar oracular she-serpent, Nehushtah, Goddess of Kadesh (meaning "Holy"), a shrine like that of the Pythonesses. Israelites apparently violated the sanctuary and raped its priestesses, but "Moses and Yahweh had to placate the angry serpent goddess of Kadesh, now deposed, by erecting her brazen image..."[3]

The serpent deity was viewed not only as male but also as female. Astour also points out the bigendered characteristic of the serpent deity, which recalls the two-sexed Mises, a Bacchic title that likewise may reflect the merger of the Dionysian cult into the Sumero-Semitic serpent cult. It should be recalled that, like Moses, Bacchus too was associated with snakes.

Son of the Cow and Healer

Added to these correspondences is the fact that Moses himself was a "son of the cow," so to speak, noteworthy since in the Canaanite myth Mŝ/Mush is said to be the son of Baal, the bull, and Anath, the heifer. A "chthonic deity identical with Mŝ" is the god Rpu-Bᶜl or Rāpiu Baal, "son of Baal and the heifer," whose name means

---

[1] Astour, 231.
[2] Strong's H5180.
[3] Walker (1988), 387, citing Betz, 119.

"Healing Baal" or "Lord Healer."[1] In this god, Astour also finds the Sumerian deity Ninazu, father of the serpentine Ningishzida,[2] as well as the later Greek hero and monster-slayer Bellerophon. We may look also to Rpu-B‘l for inferences of the Moses character.

Serpent-Goddess Mother

Another clue as to Moses's serpentine nature comes in the name of his adoptive mother in Josephus, Thermuthis/Thermouthis,[3] also the Greek moniker of the Egyptian serpent goddess Renenutet, who watched over and nursed babies, and protected grain, serving also as a goddess of wine. As such, Renenutet was the "nurse of the pharaoh,"[4] appropriate for her appearance in the Moses nativity tale.

Concerning Thermouthis/Renenutet, Dr. Roelof van den Broek, professor of Christianity at Utrecht University, remarks:

> Primarily a vegetation and fertility goddess praised for providing good crops, she was considered the giver of all necessaries of life and of the blessings that make life agreeable as well....
>
> In Hellenistic times, like so many other goddesses, Thermouthis too was interpreted as a manifestation of Isis. According to Aelian, she is the sacred viper of Isis, identical with the ureus that adorns the statues of this deity as a royal diadem.[5]

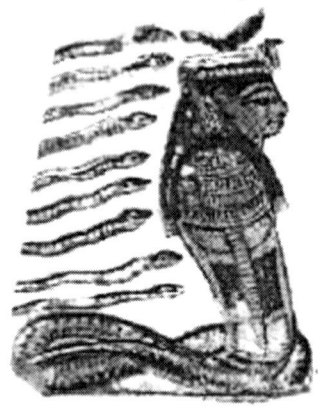

Fig. 113. Egyptian wine and snake goddess Renenutet, Renenet, Rennut, Ernutet, Thermuthis, Thermouthis, Hermouthis or Parmutit

The Egyptian fertility and childbirth goddess Isis was known in Ptolemaic times (323-30 BCE) by the epithet "Isis-Thermouthis," "Ermouthis-Isis" or other form. The cult of Isis-Thermouthis evidently existed only in Egypt, indicating it was from there that Josephus derived this Moses attribute. The serpent goddess mythology upon which this later figure was based, however, dates to hundreds or thousands of years earlier, and can be found in many places outside of Egypt. The fact that Renenutet was also a wine goddess is significant in consideration of the Moses-Dionysus connection as well.

---

[1] Astour, 233. The Hebrew root רפא *rapha'* (H7495) means "to heal." This root also can be found in the word רפאים *rephaim* (H7497), which refers to "giants" and "ancestral spirits." (See, e.g., Deut 2:11, Isa 14:9.) Schniedewind (206) cites the Ugaritic cognate of רפאים *rephaim* as the singular *rp'u*, the "god of the Netherworld/healing; shades of the dead."
[2] Astour, 229.
[3] Josephus, *Ant.* 2.9.5/2.224ff; Whiston, 56-57.
[4] Marsman, 195.
[5] van den Broek, 134.

Jebusite Serpent Cult at Jerusalem?

To reiterate, in the Bible, Moses's magical serpent staff, Nehushtan, was set up in the Jerusalem temple, to be revered as a talisman protecting against deadly snake bites, among other purposes. In this regard, it appears that there was an Amorite/Jebusite serpent cult at Jerusalem centuries before David purportedly conquered the city.[1] It is possible this talisman and its deity were called by the incantational and magical Sumero-Semitic epithet of "Mush" and/or "Mash," demoted in Yahwist times to the patriarch Mosheh/Moses.

Destruction and Salvation

According to the Bible, Moses's serpent cult fell out of favor during the reign of Hezekiah, king of Judah, who "removed the high places, and broke the pillars, and cut down the Asherah. And he broke in pieces the bronze serpent that Moses had made, for until those days the people of Israel had burned incense to it; it was called Nehushtan." (2 Ki 18:4)

Subsequent to Hezekiah's rampages, it was his great-grandson Josiah who purportedly found the Book of the Law or *torah* in the temple. Again, one wonders what ideology Hezekiah was following when he went on his brutal frenzies, which were supposedly in keeping with the (long-lost) Mosaic law but which ironically destroyed the Mosaic serpent cult.

Despite this monotheistic fanaticism, the remnants of the serpent cult survived in the Ophites and other sects. Included in this serpent cult is the perspective that the reptile is the bringer of not only wisdom but also salvation: "The best example of the serpent as savior appears in a Jewish writing from the second century BCE...the Wisdom of Solomon," in which Moses's snake is called a "symbol of salvation."[2]

Moreover, a bronze menorah dating from possibly the Roman era depicts its seven branches as serpents.[3] Indeed, in Roman times, Moses continued to be associated with the serpent in literature, as in a *haggadah*[4] evidently used by Josephus (*Ant.* 2.10.2):

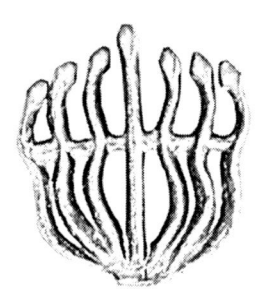

Fig. 114. Bronze menorah with seven (phallic) serpents, Roman period (?) (after Charlesworth, 16)

> Moses took the short road along the desert, deemed impassable on account of its many flying serpents ("seraphim"), and provided himself with numerous baskets filled with ibises, the

---

[1] Charlesworth, 347.
[2] Charlesworth, 256.
[3] Charlesworth, 16.
[4] The term "haggadah" refers to a "telling" at the Passover celebration.

destroyers of serpents, by the help of which he removed the dangers of the desert.[1]

Here again the patriarch possesses the snake-controlling attributes of a serpent god.

The serpent cult extended well into the common era, as related by Princeton theologian and New Testament scholar Dr. James H. Charlesworth, who refers to "Jewish, Christian and Gnostic amulets with serpents" that "often reveal the evil-eye power of the serpent…"[2]

Serpent and Cross

In the Bible, the serpent is vilified "in the beginning," then venerated, then denigrated again, and once more adored when it is associated later with Christ, as a "type of" him: "And as Moses lifted up the serpent in the wilderness, even so must the Son of Man be lifted up." (Jn 3:15) The serpent's "lifting up" is believed in Christian tradition to represent Christ's crucifixion; hence, Moses's serpent staff is Christ on the cross.

As we have seen, snake/serpent worship possibly dates back many thousands of years. It would seem that, in the Moses myth, we possess the remnants of a serpent cult, in which the god himself is identified with the snake.

Fig. 115. Robert Anning Bell, *The Brazen Serpent*, c. 1890. Reproduction of wood engraving, Wellcome Library no. 18284i

The conclusion is that, in Mŝ/Muš/Mush there appears to be another important germ for the Moses myth, the demotion of the Sumerian, Babylonian, Ugaritic and Jerusalemite serpent god to a "patriarch," as Mŝ worship in the Israel area or hill country became subordinated under Yahweh, who eventually reigned supreme, as "Most High" and "Almighty." It appears that the thrust to subordinate the serpent cult occurred at the time when the Moses myth was created, demoting the god under Yahweh but maintaining its priesthood and laws.

Mašmašu Priesthood

Along with the very ancient serpent worship would come a priesthood and rituals to propitiate the snake deity. As we have seen, the Sumerian word *maš-maš* or "mash-mash" refers to a "magician," "wonderworker" or "sorcerer,"[3] also apparently related to ritual

---

[1] Singer, Is., 9.57; Josephus/Whiston (1981), 56.
[2] Charlesworth, 216.
[3] Geller, 48ff.

washing, purification (*maš*) or baptism.[1] The term was passed along in Babylonian as *mašmašu*,[2] denoting priests and anointers of the kings,[3] and often rendered "exorcists"[4] and "charmers," as in snake-charmers and as reflecting spells and incantations. The "chief magician" in Babylon was the *rab-mašmašu*,[5] the prefix recognizable as the same as "rabbi" or "rebbe." During the reign of Assyrian king Esarhaddon (fl. 681-669 BCE), his son Ashurbanipal's chief scribe, Ishtar-shum-êresh, "ranked as a *mašmašu*."[6]

Seven Houses

In the Mesopotamian ritual of the "seven houses" called *bit rimki*, the *mašmašu* are the priests who recite in each of these chambers an incantation in Sumerian, as opposed to the Akkadian incantation invoked by the king.[7]

Dr. Joel Hamme of the Fuller Theological Seminary proposes that the biblical psalms and lamentations are modeled on the Mesopotamian *dingir.ša.dib.ba* incantations recited by these priests. Regarding the seven houses ritual, Hamme says:

> The main body of *bît rimki* is divided into seven "houses," each "house" being performed in a multi-chambered reed hut built specifically for the occasion. Each house consists of a *ki-utukam*, a Sumerian ritual prayer spoken by the *mašmašu*, a ritual priest, a *šiptu*, a ritual prayer spoken by the king, and a ritual. The prayers spoken by both the ritual priest and the king are primarily to Šamaš, although other deities are also involved...[8]

These reed huts sound similar to the booths or *sukkoth* used by pious Jews in the harvest festival and Exodus myth. It is also noteworthy that these ritual prayers were addressed mainly to Shamash, who along with Marduk was one of these priests' favored deities,[9] both called *mash-mash, mashu* or *massû*.

Marduk

One could say that this class of *mašmašu* priests was "Mosaic," possibly representing the faction of Semites who, coming into contact with others in Nineveh, Babylon, Jerusalem and elsewhere, influenced the creation of the Moses story. Since these priests revered, among others, Marduk or "Mash-Mash," one could suggest

---

[1] Morgenstern, 20. Tinney and Jones: "maš [PURE] (4x: Old Babylonian) wr. maš; maš3 'to be pure' Akk. *ellu*... Akk. *ellu* '(ritually) pure'", *PSD*.
[2] Morgenstern, 20.
[3] Hastings, et al., 10.286.
[4] Dreyer, 108.
[5] Chisholm, 22.317.
[6] Johns, 368-369.
[7] Widengren, 574.
[8] Hamme, 9.
[9] Geller, 124.

that Moses is a reflection also of that god, the "savior of the divine world" and "exorcist of the gods":

> ...in Akkadian unilingual texts, Marduk, just like Asalluḫi, is often called an "exorcist," e.g., mašmaš ilī, "exorcist of the gods."[1]

As a syncretic sun and storm god, Marduk controlled the waters and dragon/serpent of the deep, Tiamat, making of him a snake deity as well. Artifacts such as Ishtar's gate indicate that serpents signified Marduk's "power and protection."[2] Marduk's name itself apparently means "bull calf of the sun,"[3] and it could be his worship, as well, which was supplanted by the Moses cult, as the latter syncretized numerous deities in the region.

Animal Sacrifice

Like the Hebrew priests, the *mašmašu* were responsible for sacrificing animals:

> The most widely known prescriptive ritual text from Mesopotamia is that for the New Year Festival at Babylon (ANET, 331-334). It gives the order of events including sacrifices and the recital of prayers and other texts, as required for each day of the celebration. One of the most relevant for comparison with OT ritual is the act of purification performed on the fifth day. The officiating priest "...shall call a slaughterer to decapitate a ram, the body of which the mašmašu-priest shall use in performing the kuppuru-ritual for the temple." After the necessary incantations and purifications have been performed, the mašmašu-priest takes the lamb's carcass and the slaughterer takes its head; both of them proceed to the river and throw their gory burdens into it. Then they remain in the open country for seven days from the fifth to the twelfth of Nisan.[4]

Derived from the Babylonian calendar, Nisan is also a Hebrew month, named in the Babylonian-influenced biblical book of Esther, and comparable to March-April, when the Passover takes place during the seven days from the 15th to the 21st.

Lintel Blood

Part of the Babylonian sacrifice is the ritual use of the animal's blood for magical protection:

> In the ritual tablets...we read "that the mašmašu (priest's magician) is to pass forth to the gateway, sacrifice a sheep in the palace portal, and to smear the threshold and posts of the palace gateway right and left with the blood of the lamb." We are reminded of Exod. [12:7]...[5]

Exodus 12:7 describes the Hebrews in Egypt smearing lamb's blood on their door lintels, an ancient Near and Middle Eastern

---

[1] Oshima, 43.
[2] Charlesworth, 121.
[3] Mundkur, 121.
[4] "Sacrifice and Offerings."
[5] Chisholm, 22.317.

magical tradition apparently predating the supposed date of the Exodus by centuries.

Wine Priests

As we might expect, the Mesopotamian priests and religious officials were associated with wine, the drink of royalty and ritual libation: "Among later first millennium BC lists of wine consignments from Nimrud, we find officials on the wine lists being 'diviners,' 'exorcists' and 'physicians' (listed under their respective logograms...)."[1] The "exorcists" in this list are indicated by the term *maš-maš*.

Renowned Exorcists

Demonstrating how well known and important were the "*mašmaššu*-exorcists,"[2] there existed entire households of them, like the Jewish priesthood, as the tribe of Levi and family of Cohens. Geller describes how significant were these sectarians:

> The role of the Babylonian exorcist or *mašmaššu* became increasingly important within the temples in later periods and by the Hellenistic period "exorcistic arts" (*mašmaššūtu*) dominated the school curriculum, which was most confined to temples...[3]

The *maš-maš* priests continued into the fifth century BCE at Uruk, leaving behind the "largest known collection of commentaries on medical tablets..."[4] At the same time, "Uruk exorcists had become the most prominent scholars of their day."[5]

Chaldeans and Mandaeans

When all is considered, there exists good reason to suggest that this class of Semitic priests was influential in the formation of Judaism.[6] Some of these clerics apparently became the wandering "Chaldeans,"[7] the remnants of the destroyed Babylonian priesthood, who were very prominent around the Near and Middle East, and beyond.

In view of the commonalities between this Babylonian priesthood and that of the Israelites, it would be rational to suggest that the Mesopotamian system influenced the Jewish tradition, as was the case with the calendar, full of religious rituals undoubtedly inherited along with the Babylonian month-names. In this regard, it appears

---

[1] Geller, 49.
[2] Geller, 49.
[3] Geller, 50.
[4] Geller, 124.
[5] Geller, 124.
[6] See, e.g., Rudolph, 4, etc.
[7] The late, Babylonian-influenced biblical text Daniel (4:7) places together "magicians," "exorcists" or "sorcerers," "Chaldeans" and "diviners" or "soothsayers," using Aramaic terms and apparently referring to the *mašmašu* priests.

that the mašmašu may be the source of the Mosaic priesthood, with its syncretic central object of worship demoted to a patriarch under Yahweh.

In this same regard, we have seen that the book of Judith deems the Jews "Chaldeans." Philo describes the original language of the Mosaic law as "Chaldean" and "Chaldaic," even though he knows the word "Hebrew":

> ...In olden time the laws were written in the Chaldaean language, and for a long time they remained in the same condition as at first...[1]

Since Chaldean usually refers to Babylonian, the language in question probably would be Aramaic by Philo's understanding. This belief that the law was originally written in Aramaic may reflect that it was initially Babylonian, as in the Code of Hammurabi. The Mandaeans spoke a dialect of Aramaic called Mandaic, evidently derived from Amorite, as we would expect in that region. Many of the Mesopotamian priests' traditions appear to have been passed along to the Mandaeans, who inhabited the region centuries later.[2]

Conclusion

Although aspects of the Moses story certainly are very ancient, such as the Gilgamesh elements and the storm-sun god battle with the pharaoh-dragon, the earliest the Exodus tale could have been written down in Hebrew would be about 1000 BCE, with the development of the Hebrew alphabet from the Phoenician, itself created around 1050 BCE. Yet, Moses is largely if not entirely absent from pre-exilic texts, indicating he comes onto the scene after the Babylonian period. Therefore, the *terminus ad quo* or starting point for much of the Moses material may have been around the middle of the sixth century, with subsequent redactions up to the third century, along with extrabiblical texts.

If the Moses tale was created between the sixth and third centuries BCE, the story could have been based on pre-Israelite Sumero-Semitic solar, vegetation and fertility myths. Combining the Levantine solar-wine-fertility-serpent deity with Dionysus worship, along with the attributes of various other deities and heroes of the region such as Adar, Gilgamesh, Marduk, Mush, Osiris/Horus, Sargon, Shamash and Tammuz, we can see how the Moses myth was developed.

Mythicist and freethinker Thomas W. Doane (1852-1885) sums it up when he says, "Almost all the acts of Moses correspond to those of the Sun-gods."[3] Rather than serving as a historical individual with an actual exodus, in the widespread tradition of the Great God Sun, Moses himself has the earmarks of a solar deity, with the attributes

---

[1] Philo, *Moses* 2.5.26, 2.7.40; Philo/Yonge, 493, 494.
[2] Widengren, 573-574.
[3] Doane, 51.

of various gods, goddesses, lawgivers and heroes from antiquity rolled into one.

In addition, the Moses story reflects the stellar and lunar cults as well, demonstrating the dual natured "twin" myth, such as concerns Horus and Set, and the battle for supremacy between the day and night skies, as well as between the agriculturalists and nomads.

From all the evidence, it would appear that the Jewish Moses is a compilation of Sumerian, Egyptian, Greek and Semitic solar, wine, fertility and serpent deities reworked into the Israelite hero. Perhaps when Jewish priests and other elite were in Babylon, they allied with (other) wealthy wine producers and decided to create this foundational myth, demoting divine heroes/deities to a syncretic "prophet" under the god of the Yahwists and incorporating many Dionysian elements as well. These factors apparently were combined with the Muš/Maš cult that had developed in Jerusalem among the Amorites/Jebusites, centuries earlier than the Israelite presence there.

Fig. 116. French School, *Moses Receives the Tablets of the Law from God on Mount Sinai*, 19th cent. Color lithograph, Private Collection

Fig. 117. Jean-Léon Gérôme, *Moses on Mount Sinai*, revealing solar aspects, 1895-1900. Private collection, USA

Fig. 118. Moses's shining, solarized face on Mt. Sinai. Artist unknown, c. 20th cent. AD/CE

Fig. 119. Carl Heinrich Bloch, *Transfiguration of Jesus*, with Moses and Elijah, 19th cent. AD/CE

Fig. 120. Gilgamesh between two 'Bull Men with Sun-Disc,' 10th-9th cents. BCE. Relief from Kapara, Tell Halaf, Syria

GILGAMESH EPIC.	SCRIPTURES.
In the beginning of the epic the people are suffering under the tyranny of enforced labor in building the walls of the city of Erech.	The forced work of Israel when compelled to build the cities of Pithon and Ramses by Pharaoh.
The shepherd Eabani is created in order to direct the thoughts of Gilgamesh to other objects and then to deliver the opprest. He comes out from the steppes led by a harlot.	Called to be the deliverer of his people, the shepherd Moses comes with his wife from the steppes into Egypt.
Gilgamesh and Eabani become friends.	Moses finds in Aaron a friend and companion.
Gilgamesh and Eabani together go to the east to the mountains of the gods and overcome the giant Chumbaba.	Moses and Aaron go to Mt. Sinai and there conquer the Amalekites.
Istar seeks the love of Gilgamesh.	Moses is chided because he married the Cushite woman (Num. xii.).
Gilgamesh and Eabani slay the heavenly steer.	Killing of the red heifer (Num. xix.).
After this Eabani dies.	The death of Aaron.
Gilgamesh goes through the desert, where no bread is to be found, and he is compelled to eat the meat of forbidden animals, and comes to the gates of the mountains, which are guarded by a pair of scorpions, which try to prevent his passing through.	After Aaron's death Moses continues the journey through the desert with the Israelites, who murmur on account of a want and because of their unsatisfactory food, and they come to the country of the two kings, Sihon, who refuses to permit them to pass through, and Og, the giant.
Gilgamesh secures an entrance and comes to the wonderful park with the trees of the gods, on the coast of the sea, where he finds Sidari or Istar on the top of the mountain.	Moses forces his way through, comes to Chittim, and there appears the harlot woman Kosbi, the daughter of Zur, or rock.

Fig. 121. Parallels between Gilgamesh and Moses. (*Literary Digest*, 35.54)

Fig. 122. Egyptian priests and Aaron change their rods into a serpent in front of pharaoh (Exod 4:1-5). (*Foster's Bible Pictures*)

Fig. 123. Moses and the plague of fiery serpents upon Israel (Num 21:6-9). (*Treasures of the Bible*)

Fig. 124. Hezekiah removes the bronze serpent (2 Ki 18:4). (Charles Horne, *The Bible and Its Story*)

Conclusion

"In the Hebrew scriptures are many beauties, many excellent precepts, much found morality, and they deserve the attentive perusal of every scholar, every person of curiosity and taste. All those good things I admit, and admire, and would equally admire them in the writings of Plato, Tully, or Marcus Antoninus. But there are other things in great abundance that I can neither admire nor admit, without renouncing common sense and superseding reason—a sacrifice which I am not disposed to make, for any writing in the world."

Rev. Dr. Alexander Geddes, *Critical Remarks on the Hebrew Scriptures* (1.v-vi)

"A professed Egyptologist has written respecting the passage of the Red Sea: '*It would be impious to attempt an explanation of what is manifestly miraculous.*' To such a depth of degradation can Bibliolatry reduce the human mind! Such is the spirit in which the subject has been crawled over.

"These impotent attempts to convert mythology into history, dignified with the astounding title of the Book of God, have produced the most unmitigated muddle of matter ever presented to the mind of man. There has been no such fruitful case of misconception as this supposed source of all wisdom, designated the Book of God, ignorantly believed to have been communicated to man orally by an objective Deity."

Gerald Massey, *A Book of the Beginnings* (2.176)

OVER THE CENTURIES, many people have attempted to reconcile biblical persons and events with confusing ancient accounts of individuals, incursions, excursions and skirmishes involving Egypt and Canaan. These efforts frequently have been tedious and unsatisfactory in identifying Moses and explaining the Exodus story as a whole. This difficulty is so great that one is tempted to admit defeat that the "historical" Moses and Exodus are hopelessly lost, as if non-existent. Since so many aspects of the tale appear in myth, we can assume safely that the biblical account represents a fictional composite of events and individuals that cannot be considered a single historical occurrence and personage.

The fact is that the biblical story of Moses does not represent the "real history" of the leader of the "chosen people," who through supernatural events and divinely ordained laws and intervention brought the Israelites to the Promised Land. Moreover, the Pentateuch was not composed by a historical Moses but constitutes a series of pseudonymous texts written over a period of centuries and containing numerous allegorical and mythical tales interspersed with some history. In this regard, Moses cannot be discovered in history, whether as Akhenaten or another historical personage.

Instead of being founded as presented in the biblical story, the Israelites emerged from the hill country as a result of the merger of several groups of Semitic nomads, including those who had been in Sumeria, Canaan, Phoenicia, Babylon, Egypt and the southeastern Levant. Factoring in the possible Indian influence on the Syro-Jewish philosophers Josephus styled the Kalanoi, it may be that a group of Semitic Brahma worshippers from the Harappan Valley in India via Ur/Sumer had made its way to the eastern Levant during the second millennium BCE. There they encountered other Semites, El Shaddai worshippers who established superiority and demoted the immigrants' god to the patriarch Abraham. Next, this unified tribe of "Hebrews" apparently merged with the Sumero-Canaanite Mš serpent cult, joined in the hill country by Hapiru and other *bedu* followers of Baal, El and various other Semitic deities.

To this mix were added Amoritish Hyksos worshippers of Baal-Seth and Shasu followers of Yahweh familiar with Egypt. These latter eventually established supremacy and evidently subverted the Mash/Mush cult, demoting its god to a patriarch, with Hezekiah legendarily smashing its bronze serpent talisman. In this merger, the Yahwists came to dominate during the first millennium BCE and to be known as Judeans or "Jews."

Considering the abundant evidence presented here, it may be asserted that the tale of the Exodus and Conquest is not a historical account of the founding of Israel but is based largely on other *mythical* battles, sojourns in the wilderness and entries into promised lands.

As we have seen, the figure of Moses constitutes a mythical compilation of characters, the significant portion of which are solar heroes or sun gods, along with fertility, serpent, storm and wine deities and attributes. It appears that the myths of Gilgamesh, Baal and Dionysus in specific were incorporated into the patriarchal foundation/lawgiver story of the demoted god.

The scientific conclusion is that the Bible is not the literal "Word of God." Instead, the "Good Book" represents ethnic traditions and political propaganda from a particular culture and era, designed both to record ancient folklore and to establish hegemony for that especial ethnicity. To reiterate, this old tome of fabulous fairytales contains some history as well, but it should not be mistaken for a history text, in which *the* God of the cosmos actually established a "chosen people" holier than the rest of humanity.

Biblical Anachronisms and Errors

In his book *Egypt, Canaan and Israel in Ancient Times*, Egyptologist Redford expresses exasperation at the religious habit of

CONCLUSION

taking the Bible literally, in consideration of the fact that the text clearly does not represent history and makes repeated mistakes and anachronisms, revealing its folkloric nature. Firstly, he refers to the dearth of evidence from the supposedly contemporary Egyptian and Semitic sources, which barely mention Israel or "Biblical associates" before the eighth century BCE. Secondly, he points out that the Bible itself likewise lacks "any specific references betraying a knowledge of Egypt or the Levant during the second millennium B.C."[1]

Regarding the biblical account as put forth in the Hexateuch or first six books of the Bible, including the Pentateuch and Joshua, Redford next remarks:

> There is no mention of an Egyptian empire encompassing the eastern Mediterranean, no marching Egyptian armies bent on punitive campaigns, no countermarching Hittite forces, no resident governors, no Egyptianized kinglets ruling Canaanite cities, no burdensome tribute or cultural exchange. Of the latest and most disastrous migration of the second millennium, that of the Sea Peoples, the Hexateuch knows next to nothing: Genesis and Exodus find the Philistines already settled in the land at the time of Abraham.... The great Egyptian kings of the empire, the Amenophids, the Thutmosids, the Ramessides, are absent from the hundreds of pages of holy writ; and it is only in occasional toponyms unrecognized by the Hebrew writer that a faint echo of their names may be heard.... Errors persist even in periods closer in time to the period of the Biblical writers.[2]

Discussing the time of the biblical judges, from around 1456 to 1080 BCE, the Egyptologist points out that it supposedly occurred during the same period when in actuality Egyptians were dominant in the Levant, ruling over their outposts in Canaan and elsewhere. Yet, says Redford, "our Egyptian sources mention neither the patriarchs, Israel in Egypt, Joshua, nor his successors, while the Bible says absolutely nothing about the Egyptian empire in the land."[3] In other words, the biblical writers had no idea of how to depict the appropriate history of Egypt in Canaan; nor had the Egyptians ever heard of the patriarchs and judges who supposedly engaged in such dramatic behaviors as recorded in the Old Testament.

Redford proceeds to name several other errors and anachronisms, throwing his hands in the air at the devout attitude that insists on taking the Bible literally, when it clearly is not historically accurate. Says he: "Such ignorance is puzzling if one has felt inclined to be impressed by the traditional claims of inerrancy made by conservative Christianity one behalf of the Bible."[4]

---

[1] Redford (1992), 257.
[2] Redford (1992), 257-258.
[3] Redford (1992), 259.
[4] Redford (1992), 258.

Referring to the attempts by bibliolaters and others at manipulating the time periods in order to align with known history, Redford comments:

> Such manhandling of the evidence smacks of prestidigitation and numerology; yet, it has produced the shaky foundations on which a lamentable number of "histories" of Israel have been written. Most are characterized by a somewhat naïve acceptance of sources at face value coupled with the failure to assess the evidence as to its origin and reliability.[1]

Despite these efforts, we now know that the Pentateuch was composed centuries later than the time it purports to record, as proved by the many chronological errors and omissions chronicled by Redford and others here and elsewhere.

In the final analysis, high, middle, low or new chronology all rate as irrelevant when the quest is understood to reside in the realm of myth, not history. It matters not if Ramesses II, for example, flourished in the 13th century or 10th century BCE,[2] because he was not the "historical" pharaoh/dragon of the Exodus myth. Such attempts at recovering literal history from, and establishing chronology according to, *mythical* motifs remain futile, regardless of how the dates are altered and/or justified.

Brutal Literalism

In the past centuries, millions of people have taken the Bible literally, including such verses as: "Whoever sacrifices to any god, save to the LORD only, shall be utterly destroyed." (Exod 22:20) The Lord here is specifically Yahweh; hence, certain fanatical followers of the biblical god, whether Jewish or Christian, have felt the right to slaughter all nonbelievers. Another verse used to justify violence, especially against women, is Exodus 22:18: "You shall not permit a sorceress to live." The scripture at Leviticus (18:22) proscribing homosexuality is yet another of the many used to defend violence. These verses may seem of little consequence in civilized regions, but in places where superstition continues to reign supreme, such as in parts of Africa, people today suffer from these writings.

Intolerance, Cultural Bigotry and Barbarism

Although various wisdom sayings and platitudes are included in the Old Testament, Yahweh does not teach his chosen about love, charity, forgiveness, tolerance and good will to any significant extent. Instead, the lessons focus largely on enemies, adversaries, hatred, slaughter and pillage. Despite the Platonic pretensions of Yahwistic monotheism, there is little sense of godly transcendence of primitive human emotions and behaviors, as in sophisticated philosophies. On

---

[1] Redford (1992), 260.
[2] Per Rohl's "New Chronology."

the contrary, the supposedly cosmic and enlightened doctrine is full of blood and gore, on page after page, reveling in violence and retribution.

According to the Bible, the purported creator of an amazing cosmos which we now know contains, among innumerable other wonders, six-trillion-mile-high clouds of gas that give birth to stars, was obsessed not only with animal sacrifice but also with the genocide of Bronze Age, Near-Eastern tribes such as the Amalekites, Canaanites, Moabites and Midianites!

As related in the Pentateuch, this same creator of the sun, moon, planets and stars stepped down from his heavenly abode to engage in endless bloody skirmishes; yet, this violent chosen culture is supposed to be far superior to that of the barbaric Aztecs, for example. In the vast scheme of things, however, there is little difference between the latter and the biblical bloodthirstiness and pettiness.

All cultures other than the "chosen" are reduced in value biblically, as this one is raised up by the pretense of this ethnicity's myths as more sacred than all others, in spite of the fact that these myths may have been built on the stories of other cultures. In reality, the Bible itself ranks as a cultural artifact, no more sacrosanct than are the ancient religious texts of other cultures, in which various prototypical deities can be found.

In this regard, the supposedly omniscient Lord, who purportedly had been visiting Moses and Aaron for months and years on end, possessed no more knowledge than did Bronze Age shepherds and their priests, the true composers of the texts.

Misogyny and Sexism

In reworking the ancient myths of other cultures, the biblical stories often have removed completely the role of goddesses in the original tales, either demonizing the deity or demoting her to a judge, prophet, saint or other less divine role. In the frequently misogynistic and sexist texts, a number of goddesses, in fact, ended up as "whores," including Jesus's purported ancestor, Rahab. This denigration and suppression of myths about females has done a tremendous disservice not only to women and girls—one-half of humanity—but also to men, who may not experience women in their fullest potential, empowered by these divine archetypes.

The supernatural and miraculous biblical tales are no more "historical" than the predecessor myths upon which they evidently are founded. As a reflection of an ancient literary genre that used myth to record beliefs and culture, as well as possessing some history, the Bible is a valuable human artifact. As a history book, however, its value is minimal, and taking it literally has proved a great detriment to humanity.

Allegorical Fall

As we know from the remarks at the beginning of this present work and spread throughout, even in antiquity not all believers thought the Bible was entirely historical. Speaking of Philo's allegorical interpretation of the fall of mankind as found in Genesis, for example, Geddes recounted a list of others in antiquity who understood biblical tales as cosmological and allegorical, not literal:

> This allegorical mode of explaining the fall (and indeed the whole cosmogony) by the most ancient professed interpreter whose works have come down to us, appeared so ingenious and satisfactory to the more early Christian fathers, that, with some little variations, they generally adopted it. It was adopted, if we may credit Anastasius Sanita, by Papias, Pantaenus, Irenaeus, Clement of Alexandria; and we are certain it was adopted and improved upon by Origen. From Origen, it was borrowed by the Gregories of Nyssa and Nazianzum; and among the Latins, by St. Ambrose. There were not, however, wanting writers who contended for a literal meaning, and who charged the Origenists with impiety and heresy: particularly, the credulous Epiphanius, and the acrimonious Jerome....[1]

Each of these Church fathers and Christian thinkers understood that there is allegory—*myth*—in the Bible.

Political Fiction

Concerning the obfuscation during centuries of pantheon mergers and priestcraft that turned mythical or allegorical gods into historical prophets and saviors, it is important to keep in mind the words of Josephus regarding Moses (*Ant.* "Preface," §4): "Now when once he had brought them to submit to religion, he easily persuaded them to submit in all other things..."[2]

We are reminded again of the old adage, "The people like to be fooled, let them be fooled." Here we find the themes of manipulation and coercion as well as deceit, which provide some idea of one of the purposes for priestly endeavors, as the Jewish historian suggests.

As a motive for this misapprehension, in his *Critical Remarks on the Hebrew Scriptures*, Geddes refers to the "mythos of Moses" as "charming political fictions" dressed as "history":

> We have now got to the end of the *mythos* of Moses; or whoever else was the author of the wonderful production. I trust that I have done something like justice to its beauties; and that it will appear, on the whole, to be a well devised, well delineated, well executed piece: nay, that it has not equal in all the mythology of antiquity: I mean, if it be considered, not as a real history, nor as a mere mystical allegory; but, such as I have throughout exhibited it, a most charming political fiction, dressed up for excellent purposes in the garb of

---

[1] Geddes (1792), 1.viii.
[2] Josephus/Whiston, 28.

history, and adapted to the gross concepts and limited capacity of a rude, sensual and unlearned credulous people.[1]

This erudite and insightful churchman was centuries ahead of his time, this text published in the late 18th century and not "outdated" overall. For his hubris and although he remained a professed Christian—the Catholic equivalent of a Unitarian—Geddes was censured for "liberalism" in his translation of the Bible, and he lost his vocation for his subsequent *Critical Remarks*. Nevertheless, his analysis remains factual and current, with modern scholarship just now catching up with his assessment, suppressed largely because of the inculcated bias of entrenched institutions.[2]

As concerns this apparent political propaganda, a Jewish writer of the early 20th century, Marcus Eli Ravage, published an article "A Real Case Against the Jews" in *Century Magazine* that included the following taunting admission:

> Our tribal customs have become the core of your moral code. Our tribal laws have furnished the basic groundwork of all your august constitutions and legal systems. Our legends and our folk-tales are the sacred lore which you croon to your infants. Our poets have filled your hymnals and your prayer-books. Our national history has become an indispensable part of the learning of your pastors and priests and scholars. Our kings, our statesmen, our prophets, our warriors are your heroes. Our ancient little country is your Holy Land. Our national literature is your Holy Bible. What our people thought and taught has become inextricably woven into your very speech and tradition, until no one among you can be called educated who is not familiar with our racial heritage.
>
> Jewish artisans and Jewish fishermen are your teachers and your saints, with countless statues carved in their image and innumerable cathedrals raised to their memories. A Jewish maiden is your ideal of motherhood and womanhood. A Jewish rebel-prophet is the central figure in your religious worship. We have pulled down your idols, cast aside your racial inheritance, and substituted for them our God and our traditions. No conquest in history can even remotely compare with this clean sweep of our conquest over you.[3]

In the end, it appears that the story of Moses was created in order to compete with the lawgiver tales of other cultures and to give divine origin for the various laws and traditions that became definitive of the Yahwist sect of the Israelites.

---

[1] Geddes (1800), 1.49-50.
[2] For his *Critical Remarks on the Hebrew Scriptures*—in yet another example of the closed ranks of academia that also snared Dr. David F. Strauss, who lost his livelihood for his frank writings, and English minister Rev. Dr. Robert Taylor, who was imprisoned for "blasphemy"—Geddes was removed from his post as a Roman Catholic priest.
[3] Ravage, 346ff.

Moses versus Jesus Mythicism

As I say regarding the "quest for the historical Jesus," the discussion revolves around not whether or not a Moses existed but what his *myth* signifies. As a historical personage, the Moses of the Pentateuch did not exist. As a *mythical* character, however, Moses certainly *has* existed, in multiple forms in a number of cultures extending back thousands of years and developed over a period of centuries to millennia.

Various comments in the present work reveal that there has been a significant amount of Moses mythicists within academia over the past couple of centuries. Questioning Moses's historicity has become a valid exercise, in consideration of all the fabulous fairytales, supernatural events and lack of a historical and archaeological record for the biblical story. In fact, currently it appears to be almost *de rigueur* among many academicians to object to the very notion of the Exodus and the Conquest serving as history.

It should be kept in mind also that, as the tale of Moses is mythical, so too evidently are the stories of several other biblical characters, as mentioned by a number of scholars quoted here and elsewhere. These figures include Abraham, Jacob, Joshua, Noah and others.

As we can see, there exists precedent for mythical characters or fictional composites in the Bible. These fabled figures of the Old Testament are depicted as participating in supernatural events and acts. Therefore, should we not maintain our rationality, logic and skepticism when it comes to the most supernatural of all biblical characters, Jesus Christ?

The equally implausible gospel story in the New Testament likewise is full of fabulous fairytales, supernatural events and a dearth of scientific evidence. However, questioning the tale as "history"—even to the point of the historicity of the purported founder at its core, as is the case with the Moses myth—is treated as an affront to common sense.

Even with the precedent of a mythical Moses, making us suspect other biblical tales, it remains taboo to suggest as nonhistorical the virgin-born son of God who walked on water, restored sight to the blind using spit, raised the dead, turned water into wine, transfigured on a mount next to two apparitions, resurrected from death and bodily flew off into the sky, to live for all eternity omnisciently watching over every aspect of creation.

First and Second Messiahs?

Nevertheless, as might be expected, there exist many correspondences between the gospel story and that of Moses, as discussed by Dr. Burton Mack, for example, decades ago. First and foremost, both are a type of messiah for the Israelite and Jewish people. In the New Testament, Jesus is Moses's brazen serpent, erected centuries previously in the Jerusalem temple. So important is Moses in the gospel tale that he appears at Jesus's transfiguration. Moreover, the two figures naturally share many philosophical ideas, which need not emanate from a single historical individual but which could be the result of combining archetypical figureheads within religion and mythology, along with the various mysteries around the Mediterranean and beyond.

Jesus's genealogy can be traced to Moses; yet, Moses clearly is a mythical and not historical personage. We submit the same can be said of Christ. A similar process used to turn the ancient solar-serpent god and divine vine-wine legislator into a Hebrew patriarch was employed also to change the solar son of God/hero into the Jewish messiah.

In this quest, numerous passages from the Old Testament have been compiled as "messianic scriptures" purportedly predicting or foreshadowing the messiah and supposedly fulfilled in Jesus. In reality, these verses served as "blueprints" used midrashically or allegorically to *create* the gospel story and mythical messiah.[1] For example, one of the favored texts for midrash is the book of Isaiah, evidently used in the creation of not only the messianic character but also the Exodus.

It is obvious that, in emulation of other cultures with lawgivers, Moses was created in order to give divine legitimacy to the Yahwist priestly ordinances and authorities. In the same way, the "historical" Jesus was fashioned in order to unify the religions of the Roman Empire.

Preventing Armageddon

In consideration of purported plans by various "fringe" elements and governmental officials alike in Israel to rebuild the Jerusalem Temple in order to house the Ark of the Covenant[2]—an act that would require the demolition of the Muslim Dome of the Rock and possibly set off a major war—it is urgent that humanity as a whole investigate scientifically, with great scrutiny, the stories it holds sacred. Are these tales "historical events" based on God's intervention, which will lead us inexorably to Armageddon? Or, are they myths, fables and, when taken literally, deleterious fantasies?

It would be best to recognize the Pentateuch/Torah as a book of fabulous fairytales and meaningful myths, rather than insisting that such stories represent "history," for which there is no corroborating evidence, no archaeological remains, no other literary account confirming the brutal conquest of the Promised Land.

---

[1] See, e.g., the chapter "Did Jesus Fulfill Prophecy?" in my book *Who Was Jesus?*
[2] See, e.g., "Minister calls for third Temple to be built," *The Times of Israel.*

The Bible's myths have inspired the world to create great cathedrals, literature, music and art, but they should not have been taken as literal facts, as we can see from the tale of Moses and the Exodus, neither of which entities finds its place in history but both of which clearly constitute ancient mythical motifs present in other cultures.

It must be admitted that, as *mythology*, Moses and the Exodus ranks as a well-crafted tale with drama and intrigue, even if quite illogical and implausible—nay, *impossible*—as history. Devoid of the significance of the myth, however, the story appears absurd and grotesque, if taken literally. With the mythological understanding, the narrative gains greater depth, when put into its context as one of many similar stories across a variety of cultures and eras.

Taken alone as "ultimate truth" while dismissing with utter prejudice and fallacious superiority all these other myths and epics, the biblical tall tale loses its meaning and becomes debased, reflecting an insane and violent god with a megalomaniacal representative bent on tormenting and/or slaughtering hundreds of thousands of people. It is time to acknowledge this genocidal story's place in *mythology*, rather than erroneously presuming it to be history.

Nor is the Bible as literature superior to the sacred texts of other cultures, such as the *Rigveda*, *Iliad*, *Odyssey* and Norse *Eddas*. In order to progress into a more truthful and enlightened future, we must recognize these facts and adjust our attitude accordingly, for we are all one human species on a small planet far off to the side of one of countless galaxies.

The final answer to the question of "Did Moses exist?" is no and yes: No, the character of Moses in the Bible is not a historical person; and, yes, Moses exists—as a *mythical* figure. In the end, the biblical story of Moses should be understood as folklore, not literal history, similar to the legends of other cultures, and not given divine status. In an age of transparency and information, this suppressed and hidden knowledge needs to be known widely with alacrity.

Fig. 125. Moses orders the Levites to slaughter all those worshipping the Golden Calf. Woodcut by Julius Schnoor von Carolsfeld (*Das Buch der Bücher in Bilden*, 1920)

Fig. 126. James Tissot, *The Women of Midian Led Captive by the Hebrews*, 1900. Watercolor, Jewish Museum, New York.

Bibliography

"Abdi-Heba." en.wikipedia.org/wiki/Abdi-Heba
"Achelous." en.wikipedia.org/wiki/Achelous
"An *adab* to Nergal for Šu-ilīšu." etcsl.orinst.ox.ac.uk/cgi-bin/etcsl.cgi?text=t.2.5.2.1#
"Adar." en.wikipedia.org/wiki/Adar
"Aelius Aristides." en.wikipedia.org/wiki/Aelius_Aristides
"Ahmose I." en.wikipedia.org/wiki/Ahmose_I
"Akhenaten." en.wikipedia.org/wiki/Akhenaten
"Allegorical Interpretation." jewishencyclopedia.com/articles/1256-allegorical-interpretation
"Amorites." britishmuseum.org/explore/cultures/middle_east/amorites.aspx
"Amorites." en.wikipedia.org/wiki/Amorite
"Anat." en.wikipedia.org/wiki/Anat
"Ancient Jerusalem." israel-a-history-of.com/ancient-jerusalem.html
"Ancient Mesopotamia." worldology.com/Iraq/ancient_mesopotamia.htm
"Anu." en.wikipedia.org/wiki/Anu
"Atenism." en.wikipedia.org/wiki/Atenism
"Babylonian star catalogues." en.wikipedia.org/wiki/Babylonian_star_catalogues
"Bašmu/Ušum, Muš huššu, Nirah." forums.abrahadabra.com/archive/index.php/t-5826.html
"Beit She'an." jewishvirtuallibrary.org/jsource/Archaeology/Beitshean.html
"Bible Battles." History Channel
"Book of Daniel." en.wikipedia.org/wiki/Book_of_Daniel
"Book of Judith." *United States Conference of Catholic Bishops.* usccb.org/bible/scripture.cfm?bk=Judith&ch=
"Bronze Age collapse." en.wikipedia.org/wiki/Bronze_Age_collapse
"Canaan." newworldencyclopedia.org/entry/canaan
"Canaanite religion." en.wikipedia.org/wiki/Canaanite_religion
"Chaldea." en.wikipedia.org/wiki/Chaldea
"Charondas." en.wikipedia.org/wiki/Charondas
"*Chronicon* (Jerome)." en.wikipedia.org/wiki/Chronicon_(Jerome)
"Dating the Bible." en.wikipedia.org/wiki/Dating_the_Bible
"Deborah.' en.wikipedia.org/wiki/Deborah
"Dionysiaca." en.wikipedia.org/wiki/Dionysiaca
"Dionysian mysteries." en.wikipedia.org/wiki/Dionysian_Mysteries
"Documentary hypothesis." en.wikipedia.org/wiki/Documentary_hypothesis
"Early Dynastic Officials." *The Pennsylvania Sumerian Dictionary.* psd.museum.upenn.edu/cgi-bin/cdlhtml?project=ctxt&mode=ctxt&item=Q000008&line=Q000008.44&frag=Q000008.41#a.Q000008.41
"Ebla tablets." en.wikipedia.org/wiki/Ebla_tablets
"Egyptian Chariot Wheels Found at the Bottom of the Red Sea—Unproven!" truthorfiction.com/rumors/c/chariot-wheels.htm
"Elohim." en.wikipedia.org/wiki/Elohim
"Emar." en.wikipedia.org/wiki/Emar
"Enlil." en.wikipedia.org/wiki/Ellil

BIBLIOGRAPHY 503

"The Epic of Gilgamesh." *Annenberg Learner.*
 learner.org/courses/worldlit/gilgamesh/watch
"Execration texts." en.wikipedia.org/wiki/Execration_texts
"The Exodus." en.wikipedia.org/wiki/The_Exodus
"The Exodus Revelation, Part II: The Exodus."
 mysteriousworld.com/Journal/2008/Spring/Artifacts/ExodusRevelation
 Part2-TheExodus.asp
"Gaius Marcius Coriolanus."
 en.wikipedia.org/wiki/Gaius_Marcius_Coriolanus
"Gemara." en.wikipedia.org/wiki/Gemara
"Geštinanna/Belet-ṣeri (goddess)." *Ancient Mesopotamian Gods and
 Goddesses.* oracc.museum.upenn.edu/amgg/listofdeities/getinanna
"Gilgamesh: Score Transliteration: Tablet XI."
 soas.ac.uk/nme/research/gilgamesh/standard/file39599.pdf
"God Almighty."
 freethoughtnation.com/forums/viewtopic.php?p=27584#p27584
"Great Assembly." en.wikipedia.org/wiki/Great_Assembly
"The Great Hymn to the Aten."
 uta.edu/honors/faculty/petruso/HymnAten.htm
"Habiru." en.wikipedia.org/wiki/Habiru
"The Hebrew Words El, Elim, Eloah, and Elohim."
 freewebs.com/kensoffice/godhebrewgreek.htm
"Historical Philistines were not philistines, archaeologists say."
 nytimes.com/1992/09/29/science/philistines-were-cultured-after-all-
 say-archeologists.html
"History of the constellations."
 en.wikipedia.org/wiki/History_of_the_constellations
"History of wine." en.wikipedia.org/wiki/History_of_wine
"History of the wine press." en.wikipedia.org/wiki/History_of_the_wine_press
"Hyksos." en.wikipedia.org/wiki/Hyksos
"Hyksos."
 jewishvirtuallibrary.org/jsource/judaica/ejud_0002_0009_0_09361.html
"Hyksos." *Online Etymology Dictionary.*
 etymonline.com/index.php?term=Hyksos&allowed_in_frame=0?ie=UTF8
"Iah." en.wikipedia.org/wiki/Iah
"Illyrians." en.wikipedia.org/wiki/Illyrians
"Inana's descent to the nether world: translation." *The Electronic Text Corpus
 of Sumerian Literature.* etcsl.orinst.ox.ac.uk/section1/tr141.htm
"Indian wine." en.wikipedia.org/wiki/Indian_wine
"The Ipuwer Papyrus." en.wikipedia.org/wiki/Ipuwer_papyrus
"Issachar." en.wikipedia.org/wiki/Issachar
"Jerusalem." en.wikipedia.org/wiki/Jerusalem
"The 'Job motif' in earlier literature."
 en.wikipedia.org/wiki/Book_of_Job#The_.22Job_motif.22_in_earlier_liter
 ature
"John William Colenso." en.wikipedia.org/wiki/John_William_Colenso
"Kharosthi." en.wikipedia.org/wiki/Kharosthi
"Kottabos." en.wikipedia.org/wiki/Kottabos
"Koyaanisqatsi." en.wikipedia.org/wiki/Koyaanisqatsi
"Kuntillet Ajrud." en.wikipedia.org/wiki/Kuntillet_Ajrud
"A Letter from Abdu-Heba of Jerusalem." reshafim.org.il/ad/egypt/a-abdu-
 heba1.htm

"Library of Ashurbanipal." en.wikipedia.org/wiki/Library_of_Ashurbanipal
"Mari, Syria." en.wikipedia.org/wiki/Mari,_Syria
"Maš [PURE]." psd.museum.upenn.edu/epsd/epsd/e3619.html
"Maš [TWIN] wr. maš 'twin' Akk. *māšu*." *The Pennsylvania Sumerian Dictionary.* psd.museum.upenn.edu/epsd/signnames-toc-M.html
"Mašmaš [SORCERER]." psd.museum.upenn.edu/epsd/epsd/e3641.html
"Massu [LEADER]." psd.museum.upenn.edu/epsd/epsd/e3613.html
"Me (mythology)." en.wikipedia.org/wiki/Me_(mythology)
"Megasthenes." en.wikipedia.org/wiki/Megasthenes
"Melampus." en.wikipedia.org/wiki/Melampus
"Meluhha." en.wikipedia.org/wiki/Meluhha
"Menes." en.wikipedia.org/wiki/Menes
"Merneptah Stele." en.wikipedia.org/wiki/Merneptah_Stele
"Milkilu." en.wikipedia.org/wiki/Milkilu
"Minister calls for third Temple to be built." *The Times of Israel*, 7/7/2013; timesofisrael.com/minister-calls-for-third-temple-to-be-built
"Mishnah." en.wikipedia.org/wiki/Mishnah
"Mitochondrial Eve." en.wikipedia.org/wiki/Mitochondrial_Eve
"Molech." en.wikipedia.org/wiki/Moloch
"Moses." en.wikipedia.org/wiki/Moses
"Muš [SNAKE]." psd.museum.upenn.edu/epsd/e3832.html
"Muš [SNAKE]." psd.museum.upenn.edu/cgi-bin/distprof?cfgw=mu%C5%A1[SNAKE]&res=aqq&eid=e3832
"Mušhuš [MONSTER]." psd.museum.upenn.edu/epsd/e3849.html
"Muš☐uššu." en.wikipedia.org/wiki/Muš☐uššu
"Mythicist Milwaukee." mythicistmilwaukee.com
"New Chronology (Rohl)." en.wikipedia.org/wiki/New_Chronology_%28Rohl%29
"Ningishzida." en.wikipedia.org/wiki/Ningishzida
"Ningishzida's Journey to the Netherworld." etcsl.orinst.ox.ac.uk/section1/tr173.htm
"Oldest Alphabetical Written Text Found Near Temple Mount." jewishpress.com/news/oldest-alphabetical-written-text-found-near-temple-mount/2013/07/10/
"Origins of the Hyksos." en.wikipedia.org/wiki/Origins_of_the_Hyksos
"Orotalt." en.wikipedia.org/wiki/Orotalt
"Orphic Hymns." hellenicgods.org/orphic-hymns---orphikoi-hymnoi
"Osarseph." en.wikipedia.org/wiki/Osarseph
"Οι Πελασγοι Και Η Πελασγικη (Γραμμικη) Γραφη." krassanakis.gr/linear.htm
"Perseus Hopper." perseus.tufts.edu/hopper
"Phaethon." theoi.com/Titan/Phaethon.html
"Pharaoh's chariots found in the Red Sea?" wnd.com/2003/06/19382/
"Philistines, but Less and Less Philistine." nytimes.com/2007/03/13/science/13phil.html?_r=1&partner=rssnyt&emc=rss
"Plague of Athens." en.wikipedia.org/wiki/Plague_of_Athens
"The Population at the Exodus." askelm.com/secrets/sec107.htm
"Reconsidering BACCHIVS IVDAEVS." *Forum Ancient Coins.* forumancientcoins.com/board/index.php?topic=81805.0
"The Return of Hephaistos." theoi.com/Gallery/K7.4.html
"Roca dels Moros." en.wikipedia.org/wiki/Roca_dels_Moros
"Ron Wyatt." en.wikipedia.org/wiki/Ron_Wyatt

BIBLIOGRAPHY 505

"Σείρ." *Suda On Line Search.* stoa.org/sol
"Sethianism." en.wikipedia.org/wiki/Sethianism
"Shamsiel." en.wikipedia.org/wiki/Shamsiel
"Shapash, Shapshu."
    webspace.webring.com/people/nl/lilinah_haanat/mindei.html
"Shasu." en.wikipedia.org/wiki/Shasu
"Staphylus." en.wikipedia.org/wiki/Staphylus
"Story of Sinuhe." en.wikipedia.org/wiki/Story_of_Sinuhe
"Tablets of Destiny." en.wikipedia.org/wiki/Tablets_of_Destiny
"Tammuz (Hebrew month)."
    en.wikipedia.org/wiki/Tammuz_%28Hebrew_month%29
"Tannin." en.wikipedia.org/wiki/Tannin_(demon)
"Tempest Stele." en.wikipedia.org/wiki/Tempest_Stele
"Tenedos." en.wikipedia.org/wiki/Tenedos
"Teraphim." en.wikipedia.org/wiki/Teraphim
"Thutmose III." en.wikipedia.org/wiki/Thutmose_III
"Tiamat." en.wikipedia.org/wiki/Tiamat
"Torah." en.wikipedia.org/wiki/Pentateuch
"Tyana (Kemerhisar)." livius.org/tt-tz/tyana/tyana.html
"Twelve Tables." en.wikipedia.org/wiki/Twelve_Tables
Abel, Eugenius. *Orphica: Accedunt Procli Hymni. Hymni Magici.* Lipsiae: Sumptus Fecit G. Freytag, 1885.
Abusch, Tzvi, and Schwemer, Daniel. *Corpus of Mesopotamian Anti-Witchcraft Rituals,* vol. 1. Leiden: E.J. Brill, 2011.
Acharya S. *The Christ Conspiracy: The Greatest Story Ever Sold.* Illinois: AUP, 1999.
    —*Suns of God: Krishna, Buddha and Christ Unveiled.* Illinois: AUP, 2004. See also D.M. Murdock
Aeschylus. *Aeschylus,* vol. 2. tr. Herbert Weir Smyth. ed. E. Capps, T.E. Page, W.H.D. Rouse. London: William Heinemann/New York: G.P. Putnam's Sons, 1926.
Akkadian Dictionary. premiumwanadoo.com/cuneiform.languages/dictionary
Albright, William Foxwell. *Yahweh and the Gods of Canaan.* Winona Lake, IN: Eisenbrauns, 1968.
Aling, Charles, and Clyde Billington. "The Name Yahweh in Egyptian Hieroglyphic Texts." *Artifax Magazine.* biblearchaeology.org/post/2010/03/08/The-Name-Yahweh-in-Egyptian-Hieroglyphic-Texts.aspx
Allegro, John. *The Sacred Mushroom and the Cross. The Sacred Mushroom and the Cross.* Doubleday, 1970.
Allen, Don Cameron. *Mysteriously Meant: The Rediscovery of Pagan Symbolism and Allegorical Interpretation in the Renaissance.* Baltimore: Johns Hopkins Press, 1970.
Allen, James P. *Middle Egyptian: An Introduction to the Language and Culture of Hieroglyphs.* Cambridge University Press, 2000.
    —*The Ancient Egyptian Pyramid Texts.* Atlanta: Society of Biblical Literature, 2005.
Allen, Richard Hinckley. *Star-Names and Their Meanings.* New York: G.E. Stechert, 1899.
Ancient Coin Search Engine.
    acsearch.info/search.html?search=BACCHIVS&view_mode=1#28

André, Richard. *The Coloured Picture Bible for Children.* Society for Promoting Christian Knowledge, 1884.
Andrews, Ethan A., and William Freund. *A Copious and Critical Latin-English Lexicon.* New York: Harper & Brothers, 1860.
Ankerberg, John, and John Weldon. *Astrology: Do the Heavens Rule Our Destiny?* ATRI Publishing, 2010.
Apollodorus. *Apollodorus: The Library, with an English Translation by Sir James George Frazer*, vols. 1-2. Cambridge, MA: Harvard University Press, 1921.
—*The Library*, vol. 1. tr. James George Frazer. New York: G.P. Putnam's Sons, 1921.
Apuleius. *The Golden Ass, being the Metamorphoses of Lucius Apuleius.* Ed. Stephen Gaselee. London: William Heinemann; New York: G.P. Putnam's Sons, 1915.
—*The Isis-Book: Metamorphoses, Book XI.* ed. John G. Griffiths. Leiden: E.J. Brill, 1975.
—*The Metamorphoses or Golden Ass of Apuleius of Madaura*, vol. 2. tr. H.E. Butler. Oxford: Clarendon Press, 1910.
Aristides, Aelius. *Aristides. ex recensione Guilielmi Dindorfii.* Leipzig: Weidmann, 1829.
Aristophanes. *Aristophanes Comoediae*, vol. 2. ed. F.W. Hall and W.M. Geldart. Oxford: Clarendon Press, 1907.
—*Women at the Thesmophoria. The Complete Greek Drama*, vol. 2. tr. Eugene O'Neill, Jr. New York: Random House, 1938.
Aristotle. *Aristotle in 23 Volumes*, vol. 22, tr. J. H. Freese. Cambridge, MA: Harvard University Press, 1926.
—*Aristotle in 23 Volumes*, vol. 23. tr. W.H. Fyfe. Cambridge, MA: Harvard University Press, 1932.
—*Aristotle's Ars Poetica.* ed. R. Kassel. Oxford: Clarendon Press, 1966.
Armour, Robert A. *Gods and Myths of Ancient Egypt.* Cairo: American University in Cairo Press, 2001.
Armstrong, Karen. *History of God.* New York: Random House, 1993.
Arnason, Johann P., S.N. Eisenstadt, and Björn Wittrock. *Axial Civilizations and World History.* Leiden: Brill, 2005.
Arnold, Bill T., and Bryan E. Beyer. *Readings from the Ancient Near East: Primary Sources for Old Testament Study.* Grand Rapids, MI: Baker Publishing Group, 2005.
Arrian, *The Anabasis of Alexander.* tr. E.J. Chinnock. London: Hodder and Stoughton, 1884.
—*Flavii Arriani Anabasis Alexandri.* ed. A.G. Roos. Leipzig: B. G. Teubneri, 1907.
Asheri, David, Alan Lloyd, and Aldo Corcella. *A Commentary on Herodotus Books I-IV.* eds. Oswyn Murray and Alfonso Moreno. Oxford: Oxford University Press, 2007.
Assmann, Jan. *Egyptian Solar Religion in the New Kingdom: Re, Amun and the Crisis of Polytheism.* London/NY: Kegan Paul International, 1995.
—*Moses the Egyptian: The Memory of Egypt in Western Monotheism.* Cambridge, MA: Harvard University Press, 1997.
—*The Search for God in Ancient Egypt.* tr. David Lorton. Ithaca/London: Cornell University Press, 2001.
Astour, Michael C. *Hellenosemitica.* Leiden: E.J. Brill, 1967.

Athenaeus. *The Deipnosophists.* tr. Charles Burton Gulick. Cambridge, MA: Harvard University Press, 1927.
Atsma, Aaron J. "DIONYSOS WRATH 1." theoi.com/Olympios/DionysosWrath.html
Aulestia, Gorka. *Basque-English Dictionary.* ed. William A. Douglass. Reno: University of Nevada Press, 1989.
Avery-Peck, Alan J., and Jacob Leusner, eds. *Judaism and Christianity: New Directions for Dialogue and Understanding.* Leiden: E.J. Brill, 2009.
Azize, Joseph. *The Phoenician Solar Theology.* New Jersey: Gorgias Press, 2005.
Baker, Margaret. *The Great Angel: A Study of Israel's Second God.* Louisville, KY: 1992.
—*The Mother of the Lord: Volume 1: The Lady in the Temple.* New York: Bloomsbury T&T Clark, 2012.
Banks, J., tr. *The Idylls of Theocritus, Bion, and Moschus, and the War-songs of Tyrtæus.* London: Belly and Daldy, 1870.
Barclay, Joseph. *The Talmud.* London: John Murray, 1878.
Baring, Anne, and Jules Cashford. *The Myth of the Goddess: Evolution of an Image.* London: Penguin Group, 1991.
Barkay, Gabriel. "What's an Egyptian Temple Doing in Jerusalem?" *Biblical Archaeology Review* 26:03, May/Jun 2000.
Bar-Kochva, Bezalel. *The Image of the Jews in Greek Literature: The Hellenistic Period.* Berkeley: University of California Press, 2010.
Barnstone, Willis, ed. *The Other Bible.* HarperSanFrancisco, 1984.
Barton, George A. "Native Israelitish Deities." *Oriental Studies.* Boston: Ginn & Company, 1894.
Batto, Bernard F. *Mythmaking in the Biblical Tradition: Slaying the Dragon.* Louisville, KY: Westminster John Knox Press, 1992.
Baumgarten, Albert I. *The Phoenician History of Philo of Byblos.* Leiden: E.J. Brill, 1981.
Bautch, Kelley Coblentz. *A Study of the Geography of 1 Enoch 17-19.* Leiden: E.J. Brill, 2003.
Beale, Gregory K. *The Book of Revelation: A Commentary on the Greek Text.* Grand Rapids, MI: Wm. B. Eerdmans, 1999.
Becker, Carl J. *A Modern Theory of Language Evolution.* New York: iUniverse, 2005.
Becking, Bob, and Meindert Dijkstra. *On Reading Prophetic Texts: Gender-Specific & Related Studies in Memory of Fokkelien van Dijk-Hemmes.* Leiden: E.J. Brill, 1996.
Bell, John. *Bell's New Pantheon; Or, Historical Dictionary of the Gods, Demi-Gods, Heroes and Fabulous Personages of Antiquity,* vol. 1. London: J. Bell, 1790.
Bellamy, John. *The Holy Bible, Newly Translated from the Original Hebrew.* London: Longman, Hurst, Rees, et al., 1818.—"On the Origin of the Heathen Mythology." *The Classical Journal,* vol. 21. London: A.J. Valpy, 1820.
—"On the Origin of the Heathen Mythology." *The Classical Journal.* Cambridge: Cambridge University Press, 2013.
Ben-Gedalyahu, Tzvi. "Evidence of Stone Age Cultic Phallic Symbols Found in Israel." *Jewish Press* (3/13/13). jewishpress.com/news/evidence-of-stone-age-cultic-sexual-symbols-found-in-israel/2013/03/13.

Bennett, De Robigne Mortimer. *The Gods and Religions of Ancient and Modern Times*, vol. 2. New York: Liberal and Scientific Publishing House, 1881.Berchman, Robert M. *Porphyry Against the Christians*. Leiden: Brill, 2005.

Bergmann, Claudia D. *Childbirth as a Metaphor for Crisis: Evidence from the Ancient Near East, Hebrew Bible and 1QH XI, 1-18*. Berlin: Walter de Gruyter, 2008.

Berlin, Adele. *Lamentations*. Louisville, KY: Westminster John Knox Press, 2004.

Berry, Thomas. *The Religions of India: Hinduism, Yoga, Buddhism*. New York: Columbia University Press, 1992.

Betz, Walter. *God and the Gods: Myths of the Bible*. New York: Penguin Books, 1983.

Bhandarkar, Ramkrishna Gopal. *R. G. Bhāṇḍārkar Commemoration Volume*. Delhi: Bharatiya Pub. House, 1977.

The Bible Cyclopedia, vol. 1. London: John W. Parker, 1841.

Bienkowski, Piotr, and Alan Millard. *Dictionary of the Ancient Near East*. Philadelphia: University of Pennsylvania Press, 2000.

Birch, Samuel. *Records of the Past: Being English Translations of the Assyrian and Egyptian Monuments*, vol. 8. London: Samuel Bagster and Sons, 1874.

Bleeker, Claas Jouco. *Hathor and Thoth: Two Key Figures of the Ancient Egyptian Religion*. Leiden: E.J. Brill, 1973.

Blue Letter Bible. BlueletterBible.org.

Boardman, John, et al., eds. *The Cambridge ancient history. Volume III, Part 2: The Assyrian and Babylonian Empires and Other States of the Near East*. Cambridge: Cambridge University Press, 2003.

Bochart, Samuel. *Opera Omni: Hoc Est Phaleg, Canaan et Hierozoicon*. London: C. Boutesteyn and J. Luchtmans, 1692.

—*Hierozoicon: sive bipartitum opus de animalibus S. Scripturae*. Lugdunum Batavorum: Boutesteyn & Luchtmans, 1712.

Bolton, Lesley. *The Everything Classical Mythology Book*. Avon, MA: F+W Publications, 2002.

Botterweck, G. Johannes, and Helmer Ringgren, eds. *Theological Dictionary of the Old Testament*, vol. 6. William B. Eerdmans Publishing, 1990.

Boylan, Patrick. *Thoth: The Hermes of Egypt*. London: Oxford University Press, 1922.

Bowersock, Glen Warren. *Mosaics as History: The Near East from Late Antiquity to Early Islam*. Cambridge: MA: Harvard University Press, 2006.

Bradshaw, Robert I. "Archaeology & the Patriarchs." biblicalstudies.org.uk/article_archaeology.html

Braund, David, and John Wilkins. *Athenaeus and His World*. Exeter: University of Exeter Press, 2000.

Breasted, James Henry. *Development of Religion and Thought in Ancient Egypt*. New York: Charles Scribner's Sons, 1912.

—"Israel and the Monuments of the Nile." *Self Culture*, vol. 8. ed. G. Mercer Adam. Akron, OH: The Werner Company, 9/1898-2/1899.

Britt, Robert Roy. "Scientists find first known human ritual." *NBC Science News*. nbcnews.com/id/15970442

Bromiley, Geoffrey W. *The International Standard Bible Encyclopedia*, vol. 4. Grand Rapids, MI: Wm. B. Eerdmans Publishing, 1988.

Bromiley, Geoffrey W., Gerhard Kittel, and Gerhard Friedrich, eds. *Theological Dictionary of the New Testament.* Grand Rapids, MI: William B. Eerdmans, 1985.
Bronnikov, G., and Phil Krylov. "Afroasiatic and Semitica etymology." starling.rinet.ru/cgi-bin/etymology.cgi?single=1&basename=/data/semham/afaset&text_number=++50&root=config
Brown, John Pairman. *Israel and Hellas.* Berlin: Walter de Gruyter, 1995.
Brown, William P. *Seeing the Psalms: A Theology of Metaphor.* Louisville, KY: Westminster John Knox Press, 2002.
Brugsch, Heinrich Karl, and Mary Brodrick. *Egypt Under the Pharaohs.* London: John Murray, 1891.
Budge, E.A. Wallis. *The Book of the Dead: The Papyrus of Ani in the British Museum.* London: Longmans & Co, et al., 1895.
—*The Book of the Dead with 25 Illustrations.* London: British Museum Order of Trustees, 1920.
—*Osiris and the Egyptian Resurrection,* vol. 1. New York: Dover Publications, 1973.
—*A Hieroglyphic Vocabulary to the Book of the Dead.* New York: Dover, 1991.
—*Alexander the Great: An Account of His Life and Exploits from Ethiopic Sources and Other Writing.* London: Kegan Paul, 2003.
—*Egyptian Hieroglyphic Dictionary,* vol. 1 (1920). New York: Cosimo Classics, 2010.
Buitenen, Johannes Adrianus Bernardus. *The Mahābhārata.* Chicago: University of Chicago Press, 1981.
Bulletin of the American Schools of Oriental Research, vols. 81-92. Ann Arbor, MI: American Schools of Oriental Research and Scholars Press, 1941.
Burt, Richard Francis. *The Book of the Sword.* London: Chatto and Windus, Piccadilly, 1884.
Busenbark, Ernest. *Symbols, Sex and the Stars.* Escondido, CA: The Book Tree, 1997.
Butcher, S.H. *The Odyssey of Homer Done into English Prose.* New York: The Macmillan Company, 1893.
Byrne, Joseph P. *Encyclopedia of Pestilence, Pandemics, and Plagues, Volume 1: A-M.* Westport, CT: Greenwood Publishing Group, 2008.
Caiozzo, Matt. "The Secret of Making Bricks without Straw." mattcaiozzo.com/the-secret-of-making-bricks-without-straw/
Callimachus. *Works.* ed. A.W. Mair. New York: G.P. Putnam's Sons, 1921.
Campbell, Joseph. *Occidental Mythology: The Masks of God.* New York: Arkana/Penguin, 1991.
Carus, Paul, ed. *The Open Court,* vol. 15. Chicago: The Open Court Publishing Company, 1901.
—*The Monist.* vol. 15. no. 1. Chicago: The Open Court Publishing Company, 1905.
Cassius Dio Cocceianus, *Historiae Romanae.* eds. Earnest Cary, Herbert Baldwin Foster. London: William Heinemann, 1914.
Chaitanya, Satya. "Bheel Mahabharata: Kunti and the Birth of the Sun God's Child." boloji.com/index.cfm?md=Content&sd=Articles&ArticleID=1190
Charlesworth, James H. *The Good And Evil Serpent: How a Universal Symbol Became Christianized.* Yale University Press, 2011.

Chisholm, Hugh, et al., eds. *The Encyclopaedia Britannica*, vol. 22. Cambridge: Cambridge University Press, 1911.

Cicero, M. Tullius. *Of the Nature of the Gods*. tr. Thomas Francklin. London: William Pickering, 1829.

Ciholas, Paul. "Plato: The Attic Moses? Some Patristic Reactions to Platonic Philosophy." *The Classical World*, vol. 72, no. 4. Johns Hopkins University Press, 12/1978-1/1979; 217-225.

Clarke, Adam. *The Holy Bible, Containing the Old and New Testaments*, vol. 1. London: Thomas Tegg and Son, 1836.

Clay, Albert T. *The Empire of the Amorites*. New Haven: Yale University Press, 1919.

Clement. *Fathers of the Church, vol. 85: Clement of Alexandria, Books 1-3*. tr. John Ferguson. Catholic University of America Press, 2005.

Coats, George W. *The Moses Tradition*. Sheffield, England: Sheffield Academic Press, 1993.

Conder, Josiah. *The Modern Traveller*, vol. 4. London: James Duncan, 1830.

Colenso, John William. *The Pentateuch and Book of Joshua Critically Examined*, vol. 5. London: Longmans, Green and Co., 1865.

Collier, Mark, and Bill Manley. *How to Read Egyptian Hieroglyphs*. Berkeley/Los Angeles: University of California Press, 2003.

Collins, Billie Jean. *The Hittites and Their World*. Leiden: E.J. Brill, 2008.

Coogan, Michael D. *A Brief Introduction to the Old Testament*. New York/Oxford: Oxford University Press, 2009.

Cook, John Granger. *The Interpretation of the Old Testament in Greco-Roman Paganism*. Tübingen, Germany: Mohr Siebeck, 2004.

Coulter, Charles Russell, and Patricia Turner. *Encyclopedia of Ancient Deities*. New York: Routledge, 2012.

Craig, John. *A New Universal Technological, Etymological and Pronouncing Dictionary of the English Language*, vol. 2. London: Henry George Collins, 1848.

Crawford, Angus. "Tel El-Amarna, the Great Discovery." *The Virginia Seminary Magazine*, vol. 5. Fairfax, VA: Virginia Theological Seminary, 1892.

Cross, Frank M. *Canaanite Myth and Hebrew Epic*. Cambridge, MA: Harvard University Press, 1997.

Cunchillos, Jesús-Luis, Juan-Pablo Vita, José-Ángel Zamora, Rachel Cervigón, and A Lacadena. *The Texts of the Ugaritic Data Bank*. Piscaway, NJ: Gorgias Press, 2003.

Cunningham, Graham. *Deliver Me from Evil: Mesopotamian incantations 2500-1500 BC*. Rome: Editrice Pontificio Isituto Biblico, 2007.

Dalby, Andrew. *Food in the Ancient World From A to Z*. London: Routledge, 2003.

Danet, Pierre. *A Complete Dictionary of the Greek and Roman Antiquities*. London: John Nicholson, 1700.

Darlington, William. *A Catechism of Mythology; Containing a Compendious History of the Heathen Gods and Heroes*. Baltimore: William R. Lucas, 1832.

Davidovits, Joseph. "Error or forgery on the Stele of Merneptah, known as Israel Stele." davidovits.info/496/error-or-forgery-on-the-stele-of-merneptah-known-as-israel-stele

Davis, Stevan, tr. *The Secret Book of John*. 2005; gnosis.org/naghamm/apocjn-davies.html

BIBLIOGRAPHY 511

Davis, Bahir. "Hanukah: The Power of Light." *Rocky Mountain HAI.* rockymountainhai.com/2011/12/14/hanukah-the-power-of-light
Day, John. *Yahweh and the Gods and Goddesses of Canaan.* Sheffield, England: Sheffield Academic Press, 2002.
Dever, William G. *What Did the Biblical Writers Known & When Did They Know It?* Grand Rapids, MI: Wm. B. Eerdmans, 2001.
—*Who Were the Early Israelites and Where Did They Come From?* Grand Rapids, MI: William B. Eerdmans Pub. Co., 2003.
Diodorus Siculus. *The Historical Library of Diodorus the Sicilian, in Fifteen Books,* vols. 1-2. tr. G. Booth. London: W. McDowall, 1814.
—*Bibliotheca Historica,* vol. 1. ed. Ludwig Dindorf. Lipsiae: CH.F. Hartman, 1828.
—*Diodori Bibliotheca Historica,* vol. 1-2. ed. Immanuel Bekker, Ludwig Dindorf, Friedrich Vogel. Leipzig: B. G. Teubneri, 1888-1890.
—*Diodorus of Sicily,* vol. 2. tr. C.H. Oldfeather. London: W. Heinemann, 1953.
—*The Antiquities of Egypt.* New Brunswick, NJ: Transaction Publishers, Rutgers, 1990.
—*Diodorus of Sicily,* vol. 4. tr. Charles Henry Oldfeather. Cambridge, MA: Harvard University Press, 2002.
Diogenes Laertius. *Lives of Eminent Philosophers.* tr. R.D. Hicks. Cambridge, MA: Harvard University Press, 1972.
Dion, Paul E. "*Yahweh as Storm-God and Sun-God: The Double Legacy of Egypt and Canaan as Reflected in Psalm 104.*" Zeitschrift für die Alttestamentliche Wissenschaft, vol. 103. 1991; 58-65.
Dionysius of Halicarnassus. *Roman Antiquities.* tr. Edward Spelman, vol. 3. London: Booksellers of London and Westminster, 1758.
—*Dionysii Halicarnasei Antiquitatum Romanarum quae supersunt,* vol. 3. ed. Karl Jacoby. Leipzig: In Aedibus B.G. Teubneri, 1891.
Di Vito, Robert A. *Studies in Third Millennium Sumerian and Akkadian Personal Names.* Rome: Editrice Pontificio Istituto Biblico, 1993.
Doane, T.W. *Bible Myths and Their Parallels in Other Religions.* WA: Health Research, 1985.
Dollinger, André. "The Great Mendes Stela." reshafim.org.il/ad/egypt/texts/great_mendes_stela.htm
Doniger, Wendy. *Merriam-Webster's Encyclopedia of World Religions.* Springfield, MA: Merriam-Webster, 1999.
Doresse, Jean. *The Secret Books of the Egyptian Gnostics.* Rochester, VT: Inner Traditions International, 1986.
Draper, George Otis. *Searching for Truth.* London: Peter Eckler, 1902.
Dreyer, Boris, and Peter Franz Mittag. *Lokale Eliten und hellenistische Könige.* Berlin: Verlag Antike, 2011.
Duncker, Max. *The History of Antiquity,* vol. 1. tr. Evelyn Abbott. London: Richard Bentley & Son, 1877.
Dunlap, Samuel F. *The Origin of Ancient Names.* Cambridge: Metcalf and Company, 1856.
Dupuis, Charles. *The Origin of All Religious Worship.* New Orleans, 1872.
Eakin, Frank E. *The Religion and Culture of Israel: An Introduction to Old Testament Thought.* Boston: Allyn and Bacon, 1971.
Easterling, Pat, and Edith Hall. *Greek and Roman Actors: Aspects of an Ancient Profession.* Cambridge: Cambridge University Press, 2002.

Eastwick, R.W. Egerton. *The Oracle Encyclopedia*, v. IV. London: George Newnes, Ltd., 1896.
Eckenstein, Lina. *A History of Sinai*. London: Society for Promoting Christian Knowledge, 1921.
Emerton, John A., ed. *Congress Volume: Jerusalem 1986*. Leiden: E.J. Brill, 1988.
Encyclopedia Judaica. eds. Abraham Schalit, Shimon Gibson. The Gale Group, 2008; jewishvirtuallibrary.org/jsource/judaica/ejud_0002_0005_0_05245.html
Epiphanius. *The Panarion of Epiphanius of Salamis*, vol. 2. tr. Frank Williams. Leiden: E.J. Brill, 1994.
ePSD Sumerian Sign-name Index. psd.museum.upenn.edu/epsd/signnames-toc-M.html.
Epstein, Isidore, ed. *The Babylonian Talmud*. London: Soncino Press, 1952.
Epsztein, Léon. *Social Justice in the Ancient Near East and the People of the Bible*. London: SCM Press, 1986.
Estrin, Daniel. "Have the oldest human remains been found in Israel?" nbcnews.com/id/40820248/ns/technology_and_science-science/t/have-oldest-human-remains-been-found-israel
Euripides. *The Theophania or Divine Manifestation of Our Lord and Saviour Jesus Christ*. ed. Samuel Lee. Cambridge: Duncan and Malcom, 1843.
—*The Tragedies of Euripides*. tr. T. A. Buckley. London: Henry G. Bohn, 1850.
—*Eusebii Pamphili Evangelicae Praeparatione*, vol. 15. ed. E.H. Gifford. Novi Eboraci: H. Frowde, 1903.
—*Euripidis Fabulae*, vol. 2 and 3. Gilbert Murray. Oxford. Clarendon Press, Oxford. 1913.
Eusebius. *Praeparatio Evangelica (Preparation for the Gospel)*, vol. 15. tr. E.H. Gifford. Oxonii: Typographeo Academico/H. Frowde, 1903.
Evans, Arthur J. "The Palace of Minos." *Annual Report of the Board of Regents of the Smithsonian Institution*. Washington, DC: Government Printing Office, 1902.
Evelyn-White, Hugh G., tr. *The Homeric Hymns and Homerica*. Cambridge, MA: Harvard University Press, 1914.
Faber, George Stanley. *The Origin of Pagan Idolatry Ascertained from Historical Testimony*, vol. 2. London: A.J. Valpy, 1816.
Fahlbusch, E., et al. *The Encyclopedia of Christianity*, vol. 4. Grand Rapids, MI/Leiden: Wm. B. Eerdmans/Brill, 2005.
Falk, Avner. *A Psychoanalytic History of the Jews*. NJ: Associated University Presses, 1996.
Faulkner, Raymond O. *A Concise Dictionary of Middle Egyptian*. Oxford: Oxford University Press, 1962.
—*The Ancient Egyptian Coffin Texts*. Oxford: Aris & Phillips, 1973.
—*The Egyptian Book of the Dead*. ed. Ogden Goelet. San Francisco: Chronicle Books, 1998.
FawkesGlynnis, and Robert Allan. "Tale of Aqhat." kingmixers.com/CLA196/AQHAT.pdf.
Feldman, Louis H. *Studies in Hellenistic Judaism*. Leiden: E.J. Brill, 1996.
Finkel, Avraham Yaakov. *Kabbalah: Selections from Classic Kabbalistic Works from Raziel HaMalach to the Present Day*. Southfield, MI: Targum Press, 2002.

Finkelstein, and Amihai Mazar. *The Quest for the Historical Israel.* ed. Brian B. Schmidt. Atlanta, GA: Society of Biblical Literature, 2007.
Finkelstein, Israel, and Neil A. Silberman. *The Bible Unearthed.* New York: The Free Press, 2001.
Flavin, Richard D. "The Karanovo Zodiac." *Epigraphic Society Occasional Papers,* vol. 20, 1991/2, pp. 37-42; flavinscorner.com/karanovo.htm.
Flückiger-Hawker, Esther. *Urnamma of Ur in Sumerian Literary Tradition.* Zurich: University of Zurich Press, 1999.
Frank, Harry Thomas. *An Archaeological Companion to the Bible.* London: SCM Press, 1972.
Franke, William. "The Exodus Epic: Universalization of History through Ritual Repetition." *Universality and History: Foundations of Core.* eds. Don Thompson, et al. Lanham, Md. : Association and University Press of America, 2002.
Frankel, Pinchas. "The Month of 'Tammuz' and Jewish Feminism." ou.org/torah/frankel/5764/pinchas64.htm
Franklin, Michael John, ed. *Representing India: Institutes of Hindu Law, or the Ordinances of Menu.* New York: Routledge, 2000.
Frazer, James George. *The Golden Bough,* vol. 5. New York: Cambridge University Press, 2012.
Free, Joseph P. *Archaeology and Bible History.* ed. Howard F. Vos. Wheaton, IL: Scripture Press Publication, Inc., 1992.
Freedman, David Noel, ed. *Eerdmans Dictionary of the Bible.* Grand Rapids, MI: Wm. B. Eerdmans Publishing Co., 2000.
Friedman, Richard E. *Who Wrote the Bible?* New York: Perennial Library, 1989.
—*The Bible with the Sources Revealed.* New York: HarperCollins, 2003.
Furneaux, Rupert. *Myth and Mystery.* London: Allan Wingate, 1955.
Gallagher, William R. "On the Identity of Hêlēl ben Ša☐ar of Is. 14:12-15." UF, vol. 26. 1994.
Galpaz-Feller, Pnina. *Samson: The Hero and the Man.* Bern: Peter Lang AG, 2006.
Gardiner, Alan H. *Egypt of the Pharaohs.* London: Oxford University Press, 1964.
Gardner, Gregg, and Kevin L. Osterloh, eds. *Antiquity in Antiquity: Jewish and Christian Pasts in the Greco-Roman World.* Tübingen: Mohr Siebeck, 2008.
Gaster, Theodor Herzl. *Myth, Legend and Custom in the Old Testament: A Comparative Study with Chapters from Sir James G. Frazer's Folklore in the Old Testament.* New York: Harper & Row, 1969.
Gately, Iain. *Drink: A Cultural History of Alcohol.* New York: Gotham Books, 2008.
Geddes, Alexander. *The Holy Bible, or the Books Accounted Sacred by Jews and Christians,* vol. 1. London: J. Davis, 1792.
—*Critical Remarks on the Hebrew Scriptures,* vol. 1. London: Davis, Wilks and Taylor, 1800.
Geller, Markham J. *Ancient Babylonian Medicine: Theory and Practice.* Chichester: John Wiley & Sons, 2010.
George, A.R. "Bilgames and the Bull of Heaven: Cuneiform Texts, Collations and Textual Reconstruction." eprints.soas.ac.uk/8612/1/jabmv-08-george.pdf

Gesenius, William. *Gesenius's Hebrew and Chaldee Lexicon to the Old Testament Scriptures.* tr. Samuel Prideaux Tregelles. New York: John Wiley & Sons, 1893.

Gillingham, Susan, ed. *Jewish and Christian Approaches to the Psalms: Conflict and Convergence.* Oxford: Oxford University Press, 2013.

Gmirkin, Russell E. *Berossus and Genesis, Manetho and Exodus.* New York: T&T Clark, 2006.

Gnuse, Robert Karl. *No Other Gods: Emergent Monotheism in Israel.* Sheffield, England: Sheffield Academic Press, 1997.

—*No Tolerance for Tyrants.* Collegeville, MN: Liturgical Press, 2011.

Goelet, Ogden. *The Egyptian Book of the Dead.* San Francisco: Chronicle Books, 1998.

Goetz, Delia, and Sylvanus G. Morley, eds. *Popol Vuh: The Sacred Book of the Ancient Quiche Maya.* tr. Adrian Recinos. Norman, OK: University of Oklahoma Press, 1950.

Goodenough, Erwin R. *Jewish Symbols in the Greco-Roman Period: Fish, Bread and Wine.* Pantheon Books, 1968.

Gordley, Matthew E. *The Colossian Hymn in Context.* Tübingen: Mohr Siebeck, 2007.

Gordon, Cyrus H. *Ugaritic Textbook: Grammar, Texts in Transliteration, Cuneiform Selections, Glossary, Indices.* Rome: Pontificio Istituto Biblico, 1998.

Gordon, Cyrus H., and Gary A. Rendsburg, eds. *Eblaitica: Essays on the Ebla Archives and Eblaite Language*, vol. 2. Winona Lake, IN: Eisenbrauns, 1990.

—*Eblaitica: Essays on the Ebla Archives and Eblaite Language*, vol. 4. Winona Lake, IN: Eisenbrauns, 2002.

Govier, Gordon. "Biblical Archaeology's Top Ten Discoveries of 2013." *Christianity Today.* christianitytoday.com/ct/2013/december-web-only/biblical-archaeologys-top-ten-discoveries-of-2013.html

Graupner, Axel, and Michael Wolter. *Moses in Biblical and Extra-Biblical Traditions.* Berlin/New York: W. De Gruyter, 2007.

Graves, Robert. *The Greek Myths*, vol. 1. Baltimore, MD: Penguin Books, 1955.

Gray, John. *The Canaanites.* New York: Praeger, 1964.

—*The Legacy of Canaan: The Ras Shamra Texts and Their Relevance to the Old Testament.* Leiden: E.J. Brill, 1965.

Green, H.L., ed. *The Free Thought Magazine*, vol. 17. Chicago, 1899.

Greenberg, Gary. *The Bible Myth: The African Origins of the Jewish People.* New York: Citadel Press Books, 1996.

Greenberg, Moshe. "The Redaction of the Plague Narrative in Exodus." ed. H. Goedicke. *Near Eastern Studies in Honour of W.F. Albright.* Baltimore: Johns Hopkins Press, 1971; pp. 243-252.

Greenbaum, Avraham. "Hosea Chapter 11." *Know Your Bible.* azamra.org/Bible/Hosea%2011-12.htm

—"From month to month." *Know Your Bible.* azamra.org/Earth/house-11.html

Greer, Jonathan. *The Use of MZRQ in Amos 6:6: Amos 6:4-7 in Light of the MRZ Banquet.* Gordon-Conwell Theological Seminary, 2002.

Greswell, Edward. *Fasti Temporis Catholici and Origines Kalendariae*, vol. 3. Oxford: Oxford University Press, 1852.

Grethenbach, Constantine. *Secular View of the Bible*. New York: Peter Eckler, 1902.
Griffiths, John Gwyn. *The Origins of Osiris and His Cult*. Leiden: E.J. Brill, 1980.
Guénon, René. *Fundamental Symbols: the Universal Language of Sacred Science*. Cambridge: Quinta Essentia, 1995.
Habesci, Elias. *Objects Interesting to the English Nation*. Calcutta: Oriental Star-Office, 1793.
Hachlili, Rachel. *Ancient Mosaic Pavements: Themes, Issues and Trends*. Leiden: Brill, 2009.
Hadas, Moses, and Morton Smith. *Heroes and Gods: Spiritual Biographies in Antiquity*. London, Routledge and Kegan Paul, 1965.
Haldar, Alfred. *Who Were The Amorites?* Leiden: E.J. Brill, 1971.
Hall, G. Stanley. *Jesus the Christ in Light of Psychology*. New York: D. Appleton and Co., 1924.
Hallet, Jean-Pierre, and Alex Pelle. Pygmy Kitabu. New York: Random House, 1973.
Hallo, William W., and K. Lawson Younger. *The Context of Scripture: Monumental Inscriptions from the Biblical World*. Leiden: E.J. Brill, 2002.
Halperin, David M., et al. *Before Sexuality: The Construction of Erotic Experience in the Ancient Greek World*. Princeton, NJ: Princeton University Press, 1991.
Hamme, Joel. "The dingir.ša.dib.ba as an Empirical Model for the Study of the Lament of the Individual." academia.edu/3116442/The_dingir.sa.dib.ba_as_an_Empirical_Model_for_the_Study_of_the_Lament_of_the_Individual
Handwerk, Brian. "'Python Cave' Reveals Oldest Human Ritual, Scientists Suggest." *National Geographic News*. news.nationalgeographic.com/news/pf/63357644.html
Hare, A. Paul, and Gideon M. Kressel. *The Desert Experience in Israel*. Lanham, MD: University Press of America, 2009.
Harl, Kenneth W. "Chronology of New Kingdom and Post-Imperial Egypt (1570-525 B.C.)." tulane.edu/~august/chron/nkegypt.htm
Harper, Robert Francis. *The Code of Hammurabi, King of Babylon, about 2250 B.C.* Chicago: University of Chicago Press, 1904.
Harrison, Roland K. *Introduction to the Old Testament*. Grand Rapids, MI: Wm. B. Eerdmans, 1969.
Hart, George. *The Routledge Dictionary of Egyptian Gods and Goddess*. New York: Routledge, 2005.
Hasel, Michael G. *Domination & Resistance: Egyptian Military Activity in the Southern Levant, 1300-1185 BC*. Leiden: Brill, 1998.
Hastings, James, ed. *Encyclopedia of Religion and Ethics, Part 3*. Kessinger, 2003.
Hastings, James, John A. Selbie, and Louis H. Gray, eds. *Encyclopaedia of Religion and Ethics*, vol. 10. New York: Charles Scribner's Sons, 1919.
Heidel, Alexander. *The Gilgamesh Epic and Old Testament Parallels*. Chicago: University of Chicago Press, 1963.
Heiser, Michael S. "Deuteronomy 32:8 and the Sons of God." thedivinecouncil.com/DT32BibSac.pdf
—"Should the Plural אלהים of Psalm 82 Be Understood as Men or Divine Beings?"

thedivinecouncil.com/Heiser%20Elohim%20of%20Ps82%20Gods%20or%20Men%20ETS2010.pdf
Henry, Matthew. *An Exposition of the Old and New Testaments*, vol. 1. London: W. Baynes, 1804.
Herbermann, Charles G., et al., eds. *The Catholic Encyclopedia*, vol. 2. New York: The Encyclopedia Press, 1913.
Herodas, *The Mimes of Herodas*. ed. John Arbuthnot Nairn. Oxford: Clarendon Press, 1904.
Herodotus. *Herodotus*. tr. A. D. Godley. Cambridge, MA: Harvard University Press, 1920.
—*The Histories*. tr. Aubrey de Selincourt. New York: Penguin Books, 1996.
—*The Histories*. tr. Robin Waterfield. Oxford: Oxford University Press, 1998.
Hesiod. *The Homeric Hymns and Homerica with an English Translation*. tr. Hugh G. Evelyn-White. New York: Putnam, 1920.
Heskett, Randall, and Joel Butler. *Divine Vintage: Following the Wine Trail from Genesis to the Modern Age*. New York: Palgrave Macmillan, 2012.
Heyob, Sharon Kelly. *The Cult of Isis among Women in the Graeco-Roman World*. Leiden: E.J. Brill, 1975.
Higgins, Godfrey. *Anacalypsis*, vols. 1 and 2. London: J. Burns, 1874.
Hinnells, John R., ed. *Mithraic Studies*, vol. 1. Manchester: Manchester University Press, 1975.
Historical Atlas of the World. New York: Barnes & Noble Books, 1981.
Hoffmeier, James Karl. *Israel in Egypt: The Evidence for the Authenticity of the Exodus Tradition*. New York: Oxford University Press, 1996.
—"The Exodus in Light of Recent Archaeological and Geological Work in North Sinai." Lanier Library Lecture Series, May 21, 2011.
Holloway, Steven W. *Aššur is King! Aššur is King!* Leiden: E.J. Brill, 2002.
Holst, Sanford. *Phoenicians: Lebanon's Epic Heritage*. Los Angeles: Cambridge & Boston Press, 2005.
The Holy Bible: According to the Authorized Version, vol. 1. London: C. Knight, 1836.
Homer. *The Odyssey with an English Translation*, vols. 1 and 2. tr. A.T. Murray. Cambridge, MA: Harvard University Press, 1919.
— *Homeri Opera*, vols. 1-5. Oxford: Oxford University Press, 1920
—*The Iliad with an English Translation*. tr. A.T. Murray. Cambridge, MA: Harvard University Press, 1965.
Horace. *The Odes and Epodes of Horace*. ed. Edward Bulwer Lytton. New York: Harper & Brothers, 1870.
—*The Odes and Carmen Saeculare of Horace*. tr. John Conington. London: George Bell and Sons, 1882.
Horne, Charles Francis. *The Sacred Books and Early Literature of the East*. New York: Parkes, Austin and Lipscomb, 1917.
Hornung, Erik. *Conceptions of God in Ancient Egypt*. tr. John Baine. New York: Cornell University Press, 1982.
Horowitz, Wayne. *Mesopotamian Cosmic Geography*. Winona Lake, IN: Eisenbrauns, 1998.
Hort, William Jillard. *The New Pantheon; Or, an Introduction to the Mythology of the Ages*. London: Longman, Hurst, Rees, et al., 1825.
Houghton, Walter R., ed. *Neely's History of the Parliament of Religions and Religious Congresses*. Chicago/New York: F. Tennyson Neely, 1894.

BIBLIOGRAPHY

Houston, George. *The Correspondent*, vol. 1. New York: Private Printing, 1827.
Houtman, Cornelis. *Exodus*, vol. 1. Kampfen: Kok Publishing House, 1993.
Huet, Pierre Daniel. *Demonstratio Evangelica ad Serenissimum Delphinum.* Lipsiae: Apud Thomam Fritsch, 1703.
Human, Dirk J., and Cas J.A. Vos, eds. *Psalms and Liturgy.* London/New York: T&T Clark, 2004.
Humphreys, Ken. "The Gospel of Mithras." jesusneverexisted.com/gospel-mithras.html
Husain, Shahrukh. *The Goddess: Power, Sexuality and the Feminine Divine.* Ann Arbor, MI: The University of Michigan Press, 2003.
Inman, Thomas. *Ancient Faiths and Modern.* New York: J.W. Bouton, 1875.
The Israel Museum Journal, vol. 3. Jerusalem: The Museum, 1984.
Jackson, Wayne. "The Ras Shamra Discovery." apologeticspress.org/rr/reprints/Ras-Shamra.pdf
James, E.O. *The Tree of Life: An Archaeological Study.* Leiden: E.J. Brill, 1966.
Jamieson, Robert, Andrew Robert Fausset, and David Brown, eds. *A Commentary, Critical and Explanatory, on the Old and New Testaments*, vol. 1. Hartford, CT: S.S. Scranton & Company, 1871.
Jastrow, Morris. *The Religion of Babylonia and Assyria.* Boston: Ginn & Company, 1898.
Jastrow, Morris, and Albert T. Clay. *The Epic of Gilgamesh: An Old Babylonian Version.* Yale University Press, 1920.
The Jewish Encyclopedia, vol. 2. New York: Funk & Wagnalls, 1925.
Jodrell, Richard Paul. *Illustrations of Euripides on the Ion and the Bacchae.* London: J. Nichols, 1781.
Johansen, Flemming. *Statues of Gudea Ancient and Modern.* Copenhagen: Akad. Forlag, 1978.
Johns, Claude Hermann Walter. *Babylonian and Assyrian Laws, Contracts and Letters.* New York: Charles Scribner's Sons, 1904.
Jones, Alfred. *Jones' Dictionary of Old Testament Proper Names.* Grand Rapids, MI: Kregel Publications, 1990.
Jones, Benjamin Charles. *Allegories, Discourses, Dissertations, etc.* London: H.M. Pollett & Co., 1884.
Josephus, Flavius. *The Complete Works of Flavius Josephus.* tr. William Whiston. London: T. Nelson and Sons, 1860.
—*Flavii Iosephi opera.* B. Niese. Berlin: Weidmann, 1892.
—*The Complete Works of Josephus.* tr. William Whiston. Grand Rapids, MI: Kregel Publications, 1981.
Josephus, and Paul L. Maier, ed. *The New Complete Works of Josephus.* tr. William Whiston. Grand Rapids, MI: Kregel Publications, 1999.
Journal of the North China Branch of the Royal Asiatic Society, vols. 8-9. Shanghai: A.H. De Carvalho, 1874.
Kaiser, Walter C. *The Old Testament Documents; Are They Reliable & Relevant?* Downers Grove, IL: InterVarsity Press, 2001.
Kapur, Kamlesh. *History of Ancient India.* New Delhi: Sterling Publishers, 2010.
Keel, Othmar, and Christoph Uehlinger. *Gods, Goddesses, And Images of God in Ancient Israel.* Minneapolis, MN: Fortress Press, 1998.
Kelley, David H., and Eugene F. Milone. *Exploring Ancient Skies: A Survey of Ancient and Cultural Astronomy.* New York: Springer, 2011.

Kelley, Donald R., ed. *Versions of History from Antiquity to the Enlightenment.* Binghamton, NY: Yale University, 1991.
Kennard, H. Martyn. *Philistines and Israelites: A New Light on the World's History.* London: Chapman & Hall, 1893.
Kerenyi, Carl. *Dionysos: Archetypal Image of Indestructible Life.* Princeton, NJ: Princeton University Press, 1996.
Kerr, Robert. *A General History and Collection of Voyages and Travels*, vol. 18. London: T. Cadell, 1824.
Ketkar, Shridhar V. *The History of Caste in India*, vol. 1. Taylor & Carpenter, 1909.
Kimball, Sara E., Winfred P. Lehmann, and Jonathan Slocum. "Hittite Online." utexas.edu/cola/centers/lrc/eieol/hitol-8-X.html
Kitchen, Kenneth Anderson. *On the Reliability of the Old Testament.* Grand Rapids, MI: Wm. B. Eerdmans Publishing, 2003.
Kleinerman, Alexandra. *Education in Early 2nd Millennium BC Babylonia: The Sumerian Epistolary.* Leiden: Brill, 2011.
Kloos, Carola. *Yhwh's Combat with the Sea: A Canaanite Tradition in the Religion of Ancient Israel.* Leiden: E.J. Brill, 1986.
Knight, Richard Payne. *The Symbolical Language of Ancient Art and Mythology.* ed. Alexander Wilder. New York: J.W. Houton, 1876.
Kovacs, Joe. "Pharaoh's chariots found in the Red Sea?" wnd.com/2003/06/19382
Kovacs, Maureen G., tr. *The Epic of Gilgamesh.* Stanford, CA: Stanford University Press, 1989.
Kramer, Samuel Noah. *History Begins at Sumer.* Garden City, NY: Doubleday, 1959.
Kraus, Hans-Joachim. *Psalms 1-59: A Continental Commentary.* Minneapolis, MN: Fortress Press, 1993.
Kreis, Steven. "The Laws of the Twelve Tables, c.450 B.C." historyguide.org/ancient/12tables.html
Krell, Marc A. *Intersecting Pathways.* Oxford: Oxford University Press, 2003.
Kuhn, Alvin Boyd. *Who is this King of Glory?* San Diego, CA: The Book Tree, 2007.
Lacocque, André. *The Book of Daniel.* Atlanta: John Knox Press, 1979.
Ladd, Parrish B. "The Hebrews, Egypt, Moses and the Exodus." *The Humanitarian Review*, vol. 5, no. 1. Los Angeles, CA: Singleton W. Davis, 1907.
Landa, Gertrude. *Jewish Fairy Tales and Legends.* New York: Bloch Publishing Co., Inc., 1919/1943.
Langdon, Stephen. "The Assyrian Root raSAnu." *The American Journal of Semitic Languages and Literatures*, vol. 28. Chicago: University of Chicago Press, 1911-1912.
Langfur, Stephen. "Nabataeans." netours.com/content/view/143/1/
Laughlin, John C. *Fifty Major Cities of the Bible.* New York: Routledge, 2006.
Layard, Austen Henry. *Monuments of Nineveh, Second Series.* London: J. Murray, 1853.
Lazarus, M. Edgeworth. *Zend Avesta and Solar Religions: A Historical Compilation.* Kessinger Publishing, 2003.
Leeming, David Adams. *The World of Myth: An Anthology.* Oxford/New York: Oxford University Press, 1990.
—*The Oxford Companion to World Mythology.* Oxford: Oxford University

Press, 2006.
—*Creation Myths of the World*, vol. 1. Santa Barbara: ABC-CLIO, 2010.
Lemaire, André, Baruch Halpern, and Matthew J. Adams. *The Books of Kings: Sources, Composition, Historiography and Reception.* Leiden/Boston: Brill, 2010.
Lemche, Niels Peter. *Early Israel: Anthropological and Historical Studies on the Israelite Society before the Monarchy.* Leiden: E.J. Brill, 1985.
—*The A to Z of Ancient Israel.* Lanham, MD: Rowman & Littlefield Publishing, 2004.
Lemonick, Michael D. "Are the Bible's Stories True?" *TIME*, vol. 147. *TIME*, 12/18/95; 2001; content.time.com/time/magazine/article/0,9171,133539,00.html
Levinson, Bernard M. *Deuteronomy and the Hermeneutics of Legal Innovation.* Oxford: Oxford University Press, 1997.
Leviton, Richard. *Encyclopedia of Earth Myths.* Charlottesville, VA: 2005.
Liberman, Anatoly. *Word Origins and How We Know Them.* Oxford: Oxford University Press, 2005.
Lichtheim, Miriam. *Ancient Egyptian Literature: The New Kingdom*, vol. 2. Berkeley and Los Angeles: University of California Press, 2006.
Liddell, Henry George, and Robert Scott. *An Intermediate Greek-English Lexicon.* Oxford: Clarendon Press, 1900.
Lightfoot, John. *The Whole Works of the Rev. John Lightfoot, D.D.*, vol. 1. ed. John Rogers Pitman. London: J.F. Dove, 1825.
Lipiński, Edward. *Semitic Languages: Outline of a Comparative Grammar.* Leuven, Belgium: Peeters Publishers, 2001.
Literary Digest, vol. 35. New York: Funk and Wagnalls, 1907.
Littleton, Scott. *Gods, Goddesses and Mythology*, vol. 1. New York: Marshall Cavendish, 2005.
Livy. *History of Rome.* tr. Canon Roberts. New York: E. P. Dutton and Co., 1912.
—*Livy. Books III and IV with An English Translation.* Cambridge, MA: Harvard University Press, 1922.
Lockyer, Herbert. *All the Miracles of the Bible.* Grand Rapids, MI: Zondervan, 1961.
Long, Harry A. *Personal and Family Names.* London: Hamilton, Adams & Co., 1883.
Lucian. *The Works of Lucian of Samosata.* tr. H.W. Fowler. Oxford: The Clarendon Press, 1905; sacred-texts.com/cla/luc/wl3/wl316.htm
—*Works, with an English Translation.* ed. A. M. Harmon. Cambridge, MA: Harvard University Press, 1913.
Lukacher, Ned. *Time-Fetishes: The Secret History of Eternal Recurrence.* Durham, NC: Duke University Press, 1998.
Lutz, Henry Frederick. *Viticulture and Brewing in the Ancient Orient.* Leipzig: J.C. Hinrichs'sche Buchhandlung, 1922.
Lydus, John. *De Mensibus, Book 4.* tr. Andrew Eastbourne. tertullian.org/fathers/john_the_lydian_months_04.htm
Lynch, Patricia Ann, and Jeremy Roberts. *African Mythology A to Z.* New York: Chelsea House, 2010.
Macrobius. *The Saturnalia, Books 1-2.* ed. and tr. Robert A. Kaster. Cambridge, MA: Harvard University Press, 2011.
Maimonides, Moses. *The Guide for the Perplexed.* tr. M. Friedländer. London: George Routledge & Sons, 1919.

Mann, Charles C. "Gobekli Tepe: The Birth of Religion." *National Geographic.* June 2011; ngm.nationalgeographic.com/2011/06/gobekli-tepe/mann-text/2

Marsman, Hennie J. *Women in Ugarit & Israel: Their Social & Religious Position in the Context of the Ancient Near East.* Leiden: E.J. Brill, 2003.

Martin, Ralph P., and Peter H. Davids. *Dictionary of the Later New Testament and Its Developments.* Downers Grove, IL: InterVarsity Press, 1997.

Maspero, Gaston. *History of Egypt*, vol. 8. ed. A.H. Sayce. tr. M.L. McClure. London: Grolier Society, 1904.

Massey, Gerald. *A Book of the Beginnings*, vol. 2 (1881). New York: Cosimo Classics, 2007.

—*Ancient Egypt: The Light of the World, a Work of Reclamation and Restitution in Twelve Books*, vols. 1 and 2. London: T. Fisher Unwin, 1907.

—*The Natural Genesis*, vols. 1 and 2. London: Williams and Norgate, 1883.

Matthews, Danny. *Royal Motifs in the Pentateuchal Portrayal of Moses.* London: T&T Clark, 2012.

Mayo, Robert. *A New System of Mythology*, vol. 3. Philadelphia: Robert Mayo, 1819.

McCrindle, J.W., tr. *Ancient India as Described by Megasthenes and Arrian.* London: Trübner & Co., 1877.

McDermott, Gerald R. *Jonathan Edwards Confronts the Gods: Christian Theology, Enlightenment Religion, and Non-Christian Faiths.* Oxford University Press, 2000.

McDonough, Sean M. *YHWH at Patmos.* Tübingen: Mohr Siebeck, 1999.

McGovern, Patrick E. *Ancient Wine: The Search for the Origins of Viniculture.* Princeton/Oxford: Princeton University Press, 2003.

McGovern, Patrick E., Stuart J. Fleming, and Solomon H. Katz, eds. *The Origins and Ancient History of Wine.* Amsterdam: Routledge/Taylor & Francis, 1996.

Mead, George R.S. *The Gospels and the Gospel.* London: Theosophical Publishing Society, 1902.

Meissner, William W. *Psychoanalysis and Religious Experience.* Ann Arbor, MI: Yale University Press, 1984.

Mellinkoff, Ruth. *The Horned Moses in Medieval Art and Thought.* Berkeley: University of California Press, 1970.

Mellor, Enid B. *The Cambridge Bible Commentary: The Making of the New Testament*, vol. 1. London: Cambridge University Press, 1972.

Mercer Commentary on the Bible: History of Israel, vol. 2. eds. Watson E. Mills and Richard F. Wilson. Macon, GA: Mercer University Press, 1999.

Mettinger, Tryggve N.D. *The Riddle of Resurrection: "Dying and Rising Gods" in the Ancient Near East.* Stockholm: Almqvist & Wiksell International, 2001

Metzger, Bruce M., and Michael D. Coogan, eds. *The Oxford Companion to the Bible.* Oxford: Oxford University Press, 1993.

Meyer, Marvin W., ed. *The Ancient Mysteries: A Sourcebook of Sacred Texts.* Philadelphia, PA: University of Pennsylvania, 1999.

Meyer, Stephen C. "Biblical Archaeology: The Date of the Exodus According to Ancient Writers." Institute for Biblical & Scientific Studies. bibleandscience.com/archaeology/exodusdate.htm#ANCIENT%20WRITERS

Meyers, Carol L., Toni Craven, and Ross Shepard Kraemer. *Women in Scripture: A Dictionary of Named and Unnamed Women in the Hebrew Bible, the Apocryphal/Deuterocanonical Books and New Testament.* Grand Rapids, MI: Wm. B. Eerdmans Publishing, 2001.

Miller, Douglas B., and R. Mark Shipp. *An Akkadian Handbook: Paradigms, Helps, Glossary, Logograms, and Sign List.* Winona Lake, IN: Eisenbrauns, 1996.

Mintz, Zoe. "Oldest Camel Bones Undergo Carbon Dating, 'Direct Proof' Bible Was Written Centuries After Events Described." ibtimes.com/oldest-camel-bones-undergo-carbon-dating-direct-proof-bible-was-written-centuries-after-events

Möller, Lennart. *The Exodus Case: New Discoveries Confirm the Historical Exodus.* Copenhagen, Scandinavia Publishing House, 2003.

Mooney, Sharon. "The Tree of Life and Ancient Tree Worship." etb-biblical-errancy.blogspot.com/2012/03/tree-of-life-and-ancient-tree-worship.html

Morgenstern, Julian. *The Doctrine of Sin in the Babylonian Religion.* Kirchhain, NL: Zahn & Baendel, 1905.

Moscati, Sabatino. *The Phoenicians.* London/New York: I.B. Tauris, 2001.

Müller, Max, ed. *The Zend-Avesta: The Vendîdâd*, vol. 4. Oxford: Clarendon Press, 1880.

Mundkur, Balaji. *The Cult of the Serpent.* Albany, NY: State University of New York. 1983.

Murdock, D.M. "Did George Washington and Thomas Jefferson Believe Jesus was a Myth?" truthbeknown.com/washington-jefferson-mythicists.html
—"Did the Exodus Really Happen?" freethoughtnation.com/contributing-writers/63-acharya-s/772-did-the-exodus-really-happen.html
—"Dionysus: Born of a Virgin on December 25th, Killed and Resurrected after Three Days." truthbeknown.com/dionysus.html
—"Parallels between Mesoamerican and Middle Eastern/Egyptian Religion and Mythology." freethoughtnation.com/forums/viewtopic.php?p=28123
—"The Twelve in the Bible and Ancient Mythology." freethoughtnation.com/forums/viewtopic.php?f=16&t=2639
—"Was the Persian Goddess Anahita the Pre-Christian Virgin Mother of Mithra?" *Anahita: Ancient Persian Goddess and Zoroastrian Yazata.* ed. Payam Nabarz. Avalonia Books, 2013.
—"Was There a Historical 'Jesus of Nazareth?'" *Bart Ehrman and the Quest of the Historical Jesus of Nazareth.* eds. Frank R. Zindler and Robert M. Price. New Jersey: American Atheists Press, 2013.—*Michael Lockwood's Buddhism's Relation to Christianity Reviewed by D.M. Murdock.* stellarhousepublishing.com/buddhismchristianity.html
—*Jesus as the Sun throughout History.* stellarhousepublishing.com/jesusasthesun.html
—*Who Was Jesus? Fingerprints of The Christ.* Seattle: Stellar House Publishing, 2007.
—*Christ in Egypt: The Horus-Jesus Connection.* Seattle: Stellar House Publishing, 2009.
—*The Gospel According to Acharya S.* Seattle: Stellar House Publishing, 2009a.

Murdock, D.M., and N.W. Barker. *The 2012 Astrotheology Calendar.* Seattle: Stellar House Publishing, 2009.

—*The 2013 Astrotheology Calendar.* Seattle: Stellar House Publishing, 2012.
Na'aman, Nadav. *Ancient Israel's History and Historiography.* Winona Lake, IN: Eisenbrauns, 2006.
Neumann, Erich. *The Origins and History of Consciousness.* Routledge, 1999.
New International Encyclopedia, v. 20. New York: Dodd, Mead and Company, 1916.
Niditch, Susan. *Oral World and Written Word: Ancient Israelite Literature.* Louisville: Westminster John Knox Press, 1996.
Nitzan, Bilha. *Qumran Prayer & Religious Poetry,* vol. 12. Leiden: E.J. Brill, 1994.
Nohrnberg, James. *Like unto Moses: The Constituting of an Interruption.* Bloomington, IN: Indiana University Press, 1995.
Nonnos. *Dionysiaca,* vol. 2. tr. W.H.D. Rouse, et al. Cambridge, MA: Harvard University Press, 1940.
Norris, Edwin. *Assyrian Dictionary,* vol. 2. London: Williams and Norgate, 1870.
The NSRV Bible. Oxford/New York: Oxford University Press, 1999.
O'Flaherty, Wendy Doniger. *The Rigveda: An Anthology of One Hundred Eight Hymns.* New York: Penguin Classics, 1981.
Oblath, Michael D. *The Exodus Itinerary Sites: Their Locations from the Perspective of the Biblical Studies.* New York: Peter Lang, 2004.
Offord, Joseph. "The Animal Symbol of the Egyptian Deity, Set." *Nature,* vol. 99. London: Macmillan and Co., 1917.
Oldenburg, Ulf. *The Conflict Between El and Ba' al in Canaanite Religion.* Leiden: E.J. Brill, 1969.
Oort, Henricus, Isaäc Hooykaas, and Abraham Kuenen, eds. *The Bible for Learners,* vol. 1. tr. Philip H. Wicksteed. Boston: Roberts Brothers, 1878.
Origen. *Contra Celsum,* vol. 8. ed. Miroslav Marcovich. Leiden: Brill, 2001.
—*Contra Celsum.* tr. Harry Chadwick. Cambridge: Cambridge University Press, 1980/2003.
Orr, James, et al., eds. *The International Standard Bible Encyclopedia,* vol. 3. Chicago: The Howard-Severance Company, 1915.
Oshima, Takayoshi. *Babylonian Prayers to Marduk.* Tübingen: Mohr Siebeck, 2011.
Osman, Ahmed. *Moses and Akhenaten: The Secret History of Egypt at the Time of the Exodus.* Rochester, VT: Bear & Company, 2002.
—*The Hebrew Pharaohs of Egypt: The Secret Lineage of the Patriarch Joseph.* Rochester, VT: Bear & Company, 2003.
Overdorf, Jason. "Archaeologists confirm Indian civilization is 2000 years older than previously believed." globalpost.com/dispatch/news/regions/asia-pacific/india/121116/indus-civilization-2000-years-old-archaeologists
Ovid. *Metamorphoses.* tr. Davidson and Clarke. Philadelphia: William Spotswood, 1790.
—*Metamorphoses.* tr. Brookes More. Boston: Cornhill Publishing Co., 1922.
—*Fasti.* ed. James George Frazer. Cambridge, MA: Harvard University Press, 1933.
Palagia, Olga. *The Pediments of the Parthenon.* Leiden: Brill, 1998.
Palmer, A. Smythe. *Babylonian Influence on the Bible and Popular Beliefs.* London: David Nutt, 1897.

Pardes, Ilana. *Countertraditions in the Bible: A Feminist Approach.* Harvard University Press, 1992.
Parker, Janet, and Julie Stanton, et al. *Mythology: Myths, Legends and Fantasies.* Cape Town, South Africa: Struik Publishers, 2006.
Patrich, Joseph. *The Formation of Nabataean Art.* Jerusalem: The Hebrew University, 1990.
Patrick, Symon. *A Commentary upon the First Book of Moses called Genesis.* London: Rt. Chiswell, 1695.
—*A Commentary upon the Two Books of Samuel.* London: Ri. Chiswell, 1703; openlibrary.org/details/commentaryupontw00patriala
—*A Commentary upon the Historical Books of the Old Testament.* London: D. Midwinter, et al., 1738.
Paul, Shalom M., Robert A. Kraft, Eva Ben-David, Lawrence H. Schiffman, and Weston W. Fields, eds. *Emanuel: Studies in the Hebrew Bible, the Septuagint, and the Dead Sea Scrolls.* Leiden: E.J. Brill, 2003.
Pausanias. *Description of Greece,* vol. 1. tr. Thomas Taylor. London: Priestley and Weale, 1824.
—*Pausaniae Graeciae Descriptio,* vols. 1-3. Leipzig: Teubner, 1903.
—*Description of Greece,* vol. 1. tr. W.H.S. Jones, et al. New York: G.P. Putnam's Sons, 1918.
—*Description of Greece,* vols. 2-5. tr. W.H.S. Jones, et al. New York: G.P. Putnam's Sons, 1926.
—*Description of Greece,* vol. 2. ed. James George Frazer. London/New York: The Macmillan Company, 1898.
—*Description of Greece,* vol. 2. tr. Richard Earnest Wycherley. Harvard University Press, 1993.
Pearson, Birger A. "Seth in Gnostic Literature." *The Rediscover of Gnosticism: Proceedings of the Conference at Yale, March 1978,* vol. 2. Leiden: E.J. Brill, 1981.
Peck, Harry Thurston, ed. *Harper's Dictionary of Classical Literature and Antiquities.* New York: Harper & Brothers, 1897.
Pellar, Brian R. "On the Origins of the Alphabet." *Sino-Platonic Papers,* no. 196. December 2009.
—"The Foundation of Myth: A Unified Theory on the Link Between Seasonal/Celestial Cycles, the Precession, Theology, and the Alphabet/Zodiac." *Sino-Platonic Papers,* no. 219. January 2012.
Peltenburg, E.J., and Alexander Wasse. *Neolithic Revolution: New Perspectives on Southwest Asia in Light of Recent Discoveries on Cyprus.* Oxford: Oxbow Books, 2004.
Petrie, W.M. Flinders, et al. *Researches in Sinai.* New York: E.P. Dutton and Company, 1906.
Pettazzoni, Raffaele. *Essays on the History of Religions.* Leiden: E.J. Brill, 1954.
Philo. *The Works of Philo Judaeus,* vol. 3. tr. C.D. Yonge. London: Henry G. Bohn, 1855.
—*The Works of Philo Judaeus,* vol. 2. tr. C.D. Yonge London: George Bell & Sons, 1894.
—*De Confusione Linguarum. Philonis Alexandrini opera quae supersunt,* vol. 2. ed. P. Wendland. Berlin: Reimer, 1897/De Gruyter, 1962; 229–267.
—*Philo,* vol. 4. trs. F.H. Colson and G.H. Whitaker. Cambridge, MA: Harvard University Press, 1962.

—*Philo of Alexandria.* tr. David Winston. New Jersey: Paulist Press, 1981.
—*The Works of Philo: Complete and Unabridged.* tr. C.D. Yonge. ed. David M. Scholer. Hendrickson Publishers, 2000.
Philostratus. *Philostratus the Elder, Imagines. Philostratus the Younger, Imagines. Callistratus, Descriptions.* tr. Arthur Fairbanks. Cambridge, MA: Harvard University Press, 1979.
Piepkorn, Arthur Carl. *Profiles in Belief: Holiness and Pentecostal*, vol. 3. Harper & Row, 1979.
Pigault-Lebrun. *Le Citateur*, vol. 1. Paris: Gustave Barba, 1832.
Pinch, Geraldine. *Egyptian Mythology: A Guide to the Gods, Goddesses and Traditions of Ancient Egypt.* Oxford: Oxford University Press, 2002.
Pindar. *Odes of Pindar.* tr. G. West, R.B. Greene, and H.J. Pye. Chiswick: Press of C. Whittingham, 1822.
—*Pindar and Anacreon.* trs. C.A. Wheelwright and Thomas Bourne. New York: Harper & Brothers, 1837.
Plato. *Platonis Opera*, ed. John Burnet. Oxford University Press. 1903.
—*Plato in Twelve Volumes*, vol. 11. tr. Harold North Fowler, et al. Cambridge, MA: Harvard University Press, 1967.
—*Plato in Twelve Volumes*, vol. 9. tr. W.R.M. Lamb. Cambridge, MA: Harvard University Press, 1925.
Pliny the Elder. *Naturalis Historia.* ed. Karl Friedrich Theodor Mayhoff. Lipsiae: Teubner, 1906.
—*The Natural History.* tr. John Bostock and H.T. Riley. London: H. G. Bohn, 1856.
—*The Natural History*, vol. 6. tr. John Bostock and H.T. Riley. London: Henry G. Bohn, 1857.
—*Pliny's Natural History*, vol. 1. tr. Philemon Holland. London: G. Barclay, 1847-49.
Plumptre, Edward Hayes. *Master and Scholar.* New York: E.P. Dutton & Co., 1884.
Plutarch. *Plutarch's Lives*, vol. 4. tr. John Dryden, ed. A.H. Clough. Boston: Little, Brown and Company, 1885.
— *Moralia.* ed. Gregorius N. Bernardakis. Leipzig: Teubner, 1889.
—*Plutarch's Miscellanies and Essays*, vol. 3. ed. William W. Goodwin. Boston: Little, Brown and Company, 1889.
—*Plutarchi moralia*, vol. 2.3. ed. W. Sieveking. Leipzig 1935.
—*Plutarch's Lives*, vol. 7. tr. Bernadotte Perrin. Cambridge: Harvard University Press, 1958.
—*Moralia.* tr. Frank Cole Babbitt. Montana: Kessinger, 2005.
Poe, Michael. "Wine in Ancient Egypt." touregypt.net/egypt-info/magazine-mag11012000-magf2.htm
Polano, H. *The Talmud: Selections from the Contents of that Ancient Book.* London: Frederick Warne and Co., 1868.
Porphyry. *Select Works of Porphyry.* tr. Thomas Taylor. London: Thomas Rodd, 1823.
Potter, Charles Francis. *The Great Religious Leaders.* Simon and Schuster, 1958.
Price, Robert M. "Review of *Christ in Egypt* by D.M. Murdock." robertmprice.mindvendor.com/reviews/murdock_christ_egypt.htm
—"Of Myth and Men." *Free Inquiry.* Amherst, NY, 1999-2000.
Pritchard, James B. *Ancient Near Eastern Texts.* Princeton: Princeton University Press, 1969.

Proceedings of the Society of Antiquaries of Scotland, vol. 6. Edinburgh: Neill and Company, 1868.
Quispel, Gilles, R. van den Broek, and Maarten Jozef Vermaseren, eds. *Studies in Gnosticism and Hellenistic Religions Presented to Gilles Quispel on the Occasion of His 65th Birthday*. Leiden: E.J. Brill, 1981.
Rahmouni, Aicha. *Divine Epithets in the Ugaritic Alphabetic Texts*. tr. J.N. Ford. Leiden: E.J. Brill, 2008.
Rainey, Anson F. "The Kingdom of Ugarit." *The Biblical Archaeologist*, vol. 28. Jerusalem/Bagdad: The American Schools of Oriental Research, 1965.
—"Wine from the Royal Vineyards." *Bulletin of the American Schools of Oriental Research*, no. 245. Boston: The American Schools of Oriental Research, Winter, 1982; pp. 57-62.
—"Israel in Merneptah's Inscription and Reliefs." *Israel Exploration Journal*, vol. 51, no. 1. Jerusalem: Israel Exploration Society, 2001; pp. 57-75.
—"Shasu or Habiru: Who Were the Early Israelites?" *Biblical Archaeology Review* (34:06). Nov/Dec 2008.
Raleigh, Walter. *The History of the World*, vol. 1. Edinburgh: Archibald Constable and Co., 1820.
Ravage, Marcus. "A Real Case Against the Jews." *The Century Magazine*, vol. 115, no. 3. New York: The Century Co., 1928.
Rawlinson, George, et al. *The Five Great Monarchies of the Ancient Eastern World*, vol. 3. New York: Dodd, Mead and Company, 1881.
—*The History of Herodotus*, vol. 2. New York: D. Appleton and Company, 1889.
Redford, Donald B. "Aspects of Monotheism." *Biblical Archeology Review*, 1996.
—*Akhenaten: The Heretic King*. Princeton, NJ: Princeton University Press, 1987.
—*Egypt, Canaan and Israel in Ancient Times*. NJ: Princeton University Press, 1992.
Reik, Theodor. *Pagan Rites in Judaism*. New York: Noonday, 1964.
Remsburg, John E. *The Christ Myth: A Critical Review and Analysis of the Evidence of His Existence*. The Truth Seeker Company, 1909.
Renouf, Peter le Page. *The Origin and Growth of Religion as Illustrated by the Religion of Ancient Egypt*. New York: Charles Scribner's Sons, 1880.
—*The Egyptian Book of the Dead*. London: Society of Biblical Archaeology, 1904.
Retsö, Jan. *The Arabs in Antiquity: Their History from the Assyrians to the Umayyads*. New York: RoutledgeCurzon, 2003.
Rigoglioso, Marguerite. *The Cult of the Divine Birth in Ancient Greece*. New York: Palgrave Macmillan, 2009.
—*Virgin Mother Goddesses of Antiquity*. New York: Palgrave Macmillan, 2010.
Roberts, Alexander, and James Donaldson, eds. Ante-Nicene Christian Library, vol. 2. Edinburgh, T&T Clark, 1868.
—*Ante-Nicene Christian Library*, vol. 15. Edinburgh: T&T Clark, 1870.
—*Ante-Nicene Christian Library*, vol. 4. Edinburgh: T&T Clark, 1884.
Robertson, John M. *Christianity and Mythology*. London: Watts & Co., 1910.
Robbins, Manuel. *Collapse of the Bronze Age: The Story of Greece, Troy, Israel, Egypt and the Peoples of the Sea*. San Jose, CA: Authors Choice Press, 2001.

Rogers, Henry. *The Works of Jonathan Edwards*, vol. 2. London: Ball, Arnold and Co., 1840.
Rogers, John H. "Origins of the ancient constellations: I. The Mesopotamian traditions." *Journal of the British Astronomical Association*, vol. 108, no. 1. 1998; 9-28.
Rogers, Robert William. *The Religion of Babylonia and Assyria*. New York: Eaton & Mains, 1908.
Roheim, Geza. *Animism, Magic and the Divine King*. New York: Cosimo, Inc., 2005.
Rollin, Charles. *The Ancient History of the Egyptians, Carthaginians, Assyrians, Babylonians, Medes, Persians, Macedonians and Grecians*, vol. 1. Baltimore: Geo. McDowell & Son, 1852.
—*The Ancient History of the Egyptians*, vol. 2. Philadelphia: J.B. Lippincott & Co., 1869.
Rood, Michael. "The Red Sea Crossing & The Exodus Revealed." michaelrood.tv/store-1/specials/the-red-sea-crossing-the-exodus-revealed-bundle.html
Rosen, Brenda. *The Mythical Creatures Bible*. New York: Sterling Publishing Co., 2009.
Rowton, Michael B. "Dimorphic Structure and the Problem of the 'Apiru-'Ibrim." *Journal of Near Eastern Studies*, vol. 35, no. 1. University of Chicago Press, 1976; 13-20.
Ruck, Carl A.P. "The Wild and the Cultivated: Wine in Euripides' Bacchae." *Persephone's Quest: Entheogens and the Origins of Religion*. eds. R. Gordon Wasson, et al. New Haven: Yale University Press, 1986.
Ruck Carl A.P., Blaise Daniel Staples, and Clark Heinrich. *The Apples of Apollo: Pagan and Christian Mysteries of the Eucharist*. Durham, NC: Carolina Academic Press, 2001.
Rudd, Steven. "The Exodus Route." bible.ca/archeology/bible-archeology-exodus-route-population-of-jews-hebrews.htm
—"The Number of the Exodus Jews." bible.ca/archeology/bible-archeology-exodus-route-population-of-jews-hebrews.htm
Rudolph, Kurt. *Mandaeism*. Leiden: E.J. Brill, 1978.
Ruether, Rosemary Radford. *Goddesses and the Divine Feminine: A Western Religious History*. Berkeley: University of California, 2005.
Russell, Brian D. *The Song of the Sea: The Date of Composition and Influence of Exodus 15:1-21*. New York: Peter Lang, 2007.
Sale, George. *An Universal History, from the Earliest Account of Time*, vol. 17. London: C. Bathurst, 1780.
Sallust on the Gods and the World. London: Edward Jeffrey, 1793.
Sanders, Paul. *The Provenance of Deuteronomy 32*. Leiden: E.J. Brill, 1996.
Sandoval, Timothy J., and Carleen Mandolfo, eds. *Relating to the Text: Interdisciplinary and Form-Critical Insights on the Bible*. London/New York: T&T Clark, 2003.
Sarton, George. *Hellenistic Science and Culture in the Last Three Centuries B.C*. New York: Dover 1993.
Sayce, Archibald Henry. *Lectures on the Origin and Growth of Religion, as Illustrated by the Religion of the Ancient Babylonians*. London: Williams and Norgate, 1887.
—ed. *Lectures on the Origin and Growth of Religion as Illustrated by the Religion of the Ancient Babylonians*. London: Williams and Norgate, 1888.
—*Records of the Past, Being English Translations of the Ancient*

Monuments of Egypt and Western Asia, vol. 1. London: Samuel Bagster and Sons, 1888.
—"Babylonian Tablets from Tel El-Amarna, Upper Egypt." *Journal of the Transactions of the Victoria Institute*, vol. 24. ed. Francis W.H. Petrie. London: W. Thacker & Co., 1890.
—"The Cuneiform Inscriptions of Tel El-Amarna." *The Journal of the Transactions of the Victoria Institute*, vol. 24. London: Victoria Institute, 1890.
—*The "Higher Criticism" and the Verdict of the Monuments*. London: Society for Promoting Christian Knowledge, 1894.
Schlesier, Renate, ed. *A Different God? Dionysos and Ancient Polytheism*. Berlin/Boston: Walter de Gruyter, 2011.
Schniedewind, William M., and Joel H. Hunt. *A Primer on Ugaritic: Language, Culture and Literature*. Cambridge: Cambridge University Press, 2007.
Scholem, Gershom Gerhard. *On the Kabbalah and Its Symbolism*. Schocken Books, 1965.
Schwemer, Daniel. "The Storm-Gods of the Ancient Near East: Summary, Synthesis, Recent Studies, Part 1." *Journal of Ancient Near Eastern Religions*, vol. 7, no. 2. Leiden: E.J. Brill, 2007.
Scolnic, Benjamin Edidin. *If The Egyptians Drowned In The Red Sea Where Are Pharaoh's Chariots? Exploring the Historical Dimension of the Bible*. Lanham, MD: University Press of America, 2005.
Seneca, Lucius Annaeus. *Seneca's Tragediaes*, vol. 1. tr. Frank Justus Miller. New York: G.P. Putnam's Son, 1917.
Seznec, Jean. *The Survival of the Pagan Gods*. tr. Barbara F. Sessions. New York: Harper & Row, 1961.
Shaw, Robert. *Sketch of the Religions of the World*. St. Louis: Becktold & Company, 1904.
Shendge, Malati J. *The Language of the Harappans: From Akkadian to Sanskrit*. New Delhi: Abhinav Publications, 1997.
Shinan, Avigdor, ed. *Proceedings of the Sixth World Congress of Jewish Studies*. Jerusalem: World Union of Jewish Studies, 1977.
Shoham, Reuven. *Poetry and Prophecy*. Leiden: E.J. Brill, 2003.
Shushan, Gregory. *Conceptions of the Afterlife in Early Civilizations*. London/New York: Continuum International, 2009.
Sidebotham, Steven E. *Roman Economic Policy in the Erythra Thalassa*. Leiden: E.J. Brill, 1986.
de Silva, Rajpal Kumar, and Willemina G. M. Beumer, eds. *Illustrations and Views of Dutch Ceylon 1602-1796*. Leiden: E.J. Brill, 1988.
Singer, Isidore, ed. *The Jewish Encyclopedia*, vol. 9. London: Funk and Wagnalls Co., 1907.
—*The Jewish Encyclopedia*, vol. 2. London: Funk and Wagnalls Co., 1916.
—*The Jewish Encyclopedia*, vol. 2. New York: Funk & Wagnalls, 1925.
Singer, Itamar. *Hittite Prayers*. Leiden: Brill, 2002.
Sinks, Perry Wayland. "The Laws Of Plato Compared With The Laws Of Moses." *Bibliotheca Sacra*, vol. 91. Texas: Dallas Theological Seminary, 1934.
Sivertsen, Barbara J. *The Parting of the Sea: How Volcanoes, Earthquakes, and Plagues Shaped the Story of the Exodus*. New Jersey: Princeton University Press, 2009.

Smallwood, E. Mary. *The Jews Under Roman Rule: From Pompey to Diocletian.* Leiden: E.J. Brill, 1976.
Smith, George. *Assyrian Discoveries: An Account of Explorations and Discoveries on the Site of Nineveh, During 1873 and 1874.* London: Sampson Low, Marston, Low and Searle, 1875.
Smith, George Adam. *Atlas of the Historical Geography of the Holy Land.* London: Hodder and Stoughton, 1915.
Smith, Jonathan Z. *Divine Drudgery: On the Comparisons of Early Christianities and the Religions of Antiquity.* Chicago: University of Chicago Press, 1990.
Smith, Mark S. *The Ugaritic Baal Cycle*, vol. 1. Leiden: E.J. Brill, 1994.
—*The Origins of Biblical Monotheism: Israel's Polytheistic Background and the Ugaritic Texts.* Oxford/New York: Oxford University Press, 2001.
—*The Early History of God: Yahweh and the Other Deities in Ancient Israel.* Grand Rapids, MI: Wm. B. Eerdmans Publishing Co., 2002.
Smith, Mark S., and Wayne T. Pitard. *The Ugaritic Baal Cycle*, vol. 2. Leiden: Brill, 2009.
Snell, Bruno. *Scenes from Greek Drama.* Berkeley: University of California Press, 1964.
Snell, Daniel C. *Religions of the Ancient Near East.* Cambridge: Cambridge University Press, 2011.
Snodgrass, Mary Ellen. *Encyclopedia of the Literature of Empire.* New York: Facts on File, 2010.
Sparks, Brad C. "Problems with Mt. Sinai in Saudi Arabia." ldolphin.org/sinai.html
Sparks, Karen Jacobs, ed. *Encyclopaedia Britannica 2008 Book of the Year.* Chicago/London: Encyclopaedia Britannica, 2008.
Speiser, E.A. "Some Factors in the Collapse of Akkad." *Journal of the American Oriental Society*, vol. 72, no. 3. American Oriental Society, 1952.
Stackhouse, Thomas. *A History of the Holy Bible.* Glasgow: Blackie & Son, 1836.
Stehelin, J.P. *Rabbinical Literature: Or, the Traditions of the Jews, Contained in their Talmud and Other Mystical Writings*, vol. 1. London: J. Robinson, 1748.
Steila, Donald, and Thomas E. Pond. *The Geography of Soils.* Savage, MD: Rowman & Littlefield Publishers, 1989.
Stephens, Susan A. *Seeing Double: Intercultural Poetics in Ptolemaic Alexandria.* Berkeley: University of California Press, 2003.
Stewart, Charles Anthony. *Domes of Heaven.* Bloomington, IN: Indiana University, 2008.
Stone, Lee Alexander. *The Power of a Symbol.* Chicago: Pascal Covici, 1924 .
Stone, Merlin. *When God Was a Woman.* New York: Harcourt Brace Jovanovich, 1978.
Strabo. *Geographica.* ed. A. Meineke. Leipzig: Teubner, 1877.
—*The Geography of Strabo.* eds. Horace Leonard Jones and J.R. Sitlington Sterrett. Cambridge, MA: Harvard University Press, 1988.
—*The Geography of Strabo*, vol. 3. tr. Hans Claude Hamilton. London/New York: G. Bell & Sons, 1889-93.
Tacitus. *The History of Tacitus.* tr. Alfred John Church and William Jackson Brodribb. London/New York: Macmillan and Co., 1894.

Tait, John, ed. *'Never Had the Like Occurred': Egypt's View of Its Past.* London: UCL Press, 2003.
Talbot, H.F. "On the Eastern Origin of the Name and Worship of Dionysus." *Transactions of the Royal Society of Literature of the United Kingdom,* vol. 8. London: John Murray, 1866.
—"On the Religion Belief of the Assyrians." *Transactions,* vol. 2. London: Longmans, Green, Reader and Dyer, 1873.
Tarn, W.W. *Alexander the Great: Volume II: Sources and Studies.* Cambridge: Cambridge University Press, 1948/2002.
Taylor, Bernard A., ed. *Analytical Lexicon to the Septuagint.* Peabody, MA: Hendrickson Publishers, 2009.
Taylor, J. Glen. *Yahweh and the Sun: Biblical and Archaeological Evidence for Sun Worship in Ancient Israel.* Sheffield, England: Sheffield Academic Press, 1993.
—"Was Yahweh Worshiped as the Sun?" *Biblical Archaeology Review* 20/3. 1994; 53-61, 90-91.
Taylor, Robert. *The Diegesis, being a Discovery or the Origin, Evidences, and Early History of Christianity.* London: Richard Carlile, 1829.
Taylor, Thomas. *The Hymns of Orpheus, tr. from the Original Greek: With a Preliminary Dissertation on the Life and Theology of Orpheus.* London: T. Payne, 1792.
The Larousse Encyclopedia of Mythology. New York: Barnes & Noble Books, 1994.
The Saturday Review, vol. 23. London: Saturday Review Pub., 1867.
Thomassin, Louis. *La méthode d'étudier et d'enseigner Chrétiennement.* Paris: Chez François Muguer, 1682.
Tichelaar, Tyler R. *King Arthur's Children: A Study in Fiction and Tradition.* Ann Arbor, MI: Modern History Press, 2011.
Tigay, Jeffrey H. "The Evolution of the Pentateuchal Narratives in Light of the Evolution of the *Gilgamesh Epic.*" *Empirical Models for Biblical Criticism.* Philadelphia: University of Pennsylvania Press, 1985.
Tilak, Bal Gangadhar. "Chaldean and Indian Vedas." *Commemorative Essays Presented to Sir Ramkrishna Gopal Bhandarkar.* Poona: Bhandarkar Oriental Research Institute, 1917; p. 29ff.
Timmer, Daniel. "Ugaritic Ritual in Epic, Cult and Everyday." *Revue d'Etudes des Civilisations Anciennes du Proche-Orient,* vol. 14. 2008-2009.
Tod, James. *Annals and Antiquities of Rajasthan, or The Central and Western Rajput States of India,* vol. 2.
Tomlinson, Sally. *Demons, Druids and Brigands on Irish High Crosses.* Ann Arbor, MI: ProQuest, 2007.
Tsumura, David Toshio. *Creation and Destruction: A Reappraisal of the Chaoskampf Theory in the Old Testament.* Winona Lake, IN: Eisenbrauns, 2005.
—*The Earth and the Waters in Genesis 1 and 2: A Linguistic Investigation.* Sheffield, England: Sheffield Academic Press, 1989.
Turner, Frederick. *Shakespeare's Twenty-first Century Economics: The Morality of Love and Money.* Oxford/New York: Oxford University Press, 1999.
Udren, Jonathan. "Purim and the Secret of Wine." *Kabbalah Online.* chabad.org/kabbalah/article_cdo/aid/652345/jewish/Purim-and-the-Secret-of-Wine.htm
Unwin, Tim. *Wine & The Vine.* London, Routledge, 1996.

Upton, William. *The Japetic Philosophy*. London: Elliott, Lamb's, 1861.
Valpy, Abraham John, and Edmund Henry Barker, eds. *The Classical Journal*, vol. 21. Cambridge: Cambridge University Press, 2013.
van den Broek, Roelof. *Studies in Gnosticism and Alexandrian Christianity*. Leiden: E.J. Brill, 1996.
van der Toorn, Karel, Bob Becking, and Pieter W. van der Horst, eds. *Dictionary of Deities and Demons in the Bible*. Leiden: E.J. Brill, 1999.
van der Veen, Peter. "The Exodus Case questioned!" amazon.com/review/RLI2A7AX66I8N/ref=cm_cr_rdp_perm?ie=UTF8&ASIN=8772477083&linkCode=&nodeID=&tag=
—"When Pharaohs Ruled Jerusalem." *Biblical Archaeology Review* 39:2. 2013; academia.edu/2569658/When_Pharaohs_Ruled_Jerusalem_BAR_39_2_2013_
van der Veen, Peter, et al. "Israel in Canaan (Long) Before Pharaoh Merneptah? A Fresh Look at Berlin Statue Pedestal Relief 21687." *Journal of Ancient Egyptian Interconnections*. xa.yimg.com/kq/groups/12188019/1784144774/name/Jaei2-4VanDerVeenEtAl.pdf
van Goudoever, Jan. *Biblical Calendars*. Leiden: E.J. Brill, 1961.
Van Seters, John. *The Life of Moses: The Yahwist as Historian in Exodus—Numbers*. Louisville, KY: Westminster/John Knox Press, 1994.
—*Prologue to History: The Yahwist as Historian in Genesis*. Louisville, KY: Westminster John Knox, 1992.
Varro, Marcus Terentius. *The Three Books of M. Terentius Varro Concerning Agriculture*. tr. T. Owen. Oxford: Oxford University Press, 1800.
—*De lingua latina libri*. ed. Leonardus and Andreas Spengel. Berolini: Apud Weidmannos, 1885.
—du Veil, C.M. *A Commentary on the Acts of the Apostles*. ed. F.A. Cox. London, J. Haddon, 1851.
—*On the Latin Language*, vol. 2. tr. Roland G. Kent. Cambridge, MA: Harvard University Press, 1938.
Velikovsky, Immanuel. *Worlds in Collision*. LaVergne, TN: Paradigma, 2009.
Verbrugghe, Gerald P., and John M. Wickersham. *Berossos and Manetho Introduced and Translated: Native Traditions in Ancient Mesopotamia and Egypt*. University of Michigan Press, 2000.
Vergano, Dan. "Sunken cities surface in time." *USA Today*. usatoday30.usatoday.com/news/world/june01/2001-06-28-sunken-cities.htm
Vermaseren, Maarten J., and Carol Cl. van Essen. *The Excavations in the Mithraeum of the Church of Santa Prisca in Rome*. Leiden: E.J. Brill, 1965.
Vernus, Pasal, and Jean Yoyotte. *The Book of the Pharaohs*. tr. David Lorton. New York: Cornell University, 2003.
Villiers Stuart, Henry Windsor. *Egypt After the War*. London: John Murray, 1883.
Voltaire. *A Philosophical Dictionary*, vol. 1. London: J. and H.L. Hunt, 1824.
—*The Philosophy of History*. tr. Henry Wood Gandell. London: Thomas North, 1829.
von Carolsfeld, Julius Schnorr. *Das Buch der Bücher in Bilden*. Wigand, 1920.
Vossius, Gerardus. *De Theologia Gentili et Physiologia Christiana*, vols. 1-2. Francofurti: Casparis Waechtleri, 1668.

BIBLIOGRAPHY

Waardenburg, Jacques. *Classical Approaches to the Study of Religion.* Berlin: Walter de Gruyter, 1999.

Waddell, L.A. *Egyptian Civilization: Its Sumerian Origin and Real Chronology.* Kessinger, 2003.

Wagenseil, Johann Christoph. *Sota. Hoc est: Liber Mischnicus de Uxore Adulterii Suspecta.* Altdorfium Noricorum: Schönnerstädt, 1674.

Walker, Barbara G. *The Woman's Encyclopedia of Myths and Secrets.* Harper Collins, 1983.

—*The Woman's Dictionary of Sacred Symbols and Objects.* New York: HarperCollins Publishers, 1988.

Walters, Vivienne J. *The Cult of Mithras in the Roman Provinces of Gaul.* Leiden: Brill, 1974.

Walton, John H., et al. *The IVP Bible Background Commentary: Old Testament.* Downers Grove, IL, 2000.

—*Zondervan Illustrated Bible Backgrounds Commentary, vol. 5: The Minor Prophets, Job, Psalms, Proverbs, Ecclesiastes, Song of Songs.* Grand Rapids, MI: Zondervan, 2009.

Ward, William Hayes. "The Origin of the Worship of Yahwe." *The American Journal of Semitic Languages and Literatures*, vol. 25. ed. Robert Francis Harper. Chicago/New York: University of Chicago Press, 1909.

Weigall, Arthur. *The Life and Times of Akhnaton, Pharaoh of Egypt.* Montana: Kessinger Publishing, 2004.

Wells, Louise. *The Greek Language of Healing from Homer to New Testament Times.* Berlin: Walter de Gruyter, 1998.

Wenham, Gordon. "Pentateuchal Studies Today." *Themelios* 22.1 (October 1996); 3-13.

West, M.L. *Hellenica: Volume II: Lyric and Drama.* Oxford: Oxford University Press, 2013.

Wheeler, Brannon M. *Moses in the Qur'an and Islamic Exegesis.* London: RoutledgeCurzon, 2002.

Wheeler, Edward J. *Current Literature*, vol. 43. New York: The Current Literature Publishing Company, 1907.

Wheless, Joseph. *Is It God's Word?* New York: Cosimo, Inc., 2007.

Whitman, Jon, ed. *Interpretation & Allegory: Antiquity to the Modern Period.* Leiden/Boston: Brill, 2000.

Whittaker, Molly. *Jews and Christians: Volume 6: Graeco-Roman Views.* Cambridge: Cambridge University Press, 1984.

Wiener, Noah. "When Egyptian Pharaohs Ruled Bronze Age Jerusalem: Peter van der Veen investigates an Egyptian presence before the time of David." biblicalarchaeology.org/daily/biblical-sites-places/jerusalem/when-egyptian-pharaohs-ruled-bronze-age-jerusalem

Widengren, Geo. "Heavenly Enthronement and Baptism: Studies in Mandaean Baptism." *Religions in Antiquity.* Leiden: Brill, 1968.

Wilder, Alexander, and Robert A. Gunn. *The Medical Tribune.* New York: Monroe & Metz, 1878.

Wilford, John Noble. "Wine Cellar, Well Aged, Is Revealed in Israel." *The New York Times.* nytimes.com/2013/11/23/science/in-ruins-of-palace-a-wine-with-hints-of-cinnamon-and-top-notes-of-antiquity.html?_r=2&

Willis, George. *Willis's Current Notes: A Series of Articles on the Antiquities, Biography*, etc. London: George Willis, 1853.

Winckler, Hugo. *The Tell-El-Amarna Letters.* Berlin: Reuther & Reichard, 1896.

Wood, Bryan G. "The Biblical Date for the Exodus is 1446 B.C.: A Response to James Hoffmeier." *Journal of the Evangelical Theological Society* 50/2 (2007), 258-259.

Woodward, Jocelyn M. *Perseus: A Study in Greek Art and Legend.* Cambridge: Cambridge University Press, 1937/2013.

Wright, Chauncey. *Darwinism.* London: John Murray, 1871.

Wunderlich, Hans-Georg. *The Secret of Crete.* New York: Macmillan, 1974.

Yadin, Yigael. *The Art of Warfare in Biblical Lands*, vol. 1. New York: McGraw-Hill, 1963.

Yahuda, A.S. *Language of the Pentateuch in its Relation to Egyptian.* Montana: Kessinger, 2003.

Yang, Linda. *Topiaries & Espaliers: Plus Other Designs for Shaping Plants.* New York: Houghton Mifflin Company, 1999.

Zanger, Walter. "Jewish Worship, Pagan Symbols." *Bible History Daily.* biblicalarchaeology.org/daily/ancient-cultures/ancient-israel/jewish-worship-pagan-symbols.

Zavada, Jack. "What is Frankincense?" christianity.about.com/od/glossary/qt/What-Is-Frankincense.htm

Ziolkowski, Theodore. *Gilgamesh among Us: Modern Encounters with the Ancient Epic.* Ithaca, NY: Cornell University, 2012.

Index

6

600,000, 10, 76, 77, 92, 104, 106, 167, 211, 212, 213, 214, 215, 216, 221, 234

A

Aaron, 14, 28, 32, 33, 45, 48, 107, 112, 128, 317, 376, 422, 447, 464, 495
  83 years old, 30, 69, 85
  ark, 242
  Golden Calf, 112
  Horus, 242
  light bringer, 201, 242
  Miriam, 349
  priesthood, 36, 107, 113, 464
  serpent, 82, 225, 384
  staff, 382, 386, 387, 477
Abdi-Heba, 182
Abraham, 2, 9, 27, 62, 63, 75, 116, 177, 181, 264, 324, 325, 326, 402, 461, 493
  Brahma, 219, 492
  camels, 27, 28
  Chaldean, 415
  Ebla, 40
  El Shaddai, 62, 157, 408
  Gilgamesh, 461
  Melchizedek, 374
  myth, 17, 18, 75, 178, 498
  polygamy, 405
  polytheism, 61
  trial, 39, 310
  Yahweh, 63, 179, 184, 400
abyss, 213, 224, 225, 232, 474
Achaicarus, 259, 260
Acharnians, 332, 344
Acts, Book of, 173, 240, 246, 335, 339, 375, 399
Adad, Hadad, 157, 229, 248, 410, 411, 412, 418, 422, 466
Adam, 178, 198, 218, 219, 324, 372, 403
Adar, 260, 398, 399, 439, 451, 452, 454, 470, 484
Adda. *See* Adad, Hadad
Adon, Adonai, 63, 70, 71, 128, 303, 319, 395, 400, 434, 435, 436
Adonis, 70, 71, 257, 303, 319, 322, 435, 436
  river, 211, 379
Adonizedek, 159
Adummatu, 285
Aelian, 332, 478
Aeneas, 342
Aeschylus, 227, 233, 287, 289, 347, 367, 443
Afghanistan, 218, 293, 468
Africa, 16, 18, 155, 168, 229, 259, 269, 284, 336, 337
  Christianity, 494
  DNA studies, 155
  migration, 220, 270, 292
  serpent cult, 472
Africanus, 147
Aglaurus, 242, 245, 343
Ahmose I, 56, 67, 148, 152, 153, 227
Ahriman, 140, 223
Ahura Mazda, 258, 261, 265
Aion, 315
Akhenaten, 55, 59, 64, 65, 70, 71, 72, 99, 144, 161, 167, 420, 454, 492
  Amenophis, 161
  fanaticism, 64
  mediator, 60
  Mitanni wife, 454
  monotheism, 56, 58
  Osarseph, 163
  Psalm, 52, 64, 421, 442, 448
Akkad, Akkadians, 39, 156, 158, 182, 183, 225, 319
Amarna letters, 144, 393, 454
Ashurbanipal library, 453

Epic of Gilgamesh, 457, 467
hymns, 395, 459
incantations, 481
Jerusalem, 154
language, 4, 20, 40, 183
Mari tablets, 41
Mash, 453
mashu, 454, 460
maš-maš, 473
Alalakh, 93, 182
Albright, William F., 126, 147, 409, 431
Aldhouse-Green, Miranda J., 391
Alexander the Alabarch, 12
Alexander the Great, 292, 337, 366, 446
    600,000, 216
    Apollo, 446
    crossing sea, 220
    India, 293, 337
    library, 453
    New Dionysus, 366
    Zeus Ammon, 71
Alexandria, Egypt, 49, 81, 162, 277, 289, 295
    Gnostics, 173
    Jews, 53, 267
    library, 49, 76, 269, 453
    Septuagint, 49
Aling, Charles F., 187
Alisphragmuthosis, 152
Allah, 15, 60
Allat, 60, 406
Allen, Don C., 17, 317, 318, 322, 348
Allen, James P., 58
Amarna, 55, 56, 161, 443, 454
    heresy, 59
    letters, 144, 145, 154, 174, 177, 182, 184, 393, 448, 454, 456
Amasis, 67, 260
Ambrose of Milan, 268, 445, 496
Amen, Amun, 59, 145, 199, 200, 210, 241
Amenemhet I, 56, 217
Amenophis, Amenhotep, 160, 161, 167
Amenophis, Amenhotep II, 185, 189

Amenophis, Amenhotep III, 22, 144, 157, 167, 186, 454
Amenophis, Amenhotep IV, 51, 55, 56, 72, 167. *See also* Akhenaten
Amenta, 191
Ammon, 72, 79, 346
Amon-Ra, 361
Amos, 15, 140, 404
    Book of, 31, 63, 249, 370, 375, 398, 399, 408
Ampelos, Ampelus, 315, 371
Amphiaraus, 17, 259, 260
Amphictyons, 168
Amud, 18
Amurru, 156, 230
    book, 452, 459
    god, 157, 227, 230, 387, 452
    kingdom, 71, 91, 93, 129, 144, 157, 160, 184, 227
Anacreon, 4, 282, 283
Anahita, 238
Anakim, 114
Anath, 47, 132, 150, 172, 470, 477
Anatolia, 139, 159, 229, 360, 412
Andocides, 14
Andromeda, 337
Andros, 303, 338
Ani, 213
anoint, 294, 370, 450
Anthesteria, 365
Antiochus IV, 48, 164, 165, 171, 296, 432, 433, 441
Anu, 196, 265, 410, 475
Anubis, 201, 214, 322, 355
Aphrodite, 139, 285, 286, 341, 342, 364, 367, 469
Apis, 322, 324
Apocryphon of Joshua, 158
Apollo, 204, 223, 231, 232, 256, 280, 296, 312, 313, 349, 409, 431, 442, 446
    Adonis, 322
    chariot, 421, 428
    Claros, 313, 435
    Corinth, 380
    covenant, 246

INDEX 535

Delphi, 170, 258
Dionysus, 256, 288, 312, 322
far-darter, 231, 409
healer, 208
Hierapolis, 231
Horus, 201, 242, 256
Ion, 256
lawgiver, 253, 260, 261
oath, 384
Phoebus, 220, 348
plague aversion, 207
wand, 384, 442
Apollodorus, 4, 227, 239, 275, 296, 336, 383, 384, 443
Apophis, 148, 150, 169, 173, 197
Apuleius, 241, 242
Aqaba, Gulf of, 99, 100
Aqhat, Tale of, 373
Aquarius, 427, 467
Arab period, Early, 279
Arabia, 159, 332
  Adonis, 257, 322
  Dionysus, 295, 315, 325, 327
  Gilgamesh, 462
  nomads, 185
  Nysa, 323, 327, 336, 337
  Osiris, 202
  Sinai, Mount, 91
  sun god, 285, 353
  wine god, 285
Arabic, 4, 402
  Aaron, 242
  Al Kalb, 355
  astrotheology, 424
  god, 60
  Hebrew, 51
  hornet, 139
  mankind, 354
  Musa, 462, 471
  Orion, 249
  quddūsun, 16
  salaam, 249
  sun goddess, 394
  Suriya, 184
  zodiac, 423

Arad, 117, 118, 377
Arameans, 158, 178, 210, 229
Arcadia, 236
Argos, 154, 260, 287, 306
Argus, 383
Ariadne, 280, 341, 367, 368
Aries, 200, 347, 401, 467
Aristeas, 432
Aristides, 4, 14, 203
Aristobulus, 234, 267, 288, 297
Aristophanes, 4, 14, 203, 227, 246, 289, 291, 340, 344
Aristotle, 14, 203, 204, 219, 220, 232, 257, 289, 307, 402, 409, 443
Arjun, 239
Armageddon, 499
Armenia, 275, 290, 360
Arnon, 29
Arrian, 4, 292, 293, 294, 306, 337
Artapanus, 294, 295, 310, 430
Artaxerxes Longimanus, 238
Artemis, 17, 140, 204, 236, 244
  plague aversion, 207
Asclepius, 208, 236, 386, 475
Asenath, 172
Ashdad, Ashdod, 111, 343
Asherah, 43, 407, 414
  cult object, 43
  goddess, 15, 43, 139, 368, 399, 405, 406, 407, 436
  grove, 44, 110, 479
Ashoka, 199, 292
Ashtar, 15, 223, 406
Ashurbanipal, 269, 453, 454, 481
  library, 453, 456
Ashurnasirpal II, 354, 355
ass, 170, 171, 197, 198, 375, 380, 381
Assmann, Jan, 9, 55, 58, 59, 71, 147, 160, 161, 163, 168, 172
Assumption of Moses, 334, 441
Assyria, Assyrians, 39, 41, 114, 152, 156, 230, 255, 259, 260, 261, 264, 309, 319, 399, 427, 429
Astarte, 20, 43, 150, 183, 223, 406
Astoreth, 20, 223, 406

Astour, Michael C., 470, 471, 476, 477, 478
astrotheology, 72, 196, 198, 325, 443, 445, 446
   Deborah, Song of, 138
   Dionysus, 325, 367
   divine birth, 258
   dodecans, 446
   Egypt, 192
   elohim, 404
   Erigone, 316
   Ezekiel, 425
   giants, 248
   Habakkuk, 223
   Hosea, 236
   hosts of heaven, 434
   Israel, 44, 422, 424
   menorah, 446
   moon, 275
   Sabians, 367
   stars, 191
   tabernacle, 444
   twins, 123
   Venus, 329
   Yahweh, 418
Atalanta, 236
Aten, Atenism, 56, 59, 60, 64, 70, 71, 73, 161, 167, 448, 454
Aten, Great Hymn to, 64, 421, 442, 454
Atharvaveda, 236
Athena, 239, 242, 243, 342, 343, 384
Athenaeus, 446
Athenodorus, 285
Athens, 92, 239, 243, 275, 291, 344, 365, 376, 446
   Acropolis, 237, 239, 243, 344
   plague, 207, 208, 332, 344
Athyr, 244
Aṭiratu, 15
Attalus I, 250
Attica, 239, 310, 343
Atum, 80, 188
Augustine, 268
Aurignacian, 276
Avaris, 148, 153, 160, 161, 167, 168, 188

Axe, Anthony, 122
Azize, Joseph, 369
Aztecs, 495

B

Baal Cycle, 125, 129, 130, 131, 132, 133, 135, 149, 225, 236, 368
Baal, Ba'al, Balu, 154, 196, 222, 223, 225, 227, 229, 248, 253, 326, 350, 369, 395, 399, 406, 407, 409, 411, 437, 492
   'ali, 57
   2 Kings, 414
   Adad, 422
   Berith, 260, 264
   bull, 403
   Byblos, 431
   chariot, 134
   Emar temple, 183
   fertility god, 401
   four faces, 426
   Hadad, 101, 409, 411
   holy mountain, 130
   horns, 210, 248
   Hyksos, 147, 150, 170, 171, 197, 207, 227
   Jewish temple, 43
   king, 179
   Mitanni, 454
   Mush, 470, 477
   priesthood, 210
   Psalm, 129, 130
   Ras Shamra temple, 46
   resurrection, 412
   scapegoat, 140
   Seth, 132, 171, 173, 174, 178, 198, 248, 492
   seventy brothers, 403
   Shamash, 392
   storm god, 21, 221, 229, 418, 422
   sun god, 419, 425
   water god, 61
   wine jars, 368, 379
   Yahweh, 412
   Yamm, 222
   Zebub, 86

INDEX

Zephon, 100, 101, 229
Baal's Drink, 368
Babel, 39
Babylon, 31, 35, 49, 104, 156, 196, 256, 353, 399, 439, 460, 485, 492
   Amorites, 230, 416
   Cyrus, 215, 233
   Dian-nisi, 353
   Hammurabi, 260
   Ishtar Gate, 472
   library, 38, 269, 453, 457
   magicians, 481
   Marduk, 451
   marzeah, 369
   Mash, 452
   Masu, 451
   Moses, 195
   Nebo, 261
   new year festival, 482
   Nimrod, 261
   Nysa, 337
   priesthood, 481
   Revelation, 378
   Shamash, 261
   Tammuz, 376
   Thutmose III, 68
   wine, 324
Babylonian Exile, 30, 31, 34, 37, 38, 44, 47, 114, 127, 141, 172, 209, 215, 329, 417, 429
bacchantes, 291, 307, 309, 316, 370, 385
Bactria, 288, 293, 337
Baker, Margaret, 31, 415, 417
Balaam, 115
Barkay, Gabriel, 21
Bashan, 2, 116
Basques, 365
Batto, Bernard F., 35, 95, 125, 133, 134
bdellium, 102, 103
Beale, Gregory K., 378
Becker, Carl J., 274, 276, 277
Bedouins, *bedu*, 112, 141, 142, 185, 186, 188, 189, 193, 492
bee, 139
beer, 209, 274, 276, 277, 310, 312, 361, 376, 476
Beersheba, 43, 63
Beirut, 405, 431
Bel, 223, 326, 451, 470
Bel and the Dragon, 472
Bell, John, 324
Bellamy, John, 326, 327
Bellerophon, 478
Beowulf, 196, 223
Bergmann, Claudia, 257
Berossus, 49, 76
Beruta, 144
Beth Alpha, 425
Beth Shean, 278, 279
Beth Shemesh, 110, 111, 343
Bethel, 43, 47, 112, 248, 397
Billington, Clyde E., 187
bimater, 300, 310, 341
Black Sea, 18, 290, 364
Boccharis, Bocchoris, 166, 167, 260
Bochart, Samuel, 197, 318, 319, 322, 331, 343
Boeotia, 343, 344
Bonner, Campbell, 380, 434
Book of the Dead, Egyptian, 16, 213, 214, 215, 234, 265, 269, 426
Bouriant, Urbain, 454
Bourriau, Janine, 149
Brahma, 219, 220, 374, 402, 492
Brahman, 58
Braund, David, 344
Breasted, James H., 83, 143, 180
Brodribb, William J., 169
Bromius, 291
Bronze Age, 91, 117, 154, 178, 209, 423, 495
   Early, 19, 117, 247
   Intermediate, 184
   Late, 93, 100, 117, 119, 121, 150, 177, 178, 187, 192, 198, 211, 217, 247, 279, 417, 436
   Middle, 117, 155, 211, 467
Brown, John P., 383, 385, 401
Brown, William P., 443

Brugsch-Bey, Heinrich K., 199, 200
bruma, 356
Brynner, Yul, 69
Buddha, Buddhism, 199, 232, 242, 260, 265, 356
Budge, E.A. Wallis, 51, 213, 430
Bulaq, Boulaq, 199
Butler, Joel, 241, 359, 374
Byblos, 19, 20, 70, 92, 150, 157, 183, 217, 275, 319, 431
Byelobog, 223
Byrne, Joseph, 207, 208
Byzantine era, 314

C

Cadmus, Kadmos, 289, 306, 314, 318, 319
caduceus, 205, 313, 332, 386, 387, 442, 475
Caleb, 113, 116, 317, 321, 334, 355, 356
Callimachus, 236, 314
Callistratus, 168
Calmet, Dom Augustin, 446
Calypso, 383
camel, 27, 28
Campbell, Joseph, 1, 4, 23
Cana, 311, 338, 368, 379
Canis Major, Minor, 355, 415
Canopus, 255
Caprius, 299
Carbon-14, 121
Caria, Carians, 92, 93
carpenter, 20, 21
Carthage, 350
Casius, Mount, 100
Çatalhöyük, 18, 360
Catholic Encyclopedia, 398, 424
Ceres, 283, 298
Chaeremon, 165, 167, 168
Chaldeans, 111, 249, 259, 261, 326, 415, 423, 427, 432, 433, 439, 457, 483, 484
chariots, 100, 104, 133, 134, 222, 419, 421, 427, 428, 459
Charlesworth, James H., 480
Charondas, 246, 247, 260

Chaucer, 26
Chemosh, 182
Chernobog, 223
cherubim, 110, 419, 426, 427
China, 141, 322, 385
Christos, 72, 215
Church, Alfred J., 169
Cicero, 4, 299, 306, 338
Ciholas, Paul, 268
Cilicia, 93, 220
    Nysa, 337
Circe, 383, 384
Cithaeron, 309
Clarke, Adam, 206, 241, 245, 327, 343, 446
Clay, Albert T., 230, 452, 458, 459, 467
Clement of Alexandria, 4, 11, 216, 267, 307, 308, 320, 445, 496
Cleomedes, 243
Codex Sinaiticus, 7
Coffin Texts, 59, 235
Cogul, 276
Cohens, 483
Colenso, John W., 76, 433, 436, 440
Columbus, 102
Congo, 58, 261, 269, 472
Coogan, Michael, 9, 25
Copts, 50, 51, 338, 339, 433
coriander, 102, 103, 234
Cornelius Labeo, 297, 313
Crawford, Angus, 454
Crete, Cretans, 264, 287
    Dionysus, 274, 349
    Ida, 168
    Jews, 168
    Minos, 253, 258, 259, 260
    Pelasgians, 274, 287
    Philistines, 91, 92
    Typhon, 175
    viticulture, 275, 364
Creusa, 256
crocodile, 21, 232
Cross, Frank M., 35, 157, 177, 408, 417
Cunningham, Graham, 463, 472, 474
Cybele, 297, 342

INDEX   539

Cyprus, 41, 93, 220, 340, 341, 367
Cyrus, 215, 216, 233, 453

D

Dagan, Dagon, 46, 111
Dan, 112, 248, 401, 412
Dan'el, 35
Danet, Pierre, 309, 321, 322
Daniel, 223
  Book of, 34, 36, 398, 483
Dardanus, 245
Darlington, William, 328
David, 21, 34, 37, 51, 72
  Ebla, 40
  Gilgamesh, 461
  Goliath, 296
  House of, 179
  Jerusalem, 129, 154, 404, 411, 479
  Jesse, 382
  myth, 17, 129
  Orpheus, 370
  Philistines, 110
  psalmist, 131
  Star of, 421
Davids, Peter H., 17
Day, John, 421
Dead Sea Scrolls, 133, 141, 185, 191, 433
Delilah, 39, 396
Delitzsch, Friedrich, 104, 111, 416
Delphi, 170, 172, 244, 256, 258
Demeter, 139, 260, 283, 284, 339, 340
Demosthenes, 14, 246, 289, 443
Dever, William G., 10, 25, 44, 46, 75, 96, 100, 119, 122
Devil, 228, 328
Dian-nisi, 353, 354, 355, 365, 395, 444
Dijkstra, Meindert, 429
Diodorus, 4, 13, 14, 17, 258, 279, 287, 299, 301, 306, 307, 308, 310, 320
  Antiochus IV, 164
  bimater, 341
  Boccharis, 166
  covenant, 246
  cow, 294

Dionysus, 201, 295, 299, 300
  Hecataeus, 76
  Horus, 201, 256
  Hyksos, 165
  Iao, 327, 432
  India, 299, 300, 327
  Jews, 165
  lawgivers, 253, 308, 348
  lepers, 168
  Lycurgus crucifixion, 300
  Meros, 295
  Moses, 165, 170
  Mousaios, 295
  Nabateans, 285
  Nysa, 336
  Osiris, 200, 201, 202, 301, 327
  prophet, 289
  sun, 301
  tent, 443
  water to wine, 379
  Yahweh, 329, 435
Diogenes Laertius, 366
Diomedes, 280, 347
Dion, Paul E., 229, 421, 422
Dionysius, 14, 203, 446
Dios, Deus, 282
Dioscuri, 238, 242
DNA, 121, 155, 159, 219, 292, 473
Doane, Thomas W., 484
Documentary Hypothesis, 25, 34, 35, 49, 63
dodecans, 234, 412, 445, 446
Dodona, 258
dragon, 227, 475
  Bel, 472
  Ezekiel, 426
  Hebrew, 226
  Pentheus, 232, 291
  pharaoh, 227, 332, 410, 484, 494
  Revelation, 227, 228
  Sabaoth, 434
  sea, 223, 225, 226, 227, 482
  sun, 232
  Yahweh, 225
drums, 292, 294, 349, 350

Dumuzi, 342, 452, 471. *See also* Tammuz
Dumuzi's Dream, 471
Dunixi, 353, 365
Dupuis, Charles, 324, 325
Dusares, Dushara, 285, 365, 452
Dyaus Pitar, 432

E

Eakin, Frank, 61
Ebla, Eblaites, 40, 41
  Abraham, 219
  Adanu, 435
  Adda, 229
  Ashtar, 406
  Belatu, 435
  Dagan, 111
  El, 397
  Israel, name, 178, 181
  Kothar, 20
  marzeah, 369
  Mush, 471
  texts, 40, 264
ecclesia, 344
Eckenstein, Lina, 98, 99, 192, 430
Eddas, 175, 196, 500
Eden, 39, 228, 465
Edfu, 232, 242
Edom, Edomites, 79, 114, 122, 128, 136, 154, 187, 188, 191, 407
Edwards, Jonathan, 288, 324, 331
Ein Gedi, 425
El's Divine Feast, 363, 369
Elanitic Gulf, 191
Eleazar, 115
Elephantine, 25, 47, 48, 164, 172, 417
Eleusis, 339, 340
  mysteries, 286, 341, 366, 385
Eliezer, 3
Elijah, 61, 240, 439, 441
  myth, 17
Elim, 60, 97, 101, 233
elohim, 60, 61, 62, 63, 107, 127, 131, 138, 210, 395, 400, 407, 408, 421
  2606 biblical uses, 398

Ari, 60
council, 404
El, 374, 375, 398, 399, 400
  holy mountain, 402
  sons of, 114, 402, 403, 404, 405, 415
  Yahweh, 440
Elyon, El, 61, 128, 305, 308, 369, 374, 403, 404, 405, 412, 431
Elysian, Elysium fields, 214
Enki, Ea, 196, 223, 235, 237, 260, 265, 363, 474
Enkidu, 240, 456, 463, 464, 469, 474
Enkomi, 93
Enlil, 196, 260, 265, 354, 410, 412, 435, 456, 463
Enoch, 2, 3, 213, 418
  First Book of, 418, 460
  myth, 439
  Second Book of, 418
  Slavonic, 425
  Third Book of, 134, 387
Enuma Elish, 125, 130, 134, 149, 224, 231, 266, 453, 472
Eosphoros, 202, 406
Ephraim, Mount, 128, 187, 466
Epiphanius, 338, 450, 496
equinox, 312
  autumnal, 238, 334, 345, 427, 429
  vernal, 238, 334, 345, 346, 347, 427, 429, 451, 466, 467
Erech, 452, 457, 461
Erichthonius, 243, 256
Erigone, 316, 355
Erythraean Sea, 301, 318, 348
Eshcol, 373, 374
Ethiopia, Ethiopians, 111, 167, 168, 202, 283, 336, 337, 441
  Nysa, 337
Euboea, 277
Euhemeros, Evemerus, 71
Euphrates, 41, 105, 156, 158, 254, 315
Euripides, 4, 288, 289, 290, 314, 320, 329, 343, 447
  Bacchae, 288, 291
  deity manifest, 289

INDEX

dragon, 227
drums, 350
Erichthonius, 256
horns, 290
India, 337
maenads, 343
milk, honey, wine, 240, 343, 351
mysteries, 14
Pentheus, 290, 302, 343
prophet, 289
vine, 367
Eurytus, 296
Eusebius, 4, 147, 267, 268, 288, 294, 310, 404, 431
Evans, Arthur J., 264
Eve, 155, 198, 342, 372, 473
Evelyn-White, Hugh G., 281
evemerism, euhemerism, 71, 72, 125
exodos, 203, 204
exorcists, 481, 483
Ezekiel, 133, 376, 426, 427, 429
   Book of, 15, 35, 425
   four creatures, 426, 427
   holy mountain, 402
   Jerusalemites, 154, 417
   pharaoh, 227
   storm god, 422
   sun chariot, 427, 428
   sun worship, 414, 419, 429
   Tammuz, 376, 429
   temple, 428
Ezekiel the Dramatist, 440
Ezra, 28, 30, 37, 39, 45, 48, 121
   Book of, 28

F

Falk, Avner, 148
Faulkner, Raymond, 151
Feast of the Tabernacles, 105, 307, 334, 383, 429
Feldman, Louis H., 348
Finkelstein, Israel, 38, 65, 75, 118, 120, 121, 123, 147, 153, 177, 181
First Temple, 64, 128, 129, 278
Fisher-Elfert, Hans W., 218
Flavin, Richard D., 423
Franke, William, 125
Frankel, Pinchas, 376
frankincense, 190, 285
Frazer, James G., 336, 435
Free, Joseph P., 84
Freud, Sigmund, 70, 435
Friedman, Richard E., 26, 36, 45
Furneaux, Rupert, 84
Fyfe, W.H., 257

G

Gabriel, Richard A., 119
Gales, Theophilus, 319
Gardiner, Alan, 50, 99
Gately, Ian, 361
Gaza, 153, 163, 428
Geddes, Alexander, 120, 491, 496, 497
Gemara, 1, 3, 14, 23
Gemini, 459, 460
George, Saint, 224, 232
Georgia, 275, 290, 360
Germany, Germans, 263, 322
Geshtinanna, 364, 365, 476
Gezer, 144
giants, 2, 113, 114, 156, 248, 250, 253, 283, 291, 296, 302, 314, 315, 316, 478
Gibeon, Gibeonites, 117, 118, 156
Gilgal, 118
Gilgamesh, 3, 460, 484, 492
   40 days, 240
   Amorites, 156, 457
   Bible, 470
   bull, 466
   crossing the sea, 217, 465
   death, 464, 469
   giant, 467
   Gudea, 475
   Hebrew, 458
   Islam, 462
   Jensen, 461
   lawgiver, 260, 265
   Moses, 462
   snake god, 474
   sun, 458, 464, 465

wandering the desert, 232
wine, 468
Gilgamesh, Epic of, 149, 150, 196, 218, 255, 457, 461, 467, 470
  flood myth, 456
  Mashu, 455, 459
  Mush, 471
  Nineveh, 453
  snake, 474
  Sumerian, 468
Gmirkin, Russell, 25, 37, 47, 48, 49, 70, 76, 148, 151, 171, 267, 269
Gnostics, Gnosticism, 173, 224, 313, 433, 434
  amulets, 480
  First and Second Books of Ieu, 431
  IAO, 433
  Sethians, 198
  Valentinians, 433
Gnuse, Robert K., 255
Gobekli Tepe, 18, 470
Goelet, Ogden, 213, 214
Good Shepherd, 219
Goodenough, Erwin R., 359
Gordley, Matthew, 287, 288
Gordon, Cyrus, 393
Gorgon, 224
Goshen, 27, 80, 86, 188
goyim, 165
Grant Bey, James, 57, 58, 60
grasshopper, 2
Graves, Robert, 275, 276, 287, 291, 314
Gray, John, 155, 179, 210, 222, 249, 397, 398, 401, 402, 404, 405, 407, 411, 431, 442
Great Architect, 451
Greenbaum, Avraham, 200, 466
Greenberg, Gary, 171
Greenberg, Moshe, 206
Grendel, 223
Gressmann, Hugo, 172
Greswell, Edward, 423
Grethenbach, Constantine, 233
Gudea, 457, 475
Gulliver, 71, 101

Gunkel, Hermann, 172
Gymnosophists, 259

H

Habakkuk, Book of, 31, 222, 356
Habiru, Hapiru, 81, 144, 157, 177, 182, 183, 184, 185, 186, 187, 189, 192, 193, 279, 492
Hadad. *See* Adad, Hadad
Hades, 139, 209, 217, 233, 307, 313, 353, 427, 435, 465
haggadah, 479
Haifa, 19
Hallet, Jean-Pierre, 269, 270, 271
Haman, 223
Hamme, Joel, 481
Hammurabi, 32, 155, 156, 230, 260, 265, 266, 416, 458
  Code of, 16, 262, 266, 394, 442, 484
haNasi, Yehudah, 1
Harl, Kenneth W., 69
Harmonia, 228
Harpocrates, 199, 465
Hassan, Nassif M., 100
Hathor, 20, 98, 150, 209, 217, 247, 362, 363
Hatti, 209
Hazor, 419
Hebron, 118, 184, 188, 374
Hecataeus of Abdera, 76, 269, 415
Hedylus, 220
Hekate, 18
Helen of Troy, 244
Heliopolis, 81, 309
Helios, 191, 307, 313, 322, 349, 397, 421, 425, 427, 428, 435
henotheism, 57, 60, 61, 65, 138, 418
Henry, Matthew, 77, 345
Hephaestus, Hephaistos, 171, 243, 245, 296, 380, 381
Hera, 228, 275, 282, 296, 315, 316, 380, 381
Herakles, Heracles, Hercules, 21, 311, 316, 334, 395, 439, 464, 465
Herem, 47

INDEX

Hermes, 205, 206, 261, 274, 334
   Dionysus, 296, 315
   lawgiver, 253, 260, 262
   messenger, 387
   Moses, 295
   plague aversion, 207
   putting to sleep, 383
   Trismegistus, 432
   waking souls, 206
   wand, 383, 384, 386, 387, 475
Hermias, 313
Herodas, 339
Herodotus, 4, 14, 51, 174, 273, 329
   Cabeiri, 287
   Cadmus, 314, 319
   circumcision, 163, 164
   Dionysian mysteries, 286
   exodos, 203
   lawbearer, 340
   Menes, 262
   Meroe, 283
   Nysa, 336
   Orotalt, 273, 284, 353
   Palestine, 163
   pigs, 283
   Poseidon, 239
   Red Sea, 315
   reincarnation, 284
   Sesostris, 326
   tonsure, 286
   wands, 384
   Xerxes, 203
Heroöpolis, 80
Herzog, Ze'ev, 180
Heshbon, 116, 117, 118
Hesiod, 4, 227, 280, 281, 314, 329
Heskett, Randall, 359, 374
Hestia, 253
Heston, Charlton, 69
Hesychius of Alexandria, 337
Hexateuch, 33, 493
Hezekiah, 45, 48, 114, 129, 193
   destruction, 43, 46, 63, 429, 479
   Edomites, 128, 136
   LMLK, 420

Midianites, 116
Moabites, 182
Psalm, 127
serpent cult, 36, 479, 492
Solomon's proverbs, 44
wineries, 377
Hieracleopolis, 143
Hierakonpolis, 20
Hierombalos, 431
Hieronymus of Cardia, 285
Hierosolyma, Hierosolymus, 166, 168, 169, 171, 197
Higgins, Godfrey, 273, 328
Hilkiah, 38, 42, 43, 47, 268, 377
Hinnom, 43
Hipparchus, 401, 467
Hittites, 39, 156, 183, 493
   Amarna letters, 144
   Bible, 116, 154, 158, 159
   Ellil, 410
   Gilgamesh, 457, 467
   Hapiru, 182
   Indo-Europeans, 220, 457
   Jebusites, 417
   law code, 264
   plague prayers, 209
   sea peoples, 93
   storm god, 229
   Ugarit, 41
   wine, 360
Hokhmah, 173
Hollady, Carl, 295
Holst, Sanford, 319
Holy Grail, 362, 368, 378
Holy Spirit, 28, 81, 135
Homer, 4, 227, 280, 281, 287, 301, 329, 357
   Achelous, 298
   Bible, 11, 250, 307, 322
   Circe, 384
   Diomedes, 280
   Dionysus, 353
   Hermes, 206, 383
   monster, 225
   Nestor, 274

Nonnus, 314
Nysa, 327
Red Sea, 347
Solymi, 168, 169
Trojan War, 244
Homeric Hymns, 282
Homo sapiens, 18, 155, 473
honey, 240, 320, 465
  bacchantes, 291, 351
  Crete, 274
  Demeter, 139
  Dionysus, 240, 289, 301, 309, 332, 343, 349, 351
  India, 236
  Jews, 304
  manna, 28, 102, 103, 234, 331
  sacred fruits and grains, 372
  Samson, 138
  Ugarit, 235
Horace, 301, 302, 327
Horeb, Mount, 10, 62, 97, 240, 460
horns, 198, 200, 210, 226, 248, 273, 290, 302, 307, 309, 320, 334, 400, 447, 460
Horon, 242, 473
Hort, William J., 325
Horus, 57, 169, 171, 196, 197, 201, 224, 232, 247, 250, 253, 381, 442, 484, 485
  Aaron, 242, 317
  Bible, 151
  crocodile, 232
  Harpocrates, 199, 465
  Hierakonpolis, 20
  Hyksos, 151
  nativity, 256
  Osiris's brother, 201
  pharaoh, 171, 200
  resurrection, 283
  Sokar, 242
  sun, 57, 199, 242, 255, 256
  vineyard, 361
Horus Way, 81, 90, 151
Hosea, 31, 140
  Book of, 31, 35, 235, 372, 466
Huet, Pierre D., 273, 322, 323
Humash, 17

Humbaba, 467
Humphreys, Colin, 109
Humphreys, Ken, 238
Hurrians, 155, 159, 182, 183, 250
Hydaspes, 273, 302, 316, 323, 327, 333
Hyksos, 142, 155, 177, 178, 182, 186, 187, 188, 189, 193, 197, 198, 207, 218, 227, 492. See also "Hyksos and Lepers" chapter
Hyrcanus II, John, 297

I

Iacchus, 286, 306, 319, 340, 435
Iao, 13, 17, 253, 286, 313, 319, 327, 431, 432, 433, 434, 435, 436
Ieuo, 431, 433
Ikarios, 355
Iliad, 11, 196, 274, 280, 314, 347, 383, 500
Ilimilku, 145
Imhotep, 72
Inanna, Inana, 235, 260, 265, 342, 364, 471
Inanna's Descent, 235, 260, 265, 471
India, Indians, 14, 39, 120, 141, 337
  Alexander the Great, 337
  Andromeda, 337
  arks, 241
  Astacani, 293
  Buddha, 260
  Cyrus, 233
  Dionysus, 200, 273, 292, 293, 294, 299, 300, 302, 307, 308, 314, 315, 316, 332, 337, 348
  drums, 292
  drunk, 316
  ivy, 293
  Jews, 219, 220, 492
  Manu, 260
  Megasthenes, 292
  Meru, Mount, 460
  migration, 219
  Mitanni, 157, 220
  Nysa, 202, 293, 337
  Osiris, 200, 202, 301

INDEX   545

Pliny, 292
polytheism, 62
priests, 1
reincarnation, 284
Staphylus, 315
Strabo, 259
Vishnu, 460
viticulture, 294, 300
wine, 294
Indian Ocean, 348
Indra, 223, 237, 239, 292
Indus Valley, 219, 220, 294
Inman, Thomas, 9, 450
Ipuwer, 142, 143
Iran, 275, 468. See also Persia, Persians
Ireland, 14
Irenaeus, 445, 496
Iron Age, 21, 65, 93, 97, 117, 139, 162, 177, 178, 269, 419
Isaac, 62, 75, 178, 461
Isaiah, 382
  Abraham, 402
  astrologers, 138
  Book of, 31, 339, 352, 499
  Cyrus, 215
  dragon, 225, 226
  Jesse, 377, 382
  Lucifer, 406, 410
  Moses, 31
  mount of assembly, 402
  Nebo, 261
  Nile, 217
  nissi, 352
  Rahab, 226
  root, 382
  Second, 205
  storm god, 422
  Tannin, 225
  vine of Israel, 372
  wine, 370
Ishtar, 15, 139, 182, 217, 223, 342, 406, 469, 471, 475, 481, 482
Ishum, 47
Isis, 168, 171, 247, 317
  Byblos, 20, 217

Dionysus, 306, 320
Eleusis, 341
Horus nativity, 256
lawgiver, 260
Miriam, 317
Mises, 340
moon, 301
Nile, 341
Plutarch, 283
Sirius, 281
Thermouthis, 478
Islam, 108, 285
Isocrates, 14, 246
Israel, personal name, 178
Issachar, 139, 184, 381
ivy, 289, 292, 293, 294, 296, 297, 302, 303, 304, 305, 307, 309, 351, 385
  hangover cure, 303, 385

J

Jacob, 9, 62, 77, 404, 461
  12 sons, 445
  72, 234
  booths, 105
  children, 148
  Deuteronomy 32, 404
  Egypt, 80
  El Shaddai, 62
  embalming, 51, 240
  Israel, 178, 203, 401
  Issachar, 381
  loins, 293
  myth, 75, 498
  Psalm, 128, 222
  Seth, 132
  star, 138
  sun, 191
  Thutmose III, 450
Jacob's Ladder, 39
Jael, 139, 140
Jamieson, Fausset and Brown, 77, 427
Janus, 322
Japan, 111, 322
Jason, 196, 277
Jastrow, Morris, 392, 396, 467

Jebus, Jebusites, 53, 154, 158, 159, 174, 184, 417, 485
Jehovahnissi, 320, 327, 328, 351, 353, 382
Jensen, Peter, 461
Jeremiah, 268
  Book of, 31, 35, 201, 230
Jericho, 18, 109, 115, 116, 117, 118, 119, 227
Jeroboam, 112, 248, 401
Jerome, 30, 50, 215, 242, 310, 381, 397, 432, 435, 445, 447, 496
Jesse, 362, 375, 377, 382
Jesus Christ, 72, 202, 222, 223, 236, 286, 287, 325, 339, 345, 357, 375, 397, 420, 436, 499
  alpha and omega, 433
  ass and foal, 380, 381
  blood, 366, 375, 378, 388
  bread of life, 235
  carpenter, 20
  crucifixion, 345, 365
  disciples, 205, 403
  etymology, 277
  exodus of, 202, 203
  genealogy, 499
  Gilgamesh, 461, 470
  high priest, 374
  Holy Grail, 362, 368
  Jesse, 382
  Lamb of God, 275, 296, 345
  living water, 238
  mediator, 60, 410
  morning star, 406
  myth, 17, 18, 235, 238, 289, 396, 498
  nativity, 275, 303, 338, 381, 423
  Nazarene, 422
  New Dionysus, 366, 379
  passion, 204, 334
  Rahab, 119, 227, 495
  Rock, 203, 239
  sacrifice, 310
  savior, 50, 141, 190, 250, 282, 499
  second Moses, 450
  serpent, 480
  shepherd, 401
  slaughter of infants, 196
  son of God, 392, 405, 441
  storm control, 411
  sun, 228, 397, 412, 420, 442
  swine, 284
  temptation, 240
  transfiguration, 270, 418, 441, 499
  tree of life, 387
  two thieves, 238, 249
  underworld, 262
  vine, 364, 371
  water to wine, 311, 338, 368, 380
  wilderness, 232
  zodiac, 424
Jethro, 107, 114, 341
Jezreel, 181, 279
John the Baptist, 232, 442
John the Lydian. *See* Lydus
Jonah, 119, 439
  Book of, 31
Joppa, 337
Jordan, 4, 18, 285
  River, 115, 116, 117, 158, 177, 205, 221, 222, 279
  Valley, 279
Joseph, 189, 247
  bull, 466
  coffin, 244
  Egypt, 148
  Goshen, 188
  Jacob, 80
  Moses, 171, 172
  myth, 172
  Osarseph, 172
  Psalm, 128
  Serapis, 324
  Sinuhe, 218
  Taurus, 466
  Thutmose III, 450
Josephus, 4, 14, 167, 479
  Ahmose I, 152
  Alexander the Great, 220
  allegory, 445
  Amenophis, 160

Chaeremon, 167
covenant, 246
Hyksos, 147, 148, 159, 162, 164
Indian Jews, 219, 402, 492
Jewish antiquities, 152
Jewish war, 13
Lysimachus, 166
Manetho, 76, 147
menorah, 446
Moses, 496
Osarseph, 160, 161
shepherd kings, 148
tabernacle, 444
Thermuthis, 478
zodiac, 425, 445
Joshua, 116, 439, 493
  Ai, 118
  Amorites, 156
  Book of, 117, 118, 399, 449, 493
  bronze, 118
  Cadmus, 319
  Conquest, 117, 138, 177, 193, 335
  genocide, 33, 116
  god, 141
  governor, 43
  Herakles, 324
  Jordan River, 205, 222
  Judges, 136, 137
  Misheal, 450
  Mosaica, 28, 29, 38
  Moses, 441
  myth, 9, 17, 18, 439, 498
  Northern Kingdom, 140
  Rahab, 227
  savior, 50, 119, 131, 277
  solstice, 211, 323, 335, 356
  soothsayer, 289
  summer, 356
  sun, 439, 442, 451
Josiah, 36, 43, 45, 48, 114, 193
  destruction, 38, 42, 407, 429
  Deuteronomy, 44
  Edomites, 128, 136
  Isaiah, 352
  Moabites, 182
  Mosaic law, 46, 479
  myth, 47
  Pentateuch, 47
  Yahwism, 63
Judaeus, 171, 197
Judah, Rabbi, 241
Judas, Judah, 169
Jude, Epistle of, 2
Judea, Judah, 140, 158, 192, 222, 297, 457
  Amorites, 158
  Dionysus, 298
  Hebrew text, 53
  Herodotus, 163
  high places, 43, 414
  Hyksos, 151, 153, 166
  Rome, 297
  scepter, 375
  Shasu, 185
  sun horses, 43, 414
  tribe, 128, 163, 174
  viticulture, 359
  winged sun, 420
  Yahweh, 416, 436
  Yahwist, 35, 36
Judge River, 221, 222, 368
Juno, 318
Jupiter, 258
  Ammon, 166, 346
  Crete, 168
  Dionysus, 299, 303, 326
  ark, 245
  Iris, 333
  Meros, 293
  Osiris, 336
  planet, 399, 446
  ram, 309
  thigh, 293
  Yahweh, 327, 432
  See also Zeus
Justin Martyr, 4, 11, 267, 307, 321

K

Kabbalah, 133, 212
Kadesh, 68

Barnea, 27, 79, 97, 117
goddess, 477
Kalanoi, 219, 402, 492
Karanovo stamp seal, 423
Karna, 16, 254
Kaster, Robert A., 313
Kebara, 19
Keel, Othmar, 198
Kelley, David H., 433
Kenites, 114, 154, 158, 187
Kenyon, Kathleen, 119
Kerenyi, Carl, 274, 314
Keret, Krt, Kirta, Epic/Legend of, 114, 145, 210, 363
Khety I, 142
khus, 213, 214, 215, 234, 249, 426
Khyan, 155
kibotos, 242, 243, 244, 245
kiddush, 378
Kidron, 43
King James Bible, 26, 29, 101, 351
King's Highway, 90
Kitchen, Kenneth A., 449
Kloos, Carola, 130
Kore. *See* Persephone, Proserpine
Kothar, 20
Kraus, Hans-Joachim, 444
Krishna, 196, 239, 254, 292, 428
Kronos, 169, 170, 223, 228, 261, 347, 350, 398
Kuenen, Abraham, 440
Kunti, 254, 256
Kuntillet Ajrud, 48

L

Labayu, 182, 184
Lachish, 184, 198, 417, 419, 420
Ladd, Parrish B., 147, 162
Lagash, 376, 457, 471
lamb, 275, 296, 346, 347, 368
Lambert, Wilfred G., 40, 225
Laughlin, John C.H., 125
Lebanon, 4, 18, 20, 319, 379, 436, 468
Lebrun, C.A.G., 325
Leeming, David, 9, 254, 436

Lemche, Niels Peter, 31, 374
Lemonick, Michael D., 122
Lent, 240
leprosy, 160, 161, 162, 164, 165, 166, 168, 171, 190
leviathan, 133, 205, 224, 225, 226, 421, 477
Levites, 45, 48, 184, 226, 304, 305
Liber, 231, 244, 277, 279, 298, 302, 307, 312, 313, 318, 320, 366
lichen, 103
Lipiński, Edward, 103
Livy, 208, 266
LMLK seals, 377, 420
Lockwood, Michael, 199
Lockyer, Herbert, 103
Lost Tribes, 215
Louvre, 57
Lucian, 14, 203, 246, 307, 379
Lucifer, 202, 406, 410
Lucretius, 207
lulav, 383
Lulu-Ngoogounogounmbar, 228
Luwians, 92
LXX, 15,
  ampelos, 372
  ark of the covenant, 242
  Chaldaios, 249
  christos, 222
  drakon, 227
  erēmos, 233
  hiss, 352
  Holy Spirit, 135
  house of wine, 377
  ketos, 225
  kyrios, 351
  mazouroth, 422
  petra, 131
  rhabdos, 206, 382
  Sinai, 317
  veil, 448
  See also Septuagint
Lycia, Lycians, 169
Lycurgus, 17, 253, 259, 260, 261, 280, 300, 302, 315, 347, 348

INDEX

Lydia, Lydians, 92, 260, 263, 288, 309, 337, 350
Lydus, 297, 298, 432
Lynch, Patricia L., 472
Lysias, 243
Lysimachus, 165, 166, 168

M

Maat, 188, 215, 218
Maccabees, 64, 311
  First Book of, 296, 432
  Second Book of, 267, 295, 296, 297, 371, 432
  Third Book of, 295, 296
Macedonia, Macedonians, 147
Mack, Burton, 498
Macrobius, 231, 297, 312, 323, 349, 415
  Apollo, 312, 313
  Dionysus, 312, 313
  Iao, 313, 431, 435
  Liber, 231
  thyrus, 313
  winter solstice, 312
maenads, 290, 291, 296, 307, 316, 343, 349, 350, 383
Maera, Maira, 317, 322, 333, 355
Magen David, 421
magicians, 225, 483
Mahabharata, 175, 196, 254, 314
Maimonides, 1, 371
Malachi, 397
malaria, 211
Manahat, 21
Manasseh, 42, 43, 63, 110, 407
Mandaeans, 484
Mandara, 460
Manetho, 49, 76, 150, 151, 162, 166, 168
  Ahmose I, 152
  Amenophis, 161
  Arabians, 159
  Bible, 152
  Diodorus, 164, 165
  Hyksos, 148, 150, 151, 152, 153, 161, 167, 174
  Josephus, 147

Menes, 262
Osarseph, 160, 161, 162
sacred books, 149
servants of Horus, 151
Shepherd kings, 148
Manis, 260, 263
manna, 6, 10, 28, 34, 65, 79, 102, 103, 104, 105, 120, 122, 349
  allegory, 235
  aromatic gum, 189
  bread, 234, 235
  definition, 102
  Gilgamesh, 463
  oil, 235
  sabbath, 104
  who, what, 103
Mannus, 16, 260, 263
Manu, 16, 260, 263
manzaltu, 424
Marah, 101
Marathon, 216
Marcus Antoninus, 491
Marcus Aurelius, 278
Marduk, 130, 223, 224, 225, 230, 454
  Amurru, 227
  Asari, 58
  Babylon, 230
  Bible, 230
  chariot, 134
  divine judge, 354
  Enuma Elish, 231
  exorcist, 482
  Mash, 230, 452, 481
  Mordecai, 223
  Moses, 484
  Mush, 472, 475
  solar calf, 230, 247
  spring festival, 266
  sun and storm god, 230, 231, 482
  Yahweh, 224, 422
Mari, 41, 156, 157, 371
Maria, Mary, 317, 333, 367, 406
Martin, Ralph P., 17
maryannu, 134
marzeah, 46, 305, 369, 370, 371, 373, 430

Mash, 230, 440, 449, 452, 454, 458, 459, 475, 479, 492
　Adar, 470
　Amurru, 230
　El, 450, 452
　Gemini, 459
　Gilgamesh, 462
　Mashtu, 452
　Masu, 454
　Shamash, 450, 452
mashah, 67, 449, 450
mash-mash, 452, 458, 480, 481
mashu, 449, 456, 460, 481
Mashu, 440, 449, 451, 452, 455, 456, 459, 460, 462, 470
　god, 453
maš-maš, 473, 474, 483. See also mash-mash
mašmašu, 345, 452, 473, 481, 482, 483, 484
mason, 20
Massey, Gerald, 1, 33, 34, 50, 138, 139, 191, 195, 213, 328, 329, 341, 345, 449, 451, 491
Masu, 387, 399, 439, 440, 449, 451, 454, 455, 456, 462
Maunder, Walter, 423
Maya, 220
Mayor, Federico, 391
Mazar, Amihai, 75, 118, 120, 121, 123, 181
Mazzaroth, 422, 423
mazzeboth, 107
McDermott, Gerald R., 324, 331
McDonough, Sean M., 297
McGovern, Robert E., 360
Medes, 288, 453
medicine, 72, 270, 283, 285, 360, 361, 367, 475
Megasthenes, 4, 292, 293, 294
Megiddo, 68, 144, 184, 456
Meissner, William W., 35, 36, 409
Melampus, 284
Melchizedek, 159, 178, 374
Memphis, 20, 143, 149, 262

Mendes, 199, 200, 346
Menes, 16, 19, 260, 262, 263, 264
menorah, 446, 479
Menu, 16, 263
Mercurius, 17
Mercury, 205, 260, 261, 313, 322, 387, 399, 446
Meri, 317
merkabah, 133, 134, 428
Merneptah, 179, 180, 181, 182, 188
Meroe, 283, 295
Meros, 293, 295, 460
Meru, 293, 303, 460
mes, 67, 265, 339, 449, 455
Mesha Stele, Moabite Stone, 182
messiah, 386, 499
　Cyrus, 215
　Dionysus, 282
　Enkidu, 463
　etymology, 450
　House of David, 382
　Jesse, 382
　mashiyach, 215
　mesu, 450
　midrash, 205
　Moses, 498
　star of, 138
　sun of righteousness, 397
　wine-drenched, 375, 376, 377, 380, 388
Metatron, 386, 387
Mettinger, Tryggve N.D., 247, 411
Metzger, Bruce M., 37
Mexico, 79, 322
Meyer, Stephen C., 56, 142, 147, 166, 177
Micah, 31, 140
Michabo, 232
Midian, Midianites, 33, 60, 91, 114, 116, 122, 187, 316, 329, 462, 495
midrash, 12, 205, 339, 381, 425, 499
Migdol, 101
Milichus, 318
milk, 240, 289, 291, 301, 309, 315, 320, 331, 332, 343, 351, 375, 465

INDEX

Miller, Frank J., 302, 348
Miltiades, 216
Minos, 16, 17, 253, 258, 259, 260, 264, 265, 274, 280
Minucius Felix, 170
Miriam, 317, 333, 342, 349, 439
Mises, 16, 317, 318, 320, 321, 323, 325, 331, 339, 340, 477
Mishna, Mishnah, 1, 241, 371
Mitanni, 39, 41, 144, 157, 159, 182, 183, 220, 454, 457
Mitchell, Logan, 273
Mithra, Mithraism, 223, 237, 238, 249, 366, 411, 466
Moab, Moabites, 33, 79, 114, 115, 182, 187, 188, 495
Moiragenes, 277, 303
Molech, 43, 247, 350, 374, 399, 407, 408
Möller, Lennart, 65, 66, 101
Monius, 260, 318
monolatry, 57, 58, 59, 60, 61, 65
Mordecai, 223
Mordred, 196
Morenz, Ludwig D., 142, 143
Moso, 261, 317, 318
Mursilis II, 209
Musaeus, 17, 259, 261, 288, 295, 307, 310
Mush, 470, 471, 475, 477, 479, 480, 484, 492
Mutnofret, 66
Mycenae, Mycenaeans, 92, 93, 139, 274
myrrh, 190, 285
Myrrha, 436

N

Nabateans, 285, 297
nachash, 228, 473, 477
Nahum, Book of, 31
Natufians, 18, 19, 470
Nazarenes, Nazarites, 376, 382
Neanderthals, 18
Nebo, 231, 261
Nebseni, 213
Nebuchadnezzar II, 56, 353

Nectanebo II, 70
Negev, 79, 285
Nehushtan, 477, 479
Nephilim, 113, 114, 248, 249
Nergal, 209, 399, 452, 457, 458
Nestor, 274
Niditch, Susan, 10
Nile, 55, 68, 129, 151, 173, 244, 288, 320, 323, 331, 338, 341, 386
  bloody, 209, 211
  canal, 70
  Delta, 81, 148, 178, 188, 364
  drowning innocents, 196
  flood, 281, 341, 361, 379
  Isaiah, 217
  January 5/6th, 338
  migration, 18
  mud, 84
Nimrod, 196, 261, 319, 324
Nimrud, 483
Nineveh, 255, 353, 451, 452, 453, 481
Ningishzida, Ningizzida, 387, 452, 457, 458, 474, 475, 476, 478
Ninhursag, 237, 363
Ninib, 260, 398, 399, 452
Ninlil, 436
Ninurta, 229
Nippur, 260, 439, 471
Niqmaddu II, 41
Nisan, 345, 346, 356, 482
Noah, 324, 373, 456, 469
  ark, 2, 39, 119, 240, 242, 244, 257
  Bacchus, 309, 320, 322, 373
  covenant, 246
  drunk, 316, 372
  flood, 410, 470
  myth, 17, 18, 498
  sons, 263
  tiller, 372
Nones of January, 303, 338
Nonnos, Nonnus, 228, 314, 315, 316, 317, 318, 320, 321, 347, 348, 385
North America, 27
Nuzi, 183

O

Oblath, Michael D., 37, 75, 120, 126, 127, 129, 137
Oceanos, 228
Odyssey, 11, 196, 206, 274, 280, 342, 383, 384, 500
Oedipus, 196, 208
Og, 2
Oldenburg, Ulf, 250, 403
Oort, Henricus, 258
Opet Festivals, 241
Ophion, 223, 228
Origen, 1, 4, 267, 435, 445, 496
Orion, 248, 249, 281, 355, 415
Orontes, 157, 273, 302, 323, 327, 333
Orotalt, 273, 285, 365, 416
Orpheus, 17, 201, 259, 261, 287, 296, 298, 301, 307, 310, 313, 320, 321, 322, 323
    David, 370
    Moses, 295
    myth, 286
    Pelasgian, 287
Orphic Hymns, 286, 287, 321, 331, 339, 340
Osarseph, 160, 161, 162, 165, 171, 172
Osiris, 196, 202, 318, 484
    Adonis, 322, 436
    Anubis, 355
    ark, 244, 257
    birthday, 303
    bread, 235
    burial, 172
    Byblos, 319
    Dian-nisi, 444
    Dionysus, 201, 256, 283, 299, 301, 303, 306, 322, 326, 334, 336, 353, 354
    enthroned eye, 57
    etymology, 57
    exodus, 200, 202
    Horus, 201
    India, 202, 301
    Jerusalem, 21, 247
    Jesus, 202
    judge, 265, 354
    Jupiter, 336
    lawgiver, 261, 269, 270
    moon, 276, 430
    Moses, 171, 317
    nativity, 338
    Nile, 338, 341
    Nysa, 336
    Orpheus, 310
    Osarseph, 160, 171, 172
    passion, 204, 275
    prince, 201
    Ram, 200
    resurrection, 214, 284
    sepulcher, 327
    Seth, 224, 250
    Sirius, 191, 281
    slain, 20
    Sokar, 381
    staff, 386
    sun, 201, 301, 312, 465
    underworld, 458, 475
    water, 203, 244, 339, 351, 379
    wine, 335, 338, 360, 361, 365, 375, 379
    Yahweh, 432
Ovid, 4, 207, 266, 302, 327, 337, 347, 385

P

Pakistan, 41
Palestine, 33
    Amorites, 156
    Arabia, 159
    Baal, 130
    Conquest, 17, 117
    Egypt, 19
    El Shaddai, 409
    etymology, 163
    grapes, 160
    hornets, 139
    Hyksos, 155
    Raphia, 279
    Shasu, 185

INDEX

Suteans, 183
Tacitus, 169
Palmer, A. Smythe, 195, 229, 230, 232
Pamphylian Sea, 220
Pan, 140, 207, 210
Pandrosus, 242
Pantaenus, 445, 496
Papias, 445, 496
Paran, 191
Pardes, Ilana, 342
Passover, 47, 78, 88, 89, 334, 345, 347, 451, 479, 482
Patrick, Saint, 224
Patrick, Simon, 321, 343
Paul, Apostle, 286
Pausanias, 4, 14, 204, 306, 347
  Artemis, 244
  Dionysus ark, 245
  Dioscuri, 242
  exodos, 203
  giants, 250
  Hephaistos, 380
  Pelops, 243
  plagues, 207
  Semele, 306
  Trojans, 244
  vernal equinox, 346
  water miracle, 236, 306, 351
Peet, T. Eric, 84
Pegasus, 344
Peisander of Laranda, 314
Pelasgians, 92, 274, 276, 287, 314, 322, 436
Pellar, Brian R., 402, 424, 467
Pelle, Alex, 269, 270, 271
Pelops, 243
Pelusium, 167
Peneus River, 203
Pentheus, 223, 232, 240, 289, 290, 291, 301, 302, 309, 316, 332, 343, 350
Per-Atum, 188. *See also* Pithom
Pergamon, Pergamum, 250, 288
Pericles, 207, 344
Persephone, Proserpine, 257, 259, 282, 299, 306, 322, 339, 340
Perseus, 196, 224, 337
Persia, Persians, 27, 39, 147, 259
  Alexander, 220
  Dionysus, 288
  Jahi the Whore, 139
  Judith, 433
  Marathon, 216
  Moses, 322
  Nineveh, 453
  viticulture, 294, 360
  Xerxes, 163
Persian Gulf, 348
Petrie, Flinders, 98
Pettazzoni, Raffaele, 450
Pfeiffer, Charles F., 128
Philistines, 90, 91, 92, 93, 110, 111, 122, 128, 135, 137, 163, 169, 178, 279, 493
Philo of Alexandria, 12, 268
  12 tribes, 445
  Aaron, 112
  allegory, 445, 496
  Chaldeans, 484
  Golden Calf, 247
  Manetho, 147
  manna, 102
  Moses, 12, 13, 66, 257, 259, 270, 440, 441, 448
  Plato, 268
  seventy, 234
  zodiac, 233, 425
Philo of Byblos, 404, 431
Philostratus of Lemnos, 237, 239, 309, 343
Phoebus. *See* Apollo
Phoenicia, Phoenicians
  alphabet, 52, 314, 484
  Amurru, 157
  Cadmus, 314, 318
  Dionysus, 315, 316, 325
  Egypt, 20, 247
  Herakles, 21
  Herodotus, 163
  Hyksos, 150, 155
  marzeah, 369
  Poseidon, 405

sea peoples, 150
theogony, 250
wine, 362
Yamm, 132
Phosphoros, 202, 406
Phrygia, Phrygians, 260, 263, 288, 326, 340, 350
pigs, swine, 165, 167, 168, 174, 190, 283, 284, 384
Pindar, 4, 14, 283, 314, 395
pine, 300, 305, 386
Pi-Ramesses, 27, 80, 81
Pisa, 243
Pithom, 27, 79, 80, 83, 188
Plato, 4, 13, 14
  covenant, 246
  Diodorus, 348
  Dionysus, 291
  exodos, 203
  Jeremiah, 268
  Judaism, 61
  Justin, 307
  lawgiver, 261
  laws, 267, 269
  Minos, 259
  Moses, 11, 267, 268
  Philo, 268
  wine, 360
Plautius, 297
Pleiades, 139, 415
Pliny, 277, 279, 292, 302, 303, 314, 338, 446
Plumptre, Edward H., 305
Plutarch, 4, 14, 246, 278, 279, 320
  Adonis, 303
  ark, 244
  Carthage sacrifice, 350
  Cleomedes, 243
  Dionysus, 303, 305, 312, 338
  exodos, 203, 204
  Feast of the Tabernacles, 278, 305, 307
  Iao, 435
  Jews, 197, 273, 277, 303, 304, 311, 322, 329, 371

leprosy, 168
Manetho, 147
Osiris, 360
ark, 244
Dionysus, 353
priest, 170
Typhon, 197
vintage, 305
wine, 305, 379
Pluto, 322, 353
Poe, Michael, 360
Polyaenus, 308
Polyhistor, 261, 430
Pompeius Trogus, 168, 171
Popol Vuh, 196, 220
Porphyry, 4, 30, 48, 309, 310, 343, 431
Poseidon, 95, 123, 225, 237, 239, 257, 316, 344, 405
Potter, Francis, 17
Price, Robert M., 72, 439, 442
Prince Sea, 221, 222
Prometheus, 233, 237, 282
Proto-Sinaitic, 52, 98, 99
Ptah, 20, 57, 84
Ptolemy II, 49, 199, 200, 453
Purim, 373
Pygmies, 58, 228, 250, 261, 269, 270, 271, 472
Pylos, 274, 284, 351, 354
Pyramid Texts, 235, 379, 380
Pythagoras, 11, 246, 267
Python, 223, 231

Q

Qadesh, 144
  goddess, 15
qadeshim, 15, 16, 44
Qatna, 144
Qesem, 18
Quran, 441, 462

R

Ra, Re, 143, 150, 200, 209, 214, 219, 255, 430
Rafa, Rafah, Raphia, 278, 279

INDEX

Rahab, 118, 225, 226, 227, 495
Rahmouni, Aicha, 21, 387
Ra-Horakhti, 199, 255, 256
Rainey, Anson, 32, 181, 185, 187, 377
Rajputana, 218
Raleigh, Walter, 11, 250
Rama, 218, 219
Ramayana, 175, 196
Ramesses I, 56, 68, 69
Ramesses II, 22, 56, 69, 80, 81, 161, 167, 186, 494
Ramesses III, 71, 91, 93, 129, 156, 227
Rameswaram, 219
Ras Shamra, 15, 41, 46, 145, 193, 210, 398, 401, 402, 408, 411
Ravage, Marcus E., 497
Rawlinson, George, 163
Rawlinson, Henry, 353
Redford, Donald B., 19
  12 tribes, 445
  Amarna letters, 144
  Amorites, 156
  Amurru, 157
  Arabia, 159
  bedu, 185
  biblical literalism, 492, 493
  Byblians, 19
  Conquest, 117, 493
  Exodus era, 37
  Hapiru, 182
  Hurrians, 155
  Hyksos, 147, 155
  Philistines, 92, 93
  Pi-Ramesses, 80
  Pithom, 80
  Psalm, 64
  Sardes, 93
  sea peoples, 93
  Shasu, 187, 189, 190
  Thoth, 20
  Yahweh's law, 46
Reed Sea, 94, 95, 130, 134
Reik, Theodor, 391, 430
reincarnation, 284
Remsburg, John E., 439

Renaissance, 314, 316
Renan, Joseph E., 162
Renentet, Renenutet, 363, 478
Renouf, Peter, 213
Rephidim, 96, 106, 320
Rešef, Reshef, 150, 210
resurrection, 284, 365
Retenu, 185, 186
retsina, 305, 371
Rhea, 236, 350
Rigoglioso, Marguerite, 256
Rigveda, 58, 500
Ringgren, Helmer, 470
Roberts, Jeremy, 472
Rogers, John H., 392, 467
Roheim, Geza, 338
Rohl, David M., 69, 147
Romania, 277
Romulus and Remus, 123, 196, 197, 261, 322
Rosetta Stone, 5
Roth, Andrew Gabriel, 51
Rowton, Michael B., 80, 183, 185
Roy, S.B., 391
rubri maris, 302, 348
Ruck, Carl A.P., 336, 366, 385
Russell, Brian D., 37, 41, 95, 127, 130, 132, 133, 135, 350
Ruwenzori, 270

S

Sabaoth, 367, 432, 434
Sabbath, 104, 277, 304, 334, 378
Sadducees, 42
Samaria, Samaritans, 36, 63, 65, 151, 154, 158, 187, 406, 441
Samothrace, Samothracians, 242, 287
Samson, 39, 137, 394, 395, 396, 412, 414, 439, 440, 461
San, Khoisan, 472, 473
Sanchoniathon, 431
Sanders, Paul, 25, 136
Sanford, Hugh, 317, 318, 319
Sanskrit, 4, 263
Santorini, 89, 153

Sardes, Sardis, 93
Sargon, I, 3, 16, 17, 196, 254, 255, 256, 454, 484
Sasychis, 260, 261
Satan, 228, 240, 284
Saturn, 169, 175
   Adam, 324
   Adar, 399
   Carthage sacrifice, 350
   Crete, 168
   El, 398, 412
   flight, 169, 197
   Golden Age, 170
   Hyksos, 170
   Jews, 399
   Kaiwan, 398, 399
   planet, 446
   Set, Seth, 139
   Shu, 261
   Yahweh, 228
Sayce, Archibald H., 439, 449, 450, 451, 452, 454
Scandinavia, 260
Schniedewind, William M., 16, 41, 129, 130, 393
Scholem, Gershom G., 212
Scorpion King, 362
Second Temple, 128, 311, 429
Seder Olam Rabbah, 30
Seir, 191, 285, 416
Sekhmet, 21
Seleucids, 27, 164, 296, 423
Semele, 280, 281, 282, 288, 289, 291, 296, 306, 307, 309, 310, 315, 341
Seneca, 4, 169, 302, 315, 347, 348
Sennacherib, 254
Senwosret I, 218
Sepphoris, Tzippori, 311, 342, 425
Septuagint, LXX, 49, 77, 267, 443
   anachronism, 80
   Aristobulus, 267
   Christos, 72, 215
   little bird, 341
   Moyses, 339
   mysteries, 15
   On, 81
   Psonthomphanex, 50
   Red Sea, 221
   serpent, 228
   seventy, 49
   soothsayer, 289
   tauros, 466
   teletai, 14
   thigh, 293
   vine, 371
Serabit el-Khadim, 19, 98
seraphim, 426, 479
Sesoösis, 261
Sesostris, 260, 326
Set, Seth, 171, 196, 197, 224, 250
   ass, 170
   Baal, 132, 150, 173, 174, 198, 229
   biblical, 178, 198
   crocodile, 232
   flight, 169
   horns, 248
   Horus, 256
   Hyksos, 170, 198, 207, 227, 492
   Jacob, 178
   Jews, 198
   night, 276
   pestilence, 465
   sea serpent, 198
   seals, 198
   sons, 197
   storm god, 422
   Typhon, 170, 171, 175
   Yahweh, 207
Seti I, 69, 71, 171, 184, 185, 186, 189, 279
seventy, 62, 210, 233, 234, 403, 404, 412, 428, 444, 445, 446
Shaddai, El, 62, 157, 192, 400, 408, 409, 412, 492
Shahar, 202, 249, 406, 475
Shakespeare, 26
Shalim, 154, 202, 249, 475
Shamash, 51, 253, 354, 392, 393, 394, 395, 412, 418, 425, 452, 454, 481, 484
   chariot, 134, 459

INDEX

consort, 430
Dian-nisi, 444
etymology, 393
Gilgamesh, 465, 466
god of my father, 393
horns, 447
Jesus, 397
judge, 395, 444
king, 396
lawgiver, 32, 261, 262, 442, 468, 470
light bringer, 394, 396
Malachi 4
2, 397
Mash, 450, 452, 458
Masu, 451, 454
moon god, 192
Moses, 440
mušnammiru, 472
nativity, 257
Ur, 392
wine god, 369
Yahweh, 392, 396, 421
Shamshi-Adad I, 155, 410
Shamshiel, 418
Shapash, 261, 393, 394, 395, 412
Sharpe, Samuel, 317
Sharuhen, 153
Shasu, 142, 181, 186, 187, 193, 437, 492
  Amorites, 189
  aromatic gum, 189, 234
  Edomites, 188
  etymology, 186
  Goshen, 188
  Hebrews, 185
  Hyksos, 148, 160, 186
  Israelites, 187, 189, 190, 192
  Moabites, 187, 188
  northern, 186
  plunderers, 187
  prisoners of war, 185
  southeastern, 185
  Yhw, 190, 416
Shechem, 172, 179, 184, 397, 400
Shihor, 151
Shishak, Shoshenk, 326

Shiva, 239, 292
Shu, 50, 135, 156, 171, 191, 261, 328, 410, 449
Shur, 90
Sicily, 246, 260
Siduri, 464, 468, 469
Siegfried, 254
Silberman, Neil A., 38, 147, 153, 177
Simon, Richard, 26
sin, 289
  offering, 346, 347
Sin, 97, 106
  moon god, 192, 271
Sinai, 317, 318, 327, 463
  Mount, 97
  10 commandments, 270
  40 days, 108, 448, 463
  600,000, 212
  Arabia, 91
  archaeology, 79, 98, 108
  cloud, 422
  holy, 130
  Horeb, 10, 97, 240, 460
  Mishnah, 1, 241
  Mosaic law, 32, 137, 269
  Serabit el-Khadim, 98
  shining face, 447
  Sin, 271
  St. Catherine's Monastery, 97, 460
  two tablets, 447
  water miracle, 459
  Yahweh, 62, 179, 184, 192, 400
Nysa, 317, 323, 332
Peninsula, 9, 75, 77, 79, 80, 96, 99
  archaeology, 79, 108, 121, 122, 212
  cattle graffiti, 112
  crossing, 18
  Egyptian forces, 188
  geography, 79
  Kuntillet Ajrud, 406, 407
  manna, 103
  mines, 19
  moon worship, 192

routes, 90
Serabit el-Khadim, 98
slaves, 121
southern coast, 91
Stone Age, 122
thorny, 97
Sinuhe, 56, 217, 218
Sirius, 191, 281, 301, 415
Sitchinism, 6
Sivertsen, Barbara, 177, 211
Skokljeve, Antonije and Ivan, 274
smith, 114, 145, 232, 380
Smith, George, 254, 255
Smith, Mark S., 178, 179, 248, 399, 400, 404, 405, 419, 431
Snodgrass, Mary E., 468
Sokar, 242, 381
Solomon, 37, 56, 110, 406
　myth, 17, 129
　proverbs, 44
　Song of, 377
　temple, 56, 68, 128, 305
　Wisdom of, 479
Solon, 261, 348
solstice, 211, 356
　summer, 134, 231, 312, 338, 356, 376, 381, 425, 427, 442
　winter, 210, 242, 275, 312, 338, 356, 427, 442, 450, 451
sophia, 173
Sophocles, 208, 320
sorcerers, 483
Soteirichus, 314
Sparta, Spartans, 189, 261, 280, 347, 348
Speos Artemidos, 153
Spinoza, 3, 26
Sri Lanka, Ceylon, 218, 219
St. Catherine's Monastery, 460
Staphylus, 315, 367
Stephanus of Byzantium, 278, 279
Stone, Merlin, 386
Strabo, 4, 14, 17, 55, 70, 165, 203, 220, 258, 292, 320, 327
Strait of Gibraltar, 395

Strauss, David F., 497
Stuart, Henry V., 83
Suez, 159
Suidas, 191
Surya, 184, 254, 428
Suteans, 183
Swift, Jonathan, 71
Syria, 4, 41
　Amorites, 91, 156
　circumcision, 163, 164, 174
　Dionysus, 325
　Jews, 163
　lawgiver, 16
　North, 93, 158
　Nysa, 337
　Palestine, 163
　Phoenicians, 163
　Saturn, 399
　Ysir, 181

T

Taanach, 144, 419
Tabor, Mt., 2
Tacitus, 167, 168, 169, 170, 171, 197, 263, 277, 297
Talbot, William H.F., 353, 354
Talmud, 1, 2, 211, 241, 335, 371, 441, 459
tamarisk, 102, 103
Tammuz, Dumuzi, 364, 365, 375, 376, 429, 430, 435, 436, 437, 456, 457, 458, 475, 476, 484
Tanakh, 45, 48, 53, 165, 205, 371, 408
Tanen, 199
Tanis, 81
Tannin, 225, 226, 227
Tarhui, 383
Tarkhunda, 229
Tarsus, 93
Taru, 185
Taurus, 427, 451, 466, 467
Taylor, J. Glen, 425
Taylor, Robert, 328, 497
Tehom, 224
tekton, 20

INDEX

Tel Aviv, 18
Tel Kabri, 370, 371
Tell el-Daba, 155. *See also* Avaris
Tempest Stele, 153
Tenedos, 288
Tertullian, 170, 433
Tesla, Nicholas, 33
Thamti, 223
Thasos, 367
Thebes, Greece, 288, 289, 306, 314
Theodoretus, 435
Theophanes of Mytilene, 76
Theophilus of Antioch, 11
Thera, 89, 153
Thermuthis, Thermouthis, 478
Theseus, 280, 367
Thessaly, 92, 203, 287, 337
Thetis, 280, 347
Thomassin, Louis, 16, 320
Thor, 111, 401
Thoth, 20, 258, 261, 262, 270, 295, 322, 387, 432
Thrace, Thracians, 289, 312, 326, 335, 337, 364
Thrasybulus, 216
Thucydides, 203, 207, 208
Thutmose II, 56, 65
Thutmose III, 56, 67, 68, 145, 450
thyrsus, 294, 296, 304, 306, 309, 313, 323, 333, 340, 351, 352, 382, 385, 386
Tiamat, 130, 223, 224, 226, 266, 472, 482
Tiberias Julius Alexander, 12
Tibet, 241
Tigay, Jeffrey, 457, 461
Tigris, 105, 156
timbrel, 349, 350
Timmer, Daniel, 363
Titans, 275, 310
Titus, 12
Topheth, 43
Transjordan, 75, 79, 158, 187, 188, 285
Tree of Life, 139, 364, 387
trichinosis, 167, 190
Trophonius, 259, 261

Troy, Trojans, 93, 244, 245, 280
Tsaphnath phanehh, 50
Tuat, 214
Tuisco, 263
Tulán, 220
Tullus Hostilius, 208
Turkey, 4, 18, 92, 93, 157, 220, 288, 360, 456, 470
Turner, Frederick, 192, 386, 387, 417, 430
Tutankhamun, 56, 68, 362
Typhon, 138, 148, 150, 169, 170, 171, 175, 197, 198, 207, 224, 231
Tyre, 316, 362
Tyrrhenians, 259, 309

U

Udumu, 114
Uehlinger, Christoph, 198
Ugarit, Ugaritians, 16, 39, 41, 260, 261, 398, 402
  bull, 400
  Elat, 406
  Gilgamesh, 457
  Israel, name, 178
  marzeah, 369
  Mush, 471
  Orontes, 323
  scribal center, 41
  sea peoples, 93
  sun, 393
  texts, 46, 202
  wine, 362, 363, 369
  Yamm, 132
Unwin, Tim, 359, 378, 468
Ur, 63, 142, 156, 219, 262, 392, 452, 471, 492
Urania, 273, 285
Ur-Nammu, 261, 262, 395, 456
Uruk, 457, 471, 483
Ussefiyeh, 425
Utnapishtim, 410, 456, 462, 464, 470
Utu, 230, 392, 410, 447, 471
Uzziah, 377

V

Valentinus, Valentinians, 173, 433
van den Broek, Roelof, 435, 478
van der Veen, Peter, 21, 66, 179
van Essen, Claudius, 237
van Goudoever, Jan, 134, 427
Van Seters, John, 27, 36, 250
Varro, 4, 298, 306, 356, 432
Vedic, 4, 157, 184
Venus, 329, 332, 367
  goddess, 285, 341, 342, 367, 469
  planet, 154, 202, 216, 341, 342, 364, 399, 403, 406, 410, 412, 423, 446, 475
Vergil. *See* Virgil, Vergil
Vermaseren, Maarten J., 237
Vespasian, 12
Vinča symbols, 277
Virgil, Vergil, 4, 207, 298
virgin, 254
  birth, 238, 256, 312, 436, 498
  girls, 92, 115, 193, 464, 468
  mother, 150, 238, 243, 256, 282, 340, 405, 412
Vishnu, 460
Vitzliputzli, 245
Voltaire, 323, 324, 327
von Danikenism, 6
von Rad, Gerhard, 172
Vossius, Gerhard J., 273, 318, 320, 321, 373
Vritra, 223
Vulcan, 245
Vulgate Bible, 29, 50, 67, 215, 242, 302, 352, 381, 382, 423

W

Walker, Barbara G., 139, 140, 196, 236, 255, 264, 477
Way of the Wilderness, 90
Weigall, Arthur, 70
Wellhausen, Julius, 34, 35, 36, 47
Wenham, Gordon, 36
whales, 225, 228

Wheeler, Brannon M., 462
Wheless, Joseph, 26, 28, 29, 77, 78, 87, 95, 96, 105, 106, 107, 122, 128
Whybray, Roger N., 37
Wilkins, John, 344
winter, 200, 275, 313, 345, 346, 347, 356, 362, 376, 411, 442, 448. *See also* solstice
Wyatt, Ron, 100

X

xenophobia, 164, 165, 168, 169
Xenophon, 203
Xerxes, 163, 203, 443
Xikum, 139

Y

Yadin, Yigal, 100
Yahu, 140, 172, 313, 416, 417, 428, 430, 433
Yamm, 95, 130, 131, 132, 133, 135, 222, 223, 226, 248, 405, 431
Yarmuta, Yarmuth, 118, 184
Yeshua, 50, 131, 222, 410
Yhw, 186, 190, 191, 416, 437
ysril, 134

Z

Zadok, Zadokites, 42, 141
Zalmoxis, Zamolxis, 17, 253, 259, 261
Zarathustra. *See* Zoroaster
Zellentin, Holger M., 295
Zephaniah, 31
Zeus, 82, 204, 224, 307, 336, 353
  Ammon, 72
  Apollo, 384, 409
  birth, 236
  Crete, 264
  Dionysus, 281, 282, 288, 306, 312, 336
  Dios, 282
  Ethiopia, 283
  Father, 282
  India, 315
  infanticide, 196

INDEX

Jove, 431
Kasios, 100
lawgiver, 253, 258, 261, 262
lightning, 307
Pater, 432
Sabasius, 367
Silver Age, 170
storm god, 229
sun, 313, 427, 435
thigh, 293, 341
thunderbolt, 111

Yahweh, 48, 297
  See also Jupiter
Zidon, 144
Ziolkowski, Theodore, 461
Zion, Mt., 125, 128, 178
Zipporah, 329, 332, 341, 342, 469
zodiac, 233, 381, 422, 423, 424, 425, 427, 429, 445, 465, 467
Zoroaster, Zarathustra, 60, 253, 258, 261, 265

D.M. Murdock, also known as "Acharya S," majored in Classics, Greek Civilization, at Franklin & Marshall College in Lancaster, PA. She is also an alumna of the American School of Classical Studies at Athens, Greece. Ms. Murdock is the author of the controversial books *The Christ Conspiracy: The Greatest Story Ever Sold*; *Suns of God: Buddha, Krishna and Christ Unveiled*; *Who Was Jesus? Fingerprints of The Christ*; *Christ in Egypt: The Horus-Jesus Connection*; *The Gospel According to Acharya S*; and the *Astrotheology Calendar* series. Murdock's books and many of her articles can be found on her websites TruthBeKnown.com, StellarHousePublishing.com and FreethoughtNation.com.

The Christ Conspiracy: The Greatest Story Ever Sold

by Acharya S

Contrary to popular belief, there was no single man at the genesis of Christianity but many characters rolled into one. The majority of these characters were personifications of the ubiquitous solar myth, as reflected in the stories of such popular deities as Mithra, Hercules and Dionysus.

Suns of God: Krishna, Buddha and Christ Unveiled

by Acharya S

Picking up where the bestselling and controversial *The Christ Conspiracy* leaves off, *Suns of God* leads the reader through an electrifying exploration of the origin and meaning of the world's religions and popular gods. The Big Three spiritual leaders have been Christ, Krishna and Buddha, with their similar myths.

Who Was Jesus? Fingerprints of The Christ

by D.M. Murdock/Acharya S

Was Jesus Christ truly the divine Son of God who walked the earth 2,000 years ago? How can we be sure the gospel story is an accurate and infallibly related historical account? When the gospels are examined scientifically, can we truthfully uphold them as "inerrant?"

Christ in Egypt: The Horus-Jesus Connection

By D.M. Murdock/Acharya S

Destined to be a classic enjoyed by both the professional scholar and the layperson, this comparative religion book contains a startling perspective of the extraordinary history of the Egyptian religion and its profound influence upon the later Christian faith.

The Gospel According to Acharya S

by D.M. Murdock/Acharya S

What is God? Is belief in God righteous? Should we praise God? Who speaks for God? Is the Bible "God's Word?" Does prayer work? Are we born in sin? What is the origin of good and evil? Who is the Devil? Is the Bible prophetic? Do we have free will? What is the purpose in life?

Man Made God

by Barbara G. Walker, 'Foreword' by D.M. Murdock

Extraordinary independent scholar of comparative religion and mythology Barbara G. Walker takes us through a riveting journey back in time to when the Goddess and her consort/ son ruled supreme, into the era of the patriarchy.

www.StellarHousePublishing.com

Lightning Source UK Ltd.
Milton Keynes UK
UKOW04f1900251114

242177UK00001B/14/P